France

Vintage	Red Bordeaux Médoc/Graves		Pom/St–Em		White Bordeaux Sauternes & sw		Graves & dry		Alsace	
2011	7–9	♉	6–9	♉	8–10	♉	7–8	♉	5–7	�
2010	7–10	♉	6–10	♉	8–10	♉	7–9	♉	8–9	♉
2009	7–10	♉	7–10	♉	8–10	♉	7–9	♉	8–9	♉
2008	6–9	♉	6–9	♉	6–7	♉	7–8	♉	7–8	♉
2007	5–7	♉	6–7	♉	8–9	♉	8–9	♉	6–8	♉
2006	7–8	♉	7–9	♉	8–9	♉	8–9	♉	6–8	♉
2005	9–10	♉	8–9	♉	8–10	♉	8–10	♉	8–9	♉
2004	7–8	♉	7–9	♉	5–7	♉	6–7	♉	6–8	♉
2003	5–9	♉	5–8	♉	7–8	♉	6–7	◔	6–7	◔
2002	6–8	♉	5–8	♉	7–8	♉	7–8	♉	7–8	♉
2001	6–8	♉	7–8	♉	8–10	♉	7–9	♉	6–8	♉
2000	8–10	♉	7–9	♉	6–8	♉	6–8	◔	8–10	♉
1999	5–7	◔	5–8	◔	6–9	♉	7–10	♉	6–8	♉
1998	5–8	♉	6–8	♉	5–8	♉	5–9	◔	7–9	♉
1997	5–7	◔	4–7	◔	7–9	♉	4–7	◔	7–9	♉
1996	6–8	♉	5–7	◔	7–9	♉	7–10	♉	8–10	◔
1995	7–9	♉	6–9	♉	6–8	♉	5–9	◔	6–9	◔
1994	5–8	◔	5–8	◔	4–6	◔	5–8	◔	6–9	◔
1993	4–6	⏳	5–7	◔	2–5	⏳	5–7	◔	6–8	◔

France continued

Vintage	Burgundy Côte d'Or red		Côte d'Or white		Chablis		Rhône Rhône (N)		Rhône (S)	
2011	7–8	♉	7–8	♉	7–8	♉	7–8	♉	6–8	♉
2010	8–10	♉	8–10	♉	8–10	♉	8–10	♉	8–9	♉
2009	7–10	♉	7–8	♉	7–8	♉	7–9	♉	7–8	♉
2008	7–9	♉	7–9	♉	7–9	♉	6–7	♉	5–7	♉
2007	7–8	♉	8–9	◔	8–9	♉	6–8	♉	7–8	♉
2006	7–8	♉	8–10	◔	8–9	◔	7–8	♉	7–9	◔
2005	7–9	♉	7–9	♉	7–9	♉	7–8	♉	6–8	♉
2004	6–7	◔	7–8	◔	7–8	◔	6–7	♉	6–7	♉
2003	6–7	♉	6–7	◔	6–7	◔	5–7	♉	6–8	♉
2002	7–8	♉	7–8	◔	7–8	◔	4–6	♉	5–5	◔
2001	6–8	◔	7–9	◔	6–8	◔	7–8	♉	7–9	♉
2000	7–8	♉	6–9	◔	7–9	◔	6–8	♉	7–9	◔
1999	7–10	♉	5–7	◔	5–8	◔	7–9	♉	6–9	♉
1998	5–8	◔	5–7	◔	7–8	◔	6–8	♉	7–9	♉

Beaujolais 2011, 10, 09, 08. Crus will keep. **Mâcon–Villages** (white). Drink 11, 10, 09. **Loire** (Sweet Anjou and Touraine) best recent vintages: 10, 09, 07, 05, 02, 97, 96, 93, 90, 89; Bourgueil, Chinon, Saumur–Champigny: 10, 09, 06, 05, 04, 02, 00, 99. **Upper Loire** (Sancerre, Pouilly–Fumé): 10, 09, 08 **Muscadet** DYA.

HUGH JOHNSON'S

POCKET WINE BOOK

2013

MITCHELL BEAZLEY

Hugh Johnson's Pocket Wine Book 2013

Edited and designed by Mitchell Beazley,
an imprint of Octopus Publishing Group Limited, Endeavour
House, 189 Shaftesbury Avenue, London WC2H 8JY

An Hachette Livre UK Company
www.hachettelivre.co.uk

Distributed in the USA and Canada by Octopus Books USA:
c/o Hachette Book Group USA,
237 Park Avenue, New York, NY 10017

www.octopusbooksusa.com

Copyright © Octopus Publishing Group Ltd 2012

First edition published 1977

Revised editions published 1978, 1979, 1980, 1981, 1982,
1983, 1984, 1985, 1986, 1987, 1988, 1989, 1990, 1991,
1992, 1993, 1994, 1995, 1996, 1997, 1998, 1999, 2000,
2001, 2002 (twice), 2003, 2004, 2005, 2006 (twice), 2007,
2008, 2009, 2010, 2011, 2012

A CIP record for this book is available from
the British Library.

ISBN: 978-1-845-33684-4

The author and publishers will be grateful for any
information that will assist them in keeping future editions
up to date. Although all reasonable care has been taken in
preparing this book, neither the publishers nor the author
can accept any liability for any consequences arising from
the use thereof, or from the information contained herein.

General Editor **Margaret Rand**
Editoral Director **Tracey Smith**
Commissioning Editor **Hilary Lumsden**
Project Editor **Jo Wilson**
Proofreader **Jamie Ambrose**
Deputy Art Director **Yasia Williams-Leedham**
Designer **Jeremy Tilston**
Production Manager **Peter Hunt**
Printed and bound in China

HUGH JOHNSON'S

POCKET WINE BOOK

GENERAL EDITOR
MARGARET RAND

2013

Acknowledgements

This store of detailed recommendations comes partly from my own notes and mainly from those of a great number of kind friends. Without the generous help and cooperation of innumerable winemakers, merchants and critics, I could not attempt it. I particularly want to thank the following for help with research or in the areas of their special knowledge:

Sarah Ahmed, Helena Baker, Susie Barrie MW, Nicolas Belfrage MW, Philipp Blom, Jim Budd, Michael Cooper, Terry Copeland, Michael Edwards, Sarah Jane Evans MW, Rosemary George MW, Caroline Gilby MW, Annie Kay, Chandra Kurt, James Lawther MW, Konstantinos Lazarakis MW, John Livingstone-Learmonth, Wes Marshall, Campbell Mattinson, Adam Montefiore, Jasper Morris MW, Margaret Rand, Ulrich Sautter, Eleonora Scholes, Stephen Skelton MW, Paul Strang, Marguerite Thomas, Larry Walker, Simon Woods, Philip van Zyl

Contents

The top line of most entries consists of the following information:

1. Aglianico del Vulture Bas

2. r dr (s/sw sp)

3. ★★★

4. 96' 97 98 00 01' 02 (03)

1. Aglianico del Vulture Bas

Wine name and the region the wine comes from, abbreviations of regions are listed in each section.

2. r dr (s/sw sp)

Whether it is red, rosé or white (or brown/amber), dry, sweet or sparkling, or several of these (and which is most important):

r	red
p	rosé
w	white
br	brown
dr	dry*
sw	sweet
s/sw	semi-sweet
sp	sparkling

( ) brackets here denote a less important wine
* assume wine is dry when dr or sw are not indicated

3. ★★★

Its general standing as to quality: a necessarily rough-and-ready guide based on its current reputation as reflected in its prices:

★	plain, everyday quality
★★	above average
★★★	well known, highly reputed
★★★★	grand, prestigious, expensive

So much is more or less objective. Additionally there is a subjective rating:

★ etc   Stars are coloured for any wine which in my experience is usually especially good within its price range. There are good everyday wines as well as good luxury wines. This system helps you find them.

4. 96' 97 98 00 00 01' 02 (03)

Vintage information: those recent vintages that can be
recommended; and of these, which are ready to drink this year, and
which will probably improve with keeping. Your choice for current
drinking should be one of the vintage years printed in **bold** type. Buy
light-type years for further maturing.

00 etc   recommended years that may be currently available

96' etc   vintage regarded as particularly successful for the property
in question

97 etc   years in bold should be ready for drinking (those not in bold
will benefit from keeping)

98 etc   vintages in colour are those recommended as first choice
for drinking in 2012. (*See also* Bordeaux introduction, p.96.)

(02) etc provisional rating

The German vintages work on a different principle again: *see* p.157.

Other abbreviations & styles

DYA	Drink the youngest available.
NV	Vintage not normally shown on label; in Champagne this means a blend of several vintages for continuity.
CHABLIS	Properties, areas or terms cross-referred within the section; all grapes cross-ref to Grape Varieties chapter on pp.16–26.
Aiguilloux	Entries styled this way indicate wine (mid-2011–2012) especially enjoyed by Hugh Johnson.

As I sign off this book each year (this is the 36th) I always ask myself the same question: what information about wine do I actually want to carry around in my pocket? That was the original intention. My problem, from about year five, has been that the pocket has been increasingly stretched to bursting. But who can really complain that we have 20 times as many good things to drink?

So what sort of advice on wine are you really looking for? New ideas? Bargains? The latest on New Zealand? How to spell Echézeaux? How much of the known world belongs to Constellation Brands? If anyone makes any wines under 15 per cent alcohol any more? Reassurance that others share your tastes, perhaps? I know what I hope to find in books and articles, and indeed, on websites: a clear idea of where and how each bottle or brand can or might fit into my life.

It's easy enough to do this by categories: Big Reds, Feisty Whites or whatever. A tough call, though, to make it clear at what moment you should plump for a Mendoza Malbec, and when a Monthélie or a Martinborough Pinot Noir might do the business better. And of course, which one.

Don't look at me. I don't have all the answers. The fact is that we each have a palate. We each feed it information, glass by glass, to build up a set of preferences. But there is no way for it to upload stuff it has never tasted. This is why restaurant wine lists these days have taken up the idiom of the more imaginative wine critics: a long and fanciful list of flavours. You've set your heart on Thai curry, or chicken and chips. Which of these is right to wash it down: "White fruits and lime blossom nuanced with macadamia" or "Herbal notes and orange marmalade with tightly focused minerality...?"

It's easier to decide whether an 88-pointer or a 93 would fit the bill; your online bank balance will tell you. Easier still to ask the wine waiter – though harder, most people tell me, to remember what it was they rather liked last time. I used to have almost total recall for tastes and labels; there were fewer of them, then. But this is one of the things I use my little book for: ticking or circling the names and vintages of wines that have hit my spot.

As I read a list, working on my decision, I find that I subconsciously classify the wines into three categories. First, there are the Old Masters: the classic originals from the regions that made their grape varieties famous. Second come their Derivatives (if that isn't a dirty word): wines made originally to be as close to them as possible. Mistake an Oregon Pinot Noir or Napa Cabernet for a burgundy or Médoc and its maker will be tickled pink. Third are the New Talent: creators of flavours that come from their imaginations – as well as, of course, from their soil and the grapes they choose to grow. These are the blends of varieties from different regions, for example, that would make no sense in an historical context – and in France would probably be against the law. Sommeliers love this sort of wine. "You must try X's Viognier/Grüner Veltliner blend". Indeed you should, if only to find out why it's unlikely to be tried again.

Seriously, though, this sort of creative, experimental thinking is one of the most exciting new aspects of the wine world. A Nobel Prize to the person who first put Cabernet and Shiraz in the same barrel, or re-tuned his Chianti with Merlot. But another to the dogged souls who are putting varieties you never heard of on the map simply by making their wine better than it has ever been made before.

I also, not so subconsciously, consult the urges of my palate. Freshness in the first glass is an easy decision. Coolness, a little perfume, the cleansing feeling of moderate acidity, bubbles… the light touch of a Riesling. More stuffing in a wine when the palate has got going, and come to terms with good, savoury food – the Chardonnay moment. Then, with the stomach satisfied, the need for closure of some kind: the manly tannin of a serious red. The full-mouth satisfaction that comes with sugar and alcohol together in a dessert wine – or the almost-threatening burn of a Cognac or a single malt. Each has its place. You can alternate, pick and choose – but you can't reverse them. No dry after sweet. Their places in your life are pre-ordained.

These are the verities and, if not eternal, at least pretty fixed. So what are the topics of the day?

Old hands who remember bagging a couple of cases of First Growths of each good vintage are mostly living on their memories now. Each remaining bottle raises the question: "Can I justify spending hundreds on old McMurdo? Won't he think I'm after something?"

The grim fact is that the world's few wines (and perhaps everything else) with AAA ratings have floated off into investment territory, never, I fear, to return. Treasure the Musigny memories you have, if any, is my advice, and learn to love simpler fare.

Reflect, too, that the cult wines whose absurd prices you read about are a trap – and a pretty obvious one for that old figure of fun, the wine snob. Worse, they give wine in general a bad name as an ocean full of reefs, when to a reasonably savvy citizen it's (fairly) plain sailing. My worst bugbear is the cult wine with a waiting list, safe from critical scrutiny. Only members ever taste the object of their veneration, and their minds are already made up. "Organic" and "natural" wines? If that's your main concern, more important than a delicious glass, don't let me poop your party.

For the upside is that almost all wine is far better than it used to be, and there are ten, 20, who knows how many times more at the level we used to consider very good indeed. The moan a few years ago was that it all tasted the same. Perhaps it started to for a while, but that was before the current bonanza. What is same-y about Loire Chenin, about Santa Cruz, about Uruguay, the Jura, Bierzo, Bairrada, Valtellina or the Canaries? They are all making brilliant wines. It'll take you years to enjoy a fraction of them. And (best of all) the wider you range from the standard classics, the further your money goes.

Footnote

Minerality. I thought of doing a supplement on this. The word is everywhere today, in every taster's vocabulary, in every tasting note – including, I admit, a few in this book. What is it? Who started it?

It can mean the sense that you are tasting the soil as well as the grape; that some hint of mineral flavour has somehow migrated through the vine-roots into the wine. The easiest to spot and to label is saltiness – not common, but there is no argument when it's there.

It can be more of a metaphor for something crystalline; a hard, glinting presence setting off what is soft and fruity.

Most often it is just a variant on "acidic" – which never sounds very attractive, essential though it is. So for "minerality" read "sharpness", and enjoy it.

The spring of 2011 took much of Europe by surprise: so early, so warm, so beautiful, after one of the coldest winters anyone could remember. (By contrast, California was, as the song says, cold and damp.) European vines raced ahead in the hot weather, and holiday plans were put on hold as many regions seemed set for the earliest vintage ever. Then the weather changed, and July and much of August were chilly, grey and wet, at least in northern Europe.

In southern Europe heat and drought continued, but **France** and **Germany** suffered from torrential rain at the end of August. (The trade organization in **Alsace**, relentlessly positive, said that the wet July "led to good growth".) Harvest-time was a test of nerves, with those who dared to wait for the ground, and the vines, to dry out being rewarded with a warm September and October – as warm as summer should have been.

Picking times were crucial. At Veuve Clicquot they say that the date of picking was the single most important factor in the quality of the wine this year. Will it be a vintage year in **Champagne**? There will certainly be some vintage Champagnes – there are vintage Champagnes almost every year these days. Each producer's decision will depend on the quality and style of the Pinot and Chardonnay they have in front of them; some are very good, some less so.

That the wines are as good as they are is a result of the early spring, which got the vines off to a rapid start – when the poor summer set in, they had time in hand. **In Sauternes**, for example, the harvest started in some cases even earlier than in 2003, and botrytis was plentiful; the wines are rich and perfumed, and the Sauternais have smiles on their faces. And the reds of **Bordeaux**? It is noticeable that the hype machine was somewhat subdued in the autumn. "Surprisingly good" seems to be a fair assessment. There will be some lovely wines. But it will be a year to choose your producer carefully.

The **Loire** and **Burgundy** seem to have made wines with good acidity. In the **Rhône** warm weather returned in August, and reports are positive. **English** growers, their hopes raised by the very good quality of 2009 and 2010, were able to make only tiny quantities, though quality was good.

Austrian growers had their share of ups and downs, but good weather in late summer has produced good results. In **Portugal**, Port will be good and may be great. June temperatures topped 40ºC on occasion, August saw a terrific storm, and then there were five weeks of perfect weather. In **Spain** the problems were those that come with drought, so expect intense, ripe flavours and probably lowish acidity. In **Rioja** the best areas are those that are naturally cooler and have irrigation installed. Garnacha seems to have coped better than Tempranillo.

In the **USA,** West Coast producers are reporting remarkably low tannin levels after the cool, wet year just didn't give the grapes their usual oomph. Spring was late, summer unpromising and autumn patchily rainy; even though US growers have a freer hand

---

A closer look at 2010

A good vintage in Bordeaux still sets the tone, in the world's opinion, for the rest of France – and Bordeaux had a very good vintage in 2010. Convincing people that such a thing was possible was a bit tricky after 2009 had been proclaimed (by the **Bordelais,** not by the press) as the best vintage in the history of the universe, but they mostly pulled it off. Luckily it was in a very different style, so the two can stand side-by-side as non-identical twins: 2009 elegant, silky; 2010 more structured and concentrated. And, if truth be told, 2010 is a great deal less homogeneous than 2009, with overripeness and alcohol sometimes overwhelming, especially in **St-Emilion.** With the top wines only just in bottle when this book appears, it's still too early to say if they'll turn out all right or not. Wines can surprise one, and often do: oakiness can be absorbed, for example. But balance is a key indicator in young wine. I would be nervous of buying a wine to lay down for ten years or more if it wasn't balanced when I bought it. Overripeness doesn't go away any more than greenness does; neither does alcohol.

The Bordelais, in fact, are starting to take the problem, or possible problem, of excess alcohol very seriously. Château Margaux has changed the way it makes its white wine to ensure good balance; with a few exceptions Bordeaux doesn't want its wines to resemble those of Napa. This is reassuring for those of us who agree.

In **Burgundy** 2010 produced more classic structure after the lushness of 2009 – good for those who like a bit of bite to their burgundy. It was actually a superb vintage: reds with freshness, perfume and concentration; minerally whites with ripeness and acidity. **Chablis** was on song; a vintage to lay down for

than Europeans when it comes to adding tannin, the most flattering description of the year is "challenging".

Australia, picking some six months earlier, didn't have much of a time of it either. South Australia was horribly wet, and produced a huge harvest because of all the rain; rot was a big problem, and even though some of the excess will be turned into concentrate, a big harvest is just what Australia, with its problems of oversupply, doesn't need.

---

that inimitable Chablis minerality. Down in **Beaujolais** it was a vintage that confirmed the region's revival. Good growers here are making wines of more interest than I can ever remember. The **Northern Rhône** is on a roll, too, with compelling wines of great purity. As is **Alsace**, which is gradually moving back towards properly dry wines and away from the residual sugar that so confused us all. But the patchiness of the year becomes apparent when one looks at the **Loire** and, outside France, at **Germany** and **Italy.** No region here can claim uniformly good wines.

Further east the year was generally either cool (**Bulgaria**) or wet (**Hungary**). The ability and efforts of the individual producer will be what makes the difference, so check the name before you buy. **Iberia** was happier, and there'll be some delicious single-quinta Ports from the Douro.

Further west again, in **California**, it was as difficult as 2011, though drinkers with a more European palate might welcome some lighter wines the year produced. That is, if they've emerged from the wineries as light as they went in. **Oregon and Washington** had problems, too, and again the results are lighter, with less alcohol.

Australia seems to swerve from extreme to extreme, though nothing seems to dent for long the amount of wine it produces. In **New South Wales,** which recently was wondering if wine production was sustainable at all, given how little rain they'd been getting, too much rain was the problem in 2010. **Victoria** had a pause between two alarming years: bush fires in 2009, rain in 2011. But 2010 had no extremes at all – extremely moderate, perhaps. And **South Australia**, with very good Riesling and Shiraz to show, was blessing its good fortune. As was **Western Australia**, where a run of good years continues. But moderation, and a run of good years... what sort of news is that?

We all have our comfort zones, in wine as in everything else. Perhaps we'll explore outside them tomorrow, but tonight let's just have another bottle of... It's a pity. Wine is wonderfully various, and you never know what potential new favourite you're missing if you never try it. So, here are some leads to more exploratory drinking. If you love Elvis you'll love the Everly Brothers. Or maybe not, but I do, so here goes.

If you like late-harvest Tokáji, try Sercial Madeira
Good Tokáji (and quality and style do vary) has searing acidity, smoky fruit and an intense fieriness that is like nothing else – unless you swap a continent for an island, and Furmint for Sercial, which has (wait for it) searing acidity, smoky fruit and an intense preserved-lemons citrus note. Two caveats: Sercial Madeira is bone-dry, and Tokáji is sweet, though late-harvest styles, which won't be labelled with any puttonyos rating, tend to taste less obviously sweet because of their acidity. Both are utterly compelling.

If you like Médoc, try Saperavi
You know that beautiful cigar-box and plum-skins flavour of proper mature Médoc? Ripe but not overripe, balanced by good acidity, and with some bottle-age? If you can find a good Saperavi, it'll have it in spades. Saperavi is a grape we hardly know; there's a vast acreage of it in Georgia, Moldova and various places around the Black Sea, but the winemaking can be a little, shall we say, erratic. So it's not much exported. But it's worth mentioning because the odd supermarket is exploring the area, and occasional Saperavis are appearing on the shelves. They're worth a look.

If you like white burgundy, try Australian Chardonnay
"Surely not!" I hear you say. "All that butterscotch and pineapple and oak – what has that to do with Meursault or Puligny?" But times have changed, and so has Aussie Chard. Out with the oak and in with the elegance. Choose cool-climate spots like Victoria's Mornington Peninsula or the slightly warmer Yarra, close your eyes and be transported to – not any particular part of the fractured geology of the Côte d'Or, but somewhere surprisingly close.

If you like Viognier, try Fiano di Avellino
The best Viognier is not obvious or overblown, and its apricot fruit is subtle and minerally. Some of the best comes from Condrieu in the Northern Rhône, but there are contenders from as far apart as Australia and Virginia. Apricot-type fruit is not that uncommon in wine, but few combine it with Viognier's low acidity and tendency to high alcohol – making Viognier a difficult grape to grow and a difficult wine to make. Southern Italy's Fiano grape has a flavour

of honeyed peaches, which, given the traditional Italian suspicion of aromatic grapes, is subtly presented, with a little more acidity than Viognier. Avellino is not the only place to grow Fiano; Coriole makes some, and Australia's McLaren Vale does, too.

If you like Napa Cabernet, try Priorat

This is one the last bastions of very overripe grapes in a world edging nervously towards better balance. Hang-times are super-long because producers seek the most velvety tannins possible, and don't mind the low acidity and high alcohol that are inevitable side effects. It finds an echo in the raisiny, figgy fruit of Priorat in Spain, where a variety of grapes, usually involving Garnacha to some degree (usually a high one in alcoholic terms), make wines you could stand a spoon in. Priorat is not quite as massive as it was, true, and it has earthier flavours than you'll find in Napa Cab, but the profile is not dissimilar.

If you like Vin Santo, try Amontillado

Vin Santo can be a bit of a risk because while some are very good, some are not good at all. Choose a reputable producer, and enjoy the walnut pungency that takes the edge off the sweetness. It's made all over Italy (Vino Santo in Trentino) but the principle is the same: grapes are picked and left to dry on trays to concentrate their sweetness. Amontillado Sherry is made in a very different way. Here the concentration comes from long ageing in solera, while the wine oxidizes to tawny nuttiness, and gains that characteristic austere bite. Real amontillado – proper amontillado – is bone-dry, but the richness and weight of the wine balance the lack of sweetness. It is also the biggest bargain in the world of wine.

If you like Clare Riesling, try Godello

Australian Riesling has carved out its own style among Rieslings: lime-cordial fruit, complete dryness and total purity. It ages well, developing more honeyed flavours in bottle, and it always has the high, ripe acidity of Riesling. That lime-ness, that precision, finds its counterpart in Spain's Godello grape, which in turn reaches its apogee in Valdeorras. The limes can have a note of pineapple here, minerality comes singing through, and there's richness, too, to keep it all together. Godello, incidentally, is the local name for Verdelho, which in Australia's Hunter Valley gives wines of huge richness and spice, while remaining dry.

If you like red burgundy, try Langhe Nebbiolo

The burgundy I mean here is light, young and crunchy. It comes from a good grower; and probably from one of the lighter appellations of the Côte d'Or: eg. Savigny-lés-Beaune or young vines in a grander AC blended into plain Bourgogne Rouge. That same freshness and lightness is to be found in Langhe Nebbiolo, a world away from the weight and concentration of Barolo, and lighter than Nebbiolo d'Alba or Nebbiolo d'Asti (though often this is where it comes from). The wines have the same floral spiciness as young burgundy, the same freshness, the same bright moreishness.

Grape varieties

In the past two decades a radical change has come about in all except the most long-established wine countries: the names of a handful of grape varieties have become the ready-reference to wine. In senior wine countries, above all France and Italy, more complex traditions prevail. All wine of old prestige is known by its origin, more or less narrowly defined – not just the particular fruit juice that fermented. For the present the two notions are in rivalry. Eventually the primacy of place over fruit will become obvious, at least for wines of quality. But for now, for most people, grape tastes are the easy reference point – despite the fact that they are often confused by the added taste of oak. If grape flavours were really all that mattered, this would be a very short book. But of course they do matter, and a knowledge of them both guides you to flavours you enjoy and helps comparisons between regions. Hence the originally Californian term "varietal wine", meaning, in principle, from one grape variety. At least seven varieties – Cabernet Sauvignon, Pinot Noir, Riesling, Sauvignon Blanc, Chardonnay, Gewurztraminer and Muscat – taste and smell distinct and memorable enough to form international categories of wine. To these you can add Merlot, Malbec, Syrah, Sémillon, Chenin Blanc, Pinots Blanc and Gris, Sylvaner, Viognier, Nebbiolo, Sangiovese, Tempranillo. The following are the best and/or most popular wine grapes.

NOTE: all grapes and synonyms listed in this section are cross-referenced through every section in the book.

Grapes for red wine

Aghiorgitiko (Agiorgitiko) Greek; grape of Nemea, planted almost everywhere. Versatile, delicious, from soft and charming to dense and age-worthy. A must-try.

Agiorghitiko See AGHIORGITIKO.

Aglianico Southern Italian. Dark, deep and fashionable.

Aragonez See TEMPRANILLO.

Auxerrois See MALBEC, if red. White Auxerrois has its own entry in white grapes.

Băbească Neagră Traditional "black grandmother grape" of Moldova; light body and ruby-red colour.

Babić Dark grape from Dalmatia, grown in stony seaside v'yds round Sibenik. Exceptional quality potential.

Baga Portugal. Bairrada grape. Dark and tannic. Great potential but hard to grow.

Barbera Widely grown in Italy, at its best in Piedmont: high acidity, low tannin, cherry fruit. Ranges from barriqued and serious to semi-sweet and frothy. Fashionable in California and Australia; promising in Argentina.

Blauburger Austrian cross: BLAUER PORTUGIESER and BLAUFRÄNKISCH. Simple wines.

Blauburgunder See PINOT N.

Blauer Portugieser Central European, esp Germany (Rheinhessen, Pfalz, mostly for rosé), Austria, Hungary. Light, fruity reds to drink slightly chilled when young. Not for laying down.

Blauer Zweigelt See ZWEIGELT.

Blaufränkisch (Kékfrankos, Lemberger, Modra Frankinja) Originally Hungarian; now big in Austria, widely planted in Mittelburgenland: medium-bodied, peppery acidity, a characteristic salty note, berry aromas and eucalyptus. Often blended with CAB SAUV or ZWEIGELT. Lemberger in Germany (specialty of Württemberg), Kékfrankos in Hungary, Modra Frankinja in Slovenia.

Boğazkere Tannic and Turkish. Produces full-bodied wines.

Bonarda Several different grapes sail under this flag. In Italy's Oltrepò Pavese, an alias for Croatina: soft, fresh *frizzante* and still red; Piedmont's Bonarda is different. Bonarda in Lombardy and Emilia-Romagna is an alias for Uva Rara. Argentina's Bonarda can be any of these, or something else.

Bouchet See CABERNET FRANC.

Brunello Alias for SANGIOVESE, splendid at Montalcino.

Cabernet Franc [Cab Fr] The lesser of two sorts of Cab grown in Bordeaux but dominant in St-Emilion. Outperforms CAB SAUV in the Loire (Chinon, Saumur-Champigny, rosé), in Hungary (depth and complexity in Villány and Szekszárd) and often in Italy. Much of northeast Italy's Cab Fr turned out to be CARMENÈRE. Used in Bordeaux blends of Cab Sauv/MERLOT across the world.

Cabernet Sauvignon [Cab Sauv] Grape of great character: spicy, herby, tannic, with characteristic blackcurrant aroma. Main grape of the Médoc; also makes some of the best California, South American, East European reds. Vies with Shiraz in Australia. Grown almost everywhere, and led vinous renaissance in eg. Italy. Top wines need ageing; usually benefits from blending with eg. MERLOT, CAB FR, SYRAH, TEMPRANILLO, SANGIOVESE, etc. Makes aromatic rosé.

Cannonau GRENACHE in its Sardinian manifestation; can be v. fine, potent.

Carignan (Carignano, Cariñena) Low-yielding old vines now v. fashionable everywhere from south of France to Chile; best: Corbières. Lots of depth and vibrancy. Overcropped Carignan is wine-lake fodder. Common in North Africa, Spain (as Cariñena) and California.

Carignano See CARIGNAN.

Cariñena See CARIGNAN.

Carmenère An old Bordeaux variety that is now a star, rich and deep, in Chile (where it's pronounced *carmeneary*). Bordeaux is looking at it again.

Castelão *See* PERIQUITA.

Cencibel *See* TEMPRANILLO.

Chiavennasca *See* NEBBIOLO.

Cinsault (Cinsaut) A staple of southern France. V.gd if low-yielding; wine-lake stuff if not. Makes gd rosé. One of the parents of PINOTAGE.

Cornalin du Valais Swiss specialty, esp in Valais.

Corvina Dark and spicy; one of the best grapes in the Valpolicella blend. Corvinone, even darker, is a separate variety.

Côt *See* MALBEC.

Dolcetto Source of soft, seductive dry red in Piedmont. Now high fashion.

Dornfelder Deliciously light reds, straightforward, often rustic, and well-coloured, in Germany, parts of the USA, England. German plantings doubled since 2000.

Fer Servadou Exclusive to Southwest France, particularly important in Marcillac, Gaillac and St-Mont. Redolent of soft fruits and spice.

Fetească Neagră Romania: "black maiden grape" with potential as showpiece variety and being more widely planted. Needs care and low yields in v'yd, but can give deep, full-bodied wines with character.

Frühburgunder An ancient mutation of PINOT N, found mostly in Germany's Ahr but also in Franken and Württemberg, where it is confusingly known as Clevner. Lower acidity and thus more approachable than Pinot N.

Gamay The Beaujolais grape: light, v. fragrant wines, at their best young, except in Beaujolais crus (*see* France) where quality can be superb, wines for 2–10 yrs. Makes even lighter wine in the Loire Valley, in central France, in Switzerland and Savoie. "Napa Gamay" in California.

Gamza *See* KADARKA.

Garnacha (Cannonau, Garnatxa, Grenache) Becoming ultra-fashionable with *terroiristes*, who admire the way it expresses its site. Also gd for rosé and Vin Doux Naturel (esp in southern France, Spain, California) but also mainstay of beefy Priorat. Old-vine versions are prized in South Australia. Usually blended with other varieties. Cannonau in Sardinia, Grenache in France.

Garnatxa *See* GARNACHA.

Graciano Spanish; part of Rioja blend. Aroma of violets; tannic, lean structure reminiscent of PETIT VERDOT. Difficult to grow but fashionable, planted more now.

Grenache *See* GARNACHA.

Grignolino Italy: gd everyday table wine in Piedmont.

Kadarka (Gamza) Spicy, light reds in East Europe. In Hungary revived for Bikavér.

Kékfrankos Hungarian BLAUFRÄNKISCH.

Lagrein Northern Italian, deep colour, bitter finish, rich, plummy fruit. DOC in Alto Adige (*see* Italy).

Lambrusco Productive grape of the lower Po Valley. Quintessentially Italian, cheerful, sweet and fizzy red.

Lefkada Rediscovered Cypriot variety, higher quality than Mavro. Usually blended as tannins can be aggressive.

Lemberger *See* BLAUFRÄNKISCH.

Malbec (Auxerrois, Côt) Minor in Bordeaux, major in Cahors (alias Auxerrois) and the star in Argentina. Dark, dense, tannic but fleshy wine capable of real quality. High-altitude versions in Argentina are the bee's knees.

Maratheftiko Deep-coloured Cypriot grape with quality potential. Tricky to grow well but getting better as winemakers learn to manage it.

Mataro *See* MOURVÈDRE.

Mavro The most planted black grape of Cyprus. Easier to cultivate than MARATHEFTIKO, but only moderate quality. Best for rosé.

Mavrodaphne Greek; the name means "black laurel". Used for sweet fortifieds;

specialty of Patras, but also found in Cephalonia. Dry versions on the increase and show great promise.

Mavrotragano Greek, almost extinct; now revived; found on Santorini. Top quality.

Mavrud Probably Bulgaria's best. Spicy, dark, plummy late-ripener native to Thrace. Ages well.

Melnik Bulgarian grape originating in the region of the same name. Dark colour and a nice dense, tart-cherry character. Ages well.

Mencía Making waves in Bierzo, Spain. Aromatic, with steely tannins, and lots of acidity. Excellent with a gd producer.

Merlot The grape behind the great fragrant and plummy wines of Pomerol and (with CAB FR) St-Emilion. An important element in Médoc reds: soft and strong (and à la mode) in California, Washington, Chile, Australia; lighter but often gd in north Italy (can be world-class in Tuscany), Italian Switzerland, Slovenia, Argentina, South Africa, New Zealand, etc. Perhaps too adaptable for its own gd: can be v. dull; less than ripe it tastes green. Much planted in East Europe; Romania's most planted red.

Modra Frankinja See BLAUFRÄNKISCH.

Modri Pinot See PINOT N.

Monastrell See MOURVÈDRE.

Mondeuse Found in Savoie; deep colour, gd acidity. Could be same as Italy's REFOSCO.

Montepulciano Deep-coloured grape dominant in Italy's Abruzzo and important along Adriatic coast from the Marches to southern Apulia. Also name of a famous Tuscan town, unrelated.

Morellino Alias for SANGIOVESE in Scansano, southern Tuscany.

Mourvèdre (Mataro, Monastrell) Star of southern France and Australia (sometimes as Mataro) and, as Monastrell, Spain. Excellent dark, aromatic, tannic grape, gd for blending. Enjoying new interest in eg. South Australia and California.

Napa Gamay See GAMAY.

Nebbiolo (Chiavennasca, Spanna) One of Italy's best red grapes; makes Barolo, Barbaresco, Gattinara and Valtellina. Intense, nobly fruity, perfumed wine but v. tannic: improves for yrs.

Negroamaro Apulian "black bitter" red grape with potential for both high quality or high volume.

Nerello Mascalese Medium-coloured, characterful Sicilian red grape capable of making wines of considerable elegance.

Nero d'Avola Dark-red grape of Sicily. Quality levels from sublime to industrial.

Nielluccio Corsican; plenty of acidity and tannin. Gd for rosé.

Öküzgözü Soft, fruity Turkish grape, usually blended with BOĞAZKERE, rather like MERLOT in Bordeaux is blended with CAB SAUV.

Pamid Bulgarian: light, soft, everyday red.

Periquita (Castelão) Planted throughout south Portugal, esp in Península de Setúbal. Originally nicknamed Periquita after Fonseca's popular (trademarked) brand. Firm-flavoured, raspberryish reds develop a figgish, tar-like quality.

Petite Sirah Nothing to do with SYRAH; rustic, tannic, dark wine. May be blended with ZIN in California; also found in South America, Mexico and Australia.

Petit Verdot Excellent but awkward Médoc grape, now increasingly planted in CAB areas worldwide for extra fragrance. Mostly blended but some gd varietals, esp in Virginia.

Pinotage Singular South African grape (PINOT N x CINSAULT). Has had a rocky ride, but is emerging engaging, satisfying, even profound, from best producers. Gd rosé too. Fashionable "coffee Pinotage" is espresso-toned, sweetish and aimed at youth market.

Pinot Crni See PINOT N.

Pinot Meunier (Schwarzriesling) 3rd grape of Champagne, scorned by some, used by most. Softer, earlier drinking than PINOT N; useful for blending. Found in many places; vinified as a white for fizz or occasionally (eg. Germany's Württemberg, as Schwarzriesling) as still red. Samtrot is local variant in Württemberg.

Pinot Noir (Blauburgunder, Modri Pinot, Pinot Crni, Spätburgunder) [Pinot N] The glory of Burgundy's Côte d'Or, with scent, flavour and texture that are unmatched anywhere. Recent German efforts have been excellent. V.gd in Austria, esp in Kamptal, Burgenland, Thermenregion. Light wines in Hungary; light to weightier in Switzerland, where it is the main red variety and also known as Clevner. Splendid results in California's Sonoma, Carneros and Central Coast, as well as Oregon, Ontario, Yarra Valley, Adelaide Hills, Tasmania, New Zealand's South Island (Central Otago) and South Africa's Walker Bay. Some v. pretty Chileans. New French clones promise improvement in Romania. Modri Pinot in Slovenia; probably country's best red. In Italy, best in northeast and gets worse as you go south. PINOT BL and PINOT GR are mutations of Pinot N.

Plavac Mali Croatian, and related to ZIN, like so much round there. Lots of quality potential, can age well, though can also be alcoholic and dull.

Primitivo Southern Italian grape, originally from Croatia, making big, dark, rustic wines, now fashionable because genetically identical to ZIN. Early ripening, hence the name.

Refosco (Refosk) In northeast Italy possibly a synonym for Mondeuse of Savoie. Various DOCs in Italy, esp Colli Orientali. Deep, flavoursome and age-worthy wines, particularly in warmer climates. Dark, high acidity. Refosk in Slovenia and points east is genetically different but tastes similar.

Refosk See REFOSCO.

Roter Veltliner Austrian; the red version of GRÜNER VELTLINER. There is also a Frühroter and a Brauner Veltliner.

Rubin Bulgarian cross, NEBBIOLO X SYRAH. Peppery, full-bodied. Gd in blends, but increasingly used on its own.

Sagrantino Italian grape found in Umbria for powerful, cherry-flavoured wines.

St-Laurent Dark, smooth, full-flavoured Austrian specialty. Can be light and juicy or deep and structured; fashion for overextraction is over. Also in the Pfalz.

Sangiovese (Brunello, Morellino, Sangioveto) Principal red grape of west-central Italy with a reputation of being difficult to get right, but sublime and long-lasting when it is. Research has produced great improvements. Dominant in Chianti, Vino Nobile, Brunello di Montalcino, Morellino di Scansano and various fine IGT offerings. Also in Umbria generally (eg. Montefalco and Torgiano) and across the Apennines in Romagna and the Marches. Not so clever in the warmer, lower-altitude v'yds of the Tuscan coast, or in other parts of Italy despite its near ubiquity. Interesting in Australia.

Sangioveto See SANGIOVESE.

Saperavi Gd, balanced, v. long-lived wine in Georgia, Ukraine, etc. Blends v. well with CAB SAUV (eg. in Moldova). Huge potential, seldom gd winemaking.

Schiava See TROLLINGER.

Schwarzriesling PINOT MEUNIER in Württemberg.

Sciacarello Corsican, herby and peppery. Not v. tannic.

Shiraz See SYRAH.

Spanna See NEBBIOLO.

Spätburgunder German for PINOT N.

Syrah (Shiraz) The great Rhône red grape: tannic, purple, peppery wine that matures superbly. Important as Shiraz in Australia, increasingly gd under either name in Chile and South Africa, terrific in New Zealand (esp Hawke's Bay). Widely grown.

Tannat Raspberry-perfumed, highly tannic force behind Madiran, Tursan and other firm reds from Southwest France. Also rosé. Now the star of Uruguay.

Tempranillo (Aragonez, Cecibel, Tinto Fino, Tinta del País, Tinta Roríz, Ull de Llebre) Aromatic, fine Rioja grape, called Ull de Llebre in Catalonia, Cencibel in La Mancha, Tinto Fino in Ribera del Duero, Tinta Roríz in Douro, Tinta del País in Castile, Aragonez in southern Portugal. Now Australia, too. V. fashionable; elegant in cool climates, beefy in warm. Early ripening, long maturing.

Teran Close cousin of REFOSCO, same dark colour, high acidity, appetizing, esp on limestone (karst). Slovenia and thereabouts.

Teroldego Rotaliano Italian: Trentino's best indigenous variety makes serious, full-flavoured wine, esp on the flat Campo Rotaliano.

Tinta Amarela *See* TRINCADEIRA.

Tinta del País *See* TEMPRANILLO.

Tinta Negra Until recently called Tinta Negra Mole. Easily Madeira's most planted grape and the mainstay of cheaper Madeira. Now coming into its own in Colheita wines (*See* Port, Sherry & Madeira).

Tinta Roríz *See* TEMPRANILLO.

Tinto Fino *See* TEMPRANILLO.

Touriga Nacional Top Port grape in the Douro Valley, now widely used for floral, stylish table wines. Seen as Portugal's best red. Australian Touriga might be this or one of several others; California's Touriga is usually Touriga Franca.

Trincadeira (Tinta Amarela) Portugal; v.gd, spicy Alentejo. Tinta Amarela in Douro.

Trollinger (Schiava, Vernatsch) Popular pale red in Germany's Württemberg; identical with Tyrolean Vernatsch and Schiava. In Italy, snappy and brisk.

Vernatsch *See* TROLLINGER.

Xinomavro Greece's answer to NEBBIOLO. "Sharp-black"; the basis for Naoussa, Rapsani, Goumenissa, Amindeo. Some rosé, still or sparkling. Top quality can age for decades. Being tried in China.

Zinfandel [Zin] Fruity, adaptable grape of California with blackberry-like, and sometimes metallic, flavour. Can be structured and gloriously lush, aging for decades, but also makes "blush" pink, usually sweet, jammy. Genetically the same as southern Italian PRIMITIVO and Croatia's Crljenak, which is almost extinct.

Zweigelt (Blauer Zweigelt) BLAUFRÄNKISCH X ST-LAURENT, it is popular in Austria for aromatic, dark, supple, velvety wines. Also found in Hungary and Germany.

Grapes for white wine

Airén Bland workhorse of La Mancha, Spain: fresh if made well.

Albariño (Alvarinho) Fashionable and expensive in Spain: apricot-scented, gd acidity. Best in Rías Baixas; shaping up elsewhere, but not all live up to hype. Alvarinho in Portugal just as gd: aromatic Vinho Verde, esp in Monção, Melgaço.

Aligoté Burgundy's second-rank white grape. Sharp wine for young drinking, perfect for mixing with cassis (blackcurrant liqueur) to make Kir. Widely planted in East Europe, esp Russia.

Alvarinho ALBARIÑO in Portugal.

Amigne One of Switzerland's specialty grapes, traditional in Valais, esp Vétroz. Total planted: 43ha. Full-bodied, tasty, often sweet but also bone dry.

Ansonica *See* INSOLIA.

Arinto Portuguese; the mainstay of aromatic, citrusy wines in Bucelas; also adds welcome zip to blends, esp in Alentejo.

Arneis NW Italian. Fine, aromatic, appley-peachy, high-priced grape, DOCG in Roero, DOC in Langhe, Piedmont.

Arvine Rare Swiss specialty, from Valais. Also Petite Arvine. Dry and sweet, elegant, long-lasting wines with salty finish.

Assyrtiko Greek; one of the best grapes of the Mediterranean, balancing power, minerality, extract and high acid. Built to age. Could conquer the world....

Auxerrois Red Auxerrois is a synonym for MALBEC. White Auxerrois is like a fatter, spicier version of PINOT BL. Found in Alsace, much used in Crémant; also Germany.

Beli Pinot *See* PINOT BL.

Blanc Fumé *See* SAUV BL.

Boal *See* BUAL.

Bourboulenc This and the rare Rolle make some of the Midi's best wines.

Bouvier Aromatic grape indigenous to Austria. Esp gd for Beerenauslese and Trockenbeerenauslese, rarely for dry wines.

Bual (Boal) Makes top-quality sweet Madeira wines, not quite so rich as Malmsey.

Carricante Italian. Principal grape of Etna Bianco, regaining ground.

Catarratto Prolific white grape found all over Sicily, esp in west in DOC Alcamo.

Cerceal *See* SERCIAL.

Chardonnay (Morillon) [Chard] The white grape of Burgundy and Champagne, now ubiquitous worldwide, partly because it is one of the easiest to grow and vinify. Also the name of a Mâcon-Villages commune. The fashion for overoaked butterscotch versions now thankfully over. Morillon in Styria, Austria.

Chasselas (Fendant, Gutedel) Swiss (originated in Vaud). Neutral flavour, takes on local character: elegant (Geneva); refined, full (Vaud); exotic, racy (Valais). Fendant in Valais. Makes almost a third of Swiss wines but giving way, esp to red. Gutedel in Germany, grown esp in southern Baden. Elsewhere usually a table grape.

Chenin Blanc [Chenin Bl] Wonderful white grape of the middle Loire (Vouvray, Layon, etc). Wine can be dry or sweet (or v. sweet), but with plenty of acidity. Bulk wine in California. Taken v. seriously (alias Steen) in South Africa; still finding its way there, but huge potential.

Cirfandl *See* ZIERFANDLER.

Clairette Low-acid; in many southern French blends. Improved winemaking helps.

Colombard Slightly fruity, nicely sharp grape, makes everyday wine in South Africa, California and Southwest France. Often blended.

Dimiat Bulgarian: perfumed, dry or off-dry, or distilled. More synonyms than it needs.

Ermitage *See* MARSANNE.

Ezerjó Hungarian, with sharp acidity. Name means "thousand blessings".

Falanghina Italian: ancient grape of Campanian hills. Excellent dense, aromatic dry whites.

Fendant *See* CHASSELAS.

Fernão Pires *See* MARIA GOMES.

Fetească Albă / Regală (Leányka / Királyleanyka) Romania has two Feteasca grapes, both with slight MUSCAT aroma. F. Regală is a cross of F. Albă and GRAS; more finesse, gd for late-harvest wines. F. Albă is Leányka in Hungary; F. Regală is Hungary's Királyleanyka. F. Neagră is dark-skinned.

Fiano High-quality grape giving peachy, spicy wine in Campania, southern Italy.

Folle Blanche (Gros Plant, Picpoul) High acid/little flavour make this ideal for brandy. Gros Plant (Brittany), Picpoul (Armagnac). Respectable in California.

Friulano (Sauvignonasse, Sauvignon Vert) North Italian: fresh, pungent, subtly floral. Used to be called Tocai Friulano. Best in Collio, Isonzo, Colli Orientali. Found in nearby Slovenia as Sauvignonasse; also in Chile, where it was long confused with SAUV BL. Ex-Tocai in Veneto now known as Tai.

Fumé Blanc *See* SAUV BL.

Furmint (Šipon) Superb, characterful. The trademark of Hungary, both as the principal grape in Tokaji and as vivid, vigorous table wine, sometimes mineral, sometimes apricot-flavoured, sometimes both. Šipon in Slovenia. Some grown in Rust, Austria, for sweet and dry.

Garganega Best grape in Soave blend; also in Gambellara. Top, esp sweet, age well.

Garnacha Blanca (Grenache Blanc) White version of GARNACHA/GRENACHE, much used in Spain, southern France. Low acidity. Can be innocuous, or surprisingly gd.

Gewürztraminer (Traminac, Traminec, Traminer, Tramini) [Gewurz] One of the most pungent grapes, spicy with aromas of rose petals, face-cream, lychees, grapefruit. Wines are often rich and soft, even when fully dry. Best in Alsace; also gd in Germany (Baden, Pfalz, Sachsen), Eastern Europe, Australia, California, Pacific Northwest and New Zealand. Can be relatively unaromatic if just labelled Traminer (or variants). Italy uses the name Traminer Aromatico for its (dry) "Gewürz" versions. (The name takes an umlaut in German.)

Glera Uncharismatic new name for the Prosecco vine. Prosecco is now only a wine, no longer a grape.

Godello See VERDELHO.

Grasă (Kövérszőlő) Romanian; name means "fat". Prone to botrytis; v. important in Cotnari: potentially superb sweet wines. Kövérszőlő in Hungary's Tokaj region.

Graševina See WELSCHRIESLING.

Grauburgunder See PINOT GR.

Grechetto Ancient grape of central and south Italy noted for the vitality and stylishness of its wine. Blended, or used solo in Orvieto.

Greco Southern Italian: there are various Grecos, probably unrelated, perhaps of Greek origin. Brisk, peachy flavour, most famous as Greco di Tufo. Greco di Bianco is from semi-dried grapes. Greco Nero is a black version.

Grenache Blanc See GARNACHA BLANCA.

Grignolino Italy: gd everyday table wine in Piedmont.

Gros Plant See FOLLE BLANCHE.

Grüner Veltliner Austria's flagship white grape. Remarkably diverse: from simple, peppery everyday wines to others of great complexity and ageing potential. Found elsewhere in Central Europe to some extent, and now showing potential in New Zealand. The height of fashion.

Gutedel See CHASSELAS.

Hárslevelű Other main grape of Tokaji, but softer, peachier than FURMINT. Name means "linden-leaved". Gd in Somló, Eger as well.

Heida See SAVAGNIN.

Humagne Swiss specialty, older than CHASSELAS. Fresh, plump, not v. aromatic. Humagne Rouge (HR), also common in Valais, is not related but increasingly popular. HR is the same as Cornalin du Aosta; Cornalin du Valais is different. (Keep up at the back, there.)

Insolia (Ansonica, Inzolia) Sicilian; Ansonica on Tuscan coast. Fresh, racy wine at best. May be semi-dried for sweet wine.

Irsai Olivér Hungarian cross of two table varieties. Makes aromatic, MUSCAT-like wine for drinking young.

Johannisberg See SILVANER.

Kéknyelű Low-yielding, flavourful grape giving one of Hungary's best whites. Has the potential for fieriness and spice. To be watched.

Kerner Quite successful German crossing. Early ripening, flowery (but often too blatant) wine with gd acidity.

Királyleányka Aka FETEASCĂ REGALĂ.

Kövérszőlő See GRASĂ.

Laski Rizling See WELSCHRIESLING.

Leányka "Little girl". See FETEASCĂ ALBĂ.

Listán See PALOMINO.

Loureiro Best Vinho Verde variety after ALVARINHO: delicate, floral whites. Also in Spain.

Macabeo See VIURA.

Malagousia Rediscovered Greek grape for gloriously perfumed wines.

Malmsey *See* MALVASIA. The sweetest style of Madeira, from grape of same name.

Malvasia (Malmsey, Malvazija) Italy and Iberia. An ancient Greek grape planted so widely for so long that various sub-varieties often bear little resemblance to one another – can be white or red, sparkling or still, strong or mild, sweet or dry, aromatic or neutral. Slovenia's and Croatia's version is Malvazija Istarka, crisp and light, or rich, oak-aged. "Malmsey" (as in the sweetest style of Madeira) is a corruption of Malvasia.

Malvoisie Not related to MALVASIA. Covers several varieties in France, incl PINOT GR, MACABEO, BOURBOULENC, CLAIRETTE, Torbato, VERMENTINO. Pinot Gr in Switzerland.

Manseng, Gros / Petit Gloriously spicy, floral whites from Southwest France.The key to Jurançon. Superb late-harvest and sweet wines, too.

Maria Gomes (Fernão Pires) Portugal: aromatic, ripe-flavoured, slightly spicy whites in Barraida and Tejo.

Marsanne (Ermitage) Principal white grape (with ROUSSANNE) of the northern Rhône (Hermitage, St-Joseph, St-Péray). Also gd in Australia, California and (as Ermitage Blanc) the Valais. Soft, full wines that age v. well.

Melon de Bourgogne *See* MUSCADET.

Misket Bulgarian: mildly aromatic; the basis of most country whites.

Morillon CHARD in parts of Austria.

Moscatel *See* MUSCAT.

Moscato *See* MUSCAT.

Moschofilero Pink-skinned, rose-scented, high-quality, high-acid, low-alcohol Greek grape. Makes white, some pink, some sparkling.

Müller-Thurgau [Müller-T] Aromatic wines to drink young. Gd sweet wines but usually dull, often coarse, dry ones. In Germany, most common in Pfalz, Rheinhessen, Nahe, Baden, Franken. Has some merit in Italy's Trentino-Alto Adige and Friuli. Sometimes called RIES X SYLVANER (incorrectly) in Switzerland.

Muscadelle Adds aroma to white Bordeaux, esp Sauternes. In Victoria used (with MUSCAT, to which it is unrelated) for Rutherglen Muscat.

Muscadet (Melon de Bourgogne) Makes light, refreshing, v. dry wines with a seaside tang around Nantes in Brittany. Also found (as Melon) in parts of Burgundy.

Muscat (Moscatel, Moscato, Muskateller) Many varieties; the best is Muscat Blanc à Petits Grains (alias Gelber Muskateller, Rumeni Muškat, Sarga Muskotály, Yellow Muscat). Widely grown, easily recognized, pungent grapes, mostly made into perfumed sweet wines, often fortified, as in France's Vin Doux Naturel. Superb, dark and sweet in Australia. Sweet, sometimes v.gd in Spain. Most Hungarian Muskotály is Muscat Ottonel, except in Tokaj where Sarga Muskotály rules, adding perfume (in small amounts) to blends. Occasionally (eg. Alsace, Austria, parts of south Germany) made dry. Sweet Cap Corse Muscats often superb. Light Moscato fizz in Italy.

Muskateller *See* MUSCAT.

Narince Turkish; fresh and fruity wines.

Neuburger Austrian, rather neglected; mainly in the Wachau (elegant, flowery), Thermenregion (mellow, ample-bodied) and north Burgenland (strong, full).

Olaszrizling *See* WELSCHRIESLING.

Païen *See* SAVAGNIN.

Palomino (Listán) The great grape of Sherry; with little intrinsic character, it gains all from production method. Of local appeal (on a hot day) for table wine. As Listán, makes dry white in Canaries.

Pansà Blanca *See* XAREL-LO.

Pecorino Italian: not a cheese but alluring dry white from a recently near-extinct variety. IGT in Colli Pescaresi.

Pedro Ximénez [PX] Makes sweet Sherry under its own name; in Montilla, Málaga. Also grown in Argentina, the Canaries, Australia, California, South Africa.

Pinela Local to Slovenia. Subtle, lowish acidity; drink young.

Pinot Bianco See PINOT BL.

Pinot Blanc (Beli Pinot, Pinot Bianco, Weissburgunder) [Pinot Bl] Cousin of PINOT N, similar to but milder than CHARD. Light, fresh, fruity, not aromatic, to drink young. Gd for Italian spumante; potentially excellent in northeast, esp high sites in Alto Adige. Widely grown. Weissburgunder in Germany and best in south: often racier than Chard.

Pinot Gris (Pinot Grigio, Grauburgunder, Ruländer, Sivi Pinot, Szürkebarát) [Pinot Gr] Light and fashionable as Pinot Grigio in northern Italy, even for rosé, but top, characterful versions can be excellent (from Alto Adige, Friuli). Cheap versions are just that. Terrific in Alsace for full-bodied, spicy whites. Once important in Champagne. In Germany can be alias Ruländer (sweet) or Grauburgunder (dry): best in Baden (esp Kaiserstuhl) and south Pfalz. Szürkebarát in Hungary, Sivi Pinot in Slovenia (characterful, aromatic).

Pošip Croatia: mostly on Korčula. Quite characterful and citrusy; high yielding.

Prosecco See GLERA.

Renski Rizling See RIES.

Ribolla Gialla/Rebula Acidic but characterful. In Italy, best in Collio. In Slovenia, traditional in Brda. V. high quality potential in macerated and classical styles.

Rieslaner German cross (SILVANER x RIES); low yields, difficult ripening, now a rarity (less than 50ha). Makes fine Auslesen in Franken and Pfalz.

Riesling Italico See WELSCHRIESLING.

Riesling (Renski Rizling, Rhine Riesling) [Ries] As gd as CHARD, if not better, though diametrically opposite in style. Offers a range from steely to voluptuous, always positively perfumed, with more ageing potential than Chard. Great in all styles in Germany; forceful and steely in Austria; lime-cordial and toast fruit in South Australia; rich and spicy in Alsace; Germanic and promising in New Zealand, New York State, Pacific Northwest; has potential in Ontario, South Africa.

Rkatsiteli Found widely in Eastern Europe, Russia, Georgia. Can stand cold winters and has high acidity, which protects it to some degree from poor winemaking. Also grown in northeast States.

Robola In Greece (Cephalonia): top-quality, floral grape, unrelated to RIBOLLA GIALLA.

Roditis Pink grape grown all over Greece, usually producing white wines. Gd when yields are low.

Rotgipfler Austrian; indigenous to Thermenregion. With ZIERFANDLER, makes lively, lush, aromatic blend.

Roussanne Rhône grape of finesse, now popping up in California and Australia. Can age many yrs.

Ruländer See PINOT GR.

Sauvignonasse See FRIULANO.

Sauvignon Blanc [Sauv Bl] Makes distinctive aromatic, grassy-to-tropical wines, pungent in New Zealand, often minerally in Sancerre, riper in Australia. V.gd in Rueda, Austria, north Italy (Isonzo, Piedmont, Alto Adige), Chile's Casablanca Valley and South Africa. Blended with SÉM in Bordeaux. Can be austere or buxom (or indeed, nauseating). Sauvignon Gris is a pink-skinned, less aromatic version of Sauv Bl with untapped potential.

Sauvignon Vert See FRIULANO.

Savagnin (Heida, Païen) Grape of Vin Jaune from Savoie: related to GEWURZ? In Switzerland known as Heida, Païen or Traminer. Full-bodied, high acidity.

Scheurebe Grapefruit-scented German RIES x SILVANER (possibly), v. successful in Pfalz, esp for Auslese and upwards. Can be weedy: must be v. ripe to be gd.

Sémillon [Sém] Contributes the lusciousness to Sauternes but decreasingly important for Graves and other dry white Bordeaux. Grassy if not fully ripe, but can make soft, dry wine of great ageing potential. Superb in Australia; New Zealand and South Africa promising.

Sercial (Cerceal) Portugal: makes the driest Madeira. Cerceal, also Portuguese, seems to be this plus any of several others.

Seyval Blanc [Seyval Bl] French-made hybrid of French and American vines. V. hardy and attractively fruity. Popular and reasonably successful in eastern US states and England but dogmatically banned by EU from "quality" wines.

Silvaner (Johannisberg, Sylvaner) Germany's former workhorse grape, can be excellent in Rheinhessen, Pfalz, esp Franken, where its plant/earth flavours and mineral notes reach their apogee. V.gd (and powerful) as Johannisberg in the Valais, Switzerland. The lightest of the Alsace grapes.

Sipon See FURMINT.

Spätrot See ZIERFANDLER.

Sylvaner See SILVANER.

Tămâioasă Românească Romania: "frankincense" grape, with exotic aroma and taste. Belongs to MUSCAT family.

Torrontés Name given to a number of grapes, mostly with an aromatic, floral character, sometimes soapy. A specialty of Argentina; also in Spain. DYA.

Traminac / Traminec. See GEWURZ.

Traminer / Tramini Hungary. See GEWURZ.

Trebbiano (Ugni Blanc) Principal white grape of Tuscany, found all over Italy in different guises. Rarely rises above plebeian except in Tuscany's Vin Santo. Some gd dry DOCs Romagna or Abruzzo. Trebbiano di Soave or di Lugana, aka VERDICCHIO, only distantly related. Grown in southern France as Ugni Blanc, Cognac as St-Emilion. Mostly thin, bland; needs blending (and careful growing).

Ugni Blanc [Ugni Bl] See TREBBIANO.

Ull de Llebre See TEMPRANILLO.

Verdejo The grape of Rueda in Castile, potentially fine and long-lived.

Verdelho (Godello) Great quality in Australia, and in Spain as Godello – probably Spain's best white grape. Rare but gd (and medium-sweet) in Madeira.

Verdicchio Potentially gd, muscular dry wine in central-eastern Italy. Makes the wine of the same name.

Vermentino Italy: sprightly, satisfying texture and ageing capacity. Potential here.

Vernaccia Name given to many unrelated grapes in Italy. Vernaccia di San Gimignano is crisp, lively; Vernaccia di Oristano is Sherry-like.

Vidal French hybrid much grown in Canada for Icewine.

Viognier Ultra-fashionable Rhône grape, finest in Condrieu, less fine but still aromatic in Midi. Gd examples from California, Virginia, Uruguay, Australia.

Viura (Macabeo, Maccabéo, Maccabeu) Workhorse white grape of northern Spain, widespread in Rioja, Catalunya. Also in Southwest France. Gd quality potential.

Weissburgunder PINOT BL in Germany.

Welschriesling (Graševina, Laski Rizling, Olaszrizling, Riesling Italico) Not related to RIES. Light and fresh to sweet and rich in Austria; ubiquitous in Central Europe, where it can be remarkably gd for dry and sweet wines.

Xarel-lo (Pansà Blanca) Traditional Catalan grape for Cava, with Parellada, MACABEO. Neutral but clean. More character (lime cordial) in Alella, as Pansà Blanca.

Xynisteri Cyprus's most planted white grape. Can be simple and is usually DYA, but when grown at altitude makes appealing, minerally whites.

Zéta Hungarian; BOUVIER X FURMINT used by some in Tokaji Aszú production.

Zierfandler (Spätrot, Cirfandl) Found in Austria's Thermenregion; often blended with ROTGIPFLER for aromatic, orange-peel-scented, weighty wines.

Wine & food

Food these days is becoming almost as complicated as wine. We take Japanese for granted, Chinese as staple, look to Italian for comfort and then stir the pot with this strange thing called "fusion rules". Don't try to be too clever; wine you like with food you like is safest. And Riesling is the safest grape.

Before the meal – apéritifs

The conventional apéritif wines are either sparkling (epitomized by Champagne) or fortified (epitomized by Sherry in Britain, Port in France, vermouth in Italy, etc.). A glass of table wine before eating is an alternative.

Warning Avoid peanuts – they destroy wine flavours. Olives are too piquant for many wines, especially Champagne; they need Sherry or a martini. Eat almonds, pistachios, cashews or walnuts, plain crisps or cheese straws instead.

First courses

Aïoli A thirst-quencher is needed for its garlic heat. Rhône, sparkling dry white; Provence rosé, Verdicchio. And marc or grappa, too, for courage.

Antipasti Dry or medium white: Italian (Arneis, Soave, Pinot Grigio, Prosecco, Vermentino); light but gutsy red (Valpolicella, straight or *ripasso*, can handle most things).

Artichoke vinaigrette An incisive dry white: New Zealand Sauv Bl; Côtes de Gascogne or a modern Greek; young red: Bordeaux, Côtes du Rhône.
  with **hollandaise** Full-bodied, slightly crisp dry white: Pouilly-Fuissé, Pfalz Spätlese, or a Carneros or Yarra Valley Chard.

Asparagus A difficult flavour for wine, being slightly bitter, so the wine needs plenty of its own. Rheingau Ries goes well. Sauv Bl echoes the flavour. Sém beats Chard, esp Australian, but Chard works well with melted butter or hollandaise. Alsace Pinot Gr, even dry Muscat is gd, or Jurançon Sec.

Aubergine purée (*Melitzanosalata***)** Crisp New World Sauv Bl, eg. from South Africa or New Zealand; or modern Greek or Sicilian dry white. Baked aubergine dishes can need sturdier reds: Shiraz, Zin. Or try a Turkish red like the Imam.

Avocado and tiger prawns Dry to medium or slightly sharp white: Rheingau or Pfalz Kabinett, Grüner Veltliner, Wachau Ries, Sancerre, Pinot Gr; Sonoma or Australian Chard or Sauv Bl, or a dry rosé. Or premier cru Chablis.
  with **mozzarella and tomato** Crisp but ripe white with acidity: Soave, Sancerre, Greek white.

Carpaccio, beef Seems to work well with most wines, incl reds. Top Tuscan is appropriate, but fine Chards are gd. So are vintage and pink Champagnes.
  salmon Chard or Champagne.
  tuna Viognier, California Chard or New Zealand Sauv Bl.

Caviar Iced vodka. Full-bodied Champagne (eg. Bollinger, Krug). Cuvée Annamaria Clementi from Ca' del Bosco.

Ceviche Australian Ries or Verdelho, New Zealand Sauv Bl.

Charcuterie/salami Young Beaujolais-Villages, Loire reds, ie. Saumur, New Zealand or Oregon Pinot N. Lambrusco or young Zin. Young Argentine or Italian reds. Bordeaux Blanc and light Chard like Côte Chalonnaise can work well, too.

Chorizo Fino, Austrian Ries, Grüner Veltliner, but not a wine-friendly taste.

Crostini Dry Italian white such as Verdicchio or Orvieto. Or standard-grade (not Riserva) Morellino di Scansano, Montepulciano d'Abruzzo, Valpolicella.

Crudités Light red or rosé: Côtes du Rhône, Minervois, Chianti, Pinot N; or Fino Sherry. For whites: Alsace Sylvaner or Pinot Bl.

Dim sum Classically, China tea. For fun: Pinot Gr or Ries; light red (Bardolino or Loire). Non-vintage Champagne or gd New World fizz.

Eggs *See also* SOUFFLÉS. These present difficulties: they clash with most wines and can ruin good ones. But local wine with local egg dishes is a safe bet, so ★ →★★ of whatever is going. Try Pinot Bl or not too oaky Chard. As a last resort I can bring myself to drink Champagne with scrambled eggs.

    quails eggs Blanc de blancs Champagne.

    seagull (or gull) eggs Mature white Burgundy or vintage Champagne.

    oeufs en meurette Burgundian genius: eggs in red wine with glass of the same.

Escargots A comfort dish calling for Rhône reds (Gigondas, Vacqueyras). In Burgundy St-Véran or Aligoté. In the Midi, v.gd Petits-Gris ("little grey snails") go with local white, rosé or red. In Alsace, Pinot Bl or dry Muscat.

Fish terrine or fish salad Pfalz Ries Spätlese Trocken, Grüner Veltliner, premier cru Chablis, Clare Valley Ries, Sonoma Chard; or Manzanilla.

Foie gras Sweet white. In Bordeaux they drink Sauternes. Others prefer a late-harvest Pinot Gr or Ries (incl New World), Vouvray, Montlouis, Jurançon Moelleux or Gewurz. Tokaji Aszú 5 puttonyos is a Lucullan choice. Old, dry amontillado can be sublime. With hot foie gras, mature vintage Champagne. But not on any account Chard or Sauv Bl. Or red.

Goats cheese, warm Sancerre, Pouilly-Fumé, or New World Sauv Bl.

    chilled Chinon, Saumur-Champigny, or Provence rosé. Or strong red: Château Musar, Greek, Turkish, Australian sparkling Shiraz.

Guacamole Mexican beer. Or California Chard, Sauv Bl, dry Muscat, or non-vintage Champagne.

Haddock, smoked, mousse, soufflé or brandade Wonderful for showing off any stylish, full-bodied white, incl grand cru Chablis or Sonoma, South African or New Zealand Chard.

Ham, raw or cured *See also* PROSCIUTTO. Alsace Grand Cru Pinot Gr or gd, crisp Italian Collio white. With Spanish *pata negra* or *jamón*, Fino Sherry or Tawny Port. *See also* HAM, COOKED (Meat, poultry, game).

Herrings, raw or pickled Dutch gin (young, not aged) or Scandinavian *akvavit*, and cold beer. If wine essential, try Muscadet.

Mackerel, smoked An oily wine-destroyer. Manzanilla Sherry, proper dry Vinho Verde or schnapps, peppered or bison-grass vodka. Or gd lager.

Mayonnaise Adds richness that calls for a contrasting bite in the wine. Côte Chalonnaise whites (eg. Rully) are gd. Try New Zealand Sauv Bl, Verdicchio or a Spätlese Trocken. Or Provence rosé.

Mezze A selection of hot and cold vegetable dishes. Fino Sherry is in its element.

Mozzarella with tomatoes, basil Fresh Italian white, eg. Soave, Alto Adige. Vermintino from the coast. Or simple Bordeaux Blanc. *See also* AVOCADO.

Oysters, raw Non-vintage Champagne, premier cru Chablis, Muscadet, white Graves, Sancerre, or Guinness. Some like cold, light Sauternes.

    cooked Puligny-Montrachet or gd New World Chard. Champagne is gd with either.

Pasta Red or white according to the sauce or trimmings:

    cream sauce (eg. carbonara) Orvieto, Frascati, Alto Adige Chard.

    meat sauce Montepulciano d'Abruzzo, Salice Salentino, Merlot.

    pesto (basil) sauce Barbera, Ligurian Vermentino, New Zealand Sauv Bl, Hungarian Furmint.

    seafood sauce (eg. vongole) Verdicchio, Soave, white Rioja, Cirò, Sauv Bl.

    tomato sauce Chianti, Barbera, Sicilian red, Zin, South Australian Grenache.

Pastrami Alsace Ries, young Sangiovese or St-Emilion.

Pâté, chicken liver Calls for pungent white (Alsace Pinot Gr or Marsanne), a smooth red like a light Pomerol, Volnay or New Zealand Pinot N, or even Amontillado Sherry. More strongly flavoured pâté (duck, etc.) needs Châteauneuf-du-Pape, Cornas, Chianti Classico, Franciacorta or gd white Graves.

Pipérade Navarra rosado, Provence or southern French rosés. Or dry Australian Ries. For a red: Corbières.

Prawns, shrimps, or langoustines Fine dry white: burgundy, Graves, New Zealand Chard, Washington Ries, Pfalz Ries, Australian Ries – even fine mature Champagne. ("Cocktail sauce" kills wine, and in time, people.)

Prosciutto (also with melon, pears, or figs) Full, dry or medium white: Orvieto, Lugana, Grüner Veltliner, Tokaji Furmint, white Rioja, Australian Sem or Jurançon Sec.

Risotto Pinot Gr from Friuli, Gavi, youngish Sém, Dolcetto or Barbera d'Alba.
    with funghi porcini Finest mature Barolo or Barbaresco.
    nero A rich, dry white; Viognier or even Corton-Charlemagne.

Salads Any dry and appetizing white or rosé wine.
    NB Vinegar in salad dressings destroys the flavour of wine. Why don't the French know this? If you want salad at a meal with fine wine, dress it with wine or lemon juice instead of vinegar.

Salmon, smoked A dry but pungent white: fino (esp Manzanilla) Sherry, Alsace Pinot Gr, grand cru Chablis, Pouilly-Fumé, Pfalz Ries Spätlese, vintage Champagne. Vodka, schnapps or *akvavit*.

Soufflés As show dishes these deserve ★★★ wines.
    cheese Red burgundy or Bordeaux, Cab Sauv (not Chilean or Australian), etc. Or fine white burgundy.
    fish Dry white: ★★★ Burgundy, Bordeaux, Alsace, Chard, etc.
    spinach (tougher on wine) Mâcon-Villages, St-Véran or Valpolicella. Champagne can also be gd with the texture of soufflé.

Tapas Perfect with Fino Sherry, which can cope with the wide range of flavours in both hot and cold dishes. Or sake.

Tapenade Manzanilla or Fino Sherry, or any sharpish dry white or rosé.

Taramasalata A rustic southern white with personality; even possibly retsina. Fino Sherry works well. Try white Rioja or a Rhône Marsanne. A bland supermarket tarama submits to fine, delicate whites or Champagne.

Tempura The Japanese favour oaked Chard with acidity. I prefer Champagne.

Tortilla Rioja Crianza, Fino Sherry or white Mâcon-Villages.

Trout, smoked Sancerre; California or South African Sauv Bl. Rully or Bourgogne Aligoté, Chablis or Champagne. German Riesling Kabinett Feinherb.

Vegetable terrine Not a great help to fine wine, but Chilean Chard makes a fashionable marriage, Chenin Bl such as Vouvray a lasting one.

Whitebait Crisp dry whites, eg. Furmint, Greek, Touraine Sauv Bl, Verdicchio or Fino Sherry.

Fish

Abalone Dry or medium white: Sauv Bl, Côte de Beaune Blanc, Pinot Gr, Grüner Veltliner. Chinese-style: vintage Champagne (at least).

Anchovies, marinated Skip the marinade; it will clash with pretty well everything. Keep it light, white, dry and neutral.
    in olive oil or salted anchovies are fine without. A robust wine: red, white or rosé – try Rioja.

Bass, sea Weissburgunder from Baden or Pfalz. V.gd for any fine/delicate white, eg. Clare dry Ries, Chablis, white Châteauneuf-du-Pape. But strengthen the flavours of the wine according to the flavourings of the fish: ginger and spring onions need more powerful Ries.

Beurre blanc, fish with A top-notch Muscadet Sur Lie, a Sauv Bl/Sém blend, premier cru Chablis, Vouvray or a Rheingau Ries.

Brandade Premier cru Chablis, Sancerre Rouge, or New Zealand Pinot N.

Brill V. delicate: hence a top fish for fine old Puligny and the like.

Cod, roast Gd neutral background for fine dry/medium whites: Chablis, Meursault, Corton-Charlemagne, Cru Classé Graves, Grüner Veltliner, German Kabinett or Grosses Gewächs, or a gd lightish Pinot N.

black with miso sauce New Zealand or Oregon Pinot N. Or Rheingau Ries Spätlese.

Crab Crab and Ries are part of the Creator's plan.

Chinese, with ginger and onion German Ries Kabinett or Spätlese Halbtrocken. Tokaji Furmint, Gewurz.

cioppino Sauv Bl; but West Coast friends say Zin. Also California sparkling.

cold, dressed Alsace, Austrian or Rhine Ries; dry Australian Ries, or Condrieu.

softshell Chard or top-quality German Ries Spätlese.

Thai crabcakes Pungent Sauv Bl (Loire, South Africa, Australia, New Zealand) or Ries (German Spätlese or Australian).

with black bean sauce A big Barossa Shiraz or Syrah. Even Cognac.

with chilli and garlic Quite powerful Ries, perhaps German Grosses Gewächs or Wachau Austrian.

Curry A generic term for a multitude of flavours. Too much heat makes wine problematic: rosé is a gd bet. Hot-and-sour flavours (with tamarind, tomato for example) need acidity (perhaps Sauv Bl); mild, creamy dishes need richness of texture (dry Alsace Ries). But consider a big Shiraz to turn up the heat.

Eel, smoked Ries, Alsace, or Austrian or dry Tokaji Furmint. Or Fino Sherry, Bourgogne Aligoté. Schnapps.

Fish and chips, *fritto misto,* **tempura** Chablis, white Bordeaux, Sauv Bl, Pinot Bl, Gavi, Fino Sherry, Montilla, Koshu, tea; or non-vintage Champagne or Cava.

Fish baked in a salt crust Full-bodied white or rosé: Albariño, Sicily, Greek, Hungarian. Côtes de Lubéron or Minervois.

Fish pie (with creamy sauce) Albariño, Soave Classico, Alsace Pinot Gr or Ries, Spanish Godello.

Haddock Rich, dry whites: Meursault, California Chard, Marsanne, Grüner Veltliner.

Hake Sauv Bl or any fresh, fruity white: Pacherenc, Tursan, white Navarra.

Halibut As for TURBOT.

Herrings, fried/grilled Need a white with some acidity to cut their richness. Rully, Chablis, Muscadet, Bourgogne Aligoté, Greek, dry Sauv Bl. Or cider.

Kedgeree Full white, still or sparkling: Mâcon-Villages, South African Chard, Grüner Veltliner, German Grosses Gewächs or (at breakfast) Champagne.

Kippers A gd cup of tea, preferably Ceylon (milk, no sugar). Scotch? Dry Oloroso Sherry is surprisingly gd.

Lamproie à la Bordelaise 5-yr-old St-Emilion or Fronsac. Or Douro reds with Portuguese lampreys.

Lobster, richly sauced Vintage Champagne, fine white burgundy, Cru Classé Graves, California Chard or Australian Ries, Grosses Gewächs, Pfalz Spätlese.

cold with mayonnaise Non-vintage Champagne, Alsace Ries, premier cru Chablis, Condrieu, Mosel Spätlese or a local fizz.

Mackerel, grilled Hard or sharp white to cut the oil: Sauv Bl from Touraine, Gaillac, Vinho Verde, white Rioja, or English white. Or Guinness.

with spices White with muscle: Austrian Ries, Grüner Veltliner, German Grosses Gewächs.

Monkfish Often roasted, which needs fuller rather than leaner wines. Try New Zealand Chard, New Zealand/Oregon Pinot N or Chilean Merlot.

Mullet, grey Verdicchio, Rully, or unoaked Chard.

Mullet, red A chameleon, adaptable to gd white or red, esp Pinot N.

Mussels marinières Muscadet Sur Lie, premier cru Chablis, unoaked Chard.

stuffed, with garlic *See* ESCARGOTS.

Paella, shellfish Full-bodied white or rosé, unoaked Chard. Or the local Spanish red.

Perch, sandre Exquisite fish for finest wines: top white burgundy, grand cru Alsace Ries, or noble Mosels. Or try top Swiss Chasselas (eg. Dézaley, St-Saphorin).

Prawns with mayonnaise, Menetou-Salon,

with garlic Keep the wine light, white or rosé, and dry.

with spices Up to and incl chilli, go for a bit more body, but not oak: dry Ries gd.

Salmon, seared or grilled Pinot N is the fashionable option, but Chard is better. Merlot or light claret is not bad. Best is fine white burgundy, eg. Puligny- or Chassagne-Montrachet, Meursault, Corton-Charlemagne, grand cru Chablis; Grüner Veltliner, Condrieu, California/Idaho/New Zealand Chard, Rheingau Kabinett/Spätlese, Australian Ries.

fishcakes Call for similar (as for above) but less grand wines.

Sardines, fresh grilled V. dry white: Vinho Verde, Muscadet, or modern Greek.

Sashimi The Japanese preference is for white wine with body (Chablis Premier Cru, Alsace Ries) with white fish, Pinot N with red. Both need acidity: low-acidity wines don't work. Simple Chablis can be a bit thin. If soy is involved, then low-tannin red (again, Pinot). Remember sake (or Fino Sherry).

Scallops An inherently slightly sweet dish, best with medium-dry whites.

in cream sauces German Spätlese, Montrachets or top Australian Chard.

grilled or seared Hermitage blanc, Grüner Veltliner, Pessac-Léognan blanc, vintage Champagne or Pinot N.

with Asian seasoning New Zealand Chard, Chenin Bl, Verdelho, Godello, Gewurz.

Shellfish Dry white with plain shellfish, richer wines with richer sauces. Ries.

with plateaux de fruits de mer Chablis, Muscadet, Picpoul de Pinet or Alto Adige Pinot Bl.

Skate/raie with brown butter White with some pungency (eg. Pinot Gr d'Alsace or Roussanne), or a clean, straightforward wine like Muscadet or Verdicchio.

Snapper Sauv Bl if cooked with oriental flavours; white Rhône or Provence rosé with Mediterranean flavours.

Sole, plaice, etc., plain, grilled, or fried Perfect with fine wines: white burgundy or its equivalent.

with sauce According to the ingredients: sharp, dry wine for tomato sauce, fairly rich for creamy preparations.

Sushi Hot wasabi is usually hidden in every piece. German QbA Trocken wines, simple Chablis, or non-vintage brut Champagne. Or, of course, sake or beer.

Swordfish Full-bodied, dry white of the country. Nothing grand.

Tagine, with couscous North African flavours need substantial whites to balance – Austrian, Rhône – or crisp, neutral whites that won't compete. Preserved lemon demands something with acidity. Go easy on the oak.

Trout, grilled or fried Delicate white wine, eg. Mosel (esp Saar or Ruwer), Alsace Pinot Bl, Fendant.

Tuna, grilled or seared Best served rare (or raw) with light red wine: Cab Fr from the Loire, or Pinot N. Young Rioja is a possibility.

Turbot The king of fishes. Serve with your best rich, dry white: Meursault or Chassagne-Montrachet, Corton-Charlemagne, mature Chablis or its California, Australian or New Zealand equivalent. Condrieu. Mature Rheingau, Mosel or Nahe Spätlese or Auslese (not Trocken).

Meat, poultry, game

Barbecues The local wine: Australian, South African, Argentina are right in spirit. Reds need tannin.

Asian flavours (lime, coriander, etc.) Rosé, Pinot Gr, Ries.
    chilli Shiraz, Zin, Pinotage, Malbec.
    Middle Eastern (cumin, mint) Crisp, dry whites, rosé.
    oil, lemon, herbs Sauv Bl.
    red wine Cab Sauv, Merlot, Malbec, Tannat.
    tomato sauces Zin, Sangiovese.

Beef, boiled Red: Bordeaux (Bourgogne or Fronsac), Roussillon, Gevrey-Chambertin or Côte-Rôtie. Medium-ranking white burgundy is gd, eg. Auxey-Duresses. Or top-notch beer. Mustard softens tannic reds, horseradish kills everything – but can be worth the sacrifice.
    roast An ideal partner for your fine red wine of any kind. Amarone, perhaps? *See* above for mustard.
    stew, daube, Sturdy red: Pomerol or St-Emilion, Hermitage, Cornas, Barbera, Shiraz, Napa Cab Sauv, Ribera del Duero or Douro red.

Beef Stroganoff Dramatic red: Barolo, Amarone della Valpolicella, Priorat, Hermitage, late-harvest Zin – even Moldovan Negru de Purkar.

Boudin blanc **(white pork sausage)** Loire Chenin Bl, esp when served with apples: dry Vouvray, Saumur, Savennières; mature red Côte de Beaune if without.

Boudin noir **(blood sausage)** Local Sauv Bl or Chenin Bl – esp in the Loire. Or Beaujolais cru, esp Morgon. Or light Tempranillo.

Cabbage, stuffed Hungarian Cab Fr/Kadarka; village Rhône; Salice Salentino, Primitivo and other spicy southern-Italian reds. Or Argentine Malbec.

Cajun food Fleurie, Brouilly or New World Sauv Bl.
    with gumbo Amontillado.

Cassoulet Red from southwest France (Gaillac, Minervois, Corbières, St-Chinian or Fitou) or Shiraz. But best of all Beaujolais cru or young Tempranillo.

Chicken Kiev Alsace Ries, Collio, Chard, Bergerac Rouge.

Chicken/turkey/guinea fowl, roast Virtually any wine, incl v. best bottles of dry to medium white and finest old reds (esp burgundy). The meat of fowl can be adapted with sauces to match almost any fine wine (eg. *coq au vin* with red or white burgundy). With strong, spicy stuffing, Australian Shiraz.

Chilli con carne Young red: Beaujolais, Tempranillo, Zin, Argentine Malbec.

Chinese food Canton or Peking style Rosé or dry to medium-dry white – Mosel Ries Kabinett or Spätlese Trocken – can be gd throughout a Chinese banquet. Gewurz is often suggested but rarely works (though gd with ginger); Chasselas and Pinot Gr are attractive alternatives. Dry or off-dry sparkling (esp Cava) cuts the oil and matches sweetness. Eschew sweet/sour dishes but try St-Emilion ★★, New World Pinot N or Châteauneuf-du-Pape with duck. I often serve both white and red wines concurrently during Chinese meals. Champagne becomes a thirst-quencher.

Szechuan style Verdicchio, Alsace Pinot Bl or v. cold beer.

Choucroute garni Alsace Pinot Bl, Pinot Gr, Ries or lager.

Cold roast meat Generally better with full-flavoured white than red. Mosel Spätlese or Hochheimer and Côte Chalonnaise are v.gd, as is Beaujolais. Leftover cold beef with leftover vintage Champagne is bliss.

Confit d'oie/de canard Young, tannic red Bordeaux, California Cab Sauv and Merlot, and Priorat cut richness. Alsace Pinot Gr or Gewurz match it.

Coq au vin Red burgundy. Ideal: one bottle of Chambertin in the dish, two on the table.

Duck or goose Rather rich white: Pfalz Spätlese or off-dry grand cru Alsace. Or mature, gamey red: Morey-St-Denis, Côte-Rôtie, Bordeaux, burgundy. With oranges or peaches, the Sauternais propose drinking Sauternes, others Monbazillac or Ries Auslese. Mature, weighty vintage Champagne is gd, too, and handles red cabbage surprisingly well.

Peking *See* CHINESE FOOD.

  wild duck Big-scale red: Hermitage, Bandol, California or South African Cab Sauv, Australian Shiraz – Grange if you can afford it.

  with olives Top-notch Chianti or other Tuscans.

  roast breast & confit leg with Puy lentils Madiran, St-Emilion, Fronsac.

Frankfurters German/New York Ries, Beaujolais, light Pinot N. Budweiser (Budvar).

Game birds, young, plain-roasted The best red wine you can afford, but not a big Aussie one.

  older birds in casseroles Red (Gevrey-Chambertin, Pommard, Santenay or Grand Cru Classé St-Emilion, Napa Valley Cab Sauv or Rhône).

  well-hung game Vega Sicilia, great red Rhône, Château Musar.

  cold game Mature vintage Champagne.

Game pie, hot Red: Oregon Pinot N.

  cold Gd-quality white burgundy, cru Beaujolais, or Champagne.

Goulash Flavoursome young red: Hungarian Kékoportó, Zin, Uruguayan Tannat, Morellino di Scansano, Mencía, young Australian Shiraz. Or dry Tokaji.

Grouse *See* GAME BIRDS – but push the boat right out.

Haggis Fruity red, eg. young claret, young Portuguese red, New World Cab Sauv or Malbec, or Châteauneuf-du-Pape. Or, of course, malt whisky.

Ham, cooked Softer red burgundies: Volnay, Savigny, Beaune; Chinon or Bourgueil; sweetish German white (Rhine Spätlese); Tokaji Furmint or Czech Frankovka; lightish Cab Sauv (eg. Chilean), or New World Pinot N. And don't forget the heaven-made match of ham and Sherry. *See* HAM, RAW OR CURED.

Hamburger Young red: Australian Cab Sauv, Chianti, Zin, Argentine Malbec, Tempranillo. Or full-strength colas (not diet).

Hare Jugged hare calls for flavourful red: not-too-old burgundy or Bordeaux, Rhône (eg. Gigondas), Bandol, Barbaresco, Ribera del Duero, Rioja Reserva. The same for saddle, or for hare sauce with pappardelle.

Indian dishes Medium-sweet white, v. cold: Orvieto *abboccato*, South African Chenin Bl, Alsace Pinot Bl, Torrontés, Indian sparkling, Cava or non-vintage Champagne. Rosé can be a safe all-rounder. Tannin – Barolo or Barbaresco, or deep-flavoured reds such as Châteauneuf-du-Pape, Cornas, Australian Grenache or Mourvèdre, or Amarone della Valpolicella – will emphasize the heat. Soft reds can be easier. Hot-and-sour flavours need acidity.

Kebabs Vigorous red: modern Greek, Corbières, Chilean Cab Sauv, Zin, or Barossa Shiraz. Sauv Bl, if lots of garlic.

Kidneys Red: St-Emilion or Fronsac, Castillon, Nuits-St-Georges, Cornas, Barbaresco, Rioja, Spanish or Australian Cab Sauv, top Alentejo.

Lamb, roast One of the traditional and best partners for v.gd red Bordeaux – or its Cab Sauv equivalents from the New World. In Spain, the partner of the finest old Rioja and Ribera del Duero reservas; in Italy, ditto Sangiovese.

  cutlets or chops As for roast lamb, but a little less grand.

  slow-cooked roast Flatters top reds, but needs less tannin than pink lamb.

Liver Young red: Beaujolais-Villages, St-Joseph, Médoc, Italian Merlot, Breganze Cab Sauv, Zin, Tempranillo, Portuguese Bairrada.

  calves Red Rioja Crianza, Salice Salentino Riserva, Fleurie.

Meatballs Tangy, medium-bodied red: Mercurey, Crozes-Hermitage, Madiran, Morellino di Scansano, Langhe Nebbiolo, Zin, Cab Sauv.

  spicy Middle-Eastern style Simple, rustic red.

Moussaka Red or rosé: Naoussa from Greece, Sangiovese, Corbières, Côtes de Provence, Ajaccio, New Zealand Pinot N, young Zin, Tempranillo.

Mutton A stronger flavour than lamb, and not served pink. Robust but elegant red and top-notch, mature Cab Sauv, Syrah. Some sweetness of fruit suits it.

Osso bucco Low-tannin, supple red such as Dolcetto d'Alba or Pinot N. Or dry Italian white such as Soave and Lugana.

Ox cheek, braised Superbly tender and flavoursome, this flatters the best reds: Vega Sicilia, Bordeaux. Best with substantial wines.

Oxtail Rather rich red: St-Emilion, Pomerol, Pommard, Nuits-St-Georges, Barolo, or Rioja Reserva, Ribera del Duero, California or Coonawarra Cab Sauv, Châteauneuf-du-Pape, mid-weight Shiraz, Amarone.

Paella Young Spanish wines: red, dry white or rosé: Penedès, Somontano, Navarra or Rioja.

Pigeon Lively reds: Savigny, Chambolle-Musigny, Crozes-Hermitage, Chianti Classico, Argentine Malbec, or California Pinot N. Or Franken Silvaner Spätlese.

Pork, roast A gd, rich, neutral background to a fairly light red or rich white. It deserves ★★ treatment – Médoc is fine. Portugal's suckling pig is eaten with Bairrada Garrafeira; Chinese is gd with Pinot N.

    pork belly Slow-cooked and meltingly tender, this needs a red with some acidity. Italian would be gd: Dolcetto or Barbera. Loire red or lightish Argentine Malbec.

Pot au feu, bollito misto, cocido Rustic reds from the region of origin; Sangiovese di Romagna, Chusclan, Lirac, Rasteau, Portuguese Alentejo, Spain's Yecla or Jumilla.

Quail Carmignano, Rioja Reserva, mature claret, Pinot N. Or a mellow white: Vouvray or St-Péray.

Rabbit Lively, medium-bodied young Italian red or Aglianico del Vulture; Chiroubles, Chinon, Saumur-Champigny or Rhône rosé.

    with prunes Bigger, richer, fruitier red.

    as ragù Medium-bodied red with acidity.

Satay Australia's McLaren Vale Shiraz, or Alsace or New Zealand Gewurz. Peanut sauce is a problem with wine.

Sauerkraut (German) Lager or Pils. (But *see also* CHOUCROUTE GARNI.)

Sausages *See also* CHARCUTERIE, FRANKFURTERS. The British banger requires a young Malbec from Argentina (a red wine, anyway), or British ale.

Shepherd's pie Rough-and-ready red seems most appropriate, eg. Sangiovese di Romagna, but either beer or dry cider is the real McCoy.

Steak

    au poivre A fairly young Rhône red or Cab Sauv.

    filet or tournedos Any red (but not old wines with Béarnaise sauce: top New World Pinot N or Californian Chard is better).

    Fiorentina **(*bistecca*)** Chianti Classico Riserva or Brunello. The rarer the meat, the more classic the wine; the more well-done, the more you need New World, fruit-driven wines. Argentina Malbec is the perfect partner for steak Argentine style, ie. cooked to death.

    Korean *yuk whe* (the world's best steak tartare) Sake.

    tartare Vodka or light young red: Beaujolais, Bergerac, Valpolicella.

    T-bone Reds of similar bone structure: Barolo, Hermitage, Australian Cab Sauv or Shiraz.

Steak-and-kidney pie or pudding Red Rioja Reserva or mature Bordeaux.

Stews and casseroles Burgundy such as Nuits-St-Georges or Pommard if fairly simple; otherwise lusty, full-flavoured red: young Côtes du Rhône, Toro, Corbières, Barbera, Shiraz, Zin, etc.

Sweetbreads A rich dish, so grand wine: Rheingau Ries or Franken Silvaner Spätlese, grand cru Alsace Pinot Gr or Condrieu, depending on sauce.

Tagines These vary enormously, but fruity young reds are a gd bet: Beaujolais, Tempranillo, Sangiovese, Merlot, Shiraz.

Tandoori chicken Ries or Sauv Bl, young red Bordeaux, or light north Italian red served cool. Also Cava and non-vintage Champagne.

Thai dishes Ginger and lemon grass call for pungent Sauv Bl (Loire, Australia, New Zealand, South Africa) or Ries (Spätlese or Australian).

    coconut milk Hunter Valley and other ripe, oaked Chards; Alsace Pinot Bl (refreshing); Gewurz, Verdelho. Prosecco or non-vintage Champagne.

Tongue Gd for any red or white of abundant character, esp Italian. Also Beaujolais, Loire reds, Tempranillo, and full, dry rosés.

Veal, roast Gd for any fine old red that may have faded with age (eg. Rioja Reserva) or a German or Austrian Ries, Vouvray, Alsace Pinot Gr.

Venison Big-scale reds, incl Mourvèdre, solo as in Bandol or in blends. Rhône, Bordeaux or California Cab Sauv of a mature vintage; or rich white – Pfalz Spätlese or Alsace Pinot Gr. With a sharp berry sauce, try a German Grosses Gewächs Ries or a New World Cab Sauv.

Vitello tonnato Full-bodied whites: Chard; light reds (eg. Valpolicella) served cool.

Wild boar Serious red: top Tuscan or Priorat. New Zealand Syrah.

Vegetarian dishes

(see also FIRST COURSES)

Baked pasta dishes Pasticcio, lasagne and cannelloni with elaborate vegetarian fillings and sauces: an occasion to show off a grand wine, esp finest Tuscan red, but also claret and burgundy. Gavi if you want white.

Beetroot Mimics a flavour found in red burgundy. You could return the compliment.

    and goats cheese gratin Sauv Bl.

Cauliflower cheese Crisp, aromatic white: Sancerre, Ries Spätlese, Muscat, English Seyval Bl, Godello.

Couscous with vegetables Young red with a bite: Shiraz, Corbières, Minervois; or well-chilled rosé from Navarra or Somontano; or a robust Moroccan red.

Fennel-based dishes Sauv Bl: Pouilly-Fumé or one from New Zealand; English Seyval Bl or young Tempranillo.

Grilled Mediterranean vegetables Brouilly, Barbera, Tempranillo or Shiraz.

Lentil dishes Sturdy reds such as Corbières, Zin or Shiraz.

    dhal, with spinach Tricky. Soft, light red or rosé is best – and not top-flight.

Macaroni cheese As for CAULIFLOWER CHEESE.

Mushrooms (in most contexts) Gd with many reds. Pomerol, California Merlot, Rioja Reserva, top burgundy, or Vega Sicilia. On toast, best claret. Ceps/porcini, Ribera del Duero, Barolo, Chianti Rufina, Pauillac or St-Estèphe.

Onion/leek tart Fruity, off-dry or dry white: Alsace Pinot Gr or Gewurz, Canadian or New Zealand Ries, English whites, Jurançon, Australian Ries. Or Loire red.

Peppers or aubergines (eggplant), stuffed Vigorous red wine: Nemea, Chianti, Dolcetto, Zin, Bandol, Vacqueyras.

Pumpkin/squash ravioli or risotto Full-bodied, fruity dry or off-dry white: Viognier or Marsanne, demi-sec Vouvray, Gavi or South African Chenin.

Ratatouille Vigorous young red: Chianti, New Zealand Cab Sauv, Merlot, Malbec, Tempranillo; young red Bordeaux, Gigondas or Coteaux du Languedoc.

Spanacopitta (spinach and feta pie) Young Greek or Italian red or white.

Spiced vegetarian dishes See INDIAN DISHES, THAI DISHES (MEAT, POULTRY, GAME).

Watercress, raw Makes every wine on earth taste revolting. Soup is slightly easier, but doesn't require wine.

Wild garlic leaves, wilted Tricky: a fairly neutral white with acidity will cope best.

Desserts

Apple pie, strudel or tarts Sweet German, Austrian or Loire white, Tokaji Aszú or Canadian Icewine.

Apples, Cox's Orange Pippins Vintage Port (and sweetmeal biscuits) is the Saintsbury [wine] Club plan.

Bread-and-butter pudding Fine 10-yr-old Barsac, Tokaji Aszú or Australian botrytized Sem.

Cakes and gâteaux *See also* CHOCOLATE, COFFEE, GINGER, RUM. Bual or Malmsey Madeira, Oloroso or Cream Sherry.

    cupcakes Prosecco presses all the right buttons.

Cheesecake Sweet white: Vouvray, Anjou, or fizz – refreshing, nothing special.

Chocolate A talking point. Generally only powerful flavours can compete. Bual, California Orange Muscat, Tokaji Aszú, Australian Liqueur Muscat, 10-yr-old Tawny Port; Asti for light, fluffy mousses. Experiment with rich, ripe reds: Syrah, Zin, even sparkling Shiraz. Banyuls for a weightier partnership. Médoc can match bitter black chocolate. Or a tot of gd rum.

    and olive oil mousse 10-yr-old Tawny Port or as for black chocolate, above.

Christmas pudding, mince pies Tawny Port, Cream Sherry or liquid Christmas pudding itself, Pedro Ximénez Sherry. Asti or Banyuls.

Coffee desserts Sweet Muscat, Australian Liqueur Muscats, or Tokaji Aszú.

Creams, custards, fools, syllabubs *See also* CHOCOLATE, COFFEE, GINGER, RUM. Sauternes, Loupiac, Ste-Croix-du-Mont or Monbazillac.

Crème brûlée Sauternes or Rhine Beerenauslese, best Madeira or Tokaji Aszú. (With concealed fruit, a more modest sweet wine.)

Crêpes Suzette Sweet Champagne, Orange Muscat or Asti.

Fruit

    blackberries Vintage or LBV Port.

    dried fruit (and compotes) Banyuls, Rivesaltes, Maury. Tokaji Aszú.

    flans and tarts Sauternes, Monbazillac, sweet Vouvray or Anjou.

    fresh Sweet Coteaux du Layon or light, sweet Muscat.

    poached, ie. apricots, pears, etc. Tokaji Aszú, Sweet Muscatel: try Muscat de Beaumes-de-Venise, Moscato di Pantelleria or Spanish dessert Tarragona.

    salads, orange salad A fine sweet Sherry or any Muscat-based wine.

Ginger flavours Sweet Muscats, New World botrytized Ries and Sém. Late-harvest Gewurz.

Ice-cream and sorbets Fortified wine (Australian Liqueur Muscat, Banyuls). Pedro Ximénez Sherry, Amaretto liqueur with vanilla; rum with chocolate.

Lemon flavours For dishes like tarte au citron, try sweet Ries from Germany or Austria, or Tokaji Aszú; v. sweet if lemon is v. tart.

Meringues Recioto di Soave, Asti or top vintage Champagne, well-aged.

Mille-feuille A delicate sweet sparkling white, such as Moscato d'Asti or demi-sec Champagne.

Nuts (including praliné) Finest Oloroso Sherry, Madeira, Vintage or Tawny Port (nature's match for walnuts), Tokaji Aszú, Vin Santo or Setúbal Moscatel.

    salted nut parfait Tokaji Aszú, Vin Santo.

Orange flavours Experiment with old Sauternes, Tokaji Aszú. Of course California Orange Muscat.

Panettone Jurançon *moëlleux*, late-harvest Ries, Barsac, Tokaji Aszú.

Pears in red wine A pause before the Port. Or try Rivesaltes, Banyuls or Ries Beerenauslese.

Pecan pie Orange Muscat or Liqueur Muscat.

Raspberries (no cream, little sugar) Excellent with fine reds, which themselves taste of raspberries: young Juliénas, Regnié.

Rum flavours (baba, mousses, ice-cream) Muscat – from Asti to Australian Liqueur, according to weight of dish.

Salted caramel mousse/parfait Late-harvest Ries, Tokaji Aszú.

Strawberries, wild (no cream) Serve with red Bordeaux (most exquisitely Margaux) poured over.

Strawberries and cream Sauternes or similar sweet Bordeaux, Vouvray *moëlleux* or *vendange tardive* Jurançon.

Summer pudding Fairly young Sauternes of a gd vintage.

Sweet soufflés Sauternes or Vouvray *moëlleux*. Sweet (or rich) Champagne.

Tiramisú Vin Santo, young Tawny Port, Muscat de Beaumes-de-Venise, Sauternes or Australian Liqueur Muscat.

Trifle Should be sufficiently vibrant with its internal Sherry.

Zabaglione Light-gold Marsala or Australian botrytized Sem or Asti.

WINE & CHEESE

The notion that wine and cheese were married in heaven is not borne out by experience. Fine red wines are slaughtered by strong cheeses; only sharp or sweet white wines survive. Principles to remember (despite exceptions): first, the harder the cheese, the more tannin the wine can have; second, the creamier the cheese is the more acidity needed in the wine. Cheese is classified by its texture and the nature of its rind, so its appearance is a guide to the type of wine to match it. Below are examples. I try to keep a glass of white wine for my cheese.

Bloomy rind soft cheeses, pure-white rind if pasteurized, or dotted with red: Brie, Camembert, Chaource, Bougon (goats milk "Camembert") Full, dry white burgundy or Rhône if the cheese is white and immature; powerful and fruity St-Emilion, young Australian (or Rhône) Shiraz/Syrah or Grenache if it's mature.

Blue cheeses Roquefort can be wonderful with Sauternes, but don't extend the idea to other blues. It is the sweetness of Sauternes, esp old, that complements the saltiness. Stilton and Port, preferably tawny, is a classic. Intensely flavoured old Oloroso or Amontillado Sherry, Madeira, Marsala, and other fortified wines go with most blues.

Fresh, no rind – cream cheese, crème fraîche, mozzarella Light, crisp white – simple Bordeaux Blanc, Bergerac, English unoaked whites; rosé: Anjou, Rhône; v. light, young, fresh red: Bordeaux, Bardolino or Beaujolais.

Hard cheeses, waxed or oiled, often showing marks from cheesecloth – Gruyère family, Manchego and other Spanish cheeses, Parmesan, Cantal, Comté, old Gouda, Cheddar and most "traditional" English cheeses Particularly hard to generalize here; Gouda, Gruyère, some Spanish, and a few English cheeses complement fine claret or Cab Sauv and great Shiraz/Syrah wines. But strong cheeses need less refined wines, preferably local ones. Sugary, granular old Dutch red Mimolette or Beaufort are gd for finest mature Bordeaux. Also for Tokaji Aszú. But try white wines, too.

Natural rind (mostly goats cheese) with bluish-grey mould (the rind becomes wrinkled when mature), sometimes dusted with ash – St-Marcellin Sancerre, Valençay, light, fresh Sauv Bl, Jurançon, Savoie, Soave, Italian Chard, lightly oaked English whites.

Semi-soft cheeses, thickish grey-pink rind – Livarot, Pont l'Evêque, Reblochon, Tomme de Savoie, St-Nectaire Powerful white Bordeaux, Chard, Alsace Pinot Gr, dryish Ries, southern Italian and Sicilian whites, aged white Rioja, dry Oloroso Sherry. But the strongest of these cheeses kills most wines.

Washed-rind soft cheeses, with rather sticky, orange-red rind – Langres, mature Epoisses, Maroilles, Carré de l'Est, Milleens, Münster Local reds, esp for Burgundy cheeses; vigorous Languedoc, Cahors, Côtes du Frontonnais, Corsican, southern Italian, Sicilian, Bairrada. Also powerful whites, esp Alsace Gewurz and Muscat.

FOOD & FINEST WINES

With very special bottles, the wine guides the choice of food rather than the other way around. The following are based largely on the gastronomic conventions and newer experiments of the wine regions making these treasures, plus much diligent research. They should help bring out the best in your best wines.

Red wines

Red Bordeaux and other Cab Sauv-based wines (v. old, light and delicate wines: eg. pre-1959, with exceptions such as 1945). Leg or rack of young lamb, roast with a hint of herbs (but not garlic); *entrecôte*; simply roasted partridge or grouse or sweetbreads.

Fully mature great vintages (eg. Bordeaux 59 61 82 85) Shoulder or saddle of lamb, roast with a touch of garlic, roast ribs or grilled rump of beef.

Mature but still vigorous (eg. 89 90) Shoulder or saddle of lamb (incl kidneys) with rich sauce. Fillet of beef *marchand de vin* (with wine and bone-marrow). Avoid beef Wellington: pastry dulls the palate.

Merlot-based Bordeaux (Pomerol, St-Emilion) Beef as above (fillet is richest) or well-hung venison.

Côte d'Or red burgundy Consider weight and texture, which grow lighter/more velvety with age. Also consider the character of the wine: Nuits is earthy, Musigny flowery, great Romanées can be exotic, Pommard renowned for its four-squareness. Roast chicken or capon is a safe standard with red burgundy; guinea-fowl for slightly stronger wines, then partridge, grouse or woodcock for those progressively more rich and pungent. Hare and venison (*chevreuil*) are alternatives.

    great old burgundy The Burgundian formula is cheese: Epoisses (unfermented); a fine cheese but a terrible waste of fine old wines.

    vigorous younger burgundy Duck or goose roasted to minimize fat. Or *faisinjan* (pheasant cooked in pomegranate juice). Or smoked gammon.

Great Syrahs: Hermitage, Côte-Rôtie, Grange; Vega Sicilia Beef (such as the super-rich, super-tender, super-slow-cooked ox cheek I had at Vega Sicilia), venison, well-hung game; bone marrow on toast; English cheese (esp best farm Cheddar) but also hard goats milk and ewes milk cheeses such as England's Berkswell and Ticklemore.

Rioja Gran Reserva, Pesquera... Richly flavoured roasts: wild boar, mutton, saddle of hare, whole suckling pig.

Barolo, Barbaresco Risotto with white truffles; pasta with game sauce (eg. *pappardelle alla lepre*); porcini mushrooms; Parmesan.

Amarone Classically, in Verona, *risotto all'Amarone* or *pastissada*. But if your butcher doesn't run to horse, then shin of beef, slow-cooked in more Amarone.

Great vintage Port or Madeira Walnuts or pecans. A Cox's Orange Pippin and a digestive biscuit is a classic English accompaniment.

White wines

Beerenauslese/Trockenbeerenauslese Biscuits, peaches, greengages. Desserts made from rhubarb, gooseberries, quince, apples.

Supreme white burgundy (Montrachet, Corton-Charlemagne) or equivalent Graves Roast veal, farm chicken stuffed with truffles or herbs under the skin, or sweetbreads; richly sauced white fish or scallops as above. Or lobster or poached wild salmon.

Very good Chablis, white burgundy, other top-quality Chards White fish simply grilled or *meunière*. Dover sole, turbot, halibut are best; brill, drenched in butter, can be excellent. (Sea bass is too delicate; salmon passes but does little for the finest wine.)

Condrieu, Château-Grillet, Hermitage Blanc V. light pasta scented with herbs and tiny peas or broad beans.

Grand cru Alsace: Riesling *Truite au bleu*, smoked salmon, or *choucroute garni*.

Pinot Gris Roast or grilled veal. Or truffle sandwich (slice a whole truffle, make a sandwich with salted butter and gd country bread – not sourdough or rye – wrap and refrigerate overnight. Then toast it in the oven.

Gewurztraminer Cheese soufflé (Münster cheese).

Vendange tardive Foie gras or tarte tatin.

Old vintage Champagne (not blanc de blancs) As an apéritif, or with cold partridge, grouse, woodcock. The evolved flavours of old Champagne make it far easier to match with food than the tightness of young wine. Hot foie gras can be sensational. Don't be afraid of garlic or even Indian spices, but omit the chilli.

Late-disgorged old wines have extra freshness plus tertiary flavours. Try with truffles, lobster, scallops, crab, sweetbreads, pork belly, roast veal, chicken.

Rosé Pigeon.

Sauternes Simple crisp, buttery biscuits (eg. *langues de chat*), white peaches, nectarines, strawberries (without cream). Not tropical fruit. Pan-seared foie gras. Lobster or chicken with Sauternes sauce. Château d'Yquem recommends oysters. Experiment with blue cheeses. Rocquefort is classic, but needs a powerful wine.

Supreme Vouvray *moëlleux*, etc. Buttery biscuits, apples, apple tart.

Tokaji Aszú (5–6 puttonyos) Foie gras is recommended. Fruit desserts, cream desserts, even chocolate can be wonderful. It even works with some Chinese, though not with chilli – the spice has to be adjusted to meet the sweetness. Szechuan pepper is gd. Havana cigars are splendid. So is the naked sip.

France

More heavily shaded areas are
the wine-growing regions.

Abbreviations used in the text:

Al	Alsace
Beauj	Beaujolais
Burg	Burgundy
B'x	Bordeaux
Champ	Champagne
Cors	Corsica
C d'O	Côte d'Or
L'doc	Languedoc
Lo	Loire
Mass C	Massif Central
Prov	Provence
Pyr	Pyrenees
N/S Rhô	Northern/Southern Rhône
Rouss	Roussillon
Sav	Savoie
SW	Southwest
AC	appellation contrôlée
ch, chx	château(x)
dom, doms	domaine(s)

This year, more than ever, we'll be seeking value when we buy wine.
And France has it in spades; you don't even have to go far off the
beaten track. You may wonder why France, which invented fine wine
and still makes the most desired, also does value. Is it the inner passion,
the terroir, just a knack?

Let's be glad of it, however it happens. With two superb vintages
under its belt, middle-range Bordeaux is a good hunting ground;
Sauternes (except for Yquem) continues to be undervalued. Dry white
Graves with a few years of bottle age can be superb, and superb value.
Basic Bourgogne Rouge from a good producer can deliver a lot of
burgundian seduction for remarkably little money, and the 2010s are
superb. Provence is expensive, but neighbouring Languedoc, with an

array of interesting grapes, varies from underpriced to overpriced;
Alsace, even at the very top end, is underpriced for the amount of
complexity and fascination it delivers. Remember that the Rhône, even
at the top end, has yet to catch up with top Bordeaux prices, and quality
can be superb – there's been a run of good vintages here, too. The other
great river, the Loire, delivers lovely, unflashy reds and, from the Chenin
Blanc grape, whites of fine minerality. Sauvignon Blanc from Sancerre
and Pouilly can be very good, but if you want value, Chenin should be
the one on your list.

Individuals mean as much as appellations; often more. A lesser
wine from a talented, hardworking producer is better, and probably
cheaper, than a supposedly top wine from a lazy one.

France entries also cross-reference to Châteaux of Bordeaux

Recent vintages of the French classics

Red Bordeaux

Médoc/Red Graves For some wines, bottle age is optional: for these it is indispensable. Minor châteaux from light vintages need only two or three years, but even modest wines of great years can improve for 15 or so, and the great châteaux of these years can profit from double that time.

2011 Complicated year: spring drought, cool July, rain, heat, rot. Hail in St-Estèphe. Work in the vineyard counted. Be very selective.

2010 Another outstanding year. Difficult flowering and tiny berries: smaller crop than 2009. One of driest summers ever: magnificent Cab Sauv, deep-coloured, concentrated, firmly structured. At a price.

2009 Outstanding year, touted as "The Greatest". Hot, dry summer and extended sunny harvest have produced structured wines with an exuberance of fruit. Don't miss this.

2008 Much better than expected; fresh, classic flavours. Cab Sauv ripened in late-season sun. Yields down due to poor fruit set, mildew, frost. Later drinking than 2009.

2007 Miserable summer, huge attack of mildew spelled a difficult year. Easy drinking; not many will age. Be selective.

2006 Cab Sauv difficulty ripening; best fine, tasty, nervous, long-ageing. Good colour, acidity. Starting to drink.

2005 Perfect weather conditions throughout the year. Rich, balanced, long-ageing wines from an outstanding vintage. Keep all major wines.

2004 Mixed bag; top wines good, classic. Drinking now, best will age further.

2003 Hottest summer on record. Cab Sauv can be great (St-Estèphe, Pauillac). Atypical but rich, powerful at best (keep), unbalanced at worst (drink up). Be warned. Soon, for most.

2002 Saved by a dry, sunny September. Later-ripening Cab Sauv benefited most. Some good wines if selective. Drink now–2018.

2001 A cool September and rain at vintage meant Cab Sauv was not super-ripe. Some excellent fresh wines, drink now–2015.

2000 Superb wines throughout. Start tentatively on all but the top wines.

1999 Vintage rain again diluted ripe juice; so-so wines to drink now.

1998 Good (especially Pessac-Léognan), but the Right Bank is clearly the winner this year. Drink now–2015.

1997 Uneven flowering and summer rain were a double challenge. Most wines faded now.

Older fine vintages: 96 95 90 89 88 86 85 82 75 70 66 62 61 59 55 53 49 48 47 45 29 28.

St-Emilion/Pomerol

2011 Complicated as in the Médoc. Lower alcohol than 2010 and 2009. Good Cab Fr. Pomerol perhaps best overall.

2010 Outstanding. Powerful wines again with high alcohol. Small berries so a lot of concentration.

2009 Again, outstanding. Powerful wines (high alcohol) but seemingly balanced. Hail in St-Emilion cut production at certain estates.

2008 Similar conditions to the Médoc. Late harvest into November. Tiny yields helped quality, which is surprisingly good. Start to drink.

2007 Same pattern as the Médoc. Huge disparity in picking dates (up to five weeks). Extremely variable, but nothing to keep for long.

2006 Rain and rot at harvest. Earlier-ripening Pomerol a success but St-Emilion and satellites variable.

2005 Same conditions as the Médoc. An overall success. Start to drink.

2004 Merlot often better than 2003 (Pomerol). Good Cab Fr.

2003 Merlot suffered in the heat, but exceptional Cab Fr. Very mixed. Top St-Emilion on the plateau good. Most need drinking.

2002 Problems with rot and ripeness. Modest to good. Drink.

2001 Less rain than Médoc during vintage. Some powerful Merlot, sometimes better than 2000. Drinking now–2015.

2000 Similar conditions to Médoc. Less kind to Merlot, but a very good vintage.

1999 Careful, lucky growers made good wines; rain a problem. Drink.

1998 Earlier-ripening Merlot largely escaped rain. Some excellent. Now–2016.

1997 Merlot suffered in the rain. Most wines faded.

Older fine vintages: 95 90 89 88 85 82 71 70 67 66 64 61 59 53 52 49 47 45.

Red Burgundy

Côte d'Or Côte de Beaune reds generally mature sooner than grander wines of Côte de Nuits. Earliest drinking dates are for lighter commune wines – eg. Volnay, Beaune; latest for largest wines, eg. Chambertin, Romanée. Even the best burgundies are more attractive young than equivalent red Bordeaux.

2011 Some parallels with 2007, an early harvest but indifferent summer. But, thicker skins in 2011 mean more structured wine. Small crop again.

2010 Much better than expected after a fairly dismal summer. Small crop, with notably small bunches, saved the day. Fresh and classic red.

2009 Beautiful, ripe, plump reds, ready before 2005s. Beware overripe ones.

2008 Fine, fresh, structured wines from those who avoided fungal diseases, disaster for others. Pick carefully. Start drinking.

2007 Small crop of attractive, perfumed wines. Many now ready to drink.

2006 An attractive year in Côte de Nuits (less rain) with power to develop in medium term. Côte de Beaune reds good now.

2005 Best for more than a generation, outstanding everywhere. Top wines must be kept, however tempting.

2004 Lighter wines, some pretty, others spoiled by herbaceous notes. Drink up.

2003 Reds coped with the heat better than the whites. Muscular, rich. Best outstanding, others short and hot.

2002 Middleweight wines of great class with an attractive point of freshness. Now showing real class. No hurry.

2001 Just needed a touch more sun for excellence. Good to drink now.

2000 Gave more pleasure than expected, but drink up now.

1999 Big, ripe vintage; good colour, bags of fruit, steely tannins, most ready now, but top wines will improve.

1998 Ripe fruit but dry tannins. Those in balance look good now.

Older fine vintages: 96 95 93 90 88 85 78 71 69 66 64 62 61 59 (all mature).

White Burgundy

Côte de Beaune White wines now rarely made for ageing as long as they used to. Top wines should still improve for up to ten years.

2011 A large harvest; fine potential for conscientious producers, but the good old boys will have overcropped.

2010 Exciting wines with good fruit-acid balance, some damaged by September storms. Meursault and Corton-Charlemagne looking good.

2009 Fine crop of healthy grapes; definitely charming, but enough acidity to age?
2008 Small crop, ripe flavours yet high acidity. Very fine; keep best. 2012–20.
2007 Big crop – those who picked late did very well. Drink soon.
2006 Plentiful crop of charming, aromatic wines. Drink up.
2005 Small, outstanding crop of dense, concentrated wines. Give them time.
2004 Aromatic, sometimes herbaceous whites. Drink soon.
2003 Hot vintage; all but the best are falling over fast.
2002 Stylish wines showing very well, but drink up.
Mâconnais (Pouilly-Fuissé, St-Véran, Mâcon-Villages) follow a similar pattern, but don't last as long – appreciated more for their freshness than their richness.

Chablis Grand cru Chablis of vintages with both strength and acidity can age superbly for up to ten years; premiers crus proportionately less, but give them three years at least.

2011 A larger crop of potentially attractive wines.
2010 Harvested at same time as Côte d'Or, with excellent results. Fine vintage: body, powerful mineral acidity. Keepers.
2009 Rich, accessible wines, less mineral than 2007 or 2008. 2012–2016.
2008 Excellent. Small crop, powerful, juicy wines; ageing potential. 2012–20.
2007 Brilliant grands crus and premiers crus where not damaged by hail. Basic Chablis more modest. 2012–2017.
2006 An early harvest of attractive, aromatically pleasing wines. But drink up.
2005 Small but outstanding crop of dense, concentrated wines. 2012–2017.

Beaujolais 11 Third smasher in a row! 10 Compact and concentrated, very fine. 09 Wonderful, the best for years, has reignited interest in Beaujolais. 08 Tough going with widespread hail. 07 Attractive but without the heart of a really great year. 05 Concentrated wines.

Southwest France

2011 Unparalleled enthusiasm: the best year since 2005? Question mark over sweet late-harvest wines.
2010 Once again an Indian summer ensured a good crop overall.
2009 Reliable for current drinking. Reds and dry whites generally successful, but the stickies were spoilt by November rain.
2008 A moderate year. Late sunshine just about saved the day.
2007 Turned out better than expected. Sweet whites surprisingly successful.
2006 Reds now mostly at their peak. Whites won't keep much longer.
2005 Great year. Bigger wines can still improve. Sweet whites can live longer.

The Midi

2011 Coolish summer, so fresher wines, fine quality and good quantity.
2010 Fine quality throughout; yields lower than usual due to summer drought.
2009 A cool spring, a hot, dry summer. Quality is excellent.
2008 Similar to 2007; some elegant wines. Severe hail damage in Faugères.
2007 Some beautifully balanced wines with some ageing potential.
2006 Fine results from the best winemakers.

Northern Rhône

2011 Patchy, careful selection needed. Good domaines made fruity, fine wines, mid-weight, aromatic. Better than 2008. Whites variable, fresh.
2010 Wonderful. Marvellous Syrahs, balance, freshness, flair. Long, beautiful life ahead. Must-buy year. Very good Condrieu, rich whites elsewhere.

2009 Excellent. Some deeply flavoured, rich Hermitage reds, very full Côte-Rôtie. Good, lively Crozes and St-Joseph. Rather big whites that can live.

2008 Rain; wines gaining depth bit by bit. Top names best. Good, clear whites – will live (Condrieu). Reds: 8–12 years.

2007 Shapely, attractive depth. Steady gain over time. Best Hermitage, Côte-Rôtie, Cornas, St-Joseph life of 18+ years. Good whites, depth to live well.

2006 Big crop, wines of richness. Have improved well, especially Côte-Rôtie. Good acidity in robust whites, heady Condrieu.

2005 Exceptional, be in no hurry. Long ageing potential for Hermitage, Cornas and the fullest Côte-Rôtie. Whites are full, doing well now.

2004 Mid-weight; Côte-Rôtie showing well over time; fine reds from top vineyards. Superb whites singing now, a complex maturity emerging.

2003 Intense sun gave cooked "southern" flavours. Best reds show genuine richness, coming together, slight regain of terroir. 25+ yrs for best.

2002 Heavy rain. Stick to best growers. Hermitage, Cornas until 2015–18. Good whites, especially Condrieu.

2001 Lovely vintage. Reds ageing well. Top year at Côte-Rôtie. Often very good whites. Good value if available.

Southern Rhône

2011 Immediate, supple fruit, very drinkable. Challenge will be for serious, keeping wines. Ripening uneven, big crop, hence some variation. Medium-lived year. High alcohol an issue. Very good whites, rosés.

2010 Lovely year, many excellent reds. Small crop, great balance. Clear-fruited, rich wines. Interesting, full whites, too.

2009 Full reds. Drought: baked features, grainy tannins. Very ripe Châteauneuf reds; Vacqueyras, Gigondas very good; Côtes du Rhône/villages reds good now. Sound whites.

2008 Dodgy. Best have body, some charm, drinking OK now; life 15 years or so. Stay with top names. Very good, lively whites.

2007 Very good: Grenache-only wines are big, but drink with gusto. Exceptional Châteauneuf from top names. Very good Gigondas. Drink up Côtes du Rhônes, whites.

2006 Underrated; some very good reds. Rich Châteauneuf: more open than 2005, less sweet, potent than 2007. Good full whites, ideal for food.

2005 Very good. Slow ageing year. Tight-knit, concentrated. Will age well: 20+ years for top Châteauneufs. Whites best young.

2004 Good, but variable. Mineral, intricate flavours in Châteauneuf. Gigondas: best profound. Starting to drink well now. Complex whites ageing well.

2003 Slowly coming together, a surprise. Chunky, high-octane wines with baked, date/raisin flavours from the best, eg. Châteauneuf. Best can live long. Pick best names, best areas.

2002 Drink up. Simply fruited, early reds, acceptable whites. Gigondas best.

2001 Excellent classic vintage. Complex reds, lots of life ahead; be patient for top areas. Châteauneuf, Lirac on form now.

2000 Tasty, open wines, led by fruit, singing now.

1999 Very good from best names. Châteauneuf reds have moved up a step with age. Very good Gigondas, also good for top Lirac names.

Champagne

2011 Year of extremes. Warm spring and hot June, cold July and unsettled August were challenging twists. Some picked too early. Best for grand cru Pinot N and Chard.

2009 A year of ripeness, charm and refined aromas that will give great
　　　pleasure earlier than the 2008s. Sumptuous Pinot N from the Aube.
2008 Clearly one of the two best vintages of the 'noughties. Classic balance:
　　　acidity and ripeness: a real keeper, but more austere than the lovely 2002.
2006 Ripe, expressive, especially Pinot N. Supple, fine, tasting better by the day.
2005 Not a great year overall: a bit hot for real class, wines lacking dash and
　　　verve, often foursquare and pedestrian.
2004 Classic finesse. A vintage year for drinking now, but will hold.
2002 Great, graceful year: superb Pinot N and sumptuous Chard. Best released
　　　'90s vintage. Brilliant Dom Pérignon, Bollinger Grand Année. No hurry.
Older fine vintages: 2000 96 95 92 90 89 88 82.

The Loire

2011 Topsy-turvy year. Hot dry spring, vines flowering from early May. Cool
　　　wet July/August. Heat in September/October. Year of the viticulturalist,
　　　and picking date. Rot in Muscadet. Quality very variable.
2010 Big climatic variations across region. Good in Muscadet, Anjou, much of
　　　Touraine and central vineyards. Montlouis and Vouvray very difficult –
　　　rot. Fine sweets in Anjou.
2009 Generally very good, but drought in parts of Anjou-Touraine, hail damage
　　　in Menetou-Salon, Sancerre. High alcohol a problem in some Sauv Bl.
2008 Very healthy grapes, high acidity. Good age-worthy reds, excellent dry
　　　whites (Chenin Bl); sweets hit by wet November.
2007 Producer's name crucial. Austere, dry whites, really exceptional Anjou
　　　sweets. Drink up reds.
2006 Only the conscientious succeeded. Dry whites fared well, some age-
　　　worthy reds. Not great for sweet whites.
2005 Excellent. Buy without fear, though some reds quite tannic.

Alsace

2011 Warm spring, very wet July and August, summer until mid-October.
　　　Straightforward wines for early drinking.
2010 Extreme; very small crop, Excellent wines for long-keeping, most
　　　naturally dry.
2009 Great Pinot Gr and Gewurz; some fine late-harvest wines.
2008 Dry, crisp wines (Ries); a pleasing antidote to the unctuous style of late.
2007 Hot spring; cold, wet summer; sunny autumn: ripe grapes. Fine drinking
　　　2012–13.
2006 Hottest recorded July followed by coolest August. Top names made
　　　subtle, fine Ries.
2005 Ripe, well-balanced wines. Some exceptional late-harvest wines (Gewurz).
2004 Growers who picked early made some classic wines. Subtle year (Ries).

Abel-Lepitre Champ Discreet CHAMPAGNE house, improving under BOIZEL Chanoine
　　　ownership. Fine CUVÉE Idéale NV, impressive BRUT Vintage 05 06 08 09.
　　　Excellent Cuvée 134 (blend of two CHARD yrs). Widely available in France.
Abymes Sav w ★ DYA. Hilly area nr Chambéry; light, mild Vin de Savoie AC from
　　　Jacquère grape has alpine charm. SAVOIE has many such crus.
Ackerman Lo r p w (dr) (sw) (sp) ★-★★ Major négociant. Founded in 1811 – first
　　　SAUMUR sparkling wine. Alliance Loire (eight CAVE-CO-OPS) a shareholder.
　　　Ackerman group, incl Rémy-Pannier, has wines from throughout Loire, often
　　　made at its own wineries. Le Master Muscadet relaunched and Monmousseau
　　　(TOURAINE) bought in 2010. *See* its blog: Xnoir.

Agenais SW Fr r p w ★ DYA IGP of Lot-et-Garonne. Some independents, esp biodynamic ones, worth searching out in preference to co-ops. Try gd-value DOMS Lou Gaillot and Campet.

Alliet, Philippe Lo r w ★★→★★★ 02 04 05' 06 08 09' 10 (11) Top CHINON producer; CUVÉES to age. Best: oak-aged Coteau du Noire from steep slope, VIEILLES VIGNES from flat gravel and hill v'yd L'Huisserie. A little CHINON Blanc.

Aloxe-Corton r w ★★→★★★ 99' 02' 03 05' 06 07 08 09' 10' 11 Famous for its GRANDS CRUS (CORTON, CORTON-CHARLEMAGNE) but less interesting at village or PREMIER CRU level. Reds can be attractive if not overextracted. Best producers: Follin-Arbelet, PIERRE ANDRÉ, Senard, TOLLOT-BEAUT.

Alquier, Jean-Michel L'doc r w Leading FAUGÈRES producer. White MARSANNE/GRENACHE BLANC. IGP gd; also SAUV Les Pierres Blanches IGP, red CUVÉES Les Premières from younger vines, Maison Jaune and age-worthy old-vine SYRAH, Les Bastides.

Alsace Al (r) w (sw) (sp) ★★→★★★★ 00' 02' 04 05' 06 08 09' 10 11 The sheltered east slope of the Vosges Mts makes France's Rhine wines: aromatic, fruity, full-strength, mostly dry and expressive of variety. Sugar levels vary widely: dry wines now easier to find. Much sold by variety (PINOT BL, RIES, GEWURZ). Matures well (except Pinot Bl, MUSCAT) 5–10 yrs; GRAND CRU even longer. Gd-quality and -value CRÉMANT. Formerly fragile PINOT N improving fast, esp in 2010. See VENDANGE TARDIVE, SÉLECTION DES GRAINS NOBLES.

Alsace Grand Cru Al w ★★★→★★★★★ 90' 95 96 97 98 00' 02' 04 05' 06 07 08 09'10' 11 restricted to 51 (KAEFFERKOPF added in 2006) of the best named v'yds (approx 1,600ha, 800 in production) and four noble grapes (RIES, PINOT GR, GEWURZ, MUSCAT), mainly dry, some sweet. New, much-needed production rules incl higher min ripeness, ban chaptalization.

Amiel, Mas Rouss r w sw ★★★ Pioneering and innovative MAURY DOM. Others following. Warming CÔTES DU ROUSSILLON *Carérades* (r), Altaïr (w), *vin de liqueur* Plénitude from MACABEO. Vintage and cask-aged VDN. Prestige 15 yrs a star. STÉPHANE DERENONCOURT (B'X) consults.

Amirault, Yannick Lo r ★★→★★★★ 02 03 04 05' 06 08' 09' 10 (11) Top producer of both BOURGUEIL and ST-NICOLAS-DE-BOURGUEIL, now organic, and with son, Benoît. Top CUVÉES La Petite Cave and Les Quartiers in BOURGUEIL and Malagnes and La Mine in St-Nicolas; all age-worthy.

Ampeau, Robert C d'O MEURSAULT DOM with unique record for fine old vintages.

André, Pierre C d'O ★★ Sound producer, mix of négociant and grower at CH Corton-André, ALOXE-CORTON; 5ha of v'yds in and around CORTON, much improved under ownership of Ballande Group.

Anjou Lo r p w (dr) (sw) (sp) ★→★★★★ Both region and umbrella AC covering Anjou and SAUMUR. Many styles: CHENIN BL dry whites range from light quaffers to potent agers; juicy reds, incl GAMAY; juicy CAB FR-based Anjou Rouge; structured ANJOU-VILLAGES, incl CAB SAUV. Also strong, mainly dry SAVENNIÈRES; lightly sweet to luscious COTEAUX DU LAYON CHENIN BL; dry and sweet rosé and sparkling. AC Anjou v. variable; but can be excellent and v.gd value. Tiny ex-VDQS Vin de Thouarsais absorbed by AC Anjou (2011).

Anjou-Coteaux de la Loire Lo w sw s/sw ★★→★★★ 02 03 05' 07 09' 10 (11) Small (38ha) westernmost ANJOU AC for sweet whites (CHENIN BL); less rich but nervier than COTEAUX DU LAYON. Esp Delaunay, Fresche, Musset-Roullier, CH de Putille.

Anjou-Villages Lo r ★→★★★ 02 03 05' 06 08 09' 10 (11) Superior central ANJOU AC for reds (CAB FR/CAB SAUV, but a few pure Cab Sauv often top wines). Quality tends to be high and prices reasonable, esp DOMS de Brancherau, Brizé, CADY, Clos de Coulaine, Philippe Delesvaux, Bergerie, Ogereau, CH PIERRE-BISE. Sub-AC Anjou-Villages-Brissac covers the same zone as COTEAUX DE L'AUBANCE; look for Bablut, Dom de Haute Perche, Montigilet, Richou, Rochelles, Ch de Varière.

Appellation Contrôlée (AC or AOC) / AOP Government control of origin and production (not quality) of most top French wines; around 45% of the total. Now being converted to AOP (Appellation d'Origine Protegée).

Aprémont Sav w ★★ DYA One of the best villages of SAVOIE for pale, delicate whites, mainly from Jacquère grapes, but recently incl CHARD.

Arbin Sav r ★★ Deep-coloured, lively red from MONDEUSE grapes, rather like a gd Loire CAB SAUV. Ideal après-ski. Drink at 1–2 yrs.

Arbois Jura r p w (sp) ★★→★★★ Various gd and original light but tasty wines; specialty is VIN JAUNE. On the whole DYA, except Vin Jaune.

Ariège SW Fr r ★ 09 10 (11) IGP betweenToulouse and Spain. SYRAH-based red from DOM des Coteaux d'Engravies ahead of field. Also DOMS Sabarthès, Lastronques.

Arlaud C d'O ★★★ Fine MOREY-ST-DENIS estate with CHARMES-CHAMBERTIN, CLOS DE LA ROCHE, etc.; energized by new generation, now ploughing by horse. Superb BOURGOGNE Roncevie.

Arlot, Domaine de l' C d'O ★★★ Leading exponent in CÔTE DE NUITS of whole-bunch fermentation. Wines pale but aromatic and full of fruit. Look out for NUITS-ST-GEORGES, esp Clos de l'Arlot and Clos des Forêts St Georges. Gd whites, too. Will style change under new management from 2011?

Armand, Comte C d'O ★★★ Sole owner of exceptional Clos des Epeneaux, POMMARD, as well as other v'yds in AUXEY and VOLNAY. On top form since 1999. Biodynamic.

Aube Champ Southern extension of CHAMPAGNE, known as Côte des Bar. V.gd PINOT N in 2009.

Auxey-Duresses C d'O r w ★★→★★★ 99′ 02′ 03 05′ 06 07 08 09′ 10′ 11 CÔTE DE BEAUNE village tucked away out of sight. Slightly tough wines, but gd things to be had – esp mineral whites. Best: (r) COMTE ARMAND, MAISON LEROY, Prunier; (w) Lafouge, Maison Leroy (Les Boutonniers).

Aveyron SW Fr r p w (recent IGP) NATURAL winemakers (eg. ★★ Nicolas Carmarans, ★★ Patrick Rols) beginning to explore this undeveloped terroir using local grape varieties (eg. Négret de Banhars).

Avize Champ One of the top Côte des Blancs CHARD villages. Most complete wines.

Aÿ Champ One of the best PINOT N villages of CHAMPAGNE. Velvety wines.

Ayala Champ Revitalized AÿÀ-based house, owned by BOLLINGER. Fine BRUT Nature zéro *dosage* and v.gd Rosé. Excellent Prestige Perle d'Ayala (02′ 04 06 08 09).

A barrique is a Bordeaux wine barrel holding c.225 litres of wine, or 300 bottles.

Bandol Prov r p (w) ★★★ 96 97 98 99 00 01 02 03 04 05 06 07 08 09 10 11 Small coastal AC; PROVENCE's finest. Barrel-aged reds of enormous potential, predominantly MOURVÈDRE, with GRENACHE and CINSAULT; elegant rosé from young vines, and a drop of white from CLAIRETTE, UGNI BLANC and occasionally SAUV BL. Stars incl: DOMS de la Laidière, Lafran Veyrolles, La Suffrène, TEMPIER, Pibarnon, Mas de la Rouvière, La Bégude, La Bastide Blanche.

Banyuls Rouss br sw ★★→★★★ Wonderful VDN, mainly GRENACHE (Banyuls GRAND CRU, aged 2 yrs+). Newer vintage style resembles Ruby Port; far better, more original are traditional RANCIOS, aged for yrs. Think fine old Tawny Port, or even Madeira. Best: DOMS du Mas Blanc (★★★), la Rectorie (★★★), Vial Magnères, Coume del Mas (★★), la Tour Vieille (★★★). *See also* MAURY.

Barrique The B'X (and Cognac) term for an oak barrel holding 225 litres. Barrique-ageing to flavour almost any wine with oak was a craze in late 1980s. These days taste and price (of barrels) inspire caution.

Barsac Saut w sw ★★→★★★★ 83′ 86′ 88′ 89′ 90′ 95 96 97′ 98 99′ 01′ 02 03′ 05′ 07′ 09′ 10′ (11) Neighbour of SAUTERNES with similar superb botrytized wines from lower-lying limestone soil; fresher, less powerful, with more finesse. Repays long ageing. Top: CLIMENS, COUTET, DOISY-DAËNE, DOISY-VÉDRINES, NAIRAC.

Barthod, Ghislaine C d'O ★★★→★★★★ Impressive range of archetypal CHAMBOLLE-MUSIGNY. Marvellous poise and delicacy, yet depth and concentration. Nine PREMIER CRUS, incl Les Cras, Fuées, Beauxbruns.

Barton & Guestier B'X négociant now part of the group Castel (2010).

Bâtard-Montrachet C d'O w ★★★★ 99' 00 02' 04' 05' 06 07' 08' 09' 10 11 12ha GRAND CRU down-slope from MONTRACHET itself. Powerful, rich wines, occasionally a touch chunky. Also worthy siblings Bienvenues-B-M and Criots B-M. Seek out: Bachelet-Monnot, J-M BOILLOT, CARILLON, GAGNARD, FAIVELEY, LATOUR, DOM LEFLAIVE, MOREY, Pernot, Ramonet, SAUZET.

Baudry, Domaine Bernard Lo r p w ★★→★★★ 02 03 05 06 08 09' 10 (11) Excellent CHINON across the range, from CHENIN BL-based whites to CAB FR-based rosés and CHINON CUVÉES of red – from juicy Les Granges to structured Les Grézeaux, Clos Guillot and Croix Boissées. Son Matthieu now in charge.

Baudry-Dutour Lo r p w ★★→★★★ 02 03 05' 06 08 09' 10 (11) Merger in 2003 of DOMS de la Perrière and de la Roncée. CHINON's largest producer (120ha), incl CHX de St Louand and La Grille (bought 2009). Reliable quality from light, early-drinking to age-worthy reds. Modern winery at Panzoult and now la Grille.

Baumard, Domaine des Lo r p w sw sp ★★→★★★★ 03 05' 06 07' (sw) 08 09 10 (11) Leading family producer of ANJOU wine, esp CHENIN BL-based whites, incl SAVENNIÈRES (Clos St Yves, Clos du Papillon), QUARTS DE CHAUME and Clos Ste Catherine. Makes a tangy VDT from VERDELHO. Proponent of cryoextraction – freezing grapes to concentrate sugars for sweet wine. Mounting a legal challenge to Quarts de Chaume GRAND CRU?

Baux de Provence, Les Prov r p w ★★→★★★ 04 05 06 07 08 09 10 V'yds on lower slopes of dramatic bauxite outcrop of the Alpilles, topped by village of Les Baux. White mainly from Clairette, Grenache, Rolle, Roussanne. Most v'yds organic. Best estate by far is TRÉVALLON: CAB SAUV/SYRAH blend (IGP for lack of GRENACHE). Also Mas de la Dame, DOM Hauvette, Ste Berthe, CH Romanin.

Béarn SW Fr r p w ★→★★ r 09 10 (11') (w p) DYA. AOP incl rosés from MADIRAN and JURANÇON growers. Béarn and Jurançon co-ops now merged. Béarn whites dull. Best reds from ★★ DOM Lapeyre/Guilhémas.

Beaujolais Beauj r (p) (w) ★ DYA. The most basic appellation of the huge Beaujolais region, producing five million cases a yr. Some from the hills can be excellent. Will the rest be rebranded as COTEAUX BOURGUIGNONS?

Beaujolais Primeur / Nouveau Beauj The BEAUJOLAIS of the new vintage, made in a hurry (often only four to five days' fermenting) for release at midnight on the 3rd Wednesday in Nov. Ideally soft, pungent, fruity and tempting; too often crude, sharp, alcoholic. More of an event than a drink.

Beaujolais-Villages Beauj r ★★ 09' 10' 11' The middle category between straight BEAUJOLAIS and the ten named crus, such as MOULIN-À-VENT. Best locations around Beaujeu and Lantigné, worth waiting for.

Beaumes-de-Venise S Rhô r (p) (w) br ★★ (r) 05' 06 07' 08 09' 10' (MUSCAT) DYA. Since 1956 VDN Muscat, from southeast CÔTES DU RHÔNE, favourite local apéritif: sweet, honeyed, aromatic, peach/apricot flavours, rather elegant (eg. DOMS Beaumalric, Bernardins, Coyeux, Durban, JABOULET, Pigeade (v.gd), VIDAL-FLEURY, co-op. Gd with melon, rich fish, soft cheese, chocolate. Punchy, chiselled, high-altitude reds, best in ripe yrs. (CH Redortier, Doms Cassan, de Fenouillet, Durban, St-Amant.) Leave for 2–3 yrs. Simple whites (some VIOGNIER), up-tempo rosés are Côtes du Rhône.

Beaumont des Crayères Champ Côte d'Epernay co-op making excellent PINOT MEUNIER-based Grande Rés NV and v. fine Fleur de Prestige 98 02 04. Exceptional CHARD-led CUVÉE Nostalgie 02'. Fleur de Rose 02 04 05.

Beaune C d'O r (w) ★★★ 02' 03 05' 07 08 09' 10' 11 Historic wine capital of Burgundy, home to many merchants: BOUCHARD, CHAMPY, CHANSON, DROUHIN, JADOT, LATOUR, Remoissenet as well as HOSPICES DE BEAUNE. No GRAND CRU v'yds but some lovely red PREMIER CRU eg. Avaux, Bressandes, Cras, Grèves, Teurons, Clos du Roi; and an increasing amount of white, of which Drouhin's CLOS DES MOUCHES stands out.

Becker, Caves J Al ★→★★ An organic estate, progressively biodynamic. Stylish, well-balanced wines, incl exceptional GRAND CRU Froehn in GEWURZ and RIES 04 06 08 09.

Bellet Prov r p w ★★ DYA. The wine of Nice; tiny AC; v'yds within city boundary, but often ignored there. White from Rolle grape is best, with unexpected ageing potential. Braquet and Folle Noire for light red. Few producers: CH de Bellet is oldest; also Les Coteaux de Bellet, Clos St Vincent, DOM de la Source.

Bellivière, Domaine de Lo r w sw ★★→★★★ 03 05' 07 08 09' 10' (11) 13ha biodynamic DOM run by Christine and Eric Nicolas: precise CHENIN BL in JASNIÈRES and COTEAUX DU LOIR and Pineau d'Aunis.

Bergerac SW Fr r p w dr sw ★→★★★ 05' 06 07'(sw) 08 09 10 (11') Dordogne's cheaper alternative to B'X (same grapes). Best: ★★★ DOMS Clos des Verdots, *Tour des Gendres*, Jonc Blanc, Les Marnières, Monastier la Tour; ★★ CHX Belingard-Chayne, Fontenelles, Grinou, de la Mallevieille. Recommended growers in MONBAZILLAC, MONTRAVEL, PÉCHARMANT, ROSETTE, SAUSSIGNAC.

Bertrand, Gérard L'doc r p w ★★ Energetic, ex-rugger player, one of biggest v'yd owners in south; Villemajou in CORBIÈRES cru Boutenac, Laville-Bertou in MINERVOIS-LA LIVINIÈRE, l'Hospitalet in La Clape, l'Aigle in LIMOUX, la Sauvageonne in TERRASSES DU LARZAC and IGP PAYS D'OC Cigalus. Best wines: La Viala (MINERVOIS), La Forge (Corbières), l'Hospitalet (la Clape).

Besserat de Bellefon Champ Épernay house specializing in gently sparkling CHAMPAGNES (old CRÉMANT style). Part of LANSON-BCC group. Gd value.

Beyer, Léon Al ★★→★★★ V. fine, intense, dry wines that often need 10 yrs+ bottle age. Superb RIES Comtes d'Eguisheim, but no mention on label of its v'yd, GRAND CRU PFERSIGBERG. Pure, dry wines for great cuisine. Listed by many top restaurants.

Bichot, Maison Albert Burg ★★→★★★ Dynamic merchant and owner/distributor of LONG-DEPAQUIT (CHABLIS), Clos Frantin and more. Quality on the rise.

Billecart-Salmon Champ Family CHAMPAGNE house making exquisite long-lived wines, vintage CUVÉES fermented in wood. Superb Clos St-Hilaire BLANC DE NOIRS (96' 98' 99), NF Billecart (97! 98 99 00), top BLANC DE BLANCS (98' 99 00) and BRUT 04 and Extra BRUT ★★★ NV. New Cuvée Sous Bois. Exquisite *Elizabeth Salmon Rosé* 99' 02.

Bize, Simon C d'O ★★→★★★ Key producer in SAVIGNY-LÈS-BEAUNE with wide range of PREMIER CRU v'yds, esp Vergelesses; also exciting, gd-value BOURGOGNE (r w). Top wine: LATRICIÈRES-CHAMBERTIN.

Blagny C d'O r ★★→★★★ 99' 02' 03' 05' 07 08 09' 10' 11 On hill adjoining MEURSAULT. Austere reds now out of fashion as growers replant with CHARD to make Meursault-Blagny. Best red v'yds: Pièce sous le Bois, Sous le Dos d'Ane, La Jeunelotte. Best growers (r): Matrot, Martelet de Cherisey.

Blanc de Blancs Any white wine made from white grapes only, esp CHAMPAGNE. An indication of style, not of quality.

Blanc de Noirs White (or slightly pink or "blush") wine made from red grapes, esp CHAMPAGNE.

Blanck, Paul & Fils Al ★★→★★★ Grower at Kientzheim producing huge range of wines. Finest from 6ha GRAND CRU Furstentum (RIES, GEWURZ, PINOT GR) and grand cru SCHLOSSBERG (great Ries 02' 06 08 09' 10). Also gd PINOT BL.

Blanquette de Limoux L'doc w sp ★★ Fair-value, creamy fizz from cooler hilly area southwest of Carcassonne; older history than CHAMPAGNE. Base of Mauzac much improved by CHARD, CHENIN BL and, more recently, PINOT N, esp in newer AC

CRÉMANT de Limoux. Large co-op with Sieur d'Arques label. Also Rives-Blanques, Martinolles. Antech, Laurens, Fourn.

Blaye B'x r ★→★★ 03 04 05' 06 08 09' 10' Designation for top, concentrated reds (lower yields, etc.) from what used to be Premières Côtes de Blaye, now new AC (2008) BLAYE-CÔTES DE B'X (*see* box p.103).

Blaye-Côtes de Bordeaux B'x r w ★→★★ 04 05' 06 08 09' 10' Mainly red AC east of the Gironde. Formerly Premières Côtes de Blaye but new designation in 2008 (*see* box p.103). Greatly improved quality. Best CHX: Bel Air la Royère, Gigault (CUVÉE Viva), Haut-Bertinerie, Haut-Colombier, Haut-Grelot, Jonqueyres, Monconseil-Gazin, Mondésir-Gazin, Montfollet, Roland la Garde, Segonzac, des Tourtes.

Boillot C d'O Interconnected Burgundy growers. Look for Jean-Marc (POMMARD) ★★★ for fine oaky reds and whites, Henri (DOM in VOLNAY, merchant in MEURSAULT) ★★→★★★, Louis (Chambolle, married to GHISLAINE BARTHOD) ★★★ and his brother Pierre (Gevrey) ★★→★★★.

Boisset, Jean-Claude Burg New kid on the Burgundy block, now respectable after 40 yrs. Own wines and own v'yds; DOM DE LA VOUGERAIE excellent. Also owns range of other businesses, latest Rodet. Projects in Canada, California, Chile, Uruguay looked after by son Jean-Charles, now married to Gina Gallo of eponymous US giant.

Boizel Champ V.gd. mature BLANC DE BLANCS NV and *prestige* Joyau de France (02' 04 08), Joyau Rosé (02' 04 06 08). Also Grand Vintage BRUT (02' 04 06 08) and CUVÉE Sous Bois. Fine quality, easy prices.

Bollinger Champ Great classic CHAMPAGNE house, on a roll in recent vintages (viz Grande Année 95' 97 00 02). Superb GA Rosé 02. Luxury wines: RD (96' 02), VIEILLES VIGNES Françaises (02) from ungrafted PINOT N vines, La Côte aux Enfants, AŸ (02' 05 09). *See also* LANGLOIS-CH.

Bonneau du Martray, Domaine C d'O r w (r) ★★ (w) ★★★★ Scintillating, mineral CORTON-CHARLEMAGNE from hyper-meticulous producer with top holding in the heart of the AC. Red CORTON fine but pricy.

Bonnes-Mares C d'O r ★★★→★★★★ 90' 91 95 96' 98 99' 00 02' 03 05' 06 07 08 09' 10' 11 GRAND CRU (15ha) between CHAMBOLLE-MUSIGNY and MOREY-ST-DENIS. Sturdy, long-lived wines, less fragrant than Musigny. Best: Drouhin-Laroze, DUJAC, Groffier, JADOT, ROUMIER, DE VOGÜÉ, VOUGERAIE.

Bonnezeaux Lo w SW ★★★→★★★★ 89' 90' 95' 96' 97 02 03' 05' 07' 09 10 (11') Magnificently rich, almost everlasting CHENIN BL top site in COTEAUX DU LAYON. Now less rigorous than QUARTS DE CHAUME. Esp: CHX de Fesles, de Varière, DOMS les Grandes Vignes, du Petit Val.

Bordeaux (B'x) r (p) w ★→★★ 05' 08 09' 10' Catch-all AC for generic B'x (represents nearly half the region's production). Mixed quality, but usually recognizable. Most brands are in this category.

Bordeaux Supérieur B'x r ★→★★ 04 05' 08 09' 10' Superior denomination to above. Higher min alcohol, lower yield, longer ageing. Mainly bottled at the property. Make the most of the delicious 2009s.

Social *climat*

Burgundy is campaigning for UNESCO World Heritage Status for the Côte d'Or *climats* – an area that is 50km long and that covers 1,247 *climats*. What's a *climat*, you ask? It's a purely Burgundian term and means a plot of vines. Most go back centuries, even 1,000 yrs or more. The fragmented v'yds of the Côte d'Or are unique, and while they're not an exact reflection of the region's complicated geology, they're pretty close.

Borie-Manoux B'x Admirable B'x shipper, CH-owner. Chx incl BATAILLEY, BEAU-SITE, Croix du Casse, DOM DE L'EGLISE, HAUT-BAGES-MONPELOU, TROTTEVIEILLE.

Bouchard Père & Fils Burg ★★→★★★★ Huge v'yd owner – largest in CÔTE D'OR? Whites esp strong in MEURSAULT and CHEVALIER-MONTRACHET. Flagship red is BEAUNE Grèves, Vigne de L'Enfant Jésus. Part of HENRIOT Burgundian interests with WILLIAM FÈVRE (CHABLIS) and Villa Ponciago (BEAUJOLAIS).

Bouches-du-Rhône Prov r p w ★ IGP from Marseille environs. Simple, fruit-filled reds from southern varieties, plus CAB SAUV, SYRAH and MERLOT.

Bourgeois, Henri Lo ★★→★★★ 02 05 06 07 08 10 (11) Leading SANCERRE grower/merchant. V. dynamic family. Also POUILLY-FUMÉ, MENETOU-SALON, QUINCY, COTEAUX DU GIENNOIS, CHÂTEAUMEILLANT, IGP Petit Bourgeois. Top: MD de Bourgeois, La Bourgeoise (r w), Jadis, Sancerre d'Antan. Clos Henri in Marlborough, NZ.

Bourgogne Burg r (p) w ★★ (r) 05' 09' 10 11 (w) 09' 10 11 Ground-floor AC for Burgundy, ranging from mass-produced to bargain beauties from fringes of CÔTE D'OR villages, top tip for value. Sometimes comes with subregion attached, eg. CÔTE CHALONNAISE, or local would-be appellation, Chitry, Tonnerre, etc. Can also be from declassified BEAUJOLAIS crus.

Bourgogne Grand Ordinaire Burg r (w) ★ DYA. Who invented this crazy name for the most basic of Burgundy? It is about to become COTEAUX BOURGUIGNONS instead. GAMAY (r); CHARD, ALIGOTÉ, MELON DE BOURGOGNE (w).

Bourgogne Passe-Tout-Grains Burg r (p) ★ Age 1–2 yrs. The name suggests you can put any grape in, but in fact it must be a mix of PINOT N (more than 30%) and GAMAY. Can be fun from CÔTE D'OR DOMS.

Bourgueil Lo r (p) ★★→★★★(★) 96' 02 03 05' 06 08 09' 10' (11) Burly, full-flavoured TOURAINE reds and big, fragrant rosés based on CAB FR. Gd vintages can age 15 yrs. Esp AMIRAULT, Audebert, DOMS de la Butte, la Chevalerie, Delaunay, Druet, Jamet, Lamé Delisle Boucard, Minière, Nau Frères. *See* ST-NICOLAS-DE-BOURGUEIL.

Bouvet-Ladubay Lo ★ ★★★ Major sparkling SAUMUR house owned by Indian United Breweries. Barrel-fermented CUVÉE Trésor (w p) best. Also still wines mainly from ANJOU-SAUMUR. Hosts annual Journées Nationales du Livre and du Vin.

Bouzereau C d'O ★★→★★★ Family in MEURSAULT making gd whites at gd prices and improving reds. Jean-Baptiste (son of Michel B) and Vincent B are the two best.

Bouzeron Burg w ★★ CÔTE CHALONNAISE AC (since 1998) for ALIGOTÉ, with stricter rules and greater potential than straight BOURGOGNE AC. Best from A & P de Villaine.

Bouzy Rouge Champ r ★★★ 90 95 96 97 99 02 05 Still red of famous PINOT N village. Like v. light burgundy, but can last well in sunny vintages.

Brocard, J-M Chab ★★→★★★ One of the recent success stories of CHABLIS with a fine range of wines at all levels. Also on offer: a range of BOURGOGNE *blancs* from different soil types (Kimmeridgian, Jurassic, Portlandian).

Brouilly Beauj r ★★ 05' 09' 10' 11' Biggest of the ten crus of BEAUJOLAIS: fruity, round, refreshing wine, can age 3–4 yrs. Top growers: CHX de la Chaize, de Pierreux; Dubost, Martray, Michaud, Piron.

Brumont, Alain SW Fr ★★★ r w Still makes the running in MADIRAN. Oaky red, Le Tyre, CH MONTUS, DOM BOUSCASSÉ all need long keeping. Torus and ★IGPS (eg.100% GROS MANSENG, TANNAT/CAB blends) are earlier drinking.

Brut Champ Term for the dry classic wines of CHAMPAGNE.

Brut Ultra / Zéro Term for bone-dry wines in CHAMPAGNE – also known as Brut Nature – back in fashion and improved, with precision and freshness.

Bugey Sav r p w sp ★→★★ DYA VDQS for light sparkling, still, or half-sparkling wines from Roussette (or Altesse) and CHARD (gd). Best from Montagnieu; also Rosé de Cerdon, mainly GAMAY.

Burguet, Alain C d'O ★★→★★★ Compact VIGNERON for outsize GEVREY-CHAMBERTIN, esp *Mes Favorites*. Sons Eric and Jean-Luc now in charge.

FRANCE

Buxy Burg w Village in AC MONTAGNY with gd co-op for CHARD and PINOT N.

Buzet SW Fr r (p) (w) ★★ 08 09 10 (11') Powerful co-op seeks monopoly of this upstream B'X neighbour. Quirky, biodynamic independent ★★★ DOM du Pech outclasses the field. Also ★★ CHX du Frandat, De Salles.

Cabardès L'doc r ★→★★ 05 06 07 08 09 10 11 B'X CAB and MERLOT meet MIDI SYRAH and GRENACHE for original blends, 60% max B'x grapes, 40% min Midi. Best is DOM de Cabrol with Vin de l'Est, Vin d'Ouest; also Jouclary, Font Juvénal, Cazaban. CH Pennautier is largest.

Champagne growers to watch in 2013

Francis Boulard et Fille Massif St-Thierry grower making v.gd multi-vintage CUVÉE Petraea and superb all-CHARD Les Rachais (02 ★★★★★ 04 05 06 08').

Claude Cazals Exciting Extra-BRUT BLANC DE BLANCS (99 02' 04) and exceptional Clos Cazals (96 ★★★★ 99 02 04).

Richard Cheurlin One of best grower-winemakers of the Aube. Rich but balanced Carte d'Or and vintage-dated Cuvée Jeanne (02 04 05 06). New Cuvée Coccinelle & Papillon, NATURAL and chemical-free.

Pierre Cheval-Gatinois Impeccable Aÿ producer of mono-cru Champagnes and excellent still COTEAUX CHAMPENOIS (02 05 08 09).

Gonet-Médeville Exciting DOM with fine holdings in Ambonnay and LE MESNIL. Gastronomic Champagnes built to last: superb Chante Alouette Le Mesnil and Ambonnay Grandes Ruelles (both 02).

Benoît Lahaye Fine organic BOUZY grower, precise, elegant wines: excellent Essentiel NV BRUT, BLANC DE NOIRS and 05 06 08' vintage for long ageing.

Champagne Lallier Bijou AŸ producer, making exemplary Champagne from GRAND CRU grapes. Fine Tradition Brut, ★★★★ BRUT ZÉRO aged *sous liège* (clamped cork).

Jean-Luc Lallement Exceptional Verzenay grower making muscular yet exquisitely refined Blanc de Noirs. His first vintage wines will be available in 2012. Great rosé, too.

Lilbert et fils Scion of blue-chip Cramant DOM takes his GRAND CRU Chard Champagnes to higher level: great purity of flavours, great energy. Textbook 04 06 Cramant GRAND CRU.

Jacques Selosse Avize's best-known grower in top form with two exquisite releases: LE MESNIL, Les Caresses and Ambonnay Le Bout du Clos.

J-L Vergnon Fine restored LE MESNIL estate making exquisite all-Chard extra-brut cuvées, esp Confidence (02' 03 04 05).

Veuve Fourny Rising Côte des Blancs star at Vertus: ★★★★★ Extra-Brut (02' 04) and superb single-v'yd Clos du Faubourg Notre Dame (99 00 02').

Cabernet d'Anjou Lo p s/sw ★→★★ Sweetish DEMI-SEC, often derided, rosé enjoying renaissance, esp strong local demand. Once age-worthy, now DYA. CH PIERRE-BISE; DOMS de Bablut, CADY, Clau de Nell, les Grandes Vignes, Ogereau, de Sauveroy, Varière.

Cabrières L'doc (r) p ★★ DYA. Traditionally full-bodied rosé; also sound reds mostly from energetic village co-op. V'yds on schist hillsides nr Pic de Vissou.

Cadillac-Côtes de Bordeaux B'x r ★→★★ 05' 08 09' 10' Long, narrow, hilly zone on the right bank of the Garonne opposite GRAVES. Formerly Premières Côtes de Bordeaux but renamed from 2008 vintage (*see* box p.103). Medium-bodied, fresh reds. Quality extremely varied. Best: Alios de Ste-Marie, CARIGNAN, *Carsin*, CLOS Chaumont, Clos Ste-Anne, Le Doyenné, Grand-Mouëys, Lezongars, Mont-Pérat, Plaisance, Puy Bardens, REYNON and Suau.

Cady, Domaine Lo r p sw ★★→★★★ 03 04 05′ 07′ (sw) 09 10 (11′) Excellent ANJOU family grower of everything from dry whites and off-dry rosés to lusciously sweet COTEAUX DU LAYON and CHAUME. Sweet wines are strongest suit. Son Alexandre increasingly in charge.

Cahors SW Fr r ★★→★★★★ 01′ 02 05′ 06 08 09 (10) (11′) AOP. France's MALBEC stronghold; chameleon-style ranges from deeply traditional ★★★ *Clos de Gamot* (esp Vignes Centenaires and ★★★★ CLOS St-Jean), Clos Triguedina; middleweights ★★ CHX Armandière, la Coustarelle, Croze de Pys, Gaudou, Clos d'un Jour, DOMS de la Bérengeraie, Pineraie, les Rigalets, Savarines (organic); modern styles from ★★★ Chx du Cèdre, Lamartine, La Reyne, ★★ la Caminade, Eugénie, best of all worlds from cult ★★★★ Dom Cosse-Maisonneuve. Easy-drinking from ★★ Chx Latuc, Paillas, Clos Coutale, Dom Boliva.

Cailloux, Les S Rhô r (w) ★★★ 78′ 79′ 81′ 85′ 89′ 90 95′ 96′ 98′ 99 00′ 01 03′ 04′ 05′ 06′ 07′ 09′ 10′ (11) 18ha CHÂTEAUNEUF DOM; precise, stylish, gd-value hand-made reds of breeding, elegance. V. consistent, true. Special wine Centenaire, with oldest GRENACHE 1889, pure and flowing. Also André Brunel and Féraud-Brunel CÔTES DU RHÔNE merchant range: "correct", not more.

Cairanne S Rhô r p w ★★→★★★ 01′ 03 04′ 05′ 06′ 07′ 09′ 10′ (11) Easily best of the 17 CÔTES DU RHÔNE-VILLAGES: wines of character, bristling fruit, smoky herbs and tannins, esp DOMS Alary, Ameillaud, Armand, Brusset, Escaravailles, Grosset, Hautes Cances (traditional), Oratoire St-Martin (classy), Présidente, Rabasse-Charavin, Richaud (great fruit), Famille Perrin. Food-suited, gd-depth whites.

Canard-Duchêne Champ Improving house owned by ALAIN THIÉNOT. BRUT Vintage 02 04 06 08. Fine CUVÉE Charles VII and Cuvée Léonie.

Canon-Fronsac B'x r ★★ →★★★ 98 00′ 01 03 05′ 06 08 09′ 10′ Small enclave within FRONSAC – otherwise same wines. Best are rich, full and finely structured. Try CHX Barrabaque, Canon Pécresse, Cassagne Haut-Canon la Truffière, la Fleur Cailleau, DU GABY, Grand-Renouil, Haut-Ballet, Haut-Mazeris, MOULIN PEY-LABRIE, Pavillon, Vrai Canon Bouché.

Sangiovese, Italian to its toes, is now being planted in the Languedoc.

Caramany L'doc r (w) ★ Theoretically superior AC for CÔTES DU ROUSSILLON-VILLAGES.

Carillon, Louis C d'O ★★★ Sensibly priced and consistently fine PULIGNY producer, esp Combettes, Perrières, Referts. As from 2010 vintage brothers Jacques and François have gone their separate ways.

Cassis Prov (r) (p) w ★★ DYA. Pleasure port east of Marseille with traditional reputation for dry whites from CLAIRETTE, MARSANNE. Delicious with bouillabaisse, but expensive (eg. DOM de la Ferme Blanche, CLOS Ste Magdeleine, Paternel, Fontcreuse). Growers fighting rearguard action with property developers.

Castillon-Côtes de Bordeaux B'x r ★★ →★★★ 00′ 01 02 03 04 05′ 08 09′ 10′ Previously Côtes de Castillon, renamed 2008 (*see* box p.103). Flourishing region east of ST-EMILION; similar wines, usually less plump, with ageing potential; much recent investment. Top: DE L'A, d'Aiguilhe, Ampélia, Cap de FAUGÈRES, La Clarière-Laithwaite, CLOS l'Eglise, Clos Les Lunelles, Clos Puy Arnaud, Joanin Bécot, Montlandrie, Poupille, Robin, Veyry, Vieux CH Champs de Mars.

Cathiard C d'O ★★★★ Brilliant VOSNE-ROMANÉE producer on top form since the late 1990s. Perfumed, sensual wines are charming young but will age. Vosne Malconsorts best.

Cave Cellar, or any wine establishment.

Cave coopérative Wine-growers' co-op winery; over half of all French production. Often well-run, well-equipped, and wines gd value for money, but many disappearing in the economic crisis.

Cazes, Domaine Rouss r p w sw ★★ Large organic producer in ROUSSILLON. IGP pioneer, with MERLOT and CAB SAUV, esp for brands Le Canon du Maréchal and Le Crédo, also CÔTES DU ROUSSILLON-VILLAGES Ego and Alter, and delicious aged RIVESALTES. Now part of Advini, but still family-run. Excellent value.

Cépage Grape variety. *See* pp.16–26 for all.

Cérons B'x w sw ★★ 99' 01' 02 03' 05' 07 09' 10' Almost abandoned sweet AC next to SAUTERNES. Less intense wines: CHX de Cérons, CHANTEGRIVE, DOM du Grand Enclos.

Chablis Chab w ★★→★★★ 05' 06 07' 08' 09 10' 11 Lean but lovely northern burgundy CHARD so famous that it has been widely imitated round the world. My default white. Mostly unoaked. But too much is mass-produced, early bottled, anonymous Chard.

Chablis Grand Cru Chab w ★★★→★★★★ 95' 96' 99 00' 02' 05' 06 07' 08' 09 10' 11 A small block of v'yds on a steep slope on the right bank of river Serein. The richest CHABLIS is comparable to fine CÔTE DE BEAUNE whites. Needs age for minerality and individual style to develop. V'yds: Blanchots, Bougros, Les CLOS, Grenouilles, Preuses, Valmur, Vaudésir (plus brand La Moutonne). Clos and Vaudésir are best.

Chablis Premier Cru Chab w ★★★ 00' 02' 05' 07' 08' 09 10' 11 Better sites on the rolling hillsides; more white-flower character on the left bank of the river Serein (Vaillons, Montmains, Côte de Léchet), yellow fruit on the right bank (Fourchaume, Mont de Milieu, Montée de Tonnerre). Well-worth the premium over straight CHABLIS.

Chambertin C d'O r ★★★★ 88 89 90' 93 95 96' 98 99' 01 02' 03 05' 06 07 08 09' 10' 11 13ha (or 28ha incl C-CLOS DE BÈZE) of Burgundy's most imperious wine; amazingly dense, sumptuous, long-lived and expensive. Not everybody up to standard, but try from BOUCHARD PÈRE & FILS, Charlopin, Damoy, DROUHIN, DOM LEROY, MORTET, PRIEUR, Rossignol-Trapet, ROUSSEAU, TRAPET.

Chambertin-Clos de Bèze C d'O r ★★★★ 88 89 90' 93 95 96' 98 99' 01 02' 03 05' 06 07 08 09' 10' 11 May be sold under the name of neighbouring CHAMBERTIN. Splendid wines, may be more accessible in youth. Best CLAIR, Damoy, DROUHIN, Drouhin-Laroze, FAIVELEY, Groffier, JADOT, Prieuré-Roch, ROUSSEAU.

Chambolle-Musigny C d'O r ★★★→★★★★ 90' 93 95' 96' 98 99' 02' 03 05' 07 08 09' 10' 11 CÔTE DE NUITS village (170ha): fragrant, complex but never heavy wine. Best v'yds: Amoureuses, BONNES-MARES, Charmes, Cras, Fuées, MUSIGNY. Growers to note: Amiot-Servelle, BARTHOD, Digioia-Royer, DROUHIN, Felletig, Groffier, MUGNIER, RION, ROUMIER, DE VOGÜÉ.

Champagne Sparkling wines of PINOTS N and MEUNIER and/or CHARD, and region (34,000ha, 145km east of Paris); made by *méthode traditionnelle*. Bubbles from elsewhere, however gd, cannot be Champagne.

Champagne le Mesnil Champ Top-flight co-op in greatest GRAND CRU CHARD village. Exceptional CUVÉE Sublime (04 08' 11') from finest sites. Real value.

Champs-Fleuris, Domaine des Lo r p w sw ★★→★★★ 05' 06 08 09' 10 (11) Dynamic DOM with v.gd SAUMUR Blanc; SAUMUR-CHAMPIGNY, incl screwcapped Audace; fine CRÉMANT. When vintage warrants, COTEAUX DE SAUMUR CUVÉE Sarah.

Champy Père & Cie Burg ★★→★★★ Ancient négociant house (1720) revitalized by Meurgey family. Own biodynamic DOM of 27ha, incl former Dom Laleure-Piot strong in BEAUNE and around CORTON.

Chandon de Briailles, Domaine C d'O r ★★→★★★ Unfashionable but fine, light reds, esp PERNAND-VERGELESSES, Île de Vergelesses and CORTON Bressandes. Biodynamic farming, lots of stems and no new oak define the style.

Chanson Père & Fils Burg ★→★★★ Un-pushy BEAUNE-based merchant of increasing quality. CLOS des Fèves (r), CORTON-Vergennes (w). Wines to follow for value.

Chapelle-Chambertin C d'O r ★★★ 90′ 93 95 96′ 98 99′ 01 02′ 03 05′ 07 08 09′ 10′ 11 A 5.2ha neighbour of CHAMBERTIN. Wine more "nervous", less meaty. V.gd in cooler yrs. Top producers: Damoy, Drouhin-Laroze, JADOT, Rossignol-Trapet, TRAPET, Tremblay.

Chablis

There is no better expression of the all-conquering CHARD than the full but tense, limpid but stony wines it makes on the heavy limestone soils of CHABLIS. Chablis terroir divides into three quality levels (four, incl PETIT CHABLIS) with great consistency. Best makers use little or no new oak to mask the precise definition of variety and terroir: Barat, Bessin ★, Billaud-Simon ★, BOUCHARD PÈRE & FILS, Boudin ★, J-M BROCARD, J Collet ★, D Dampt, R/V DAUVISSAT ★, J Dauvissat, B, D et E and J Defaix, Droin, DROUHIN ★, Duplessis, DURUP, FÈVRE ★, Geoffroy, J-P Grossot ★, LAROCHE, LONG-DEPAQUIT, DOM des Malandes, L Michel, Christian MOREAU ★, Picq ★, Pinson, RAVENEAU ★, G Robin ★, Servin, Tribut, Vocoret. Simple, unqualified "Chablis" may be thin; best is PREMIER CRU or GRAND CRU. The co-op, La Chablisienne, has high standards (esp Grenouille ★) and many different labels (it makes one in every three bottles). (★ = outstanding.)

Chapoutier N Rhô ★★→★★★★ Owner of top Northern Rhône v'yds, esp HERMITAGE; also merchant. Intense wines; biodynamic. Note low-yield, special plot-specific CUVÉES, ripe, dense CHÂTEAUNEUF: Barbe Rac, Croix de Bois (r); CÔTE-RÔTIE La Mordorée; Hermitage: L'Ermite (outstanding), Le Pavillon (r), L'Ermite, Cuvée de l'Orée, Le Méal (w). Also ST-JOSEPH Les Granits (r w). Long-lived MARSANNE N Rhône whites, perfect with fine dishes. Gd-value *Meysonniers Crozes*. Also holdings in COTEAUX D'AIX-EN-PROVENCE, CÔTES DU ROUSSILLON-VILLAGES (gd DOM Bila-Haut), RIVESALTES. Michel has ALSACE venture (Schieferkopf, schist soil). Active Australian joint ventures: esp DOMS Tournon and Terlato & Chapoutier (fine style), and Portuguese: Estremadura.

Charbonnière, Domaine de la S Rhô r (w) ★★★ 95′ 98 99′ 00 01′ 03 04 05′ 06′ 07′ 09′ 10′ (11) Gd 17ha CHÂTEAUNEUF estate run by sisters. Decent Tradition wine, notable, authentic Mourre des Perdrix, also Hautes Brusquières, new L'Envol, VIEILLES VIGNES. Steady white, genuine VACQUEYRAS red slay.

Chardonnay As well as a white wine grape, also the name of a MÂCON-VILLAGES commune – hence Mâcon-Chardonnay.

Charmes-Chambertin C d'O r ★★★ 90′ 93 95 96′ 98 99′ 01 02′ 03 05′ 06 07 08 09′ 10′ 11 31ha, incl neighbour MAZOYÈRES-CHAMBERTIN, of mixed quality. Best has intense, ripe, dark-cherry fruit and fragrant finish. Try ARLAUD, Bachelet, DROUHIN, DUGAT, DUJAC, LEROY, Perrot-Minot, Roty, ROUMIER, ROUSSEAU, VOUGERAIE.

Chassagne-Montrachet C d'O r w ★★→★★★★ (w) 00 02′ 04 05′ 06′ 07 08′ 09′ 10 11 Large village at south end of CÔTE DE BEAUNE. Great whites from eg. Caillerets, La Romanée, Blanchots and GRANDS CRUS. Best reds from Morgeot, CLOS St-Jean, others more rustic. Production dominated by clans Coffinet, COLIN, GAGNARD, MOREY, Pillot plus top DOMS Niellon, Ramonet, CH de Maltroye.

Château (Ch/x) Means an estate, big or small, gd or indifferent, particularly in B'X (*see* Châteaux of Bordeaux). In France, château tends to mean, literally, castle or great house. In Burgundy, DOM is the usual term.

Château d'Arlay Jura ★→★★ Major Jura estate; 65ha in skilful hands. Wines incl: v.gd VIN JAUNE, VIN DE PAILLE, PINOT N and MACVIN.

Château de Beaucastel S Rhô r w ★★★★ 78' 79 81' 83 85 86' 88 89' 90' 94' 95' 96' 97 98' 99' 00' 01' 03' 04 05' 06' 07' 08 09' 10' 11 Dynamic, organic, top CHÂTEAUNEUF estate; old MOURVÈDRE, plus 100-yr ROUSSANNE. Also excellent Famille Perrin Southern Rhône business (320ha+). Smoky, dark, complex wines, drink at 2 yrs or from 7–8 yrs; live well. Recent vintages are softer in style. Top-grade 60% Mourvèdre Hommage à Jacques Perrin (r). *Wonderful old-vine Roussanne*: keep 5–25 yrs. Polished CÔTES DU RHÔNE Coudoulet de Beaucastel (r), will live 8 yrs+. Famille Perrin CAIRANNE (gd value), GIGONDAS, RASTEAU, VINSOBRES all v.gd, genuine. V.gd organic Perrin Nature Côtes du Rhône (r w). (*See also* Tablas Creek, California.)

Château du Cèdre SW Fr r w ★★★ 01' 02 04 06 08 (09) (10) (11') The Verhaeghe brothers lead the modern CAHORS school. "Le Prestige" quicker-maturing than hefty top growths. Delicious VIOGNIER IGP.

Château de la Chaize Beauj r ★★★ Magnificent CH, seventh-generation ownership, also fine gardens, with 99ha of BROUILLY all in one block.

Château-Chalon Jura w ★★★ Not a CH but AC and village. Unique dry, yellow, Sherry-like wine (SAVAGNIN grape). Develops *flor* (*see* "Port, Sherry & Madeira") while ageing in barrels for min 6 yrs. Ready to drink when bottled (62cl *clavelin* bottle), but ages almost forever. A curiosity.

Château Fuissé Burg w ★★→★★★ Substantial producer with some of the best terroirs of POUILLY-FUISSÉ. Esp Les CLOS, Combettes. Also négociant lines.

Château-Grillet N Rhô w ★★★ 91' 95' 98' 00' 01' 04' 05 06' 07 08 09' 10' (11) 3.6ha Northern Rhône terraced granite v'yd, own AC. Bought by F Pinault of CH LATOUR (spring 2011), prices rising fast. Smooth take on VIOGNIER now – subtle, can be big, always drink with food. Elegance is the word since mid-2000s. Can take 3 yrs+ to open. Decant.

Châteaumeillant Lo r p ★→★★ DYA. A small, new AC area (90ha), promoted Nov 2010, southwest of Bourges in Georges Sand country. GAMAY and PINOT N for light reds, VIN GRIS and rosés. Foolishly 100% Pinot N no longer allowed. Look for: Chaillot, Geoffrenet-Morval, Siret-Courtaud.

Château de Meursault C d'Or w ★★ 61ha estate owned by PATRIARCHE; gd v'yds and wines in BEAUNE, MEURSAULT, POMMARD, VOLNAY. Cellars open to public.

Château Montus SW Fr r w ★★★ 00 01' 02 04 05' 06 08 (09) (10) (11') ALAIN BRUMONT's all-TANNAT flagship still leads in MADIRAN. Time and food required to soften hefty tannins. Suits rugby players.

Château la Nerthe S Rhô r w ★★★ 78' 81' 89' 90' 95' 96' 97 98' 99' 00 01 03 04' 05' 06' 07' 09' 10' (11) V.gd 90ha CHÂTEAUNEUF estate. Sleek, polished wines, sadly more pristine, international lately. Special CUVÉES delicious Cadettes (r), oaked Beauvenir (w). Also runs v.gd TAVEL Prieuré Montézargues, gd-value DOM de la Renjarde CÔTES DU RHÔNE, CH Signac CHUSCLAN.

Châteauneuf-du-Pape S Rhô r (w) ★★★ 78' 81' 83 85 86 88 89' 90' 94 95' 96 98' 99' 00' 01' 03' 04' 05' 06' 07' 09' 10' (11) 3,230ha nr Avignon, around 45 really gd DOMS for best wines (remaining 85 inconsistent or poor). Up to 13 red and white varieties, led by GRENACHE, plus SYRAH, MOURVÈDRE, Counoise. Warm, heady, long-lived, should be fine, but too many heavy, sip-only wines (Parker taste) lately. Small, traditional names can be gd value (esp 2010), while prestige wines (old vines, late-harvest, new oak) are too pricey. Whites fresh, fruity, or sturdy, best can age 15 yrs. Top growers: CHX DE BEAUCASTEL, Fortia, Gardine, Mont-Redon, LA NERTHE, RAYAS, Vaudieu; DOMS de Beaurenard, Bois de Boursan, Bosquet des Papes, LES CAILLOUX, Chante Cigale, CHARBONNIÈRE, Charvin (terroir), Cristia, Font-de-Michelle, Grand Veneur (oak), Marcoux (fantastic VIEILLES VIGNES), Monpertuis, Pegaü, Roger Sabon, VIEUX TÉLÉGRAPHE, Henri Bonneau, CLOS du Mont-Olivet, CLOS DES PAPES, Clos St-Jean (sip), CUVÉE du Vatican, P Usseglio, Vieux Donjon.

Château Pierre-Bise Lo r p w ★★→★★★★ 02 03 04 05' 06 07' (sw) 08 09 10 (11) COTEAUX DU LAYON, incl Chaume, QUARTS DE CHAUME and SAVENNIÈRES, esp CLOS de Grand Beaupréau and ROCHE-AUX-MOINES. V.gd concentrated ANJOU-GAMAY, ANJOU-VILLAGES – both CUVÉE Schist and Spilite, and Anjou Blanc Haut de la Garde. New generation taking over.

Château Rayas S Rhô r w ★★★→★★★★ 78' 79 81' 85 86 88' 89 90' 93 94 95' 96' 98' 99 00 01 03 04' 05' 06' 07' 08 09' 10' 11 Caressing wines, v. traditional 12ha CHÂTEAUNEUF estate. Complex reds (100% GRENACHE) age superbly. White Rayas (GRENACHE BL, CLAIRETTE) v.gd over 18 yrs+. Gd-value second wine: *Pignan*. Supreme CH Fonsalette CÔTES DU RHÔNE. Decant all. Gd Ch des Tours VACQUEYRAS.

Château Simone Prov r p w ★★ Historic estate where Winston Churchill painted Mont St-Victoire. Same family for over two centuries. Virtually synonymous with AC PALETTE. Warming, soft reds, incl rare grape varieties; white repays bottle-ageing. Full-bodied rosé.

Château de Villeneuve Lo r w ★★→★★★★ 96 99 03 05 06 07 08' 09' 10 (11) Meticulous producer. Wonderful SAUMUR Blanc (esp Les Cormiers) and SAUMUR-CHAMPIGNY (esp VIEILLES VIGNES, Grand CLOS). Top CUVÉES only made in gd vintages. Clos de Bienboire is new easy-drinking red.

Chave, Domaine Jean-Louis N Rhô r w ★★★★ 85' 86 88' 89' 90' 91' 94 95' 96 97 98' 99' 00 01' 03' 04 05' 06' 07' 08 09' 10' 11 The best-quality HERMITAGE family DOM. Astute blending from foremost hillside sites. Classy, generous, long-lived wines, esp white (mainly MARSANNE); also ace, occasional VIN DE PAILLE. Improving Dom ST-JOSEPH red (bought 6ha+ DOM Florentin 2009), fruity J-L Chave brand St-Joseph Offerus, decent merchant Hermitage (r w).

Chavignol Lo SANCERRE village with famous steep v'yds, Les Monts Damnés and Cul de Beaujeu. Clay-limestone soil gives full-bodied, minerally wines that age 10 yrs (or longer); esp from Boulay, BOURGEOIS, Cotat, DAGUENEAU, Thomas Laballe, Yves and Pierre Martin, Paul Thomas.

Chénas Beauj r ★★★ 09' 10' 11' Smallest BEAUJOLAIS cru, one of the weightiest; neighbour to MOULIN-À-VENT and JULIÉNAS. Growers: Aufranc, Charvet, DUBOEUF, Lapierre, Piron, Robin, Trichard, co-op.

Chevalier-Montrachet C d'O W ★★★★ 99' 00' 02' 04 05' 06' 07' 08 09' 10 11 Just above MONTRACHET geographically, just below in quality, though still capable of brilliant, long-lived, minerally wines. Best sectors are Les Demoiselles (JADOT, LATOUR) and La Cabotte (BOUCHARD). Other top growers: Chartron, Dancer, LEFLAIVE, Niellon, CH de Puligny.

Cheverny Lo r p w ★→★★ 05' 06 08 09' 10 (11) Loire AC (534ha) nr Chambord. Pungent dry white from SAUV BL and CHARD. Generally light reds mainly GAMAY, PINOT N (also CAB FR, CÔT). Richer, rarer and more age-worthy *Cour-Cheverny* (48ha) local Romorantin grape only. Sparkling uses CRÉMANT de Loire and TOURAINE ACs. Esp Cazin, CLOS Tue-Boeuf, Gendrier, Huards, Philippe Tessier; DOMS de la Desoucherie, du Moulin, Veilloux, Villemade.

Chevillon, R C d'O ★★★ Delicious, approachable NUITS-ST-GEORGES with v'yds in the best sites, esp Les St-Georges, Cailles, Vaucrains, Roncières.

Chidaine, François Lo (r) w dr sw sp ★★★ 02' 05' 07 08' 09 10 (11) Biodynamic producer of minerally, v. precise MONTLOUIS and VOUVRAY. In 2002, took over historic Vouvray CLOS Baudoin (formerly Prince Poniatowski) – renewing v'yd. Concentrates on dry and DEMI-SEC styles. AC TOURAINE at Chissay in the Cher Valley.

Chignin Sav w ★ DYA. Light, soft white from Jacquère grapes for alpine summers. Chignin-Bergeron (with ROUSSANNE grapes) is best and liveliest.

Chinon Lo r p (w) ★★→★★★ 95 96' 97 02 03 05' 06 08 09' 10 (11) Big range: light to rich TOURAINE CAB FR, 10% rosé. Top vintages from top growers can age 20 yrs+. Some steely, dry CHENIN BL. ALLIET, BAUDRY, BAUDRY-DUTOUR, Couly-Dutheil, Couly

(Pierre and Bertrand), Grosbois, JM Raffault; CHX de la Bonnelière, de Coulaine, DOM de la Noblaie.

Chiroubles Beauj r 09' 10' 11' Rarely seen BEAUJOLAIS cru in the hills above FLEURIE: fresh, fruity, silky wine for early drinking (1–3 yrs). Growers: Cheysson, DUBOEUF, Fourneau, Métrat, Passot, Raousset, Trenel.

Chorey-lès-Beaune C d'O r (w) ★★ 99' 02' 05' 06 07 08 09' 10' 11 Pleasurable, affordable burgundy adjoining BEAUNE; look for CH de Chorey (Germain), Loichet, *Tollot-Beaut*.

Chusclan S Rhô r p w →★★ 07' 09' 10' CÔTES DU RHÔNE-VILLAGES, with gd-quality LAUDUN-Chusclan co-op. Soft reds, lively rosés. Best co-op labels CUVÉE de Marcoule, Seigneurie de Gicon. Also gd CH Signac (can age) and special cuvées from *André Roux*. Drink most young.

Clair, Bruno C d'O ★★★→★★★★ Terrific MARSANNAY estate with major holdings in GEVREY-CHAMBERTIN (esp CLOS de Bèze, CLOS ST-JACQUES, Cazetiers), FIXIN, MOREY-ST-DENIS and old-vine SAVIGNY La Dominode.

Clairet Between rosé and red. B'X Clairet is AC. Try CHX Fontenille, Penin, Turcaud.

Clairette de Bellegarde L'doc w ★ DYA. AC nr Nîmes: understated, dry white from CLAIRETTE, esp stylish Mas Carlot.

Clairette de Die N Rhô w dr s/sw sp ★★ NV Crisp, flinty or (better) semi-sweet, easy-drinking. Underrated, traditional, sweetly fruited, low-degree MUSCAT sparkling wine from low Alps in east Rhône; or dry CLAIRETTE, can age 3–4 yrs. Fun, unusual apéritif. Achard-Vincent, Poulet et fils, J-C Raspail.

Clairette du Languedoc L'doc w ★ DYA. V. small white AC of the MIDI, from the CLAIRETTE grape. Original identity was soft and creamy; now some oak-ageing and even late-harvest *moëlleux* and RANCIO.

In 1980 Languedoc had seven ACs – now it has over 20.

Clape, Auguste, Pierre, Olivier N Rhô r (w) ★★★→★★★★ 90' 95' 97 98' 99' 00 01' 02 03' 04' 05' 06' 07' 08 09' 10' 11 *The kings of Cornas*. Supreme 5ha+ SYRAH central v'yd at CORNAS, many old vines. Deep, fine, backward, v. consistent reds, a reminder of an unhurried era, need 6 yrs+. Perky, young-vines Renaissance. Gd CÔTES DU RHÔNE, ST-PÉRAY, VDT.

Clape, la L'doc r p w ★★→★★★ Potential Cru du L'DOC; *see* COTEAUX DU L'DOC. Warming, spicy reds from sun-soaked hills between Narbonne and the Med. *Tangy, salty whites* age surprisingly well. Gd: CHX l'Hospitalet, Moyau, La Négly, Pech-Céléyran, Pech-Redon, *Rouquette-sur-Mer*, Ricardelle, Anglès, Mas du Soleila, Camplazens.

Climat Burg Burgundian word for individually named v'yd, eg. MEURSAULT Tesson.

Clos A term carrying some prestige, reserved for distinct (walled) v'yds, often in one ownership (esp Burgundy, CHAMPAGNE, ALSACE).

Clos de Gamot SW Fr ★★★ 90' 95 98' 00 01' 02' 04 05' 06 08 (09) (10) (11') Archetypal CAHORS from 400-yr-old DOM. The Jouffreau family's long-living ★★★ Cuvée Vignes Centenaires (made best yrs only) and hilltop ★★★★ CLOS St-Jean miraculously survive modern fashions. How MALBEC should really taste.

Clos de la Roche C d'O r ★★★ 90' 93' 95 96' 98 99' 01 02' 03 05' 06 07 08 09' 10' 11 Arguably the finest GRAND CRU of MOREY-ST-DENIS, with as much grace as power. Best: Amiot, ARLAUD, DUJAC, LEROY, LIGNIER, PONSOT, ROUSSEAU.

Clos de Tart C d'O r ★★★★ 90' 96' 99' 01' 02' 03 05' 06 07 08' 09 10 11 MOREY-ST-DENIS GRAND CRU, upgraded substantially in quality and price on the watch of director Sylvain Pitiot. Often most exciting in less ripe yrs.

Clos de Vougeot C d'O r ★★★ 90' 93' 96' 98 99' 01 02' 03' 05' 06 07 08 09' 10' 11 A 50ha CÔTE DE NUITS GRAND CRU, with many owners. Occasionally sublime. Maturity depends on grower's philosophy, technique and position. Top growers:

CH de la Tour, DROUHIN, EUGÉNIE, FAIVELEY, GRIVOT, GROS, HUDELOT-Noëllat, JADOT, LEROY, LIGER-BELAIR, MÉO-CAMUZET, MUGNERET, *Vougeraie*.

Clos des Lambrays C d'O r ★★★ 90′ 95 99′ 00 02 03 05′ 06 07 09′ 10′ 11 GRAND CRU v'yd (8.8ha) at MOREY-ST-DENIS. A virtual monopoly of the DOM du CLOS des Lambrays, invigorating wine in an early-picked, spicy, stemmy style – in total contrast to neighbour Clos de Tart.

Clos des Mouches C d'O r w ★★★ Splendid PREMIER CRU BEAUNE v'yd, largely owned by DROUHIN. Whites and reds, spicy and memorable – and consistent. Little-known v'yds of the same name exist in SANTENAY and MEURSAULT, too.

Clos des Papes S Rhô r w ★★★★ 90′ 95 98′ 99′ 00 01′ 03′ 04′ 05′ 06′ 07′ 08 09′ 10′ 11 Top 32ha (18 plots) CHÂTEAUNEUF estate of Avril family for centuries. Rich, long, complex red, more obviously ripe recently (mainly GRENACHE, MOURVÈDRE, drink at 2–3 yrs or from 8 yrs) and *great white* (classy, deserves fine cuisine; 5–18 yrs), both reward patience.

Clos du Roi C d'O r ★★→★★★ The best v'yd in GRAND CRU CORTON, PREMIER CRU v'yd in BEAUNE and top site in MARSANNAY. The king usually chose well.

Clos Rougeard Lo r w (sw) ★★★★ 03 04 05′ 06 07 08 09′ 10 (11) Small, iconic DOM run by Foucault brothers – benchmark SAUMUR-CHAMPIGNY, fine SAUMUR Blanc, luscious COTEAUX DE SAUMUR. Making NATURAL wine before it was fashionable.

Clos St-Denis C d'O r ★★★ 90′ 93′ 95 96′ 98 99′ 01 02′ 03 05′ 06 07 08 09′ 10′ 11 GRAND CRU at MOREY-ST-DENIS (6.4ha). Splendid sturdy wine growing silky with age. Growers incl: ARLAUD, Bertagna, DUJAC, PONSOT.

Looking for more information on grapes? Try the "Grapes" section on pp.16–26.

Clos St-Jacques C d'O r ★★★ 90′ 93 95′ 96′ 98 99′ 01 02′ 03 05′ 06 07 08 09′ 10′ 11 6.7ha hillside PREMIER CRU in GEVREY-CHAMBERTIN, with perfect southeast exposure. Five excellent producers: CLAIR, ESMONIN, FOURRIER, JADOT, ROUSSEAU; powerful, velvety reds often ranked above many GRANDS CRUS.

Clos Ste-Hune Al w ★★★★ A TRIMBACH wine from GRAND CRU ROSACKER. Greatest RIES in ALSACE (00′ 02′ 04 05 06 08′ 09′ 10′). V. fine, initially austere; needs 5–10 yrs+ ageing.

Coche-Dury C d'O ★★★★ Superb 11.5ha MEURSAULT DOM led by Jean-François Coche and son Raphaël. Exceptional whites from ALIGOTÉ to CORTON-CHARLEMAGNE and v. pretty reds, too. Hard to find.

Colin C d'O ★★★ Leading CHASSAGNE-MONTRACHET and ST-AUBIN family, with the next generation making waves, especially Pierre-Yves (son of Marc). Try also Bruno or Philippe C (sons of Michel Colin-Deleger).

Collines Rhôdaniennes N Rhô r w ★★ Quality Rhône IGP, clear-fruited, granite, hill-based reds v.gd value. Can contain young-vine CÔTE-RÔTIE, also recent v'yds at Seyssuel (gd, expensive). Mainly red, mostly SYRAH (best), also MERLOT, GAMAY, authentic VIOGNIER (best), CHARD. Reds: Barou, Bonnefond, L Cheze, J-M Gérin, Jamet (v.gd), Jasmin, Monier, M&S Ogier. Whites: Alexandrins, Barou, Y Cuilleron, Perret (v.gd), G Vernay.

Collioure Rouss r p w ★★ Table-wine twin of BANYULS, with most producers making both. Warm, gutsy red, mainly GRENACHE, from dramatic terraces overlooking the Med. Also rosé and white (since 2002), based on GRENACHE BLANC. Top: Les CLOS de Paulilles, DOMS du Mas Blanc, de la Rectorie, La Tour Vieille, Vial-Magnères, Madeloc, Coume del Mas.

Comté Tolosan SW Fr r p w ★ Mostly DYA IGP found all over the southwest, incl luscious, sweet PETIT MANSENG from ★★★ CH de Cabidos, ★★ DOM de Moncaut, ★★ Dom DE RIBONNET. Now an umbrella for smaller IGPs, incl PYRÉNÉES-ATLANTIQUES and COTEAUX ET TERRASSES DE MONTAUBAN.

Condrieu N Rhô w ★★★ 04′ 05 07 08′ 09 10′ 11 Full, oily, freesia-scented white wine from home of VIOGNIER, many granite slopes. Best are mineral-tinted, pure, with a light touch. Has expanded to 125ha, 75 growers; means quality varies (except marvellous 2004, v.gd 2008, lovely 2010); oak, alcohol can be excessive. Best producers: CHAPOUTIER, Y Cuilleron, DELAS, Gangloff, GUIGAL, F Merlin, Niéro, A Perret, C Pichon, ROSTAING, G Vernay (esp top-notch, long-lived Coteau de Vernon), F Villard.

Corbières L'doc r (p) (w) ★★→★★★ 04 05' 06 07' 08 09 10 11 Largest AC of the L'DOC, with cru of Boutenac. Wines like the scenery: sun-soaked and rugged. Best: CHX Aiguilloux, de Cabriac, Les CLOS Perdus, Lastours, Ollieux Romanis, Les Palais, Pech-Latt, de la Voulte Gasparet, DOMS du Grand Crès, de Fontsainte, Trillol, du Vieux Parc, de Villemajou, Villerouge. Co-ops: Camplong, Embrès-et-Castelmaure, Tuchan.

Cornas N Rhô r ★★★ 78' 83' 85' 88' 89' 90' 91' 94' 95' 96 97' 98' 99' 00' 01' 02 03' 04 05' 06' 07' 08 09' 10' 11 Exciting Northern Rhône Syrah. Deep, boldly fruited, mineral-lined, needs to age 5–15 yrs. Younger growers making more accessible wines. Stunning 2010. Top: Allemand, Balthazar (traditional), *Clape* (benchmark), Colombo (new oak), Courbis (modern), *Delas*, J & E Durand, JABOULET (St-Pierre CUVÉE), Lemenicier, V Paris, Tardieu-Laurent (oak), DOM *du Tunnel*, Voge (oak).

Corsica / Vin de Corse Cors r p w ACS Ajaccio, PATRIMONIO; better crus Coteaux du Cap Corse, Sartène and Calvi. IGP: Île de Beauté. Light, spicy reds from SCIACARELLO and more structured, tannic wines from NIELLUCCIO; gd rosés; delicious *tangy, herbal whites from Vermentino*. Top growers: Abbatucci, Antoine Arena, CLOS d'Alzeto, Clos Capitoro, Gentile, Yves Leccia, Montemagni, Peraldi, Vaccelli, Saperale, Fiumicicoli, Torraccia. Original wines that rarely travel.

Corton C d'O r (w) ★★★ 90' 95 96' 98 99' 01 02' 03' 05' 06 07 08 09' 10' 11 The 160ha classified as GRAND CRU is much too much – only a few v'yds (CLOS DU ROI, Bressandes, Le Rognet) deserve it. These have weight and structure; others make appealing, softer reds. DRC involvement since 2009 has increased interest. Look for: d'Ardhuy, BONNEAU DU MARTRAY, CHANDON DE BRIAILLES, DOM des Croix, Dubreuil-Fontaine, FAIVELEY, Camille Giroud, MÉO-CAMUZET, Senard, TOLLOT-BEAUT. Occasional whites (eg. HOSPICES DE BEAUNE) rarely as interesting as CORTON-CHARLEMAGNE.

Corton-Charlemagne C d'O w ★★★★ 99' 00' 02' 03 04 05' 06 07' 08 09' 10' 11 Southwest and west exposure of hill of CORTON, plus a band round the top, all more suited to white wines. Intense minerality and great ageing potential, often insufficiently realized. Top growers: BONNEAU DU MARTRAY, COCHE-DURY, FAIVELEY, HOSPICES DE BEAUNE, JADOT, P Javillier, LATOUR, Rapet, Rollin, VOUGERAIE.

Costières de Nîmes S Rhô r p w ★→★★ 07' 09' 10' Underrated Rhône region, southwest of CHÂTEAUNEUF. Red: full, dark, spiced, ages 5–8 yrs, gd value. Top names: CHX de Campuget, Grande Cassagne, Mas des Bressades (gd fruit), Mas Carlot, Mas Neuf, Mourgues-du-Grès, Nages, d'Or et des Gueules, Roubaud, de la Tuilerie; DOMS de la Patience, Tardieu-Laurent, du Vieux Relais. Fun, fresh rosés, stylish whites (ROUSSANNE).

Côte Chalonnaise Burg r w sp ★★ Region immediately south of CÔTE D'OR v'yds; lower prices. BOUZERON for ALIGOTÉ, *Mercurey*, GIVRY for structured reds, interesting whites; RULLY for lighter wines in both colours; MONTAGNY for its leaner CHARD.

Côte d'Or Burg *Département* name applied to the central and principal Burgundy v'yd slopes: CÔTE DE BEAUNE and CÔTE DE NUITS. Not used on labels. BOURGOGNE Côte d'Or AC arrives in 2012.

Côte de Beaune C d'O r w ★★ →★★★★ Used geographically: the southern half of the CÔTE D'OR. Also an AC in its own right applying to top of hill above BEAUNE itself.

Côte de Beaune-Villages C d'O r ★★ 05' 07 08 09' 10 11 Red wines from the lesser villages of the southern half of the CÔTE D'OR. Rarely exciting.

Côte de Brouilly Beauj r ★★ 05' 09' 10' 11' Flanks of the hillside above BROUILLY provide one of the richest BEAUJOLAIS cru. Deserves to be much better-known. Try J-P Brun, L Martray, CH Thivin.

Côte de Nuits C d'O r (w) ★★→★★★★ Northern half of CÔTE D'OR. Mostly red wine.

Côte de Nuits-Villages C d'O r (w) ★★ 02' 03 05' 06 07 08 09' 10' 11 A junior AC for extreme north and south ends of CÔTE DE NUITS; well-worth investigating for bargains. Single-v'yd versions beginning to appear. Try Ardhuy, Jourdan, Chopin, Gachot-Monot.

Côte Roannaise Lo r p ★★ 08 09' 10 11 Small AC on lower slopes of the high granite hills west of Roanne; cousin of BEAUJOLAIS. Silky, focused GAMAY. Producers: Desormière, Fontenay, Lapandéry, Paroisse, Perrières, Robert Sérol, Vial. Also white IGP from CHARD and increasingly VIOGNIER.

Côte-Rôtie N Rhô r ★★★→★★★★ 78' 85' 88' 89' 90' 91' 94' 95' 98' 99' 00 01' 03' 04 05' 06' 07' 08 09' 10' 11 Finest Rhône red, mainly SYRAH, splash of VIOGNIER, connects to Burgundy. Aromatic, restrained, complex, v. fine with age (esp 15-20 yrs+). Fab 2010. Top: Barge (traditional), Bernard, Bonnefond (oak), Bonserine (GUIGAL-owned), CHAPOUTIER, Clusel-Roch (organic), DELAS, Duclaux, Gaillard (oak), Garon, J-M Gérin (oak), GUIGAL, Jamet (wonderful), Jasmin, M&S Ogier (oak), ROSTAING (fine), J-M Stéphan (organic), VIDAL-FLEURY (La Chatillonne).

Coteaux Bourguignons ★ DYA. New AC from 2012 replacing BOURGOGNE GRAND ORDINAIRE. Main take-up will be unsaleable basic BEAUJOLAIS that may be reclassified under this sexier name.

Coteaux Champenois Champ r w (p) ★★★ (w) DYA. AC for non-sparkling wines of CHAMPAGNE, eg. BOUZY. Vintages as for Champagne. Reds are getting better with climate change.

Coteaux d'Aix-en-Provence Prov r p w ★★→★★★ Sprawling AC from hills north of Aix and on plain around Etang de Berre. A fruit-salad of grapes, both Bordelais and MIDI. Reds are best, esp from CHX Beaupré, Calissanne, Revelette, les Bastides, la Realtière, les Béates, DOM de Château Bas. See also LES BAUX-EN-PROVENCE. Can lack real identity.

Coteaux d'Ancenis Lo r p w (sw) ★→★★ Generally DYA. AOP, region between Nantes and Anjou. Chiefly for dry, DEMI-SEC, sweet CHENIN BL, plus age-worthy MALVOISIE; also light reds and rosés, mainly GAMAY, plus CABS FR and SAUV. Esp Athimon et ses Enfants, Guindon, Quarteron.

Coteaux de Chalosse SW Fr r p w ★ DYA. Modest IGP from local grapes. Co-op dominates, now merged with TURSAN. Mainly found locally.

Coteaux de Glanes SW Fr r r p ★★ DYA. Easy, gd-value IGP from nr Beaulieu-sur-Dordogne. Eight-member co-op makes a local best-seller, incl the rare Ségalin grape in blend.

Coteaux de l'Ardèche S Rhô r p (w) ★→★★ Valley area west of Rhône, wide choice, gd value. New DOMS; fresh reds, some oaked; VIOGNIER (eg. Mas de Libian, CHAPOUTIER) and MARSANNE. Best from SYRAH, also GAMAY (often old vines), CAB SAUV (Serret). Burgundian-style Ardèche CHARD by LOUIS LATOUR; Grand Ardèche from mature vines, but oaked. DOMS du Colombier, J & E Durand, Favette, Flacher, Grangeon, Mazel, Vigier, CH de la Selve.

Coteaux de l'Aubance Lo w sw ★★→★★★★ 89' 90' 95' 96' 97' 02 03 05' 07' 09 10 (11') Small AC for sweet whites from CHENIN BL. Nervier, less rich than COTEAUX DU LAYON except SÉLECTION DES GRAINS NOBLES. Close to Angers, slopes more gentle than in Layon. Often gd value. Esp Bablut, Haute-Perche, Montgilet, CH Princé, Richou, Rochelles.

Coteaux de Pierrevert Prov r p w ★ Cool area producing easy-drinking wines from high v'yds nr Manosque. Off the beaten track. DOM la Blaque, CH Régusse, Ch Rousset. AC since 1998.

FRANCE

Coteaux de Saumur Lo w sw ★★→★★★ 03, 05, 07' 09 10 (11) Sweet CHENIN BL. A tradition revived since 1989 – resembles COTEAUX DU LAYON but less rich and more citric. Esp DOM DES CHAMPS FLEURIS, CLOS ROUGEARD, Régis Neau (Dom de Nerleux), Targe, Vatan (CH de Hureau).

Coteaux des Baronnies S Rhô r p w ★ DYA. Rhône VDP in high hills nr VINSOBRES. SYRAH, CAB SAUV, MERLOT, CHARD, plus GRENACHE, CINSAULT, etc. Light reds, also fresh VIOGNIER. Note DOMS du Rieu-Frais, Rosière.

Coteaux du Giennois Lo r p w ★★→★ DYA. Small appellation north of POUILLY. Scattered v'yds – Cosne to Gien. Light reds hampered by unconvincing, imposed blend of GAMAY and PINOT N; SAUV BL like a junior SANCERRE and better than the reds. Best: Emile Balland, BOURGEOIS, Catherine & Michel Langlois, Paulat, Treuillet, Villargeau.

Coteaux du Languedoc L'doc r p w ★★→★★★ 04 05 06 07 08 09 10 11 A sprawling AC from Narbonne to Nîmes, with various sub-divisions. Enormous quality range. Now destined to disappear in 2017, in favour of even larger AC L'DOC (created 2007). Potential new hierachy of crus, such as GRÈS DE MONTPELLIER, TERRASSES DU LARZAC, PÉZENAS, Sommières. New estates galore demonstrating exciting potential of the MIDI.

Coteaux du Layon Lo w sw ★★→★★★★ 89 90 95 96 97 02 03 05' 07' 09 10 (11) Heart of ANJOU: sweet CHENIN BL varying considerably in sweetness but with admirable acidity, best nearly immortal. Seven villages can add name to AC. Top ACs: BONNEZEAUX, QUARTS DE CHAUME. Growers: Baudouin, BAUMARD, Delesvaux, des Forges, DOM les Grands Vignes, Guegniard, Dom de Juchepie, Ogereau, Papin (CH PIERRE-BISE), Pithon-Paillé.

Coteaux du Loir Lo r p w dr sw ★→★★★ 03 05' 07 08 09' 10 (11) Northern tributary of the Loire, Le Loir is small but dynamic region with Coteaux du Loir and JASNIÈRES. Steely, fine, apple-scented CHENIN BL, GAMAY, peppery Pineau d'Aunis occasionally sparkling, plus Grolleau (rosé), CAB and CÔT. Top growers: Ange Vin, DOM DE BELLIVIERE, Régis Breton, Le Briseau, Fresneau, Gigou, Pascal Janvier, Les Maisons Rouges, de Rycke.

Coteaux du Lyonnais Beauj r p (w) ★ DYA Junior BEAUJOLAIS. Best *en primeur*.

Coteaux du Quercy SW Fr r p ★ 05' 06 08 09 (10) (11') AOP south of CAHORS. Gutsy wines, based on CAB FR; best from ★★ DOM du Merchien, ★ Doms d'Ariès, de Guyot, de Lafage, Lagarde. ★ Co-op makes gd-value range Bessey de Boissy.

Coteaux du Vendômois Lo r p w ★→★★ DYA. AC west of Vendôme along Le Loir Valley. Most characteristic wines are VIN GRIS from Pineau d'Aunis grape, which also gives peppery notes to red blends alongside CAB FR, PINOT N, GAMAY. Whites based on CHENIN BL and CHARD. Producers: Patrice Colin, Four à Chaux, J Martellière, Montrieux, Cave du Vendôme-Villiers.

DOP and IGP: what's happening in France
The appellations and VDPs of France are converting to AOP (Appellation d'Origine Protegée) and IGP (Indication Géographique Protegée). This means that anywhere aspiring to an appellation is likely now to become AOP rather than AOC. IGP will become more specific when the all-embracing category of VIN DE FRANCE finally comes on-stream – it allows wines to state their vintage and grape variety, information previously denied to VDT. This book now uses IGP for all former VDP.

Coteaux et Terrasses de Montauban SW Fr r p w IGP ★→★★ DYA ★★ Dynamic DOM de Montels makes huge range of wines. Also ★ Dom Biarnès. The co-op at Lavilledieu-du-Temple shows no sign of reopening.

Coteaux Varois-en-Provence Prov r p w ★→★★ 04 05' 06 07 08 09 10 11 Sandwiched between COTEAUX D'AIX and CÔTES DE PROVENCE. Gd source of warming reds and fresh rosés; deserves better reputation but still lacks a leader. Try CHX la Calisse, Miraval, DOM les Alysses, du Deffends, du Loou, des Chaberts.

Côtes Catalanes Rouss r p w ★→★★ The best IGP of ROUSSILLON, covering most of area. Exciting source of innovation and investment. Growers: Matassa, La Préceptorie Centernach, CH de Casenove, DOMS GÉRARD GAUBY, Olivier Pithon, Padié, des Soulanes, le Soula.

Côtes d'Auvergne Mass C r p (w) →→★★ Generally DYA. Small AC (412ha), promoted 2010. Mainly GAMAY, but some PINOT N (stupidly blend only allowed) and CHARD. Best reds improve 2–3 yrs. Best villages: Boudes, Chanturgue, Châteaugay, Madargues (r); Corent (p). Producers: Cave St-Verny, Maupertuis, Sauvat.

Côtes de Bordeaux B'x ★ New appellation launched in 2008 (see box p.103). Mainly red. Embraces and permits cross-blending between CASTILLON, FRANCS, BLAYE and CADILLAC (formerly Premières Côtes de Bordeaux).

Côtes de Bourg B'x r w ★→★★ 04 05' 08 09' 10' Solid, sappy reds, a little white wine from the east bank of Gironde. Independent of new CÔTES DE BORDEAUX AC. Top CHX: Brûlesécaille, Bujan, Civrac, *Falfas*, Fougas, Grand-Maison, Haut-Guiraud, Haut-Maco, Haut Mondésir, Macay, Mercier, Nodoz, *Roc de Cambes*, Rousset, Sociondo.

Côtes de Duras SW Fr r p w ★→★★★ 08 09 10 (11') AOP. Biodynamism suddenly fashionable in this eastern B'x satellite. ★★★ DOMS Mouthes-les-Bihan, ★★ Petit Malromé show the way to ★★ Dom Mont Ramé, Les Hauts de Riquet, Les Cours, Nadine Lussau and even the dull old Berticot co-op. Still reliable are ★★ des Allegrets and Laulan. ★★★ CH Condom Perceval's Doux still tops.

Côtes de Gascogne SW Fr (r) (p) w ★★ DYA IGP. Quaffable theatre-interval style makes these whites hugely successful. Beyond ★★ PRODUCTEURS PLAIMONT and Tariquet try ★★ DOMS d'Arton, Chiroulet, Ménard, Millet, Pellehaut, de San Guilhem. Otherwise ★ CH Monluc, des Cassagnoles, Higuière, de Jöy, de Laballe, de Lauroux, de Magnaut, Papolle, St Lannes, Sédouprat (esp red CUVÉE Sanglier). Also from growers in MADIRAN; plus some nearby IGPS prefer to use the Gascon name.

Côtes de Millau SW Fr r p w IGP DYA. Enthusiastic co-op; six independents, incl ★ DOM du Vieux Noyer: evangelists for this once-enormous v'yd in the Tarn Valley.

Côtes de Montravel SW Fr w dr sw ★★ 05' 07 09 10 (11') Sub-AOP of BERGERAC; drop in popularity of the *moelleux* style sadly squeezes these pretty wines between MONTRAVEL SEC and the really sweet HAUT-MONTRAVEL.

Côtes de Provence Prov r p w ★→★★★ 05 06 07 08 09 10 11 (p w) DYA. Large AC known mainly for rosé; enjoying a huge leap in quality, thanks to investment and improvement in winemaking. Satisfying reds and herbal whites. STE-VICTOIRE, Fréjus and La Londe subzones; Pierrefeu coming soon. Leaders incl: Castel Roubine, Commanderie de Peyrassol, DOMS Bernarde, de la Courtade, Léoube, *Gavoty* (superb), CHX *d'Esclans*, de Selle and CLOS Mireille, des Planes, Rabiéga, *Richeaume*, Rimauresq. See COTEAUX D'AIX, BANDOL.

Côtes de Thongue L'doc r p w ★★ (p w) DYA. Most dynamic IGP of HÉRAULT. Intriguing blends in preference to single varietals. Reds will age. DOMS Arjolle, les Chemins de Bassac, la Croix Belle, Magellan, Monplézy, des Henrys.

Côtes de Toul Al r p w ★ DYA. V. light wines from Lorraine; mainly VIN GRIS.

Côtes du Brulhois SW Fr r p (w) ★→★★ 06 08 09 10 (11'). Promoted AOP, nr Agen. Reds (so-called "black wine") must incl some TANNAT. ★ Co-op works with, not against, independents, ★★ DOM des Thermes, le Bois de Simon, ★ CH la Bastide, CLOS Pountet, DOM Coujétou-Peyret.

Côtes du Couchois Burg ★→★★ 05' 09' 10 Subdistrict of BOURGOGNE Rouge at southern end of CÔTE D'OR v'yds. Powerful reds on the tannic side. Best grower: Alain Hasard.

Côtes du Forez Lo r p (sp) ★ DYA. Southernmost Loire AC nr St-Etienne. GAMAY reds and rosés. Les Vignerons Foréziens, Le CLOS de Chozieux, Verdier et Logel. IGP: CHARD, PINOT GR, VIOGNIER.

Côtes du Jura Jura r p w (sp) ★ DYA Many light tints and tastes. ARBOIS wines are more substantial.

Côtes du Rhône S Rhô r p w ★→★★ 09' 10' 11 Vast zone across 170 communes in Southern Rhône. Big split between handmade quality and mass-produced. Fruit quality rising (prices, too). Mainly GRENACHE, also SYRAH, CARIGNAN. Best drunk young. Vaucluse area best, then GARD (Syrah).

Côtes du Rhône-Villages S Rhô r p w ★→★★ 07' 09' 10' 11 Punchy, freewheeling wine from 7,700ha, incl the 17 best Southern Rhône villages. Best are exciting – abdundant fruit, spice, gd value, keen growers behind them. Red core is GRENACHE, with SYRAH, MOURVÈDRE support. Improving whites, often have VIOGNIER, ROUSSANNE added to CLAIRETTE, GRENACHE BLANC – gd with food. *See* CAIRANNE, CHUSCLAN, LAUDUN, ST-GERVAIS, SABLET, SÉGURET, VISAN. New villages from 2005: MASSIF D'UCHAUX (gd), PLAN DE DIEU (robust), PUYMÉRAS, SIGNARGUES. Note: CHX Fontségune, Signac, DOMS Aphillantes, Cabotte, Chaume-Arnaud, Coulange, Grand Moulas, Grand Veneur, Jérome, Montbayon, *Mourchon*, Rabasse-Charavin, Renjarde, Romarins, Ste-Anne, St Siffrein, Saladin, Valériane, Vieux Chêne, Viret (cosmopolitan), Mas de Libian, Cave Estézargues, Cave Rasteau.

Côtes du Roussillon Rouss r p w ★ →★★ 05' 06 07' 08 09 10 11 East Pyrénées AC, covers v'yds of Pyrénées-Orientales behind Perpignan. Dominated by co-ops, notably VIGNERONS Catalans. Warming red is best, predominantly from old-vine CARIGNAN and GRENACHE.

Côtes du Roussillon-Villages Rouss r ★★ 05 06 07 08 09 10 11 28 villages form best part of region. Dominated by co-ops and VIGNERONS Catalans. Best labels: DOMS des Chênes, CAZES, *la Cazenove*, GAUBY (also characterful white IGP), Piquemal, CH de Jau, Mas Crémat.

Côtes du Tarn SW Fr r p w ★ DYA. IGP overlaps GAILLAC; ★★ DOMS d'en Segur (esp off-dry SAUV BL) and Vignes de Garbasses outside GAILLAC area are fine growers.

Côtes du Vivarais S Rhô r p w ★ 09' 10' DYA. Almost 500ha in hilly Ardèche country west of Montélimar. Improving, gluggable wines based on GRENACHE, SYRAH; some more robust, oak-aged reds. Note: Mas de Bagnols, VIGNERONS de Ruoms.

Coulée de Serrant Lo w dr sw ★★ 95 96 97 98 99 02 03 04 05 07 08 09 10 (11) A 7ha CHENIN BL v'yd at SAVENNIÈRES. High priest of biodynamics, Nicolas Joly's wines have been below par (failed to match the theory), improving now daughter Virginie in charge. Don't chill; decant. Old vintages can be sublime.

Courcel, Domaine de C d'O ★★★ Leading POMMARD estate – top PREMIERS CRUS Rugiens and Epenots, plus interesting Croix Noires. Wines age well.

Crémant In CHAMPAGNE, meant "creaming" (half-sparkling): now called *demi-mousse/ perle*. Since 1975, an AC for quality classic-method sparkling from ALSACE, Loire, B'X, BOURGOGNE, and most recently LIMOUX.

Crépy Sav w ★★ DYA. Light, soft, Swiss-style white from south shore of Lake Geneva. "Crépitant" has been coined for its faint fizz.

Crozes-Hermitage N Rhô r w ★★ 05' 06 07 09' 10' 11 SYRAH on granite hill/low plain v'yds next to HERMITAGE hill. Plain gives fun, early-drinking wines (2–5 yrs). Best (simple CUVÉES) have dashing black fruit, tar. Some oaked, gritty techno wines cost more. Top: Belle, Y Chave, CH Curson, Darnaud, DOMS du Colombier, Combier, des Entrefaux (oak), *A Graillot* (benchmark), Hauts-Chassis, Lises (fine), Mucyn, du Pavillon-Mercurol, de Thalabert of JABOULET, *Chapoutier*, *Delas* (Tour d'Albon, Le CLOS v.gd). Drink white (MARSANNE) early, v.gd 2010.

Cuve close Short-cut method of making sparkling wine in a tank. Sparkle dies away in glass much quicker than with *méthode traditionnelle* wine.

Cuvée Wine contained in a *cuve*, or vat. Word of many uses, incl synonym for "blend" and first-press wines (as in CHAMPAGNE). Often just refers to a "lot" of wine.

d'Angerville, Marquis C d'O ★★★★ A superstar in VOLNAY, esp CLOS des Ducs (MONOPOLE), Champans and Taillepieds. Quality is rising still further of late. Biodynamic producer.

d'Eguisheim, Cave Vinicole Al ★★ V.gd ALSACE co-op for its size. Excellent value: fine GRANDS CRUS Hatschbourg, HENGST, Ollwiller, Spiegel. Owns Willm. Top label: WOLFBERGER. Best: Grande Rés, Sigillé, Armorié. Gd CRÉMANT and PINOT N (esp 09 10′ 11).

The top Côtes du Rhône producers

La Courançonne, Domazan, l'Estagnol, Fonsalette (beauty), Grand Moulas, Haut-Musiel, Hugues, Montfaucon, St-Estève, Trignon (incl VIOGNIER); co-ops CAIRANNE, Chantecotes (Ste-Cécile-les-Vignes), PUYMÉRAS, RASTEAU, Villedieu (esp white); Cave Estézargues, DOMS Bramadou, Charvin (terroir), Combebelle, Coudoulet de BEAUCASTEL (classy r), Cros de la Mûre (great value), M Dumarcher, Espigouette, Ferrand, Gourget, Gramenon (biodynamic), Janasse (old GRENACHE), Jaume, Famille Perrin, Manarine, Réméjeanne (w also), Romarins, Rouge-Bleu (organic, clear), Soumade, Vieille Julienne, Vieux Chêne; DUBOEUF, GUIGAL, JABOULET.

Dagueneau, Didier Lo ★★★→★★★★ 02 03 04 05′ 07 08′ 09′ 10 (11) Best producer of POUILLY-FUMÉ. World reference for stunningly pure, precise SAUV BL. Son Louis-Benjamin in charge, similar quality. Top CUVÉES: Pur Sang, Silex and ungrafted and astronomically priced Asteroide. Also SANCERRE – small v'yd in CHAVIGNOL; JURANÇON.

Dauvissat, Vincent Chab ★★★ Great CHABLIS producer using old methods for v.-long-lived CHABLIS. Cousin of RAVENEAU. Best: Forest, Preuses, Les CLOS.

Degré alcoolique Degrees of alcohol, ie. % by volume.

Deiss, Dom Marcel Al ★★★ High-profile biodynamic grower at Bergheim. Favours blended wines from individual v'yds, often co-planted. Best wines: GEWURZ, RIES Schoenenbourg. More consistency now.

Delamotte Champ BRUT; *Blanc de Blancs* (99 02 04 07); CUVÉE Nicholas Delamotte. Fine small CHARD-dominated CHAMPAGNE house at LE MESNIL. V.gd *saignée* Rosé. Managed with SALON by LAURENT-PERRIER. "Library" stock of old vintages.

Delas Frères N Rhô ★→★★★ Precise quality and v. deep range. Northern Rhône merchant, with CONDRIEU, CROZES-HERMITAGE, CÔTE-RÔTIE, HERMITAGE v'yds. Top wines incl: Condrieu (CLOS Boucher), Côte-Rôtie Landonne, Hermitage DOM des Tourettes (r), M de la Tourette (r w), Les Bessards (v. fine, long life). Owned by CHAMPAGNE'S ROEDERER.

2010 in the Northern Rhône comes close to rivalling the legendary 1978.

Demi-sec "Half-dry": in practice more like half-sweet (eg. of CHAMPAGNE).

Deutz Champ BRUT Classic NV; Rosé NV; Brut (00 02 04). Top-flight CHARD CUVÉE Amour de Deutz (99 02). One of top small CHAMPAGNE houses, ROEDERER-owned. V. dry, classic wines. *Superb Cuvée William Deutz* (02′ 08′).

Dom Pérignon Champ Superb 02′, fine 03 (against the odds); rosé 02 04 06. Luxury CUVÉE of MOËT & CHANDON, named after iconic cellarmaster who first blended CHAMPAGNE. Astonishingly *consistent quality* and creamy character, esp with 10–15 yrs bottle age. Late-disgorged *Oenothèque* releases 95' 88 and magical rosé 90'.

Domaine (Dom) Property, particularly in Burgundy and rural France. *See* under name, eg. TEMPIER, DOM.

Domaine Bouscassé SW Fr ★★★ 95 98 00 01 02 04 05 (06) ALAIN BRUMONT's home base in MADIRAN making just as sturdy wines as his CH Montus.

Dopff & Irion Al ★→★★ 17th-century firm at Riquewihr, now part of PFAFFENHEIM. MUSCAT Les Amandiers, GEWURZ Les Sorcières. Fair quality.

Dopff au Moulin Al ★★★ Ancient, top-class family producer at Riquewihr. Best: GEWURZ GRANDS CRUS Brand, Sporen (08); RIES SCHOENENBOURG (09 10); *Sylvaner de Riquewihr*. Pioneers of Alsace CRÉMANT; gd CUVÉES: Bartholdi, Julien. All wines esp gd in vintages favouring dry wines; not all Alsace vintages are.

Dourthe, Vins & Vignobles B'x merchant; wide range and quality emphasis: gd, notably CHX BELGRAVE, LE BOSCQ, LA GARDE. Grand Barrail Lamarzelle Figeac improving ST-EMILION. Pey La Tour, *Dourthe No 1* are well-made generic B'x.

Drappier, André Champ Outstanding family-run AUBE CHAMPAGNE house. *Pinot-led NV*, BRUT ZÉRO, Rosé Saignée, Signature BLANC DE BLANCS (02 04), Millésime d'Exception (02 04), superb Prestige CUVÉE Grande Sendrée (99 02 04). Cuvée Quatuor (four *cépages*). Superb older vintages 95 85 82.

DRC C d'O The wine geek's shorthand for DOM DE LA ROMANÉE-CONTI.

Drouhin, J & Cie Burg ★★★ Deservedly prestigious grower and merchant. Cellars in BEAUNE; v'yds (45ha, all biodynamic) esp in BEAUNE, CHABLIS. Attractive whites, Beaune *Clos des Mouches* and LAGUICHE wines best. Notably fragrant reds from pretty CHOREY-LÈS-BEAUNE to majestic MUSIGNY, GRANDS-ECHÉZEAUX, etc. Also DDO (Domaine Drouhin Oregon), *see* North America.

Duboeuf, Georges Beauj ★★→★★★ Most famous name of BEAUJOLAIS, proponent of Nouveau. Huge range of CUVÉES and crus, consistent over many yrs.

Duclot B'x négociant; top-growth specialist. Same owner as PÉTRUS.

Dugat C d'O ★★★ Cousins Claude and Bernard (Dugat-Py) make excellent, deep-coloured GEVREY-CHAMBERTIN, respective labels. Tiny volumes, huge prices.

Dujac, Domaine C d'O ★★★→★★★★ MOREY-ST-DENIS grower now with exceptional range of GRANDS CRUS. Lighter colours but intense fruit; smoky, strawberry character from use of stems. Also DOM Triennes in COTEAUX VAROIS.

Dulong B'x merchant. Part of Grands Chais de France.

Dureuil-Janthial Burg ★★ Top DOM in RULLY in capable hands of Vincent D-J, *fresh, punchy whites*, juicy reds. Try Maizières (r w) or PREMIER CRU Meix Cadot (w).

Durup, Jean Chab ★★ Volume CHABLIS producer as DOM de l'Eglantière and CH de Maligny now allied by marriage to Dom Colinot in IRANCY.

Duval-Leroy Champ Dynamic Côte des Blancs CHAMPAGNE house. 200ha of family-owned v'yds source of gd Fleur de Champagne NV, fine Blanc de CHARD (99 00 02 04), and excellent prestige *Femme de Champagne* (96' 02). New single-village/-v'yd bottlings, esp Authentis Cumières (04 06 09).

Echézeaux C d'O r ★★★ 90' 93 96' 99' 02' 99' 02' 03 05' 06 07 08 09' 10' 11 GRAND CRU (37.7ha) next to CLOS DE VOUGEOT. Middling weight, but can have exceptionally intricate flavours and startling persistence. Best from Arnoux, DRC, DUJAC, EUGÉNIE, GRIVOT, GROS, Lamarche, LIGER-BELAIR, MUGNERET-Gibourg, ROUGET.

Ecu, Domaine de l' Lo (r) w dr (sp) ★★★ 95 96 97 02 03 04 05 06 09' 10 (11) Guy Bossard, meticulous biodynamic MUSCADET-SÈVRE-ET-MAINE producer (esp mineral-rich CUVÉE Granite); also GROS PLANT, incl sparkling from GROS PLANT, plus excellent CAB FR. 2007, 2008 tiny production; 2009, 2010 normal. Estate now for sale.

Edelzwicker Al w ★ DYA. Blended light white. Delicious CH d'Ittenwiller (09).

Entraygues et du Fel and Estaing SW Fr r p w ★ DYA. Tiny twin AOPS. Cool-as-mtn-stream wines. Zinging white CHENIN. ★★ DOM Méjanassère, Laurent Mousset, esp La Pauca red (will keep). Richer whites, ★★ from Nicolas Carmarans. Alaux (r) and Fages (w) best Estaing growers.

Entre-Deux-Mers (E-2-M) B'x w ★→★★ DYA. Gd-value, dry white B'x from between the rivers Garonne and Dordogne. Best CHX BONNET, Castenet Greffier, Fontenille, Landereau, Marjosse, La Mothe du Barry French Kiss, Nardique-la-Gravière, Sainte-Marie, *Tour de Mirambeau*, Toutigeac, Turcaud.

Esmonin, Domaine Sylvie C d'O ★★★ Rich, dark wines from fully ripe grapes, esp since 2000. Notable GEVREY-CHAMBERTIN VIEILLES VIGNES and CLOS ST-JACQUES. Cousin Frédéric has Estournelles St-Jacques.

Eugénie, Domaine C d'O New owner of former Dom Engel, bought by François Pinault of CH LATOUR in 2006. Now more concentrated wines at higher prices. CLOS VOUGEOT and GRANDS-ECHÉZEAUX best.

Faiveley, J Burg ★★→★★★★ More grower now than merchant, with big holdings in CÔTE CHALONNAISE plus top v'yds in CHAMBERTIN-CLOS DE BÈZE, CHAMBOLLE-MUSIGNY, CORTON, NUITS and recent acquisitions in MEURSAULT and PULIGNY. Hugely revitalized since 2007.

Red burgundy has never been so popular the world over – where will prices go?

Faller, Théo / Domaine Weinbach Al ★★→★★★★ Founded by Capuchin monks in 1612, now run by Colette Faller and two daughters. Outstanding wines now often drier, esp GRANDS CRUS SCHLOSSBERG (Ries, esp 02 06), Furstentum (Gewurz 05). Wines of great *character and elegance*. Great CUVÉE Sainte Catherine Sélection des Grains Noble Gewurz 02.

Faugères r (p) (w) ★→★★ 05' 06 07 08 09' 10 11 Leading L'DOC area. Warm, spicy reds from SYRAH, GRENACHE, CARIGNAN, plus MOURVÈDRE and CINSAULT, grown on schist hills; whites are MARSANNE, ROUSSANNE, Rolle. Drink DOMS JEAN-MICHEL ALQUIER, Léon Barral, des Trinités, St Antonin, Ollier-Taillefer, Cebène, Mas d'Alézon.

Fèvre, William ★★★ Star turn in CHABLIS since HENRIOT purchase (1998). Largest GRANDS CRUS owner. Les CLOS outstanding. No expense spared, priced accordingly.

Fiefs Vendéens Lo r p w ★→★★★ Mainly DYA AC. Wines from the Vendée nr Sables d'Olonne vary from easy-drinking tourist wines to serious and age-worthy. CHARD, CHENIN BL, SAUV BL, MELON (whites), Grolleau Gris, CAB FR, CAB SAUV, GAMAY, Negrette, PINOT N (r p). Producers: Aloha, Coirier, CH Marie du Fou, Michon/DOM St-Nicolas.

Fitou L'doc r w ★★ 05' 06 07' 08 09 10 11 Powerful red, from schist hills south of Narbonne as well as coastal v'yds. The MIDI's oldest AC for table wine, created in 1948, 11 mths' barrel-ageing and benefits from bottle-age. Co-op at Tuchan remains a pacesetter. Experiments with MOURVÈDRE. Gd estates incl: CH de Nouvelles, DOM Bergé-Bertrand, Lérys, Rolland.

Fixin C d'O r (w) ★★★ 99' 02' 03 05' 06 07 08 09' 10' 11 Worthy and undervalued northern neighbour of GEVREY-CHAMBERTIN. Sometimes splendid reds. Best v'yds: CLOS de la Perrière, Clos du Chapitre, Clos Napoléon. Growers: CLAIR, FAIVELEY, Gelin, Guyard, MORTET and revitalized Manoir de la Perrière.

Fleurie Beauj r ★★★ 09' 10' 11' Top BEAUJOLAIS cru for perfumed, strawberry fruit and silky texture to tingle the pleasure centres. Racier from La Madone hillside, richer below. Look for Chapelle des Bois, Chignard, Clos de la Roilette, Depardon, Desprès, DUBOEUF, CH de Fleurie, Métrat, Villa Ponciago, co-op.

Floc de Gascogne SW Fr r w Locally invented Gascon answer to PINEAU DE CHARENTES. Unfermented grape juice blended with Armagnac.

Fourrier, Jean-Claude C d'O ★★★ Jean-Marie Fourrier has taken this quiet GEVREY-CHAMBERTIN DOM to new heights for profound yet succulent reds – esp Combe aux Moines, CLOS ST-JACQUES.

Francs-Côtes de Bordeaux B'x r w ★★ 03 04 05' 08 09' 10' Fringe B'x next to

CASTILLON. Previously Côtes de Francs but new AC name from 2008 (*see* box p.103). Mainly red but some white: can be tasty and attractive. Reds can age a little. Top CHX: Charmes-Godard, Francs, Laclaverie, Marsau, Pelan, La Prade, PUYGUERAUD.

Fronsac B'x r ★★→★★★ 98 00' 01 03 05' 06 08 09' 10' Underrated hilly AC west of ST-EMILION; some of the best-value reds in B'x. Top CHX: DALEM, *la Dauphine*, Fontenil, la Grave, Haut-Carles, Mayne-Vieil, *Moulin-Haut-Laroque*, Richelieu, *la Rivière*, la Rousselle, Tour du Moulin, les Trois Croix, LA VIEILLE CURE, Villars. *See also* CANON-FRONSAC.

Fronton SW Fr r p ★★ 08 09 10 (11') AOP Local specialty Négrette grape (almost exclusive to Fronton) yields cherries, violet, liquorice character; quaffable "BEAUJOLAIS of Toulouse" ideal with cassoulet. Watch for ★★ CHX Baudare, *Bellevue-la-Forêt*, Caze, du Roc, Plaisance, DOM Viguerie de Belaygues, ★ Chx Joliet, *Bouissel*, Boujac, Cransac.

Gagnard C d'O ★★★→★★★★ Well-known clan in CHASSAGNE-MONTRACHET. Long-lasting wines, esp Caillerets, Bâtard from Jean-Noël Gagnard; while Blain-G and Fontaine G have full range as far as MONTRACHET itself. All fairly priced.

Gaillac SW Fr r p w d sw sp (r, esp oaked) 05' 06 08 09 10 (11') (w sw) 05' 07' 08 09 10 (11') ★ →★★★ (p w dr) DYA. AOP. Ancient v'yd in full revival; lightish wines. ★★★ PLAGEOLES, Causse-Marines, de la Ramaye, Peyres-Roses (all biodynamic); ★★ DOMS de Brin, La Chanade, d'Escausses, Gineste, Larroque, Lamothe, Laubarel, L'Enclos des Roses, Mas Brunet, Mayragues (biodynamic), Rotier, Sarrabelle, CHX Bourguet (esp sw w). Gd all-rounders ★★ Mas Pignou, Doms de Labarthe, La Vayssette.

Garage *Vins de garage* are (usually) B'x made on a v. small scale. 1990s phenomenon. Only best remain (VALANDRAUD).

Gard, Vin de Pays du L'doc ★ The Gard *département* west of the Rhône estuary gives sound IGP reds, incl: Cévennes, du Pont du Gard. Duché d'Uzès an aspiring AOP.

Gauby, Domaine Gérard Rouss r w ★★★ Pioneering producer, biodynamic. IGP CÔTES CATALANES Les Calcinaires (w); Coume Gineste; CÔTES DU ROUSSILLON-VILLAGES Muntada (r); Les Calcinaires VIEILLES VIGNES. Associated with DOM Le Soula. Dessert wine Le Pain du Sucre. Son Lionel developing new CUVÉES.

Gers SW Fr r p w ★ DYA. VDP indistinguishable from nearby CÔTES DE GASCOGNE.

Gevrey-Chambertin C d'O r ★★★ 90' 96' 98 99' 01 02' 03 05' 06 07 08 09' 10' 11 Village containing the great CHAMBERTIN, its GRAND CRU cousins and many other noble v'yds – eg. PREMIERS CRUS Cazetiers, Combe aux Moines, Combottes, CLOS ST-JACQUES. Top growers incl: Bachelet, L BOILLOT, BURGUET, Damoy, DROUHIN, Drouhin-Laroze, DUGAT, Dugat-Py, ESMONIN, FAIVELEY, FOURRIER, Géantet-Pansiot, Harmand-Geoffroy, JADOT, LEROY, MORTET, Rossignol-Trapet, Roty, ROUSSEAU, SÉRAFIN, TRAPET, Varoilles.

Gigondas S Rhô r p ★★→★★★ 78' 89' 90' 95' 98' 99' 00' 01' 03' 04' 05' 06' 07' 08 09' 10' (11) Limestone hill, clay-sand plain east of Avignon; GRENACHE, plus SYRAH, MOURVÈDRE. Robust, smoky wines, best with clear fruit. Ace 2010s. Increase in oak, esp for US market, and in prices, but genuine local feel in many. Try: CH de Montmirail, St-Cosme, CLOS du Joncuas, P Amadieu, DOM Boissan, Bouïssière, Brusset, Cassan, Espiers, Goubert, Gour de Chaulé, Grapillon d'Or, *les Pallières*, Pesquier, Raspail-Ay, Roubine, St Gayan, Santa Duc, *Famille Perrin*. Heady rosés.

Ginestet Go-ahead B'x négociant. Quality controls for grape suppliers. Principal brands G de Ginestet, Marquis de Chasse, Mascaron.

Girardin, Vincent C d'O r w ★★→★★★ Changes afoot at this widely distributed grower and négociant – he has just sold his merchant business.

Givry Burg r (w) ★★ 05' 07 08 09' 10' 11 Top tip in CÔTE CHALONNAISE, for tasty reds that can age. Some pretty whites, too. Best: JOBLOT, CLOS Salomon, F Lumpp.

Gosset Champ Old house founded in 16th century, making CHAMPAGNES in vinous style. Now works out of new premises in Épernay. V.gd CUVÉE Elegance NV. Traditional Grand Millésime (99 02 04). Gosset Celebris (99 02 04) is finest cuvée. Remarkable Celebris Rosé (03 04).

Gouges, Henri C d'O ★★★ Grégory G continuing success of previous generation with rich, meaty, long-lasting NUITS-ST-GEORGES from a range of PREMIER CRU v'yds. Try Vaucrains, Les St Georges, or Chaignots. Interesting white, too.

Grand Cru Means different things in different areas. One of top Burgundy v'yds with its own AC. In ALSACE, one of 51 top v'yds. In ST-EMILION, 60% of production is St-Emilion Grand Cru, often run-of-the-mill. In the MÉDOC there are five tiers of Grands Crus Classés. In CHAMPAGNE top villages are grand cru. Now a new designation in Loire for QUARTS DE CHAUME.

Grande Champagne SW Fr AC of the best area of Cognac. Nothing fizzy about it.

Grande Rue, La C d'O ★★★ 90' 95 96' 98 00 02' 03 05' 06 07 08 09' 10' 11 GRAND CRU MONOPOLE of DOM Lamarche, a narrow strip between LA TÂCHE and ROMANÉE-CONTI, if not quite in same league or price.

Grands-Échézeaux C d'O ★★★★ 90' 93 95 96' 99' 00 02' 03 05' 06 07 08 09' 10' 11 Superlative 9ha GRAND CRU next to CLOS DE VOUGEOT, may be more akin to MUSIGNY. Wines not weighty but aromatic. Viz DRC, DROUHIN, EUGÉNIE, GROS, Lamarche, Mongeard-MUGNERET.

Grange des Pères, Domaine de la L'doc r w ★★★ IGP PAYS DE L'HÉRAULT. Cult estate neighbouring MAS DE DAUMAS GASSAC, created by Laurent Vaillé for first vintage 1992. Red from SYRAH, MOURVÈDRE, CAB SAUV; white 80% ROUSSANNE, plus MARSANNE, CHARD. Original, stylish wines; well worth seeking out.

Gratien, Alfred and Gratien & Meyer Champ ★★→★★★ BRUT 97' 98 02 04 06 08; Brut NV. Superb Prestige CUVÉE Paradis Brut and Rosé (blend of fine yrs). Excellent quirky CHAMPAGNE house, now German-owned. Fine, v. dry, lasting, barrel-fermented wine, incl *The Wine Society's house Champagne*. Gratien & Meyer is counterpart at SAUMUR. (Gd Cuvée Flamme.)

Graves B'x r w ★→★★ 00 01 04 05' 06 08 09' 10' Region south of B'x city. Source of improving reds and classic, clean, dry whites. Gd value. Top CHX: ARCHAMBEAU, Brondelle, CHANTEGRIVE, *Clos Floridene*, Crabitey, Ferrande, Fougères, Haura, l'Hospital, Léhoul, Magneau, Rahoul, Respide, *Respide-Médeville*, St-Robert CUVÉE Poncet Deville, Venus, *Vieux Ch Gaubert*, Villa Bel Air.

Graves de Vayres B'x r w ★ DYA. Tiny AC in E-2-M zone. Mainly red, drunk locally.

Grès de Montpellier L'doc r p w Recently recognized subzone of AC L'DOC and aspiring cru. Sprawling v'yds in the hills behind Montpellier, incl: St-Georges d'Orques, La Méjanelle, St-Christol, St-Drézery. Try DOMS Clavel, Terre Megère, de la Prose; CHX L'Engarran, de Flaugergues and Grès St-Paul.

Grignan-les-Adhémar S Rhô r (p) w ★→★★ 07' 09' 10' Complicated name-change from Tricastin, due to nearby nuclear-plant troubles 2008–9. Mid-Rhône AC; limited core of quality; best reds full, tangy, herbal. Leaders: DOMS de Bonetto-Fabrol, Grangeneuve best (esp VIEILLES VIGNES), de Montine (gd white), St-Luc, CH La Décelle (incl white CÔTES DU RHÔNE).

Griotte-Chambertin C d'O ★★★★ 90' 95 96' 99' 00 02' 03 05' 06 07 08 09' 10' 11 Small GRAND CRU next to CHAMBERTIN. Less weight but brisk red fruit and ageing potential, at least from DUGAT, DROUHIN, FOURRIER, *Ponsot*.

Grivot, Jean C d'O ★★★→★★★★ Huge improvements at this VOSNE-ROMANÉE DOM in the past decade. Superb range topped by GRANDS CRUS CLOS DE VOUGEOT, ÉCHÉZEAUX, RICHEBOURG.

Gros, Domaines C d'O ★★★→★★★★ Fine family of VIGNERONS in VOSNE-ROMANÉE comprising (at least) DOMS Jean, Michel, Anne, Anne-Françoise Gros and Gros Frère & Soeur. Wines range from HAUTES-CÔTES DE NUITS to RICHEBOURG.

Gros Plant du Pays Nantais Lo w ★ DYA. AC from GROS PLANT, best crisply citric

– great with oysters and other shellfish. Try: Basse Ville, Bossard, Herbauges, Luneau-Papin, de la Preuille.

Guigal, Ets E N Rhô ★★→★★★★ Global-name grower-merchant: 31ha CÔTE-RÔTIE is base, plus CONDRIEU, CROZES-HERMITAGE, HERMITAGE, ST-JOSEPH v'yds. Merchant: CONDRIEU, Côte-Rôtie, Crozes-Hermitage, Hermitage, Southern Rhône. Owns DOM de Bonserine, VIDAL-FLEURY (quality up). Top Côte-Rôties La Mouline, La Landonne, La Turque (profound, rich, new oak for 42 mths, so atypical); all reds have packed flavours. Standard wines: gd value, consistent, esp v.gd-value red; also white, rosé CÔTES DU RHÔNE. Plus fat, oaky Condrieu La Doriane, authentic Hermitage white.

Haut-Médoc B'x r ★★→★★★ 98 00' 01 02 03 04 05' 06 08 09' 10' Prime source of minerally, digestible CAB/MERLOT reds. Some variation in soils and wines: sand and gravel in south; heavier clay and gravel in north; sturdier. Need age. Five classed growths (BELGRAVE, CAMENSAC, CANTEMERLE, LA LAGUNE, LA TOUR-CARNET). Other top CHX: D'AGASSAC, Belle-Vue, LANESSAN, SÉNÉJAC, SOCIANDO-MALLET.

Haut-Montravel SW F r w sw ★★★ 03 05' 06 07 08 09 10 (11') Sweetest of the three MONTRAVEL sub-aops of BERGERAC. More minerally than MONBAZILLAC or SAUSSIGNAC. Best (esp when kept) are ★★ CH Puy-Servain-Terrement, ★★ DOMS Moulin Caresse and Libarde.

Haut-Poitou Lo r p w sp ★→★★ Top age 3-4 yrs. AC from CAB SAUV, CAB FR, GAMAY, CHARD, PINOT N, SAUV BL. Cave du Haut-Poitou is largest producer (60%+); top wines Brizay, La Fuye). Ampelidae consists of 32 growers using IGP.

Hautes-Côtes de Beaune / Nuits C d'O r w ★★ (r) 05' 09' 10 11 (w) 09' 10' 11 ACS for the villages in the hills behind the CÔTE DE BEAUNE. Attractive lighter reds and whites for early drinking. Best: Carré, Cornu, Devevey, Duband, Féry, GROS, Jacob, Mazilly, Naudin-Ferrand, Verdet. Also useful large co-op nr BEAUNE.

Heidsieck, Charles Champ V. fine CHAMPAGNE house, now under enlightened new owners. BRUT Rés NV. Vintage 00 02' 08'. Outstanding Blanc des Millénaires (95' 08'). *See also* PIPER-HEIDSIECK.

Heidsieck Monopole Champ Once-illustrious CHAMPAGNE house. Fair quality. Silver Top (02 04 06 08) best wine.

Hengst Al ALSACE GRAND CRU. Excels with top GEWURZ from ZIND-HUMBRECHT and JOSMEYER; also AUXERROIS, CHASSELAS and PINOT N (latter not grand cru).

Henriot Champ BRUT Souverain NV; BLANCS DE BLANCS de CHARD NV; Brut 02 04 06 08; Brut Rosé 04. Fine family CHAMPAGNE house. Elegant, fresh, creamy style. Outstanding Prestige CUVÉE Les Enchanteleurs (88' 95' 02 04 08). Also owns BOUCHARD PÈRE & FILS, FÈVRE.

Hérault L'doc Largest v'yd *département*: 91,700ha (in 2010), incl FAUGÈRES, ST-CHINIAN, PIC ST-LOUP, PICPOUL DE PINET, Grès de Pinet, Grès de Montpellier, PÉZENAS, TERRASSES DU LARZAC and L'DOC. Source of IGP PAYS de l'Hérault encompassing full quality spectrum, from pioneering and innovative to basic. Also VDT.

Hermitage N Rhô r w ★★★ →★★★★ 61' 66' 78' 83' 85' 88 89' 90' 91' 95' 96 97' 98' 99' 00 01' 03 04 05' 06' 07' 09' 10' 11 Lingering, rich, structured SYRAH from imposing 133ha granite hill on east bank of Rhône. Red, white reward ageing over 20 yrs+. Full, complex, fascinating white (MARSANNE, some ROUSSANNE) best left for 6–7 yrs+. Best: Belle, CHAPOUTIER, J-L CHAVE, Colombier, DELAS, Desmeure (oak), Faurie (pure wines), GUIGAL, Habrard (w), JABOULET, M Sorrel, Tardieu-Laurent (oak). TAIN co-op gd (esp Epsilon, Gambert de Loche).

Hortus, Domaine de l' L'doc r p w ★★★ Pioneering producer of PIC ST-LOUP. White IGP Val de Montferrand. Stylish wines; reds Bergerie and oak-aged Grande Rés. Also red CLOS du Prieur in TERRASSES DU LARZAC.

Hospices de Beaune C d'O Medieval foundation with many fine v'yds; holds grand charity auction on 3rd Sunday in Nov, revitalized since 2005 by Christie's.

Individuals can now buy as well as trade. Standards more consistent under stewardship of Roland Masse; look out for gd-value BEAUNE CUVÉES or expensive GRANDS CRUS, eg. CLOS DE LA ROCHE, CORTON (r), BÂTARD-MONTRACHET (w).

Hudelot C d'O ★★★ VIGNERON family in CÔTE DE NUITS. New life breathed into H-Noëllat (VOUGEOT), while H-Baillet (CHAMBOLLE) challenging hard. Former more stylish, latter more punchy.

Huet Lo ★★★★ 88 89' 90' 95' 96' 97' 02' 03' 05' 06 07 08' 09' 10 VOUVRAY biodynamic estate. Anthony Hwang (owner) also has Királyudvar estate in Tokaji (*see* Central & SE Europe). Three single v'yds: Le Haut Lieu, Le Mont, CLOS du Bourg. Top-quality, precision, great agers: look for vintages such as 1919, 1921, 1924, 1947, 1959, 1989, 1990. Also *pétillant*. A benchmark for CHENIN BL. Noël Pinguet, who ran the estate from 1976, left abruptly early 2012.

Hugel & Fils Al ★★→★★★ Big house making superb late-harvest wines. Three quality levels: Classic, Tradition, Jubilee. Top wines, from GRANDS CRUS, never state grand cru on label.

IGP / Indication Géographique Protegée The successor to VDP. No difference in status, only in unhelpful name.

Irancy Burg r (p) ★★ 05' 09' 10 11 Light red, made nr CHABLIS from PINOT N and local César. Best v'yds: Palotte, Mazelots. Best growers: *Colinot*, Richoux, Goisot.

Irouléguy SW Fr r p (w) ★→★★★ 05' 06 08 09 10 (11') Basque AOP, MADIRAN's younger sister, but still a fitting match for *pelota*, bull-fighting and rugby. TANNAT/CAB-FR-based. Best: ★★★ Ameztia, Arretxea, Brana, Ilarria and ★★ Abotia, Bordathio, Etchegaraya, Mourguy. Excellent co-op (note ★★★ Xuri d'Ansa white). Gd rosés to take to the beach.

Jaboulet Aîné, Paul N Rhô 19th-century owner-merchant at Tain, sold to Swiss investor early 2006, prices up, wines lack inspiration, are international. Once leading maker of HERMITAGE (esp La Chapelle ★★★, quality varies 1990s on), CORNAS St-Pierre, CROZES Thalabert, Roure (sound); merchant of other Rhônes, notably CÔTES DU RHÔNE Parallèle 45, CONDRIEU, VENTOUX, VACQUEYRAS. Whites short on Rhône body, drink most young. Branded-goods emphasis, incl new v. expensive La Chapelle white.

Jacquart Champ BRUT NV; Brut Rosé NV (Carte Blanche, CUVÉE Spéciale); Brut 00 02 04 Co-op-based CHAMPAGNE brand; in quantity, sixth largest. Improving quality. Luxury brands: Cuvée Nominée Blanc 00 02' 04. Fine Mosaïque BLANC DE BLANCS 02 04 06 and Rosé 02 04 06. *Oenothèque* older vintages (90) now launched.

Jacquesson Champ Bijou Dizy CHAMPAGNE house, lovely, precise wines. Outstanding single-v'yd Avize Champ Caïn 02'; white (95 96' 02); new *saignée* Rosé Terre Rouge (04). Corne Bautray, Dizy 02 04, and *excellent numbered NV cuvées* 728, 730', 731, 732, 733, 734, 735.

Jadot, Louis Burg ★★→★★★★ High-performance merchant house across the board with significant v'yd holdings in CÔTE D'OR and expanding fast in MÂCON and BEAUJOLAIS; esp POUILLY-FUISSÉ (DOM Ferret) and MOULIN-À-VENT (CH des Jacques, Clos du Grand Carquelin). Mineral whites as gd as structured reds.

Jasnières Lo w dr (sw) ★★→★★★ 02 03 05' 06 07 08' 09' 10 (11) VOUVRAY-like wine (CHENIN BL), both dry and off-dry from tiny but dynamic v'yd north of Tours on south-facing slopes. Growers: Bénédicte de Rycke, DOMS Aubert la Chapelle, de L'Ange Vin, DE BELLIVIÈRE, Breton, le Briseau, de la Charriére, Janvier, les Maisons Rouges.

Jobard C d'O VIGNERON family in MEURSAULT. Antoine, son of François, for long-lived Genevrières, etc. Cousin Rémi for more immediate class. Both ★★★.

Joblot Burg ★★★ Outstanding GIVRY DOM with v. high viticultural standards. Try PREMIER CRU La Servoisine in both colours.

Joseph Perrier Champ Excellent smaller CHAMPAGNE house at Châlons with gd v'yds in Marne Valley. Supple, fruity style; top Prestige CUVÉE Joséphine 02 ★★★★.

Improved Cuvée Royale BRUT NV with lower *dosage*; Cuvée Royale BLANC DE BLANCS 02 04; Cuvée Royale Rosé NV; Brut 99 00 02

Josmeyer Al ★★→★★★ Fine, elegant, long-lived, organic dry wines. Superb RIES *grand cru Hengst* (06 08 09'). Also v.gd lesser varieties, esp AUXERROIS. Smart biodynamist, rigorous but realistic.

Juliénas Beauj r ★★★ 05' 09' 10' 11' Leading cru of BEAUJOLAIS, deserves to be better-known. Vigorous, fruity wine to keep 2–3 yrs. Growers: Aufranc, Santé, Michel Tête, Trenel.

Jurançon SW Fr w d r sw ★→★★★ (sw) 97' 03 04' 05' 06 07' 10' (11') (dr) 04' 05' 06 07 08 09 10' (11') Sweet and dry have separate ACS. The pride of Béarn, mostly from GROS and PETIT MANSENG grapes. Boutique ★★★★ Jardins de Babylon (DAGUENEAU) in class (and price) of its own. ★★★ DOMS Bellegarde, Bordenave, Castéra, *Cauhapé*, Lapeyre, Larrédya, de Souch, Thou, Uroulat, ★★ CH Jolys, Doms Bellauc, Capdevielle, Nigri, Guirardel, Clos Benguères. ★ Gd-value dry whites from co-op.

"Red Graves and Médoc are like matt and glossy prints of the same photograph." (Maurice Healy).

Kaefferkopf Al w dr (sw) ★★★ The 51st GRAND CRU of ALSACE at Ammerschwihr. Permitted to make blends as well as varietal wines, unlike other grands crus.

Kientzler, Andre Al ★★→★★★ Small, v. fine grower at Ribeauvillé. V.gd RIES from GRANDS CRUS Osterberg and Geisberg (02 06 08 09) and lush GEWURZ from grand cru Kirchberg (09). Rich, aromatic sweet wines.

Kreydenweiss, Marc Al ★★→★★★ Fine biodynamic grower, esp for PINOT GR (v.gd GRAND CRU Moenchberg), PINOT BL and RIES. Top wine: grand cru Kastelberg (ages 20 yrs); also fine AUXERROIS Kritt Klevner and gd VENDANGE TARDIVE. One of first in Alsace to use new oak – now older casks, too. Gd Ries/Pinot Gr blend CLOS du Val d'Eléon. Also in Rhône Valley.

Krug Champ Grande CUVÉE; Vintage 90 96 98' 00; Rosé; CLOS du Mesnil (BLANC DE BLANCS) 90 92 95' 00; Krug Collection 76' 81 85. Small, supremely prestigious CHAMPAGNE house. Rich, nutty wines, oak-fermented: long ageing, superlative quality, soaring price. Vintage BRUT great in 98', a challenging yr. Clos d'Ambonnay (95' 96 98) is for billionaires.

Kuentz-Bas Al ★→★★★ Famous grower/merchant at Husseren-les-Château, esp PINOT GR, GEWURZ. Gd VENDANGES TARDIVES. Owned by Caves J-B Adam.

L'Etoile Jura w dr (sw) sp ★★ Subregion of the Jura known for stylish whites, incl VIN JAUNE, similar to CH CHALON; gd sparkling.

Ladoix C d'O r (w) ★★ 02' 03 05' 07 08 09' 10' 11 Village at north end of CÔTE DE BEAUNE, incl some CORTON and CORTON-CHARLEMAGNE. After yrs in shadow of ALOXE, now undergoing revival in the hands of Claude Chevalier, Michel Mallard, Sylvain Loichet. Exuberant wines of interest, too.

Ladoucette, de Lo (r) (p) w ★★→★★★ 06 07 08 09 10 (11) Largest individual producer of POUILLY-FUMÉ, based at CH de Nozet. Expensive deluxe brand Baron de L. SANCERRE Comte Lafond, La Poussie (wonderful vy'd severely eroded); VOUVRAY Marc Brédif. Owns Albert Pic (CHABLIS).

Lafarge, Michel C d'O ★★★★ Classic VOLNAY estate run biodynamically by Frédéric L, son of ever-present Michel. Outstanding, long-lived PREMIERS CRUS *Clos des Chênes*, Caillerets, CLOS du CH des Ducs. Also fine BEAUNE and POMMARD.

Lafon, Domaine des Comtes Burg ★★★→★★★★ Iconic DOM for great MEURSAULT and MONTRACHET, with red VOLNAY (esp Santenots) equally outstanding. Try separate Mâconnais dom for value, while Dominique L also has own label in MEURSAULT.

Laguiche, Marquis de C d'O ★★★→★★★★ Largest owner of MONTRACHET and a fine PREMIER CRU CHASSAGNE, both made by DROUHIN.

Lalande de Pomerol B'x r ★★ 98 99 00' 01' 04 05' 06 07 08 09' 10' Northerly neighbour of POMEROL. Similar style but variations with soils and winemaking. New investors and younger generation a bonus. Top CHX: Belles-Graves, BERTINEAU ST-VINCENT, Chambrun, Les Cruzelles, La Fleur de Boüard, Garraud, Grand Ormeau, Jean de Gué, Haut-Chaigneau, Les Hauts Conseillants, Laborderie-Mondésir, Perron (La Fleur), La Sergue, Siaurac, TOURNEFEUILLE.

Landron (Domaines) Lo w dr sp ★★→★★★ 05 09 10 (11) Top producer of biodynamic MUSCADET-SÈVRE-ET-MAINE with several terroir CUVÉES, incl Amphibolite, age-worthy Fief du Breil, Clos de la Carizière and gd sparkling – GROS PLANT/PINOT N.

Langlois-Château Lo ★★→★★★ Top SAUMUR sparkling (CRÉMANT only) house, BOLLINGER-owned. Also still wines, esp v.gd age-worthy Saumur Blanc VIEILLES VIGNES.

Languedoc r p w General term for the MIDI, and now AC enlarging COTEAUX DU L'DOC to incl MINERVOIS, CORBIÈRES, ROUSSILLON. Rules the same as for Coteaux du L'doc, with period for name-changing extended to May 2017. The bottom of the pyramid of Midi ACs. A hierachy of crus and even better cru classés in the pipeline.

Lanson Champ Black Label NV; Rosé NV; BRUT 99 02. Improving CHAMPAGNE house, part of LANSON-BCC group. Long-lived luxury brand: Noble CUVÉE as BLANC DE BLANCS, rosé and vintage (98' 99 02). New single-vyd CLOS Lanson (07 08 09). New Extra Age (blend of 99 02 03) – fair quality. Bought a biodynamic v'yd in 2011, and will keep it bio.

Vintage Champagne comprises only around 6% of total Champagne production.

Lanson-BCC Champ Owner of LANSON, BOIZEL, Chanoine Frères, Philipponat, BESSERAT DE BELLEFON, DE VENOGE, Alexandre Bonnet.

Lapierre, Marcel Beauj ★★★ Cult MORGON DOM run by Mathieu L, in succession to his late father, pioneer of sulphur-free winemaking in the BEAUJOLAIS.

Laroche Chab ★★ Change of ownership in 2009 for large-scale CHABLIS grower and merchant with interests in south of France, Chile, South Africa. Majority owner now Groupe Jeanjean. Try GRAND CRU Rés de l'Obédiencerie.

Latour de France Rouss r (w) ★→★★★ Theoretically superior village in CÔTES DU ROUSSILLON-VILLAGES. Esp CLOS de l'Oum, Clos des Fées. Best wines often IGP CÔTES CATALANES. Old vines are inspiring new producers.

Latour, Louis Burg ★★→★★★ Famous traditional family merchant making sound whites from CÔTE D'OR v'yds (esp CORTON, CORTON-CHARLEMAGNE), Mâconnais and the ARDÈCHE (all CHARD) and less exciting reds (all PINOT) from CÔTE D'OR and Coteaux du Verdon. Now also owns Henry Fessy in BEAUJOLAIS.

Latricières-Chambertin C d'O r ★★★ 90' 93 95 96' 99' 02' 03 05' 06 07 08 09' 10' 11 GRAND CRU (7.35ha) next to CHAMBERTIN, rich if not quite as intense. Best from BIZE, Drouhin-Laroze, Duband, FAIVELEY, LEROY, Rossignol-Trapet, TRAPET.

Laudun S Rhô r p w ★→★★★ 07' 09' 10' (11) Front-rank CÔTES DU RHÔNE-VILLAGE, west bank. Early, clear reds (lots of SYRAH), go-go rosés, stylish whites (apéritif and food). Immediate flavours from Serre de Bernon co-op. DOM Pelaquié best, esp grand white. Also CHX de Bord, Courac, Juliette, Marjolet, St-Maurice, Dom Duseigneur, Prieuré St-Pierre.

Laurent-Perrier Champ V.gd BRUT NV; Rosé NV; Brut 02 04 Dynamic family-owned CHAMPAGNE house at Tours-sur-Marne. Fine, minerally NV; excellent luxury brands: Grand Siècle la CUVÉE Lumière du Millésime (the extra-special version of Grand Siècle: 90 96) Grand Siècle Alexandra Brut Rosé (98 02). But Ultra Brut fails to impress.

Leflaive, Domaine Burg ★★★★ Top biodynamic white burgundy producer in PULIGNY-MONTRACHET with a clutch of GRANDS CRUS, incl MONTRACHET, Chevalier. *Fabulous premiers crus*, such as Pucelles, Combettes, Folatières. MÂCON for value (since 2004).

Leflaive, Olivier C d'O ★★→★★★ High-quality négociant at PULIGNY-MONTRACHET, cousin of the previous entry. Reliable wines, mostly white, but drink young. V'yd holdings now expanded with Olivier's share from family DOM.

Leroy, Domaine C d'O ★★★★ DOM built around purchase of Noëllat in VOSNE-ROMANÉE in 1988. Extraordinary quality (and prices) from tiny biodynamic yields. Also original Leroy family holding Dom d'Auvenay.

Leroy, Maison C d'O ★★★★ Burgundy's ultimate NÉGOCIANT-ÉLEVEUR at AUXEY-DURESSES. Small parcels of grand old wines at prices to make you rub your eyes.

Liger-Belair C d'O ★★★→★★★★ Two recently re-established DOMS of high quality. Vicomte Louis-Michel L-B makes brilliantly ethereal wines in VOSNE-ROMANÉE, while cousin Thibault makes plump reds in NUITS-ST-GEORGES.

Lignier C d'O ★★→★★★ Family in MOREY-ST-DENIS. Best is Hubert (eg. CLOS DE LA ROCHE), but watch Virgile L-Michelot and DOM Lucie & Auguste L.

Limoux Rouss r w ★★ AC for great-value sparkling BLANQUETTE DE LIMOUX or better *Crémant de Limoux*, also unusual *méthode ancestrale*. Oak-aged CHARD, also CHENIN, Mauzac for white Limoux AC. A potential Cru du L'DOC. Red AC (2003) based on MERLOT, plus SYRAH, GRENACHE, CABS, CARIGNAN. PINOT N for CRÉMANT and IGP. Growers: DOMS de Fourn, Laurens, des Martinolles, de Mouscaillo, Rives Blanques.

Lirac S Rhô r p w ★★ 05′ 06′ 07′ 09′ 10′ (11) Lesser- known neighbour of TAVEL. Lacks spread of quality. Fair-bodied, spiced red (can age 5 yrs+), impetus from recent CHÂTEAUNEUF-DU-PAPE owners bringing improved fruit, more style. Reds best, esp DOMS Beaumont, Duseigneur, Giraud, Joncier, Lafond Roc-Epine, Lorentine, Maby (Fermade), André Méjan, de la Mordorée (best), Rocalière, Rocca Maura, R Sabon, CHX Bouchassy, Manissy, Mont-Redon, St-Roch, Ségriès. Whites combine freshness, body (5 yrs).

Listrac-Médoc H-Méd r ★★→★★★ 98 00′ 01 03 05′ 06 08 09′ 10′ Neighbour of MOULIS in the southern MÉDOC. Firm, styled clarets now often rounded-out with more MERLOT. A little white. Best CHX: Cap Léon Veyrin, CLARKE, DUCLUZEAU, FONRÉAUD, FOURCAS-DUPRÉ, FOURCAS-HOSTEN, Mayne-Lalande, Reverdi, SARANSOT-DUPRÉ.

Long-Depaquit Chab ★★★ BICHOT-owned CHABLIS DOM, incl flagship GRAND CRU brand La Moutonne.

Lorentz, Gustave Al ★★→★★★ Grower and merchant at Bergheim. Esp GEWURZ, RIES from GRANDS CRUS Altenberg de Bergheim, Kanzlerberg. As fine for aged DOM as young-volume wines.

Lot SW Fr Departmental IGP useful for growers in AOP areas whose rules do not allow white wines, and for others outside to make wine in all colours. Some are quite ambitious, eg. ★★ DOMS Belmont, Sully.

Loupiac B'x w sw ★★ 98 99′ 01′ 02 03′ 05′ 07 09′ 10′ Faces SAUTERNES across the Garonne River. Lighter and fresher in style. Top CHX: CLOS-Jean, LOUPIAC-DAUDIET, Noble, DE RICAUD, Les Roques.

Lubéron S Rhô r p w ★→★★★ 09′ 10′ Touristy, new money area, 2,500ha v'yds annex to Southern Rhône. Only fair terroir, and modern, technical wines. SYRAH emphasis. Many wannabes. Bright star is CH de la Canorgue. Also gd: DOM de la Citadelle, Ch Clapier, Edem, Fontvert, O Ravoire, St-Estève de Neri (improving), Tardieu-Laurent (rich, oak), Cellier de Marrenon, Val-Joanis, LA VIEILLE FERME (gd-value white).

Lussac-St-Emilion B'x r ★★ 98 00′ 01 03 05′ 08 09′ 10′ The lightest of the ST-EMILION satellites. Co-op the main producer. Top CHX: Barbe Blanche, Bel Air, Bellevue, Courlat, la Grenière, DE LUSSAC, DU LYONNAT, Mayne-Blanc, La Rose-Perrière.

Macération carbonique Traditional fermentation technique – whole bunches of unbroken grapes in a closed vat. Fermentation inside each grape eventually bursts it, giving vivid, fruity, mild wine, but not for ageing. Esp in BEAUJOLAIS, but not for best wines; now much used in the MIDI and elsewhere, even CHÂTEAUNEUF.

Mâcon Burg r (p) w DYA. Sound, usually unremarkable reds (from GAMAY), tasty dry (CHARDY) whites.

Mâcon-Lugny Burg w ★★ 09' 10 11 Leading Mâconnais village. Try Les Charmes from excellent co-op or Genevrières from LATOUR.

Mâcon-Villages Burg w ★★→★★★ 09' 10' 11 Catch-all name for better Mâconnais wines that may also use own names eg. MÂCON-LUGNY, La Roche Vineuse, etc. Quality individual growers. Try DOMS André Bonhomme, Guillot-Broux, les Héritiers du Comte Lafon, Nicolas Maillet, Merlin; co-ops at Lugny, Prissé, Viré.

Macvin Jura sw sw ★★ AC for "traditional" MARC and grape-juice apéritif.

Madiran SW Fr r ★★→★★★ 00' 01 02 04 05' 06 08 09 10 (11') Gascon AOP. Despite efforts to make quicker-maturing wines, real Madiran remains inescapably big and must be kept. ★★★ CHX *Montus* and BOUSCASSÉ increasingly rivalled by DOMS Berthoumieu, Capmartin, Chapelle Lenclos, CLOS Basté, Labranche-Laffont, Laffitte-Teston and *Laplace*. Also gd: ★★ Barréjat, Crampilh, Damiens, Dou Bernés.

Mähler-Besse B'x 1st-class Dutch négociant in B'X. Loads of old vintages. Has share in CH PALMER.

Mailly-Champagne Champ ★★★ Top CHAMPAGNE co-op, all GRAND CRU grapes. Prestige CUVÉE des *Echansons* (02') great wine for long ageing. V. refined L'Intemporelle (95 99).

Maire, Henri Jura ★→★★ The biggest grower/merchant of Jura wines, with half of the entire AC. Some top wines, many cheerfully commercial. Fun to visit.

Malepère L'doc r ★ DYA. Originally Côtes de la Malepère, now plain Malepère AC, nr LIMOUX, for reds that combine B'X and the MIDI: fresh, with a touch of rusticity. Gd, original drinking, esp CH Guilhem, de Cointes, DOM le Fort.

Mann, Albert Al ★→★★★ Top grower at Wettolsheim: rich, elegant wines. V.gd PINOT BL, AUXERROIS, PINOT N, and gd range of GRAND CRU wines from SCHLOSSBERG, HENGST, Furstentum and Steingrubler. Immaculate biodynamic v'yds.

Maranges C d'O r (w) ★★ 02' 03' 05' 07 08 09' 10 11 Southernmost AC of CÔTE DE BEAUNE with relatively tannic reds. Gd value from PREMIER CRU. Best growers: Bachelet-Monnot, Contat-Grangé, Chevrot.

Marc Grape skins after pressing; the strong-smelling brandy made from them.

Marcillac SW Fr r r p ★★ Characterful love-or-hate AOP from the red soil of Aveyron, producing blue-tinged, spicy, soft-fruit character from the FER SERVADOU grape (here called Mansois). ★★ DOMS du Cros, Costes, Vieux Porche and gd co-op lead the way. Best at 3 yrs old.

Margaux H-Méd r ★★→★★★★ 95 96 98 00' 01 02 04 05' 06 08 09' 10' Large communal AC in the southern MÉDOC famous for its elegant, fragrant style. Once somnolent; now much improved. Top CHX: BRANE-CANTENAC, DAUZAC, FERRIÈRE, GISCOURS, KIRWAN, LASCOMBES, MALESCOT-ST-EXUPÉRY, MARGAUX, PALMER, RAUZAN-SÉGLA, SIRAN, DU TERTRE.

Marionnet, Henry Lo r w ★★→★★★ 08' 09' 10 (11) Henry and Jean-Sébastien at eastern extremity of TOURAINE, fascinated by grape varieties. Wines incl: SAUV BL (M de Marionnet – gd vintages) and *Gamay*, esp the unsulphured Première Vendange, Provignage (from ungrafted Romorantin vines planted 1850). Ungrafted wines, incl juicy *Côt* and minerally CHENIN BL.

Marmande SW Fr r p (w) ★→★★★ 05' 06 08 09 (10) (11') Blossoming AOP on threshold of Gascony. ★★★ DOM Elian da Ros is idiosyncratic cult grower, but try ★★ *Ch de Beaulieu*, ★ Dom Bonnet et Laborde and CH Lassolle. Co-op struggles to keep up.

Marque déposée Trademark.

Marsannay C d'O r p (w) ★★ 05' 06 08 09' 10 11 Far north of CÔTE DE NUITS. Easy-to-drink wines of all three colours. Best are reds from gifted producers, eg.

Audoin, Charlopin, CLAIR, Fournier, *Pataille* and TRAPET. No PREMIERS CRUS yet, but plans afoot. Rosé gd with 1–2 yrs age.

Mas de Daumas Gassac L'doc r p w ★★→★★★ 00 01 02 03 04 05 06 07 08 09 10 Pioneering IGP set new standards in the MIDI, with CAB-based reds from apparently unique, wind-borne, glacial soil. Quality now surpassed by others, eg. neighbouring GRANGE DES PÈRES. Best wine: a deliciously fragrant white, to drink at 2–3 yrs. Also super-CUVÉE Emile Peynaud, rosé Frizant, intriguing sweet wine Vin de Laurence (MUSCAT, SERCIAL).

Mas, Domaines Paul L'doc r p w ★★ Big player in the south; 170ha of own estates and controls 700ha nr Pezenas and also Limoux. Owns DOM Astruc. Mainly IGP. Innovative marketing. Known for Arrogant Frog IGP range; La Forge, les Tannes, Les Vignes de Nicole. Also recent purchase of Dom Crès Ricards.

Bordeaux plans to reduce the number of growers of basic Bordeaux by 26%.

Massif d'Uchaux S Rhô r ★★ 09' 10' Cool, wooded-area Rhône village with talented growers, decisively fruited wines. Note: CH St-Estève, DOMS La Cabotte, Chapoton, Cros de la Mûre (v.gd, gd value), de la Guicharde, Renjarde.

Mau, Yvon B'x Négociant, now part of Freixenet. Original Mau-family owners kept CHX Brown (PESSAC-LÉOGNAN) and Preuillac (MÉDOC).

Maury Rouss r sw ★★ NV red VDN from ROUSSILLON. GRENACHE grown on island of schist in limestone hills. Much recent improvement, esp at *Mas Amiel*. Several new estates, eg. DOM of the Bee; sound co-op. RANCIOS age beautifully. Gd, potent red table wines.

Mazis- (or Mazy-) Chambertin C d'O r ★★★ 90' 93 95 96' 99' 02' 03 05' 06 07 08 09'10'11 Northernmost GRAND CRU (9ha) of GEVREY-CHAMBERTIN, top-class in upper part; *heavenly wines*. Best from DUGAT-PY, FAIVELEY, HOSPICES DE BEAUNE, LEROY, Maume, ROUSSEAU.

Mazoyères-Chambertin C d'O *See* CHARMES-CHAMBERTIN.

Méditerranée, Vin de Pays de L'doc Regional IGP from Southern Rhône/PROVENCE. Quaffable reds, characterful whites: VIOGNIER. Originally Portes de la Méditerranée.

Médoc B'x r ★★→★★★ 98 00' 02 03 04 05' 06 08 09' 10' AC for reds in the flatter, northern part of the Médoc peninsula. Gd if you're selective. Earthy, with MERLOT adding flesh. Top CHX: Goulée, GREYSAC, LOUDENNE, Lousteauneuf, LES ORMES-SORBET, POTENSAC, Rollan-de-By (HAUT-CONDISSAS), LA TOUR-DE-BY, TOUR HAUT-CAUSSAN.

Meffre, Gabriel S Rhô ★★ Big Rhône merchant under BOISSET/Eric Brousse control since 2009. Owns GIGONDAS DOM Longue-Toque. Recent progress: modern fruity wines sought. Also bottles, sells small CHÂTEAUNEUF doms. Reliable Northern Rhône Laurus (new oak) range, esp CROZES-HERMITAGE, ST-JOSEPH.

Mellot, Alphonse Lo r p w ★★→★★★ 03 05 06 07 08' 09' 10 (11) V.gd range of SANCERRE (w, esp r) from leading grower, biodynamic since 2009: La Moussière (r w), CUVÉE Edmond, Génération XIX (r w), Single-v'yds: Les Demoiselles and En Grands Champs (r), Romains, *Satellite* (w). Les Pénitents (Côtes de La Charité IGP) CHARD and PINOT N.

Menetou-Salon Lo r p w ★★ 05 06 07 08 10 (11) AC southwest of SANCERRE; similar if lighter whites (SAUV BL) from v'yds on gentler hills. Also some gd reds (PINOT N). Best producers: BOURGEOIS, *Clement* (Chatenoy), Gilbert (biodynamic), Jacolin, *Henry Pellé*, Jean-Max Roger, Teiller, Tour St-Martin.

Méo-Camuzet C d'O ★★★★ V. fine DOM in VOSNE-ROMANÉE (note: Brûlées and Cros Parantoux), plus GRANDS CRUS CORTON, CLOS DE VOUGEOT, RICHEBOURG. Also less expensive négociant CUVÉES.

Mercier & Cie Champ BRUT NV, Brut Rosé NV, DEMI-SEC Brut. One of biggest CHAMPAGNE houses at Épernay. Controlled by MOËT & CHANDON. Sold mainly in France. Full-bodied, PINOT N-led CUVÉE Eugene Mercier.

Mercurey Burg r (w) ★★→★★★ 03 05' 06 08 09' 10 11 Leading red wine village of CÔTE CHALONNAISE. Gd, middle-rank burgundy, incl improving whites. Try CH de Chamirey, FAIVELEY, M Juillot, Lorenzon, Raquillet, de Suremain.

Mesnil-sur-Oger, Le Champ ★★★★ One of the top Côte des Blancs villages. Structured CHARD for v. long ageing.

Méthode champenoise Champ Traditional method of putting bubbles into CHAMPAGNE by refermenting wine in its bottle. Outside Champagne region, makers must use terms "classic method" or *méthode traditionnelle*.

Meursault C d'O w (r) ★★★→★★★★ 99' 00' 02' 04 05' 06 07' 08 09' 10' 11 CÔTE DE BEAUNE village with some of world's greatest whites: savoury, dry, nutty, mellow. Best v'yds: Charmes, Genevrières, Perrières. Also: Goutte d'Or, Meursault-Blagny, Poruzots, Narvaux, Tesson, Tillets. Producers incl: *Ampeau*, J-M BOILLOT, M BOUZEREAU, V BOUZEREAU, Boyer-Martenot, CH DE MEURSAULT, COCHE-DURY, Ente, Fichet, GIRARDIN, *Javillier*, Jobard, *Lafon*, Latour-Labille, Martelet de Cherisey, Matrot, Mikulski, *P Morey*, PRIEUR, ROULOT. See also BLAGNY.

Midi Broad term covering L'DOC, ROUSSILLON and even PROVENCE. A melting pot; extremes of quality – level improving with every vintage. Brilliant promise, but of course, no guarantee.

Minervois L'doc r (p) (w) br sw ★★ 04 05' 06 07' 08 09 10 11 Hilly AC region; lively reds, esp CHX Bonhomme, Coupe-Roses, Faiteau, la Grave, Oupia, *Ste-Eulalie*, St-Jacques d'Albas, La Tour Boisée, Villerambert-Julien, CLOS Centeilles, DOM Borie-de-Maurel; co-ops La Livinière, de Peyriac, Pouzols. See ST-JEAN DE MINERVOIS. New wines from Burgundians GROS and Tollot should raise the bar.

Minervois-La Livinière L'doc r ★★→★★★ Quality village and Cru du L'DOC. Stricter selection and longer ageing than MINERVOIS. Best growers: Abbaye de Tholomies, Borie de Maurel, Combe Blanche, *Ch de Gourgazaud*, Clos Centeilles, Laville-Bertrou, *Ste-Eulalie*, Dom l'Ostal Cazes, co-op La Livinière.

Mis en bouteille au château / domaine Bottled at the CH, property, or estate. Note: *dans nos caves* (in our cellars) or *dans la région de production* (in the area of production) are often used but mean little.

Moët & Chandon Champ By far the largest CHAMPAGNE house; enlightened leader of v'yd research and development. Now owns 1,500ha, often in the best sites. Greatly improved BRUT NV, recent fine run of grand *solaire* vintages: esp 92 95 and awesome 02'. Impressive DOM PÉRIGNON. Branches across Europe and the New World.

Mommessin, J Burg Family still owns CLOS DE TART in MOREY-ST-DENIS but sold BEAUJOLAIS-based merchant business to BOISSET. CH de Pierreux, BROUILLY, a specialty.

Monbazillac SW Fr w sw ★★→★★★★ 90' 95' 01' 03' 05' 06 07' 09 10 (11') This BERGERAC AOP now makes some of the best sweet whites in France, Sauternes-style, incl ★★★★ CH *Tirecul-la-Gravière*. ★★★ DOM de L'Ancienne Cure, CLOS des Verdots, La Grande Maison and Les Hauts de Caillavel not far behind. Also ★★ CHX de Belingard-Chayne, Le Fagé, Poulvère, Theulet and the co-op's *Ch de Monbazillac*.

Mondeuse Sav r ★★ DYA. SAVOIE red grape and wine. Potentially gd, deep-coloured wine. Possibly same as Italy's Refosco. Don't miss a chance, eg. *G Berlioz*.

Monopole A v'yd that is under single ownership.

Montagne-St-Emilion B'x r ★★ 95 98 00' 01 03 05' 08 09' 10' Largest and possibly best satellite of ST-EMILION. Similar style of wine. Top CHX: Beauséjour, Calon, La Couronne, Croix Beauséjour, Faizeau, La Fleur-Carrère, Haut Bonneau, Maison Blanche, Roudier, Teyssier, *Vieux Ch St-André*.

Montagny Burg w ★★ 09' 10 11 CÔTE CHALONNAISE village with crisp whites, mostly in hands of Cave de Buxy and négociants. Top grower: Aladame.

Monthélie C d'O r (w) ★★→★★★ 99' 02' 03' 05' 08 09' 10' 11 Up the hill from VOLNAY but a touch more rustic. Best v'yds: Champs Fulliot, Duresses. Best from BOUCHARD PÈRE & FILS, COCHE-DURY, Darviot-Perrin, Garaudet, LAFON, CH de Monthélie (Suremain).

Montille, de C d'O ★★★ Hubert de Montille made long-lived VOLNAY, POMMARD. Son Etienne has expanded DOM with purchases in BEAUNE, NUITS-ST-GEORGES and potentially outstanding VOSNE-ROMANÉE Malconsorts. Etienne also runs CH de Puligny. Also Deux Montille (white wines) négociant venture with sister Alix.

Montlouis Lo w dr sw sp ★★→★★★ 89' 90' 95' 96' 97' 02' 03' 05' 07 08' 09 10 (11) Sister AC to VOUVRAY on south side of Loire, similar range of CHENIN BL wines. 55% sparkling. *Currently one of the Loire's most exciting ACs.* Top growers: Berger, CHANSON, CHIDAINE, Delecheneau, Jousset, Moyer, Frantz Saumon, TAILLE-AUX-LOUPS, Weisskopf.

Montrachet C d'O w ★★★★ 92' 93 95 96' 97 99 00' 01 02' 04 05' 06 07 08 09' 10 11 GRAND CRU v'yd (8.01ha) in both PULIGNY- and CHASSAGNE-MONTRACHET. Potentially the greatest white burgundy: strong, perfumed, intense, dry yet luscious. Top wines: LAFON, LAGUICHE (DROUHIN), LEFLAIVE, Ramonet, ROMANÉE-CONTI. DOM THÉNARD improving?

Montravel SW Fr p w dr ★★ (r) 02' 04 05' 06 08 09 (10) (11') (w p) DYA. Sub-AOP of BERGERAC. Hefty reds (mostly MERLOT) in modern style. Best are ★★ DOMS de Bloy, de Krevel, CHX Jonc Blanc, Laulerie, Masburel, Masmontet, Moulin-Caresse. Dry white ★★ in B'X style from same growers. For sweet styles *see* CÔTES DE MONTRAVEL and HAUT-MONTRAVEL.

Moreau ★★→★★★ Noted CHABLIS family with top-class wines, esp *Dom Christian M* (try CLOS des Hospices) and DOM M-Naudet. Dom Moreau in CHASSAGNE is separate family, also v.gd.

Morey, Domaines C d'O ★★★ VIGNERON family in CHASSAGNE-MONTRACHET, esp Jean-Marc, Marc, Thomas, Vincent, Michel M-Coffinet. Also Pierre Morey in MEURSAULT. All better known for whites than reds.

Looking for more information on grapes? Try the "Grapes" section on pp.16–26.

Morey-St-Denis C d'O r (w) ★★★ 90' 93 95 96' 98 99' 02' 03 05' 06 07 08 09' 10' 11 Small village with four GRANDS CRUS between GEVREY-CHAMBERTIN and CHAMBOLLE-MUSIGNY. Glorious wine often overlooked. Amiot, ARLAUD, CLOS DE TART, CLOS DES LAMBRAYS, DUJAC, LIGNIER, Perrot-Minot, PONSOT, ROUMIER, Taupenot-Merme.

Morgon Beauj r ★★★ 05' 06 09' 10' 11' Firm, tannic BEAUJOLAIS cru, esp from Côte du Py hillside. Becomes meaty with age. Les Charmes is softer for earlier drinking. Try Burgaud, Desvignes, Foillard, Gaget, Lafont, LAPIERRE, CH de Pizay.

Mortet, Denis C d'O ★★★→★★★★ Arnaud M adds a touch of elegance to late father's powerful, deep-coloured wines from BOURGOGNE Rouge to GRAND CRU CHAMBERTIN. Various GEVREY-CHAMBERTIN CUVÉES to look out for.

Moueix, J-P et Cie B'x Libourne-based merchant and proprietor named after legendary founder. Son Christian runs company. CHX incl: LA FLEUR-PÉTRUS, HOSANNA, MAGDELAINE, Providence, TROTANOY. BELAIR-MONANGE acquired in 2008. Distributes PÉTRUS. *See also* Dominus, California.

Moulin-à-Vent Beauj r ★★★ 99 03 05' 09' 10' 11' Biggest and potentially best wine of BEAUJOLAIS. Can be powerful, meaty, long-lived; can even taste like fine Rhône or burgundy. Many gd growers: CHX du Moulin-à-Vent, *des Jacques*, Janin, Janodet, Merlin. Watch recent investment from COTE D'OR (JADOT, LIGER-BELAIR).

Moulis H-Méd r ★★→★★★ 98 00' 01 02 03 04 05' 06 08 09' 10' Tiny inland AC in the south MÉDOC, with some honest, gd-value wines. Top CHX: Anthonic, Biston-Brillette, Branas Grand Poujeaux, BRILLETTE, CHASSE-SPLEEN, Duplessis, Dutruch Grand Poujeaux, MAUCAILLOU, POUJEAUX.

Mouton Cadet B'x Biggest-selling red B'X brand (12 million bottles). Same owner as MOUTON ROTHSCHILD. Also white, rosé and Rés GRAVES, MÉDOC, ST-EMILION, SAUTERNES.

Mugneret C d'O ★★★ VIGNERON family in VOSNE-ROMANÉE. Dr Georges M-Gibourg best (esp ECHÉZEAUX), also Gérard M, Dominique M and returning to form DOM Mongeard-M.

Mugnier, J-F C d'O ★★★→★★★★ Outstanding grower of CHAMBOLLE-MUSIGNY *les Amoureuses* and MUSIGNY at CH de Chambolle. Winery rebuilt to accommodate 9ha NUITS-ST-GEORGES CLOS de la Maréchale (since 2004).

Mumm, G H & Cie Champ Cordon Rouge NV; Mumm de Cramant NV; Cordon Rouge 98 00(★★★★) 02 04; Rosé NV. Major grower/merchant, owned by Pernod-Ricard. Marked rise in quality recently, esp in CUVÉE R Lalou 99 and GRAND CRU Verzenay.

Muré, Clos St-Landelin Al ★★→★★★ One of ALSACE's great names; esp fine, full-bodied GRAND CRU *Vorbourg Ries* and PINOT GR. The PINOT N CUVÉE "V" (04 05 09 10), ripe and vinous, is the region's best. Exceptional 2009s across the range.

Muscadet Lo w ★→★★★ DYA. (but *see* below) Popular, often delicious bone-dry wine from nr Nantes. Should never be sharp, but always refreshing. Perfect with fish and seafood. Choose a SUR LIE. Best from zonal ACS: MUSCADET-COTEAUX DE LA LOIRE, MUSCADET CÔTES DE GRAND LIEU, MUSCADET-SÈVRE-ET-MAINE. Often v.gd value but many growers struggling financially.

Muscadet-Coteaux de la Loire Lo w ★→★★ 09 10 11 Small MUSCADET zone east of Nantes (best SUR LIE). Esp Guindon, CH du Ponceau, Quarteron, Les Vignerons de la Noëlle.

Muscadet Côtes de Grand Lieu Lo ★→★★ 09 10 11 Most westerly of MUSCADET's zonal ACS, closest to Atlantic. Best are SUR LIE from eg. Eric Chevalier, Choblet (DOM des Herbauges), Malidain.

Vine roots have been measured (in the Rhône Valley) as far as 140 metres below the surface.

Muscadet-Sèvre-et-Maine Lo ★→★★★ 02 03 05' 06 09' 10 11 Largest and best of MUSCADET's delimited zones. Top: Brégeon, Bonnet-Huteau, Bernard Chereau, Cormerais, Delhommeau, Douillard, DOM DE L'ECU, Gadais, Dom de la Haute Fevrie, LANDRON, Luneau-Papin, Louis Métaireau, Marc Olivier, Sauvion. Wines from these properties can age beautifully – try 1989 or 1999. New *crus communaux* – higher quality, extra lees ageing. Three so far.

Muscat de Frontignan L'doc sw ★★ NV Small AC outside Sète for MUSCAT VDN. Experiments with late-harvest, unfortified and oak-aged IGP wines. Quality steadily improving. Leaders: CHX la Peyrade, de Stony, DOM du Mas Rouge.

Muscat de Lunel L'doc sw ★★ NV Tiny AC based on MUSCAT VDN, luscious, sweet. Experimental late-harvest IGP wines. Look for Mas de Bellevue, CH Grès St Paul.

Muscat de Mireval L'doc sw ★★ NV Tiny MUSCAT VDN AC nr Montpellier. A handful of producers.

Muscat de Rivesaltes Rouss sw ★★ NV Sweet, fortified MUSCAT VDN AC wine nr Perpignan. Popularity fading, but worth seeking out Muscat SEC IGP instead; best from DOM CAZES, CH de Jau, Baixas co-op.

Musigny C d'O r (w) ★★★★★★) 85' 88' 89' 90' 91 93 95 96' 98 99' 01 02' 03 05' 06 07 08 09' 10' 11 GRAND CRU in CHAMBOLLE-MUSIGNY (11ha). Can be the most beautiful, if not the most powerful, of all red burgundies. Best growers: DROUHIN, JADOT, LEROY, MUGNIER, PRIEUR, ROUMIER, DE VOGÜÉ, VOUGERAIE.

Napoléon Champ Brand name of PRIEUR family's Vertus CHAMPAGNE house, now owned by British wine merchant. Seek out mature vintages 90 95 96.

Natural wine Undefined, but cultish: no chemicals, minimal sulphur (whatever that means); embraces organic and biodynamic, even macerated whites. Can be v. fine, but intentionally oxidative wines can be challenging. Made worldwide, but this entry has to go somewhere...

Nature "Natural" or "unprocessed" – esp of still CHAMPAGNE.

Négociant-éleveur Merchant who "brings up" (ie. matures) the wine.

Nuits-St-Georges C d'O r ★★→★★★★ 90' 93 96' 98 99' 02' 03 05' 06 07 08 09' 10' 11 Important wine town: underrated wines, typically sturdy, tannic, need time. Best v'yds: Cailles, Vaucrains, Les St-Georges south of Nuits; Boudots, Murgers by VOSNE; CLOS de la Maréchale, Clos St-Marc in Prémeaux. Many merchants and growers: Ambroise, L'ARLOT, J Chauvenet, R CHEVILLON, Confuron, *Faiveley*, GOUGES, GRIVOT, Lechéneaut, LEROY, *Liger-Belair*, Machard de Gramont, Michelot, MUGNIER, *Rion*.

Orléans Lo r p w ★ DYA. Recent (2006) 90ha AC for white (chiefly CHARD), VIN GRIS, rosé and reds (PINOT N and esp MEUNIER) from small area around Orléans.

Orléans-Clery Lo r ★ DYA. 30ha separate AC for for simple CAB FR reds from same zone as AC ORLÉANS.

Pacherenc du Vic-Bilh SW F w dr sw ★★→★★★ Separate AOP for MADIRAN-based whites, dry (DYA) and sweet (oaked versions better kept); esp ★★★ CH MONTUS (oaked) and BOUSCASSÉ (not), ★★ Ch Laffitte-Teston, DOMS Barréjat, Berthoumieu, Capmartin, Crampilh, Damiens, Labranche-Laffont, Poujo.

Paillard, Bruno Champ BRUT Première CUVÉE NV; Rosé Première Cuvée; CHARD Rés Privée, Brut 96' 99. New vintage BLANC DE BLANCS 95' 96. Superb Prestige Cuvée Nec-Plus-Ultra (90 95 96 02). Youngest grand CHAMPAGNE house. Fine quality. Refined, v-dry style best expressed in Blanc de Blancs Rés Privée and Nec-Plus-Ultra (the 90' only now fully mature). Bruno Paillard heads LANSON-BCC and owns CH de Sarrin, PROVENCE.

Palette Prov r p w ★★★ Tiny AC nr Aix-en-Provence. Full reds, fragrant rosés and intriguing whites, traditional CH SIMONE, now challenged by Ch Henri Bonnaud.

Patriarche Burg ★→★★ One of the bigger BEAUNE-based Burgundy merchants, purchased by Castel in 2011. Main brand is sparkling Kriter.

Patrimonio Cors r p w ★★→★★★ AC Some of the island's best, from dramatic limestone hills in north CORSICA. Characterful reds from NIELLUCCIO, intriguing whites, even late-harvest, from VERMENTINO. Top growers: Antoine Arena, Clos de Bernardi, Gentile, Yves Leccia at E Croce, Pastricciola, Montemagni.

Pauillac H-Méd r ★★★→★★★★ 89' 90' 94 95' 96' 98 00' 01 02 03' 04' 05' 06 08' 09' 10' Communal AC in the MÉDOC with three First Growths (LAFITE, LATOUR, MOUTON). Famous for its powerful, long-lived wines, stressing CAB SAUV. Other top CHX: D'ARMAILHAC, CLERC MILON, GRAND-PUY-LACOSTE, LYNCH-BAGES, PICHON-LONGUEVILLE, PICHON-LALANDE, PONTET-CANET.

Pays d'Oc, IGP L'doc r p w ★→★★ Largest IGP, formerly VDP d'Oc, covering the whole of L'DOC-ROUSSILLON, with focus on varietal wines. Tremendous recent technical advances. Main producers: Jeanjean, VAL D'ORBIEU, DOMS PAUL MAS, village co-ops, plus numerous small individual growers. Some exciting wines, some v. dull.

Pécharmant SW Fr r ★★→★★★ 01' 04 05' 06 08 09(10)(11') Inner AOP of BERGERAC, where ferrous soil ("tran") provides depth and minerality. Best: ★★★ *Ch de Tiregand*, Les Chemins d'Orient, DOM du Haut-Pécharmant, ★★ CLOS des Côtes, Terre Vieille. Modern style from Dom des Costes. Former stars La Métairie, Dom des Bertranoux, CH de Biran emerging from v'yd makeovers.

Pernand-Vergelesses C d'O r w ★★★ (r) 99' 02' 03' 05' 06 07 08 09' 10' 11 Village next to ALOXE-CORTON containing part of the great CORTON-CHARLEMAGNE and CORTON v'yds. Île des Vergelesses also first rate. Growers: CHANDON DE BRIAILLES, CHANSON PÈRE & FILS, Delarche, Dubreuil-Fontaine, JADOT, LATOUR, Rapet, Rollin.

Perrier-Jouët Champ BRUT NV; Blason de France NV; Blason de France Rosé NV; Brut 02 Historic house at Épernay, one of first to make dry CHAMPAGNE; now best for gd vintage wines and de luxe Belle Epoque (85' 95' 96 98 02') (Rosé 02) in a painted bottle. Cramant de Mumm for fine drinking in 2012–3.

Pessac-Léognan B'x r w ★★★→★★★★ 90' 95 96 98 00' 01 02 04 05' 06 08 09' 10' AC created in 1987 for the best part of north GRAVES, incl all the GRANDS CRUS: HAUT-BAILLY, HAUT-BRION, LA MISSION-HAUT-BRION, PAPE-CLÉMENT, DOM DE CHEVALIER, etc. Plump, minerally reds and B'x's finest barrel-fermented dry whites.

Petit Chablis Chab w ★ DYA. Fresh and easy, lighter almost-CHABLIS from outlying v'yds. La Chablisienne co-op is gd.

Pézenas L'doc r p w ★★→★ L'DOC subregion from v'yds around Molière's town, set to become a Cru du L'doc.Try: Prieuré de St-Jean-de-Bébian, DOMS du Conte de Bébian, des Aurelles, Stella Nova, Monplézy, Trinités.

Pfaffenheim Al ★→★★ Respectable ALSACE co-op. Rather foursquare wines.

Pfersigberg Al GRAND CRU in two parcels; v. aromatic wines. GEWURZ does v. well. RIES, esp Paul Ginglinger, Bruno Sorg, LÉON BEYER Comtes d'Eguisheim. Top grower: KUENTZ-BAS.

Burgundians love *oeufs en meurette*: eggs cooked in red wine.

Philipponnat Champ NV; Rosé NV; BRUT 99 02 CUVÉE 1522 02; CLOS des Goisses 85' 91 95 96 99 02 Small house known for well-structured wines and now owned by LANSON-BCC group. Remarkable single-v'yd *Clos des Goisses* and charming rosé.

Pic St-Loup L'doc r (p) ★★→★★★ 04 05 06 07 08 09 10 11 One of northernmost L'DOC v'yds, based on SYRAH, and in line for Cru du L'doc status. Growers: Cazeneuve, Clos Marie, de Lancyre, Lascaux, Mas Bruguière, DOM DE L'HORTUS, Valflaunès. Numerous newcomers. Some of the MIDI's best: stylish and long-lasting.

Picpoul de Pinet L'doc w ★→★★ DYA. Potential Cru du L'DOC, exclusively from the old variety Picpoul. Best growers: St Martin de la Garrigue, Félines-Jourdan, co-ops Pomerols and Pinet. Gd *with an oyster*.

Pineau des Charentes SW Fr Strong, sweet apéritif: white grape juice and Cognac.

Pinon, François Lo w sw sp ★★★ 89 90 95 96 97 02 03 04 05 08 09 10 Benchmark organic producer of v. pure VOUVRAY in all its expressions, incl a v.gd *pétillant*.

Piper-Heidsieck CHAMPAGNE house now with gd new owner. Much-improved BRUT NV and fruit-driven Brut Rosé Sauvage 04; Brut 00 02 04. V.gd CUVÉE Sublime DEMI-SEC, rich yet balanced. Piper Heidsieck Rare (esp 99 02') is one of Champagne's best-kept secrets.

Plageoles, Robert and Bernard SW Fr Bernard has now taken over from his father Robert, concentrating on the lost grape varieties of GAILLAC. Ondenc yields the fantastic ★★★★ Vin d'Autan, ★★★ Prunelard (a deep, fruity red), Verdanel (dry white of unusual personality), Duras (spicy red) and a sparkling Mauzac NATURE.

Plan de Dieu S Rhô r ★→★★ 09' 10' Recent Rhône village, powerful, authentic, mainly GRENACHE wines from v. stony, windy plain south of RASTEAU. Best: CH la Courançonne, DOMS Aphillantes, Durieu, Espigouette, Pasquiers, St-Pierre, Vieux-Chêne.

Pol Roger Champ BRUT White Foil renamed Brut Rés NV; Brut 96' 98 00 02; Rosé 02; Blanc de CHARD 02, family-owned Épernay house now with vines in AVIZE joining 85ha of family v'yds. V. fine, floral NV, new Pure Brut (*zero dosage*) great with seafood. Sumptuous CUVÉE Sir Winston Churchill (96' 02).

Pomerol B'x r ★★★→★★★★ 89' 90' 94 95 96 98' 00' 01 04 05' 06' 08 09' 10' Tiny AC bordering ST-EMILION but no limestone; only clay, gravel, sand. Famed MERLOT-dominated, unctuous style. Top estates: LA CONSEILLANTE, L'ÉGLISE-CLINET, L'ÉVANGILE, LA FLEUR-PÉTRUS, HOSANNA, LAFLEUR, PÉTRUS, LE PIN, TROTANOY, VIEUX-CH-CERTAN.

Pommard C d'O r ★★★ 90' 96' 98 99' 02' 03 05' 06 07 08 09' 10' 11 The biggest CÔTE D'OR village. Few superlative wines, but many potent, tannic ones to age 10 yrs+. Best v'yds: Epenots, Rugiens. Growers: COMTE ARMAND, Billard-Gonnet,

J-M BOILLOT, COURCEL, HOSPICES DE BEAUNE, Huber-Vedereau, LEROY, Machard de Gramont, DE MONTILLE, CH de Pommard, Pothier-Rieusset.

Pommery Champ BRUT NV; Rosé NV; Brut 82' 00 02 Historic house; brand now owned by VRANKEN. Outstanding *Cuvée Louise* (89' 90' 02) and supple, wintertime BLANC DE NOIRS.

Ponsot C d'O ★★→★★★★ Idiosyncratic top-quality MOREY-ST-DENIS DOM with great range of GRANDS CRUS, esp CLOS DE LA ROCHE. Extra kudos for Laurent Ponsot's fight against fraudulent bottles.

Potel, Nicolas C d'O ★★→★★★ Brand belonging to Cottin Frères (Labouré Roi), but since 2009 without eponymous Nicolas, who now has own businesses, DOM de Bellene and Maison Roche de Bellene in BEAUNE.

Pouilly-Fuissé Burg w ★★→★★★ 05' 06 07 08 09' 10' 11 Top AC of MÂCON region now exploring PREMIER CRU classification. Stylistic differences according to location. Wines from Chaintré the softest, Fuissé the most powerful, Vergisson for minerality. Top names: Barraud, de Beauregard, Cornin, Ferret, Forest, CH DE FUISSE, Merlin, Ch des Rontets, Saumaize, VERGET.

Pouilly-Fumé Lo w ★ →★★★★ 05' 07 08 09' 10 (11) Sometimes disappointing SAUV BL from central region, nr SANCERRE. Best is round and full-flavoured. Top CUVÉES can improve 5–6 yrs. Growers: Bain, BOURGEOIS, Alain Cailbourdin, Chatelain, DIDIER DAGUENEAU, Serge Dagueneau & Filles, CH de Favray, Edmond and André Figeat, Masson-Blondelet, Jean Pabiot, Redde, Tabordet, Ch de Tracy, Treuillet.

Pouilly-Loché Burg w ★★ 09' 10' 11 Usually sold as POUILLY-VINZELLES. CLOS des Rocs, Tripoz, Bret Bros offer Loché bottlings. Cave des GRANDS CRUS Blancs co-op dominant for volume.

Pouilly-sur-Loire Lo w ★ DYA. Historic but neutral, non-aromatic wine from same v'yds as POUILLY-FUMÉ, but different grape: CHASSELAS. Now only 30ha in production. Best producers: Serge Dagueneau & Filles, Landrat-Guyollot, Michel Redde.

Pouilly-Vinzelles Burg w ★★ 07 09' 10' 11 Superior neighbour to POUILLY-LOCHÉ. Best v'yd: Les Quarts. Best producers: Bret Bros, Valette. Volume from Cave des GRANDS CRUS Blancs.

Premier Cru B'x First growth in B'x; second rank of v'yds (after GRAND CRU) in Burgundy. New second rank in Loire: one so far, COTEAUX DU LAYON Chaume; expect legal challenges.

Premières Côtes de Bordeaux B'x w sw ★→★★ 05 07 09' 10' Same geographical zone as CADILLAC-CÔTES DE BORDEAUX but for sweet white wines only. Usually *moelleux* or gently sweet in style rather than full-blown, noble-rotted *liquoreux*. Quality varies. Best CHX: Crabitan-Bellevue, Fayau, du Juge, Suau.

Prieur, Domaine Jacques C d'O ★★★ MEURSAULT estate with exceptional range of GRANDS CRUS from MONTRACHET to MUSIGNY. Style aims at weight more than finesse.

Primeur "Early" wine for refreshment and uplift; esp from BEAUJOLAIS; VDP, too. Wine sold *en primeur* is still in barrel, for delivery when bottled – buy only from established and reputable companies.

Producteurs Plaimont SW Fr Brilliant co-op reinforces identity using only authentic Gascon grapes – it has a nursery for varieties that have been "lost". Huge range of wines in all colours, mostly ★★. MADIRAN, ST-MONT, CÔTES DE GASCOGNE.

Propriétaire récoltant Owner-operator, literally owner-harvester.

Provence Prov See CÔTES DE PROVENCE, CASSIS, BANDOL, LES BAUX-EN-PROVENCE, BOUCHES-DU-RHÔNE, COTEAUX D'AIX-EN-PROVENCE, COTEAUX DE PIERREVERT, COTEAUX VAROIS-EN-PROVENCE, PALETTE.

Puisseguin St-Emilion B'x r ★★ 98 00' 01 03 05' 08 09' 10' Satellite neighbour of ST-EMILION; wines firm and solid in style. Top CHX: Bel Air, Branda, Durand-Laplagne, Fongaban, Guibot la Fourvieille, DES LAURETS, La Mauriane, Soleil. Also Roc de Puisseguin from co-op.

Puligny-Montrachet C d'O w (r) ★★★→★★★★ 02' **04 05' 06** 07 08 09' 10' 11 Smaller neighbour of CHASSAGNE-MONTRACHET: potentially even finer, more vital, floral and complex wine (apparent finesse can signal overproduction). V'yds: BÂTARD-MONTRACHET, Bienvenues-Bâtard Montrachet, Caillerets, CHEVALIER-MONTRACHET, Combettes, Folatières, MONTRACHET, Pucelles. Producers: AMPEAU, J-M BOILLOT, BOUCHARD PÈRE & FILS, CARILLON, CH de Puligny, Chavy, DROUHIN, JADOT, LATOUR, DOM LEFLAIVE, O LEFLAIVE, Pernot, SAUZET.

Puyméras r w 10' 09' Respectable Southern Rhône village, high v'yds, unpretentious reds, decent-quality co-op, sound whites. Try Cave la Comtadine, DOM du Faucon Doré, Puy du Maupas.

Pyrénées-Atlantiques SW Fr DYA. IGP for wines not qualifying for local AOPS in the far southwest. Esp ★★★ CH Cabidos (superb PETIT MANSENG: SW w) ★★ DOM Moncaut and ★ BRUMONT varietals. To watch.

New Grand Cru, new lawsuit: Dom de Baumard vs Quarts de Chaume.

Quarts de Chaume Lo w sw ★★★→★★★★ 89' 90' 95' 96' 97' 02 03 **04 05**' 07' 09 10 (11') Tiny, exposed slopes close to Layon devoted to CHENIN BL. Loire's first GRAND CRU – v. strict rules. Esp Baudouin, BAUMARD, Branchereau, FL, Yves Guegniard, CH PIERRE-BISE, Pithon-Paillé, Suronde.

Quatourze L'doc r (p) w ★★ DYA. Tiny potential Cru du L'DOC by Narbonne. Reputation maintained almost single-handedly by CH Notre-Dame du Quatourze.

Quincy Lo w ★→★★ Drink within 3 yrs. Small area on gravel west of Bourges in Cher Valley. SANCERRE-style SAUV BL. Hail-prone. Growers: Mardon, Portier, Rouzé, Siret-Courtaud, Tatin-Wilk (DOMS Ballandors, Tremblay).

Rancio Rouss The most original, lingering and delicious style of VDN, reminiscent of Tawny Port, in BANYULS, MAURY, RIVESALTES, RASTEAU, wood-aged and exposed to oxygen and heat. Same flavour is a fault in table wine.

Rangen Al Most southerly GRAND CRU of ALSACE at Thann. Extremely steep (average 90%) slopes, volcanic soils. Top wines: powerful RIES and PINOT GR from ZIND-HUMBRECHT (CLOS St-Urbain **05** 06 **08** 09') and SCHOFFIT.

Rasteau S Rhô r (p) (w) br (dr) sw ★★ 07' 09' **10**' (11) Own red-wine appellation since 2009. Big-flavoured, hearty reds, can be powerful, mainly GRENACHE, esp Beaurenard, *Cave des Vignerons* (gd), CH du Trignon, DOMS Beau Mistral, Didier Charavin, Collière, Escaravailles, Girasols, Gourt de Mautens (low yields), Rabasse-Charavin, Soumade, St-Gayan, Famille Perrin. Grenache dessert wine VDN quality on rise (Doms Banquettes, Escaravailles).

Ratafia de Champagne Champ Sweet apéritif made in CHAMPAGNE of 67% grape juice and 33% brandy. Not unlike PINEAU DES CHARENTES.

Raveneau Chab ★★★★ Great CHABLIS producer using old methods for *extraordinary long-lived wines*. Cousin of DAUVISSAT. Blanchots, Les CLOS, Vaillons best.

Regnié Beauj r ★★ 09' 10 **11**' The most recently promoted and often the lightest of the BEAUJOLAIS crus, with sandy soil making fruity, approachable wines. Try Burgaud, DOMS de la Plaigne, Rochette.

Reuilly Lo r p w ★→★★★ 05' 08 09' 10 (11) A small, improving AC west of Bourges for SAUV BL whites, plus rosés and *vin gris* made from PINOT N and/or PINOT GR as well as reds made from Pinot N. Best incl: Jamain, Claude Lafond, Mardon, Rouze, Sorbe.

Ribonnet, Domaine de SW Fr ★★ Heretic Christian Gerber (godfather to the IGP ARIÈGE) uses grape varieties from all over Europe to make a fascinating range of varietals and blends in all colours.

Riceys, Rosé des Champ p ★★★ DYA. Minute AC in AUBE for a notable PINOT N rosé. Principal producers: *A Bonnet*, Jacques Defrance.

Richebourg C d'O r ★★★★ 90' **93**' 95 96' **98** 99' **00 02**' **03** 05' 06 **07** 08 09' 10'

II VOSNE-ROMANÉE GRAND CRU. 8ha. Fabulous, magical burgundy; vastly expensive. Growers: DRC, GRIVOT, GROS, HUDELOT-Noëllat, LEROY, LIGER-BELAIR, MÉO-CAMUZET.

Rimage Rouss Increasingly fashionable trend for a vintage VDN. Super-fruity for drinking young. Think gd Ruby Port.

Rion, Patrice C d'O ★★★ Prémeaux-based DOM with excellent NUITS-ST-GEORGES holdings, esp Clos des Argillières, Clos St Marc and CHAMBOLLE. Cousins B & A Rion in Vosne-Romanée also gd.

Rivesaltes Rouss r w br dr sw ★★ NV. Fortified wine made nr Perpignan. A struggling but rewarding tradition. Top producers well-worth seeking out: DOM CAZES, CH de Jau, Sarda-Malet, des Schistes, Vaquer. The best are delicious and original, esp old RANCIOS. *See* MUSCAT DE RIVESALTES.

Roche-aux-Moines, La Lo w sw ★★→★★★ 89' 90' 95' 96' 97' 99 02 03 05' 06 07 08' 09 10' (II) A 33ha cru of SAVENNIÈRES, ANJOU. Potentially powerful, intensely minerally wine; age or drink young "on the fruit". Growers incl: Le CLOS de la Bergerie (Joly), DOM des Forges, FL, Damien Laureau, CH PIERRE-BISE.

Roederer, Louis Champ BRUT Premier NV; Rich NV; Brut 00 02' 04 05; BLANC DE BLANCS 97 99 00 02; Brut Rosé 06' 07 Top-drawer family-owned house with enviable 218ha estate of top v'yds. Magnificent Cristal (can be greatest of all prestige CUVÉES, viz 88' 90' 95 02' 04) and Cristal Rosé (02' 04 05). New Brut NATURE from 2010. Also owns DEUTZ, DELAS, CHX DE PEZ, PICHON-LALANDE. *See also* California.

Rolland, Michel B'x Ubiquitous and fashionable consultant winemaker and MERLOT specialist working in B'X and worldwide; favours super-ripe flavours as recommended by RP, Jr.

Rolly Gassmann Al ★★ Distinguished grower at Rorschwihr, esp from Moenchreben. Off-dry house style culminates in great rich GEWURZ CUVÉE Yves (05 06 08 09 10). Now biodynamic, and finer for it.

Romanée, La C d'O r ★★★★ 96' 99' 00 01 02' 03 05' 06 07 08 09' 10' II Tiniest GRAND CRU in VOSNE-ROMANÉE (0.85ha). MONOPOLE of DOM DU COMTE LIGER-BELAIR. Exceptionally fine, perfumed, intense and understandably expensive.

Romanée-Conti, Domaine de la / DRC C d'O ★★★★ Grandest estate in Burgundy. Incl the whole of ROMANÉE-CONTI and LA TÂCHE, major parts of ECHÉZEAUX, GRANDS-ECHÉZEAUX, RICHEBOURG, ROMANÉE-ST-VIVANT and a tiny part of MONTRACHET. Crown-jewel prices (if you can buy them at all). Keep top vintages for decades.

Romanée-Conti, La C d'O r ★★★★ 78' 85' 88' 89' 90' 93' 95 96' 97 98 99' 00 01 02' 03 05' 06 07 09' 10' II A 1.8ha MONOPOLE GRAND CRU in VOSNE-ROMANÉE; 450 cases per annum. The most celebrated and expensive red wine in the world, with reserves of flavour beyond imagination. Cellar for decades for best results.

Romanée-St-Vivant C d'O r ★★★★ 90' 93 95 96' 99' 02' 03 05' 06 07 08 09' 10' II GRAND CRU in VOSNE-ROMANÉE (9.4ha). Down-slope from LA ROMANÉE-CONTI, hauntingly perfumed, with intensity more than weight. Growers: ARLOT, CATHIARD, JJ Confuron, DRC, DROUHIN, DUJAC, HUDELOT-Noëllat, LATOUR, LEROY.

Looking for more information on grapes? Try the "Grapes" section on pp.16–26.

Rosacker Al GRAND CRU at Hunawihr. Makes some of best RIES in ALSACE (CLOS STE-HUNE, SIPP-MACK).

Rosé d'Anjou Lo p ★→★★ DYA. Pale, slightly sweet rosé (Grolleau dominates) generally sold on price but there are some gd examples, esp: Mark Angeli, Clau de Nell, DOMS de la Bergerie, les Grandes Vignes, des Sablonnettes.

Rosé de Loire Lo p ★→★★ DYA. The driest of ANJOU's rosés: six permitted varieties, esp GAMAY and Grolleau. AC technically covers SAUMUR and TOURAINE, too. Best: Bablut, Ogereau, CH PIERRE-BISE, Richou.

Rosette SW Fr w s/sw ★★ DYA. Dwarf AOP, the original heart of BERGERAC, makes enchanting MOËLLEUX apéritif wines, perfect partners to foie gras or mushrooms. Try ★★ CLOS Romain, CH Puypezat-Rosette, DOMS de la Cardinolle, de Coutancie.

Rostaing, René N Rhô ★★★ 95' 99' 01' 05' 06' 07' 09' 10' 11 CÔTE-RÔTIE 8ha dom: old, central v'yds; three v. tight, precise wines, all v. fine, wait 4–5 yrs. Enticing Côte Blonde (5% VIOGNIER), also La Landonne (grounded, dark fruits, 15–20 yrs). Pure fruit, some refined new oak. Decant. Intricate, unshowy CONDRIEU, also L'DOC DOM Puech Noble (r w).

Rouget, Emmanuel C d'O ★★★★ Inheritor of the legendary estate of Henri Jayer in ECHÉZEAUX, NUITS-ST-GEORGES and VOSNE-ROMANÉE. Top wine: Vosne-Romanée Cros Parantoux.

Roulot, Domaine C d'O ★★★→★★★★ Outstanding MEURSAULT producer; fine range of v'yd sites, esp Tessons CLOS de Mon Plaisir and PREMIERS CRUS, eg. Bouchères, Perrières. More v'yds from 2011.

Roumier, Georges C d'O ★★★★ Reference DOM for BONNES-MARES and other *brilliant Chambolle* wines in capable hands of Christophe R. Long-lived wines but still attractive early.

Rousseau, Domaine Armand C d'O ★★★★ Unmatchable GEVREY-CHAMBERTIN DOM: thrilling CLOS ST-JACQUES, GRANDS CRUS. Fragrant PINOT of extraordinary intensity.

Roussette de Savoie Sav w ★★ DYA. Tastiest fresh white from south of Lake Geneva.

Roussillon Rouss Leading region for traditional VDN (eg. MAURY, RIVESALTES, BANYULS). Younger vintage RIMAGE wines are competing with aged RANCIO wines. Also fine table wines. *See* CÔTES DU ROUSSILLON (and CÔTES DU ROUSSILLON-VILLAGES), COLLIOURE and IGP CÔTES CATALANES. Region incl under AC L'DOC.

Ruchottes-Chambertin C d'O r ★★★★ 90' 93' 95 96' 98 99' 00 02' 03 05' 06 07 08 09' 10' 11 Tiny (3.3ha) GRAND CRU neighbour of CHAMBERTIN. Less weighty but ethereal, intricate, lasting wine of great finesse. Top growers: MUGNERET-Gibourg, ROUMIER, ROUSSEAU.

Ruinart Champ "R" de Ruinart BRUT NV; Ruinart Rosé NV; "R" de Ruinart Brut (99 02' 04). Oldest house, owned by Moët-Hennessy. Already high standards going higher still with first-class cellar master. Rich, elegant wines. Prestige CUVÉE *Dom Ruinart* is one of the two best vintage BLANC DE BLANCS in CHAMPAGNE (viz 88' 90 95' 96 02'). DR Rosé also v. special (90' 96 02').

Rully Burg r w ★★ (r) 08 09' 10' (w) 09' 10' CÔTE CHALONNAISE village. Whites are light, fresh, tasty, gd value. Reds also fruit-forward. Try DOMS Devevey, DUREUIL-JANTHIAL, FAIVELEY, Jacqueson, C Jobard, Ninot, Rodet, Sounit.

Sables du Golfe du Lion L'doc r p w ★ DYA. IGP from Mediterranean coastal sand-dunes: esp pink Gris de Gris from CARIGNAN and CINSAULT. Giant Listel dominates.

Sablet S Rhô r (p) w ★★ 09' 10' (11) Drink-and-go fun wines at this improving CÔTES DU RHÔNE-VILLAGE. Sandy soils; often approachable, red-berry-fruited reds, esp DOMS de Boissan, Espiers, Les Goubert, Piaugier, Roubine. Gd full whites for apéritif and food.

Salon Champ ★★★★ The original BLANC DE BLANCS, from LE MESNIL in the Côte des Blancs. Tiny quantities. Awesome reputation for long-lived wines – in truth, sometimes inconsistent but on song recently, viz 90 96' 97' 99 02'.

Sancerre Lo (r) (p) w ★→★★★ 05' 08' 09 10 (11) Benchmark for SAUV BL, often more aromatic and vibrant than POUILLY-FUMÉ. Best wines can age 10 yrs+. Top growers making memorable reds (PINOT N). Sancerre rosé rarely worth expense. Best: Boulay, BOURGEOIS, Cotat, François Crochet, Lucien Crochet, André Dezat, Dionysia, Fouassier, Thomas Laballe, ALPHONSE MELLOT, Merlin Cherrier, Mollet, Vincent Pinard, Pascal & Nicolas Reverdy, Claude Riffault, Jean-Max Roger, Roblin, Vacheron, André Vatan, Michel Vattan.

Santenay C d'O r (w) ★★★ 99' 02' 03 05' 06 07 08 09' 11 Sturdy reds from spa village south of CHASSAGNE-MONTRACHET. Best v'yds more succulent: La Comme,

Les Gravières, CLOS de Tavannes. Top growers: GIRARDIN, Jessiaume, Lequin-Colin, Muzard, Vincent.

Saumur Lo r p w sp ★→★★★ 05′ 06 07 08 09′ 10 (11) Umbrella AC for whites varying light to serious; mainly easy-drinking reds except SAUMUR-CHAMPIGNY zone; pleasant rosés; major sparkling production: CRÉMANT and SAUMUR Mousseux. Saumur-Le-Puy-Notre-Dame new AC for CAB FR reds covering over-wide area – 17 communes. Producers: BOUVET-LADUBAY, CHAMPS FLEURIS, CLOS Mélaric, CLOS ROUGEARD, Antoine Foucault, René-Hugues Gay, Guiberteau, Paleine, St-Just, CH DE VILLENEUVE, Cave des Vignerons de Saumur.

Southwest growers to watch in 2013

Nicholas Carmarans (VDP Aveyron) ★★ Characterful biodynamic vines from ex-Paris bistro-owner. Dry white seeking entry to AOP ENTRAYGUES ET DU FEL and ESTAING.

Patrice Lescarret (VIN DE FRANCE, probably) This GAILLAC *enfant terrible* is about to launch PETIT MANSENG from micro-v'yd nr Marcillac. Wild, but could be fabulous.

Dom Laubarel (GAILLAC) New owners making huge improvements after only 2 yrs of restructuring a formerly mediocre v'yd and *chai*.

Domaine de Lancement. (IGP THÉZAC-PERRICARD) Sandrine Annibal is proving her early promise. Much better than many so-called "CAHORS Nouveaux".

Domaine Carcenac (GAILLAC) Try the light-style and v. quaffable ★★ Prunelard. The rest of the range is pretty gd too.

Vignes de Garbasses (IGP CÔTES DU TARN) A serious range of ★ wines that do not qualify as GAILLAC, being outside the AOP area nr Lavaur.

Domaine Mont Ramé (CÔTES DE DURAS) Exciting father-and-son DOM converting to biodynamism. Gd reds, superb sweet white. ★★ Tantelys from 100% SAUV BL.

Domaine Poujo (PACHERENC DU VIC-BILH) Lovely ★★ sweet white rivalling the best of the appellation.

Domaine Bellauc (JURANÇON). Pocket-sized 2ha DOM making award-winning wines, dry and sweet.

Saumur-Champigny Lo r ★★→★★★★ 95 96′ 97 02′ 03 05′ 06 08′ 09′ 10 (11) Popular nine-commune AC for quality CAB FR, ages well in gd vintages. Look for Bruno Dubois, CHX de Targé, DE VILLENEUVE; CLOS Cristal, Clos ROUGEARD, CHAMPS FLEURIS, de la Cune, Filliatreau, Hureau, Legrand, Nerleux, Roches Neuves, St-Just, Antoine Sanzay, Vadé, Val Brun; Cave des Vignerons de Saumur.

Saussignac SW Fr w sw ★★→★★★ 05′ 06 07′ 09 10 (11′) AOP. Wines sometimes with more bite than neighbouring MONBAZILLAC. Best: ★★★ DOMS de Richard, La Maurigne, Les Miaudoux, *Clos d'Yvigne*, ★★ CHX Le Chabrier, Court-les-Mûts, Le Payral, Le Tap, Lestevénie, Tourmentine.

Sauternes B'x w sw ★★→★★★★★ 83′ 86′ 88′ 89′ 90′ 95 96 97′ 98 99′ 01′ 02 03′ 05′ 07′ 09′ 10′ (11) District of five villages (incl BARSAC) that make France's best sweet wine. Strong, luscious, golden. Spate of great yrs recently. Still undervalued and underappreciated. Top CHX: d'YQUEM, GUIRAUD, LAFAURIE-PEYRAGUEY, RIEUSSEC, SUDUIRAUT, LA TOUR BLANCHE, etc. Dry wines cannot be sold as Sauternes.

Sauzet, Etienne C d'O ★★★ Leading PULIGNY DOM with superb PREMIERS CRUS (Combettes, Folatières) and GRANDS CRUS (BÂTARD), etc). Fresh, lively wines.

Savennières Lo w dr sw ★★★→★★★★ 89′ 90′ 95 96′ 97′ 99 02′ 03 05′ 06 07 08′ 09 10 (11) Small ANJOU district for elegant, extremely mineral, long-lived whites

(CHENIN BL). BAUMARD, Closel, CLOS de Coulaine (*see* CH PIERRE-BISE), Ch d'Epiré, DOM FL, Yves Guegniard, Damien Laureau, Eric Morgat, Vincent Ogereau, Pithon-Paillé, Ch Soucherie, Mathieu-Tijou. Top sites: COULÉE DE SERRANT, ROCHE-AUX-MOINES, Clos du Papillon.

Savigny-lès-Beaune C d'O r (w) ★★★ 99' 02' 03 05' 07 08 09' 10' 11 Important village next to BEAUNE; similar mid-weight wines, should be delicious and lively; can be rustic. Top v'yds: Dominode, Guettes, Lavières, Marconnets, Vergelesses; growers incl: *Bize*, Camus, CHANDON DE BRIAILLES, CLAIR, Ecard, Girard, Guyon, LEROY, Pavelot, TOLLOT-BEAUT.

Savoie r w sp ★★ DYA. Alpine area with light, dry wines like some Swiss or minor Loires. APRÉMONT, CRÉPY, SEYSSEL best-known whites; Roussette more interesting. *Also gd Mondeuse red.*

Schlossberg Al GRAND CRU at Kientzheim famed since 15th century. Glorious, compelling RIES from FALLER.

Schlumberger, Domaines Al ★→★★★ Vast, top-quality ALSACE DOM at Guebwiller owning approx 1% of all ALSACE v'yds. Holdings in GRANDS CRUS Kitterlé, Kessler, Saering and Spiegel. Rich wines. Rare RIES, signature CUVÉE Ernest and now PINOT GR Grand Cru Kessler (09 10).

Schoenenbourg Al V. rich, successful Riquewihr GRAND CRU: PINOT GR, RIES, v. fine VENDANGE TARDIVE and SÉLECTION DES GRAINS NOBLES, esp from DEISS and DOPFF AU MOULIN. Also v.gd MUSCAT.

Schoffit, Domaine Al ★★→★★★ Eclectic Colmar grower. Excellent VENDANGE TARDIVE GEWURZ GRAND CRU RANGEN CLOS St Theobald (00 05) on volcanic soil. Also rare, gd CHASSELAS, fine RIES Sonnenberg (06 08 09').

Schröder & Schÿler B'x Old B'x merchant, owner of CH KIRWAN.

Sec Literally means dry, though CHAMPAGNE so-called is medium-sweet (and better at breakfast, teatime and weddings than BRUT).

Séguret S Rhô r p w ★★ 07' 09' 10' Picturesque hillside village nr GIGONDAS. Mainly GRENACHE, peppery, direct reds – styles can differ; clear-fruited whites. Esp CH la Courançonne, DOMS de l'Amauve (fine), de Cabasse (elegant), J David (bold, organic), Garancière, *Mourchon* (robust), Pourra, Soleil Romain.

Sélection des Grains Nobles Al Term coined by HUGEL for ALSACE equivalent to German Beerenauslese, and subject to ever-stricter regulations (since 1984). *Grains nobles* are individual grapes with "noble rot".

Sérafin C d'O ★★★ Christian Sérafin has gained a cult following for his intense GEVREY-CHAMBERTIN VIEILLES VIGNES, CHARMES-CHAMBERTIN. Plenty of new wood here.

Seyssel Sav w sp ★★ NV Delicate white, pleasant sparkling, eg. Corbonod.

France drinks two-thirds of all Champagne. Of the rest, UK drinks nearly one-third.

Sichel & Co B'x One of B'x's most respected merchant houses (Sirius a top brand): interests in CHX D'ANGLUDET, PALMER and in CORBIÈRES.

Signargues ★→★★ CÔTES DU RHÔNE village in four areas between Avignon and Nîmes (west bank). Freely fruited reds, most to drink inside 4 yrs. Note: la Font du Vent (best, deepest), CH Haut-Musiel, DOM Valériane.

Sipp, Louis Al ★★→★★★ Grower/négociant in Ribeauvillé. V.gd RIES GRAND CRU Kirchberg, superb grand cru Osterberg GEWURZ VENDANGE TARDIVE (esp 05').

Sipp-Mack Al ★★→★★★ Excellent DOM at Hunawihr. Great RIES from GRANDS CRUS ROSACKER (02 07 08 10') and Osterberg; also v.gd PINOT GR.

Sorg, Bruno Al ★★→★★★ First-class small grower at Eguisheim for GRANDS CRUS Florimont (RIES 08 09 10) and PFERSIGBERG (MUSCAT). Immaculate eco-friendly v'yds. Winemaking with feeling.

St-Amour Beauj r ★★ 09' 10' 11' Northernmost cru of BEAUJOLAIS: light, fruity, resistible (except on 14 Feb). Growers to try: Janin, *Patissier*, Revillon.

St-Aubin C d'O r w ★★★ (r) 05' 06 07 08 09' 10' 11 (w) 07 08 09' 10 11 Fine source for *lively, refreshing whites*, adjacent to PULIGNY and CHASSAGNE, also pretty reds. Best v'yds: En Remilly, Murgers Dents de Chien. Best growers: J C Bachelet, COLIN, Lamy, Prudhon.

St-Bris Burg w ★ DYA. Neighbour to CHABLIS. Unique AC for SAUV BL in Burgundy. Fresh, lively, worth keeping from J-H Goisot.

St-Chinian L'doc r ★→★★★ 04 05' 06 07' 08 09' 10 11 Hilly area of growing reputation in L'DOC. AC for red (since 1982) and for white (since 2005). Includes crus of Berlou and Roquebrun. Warm, spicy southern reds, based on SYRAH, GRENACHE, CARIGNAN. Gd co-op Roquebrun; CH de Viranel, DOMS Canet Valette, Madura, Rimbaud, Navarre, Borie la Vitarèle, Mas Champart, and many others, both newcomers and established estates.

St-Emilion B'x r ★★→★★★★ 95 96 98' 00' 01 03 04 05' 08 09' 10' Large MERLOT-dominated district on B'x's Right Bank. ST-EMILION GRAND CRU AC the top designation. Warm, full, rounded style (can drink early); the best firm and long-lived. Top CHX: ANGÉLUS, AUSONE, CANON, CHEVAL BLANC, FIGEAC, MAGDELAINE, PAVIE. Also GARAGISTES LA MONDOTTE and VALANDRAUD. Gd co-op.

St-Estèphe H-Méd r ★★→★★★★ 89' 90' 94 95' 96' 98 00' 01 02 03 04 05' 06 08 09' 10' Most northerly communal AC in the MÉDOC. Solid, structured wines. Hail damage for some in 2011. Top CHX: COS D'ESTOURNEL, MONTROSE, CALON-SÉGUR. Also many gd unclassified estates eg. HAUT-MARBUZET, MEYNEY, ORMES-DE-PEZ, DE PEZ, PHÉLAN-SÉGUR.

St-Gall Champ BRUT NV; Extra Brut NV; Brut BLANC DE BLANCS NV; Brut Rosé NV; Brut Blanc de Blancs 02 04; CUVÉE Orpale Blanc de Blancs 95 96' 02. Brand used by Union-Champagne CO-OP: top CHAMPAGNE growers' co-op at AVIZE. Fine-value *Pierre Vaudon NV*.

St-Georges-St-Emilion B'x r ★★ 00' 01 03 05' 08 09' 10' Miniscule ST-EMILION satellite. Usually gd quality. Best CHX: Calon, MACQUIN-ST-GEORGES, ST-GEORGES, TOUR DU PAS-ST-GEORGES, Vieux Montaiguillon.

St-Gervais S Rhô r (p) (w) ★ 09' 10' Mid-level quality west bank Rhône village. Steady co-op, but clear best is top-grade, long-lived (10 yrs+) DOM Ste-Anne red (firm, strong MOURVÈDRE liquorice flavours); gd VIOGNIER.

St-Jean de Minervois L'doc w sw ★★ Fine, sweet VDN MUSCAT. Much improvement recently, esp from DOM de Barroubio, Michel Sigé, Clos du Gravillas, Clos Bagatelle, village co-op.

St-Joseph N Rhô r w ★★ 99' 01' 03' 05' 06' 07' 09' 10' 11 65km of granite v'yds lining west bank of Northern Rhône. SYRAH reds. Oldest zone nr Tournon: stylish, red-fruited wines; elsewhere darker, peppery flavours, more new oak. More complete, serious wines than CROZES-HERMITAGE, esp from CHAPOUTIER (Les Granits), Gonon (top class), *B Gripa*, GUIGAL (*lieu-dit* St-Joseph); also J-L CHAVE, Chèze, Courbis, Coursodon, Cuilleron, *Delas*, J & E Durand, B Faurie, Faury, Gaillard, P Marthouret, Monier-Perréol, A Perret, Nicolas Perrin, Vallet, F Villard. Gd food-friendly *white (mainly Marsanne)*, esp Barge, CHAPOUTIER (Les Granits), Cuilleron, Gonon (fab), B Gripa, Faury, A Perret.

St-Julien H-Méd r ★★★→★★★★ 89' 90' 94 95' 96' 98 00' 01 02 03 04 05' 06 08 09' 10' Small mid-MÉDOC communal AC dominated by 11 classified (1855) estates, incl three LÉOVILLES, BEYCHEVELLE, DUCRU-BEAUCAILLOU, GRUAUD-LAROSE, etc. The epitome of harmonious, fragrant, savoury red wine.

St-Mont SW Fr r p w ★★ (r) 09 10 (p w) DYA. AOP in Gers, almost a *monopole* of PRODUCTEURS PLAIMONT, the most successful co-op in the southwest. Gd red from DOM des Maouries on Madiran borders. Same grapes as MADIRAN and PACHERENC.

St-Nicolas-de-Bourgueil Lo r p ★→★★★ 89' 90' 95 96' 02' 03 05' 06 08 09' 10 (11) Companion appellation to BOURGUEIL making identical wines from CAB FR. High proportion of gravel soils. Ranges from easy-drinking (sand/gravel) to age-worthy (limestone). Try: YANNICK AMIRAULT, Cognard, Lorieux, Frédéric Mabileau, Laurent Mabileau, Mabileau-Rezé, Taluau-Foltzenlogel, Gerard Vallée.

St-Péray N Rhô w sp ★★ o6' o7' o8' o9' 10' 11 Underrated white Rhône (mostly MARSANNE) from 60ha granite hill v'yds opposite Valence. New planting interest. A little *méthode Champenoise – worth trying* (J-L Thiers). Still white has cut, is stylish; some are fat from v. ripe fruit, plus oak. Best: S Chaboud, CHAPOUTIER, CLAPE, Colombo, B Gripa (v.gd), J-L Thiers, TAIN co-op, du Tunnel, Voge (oak).

St-Pourçain Mass C r p w ★→★★ DYA. AC north of Vichy. Light red and rosé from GAMAY and PINOT N (AC rules stupidly forbids 100% PINOT N), white from local Tressalier and/or CHARD or SAUV BL. Growers: DOM de Bellevue, Grosbot-Barbara, Laurent, Nebout, Pétillat, Ray, and gd co-op (VIGNERONS de St-Pourçain) with range of styles, incl drink-me-up CUVÉE Ficelle.

St-Romain C d'O r w ★★ (w) o9' 10' 11 *Crisp, minerally whites* and clean-cut reds from vines tucked away in the back of the CÔTE DE BEAUNE. PREMIER CRU v'yds expected soon. Alain Gras best. Also Buisson, De Chassorney.

St-Sardos SW Fr r p w DYA (unless oaked). AOP nr Montauban. ★ DOM de la Tucayne only independent, owner-founded, ambitious ★ co-op. Gd-value SYRAH-based wines.

St-Véran Burg w ★★ o9' 10 11 AC outside POUILLY-FUISSÉ with variable results, depending on soil and producer. Best are exciting. DUBOEUF, Deux Roches, Poncetys for value, Cordier, Corsin, Merlin for top quality.

Ste-Croix-du-Mont B'x w sw ★★ 97' 98 99' o1' o2 o3' o5' o7 o9' 10' Sweet-white AC facing SAUTERNES across the river Garonne. Worth trying the best, ie. CHX Crabitan-Bellevue, *Loubens*, du Mont, Pavillon, la Rame.

Ste-Victoire Prov r p ★★ Subzone of CÔTES DE PROVENCE from the southern slopes of the Montagne Ste-Victoire. Dramatic scenery goes with gd wine. Try Mas de Cadenet, Mauvan.

Sur lie "On the lees". MUSCADET is often bottled straight from the vat, for max zest, body and character.

Tâche, La C d'O r ★★★★ 90' 93' **95** 96' **98** 99' oo o1 o2' o3 o5' o6 o7 o9' 10' 11 A 6ha (1,500 case) GRAND CRU of VOSNE-ROMANÉE, MONOPOLE of DRC. One of best v'yds on earth: full, perfumed, luxurious wine, tight in youth.

> **Grand application**
> The village of Pommard in Burgundy has officially applied for GRAND CRU status for its Rugiens and Epenots v'yds. The decision will depend on the v'yds' history, terroir and the price of the wines compared to that of other grands and PREMIERS CRUS. One complication, however, will be that Rugiens is divided into Rugiens Bas and Rugiens Haut, and Epenots into Grands- and Petits-Epenots.

Taille-aux-Loups, Domaine de la Lo w sw sp ★★★ o2' o3' o5' **o6 o7' o8' o9** 10 (11) Jacky Blot is one of the Loire's leading, most dynamic producers: barrel-fermented MONTLOUIS and VOUVRAY, from dry to richly sweet; Triple Zéro MONTLOUIS pétillant, plus Triple Zéro Rosé and fine reds from DOM de la Butte BOURGUEIL. Acquired CLOS Mosny (Montlouis) late 2010.

Tain, Cave de N Rhô ★★ Top, improving Northern Rhône co-op, 290 members, many mature v'yds, incl 25% of HERMITAGE. Decent red Hermitage, esp Epsilon, Gambert de Loche, gd white Hermitage Au Coeur des Siècles; modern reds, esp CROZES. MARSANNE whites gd value, accomplished VIN DE PAILLE.

Taittinger Champ BRUT NV; Rosé NV; Brut **90 95' o2'** o4; Collection Brut **90 95** 96. Once-fashionable Reims grower and merchant sold to Crédit Agricole group

FRANCE

(2006). Distinctive silky, flowery touch, though not always consistent, often noticeably dosed. Excellent luxury brand Comtes de Champagne BLANC DE BLANCS (95' 96' 02) and Rosé (96 02), also gd, rich PINOT Prestige Rosé NV. New CUVÉES Nocturne and Prélude. Also excellent new single-v'yd La Marquetterie. *See also* California: Dom Carneros.

Tavel S Rhô r p w ★★ DYA. GRENACHE-based Rhône rosé, formerly all robust, full Mediterranean dishes suited. Now many PROVENCE-style wines, often for apéritif. Best growers: DOM Corne-Loup, GUIGAL, Lafond Roc-Epine, Maby, Dom de la Mordorée (full), Prieuré de Montézargues (fine), Moulin-la-Viguerie, Rocalière (fine), CH de Manissy, Trinquevedel (fine).

Early signs Southern Rhône is turning away from oppressive opulence? Just maybe.

Tempier, Domaine Prov r w ★★★★ Once the pioneering estate of BANDOL. Wines of considerable elegance and longevity. Excellent quality now challenged by several others.

Terrasses du Larzac L'doc r p w ★★→★★★ Northern part of AC L'DOC. Wild, hilly region from the Lac du Salagou towards Aniane. Cooler temperatures make for fresher wines. In line to be a Cru du L'doc. Several established stars, as well as rising stars, incl: Mas de l'Ecriture, CLOS des Serres, Cal Demoura, Montcalmès, *Mas Jullien*.

Terroirs Landais SW Fr r p w ★ VDP, an appendix to CÔTES DE GASCOGNE, a name that many growers prefer to use. DOM de Laballe most seen eg.

Thénard, Domaine Burg Major grower of the GIVRY appellation, but best-known for his substantial portion (1.6ha) of MONTRACHET. Signs of improvement?

Thévenet, Jean Burg ★★★ Mâconnais purveyor of rich, some semi-botrytized, wines eg. CUVÉE Levroutée at DOM de la Bongran. Also Dom Emilian Gillet.

Thézac-Perricard SW Fr r r p ★★ 09 10 (11') MALBEC-based IGP adjoining CAHORS. Made for earlier drinking. ★★ DOM de Lancement keeps co-op on its toes.

Thiénot, Alain Champ New generation takes this firm forward. Ever-improving quality across the range. Impressive, fairly priced BRUT NV. Rosé NV Brut. Vintage Stanislas (02 04 05 06 08) and voluminous Vigne aux Gamins (single-v'yd AVIZE 99 02). Top Grande CUVÉE 96' 98 02'. Also owns Marie Stuart and CANARD-DUCHÊNE in CHAMPAGNE, CH Ricaud in LOUPIAC.

Thomas, André & fils Al ★★★ V. fine grower at Ammerschwihr, rigorously organic. An artist-craftsman in the cellar: v.gd RIES Kaefferkopf (08 10') and magnificent GEWURZ VIEILLES VIGNES (05 09').

Thorin, J Beauj ★ Major BEAUJOLAIS négociant owned by BOISSET.

Tollot-Beaut C d'O ★★★ Stylish, consistent Burgundy grower with 20ha in CÔTE DE BEAUNE, incl v'yds at BEAUNE (Grèves, Clos du Roi), CORTON, SAVIGNY (Les Champs Chevrey) and at its CHOREY-LÈS-BEAUNE base.

Touraine Lo r p w dr sw sp ★→★★★★ 08 09' 10 (11) Huge region with many ACS (eg. VOUVRAY, CHINON and BOURGUEIL), it is also an umbrella AC of variable quality – zesty reds (CAB FR, CÔT, GAMAY and PINOT N), pungent whites (SAUV BL and CHENIN BL), rosés and mousseux. Often gd value. Gd producers: CLOS Roussely, DOMS des Bois-Vaudons, Corbillières, Joël Delaunay, de la Garrelière, Gosseaume, Clos Roche Blanche, Mandard, Jacky Marteau, *Marionnet*; Morantin, Oisly & Thesée, Presle, Puzelat, Petit Thouars, Ricard, Clos de Tue-Boeuf. Ill-conceived reforms proposed for new overlarge ACs Touraine-Chenonceaux and Touraine-Oisly.

Touraine-Amboise Lo r p w ★→★★ TOURAINE sub-appellation. François 1er is entry-level local blend (GAMAY/CÔT/CAB FR). CHENIN BL for whites. Too many poor wines using Amboise name. Best: Closerie de Chanteloup, Delecheneau, DOM des Bessons, Dutertre, Xavier Frissant, de la Gabillière.

Touraine-Azay-le-Rideau Lo p w ★→★★ Small TOURAINE sub-appellation for CHENIN BL-based dry, off-dry white and Grolleau-dominated rosé. Producers: CH de l'Aulée, Nicolas Paget, Pibaleau.

Touraine-Mesland Lo r p w ★→★★ Small TOURAINE sub-appellation red blends (GAMAY/CÔT/CAB FR). Not obviously better than Touraine. Whites are mainly CHENIN with a little CHARD. CH Gaillard, Clos de la Briderie.

Touraine-Noble Joué Lo p ★→★★ DYA. Ancient but now revived rosé from three PINOTS (N, GR, MEUNIER). AC (2001), now 28ha mainly in Esvres-sur-Indre just south of Tours. Esp Cosson, ROUSSEAU, Sard.

Trapet C d'O ★★→★★★ A long-established GEVREY-CHAMBERTIN DOM now enjoying new life and sensual wines with biodynamic farming. Ditto cousins Rossignol-Trapet – slightly more austere wines.

Trévallon, Domaine de Prov r w ★★★ 95 96 97 98 99 00' 01 03 04 05 06 07 08 09 10 Pioneering estate in LES BAUX DE PROVENCE, but IGP Bouches du Rhône because it lacks GRENACHE. Fully deserving its huge reputation. Intense CAB SAUV/SYRAH able to age. *Barrique-aged white* from MARSANNE and ROUSSANNE, a drop of CHARD and now GRENACHE BL. Well-worth seeking out.

Tricastin S Rhô *See* GRIGNAN-LES-ADHÉMAR.

Trimbach, F E Al ★★★→★★★★ Matchless growers of ALSACE RIES on limestone soils around Ribeauvillé; magnificent CLOS STE-HUNE (06 08 09'10); almost-as-gd (and much cheaper) *Frédéric Emile* (06 08). Dry, elegant wines for great cuisine.

Tursan SW Fr r p w ★★→★★★ (Mostly DYA.) Lively ★ co-op, now twinned with COTEAUX DE CHALOSSE, is a bit outclassed by master chef Michel Guérard's lovely but atypical ★★ wines. More authentic ★★ DOM de Perchade is pretty gd, too.

In the Médoc claret is drunk with roast lamb; in St-Emilion it's lampreys stewed in red wine.

Vacqueyras S Rhô r (p) w ★★ 01' 03 04' 05' 06' 07' 09' 10' 11 Robust, full, peppery, GRENACHE-led neighbour of GIGONDAS. Earlier, hotter v'yds, so can be fired up. Lives 10 yrs+. Note: Arnoux Vieux Clocher, JABOULET, CHX de Montmirail, des Tours (v. fine), VIDAL-FLEURY; CLOS des Cazaux (gd value), DOMS Amouriers, Archimbaud-Vache, Charbonnière, Couroulu (v.gd, traditional), Font de Papier, Fourmone, Garrigue, Grapillon d'Or, Monardière (v.gd), Montirius (organic), Montvac, Famille Perrin, Roucas Toumba (organic), Sang des Cailloux (v.gd). Full whites (Clos des Cazaux, Sang des Cailloux).

Val de Loire Lo r p w DYA. One of France's four regional IGPS, formerly Jardin de la France. There are a wide range of single varietals, incl CHARD, CAB FR, GAMAY, SAUV BL.

Val d'Orbieu, Vignerons du L'doc ★★ Association of some 200 growers and co-ops in CORBIÈRES, L'DOC, MINERVOIS, ROUSSILLON, etc., marketing a sound range of AC and IGP wines. Red CUVÉE Mythique is flagship.

Valençay Lo r p w ★→★★ AC in east TOURAINE; light, easy-drinking, from similar range of grapes as neighbouring TOURAINE, esp SAUV BL, usually CHARD in the blend. CLOS Delorme, Jacky Preys, Hubert & Olivier Sinson, Sébastien Vaillant.

Valréas S Rhô r (p) (w) ★★ 07' 09' 10' Modest, late-ripening CÔTES DU RHÔNE-VILLAGES in north Vaucluse black-truffle area; large co-op, but lacks range of quality DOMS. Pebbly, can be heady, fair-depth red (mainly GRENACHE), improving white. Esp Emmanuel Bouchard, Dom des Grands Devers, Séminaire, CH la Décelle.

Varichon & Clerc Sav Principal makers and shippers of SAVOIE sparkling wines.

VDQS *Vins délimité de qualité supérieure.* Being phased out.

Vendange Harvest. **Vendange tardive:** late-harvest; ALSACE equivalent of German Auslese but usually higher alcohol.

Venoge, de Champ Venerable house now revitalized under LANSON-BCC ownership.

Gd, niche blends: Cordon Bleu Extra-brut, Vintage BLANC DE BLANCS (00 02), CUVÉE 20 ans and Prestige CUVÉE Louis XV, a 10-yr-old BLANC DE NOIRS.

Ventoux S Rhô r p (w) ★★ 07' 09' 10' (11) Widespread 6,000ha+ AC around Mont Ventoux between Rhône and PROVENCE for juicy, enjoyable, clear red (GRENACHE/ SYRAH, café-style to fuller, deeper), rosé and gd white (more use of oak). Altitude supplies welcome cool flavours for some. Best: Gonnet, *La Vieille Ferme* (r) owned by BEAUCASTEL, CHX Unang, Valcombe, co-op Bédoin, Goult, St-Didier, DOMS Anges, Berane, Brusset, Cascavel, Champ-Long, Croix de Pins, Fondrèche, Font-Sane, Grand Jacquet, JABOULET, Martinelle, Murmurium, *Pesquié* (excellent), Pigeade, Terres de Solence, Verrière, VIDAL-FLEURY.

Verget Burg ★★→★★★ Jean-Marie Guffens' Mâconnais-based white wine-merchant venture, nearly as idiosyncratic as his own DOM. Fine quality, plans for reds, too.

Veuve Clicquot Champ Yellow Label NV; White Label DEMI-SEC NV; Vintage Rés 98' 02' 04; Rosé Rés 02' 04. Historic house of highest standing, owned by LVMH. Full-bodied, almost rich: one of CHAMPAGNE's surest things. Luxury brands: La Grande Dame (95' 98), Rich Rés (96 99 02), La Grande Dame Rosé (95 98). Part-oak-fermented vintages from 2008. New Cave Privée re-release of old vintages in several formats: superb 1985 and 1978 Rosé.

Veuve Devaux Champ Premium brand of the powerful Union Auboise co-op. Excellent aged Grande Rés NV, Oeil de Perdrix Rosé, Prestige CUVÉE D (02) and BRUT Vintage (04).

Vézelay Burg r w ★→★★ Age 1–2 yrs. Up-and-coming subdistrict of generic BOURGOGNE for reds (Pinot). Flavoursome whites from CHARD or MELON sold as BOURGOGNE GRAND ORDINAIRE. Try DOM de la Cadette, des Faverelles, Maria Cuny, Elise Villiers.

Vidal-Fleury, J N Rhô ★★ New cellars, gd changes at GUIGAL-owned merchant of Rhône wines and grower of CÔTE-RÔTIE, top notch, v. elegant *La Chatillonne* (12% VIOGNIER; wait min 5 yrs). Range sharply on the up. Gd CÔTES DU RHÔNE VIOGNIER, VENTOUX, MUSCAT DE BEAUMES-DE-VENISE, VACQUEYRAS.

Vieille Ferme, La S Rhô r w ★★ Often a great-value brand; esp VENTOUX (r) and LUBÉRON (w) made by Famille Perrin of CH DE BEAUCASTEL. Lots of fruit, authentic local appeal.

Vieilles Vignes Old vines, which should make the best wine. Eg. COMTE GEORGES DE VOGÜÉ, MUSIGNY, VIEILLES VIGNES. But no rules about age and can be a tourist trap.

Vieux Télégraphe, Domaine du S Rhô r w ★★★ 78' 81' 85 88 89' 90 94' 95' 96' 97 98' 99' 00 01' 03' 04' 05' 06' 07' 09' 10' 11 Front rank, large estate, maker of smoky, complex, long-lived red CHÂTEAUNEUF, and rich white (more chubby since 1990s; excellent with food, always gd in lesser yrs). Second DOM: de la Roquète: pure fruit, reds becoming deeper, fresh whites, both on the rise. Owns fine, slow-ageing, understated *Gigondas Dom Les Pallières* with US importer Kermit Lynch.

Vigne or vignoble Vineyard (v'yd), vineyards (v'yds).

Vigneron Vine-grower.

Vin de France Replaces VDT. Allows mention of grape variety and vintage. Often blends of regions with brand name. Can be source of unexpected delights if talented winemaker uses this category to avoid bureaucractic hassle.

Vin de paille Wine from grapes dried on straw mats, so v. sweet, like Italian passito. Esp in the Jura. *See also* CHAVE, VIN PAILLÉ DE CORRÈZE.

Vin de Pays (VDP) Potentially most dynamic category in France (with over 150 regions), allowing scope for experimentation. Renamed IGP (*Indication Géographique Protegée*) from 2009 vintage, but position unchanged and new terminology still not accepted by every area. The zonal names are most individual: eg. CÔTES DE GASCOGNE, CÔTES DE THONGUE, Haute Vallée de l'Orb,

Duché d'Uzès, among others. Enormous variety in taste and quality but never ceases to surprise.

Vin de table (VDT) Category of standard everyday table wine now replaced by VIN DE FRANCE.

Vin doux naturel (VDN) Rouss Sweet wine fortified with wine alcohol, so the sweetness is natural, not the strength. This is the specialty of ROUSSILLON and is based on either GRENACHE or MUSCAT. Top wines, esp RANCIOS, can provide fabulous drinking.

Vin gris "Grey" wine is v. pale pink, made of red grapes pressed before fermentation begins – unlike rosé, which ferments briefly before pressing. "Œil de Perdrix" means much the same; so does "blush".

Vin Jaune Jura w ★★★ Specialty of ARBOIS: odd yellow wine like Fino Sherry. Normally ready when bottled (after at least 6 yrs). Best: CH-CHALON. *See also* PLAGEOLES. A halfway-house oxidized white is sold locally as *vin typé*.

Vin paillé de Corrèze SW Fr r w Made nr Beaulieu-sur-Dordogne by 25 keen growers and small co-op. Modern grapes and cellar techniques preferred by most growers, gradually replacing the older style (once said to have been prescribed for breast-feeding mothers). An acquired taste. Try ★ Christian Tronche.

Vinsobres S Rhô r (p) (w) ★→★★ 07' 09' 10' (11) SYRAH-leaning appellation, marked by strong winds and altitude, nr Nyons. The top reds offer direct fruit and punchy body. Leaders incl: Cave la Vinsobraise, DOMS les Aussellons, Bicarelle, Chaume-Arnaud, Constant-Duquesnoy, Coriançon, Deurre (traditional), Jaume (modern), Moulin (traditional), Famille Perrin (v.gd value), Peysson, CH Rouanne.

Viré-Clessé Burg w ★★ 09' 10' 11 AC based around two of best white villages of MÂCON. Extrovert style, though residual sugar originally forbidden. Try A Bonhomme, Bret Bros, Chaland, LAFON, Michel, THÉVENET, co-op.

Visan S Rhô r (p) (w) ★★ 07' 09' 10' Young growers bringing quality impetus to Rhône village for medium-full reds sprinkled with direct fruit, freshness. Acceptable whites. Best: DOMS Coste Chaude, Florane, Fourmente (esp NATURE), des Grands Devers, Roche-Audran.

Vogüé, Comte Georges de C d'O ★★★★ Iconic CHAMBOLLE estate, incl lion's share of MUSIGNY. Heralded vintages from 1990s taking time to come round.

Volnay C d'O r ★★★ →★★★★ 90' 95 96' 98 99' 02' 03 05' 06 07 08 09' 10' 11 Village between POMMARD and MEURSAULT: often the best reds of the CÔTE DE BEAUNE; structured and silky. Best v'yds: Caillerets, Champans, CLOS des Chênes, Santenots, Taillepieds, etc. Best growers: D'ANGERVILLE, BOILLOT, HOSPICES DE BEAUNE, LAFARGE, LAFON, DE MONTILLE, Rossignol.

Volnay-Santenots C d'O r ★★★ Best red-wine v'yds of MEURSAULT sold under this name. Indistinguishable from other PREMIER CRU VOLNAY, unless more body, less delicacy. Best growers: AMPEAU, HOSPICES DE BEAUNE, LAFON, LEROY, PRIEUR.

Vosne-Romanée C d'O r ★★★ →★★★★ 90' 93 95 96' 98 99' 02' 03 05' 06 07 08 09' 10' 11. Village with Burgundy's grandest crus (eg. ROMANÉE-CONTI, LA TÂCHE) and outstanding PREMIERS CRUS Malconsorts, Suchots, Brûlées, etc. There are (or should be) no common wines in Vosne. Many gd growers, incl: Arnoux, CATHIARD, Clavelier, DRC, EUGÉNIE, GRIVOT, GROS, Lamarche, LEROY, LIGER-BELAIR, MÉO-CAMUZET, MUGNERET, ROUGET, Tardy.

Ch Lafite is first of the First Growths only because F comes before T in the alphabet.

Vougeot C d'O r w ★★★ 90' 93 95' 96' 98 99' 02' 03 05' 06 07 08 09' 10' 11 Mostly GRAND CRU as CLOS DE VOUGEOT but also village and PREMIER CRU, incl outstanding white MONOPOLE, *Clos Blanc de V.* HUDELOT-Noellat and VOUGERAIE best.

Vougeraie, Domaine de la C d'O r w ★★→★★★ DOM uniting all BOISSET's v'yd holdings (since 1999). Gd-value BOURGOGNE Rouge up to fine MUSIGNY GRAND CRU and unique white CLOS Blanc de VOUGEOT.

Vouvray Lo w dr sw sp ★★→★★★★ (dr) 89 90 96' 97 02' 03 05' 07 08' **09** 10 (sw) 89' 90' 95' 96' 97' 03' 05' 08 09' Important AC east of Tours: still wines from top producers increasingly gd and reliable. DEMI-SEC is classic style, but in gd yrs *moëlleux* can be intensely sweet, almost immortal. Variable sparkling (60% of production): look out for *pétillant*. Producers: Allias, Bonneau, Brunet, Carême, *Champalou*, CLOS Baudoin, Dhoye-Deruet, Foreau, Fouquet (DOM des Aubuisières), CH Gaudrelle, *Huet*, Pinon, *Dom de la Taille-aux-Loups*, Vigneau-Chevreau. Ancient vintages – ie. 1921, 1924, 1947, 1959 – a must-try.

Vranken Champ Ever-more-powerful CHAMPAGNE group. Sound quality. Leading brand: Demoiselle. Owns HEIDSIECK MONOPOLE and POMMERY.

Wolfberger Al ★★ Principal label of Eguisheim co-op. Exceptional quality for such a large-scale producer. V. important for CRÉMANT.

"Y" B'x (pronounced "ygrec") 80' 85 86 88 94 96 00 02 04 05 06 07 08 09 10 (11) Intense dry white wine produced at CH d'YQUEM, now on a yearly basis. Enticing young but interesting with age. Dry style in 2004; otherwise in classic off-dry mould, but recently purer and fresher than in the past.

Zind Humbrecht, Domaine Al ★★★★ Leading biodynamic DOM sensitively run by Olivier Humbrecht, great winemaker and thinker: rich yet balanced wines, drier, more elegant than before, v. low yields. Top wines from single-v'yds *Clos St-Urbain*, Jebsal (superb PINOT GR 02 08 09 10) and Windsbuhl (esp GEWURZ 05 08 09'), plus GRANDS CRUS RANGEN, HENGST, Brand, Goldert.

An oeuf's enough?

New-ageism is becoming mainstream. The concrete egg-shaped fermenters beloved of biodynamicists, which looked wacky only a few years ago, are now a must-have piece of kit – they keep the lees in gentle circulation in the wine, which is A Good Thing. But the really new accessory is called (perhaps) Dobbin, pulls a plough and doesn't compact the soil. A quick and extremely unscientific survey of v'yds visited last spring revealed horses popping up all over the place. Could it be the price of diesel?

Châteaux of Bordeaux

Abbreviations used in the text:

B'x	Bordeaux
Bar	Barsac
E-2-M	Entre-Deux-Mers
Grav	Graves
H-Méd	Haut-Médoc
L de P	Lalande de Pomerol
List	Listrac
Mar	Margaux
Méd	Médoc
Mou	Moulis
Pau	Pauillac
Pe-Lé	Pessac-Léognan
Pom	Pomerol
St-Em	St-Emilion
St-Est	St-Estèphe
St-Jul	St-Julien
Saut	Sauternes
AC	appellation contrôlée
ch(x)	château(x)
dom(s)	domaine(s)

More heavily shaded areas are the wine-growing regions.

The euphoria couldn't last for ever. After the unprecedented vintages of 2009 and 2010, Bordeaux had to deal with a changeable and tortuous 2011. A heatwave in the spring, variable summer, late-season rot and local-ized hail tested producers' skills, energy and patience. The resulting wines are consequently extremely variable (though selectively there are some stars). But don't worry – at least not yet. In the cellars and shops are a hat-trick of golden years: 2008, 2009 and 2010. The last two are among the region's greatest. The top of the range disappeared into the luxury goods category years ago, but humbler Bordeaux remains perfectly realistic, indeed good

Châteaux of Bordeaux entries also cross-reference to France

value compared with its international Cabernet/Merlot competition. And the delicious 2009s are so supple and seductive there's the choice to cellar or drink. 2010, 2008 and 2006 still need ageing but 2005s, at *petit château* level in appellations such as Blaye, Fronsac, Lalande de Pomerol, Listrac and Haut-Médoc, are opening up and drinking beautifully. The grands crus of 2001, 2002, 2004 are the ones to look for now; these are classic years, destined to be enjoyed at the table while we wait for the 2005s and the great wines of 2000.

You can drink the foothills, but I don't think the 2000s have reached their peak yet. But 1998, a bit tough on the Left Bank, was a great year on the Right Bank and is now a handsomely mature vintage. Dry white Bordeaux continues to be consistent and good value (even 2011 has pulled off some surprises) and Sauternes is piling up excellent years (2010, 2009, 2007, 2005, 2003, 2002, 2001). Someone has to drink and appreciate them.

L'A, Domaine de r ★★ 02 03 04 05' 06 07 08 09' 10' Owned by winemaking consultant STÉPHANE DERENONCOURT and one of the best in CASTILLON-CÔTES DE BORDEAUX. Biodynamically run. More finesse than usual for the AC.

d'Agassac H-Méd r ★★ 00' 02 03 04 05 06 07 08 09' 10' "Sleeping Beauty" 14th-century moated fort. Southern HAUT-MÉDOC v'yd. Modern, accessible wine.

Andron-Blanquet St-Est r ★★ 98 00' 01 03 04 05' 06 08 09' 10' Sister CH to COS-LABORY. Unfashionable but gd value.

Angélus St-Em r ★★★★ 89' 90' 92' 95 96 98' 99 00' 01 02 03' 04 05 06 07 08 09' 10' 11 Leading PREMIER GRAND CRU CLASSÉ on ST-EMILION CÔTES. Pioneer of the modern style; dark, rich, sumptuous. Lots of 60-yr-old CAB FR. Major winery renovation in 2012. Second wine: Le Carillon de L'Angélus. Fleur de Boüard in LALANDE DE POMEROL and Bellevue in ST-EMILION same ownership.

d'Angludet Mar r ★★★ 90 95 96' 98' 00 02 04 05 06 08 09' 10' Owned and run by négociant SICHEL. Lively, fragrant, stylish, popular in the UK. Gd value.

Archambeau Grav r w dr (sw) ★★ (r) 00 02 04 05 06 08 09 10 (w) 04 05 06 07 08 09 10 Property at Illats owned by branch of Dubourdieu family. Gd *fruity dry white*; fragrant barrel-aged reds. Improving BARSAC-classed-growth CH Suau in same stable.

d'Arche Saut w sw ★★ 96 97' 98 99 00 01' 02 03' 05 07 09' 10' 11 Much-improved Second Growth. Top vintages are creamy. CH d'Arche-Lafaurie is a richer micro-CUVÉE. Also bed-and-breakfast in 17th-century chapter house.

d'Armailhac Pau r ★★★ 95' 96' 98 99 00 01 02 03 04 05' 06 07 08 09' 10' 11 Substantial Fifth Growth under (MOUTON) ROTHSCHILD ownership. Top-quality, more finesse than sister CLERC MILON; 15–20% CAB FR. On top form since 2004 and well-priced.

l'Arrosée St-Em r ★★★ 00 01 02 03 04 05' 06' 07 08 09' 10' 11 Classed-growth côtes estate opposite ST-EMILION CO-OP. Since 2003 (new ownership) on top form. Aromatic, structured wines with plenty of CAB FR and CAB SAUV (40%).

Ausone St-Em r ★★★★ 86' 88 89' 90 95 96' 97 98' 99 00' 01' 02 03' 04 05' 06' 07 08 09' 10' 11 Tiny but illustrious First Growth (about 1,500 cases); best position on the côtes with famous rock-hewn cellars. On superb form since 1996 (thanks to Vauthier family), hence astronomical price. Long-lived wines with volume, texture and finesse. Second wine: Chapelle d'Ausone (500 cases) also excellent.

Balestard la Tonnelle St-Em r ★★ 98' 00' 01 03 04 05 06 08 09 10 Historic classed growth on limestone plateau. Associate of MICHEL ROLLAND consults. Richer and riper since 2003.

Barde-Haut St-Em r ★★ 98 99 00 01 02 03 05' 06 07 08 09 10 11 Sister property of CLOS L'EGLISE and HAUT-BERGEY. New ecological winery in 2011. Rich, modern and opulent in style.

Bastor-Lamontagne Saut w sw ★★ 96′ 97′ 98 99 01′ 02 03′ 05 07 09′ 10 11 Large Preignac sister to BEAUREGARD. Gd value; pure, harmonious style. Second label: Les Remparts de Bastor. Fruity Caprice (from 2004) for early drinking. Also CH St-Robert at Pujols: GRAVES (r w).

Batailley Pau r ★★★ 95 96 98 00′ 02 03 04 05′ 06 08 09′ 10′ Fifth Growth property bordering PAUILLAC and ST-JULIEN. Fine, firm, strong-flavoured. *Gd-value Pauillac* on steady form. Denis Dubourdieu consults.

Beaumont H-Méd r ★★ 98 00′ 02 04 05′ 06 07 08 09 10′ One of the largest estates in the MÉDOC peninsula; large volume, early maturing, *easily enjoyable wines*. Second label: CH Moulin d'Arvigny. In the same hands as BEYCHEVELLE.

Beauregard Pom r ★★★ 96′ 98′ 00′ 01 02 03 04 05′ 06 08 09′ 10′ Large (for POMEROL) estate: fine 17th-century CH nr LA CONSEILLANTE. Harmonious rather than full style. Consistent. Second label: Benjamin de Beauregard.

Beau-Séjour-Bécot St-Em r ★★★ 89′ 90′ 95′ 96 98′ 99 00′ 01 02 03 04 05′ 06 07 08 09′ 10′ 11 PREMIER GRAND CRU CLASSÉ on the limestone plateau. On top form since 1996. Seductive wines with more finesse from 2001. GRAND-PONTET and LA GOMERIE in same family hands.

Beauséjour-Duffau St-Em r ★★★ 95 96 98 99 00 01 02 03 04 05′ 06 08 09′ 10′ 11 Tiny PREMIER GRAND CRU CLASSÉ estate on west slope of the côtes, owned by the Duffau-Lagarrosse family. It has moved up a gear from 2009: STÉPHANE DERENONCOURT consults.

Beau-Site St-Est r ★★ 98 00 03 04 05 06 08 09 10 CRU BOURGEOIS (2009) property in same hands as BATAILLEY, etc. 70% CAB SAUV. Average wine but more flesh in recent yrs.

Belair-Monange St-Em r ★★★ 89′ 90′ 94 95′ 96 98 99 00′ 01 02 03 04 05′ 06 08 09′ 10′ 11 Classed-growth neighbour of AUSONE. Name changed from 2008 (used to be plain Belair), and new label. Négociant J-P MOUEIX owner since 2008 and new investment. Fine, fragrant, elegant style; more concentration since 2008.

Belgrave H-Méd r ★★ 98′ 00′ 02′ 03 04′ 05′ 06 07 08 09′ 10′ 11 Sizeable Fifth Growth, well-managed by CVBG-DOURTHE (*see* LA GARDE, REYSSON). Modern-classic in style. Now consistent quality. Second label: Diane de Belgrave.

Bellefont-Belcier St-Em r ★★ 00 01 02 03 04 05′ 06 07 08′ 09′ 10′ 11 GRAND CRU CLASSÉ justifiably promoted in 2006. Neighbour of LARCIS-DUCASSE on the côtes at St-Laurent-des-Combes. Suave, fresh and refined. Recent vintages v.gd.

Bel-Orme-Tronquoy-de-Lalande H-Méd r ★★ 96 98′ 00 02 03 04 05 08 09 10 Northern HAUT-MÉDOC estate. Clay-limestone soils, so MERLOT (60%) dominates. Firm, muscular style. Same owner as CROIZET-BAGES, RAUZAN-GASSIES.

Berliquet St-Em r ★★ 98′ 99 00′ 01 02 04 05′ 06 08 09 10 Tiny GRAND CRU CLASSÉ on the côtes. Steady progress since 1996. DERENONCOURT consultant from 2008.

Bernadotte H-Méd r ★★ 99 00′ 01 02 03 04 05′ 06 07 08 09′ 10′ V'yd close to PAUILLAC. ROEDERER owner since 2006. Same management and technical team as PICHON-LALANDE. Structured wines. Recent vintages have more finesse.

Bertineau St-Vincent r ★★ 98 99 00′ 01 04 05 06 08 09 10 Top enologist MICHEL ROLLAND owns this tiny estate in Lalande-de-Pomerol. Old vines, fairly consistent. (*See also* LE BON PASTEUR.)

Beychevelle St-Jul r ★★★ 98 99 00′ 01 02 03 04 05′ 06 07 08 09′ 10′ Fourth Growth with eye-catching boat label. Castel (since 2011) and Suntory (LAGRANGE) owners. Wines of consistent elegance rather than power. On top form since late 1990s. Second wine: Amiral de Beychevelle.

Biston-Brillette Mou r ★★ 00 01 02 03 04 05′ 06 08 09 10′ Well-managed, family-owned. Attractive, fruit-bound wines. Consistent quality and value.

Bonalgue Pom r ★★ 98′ 99 00 01 04 05 06 08 09 10 Dark, rich, meaty. As gd value as it gets. MICHEL ROLLAND consults. Sister estate CLOS du Clocher.

BORDEAUX

Bonnet r w ★★ (r) 05 06 08 09 10 (w) DYA. Owned by octogenarian André Lurton. Big producer of some of the best E-2-M and red B'X. *Prestige* red and white CUVÉE, Divinus. LA LOUVIÈRE, COUHINS-LURTON, ROCHEMORIN same stable.

Bon Pasteur, le Pom r ★★★ 95 96' 98' 99 00 01 02 03 04 05' 06 08 09' 10' Excellent property on ST-EMILION border, owned by MICHEL ROLLAND. Ripe, opulent, seductive wines guaranteed. (*See also* BERTINEAU ST-VINCENT.)

Boscq, le St-Est r ★★ 00 01 03 04 05' 06 08 09' 10 Quality-driven estate owned by CVBG-DOURTHE. MERLOT-dominated (60%). Excellent value.

Bourgneuf-Vayron Pom r ★★ 98' 99 00 01' 03 04 05' 06 08 09 10 Vayron name dropped from 2010. Ample and firm-edged, with more fruit and precision from 2008.

Bouscaut Pe-Lé r w ★★ (r) 95 98 00 01 02 04 05' 06 07 08 09 10' 11 (w) 00 01 02 03 04 05' 06 07 08 09 10' 11 Classed growth owned by sister of BRANE-CANTENAC's Henri Lurton. MERLOT-based reds. Sappy, age-worthy whites.

Boyd-Cantenac Mar r ★★★ 96' 98' 00 02 03 04 05' 06 07 08 09' 10' Little-known Third Growth on top form these days. CAB SAUV-dominated with a little peppery PETIT VERDOT. *Stupendous 2010.* Second wine: Jacques Boyd. *See also* POUGET.

Branaire-Ducru St-Jul r ★★★ 95 96 98 99 00' 01 02 03 04 05' 06 08 09' 10' 11 Fourth Growth with v'yd scattered around AC. "Fruit, freshness, finesse" the motto here. Less power and concentration than its peers. Second label: Duluc.

Brane-Cantenac Mar r ★★★ 96 98 99 00' 01 02 03 04 05' 06 07 08 09' 10' 11 Large Second Growth in Cantenac. Astutely managed by owner Henri Lurton. Dense, fragrant. Second label: Baron de Brane.

Brillette Mou r ★★ 98 00 02 03 04 05 06 08 09 10 V'yd on gravelly soils. Wines of gd depth and fruit. MICHEL ROLLAND consults. Second label: Berthault Brillette.

Cabanne, La Pom r ★★ 95 96 98' 00 04 05 06' 08 09 10 V'yd west of the POMEROL plateau. Rustic in style; could do better. Cellar fire in 2010; large quantity of wine lost. Second wine: DOM de Compostelle.

Looking for more information on grapes? Try the "Grapes" section on pp.16–26.

Cadet-Piola St-Em r ★★ 95 98 00 01 03 04 05 06 08 09 10 GRAND CRU CLASSÉ under same ownership/management as SOUTARD and LARMANDE from 2009. Fresh, firm, long-lived wines. 2010 more modern.

Caillou Saut w sw ★★ 89' 90' 95 96 97 98 99 01' 02 03' 05' 07 09' 10' Well-run, second-rank BARSAC for firm, fruity wine. 2010 best ever. CUVÉE Reine is a top selection, Prestige Cuvée another.

Calon-Ségur St-Est r ★★★ 90' 94 95 96' 98 99 00' 01 02 03' 04 05' 06 07 08' 09' 10' 11 Third Growth with great historic reputation. Redoubtable owner Mme Capbern-Gasqueton died in 2011. Her daughter (Hélène de Baritault) now in charge. Estate really flying since 2008. Second label: Marquis de Calon.

Cambon la Pelouse H-Méd r ★★ 00 01 02 03 04 05' 06 07 08 09 10' Big, supple, accessible southern HAUT-MÉDOC cru. L'Aura, a micro-CUVÉE from MARGAUX.

Camensac H-Méd r ★★ 96' 98 01 02 03 05 06 08 09 10' Fifth Growth in northern HAUT-MÉDOC. New owner (2005) has CHASSE-SPLEEN connection; change for the better from 2006; riper fruit. Second label: La Closerie de Camensac.

Canon St-Em r ★★★ 96 98' 99 00 01 02 03 04 05' 06 07 08' 09' 10' 11 Famous first-classed growth with walled-in v'yd on plateau west of the town, bought in 1996 by owners of RAUZAN-SÉGLA. Plenty of investment and replanting. Elegant, long-lived wines. Acquired neigbouring CH Matras in 2011. Second label: clos Canon.

Canon-de-Brem r ★★ 00 01 03 04 05' RIP from 2006. Bought by Jean Halley of Carrefour supermarkets in 2000, wine now absorbed into CH DE LA DAUPHINE. Massive recent investment. Firm, pure expression.

Canon la Gaffelière St-Em r ★★★ 95 96 98' 99 00' 01 02 03 04 05' 06 08 09' 10' 11 Leading GRAND CRU CLASSÉ on the lower slopes of the côtes. Same ownership as CLOS DE L'ORATOIRE, LA MONDOTTE and Aiguilhe in Castillon. Stylish, upfront, impressive wines with 40% CAB FR and 5% CAB SAUV.

Cantegril Grav r Saut w sw ★★ (r) 05 06 08 09 10 (w) 02 03 04 05' 06 07 09 10 Supple red, fine BARSAC-SAUTERNES from DOISY-DAËNE and CLOS FLORIDÈNE connection. Value.

Cantemerle H-Méd r ★★★ 95 96' 98 00 01 02 03 04 05' 06' 07 08 09' 10' Large property in southern HAUT-MÉDOC. Now merits its Fifth Growth status. Sandy/gravel soils give finer style. Second label: Les Allées de Cantemerle.

Cantenac-Brown Mar r ★★ →★★★ 95 96 98 99 00 01 02 03 04 05' 06 08 09' 10' Third Growth sold in 2006 to private investor; owned since late 1980s by AXA Millésimes. Previously robust style being steadily refined (v.gd 2009, 2010). Second label: Brio du CH Cantenac Brown.

Capbern-Gasqueton St-Est r ★★ 98 00 02 03 04 05 06 08' 09' 10' 11 Same stable and standards as CALON-SÉGUR. New cellars in 2010. Raised its game since 2008 – solid but polished wines.

Cap de Mourlin St-Em r ★★ →★★★ 98' 99 00 01 03 04 05 06 08 09 10 Well-known property of the Capdemourlin family, also owners of CH BALESTARD LA TONNELLE and Ch Roudier. Riper and more concentrated than in the past.

Carbonnieux Pe-Lé r w ★★★ 96 98 99 00 01 02 04 05' 06 07 08 09' 10 11 Large, historic estate at Léognan for sterling red and white, run by Eric and Philibert Perrin. *The whites*, 65% SAUV BL (eg. 98 99 00 01 02 03 04 05 06 07 08 09 10 11), can age 10 yrs or more. CHX Haut-Vigneau, Lafont Menaut and Le Sartre are also in the family. Second label: La Tour-Léognan.

101 of the 246 Crus Bourgeois (2009 vintage) were included in the original 1932 list and the annulled 2003 classification.

Carles, de r ★★ →★★★ 99 00 01 02 03 04 05' 06' 07 08 09 10 FRONSAC. Haut Carles (★★★) is the top selection here with its own modern, gravity-fed cellars. Investment and aspirations of a top growth. Superb from 2006.

Carmes Haut-Brion, les Pe-Lé r ★★★ 95 96 98 99 00 01 02 03 04 05' 06 07 08 09' 10' Tiny walled-in neighbour of HAUT-BRION with classed-growth standards. 55% MERLOT. New ownership in 2010.

Caronne-Ste-Gemme H-Méd r ★★ 00 01 02 04 05 06 08 09' 10' Go-ahead estate. Olivier Dauga consults. Recent vintages show more depth and class.

Carruades de Château Lafite Pau The second wine of CH Lafite is a relatively easy-drinker (40% MERLOT). Its price has gone ballistic thanks to Chinese demand.

Carteau Côtes-Daugay St-Em r ★★ 00 01 02 03 04 05 08 09 10 Consistent, gd-value ST-EMILION GRAND CRU; full-flavoured wines with freshness and elegance as well.

Certan-de-May Pom r ★★★ 95 96 98 00' 01' 04 05' 06 08 09' 10' 11 Tiny property on the POMEROL plateau opposite VIEUX-CH-CERTAN. Solid wines, ageing potential.

Certan-Marzelle Pom Little J-P MOUEIX estate for *fragrant, light, juicy Pomerol.*

Chantegrive Grav r w ★★ →★★★ 00 01 02 03 04 05' 06 07 08 09' 10' 11 The largest in the AC; modern and v.gd quality. Reds rich and finely oaked. Cuvée Caroline is top, fragrant white (02 03 04 05' 06 07 08 09 10).

Chasse-Spleen Mou r (w) ★★★ 98 99 00 01 02 03 04 05' 06 07 08 09' 10' 11 Big MOULIS estate at classed-growth level. Consistently gd, often outstanding, long-maturing wine. Second label: L'Heritage de Chasse-Spleen. One of the surest things in B'X. Makes a little white. *See also* CAMENSAC and GRESSIER-GRAND-POUJEAUX.

Chauvin St-Em r ★★ 00 01 03 04 05 06 08 09 10' Family-owned GRAND CRU CLASSÉ in northwest ST-EMILION. Steady performer; increasingly serious. New winemaker in 2008.

Cheval Blanc St-Em r ★★★★ 88 89 90' 93 94 95 96' 97 98' 99 00' 01' 02 03 04 05' 06 07 08 09' 10' 11 PREMIER GRAND CRU CLASSÉ (A) of ST-EMILION. High percentage of CAB FR (60%). Firm, fragrant, vigorous wines with some of the voluptuousness of neighbouring POMEROL. Delicious young; lasts a generation – or two. Same ownership and management as YQUEM and TOUR DU PIN (ST-EMILION). 1947 is a candidate for best claret ever. Stylish, new eco-friendly winery inaugurated in 2011. Second wine: Le Petit Cheval.

Chevalier, Domaine de Pe-Lé r w ★★★★ 95 96' 98' 99' 00' 01' 02 03 04' 05' 06 07 08 09' 10' 11 Superb estate in Léognan. Impressive since 1998, the red has gained in finesse, fruit, texture. Complex, long-ageing white has remarkable consistency and develops rich flavours (94 95 96' 97 98' 99 00 01 02 03 04 05' 06 07' 08' 09' 10' 11). Second wine: Esprit de Chevalier. Look out for DOM de la Solitude, PESSAC-LÉOGNAN.

China shops for châteaux

The Chinese are not only buying wine from B'X but CHX as well. Properties currently in the hands of Chinese investors include Chx Latour-Laguens (B'X), Lezongars (CADILLAC-CÔTES DE BORDEAUX), Laulan Ducos (MÉDOC), Chenu-Lafitte (BOURG), de la Salle (BLAYE), Richelieu (FRONSAC), Viaud (LALANDE DE POMEROL) and Monlot (ST-EMILION). And the list looks likely to grow – particularly if the estate is pleasing to the eye.

Cissac H-Méd r ★★ 95 96' 98 00 02 03 04 05 08 09 10 *Cru* west of PAUILLAC. Firm, tannic wines that need time. Recent vintages less rustic. Second wine: Reflets du CH Cissac.

Citran H-Méd r ★★ 96 98 99 00 02 03 04 05' 06 08 09 10' Large estate owned by Villars-Merlaut family since 1996 (*see* CHASSE-SPLEEN, CAMENSAC). Modern, ripe and oaky through the 2000s. Lately a touch more finesse. Second label: Moulins de Citran.

Clarence de Haut-Brion, le Pe-Lé r ★★★ 89' 90 94 95 96' 98 99 00 01 02 03 04 05' 06 07 08 09' 10' 11 The second wine of CH HAUT-BRION, known as Bahans Haut-Brion until 2007. Blend changes considerably with each vintage but style follows that of the *grand vin*.

Clarke List r (p) (w) ★★ 98' 99 00 01 02 03 04 05' 06 08 09' 10' Large estate, massive (Edmond) Rothschild investment. Now v.gd MERLOT-based red. Consistent style since 2000: dark fruit and fine tannins. Also a dry white: Le Merle Blanc du CH Clarke. Ch Malmaison in MOULIS same connection.

Clerc Milon Pau r ★★★ 89' 90' 94 95 96' 98' 99 00 01 02 03 04 05' 06 07 08 09' 10' 11 Once-forgotten Fifth Growth owned by (MOUTON) Rothschilds. Broader and weightier than sister D'ARMAILHAC. New, eco-friendly cellar in 2011.

Climens Saut sw sw ★★★★ 85' 86' 88' 89 90' 95 96 97' 98 99' 00 01' 02 03' 04 05' 06 07 09' 10' BARSAC classed growth making some of the world's most stylish wine. Concentrated, but with vibrant acidity giving balance; ageing potential guaranteed. Biodynamic conversion from 2009. Second label: Les Cyprès. Owned by Bérénice Lurton (sister of Henri at BRANE-CANTENAC).

Clinet Pom r ★★★★ 95 96 98' 99 00 01 02 03 05' 06 07 08 09' 10 11 Made a name for intense, sumptuous wines in the 1980s ('89 and '90 legendary). Back on same form with 2008 and 2009. MICHEL ROLLAND consults. Second label: Fleur de Clinet introduced in 1997, but now a négociant brand.

Clos l'Eglise Pom r ★★★ 96 98 99 00' 01 02 03 04 05' 06 07 08 09' 10 11 Well-sited, plateau v'yd. Rich, round and modern style since 1998. Same family owns HAUT-BERGEY, Branon and BARDE-HAUT.

Clos Floridène Grav r w ★★ (r) 01 02 03 04 05 06 08 09' 10' (w) 01' 02 03 04' 05' 06 07 08' 09 10 A sure thing from one of B'X's most famous makers of white wines, Denis Dubourdieu. SAUV BL/SÉM from limestone allows the wine to age well; much-improved red. *See also* CHX CANTEGRIL, DOISY-DAËNE and REYNON.

Clos Fourtet St-Em r ★★★ 95 96 98 99 00 01 02 03 04 05' 06 07 08 09' 10' 11 First Growth on the limestone plateau, its cellars are almost in the town. New owner and investment from 2001; on stellar form. Location for French film *Tu Seras Mon Fils* (*You Will Be My Son*). Also owns POUJEAUX. Second label: DOM de Martialis.

Clos Haut-Peyraguey Saut w sw ★★★ 89 90' 95' 96 97' 98 99 00 01' 02 03' 04 05' 06 07 09' 10' 11 Family DOM on "upper" part of the original Peyraguey estate. Elegant, harmonious wines. Haut-Bommes same stable.

Clos des Jacobins St-Em r ★★→★★★ 95 96 98 00 01 02 03 04 05' 06 07 08 09' 10' 11 Côtes classed growth with greater stature since 2000. New ownership from 2004; new creamy style. ANGÉLUS owner consults. Same family owns CH La Commanderie and FLEUR CARDINALE.

Clos du Marquis St-Jul r ★★ →★★★ 98 99 00 01 02 03 04 05' 06 07 08 09' 10' 11 As of 2007 no longer considered the second wine of LÉOVILLE-LAS-CASES but a separate wine and v'yd (as has always been the case). As gd as many classed growths.

Clos de l'Oratoire St-Em r ★★ 96 98 99 00' 01 03 04 05' 06 07 08 09 10' Serious performer on the northeastern slopes of ST-EMILION. From same stable as CANON-LA-GAFFELIÈRE and LA MONDOTTE, polished and reasonable value. Small crop in 2009 (due to hail).

Clos Puy Arnaud r ★★ 00 01' 02 03 04 05' 06 08 09' 10 Biodynamic estate. Leading light in CASTILLON-CÔTES DE BORDEAUX. Wines of depth and distinction. Owner formerly connected to PAVIE.

Clos René Pom r ★★ 98' 00' 01 04 05' 06 08 09 10 MERLOT-dominated wine with a little spicy MALBEC from sandy/gravel soils. Less sensuous than top POMEROL but gd value. Alias CH Moulinet-Lasserre.

In 2011 China imported more Bordeaux than any other country. Will it drink it?

Clotte, la St-Em r ★★ 96 98' 99 00' 01 02 03 04 05 06 08 09' 10' Tiny côtes GRAND CRU CLASSÉ: fine, perfumed, supple wines. Confidential but gd value.

Colombier-Monpelou Pau r ★★ 00' 02 03 04 05 06 08 Owned since 2007 by (MOUTON) Rothschilds. Almost RIP. Grapes now destined for other brands.

Conseillante, la Pom r ★★★★ 89 90' 94 95' 96' 98' 99 00' 01 02 03 04 05' 06' 07 08 09' 10' 11 Historic property on plateau between PÉTRUS and CHEVAL BLANC. Some of the noblest and most fragrant POMEROL; almost Médocain in style; long-ageing. New *cuvier* in 2012. Second wine (from 2007): Duo de Conseillante.

Corbin St-Em r ★★ 98 00' 01 02 04 05 07 08 09' 10' 11 Much improved GRAND CRU CLASSÉ on sand and clay soils. Now consistent and gd value. Elegant with fine tannic frame.

Corbin-Michotte St-Em r ★★ 00 01 02 04 05 06 08 09 10 Competent rather than exciting classed growth located close to POMEROL. Medium-bodied, classic wines rather than modern. In same hands as CHX Calon and Cantelauze.

Cordeillan-Bages Pau r ★★→★★★ A mere 1,000 cases of savoury PAUILLAC made by the LYNCH-BAGES team. Rarely seen outside B'X. Better known for its luxury restaurant and hotel.

Cos d'Estournel St-Est r ★★★★ 89' 90' 94 95 96' 98' 00 01 02 03 04 05' 06 07 08 09' 10' 11 Fashionable Second Growth with eccentric pagoda *chai*. Most refined ST-ESTÈPHE. New (wildly expensive) state-of-the-art cellars in 2008. Pricey white from 2005. Badly hit by hail in 2011. Second label: Les Pagodes de Cos (and CH MARBUZET for some markets). Same owner as super-modern Goulée (MÉDOC).

Cos-Labory St-Est r ★★ 90' 94 95 96' 98' 99 00 02 03 04 05' 06 07 08 09' 10' Inconsistent Fifth Growth neighbour of COS D'ESTOURNEL. Recent vintages have more depth and structure. Gd value. ANDRON-BLANQUET is sister CH.

Coufran H-Méd r ★★ 98 99 00 01 02 03 04 05 06 08 09 10' Coufran and VERDIGNAN, in extreme north of the HAUT-MÉDOC, are co-owned. Coufran is mainly MERLOT for supple wine. SOUDARS is another, smaller sister.

Couhins-Lurton Pe-Lé r w ★★ →★★★ (r) 02 03 04 05 06 09 10 (w) 98' 99 00 01 02 03 04 05 06 07 08' 09 10' Fine, minerally, long-lived, classed-growth white made from SAUV BL. Supple, MERLOT-based red from 2002. Same family as LA LOUVIÈRE and BONNET.

Couspaude, la St-Em r ★★★ 98 99 00' 01 02 03 04 05 06 07 08 09' 10' 11 Classed growth well-located on the plateau. Modern style: rich and creamy with lashings of spicy oak. MICHEL ROLLAND consults.

Coutet Saut w sw ★★★ 88' 89' 90' 95 96 97' 98' 99 01' 02 03' 04 05 07 09' 10' 11 Traditional rival to CLIMENS, but zestier style. Largest estate in BARSAC. Consistently v. fine. CUVÉE Madame is a v. rich selection in certain yrs (89 90 95).

Couvent des Jacobins St-Em r ★★ 98' 99 00' 01 03 04 05 06 08 09' 10 GRAND CRU CLASSÉ vinified within the walls of the town. Splendid cellars. Lighter, easy style. Denis Dubourdieu consults. Second label: Le Menut des Jacobins.

Crock, le St-Est r ★★ 98 99 00' 01 02 03 04 05 06 07 08 09' 10 V. fine property in the same family (Cuvelier) as LÉOVILLE-POYFERRÉ. Solid, fruit-packed.

Croix, la Pom r ★★ 95 96 98 99 00 01 04 05 06 07 08 09 10 Owned by négociant Janoueix. Appealing, rich, plummy. La Croix-St-Georges and HAUT-SARPE in ST-EMILION same stable.

Croix-de-Gay, la Pom r ★★★ 95 96 98 99 00' 01' 02 04 05 06 09' 10' 11 Situated in the best part of the commune. Round, elegant style. LA FLEUR-DE-GAY is made from the best parcels. Same ownership as Faizeau (MONTAGNE ST-EMILION).

Croix du Casse, la Pom r ★★ 98 99 00' 01' 04 05 06 08 09 10 Located on sandy/ gravel soils in the south of POMEROL. Since 2005, owned by BORIE-MANOUX; investment and improvement from 2008. Medium-bodied; better value now.

Croizet-Bages Pau r ★★→★★★ 95 96' 98 00' 02 03 04 05 06 07 08 09 10 Underperforming Fifth Growth. Same owners as RAUZAN-GASSIES. New regime in cellar is producing richer, more serious wines. Steady improvement from 2006.

Croque-Michotte St-Em r ★★ 98 00 01 03 04 05 08 09 10 Located on the sandy-gravel soils of the POMEROL border. Standard ST-EMILION.

Côtes de Bordeaux – all change

From 2009 the new appellation CÔTES DE BORDEAUX for red (mainly) and dry white wines became obligatory on labels, replacing ACS Côtes de Castillon, Côtes de Francs, Premières Côtes de Blaye and PREMIÈRES CÔTES DE BORDEAUX. Cross-blending of wines from these regions is allowed but for those stalwarts wanting to maintain the identity of a single terroir, stiffer controls permit the mention BLAYE, CASTILLON, FRANCS and CADILLAC (for the Premières Côtes de Bordeaux) before Côtes de Bordeaux. The CÔTES DE BOURG is not part of the new designation.

Cru Bourgeois *See* Cru Bourgeois box, p.106.

Cruzeau, de Pe-Lé r w sw ★★ (r) 00 01 02 04 05 06 08 09 10 (w) 02 03 04 05 06 07 08 09 10 Large (two-thirds red) v'yd developed by André Lurton of LA LOUVIÈRE and COUHINS-LURTON. Gd-value wines. SAUV BL-dominated white.

Dalem r ★★ 00 01 02 03 04 05' 06 08 09' 10' 11 Was a full-blooded FRONSAC. A feminine touch has added vibrancy and charm since 2003. 85% MERLOT.

Dassault St-Em r ★★ 98' 99 00 01 02 03 04 05' 06 08 09' 10 11 Consistent, modern, juicy GRAND CRU CLASSÉ. Owning family of Dassault aviation fame. Also La Fleur in ST-EMILION and ventures in Chile and Argentina.

Dauphine, de la r ★★→★★★ 00 01 03 04 05 06' 08 09' 10' 11 FRONSAC. Total makeover since purchased by new owner in 2000. Renovation of CH and v'yds plus new, modern winery in 2002. Stablemate CANON-DE-BREM integrated in 2006; more refined and structured since. Second wine: Delphis (from 2006).

Dauzac Mar r ★★→★★★ 89' 90' 94 95 96 98' 99 00' 01 02 04 05 06 08' 09' 10' Fifth Growth; now dense, rich, dark wines. Owned by insurance company; managed by Christine Lurton, daughter of André, of LA LOUVIÈRE. Second wine: La Bastide Dauzac.

Derenoncourt, Stéphane Leading consultant winemaker; self-taught, focused on terroir, fruit, balance. Own property, *Dom de l'A*, in CASTILLON.

Desmirail Mar r ★★→★★★ 00' 01 02 03 04 05 06 07 08 09' 10' Third Growth owned by Denis Lurton, brother of Henri (BRANE-CANTENAC). Fine, delicate style.

Destieux St-Em r ★★ 98 99 00' 01 03' 04 05' 06 07 08 09' 10' 11 Promotion to GRAND CRU CLASSÉ in 2006. Located to the east of ST-EMILION at St-Hippolyte. ROLLAND consults. Bold, powerful style; consistent.

Doisy-Daëne Bar (r) w dr sw ★★★ 88' 89' 90' 95 96 97' 98' 99 01' 02 03 04 05' 06 07 09 10' 11 Family-owned (Dubourdieu) estate; age-worthy, dry white and CH CANTEGRIL, but above all renowned for its notably *fine, sweet Barsac*. L'Extravagant (90 96 97 01 02 03 04 05 06 07 09 10) is an intensely rich and expensive CUVÉE.

Doisy-Dubroca Bar w sw ★★ 90' 95 96 97' 08 09 Tiny classed growth allied to CLIMENS. Limited production.

Doisy-Védrines Saut w sw ★★★ 89' 90 95 96 97' 98 99 01' 03' 04 05 07 09 10' 11 BARSAC Second Growth owned by Casteja family (Joanne négociant). Delicious, sturdy, rich: ages well. A sure thing for many yrs.

Dôme, le St-Em r ★★★ 04 05 06 08 09 10' 11 Micro-wine that used to be super-oaky but is now aimed at elegance and terroir expression (from 2004). Two-thirds old-vine CAB FR. Owned by Jonathan Maltus, who has a string of other ST-EMILIONS (eg. CH Teyssier, Le Carré, Les Astéries, Vieux-Ch-Mazerat) and wines from California's Napa Valley (World's End).

Dominique, la St-Em r ★★★ 89' 90' 94 95 96 98 99 00' 01 04 05' 06 08 09' 10' 11 Classed growth adjacent to CHEVAL BLANC. Solid value until 1996 then went off the boil. Back on form since 2006. New cellars in 2012 (architect Jean Nouvel). 2010 best since 1989. Second label: St Paul de Dominique.

Ducluzeau List r ★★ 00 01 03 04 05 06 08 09 10 Tiny sister property of DUCRU-BEAUCAILLOU. 50/50 MERLOT/CAB SAUV. Round, well-balanced wines.

Ducru-Beaucaillou St-Jul r ★★★★ 85' 94 95' 96' 98 99 00' 01 02 03 04 05' 06 07 08 09' 10' 11 Outstanding Second Growth, excellent form except for a patch in the late 1980s. Added impetus from owner Bruno Borie from 2003. Classic cedar-scented claret, suited to long ageing. Second wine: Croix de Beaucaillou (Jade Jagger – daughter of Sir Mick – designed label from 2010).

Duhart-Milon Rothschild Pau r ★★★ 95 96' 98 00' 01 02 03 04' 05' 06 07 08 09' 10' Fourth Growth stablemate of LAFITE. Greater precision from 2002; increasingly fine quality. Price surge with Chinese hunger for the Rothschild (LAFITE) brand. Second label: Moulin de Duhart.

Durfort-Vivens Mar r ★★★ 89' 90 94 95 96 98 99 00 02 03 04 05' 06 08 09' 10' Second Growth owned and improved by Gonzague Lurton. Recent wines have structure (lots of CAB SAUV) and finesse. Also co-owner of CH Domeyne in ST-ESTÈPHE.

Echo de Lynch-Bages Pau r ★★ 00 01 02 03 04 05 08 09 10 The second wine of LYNCH-BAGES. Until 2008 known as Haut-Bages-Averous. Tasty drinking and fairly consistent.

l'Eglise, Domaine, de Pom r ★★ 95 96 98 99 00 01 02 03 04 05' 06 07 08 09 10' 11 Small property on the clay-gravel plateau: stylish, resonant wine. Denis Dubourdieu consults. Same stable as TROTTEVIEILLE and CROIX DU CASSE.

l'Eglise-Clinet Pom r ★★★→★★★★ 89' 90' 93' 94 95 96 98' 99 00' 01' 02 03 04 05' 06 07 08 09' 10' 11 Tiny but top-flight estate with great consistency; full, concentrated, fleshy wine. Owner-winemaker Denis Durantou excels. Expensive and limited quantity. Second label: La Petite Eglise.

l'Evangile Pom r ★★★★ 88' 89' 90 95 96 98' 99 00' 01 02 03 04' 05' 06 07 08 09' 10' 11 Neighbour of CH LA CONSEILLANTE. Rich, opulent style. Investment by owners (LAFITE) Rothschild greatly improved quality. 2009 and 2010 best of the modern era. Second wine: Blason de l'Evangile.

Fargues, de Saut w sw ★★ 88 89 90 95 96 97 98 99' 01 02 03' 04 05' 06 07 09' 10' 11 V'yd attached to ruined castle. Owned by Lur-Saluces, ex-owner of YQUEM. Techniques used are same. Rich, unctuous; but balanced. Long ageing potential.

Faugères St-Em r ★★→★★★ 98 99 00' 02 03 04 05 06 07 08 09' 10' 11 Dark, fleshy, modern. CUVÉE Péby (100% MERLOT) is the garage wine, but on a large scale. Stunning Mario Botta-designed winery opened 2009. Sister to *Cap de Faugères* in CASTILLON and Chambrun in LALANDE DE POMEROL.

Faurie-de-Souchard St-Em r ★★ 98' 00 03 04 05 06 07 08 09 10 Previously underperforming CH on the côtes. Escaped declassification in 2006. Recent investment and greater effort from new generation. STÉPHANE DERENONCOURT consults. To watch.

de Ferrand St-Em r ★★ 98 00 01 03 04 05 06 08 09' 10' Big St-Hippolyte estate owned by Baron Bich (Bic pens) family. Recent investment and improvement. Wines released with 5 yrs age.

24 bottles of Bordeaux are now bought every second around the world.

Ferrande Grav r (w) ★★ 01 02 04 05 06 08 09 10 Major estate at Castres owned by négociant Castel. Steady improvement. Easy, enjoyable red; clean, fresh white.

Ferrière Mar r ★★→★★★ 96' 98 99 00' 02 03 04 05 06 08 09' 10' Tiny Third Growth with a CH in MARGAUX village restored by same capable hands as LA GURGUE and HAUT-BAGES-LIBÉRAL. Dark, firm, perfumed wines need time.

Feytit-Clinet Pom r ★★ 95 96 98 99 00 01 03 04 05' 06 07 08 09' 10' Tiny property once managed by J-P MOUEIX; back with owning Chasseuil family (since 2000). On great form since. Rich, full POMEROL with ageing potential.

Fieuzal Pe-Lé r (w) ★★★ (r) 98' 00 01 06 07 08 09' 10' (w) 98' 99 01 02 03 05 06 07 08 09' 10' 11 Classed growth at Léognan. Red form dipped from the heights of the mid-1980s but improvements from 2006. White more consistent. New gravity-fed winery from 2011. ANGÉLUS owner consults for reds.

Figeac St-Em r ★★★★ 95' 96 98' 99 00' 01' 02 03 04 05' 06 07 08 09' 10' 11 First Growth; gravelly v'yd with unusual 70% CAB FR and CAB SAUV. Rich but always elegant wines; deceptively long-ageing. Legendary owner Thierry Manoncourt (63 vintages) died in 2010. Son-in-law Eric d'Aramon continues the gd work. Second wine: Grange Neuve de Figeac.

Filhot Saut w dr sw ★★ 95 96' 97' 98 99 01' 02 03' 04 05 07 09' 10' 11 Second-rank classed growth with splendid CH, extensive v'yd. Difficult young, more complex with age. Richer and purer from 2009.

Fleur Cardinale St-Em r ★★ 98 99 00 01 02 03 04 05' 06 07 08 09' 10' 11 GRAND CRU CLASSÉ east of ST-EMILION. Gd from the 1980s but into overdrive since 2001, with new owner and *chai*. Ripe, unctuous, modern style.

Fleur-de-Gay, la Pom r ★★★ 1,000-case super-CUVÉE of CH LA CROIX-DE-GAY. Wines are 100% MERLOT.

Fleur-Pétrus, la Pom r ★★★★ 90' 94 95 96 98' 99 00' 01 02 03 04 05' 06 08 09'

10' 11 J-P MOUEIX property; v'yd opposite LAFLEUR. Laser-optical sorter used from 2009: gives v. precise selection of grapes. Finer style than PÉTRUS or TROTANOY. Needs time.

Fombrauge St-Em r ★★ →★★★ 98 99 00' 01 02 03 04 05 06 08 09' 10' A Bernard Magrez wine (*see* PAPE-CLÉMENT, TOUR-CARNET), so don't expect restraint. Big estate east of ST-EMILION. Since 1999, rich, dark, chocolatey, full-bodied wines. Magrez-Fombrauge is its GARAGE wine.

Fonbadet Pau r ★★ 98' 00' 01 02 03 04 05' 06 08 09' 10' Family-owned estate. Eric Boissenot consults. Reliable, gd value and typically PAUILLAC. Finer since 2007.

Fonplégade St-Em r ★★ 96 98 00' 01 03 04 05 06' 07 08 09' 10 GRAND CRU CLASSÉ owned by American Stephen Adams. Progression since 2004: riper, more elegance. MICHEL ROLLAND consults. CH L'Enclos in POMEROL same owner since 2007.

Fonréaud List r ★★ 98 00' 02 03 04 05 06 08 09' 10' One of the bigger and better LISTRACS making savoury, mouth-filling wines. Small volume of dry white: Le Cygne, barrel-fermented. *See* LESTAGE. Gd value.

Fonroque St-Em r ★★★ 96 98 01 03 04 05 06 08 09' 10' 11 GRAND CRU CLASSÉ on the plateau north of ST-EMILION. Biodynamic techniques (since 2008) paying off; more elegance recently. Managed by Alain Moueix (*see* MAZEYRES). MOULIN DU CADET sister estate.

Fontenil Fronsac r ★★ 00' 01' 02 03 04 05 06 08 09' 10' Leading FRONSAC, owned by ROLLAND (1986). Ripe, opulent, balanced. GARAGE: Défi de Fontenil.

Forts de Latour, les Pau r ★★★ →★★★★ 89' 90' 94 95' 96' 98 99 00' 01 02 03 04' 05' 06 07 08 09' 10' 11 The (worthy) second wine of CH LATOUR; authentic flavour in slightly lighter format at Second Growth price. From enlarged v'yds outside the central *Enclos*.

Fourcas-Dupré List r ★★ 98' 99 00' 01 02 03 04 05 06 08 09 10' Well-run property making fairly consistent wine in tight LISTRAC style. Better with bottle age. Second label: CH Bellevue-Laffont.

Fourcas-Hosten List r ★★ →★★★ 00 01 02 03 05 06 08 09 Large estate with new owners (Hermès fashion connection) from 2006: considerable investment and improvement since then. More precision and finesse. To watch.

France, de Pe-Lé r w ★★ (r) 00 02 03 04 05 06 08 09 10' (w) 01' 02 03 04 05 06 07 08 09 10 Neighbour of FIEUZAL making consistent wines in a ripe, modern style. Fire in 2011 destroyed *chai* and part of 2010 vintage.

Franc-Mayne St-Em r ★★ 96 98' 99 00' 01 03 04 05 06 08 09 10' Small GRAND CRU CLASSÉ on the côtes. New owners in 2004 (sister properties CH DE LUSSAC and Vieux Maillet in POMEROL). Investment and renovation. Luxury accommodation as well. Fresh, fruity and structured style. Round but firm wines.

Gaby, du r ★★ 00' 01' 03 04 05 06 07 08 09 10 Splendid south-facing slopes in FRONSAC. New owners in 1999 and again in 2006 (Canadian). Serious wines.

Cru Bourgeois – still middling

The new CRU BOURGEOIS label – now a certificate awarded annually, administered by an independent body, Bureau Véritas – was awarded to 246 CHX for the 2009 vintage. This is three more than in 2008, although the volume of wine increased by 30%. The HAUT-MÉDOC and MÉDOC ACS again provided the lion's share with 184 CHX. The 304 rejects can apply in subsequent vintages. Quality standards continue to vary and there is clearly the need for a hierarchy. A number of high-profile chx withdrew from the selection process in understandable dudgeon. These incl the nine Crus Bourgeois Exceptionnels in the annulled 2003 classification.

Gaffelière, la St-Em r ★★★ 89' 90' 94 95 96 98' 99 00' 01 03 04 05' 06 07 08 09' 10' 11 First Growth at foot of the côtes. Elegant, long-ageing wines. More precision and purity from 2000. DERENONCOURT consulting from 2004.

Galius St-Em r ★★ Oak-aged selection of wines from ST-EMILION co-op, usually to a high standard.

Garde, la Pe-Lé r w ★★ (r) 98' 99 00 01' 02 04 05 06 07 08 09' 10' (w) 01 02 04 05 06 07 08 09 10' Substantial property owned by négociant CVBG-DOURTHE; reliable, supple reds. Tiny production of SAUV BL/Sauv Gris-based white.

Gay, le Pom r ★★★ 95 96 98 99 00 01 03 04 05' 06 07 08 09' 10' 11 Fine v'yd on northern edge of POMEROL. Major investment, with MICHEL ROLLAND consulting. Now v. ripe and plummy in style. Improvements from 2003. CH Montviel and La Violette same stable and AC. Owner has Cristal d'Arques glassware origins.

Gazin Pom r ★★★ 90' 94' 95 96 98' 99 00' 01 02 03 04 05' 06 07 08 09' 10' Large (for POMEROL), family-owned neighbour of PÉTRUS. Well-distributed and now on v.gd form. Second label: L'Hospitalet de Gazin.

Gilette Saut w sw ★★★ 53 55 59 61 67 70 71 75 76 78 79 81 82 83 85 86 88 89 Extraordinary small Preignac CH stores its sumptuous wines in concrete vats for 16–20 yrs. Only around 5,000 bottles of each. Some bottle age still advisable. Ch Les Justices is its sister (99 01 02 03' 05 07 09 10').

Giscours Mar r ★★★ 89' 90 95 96' 98 99 00' 01 02 03 04 05' 06 07 08' 09' 10' 11 Splendid Third Growth south of Cantenac. V.gd, vigorous wine in 1970s and now. 1980s were v. wobbly; new (Dutch) ownership from 1995 and revival since 1999. Cellar-door operation as well. Second label: La Sirène de Giscours. CH La Houringue is baby sister, DU TERTRE stablemate.

British artist Anish Kapoor designed the 2009 Mouton Rothschild label and the sculpture for the London 2012 Olympics

Glana, du St-Jul r ★★ 98 99 00 02 03 04 05 06 08 09 10' Large estate, expanded by acquisition of parcels of land from CH LAGRANGE. Undemanding; undramatic; value. Same owner as Bellegrave in PAUILLAC. Second wine: Pavillon du Glana.

Gloria St-Jul r ★★ →★★★ 98 99 00' 01 02 03 04 05' 06 07 08 09' 10' 11 A widely dispersed estate with v'yds among the classed growths. Same ownership as ST-PIERRE. Regularly overperforms. Second label: Peymartin.

Gomerie, la St-Em r ★★→★★★ 09' 10' 1,000 cases, 100% MERLOT; GARAGE. *See* BEAU-SÉJOUR-BÉCOT.

Grand-Corbin-Despagne St-Em r ★★ →★★★ 95 96 98 99 00' 01 03 04 05 06 08 09' 10' 11 Demoted from GRAND CRU CLASSÉ in 1996 but reinstated in 2006. In between: investment and hard graft. Aromatic wines now with a riper, fuller edge. Still gd value. Also CH Maison Blanche, MONTAGNE ST-EMILION and Ch Ampélia, CASTILLON. Second label: Petit Corbin-Despagne.

Grand Cru Classé *See* ST-EMILION classification box, p.108.

Grand-Mayne St-Em r ★★★ 89' 90' 94 95 96 98 99 00' 01' 02 03 04 05' 06 07 08 09' 10' 11 Leading, family-owned (Nony since 1934) GRAND CRU CLASSÉ on western côtes. Consistent, firm, full, savoury wines.

Grand-Pontet St-Em r ★★★ 98' 99 00' 01 02 03 04 05 06 08 09 10 GRAND CRU CLASSÉ on the côtes. Powerful and generous style. Family connection to BEAU-SÉJOUR-BÉCOT.

Grand-Puy-Ducasse Pau r ★★★ 95 96' 98' 99 00 01 02 03 04 05' 06 07 08 09' 10' 11 Fifth Growth owned by a bank; stop-start quality. But more consistent since 2005. New winemaker 2010. Denis Dubourdieu consults. Second label: CH Artigues-Arnaud.

Grand-Puy-Lacoste Pau r ★★★ 86' 88' 89' 90' 94 95' 96' 98 99 00' 01 02 03 04 05' 06 07 08' 09' 10' 11 Fifth Growth famous for CAB SAUV-driven PAUILLAC to lay down. Same owner as HAUT-BATAILLEY. Recent investment. Second label: Lacoste-Borie.

Grave à Pomerol, la Pom r ★★★ 95 96 98' 00 01 02 04 05 06 08 09' 10 Small property facing LALANDE-DE-POMEROL. Owned by Christian MOUEIX. Accessible, medium richness. Formerly known as La Grave Trigant de Boisset.

Gressier-Grand-Poujeaux Mou r ★★ 90 94 95 96 98 00 01 04 05 09 10' Since 2003, same owner as CHASSE-SPLEEN. 5,000 cases average. Little visibility. Solid in the past and in need of ageing.

> **St-Emilion classification – 2012 version**
>
> A total of 96 CHX have applied for classification in 2012: 28 for Premier GRAND CRU CLASSÉ status and 68 for Grand Cru Classé. The new classification, now legally considered an exam rather than a competition, will be conducted by a commission of seven wine professionals nominated by INAO, none from B'X. All candidates will be visited and the tastings of ten vintages (1999–2008) administered by an independent body (15 vintages will be tasted if promotion from Grand Cru Classé to Premier Grand Cru Classé is being sought). The tastings will represent 50% of the mark for Grand Cru Classé status. Fame, management and terroir will make up the other 50%. Fame and terroir will be given greater consideration at Premier Grand Cru Classé level and will represent 65% of the mark. There are currently 15 Premiers Grands Crus Classés and 57 Grands Crus Classés. It is tempting to ask how much the customer cares.

Greysac Méd r ★★ 98 00' 02 03 04 05' 06 08 09 10' Elegant estate owned by Agnelli (Fiat) family. Same management as CANTEMERLE. Fine, with consistent quality.

Gruaud-Larose St-Jul r ★★★★ 88 89' 90' 95' 96' 98 99 00' 01 02 04 05' 06 07 08 09' 10' 11 One of the largest, best-loved Second Growths. Smooth, rich and vigorous claret; ages 20+ yrs. More finesse from 2007. Second wine: Sarget de Gruaud-Larose.

Guadet St-Em ★★ 01 04 05 06 08 09 10 Known as Guadet-St-Julien until 2005. Narrowly missed demotion from GRAND CRU CLASSÉ in 2006. Some improvement since. Organic certification from 2010.

Guiraud Saut (r) w (dr) sw ★★★ 89' 90' 95 96' 97' 98 99 01' 02 03 04 05' 06 07 09' 10' 11 Top-quality classed growth. New owning consortium from 2006 includes long-time manager, Xavier Planty and Peugeot (cars) family. More SAUV BL than most. Dry white G de Guiraud. Second label: Petit Guiraud (from 2005).

Gurgue, la Mar r ★★ 98 00' 01 02 03 04 05' 06 08 09' 10 Well-placed property. Same management as FERRIÈRE and HAUT-BAGES-LIBÉRAL. Fine. Gd value.

Hanteillan H-Méd Cissac r ★★ 00' 02 03 04 05' 06 09' 10 Huge northern v'yd: v. fair wines, early-drinking. 50% MERLOT. Second wine: CH Laborde.

Haut-Bages-Libéral Pau r ★★★ 96' 98 99 00 01 02 03 04 05' 06 08 09' 10' 11 Lesser-known Fifth Growth (next to LATOUR) in same stable as FERRIÈRE and LA GURGUE. Results are excellent, full of PAUILLAC vitality. Usually gd value.

Haut-Bages-Monpelou Pau r ★★ 98 99 00 03 04 05 06 08 09 10 Stablemate of BATAILLEY on former DUHART-MILON land. Could improve.

Haut-Bailly Pe-Lé r ★★★★ 89' 90' 95 96' 98' 99 00' 01 02 03 04 05' 06 07 08' 09' 10' 11 Léognan classed growth. Since 1979 some of the best savoury, intelligently-made red GRAVES. US ownership and investment from 1998 have taken it to greater heights. Denis Dubourdieu consults. Second label: La Parde de Haut-Bailly.

Haut-Batailley Pau r ★★★ 95 96' 98 99 00 02 03 04 05' 06 07 08 09' 10' Smaller part of divided Fifth Growth BATAILLEY. Gentler than sister GRAND-PUY-LACOSTE. New cellar in 2005; more precision. Second wine: La Tour-l'Aspic.

Haut-Beauséjour St-Est r ★★ 00 01 03 04 05 08 09 10 Property revitalized by owner CHAMPAGNE ROEDERER. Supple, round style. *See also* DE PEZ.

Haut-Bergey Pe-Lé r (w) ★★ (r) 98 99 00 01 02 04 05 06 07 08 09 10 11 (w) 04 05 06 07 08 09 10 11 Property of sister of owner of SMITH-HAUT-LAFITTE. Completely renovated in the 1990s. Rich, modern GRAVES with oak overlay. Also a little dry white. BARDE-HAUT, CLOS L'EGLISE and CH Branon same stable.

Haut-Brion Pe-Lé r ★★★★ (r) 82' 83' 85' 86' 88' 89' 90' 93 94 95' 96' 97 98' 99 00' 01 02 03 04 05' 06 08 09' 10' 11 Oldest great CH of B'X and only non-MÉDOC First Growth of 1855, owned by American Dillon family since 1935. Deeply harmonious, never aggressive wine with endless, honeyed, earthy complexity. Consistently great since 1975. A little dry, sumptuous *white*: 90 93 94 95 96 98 99 00' 01 02 03 04 05' 06 07 08' 09 10' 11. *See* LE CLARENCE DE HAUT-BRION, LA MISSION-HAUT-BRION, LAVILLE-HAUT-BRION.

Haut-Condissas Méd r ★★★ 00 01 02 03 04 05 06 07 08 09' 10' MÉDOC with an international flavour. Sister to CH Rollan-de-By. Rich, concentrated and oaky. MERLOT (60%) and PETIT VERDOT (20%) the essential components.

Haut-Marbuzet St-Est r ★★→★★★ 96' 98 99 00' 01 02 03 04 05' 06 07 08 09' 10' Leading non-classified estate. Rich, unctuous wines that age well. M Duboscq has reassembled ancient DOM de Marbuzet. Also owns Chambert-Marbuzet, MacCarthy and Tour de Marbuzet. Haut-Marbuzet is 60% MERLOT, seductive and remarkably consistent. CH Layauga-Duboscq in MÉDOC is a more recent venture (2005).

Haut-Pontet St-Em r ★★ 00 01 03 04 05 09 10 Tiny MERLOT-dominated v'yd on the côtes. Owned by Janoueix (*see* next entry) from 2007.

Haut-Sarpe St-Em r ★★ 95 96 98 00' 01 04 05 06 08 09 10 GRAND CRU CLASSÉ with elegant v'yd and park, 70% MERLOT. Same owner (Janoueix) as CH LA CROIX, POMEROL. Rich, dark, modern style.

Hosanna Pom r ★★★★ 99 00 01 03 04 05' 06 07 08 09' 10' 11 Formerly Certan-Guiraud until purchased and renamed by J-P MOUEIX in 1999. Only best part retained. First vintages confirm power, complexity and class. New cellar in 2008, shared with Providence. Stablemate of TROTANOY.

d'Issan Mar r ★★★ 98 99 00' 01 02 03 04' 05' 06 07 08 09' 10' 11 Third Growth v'yd with moated CH. Fragrant wines; more substance since late 1990s. Owner Emmanuel Cruse is the grand master of the Commanderie de Bontemps Confrérie. Second label: Blason d'Issan.

Looking for more information on grapes? Try the "Grapes" section on pp.16–26.

Kirwan Mar r ★★★ 95 96 98 99 00' 01 02 03 04 05' 06 07 08 09 10' 11 Third Growth majority-owned by SCHRÖDER & SCHŸLER (since 1997). Former PALMER winemaker applying more finesse from 2007. To watch. Second label: Les Charmes de Kirwan.

Labégorce Mar r ★★→★★★ 00 01 02 03 04 05' 07 08 09 10' In 2009 absorbed neighbouring LABÉGORCE-ZÉDÉ; returning to its 18th-century form. Solid, long-lived. CH MARQUIS-D'ALESME same stable.

Labégorce-Zédé Mar r ★★→★★★ 95 96' 98 99 00' 01 02 03 04 05' 06 07 RIP. From 2009, part of CH LABÉGORCE (*see* previous entry). Old vintages classic and fragrant in style.

Lafaurie-Peyraguey Saut w sw ★★★ 83' 85 86' 88' 89' 90' 95 96' 97 98 99 01' 02' 03' 04 05' 06 07 09' 10' 11 Fine classed growth at Bommes; owners Groupe Banque Suez. Consistent form since 1983. New manager in 2006, formerly at PAPE-CLÉMENT. Second wine: La Chapelle de Lafaurie.

Lafite-Rothschild Pau r ★★★★ 85 86' 88' 89' 90' 93 94 95 96' 97 98' 99 00' 01'
02 03' 04' 05' 06 07 08' 09' 10' 11 First Growth of famous elusive perfume and
style, but never great weight, although more density and sleeker texture from
1996. Great vintages need keeping for decades; insatiable demand from China
has driven the price sky-high. Joint ventures in Chile (1988), California (1989),
Portugal (1992), Argentina (1999), now the MIDI, Italy – even China. Second
wine: CARRUADES DE LAFITE. Also owns CHX DUHART-MILON, L'EVANGILE, RIEUSSEC.

Current top price for a single ha of eg. Pauilliac v'yd? €1.5 million.

Lafleur Pom r ★★★★ 85' 86 88' 89' 90' 93 94 95 96 98' 99' 00' 01' 02 03 04' 05'
06' 07 08 09' 10' 11 Superb family-owned and -managed property, cultivated
like a garden. Elegant, intense wine for maturing. 50% CAB FR. Second wine:
Pensées de Lafleur.

Lafleur-Gazin Pom r ★★ 98 00 01 04 05 06 08 09 10 Small J-P MOUEIX estate located
between LAFLEUR and GAZIN. Lighter style.

Lafon-Rochet St-Est r ★★★ 89' 90' 94 95 96' 98 99 00' 01 02 03' 04 05' 06 08 09'
10' Fourth Growth neighbour of COS D'ESTOURNEL. Distinctive yellow cellars (and
label). Same family ownership as PONTET-CANET. A higher percentage of MERLOT
has made this ST-ESTÈPHE more opulent since 1998. Gd value. Second label: Les
Pèlerins de Lafon-Rochet.

Lagrange St-Jul r ★★★ 90' 94 95 96 98 99 00' 01 02 03 04 05' 06 08 09'
10' 11 Formerly neglected Third Growth owned by Suntory (since 1983). Now
in tip-top condition with wines to match. Managed by Bruno Eynard since the
retirement of Marcel Ducasse in 2007. More investment since. Dry white Les
Arums de Lagrange (since 1997). Second wine: Les Fiefs de Lagrange (gd value).

Lagrange Pom r ★★ 95 96 98 00 01 04 05 06 09 10 Tiny v'yd in the centre of
POMEROL run by the ubiquitous house of J-P MOUEIX. Mainly MERLOT. Gd value but
not in the same league as HOSANNA, LA FLEUR-PÉTRUS, etc.

Lagune, la H-Méd r ★★★ 90' 95 96' 98 00' 02 03 04 05' 07 08 09' 10' Third
Growth with sandy/gravel soils. Dipped in 1990s but now on form. Fine-edged
with added structure and depth. Laser-optical sorter used from 2010: precise
selection of grapes. Owned by J-J Frey; *see also* JABOULET AÎNÉ. Daughter Caroline
is the winemaker.

Lalande-Borie St-Jul r ★★ 00 01 02 03 04 05 06 07 08 09' 10' A baby brother of
the great DUCRU-BEAUCAILLOU created from part of the former v'yd of CH LAGRANGE.
Gracious, easy-drinking wine.

Lamarque, de H-Méd r ★★ 98 99 00' 02 03 04 05' 06 08 09' 10' Central HAUT-
MÉDOC v'yd with splendid medieval fortress. Competent, mid-term wines.
Second wine: D de Lamarque.

Lamothe Bergeron H-Méd r ★★ 98' 00 02 03 04 05 09' 10' Large estate in Cussac-
Fort-MÉDOC. Owned by Cognac houses Hardy and Mounier (since 2009).
Reliable if unexceptional, but improving.

Lanessan H-Méd r ★★ 98 00' 02 03 04 05 08 09' 10' Distinguished property just
south of ST-JULIEN. Former Calvet and Cordier-Mestrezat winemaker, Paz Espejo,
now in charge – improvements since 2009. Horse museum and tours.

Langoa-Barton St-Jul r ★★★ 90' 94 95' 96' 98 99 00' 01 02 03 04' 05' 06 07 08
09' 10' 11 Third Growth sister CH to LÉOVILLE-BARTON. Home to Anthony Barton;
impeccable standards, gd value. Second wine: Réserve de Léoville-Barton.

Larcis-Ducasse St-Em r ★★★ 89' 90' 94 95 96 98 00 02 03 04 05' 06 07 08
09' 10' 11 Classed growth of St-Laurent, eastern neighbour of ST-EMILION, on the
côtes. Spectacular rise in quality (and price) since 2002. Same management as
PAVIE-MACQUIN.

Larmande St-Em r ★★ 98' 00' 01 03 04 05 07 08 09' 10 Substantial property owned by Le Mondiale insurance (as are SOUTARD, CADET-PIOLA). Replanted, re-equipped, and now making consistently solid wines. All-female winemaking and management team. Second label: le Cadet de Larmande.

Laroque St-Em r ★★→★★★ 95 96 98 99 00' 01 03 04 05 06 08 09' 10' Large classified growth at St-Christophe-des-Bardes. 17th-century CH. Fresh, terroir-driven wines.

Larose-Trintaudon H-Méd r ★★ 01 02 03 04 05 06 07 09' 10 The largest v'yd in the MÉDOC (190ha). Sustainable viticulture. Previously light and easy-drinking but improved quality from 2007. Second label: Larose St-Laurent. Special CUVÉE (from 1996) – Larose Perganson – from separate parcels.

Laroze St-Em r ★★ 96' 98' 99 00 01 05 06 07 08 09' 10' Large v'yd west of ST-EMILION. Lighter-framed wines from sandy soils, more depth from 1998; approachable when young. New *tribaie* grape-sorting machine (v. ingenious, sorts according to specific gravity, and thus ripeness) in use. Second label: La Fleur Laroze.

Larrivet-Haut-Brion Pe-Lé r w ★★★ (r) 96' 98' 00 01 02 03 04 05' 06 07 08 09 10' Substantial Léognan property with classed-growth aspirations. Rich, modern red. Also SAUV BL/SÉM barrel-fermented white (01 02 04' 05 06 07 08 09 10'). New barrel cellar and tasting room. Former MONTROSE manager in charge since 2007. Second wine: Les Demoiselles de Larrivet-Haut-Brion.

Lascombes Mar r (p) ★★★ 96' 98' 99 00 01 02 03 04 05' 06 07 08 09' 10' Second Growth owned by French insurance group (2011). Wines were wobbly, but real improvements from 2001. MICHEL ROLLAND consults. Winemaker previously with L'EVANGILE. Modern style. Second label: Chevalier de Lascombes.

Latour Pau r ★★★★(★) 82' 85 86 88' 89 90' 91 93 94 95' 96' 97 98 99 00' 01 02 03' 04' 05' 06 07 08 09' 10' 11 First Growth considered the grandest statement of the MÉDOC. Profound, intense, almost immortal wines in great yrs; even weaker vintages have the characteristic note of terroir and run for many yrs. Recently enlarged but the *grand vin* still from historical "Enclos" v'yd. Latour always needs 10 yrs to show its hand. New state-of-the-art *chai* (2003) allows more precise vinification. Around 10% of the v'yd now organic. Second wine: LES FORTS DE LATOUR; *third wine: Pauillac.*

"Latour" apparently means "to fall down" in Cantonese.

Latour-Martillac Pe-Lé r w ★★ (r) 98 00 01 02 03 04 05' 06 08 09' 10' 11 Family-owned, classed-growth property in Martillac. Regular quality (r w); gd value at this level. White can age as well (00 01 02 03 04 05 06 07 08 09 10' 11).

Latour-à-Pomerol Pom r ★★★ 88' 89' 90' 94 95 96 98' 99 00' 01 02 04 05' 06 07 08 09' 10' Top growth on plateau under J-P MOUEIX management. Rich, well-structured wines that age. Rarely disappoints.

Laurets, des St-Em r ★★ 01 03 04 05 06 08 09 10 Major property in PUISSEGUIN-ST-EMILION and MONTAGNE-ST-EMILION, with v'yd evenly split on the côtes (40,000 cases). Owned by Benjamin de Rothschild of CH CLARKE (2003).

Laville-Haut-Brion Pe-Lé w ★★★★ 92 93' 94 95' 96' 98 00' 01 02 03 04' 05' 06 07 08' Former name for LA MISSION HAUT-BRION Blanc (renamed in 2009). Only 8,000 bottles/yr of v. best white GRAVES for long, succulent maturing. Great consistency. Mainly SÉM. Second wine: La Clarté de Haut-Brion (formerly Les Plantiers); also includes wine from HAUT-BRION.

Léoville-Barton St-Jul r ★★★★ 88' 89' 90' 94' 95' 96' 98 99 00' 01 02 03' 04 05' 06 07 08' 09' 10' 11 Once part of the vast Second Growth Léoville estate; in Anglo-Irish hands of the Barton family for over 180 yrs (Anthony Barton is present incumbent). Harmonious, classic claret; traditional methods, fair prices. Investment raised v.-high standards to Super Second. *See* LANGOA-BARTON.

Léoville-las-Cases St-Jul r ★★★★ 83' 85' 86' 88 89' 90' 93 94 95' 96' 97 98 99 00'
01 02 03' 04' 05' 06 07 08 09' 10' 11 The largest Léoville; *grand vin* produced
from *grand enclos* v'yd. Elegant, complex, powerful wines, for immortality. Second
wine: Le Petit Lion (2007); previously CLOS DU MARQUIS but latter now considered
a separate wine. Laser-optical grape sorting from 2009 for greater precision.

Léoville-Poyferré St-Jul r ★★★ 86' 88 89' 90' 94 95 96' 98 99 00' 01 02 03' 04
05' 06 07 08 09' 10' 11 The best part of the v'yd lies opposite the *grand enclos* of
LÉOVILLE-LAS-CASES. Now at Super Second level with dark, rich, spicy, long-ageing
wines. ROLLAND consults at the estate. Second label: CH Moulin-Riche.

Lestage List r ★★ 98 00 02 03 04 05 06 08 09 10 LISTRAC estate in same hands as
CH FONRÉAUD. Firm, slightly austere claret. Second wine: La Dame de Coeur de
CH Lestage.

Lilian Ladouys St-Est r ★★ 96 98 00 02 03 04 05 06 07 08 09' 10' Created in
the 1980s, the v'yd has 100 parcels of vines. Firm, sometimes robust wines;
recent vintages more finesse. New owner in 2008 (owner of rugby club Racing
Métro 92 and, since 2009, PEDESCLAUX). Same management as Belle-Vue in
HAUT-MÉDOC.

Liot Bar w sw ★★ 95 96 97' 98 99 01' 02 03 05 07 09 10 BARSAC neighbour of
CLIMENS. Consistent, fairly light, golden wines. Easy-drinking and inexpensive.

Liversan H-Méd r ★★ 96 98 00 02 03 04 05 07 08 09 10 Property inland from
PAUILLAC. Same owner – Jean-Michel Lapalu – as PATACHE D'AUX. Quality-oriented;
delicate style. Second wine: Les Charmes de Liversan.

Loudenne Méd r ★★ 00' 01 02 03 04 05 06 09' 10' Beautiful, pink, riverside CH
owned for a century by Gilbeys, since 2000 by Lafragette family. Daughter
Florence is the manager. Ripe, round reds. Also an oak-scented SAUV BL white
(04 05 06 07 08 09 10). Accommodation as well.

Loupiac-Gaudiet w sw ★★ 98 99 01 02 03' 05 07 09 10 A reliable source of gd-value
"almost SAUTERNES", just across river Garonne in LOUPIAC AC.

Louvière, la Pe-Lé r w ★★★ (r) 98 99 00' 01 02 04' 05' 06 07 08 09' 10' 11 (w) 00
01 02 03 04' 05' 06 07 08 09' 10' 11 André Lurton's pride and joy. CH classed
as historical monument. Excellent *white* and red wines of classed-growth
standard. New barrel cellar (2009). *See also* BONNET, COUHINS-LURTON, DE CRUZEAU,
DE ROCHEMORIN.

Lussac, de St-Em r ★★ 00 03 04 05 06 07 08 09 10 One of the best estates in
LUSSAC-ST-EMILION. New owners and technical methods since 2000. Same stable
as FRANC-MAYNE and Vieux Maillet in POMEROL.

Lynch-Bages Pau r (w) ★★★★ 85' 86' 88' 89' 90' 94 95' 96' 98 99 00' 01 02
03 04' 05' 06 07 08 09' 10' 11 Always popular, now a regular star, far higher
than its Fifth Growth rank. Rich, robust wine: deliciously dense. *See* ECHO DE
LYNCH-BAGES. Third wine from 2009. Fresher styled white, Blanc de Lynch-Bages
(since 2007). Same owners (CAZES family; new generation – Jean-Charles – now
in charge) as LES ORMES-DE-PEZ and Villa Bel-Air.

Lynch-Moussas Pau r ★★ 95' 96' 98 00' 01 02 03 04 05' 07 08 09 10' Fifth Growth
owned by BORIE-MANOUX. Lighter, fruitier PAUILLAC. Steady improvement.

Lyonnat, du St-Em r ★★ 00' 01 03 04 05 06 08 09 10 Property in LUSSAC-ST-EMILION.
Reliable wine. The Rhône's J-L Colombo is the consulting enologist.

Macquin-St-Georges St-Em r ★★ 98 99 00 01 03 04 05 06 08 09 10 Producer of
delicious, not weighty, satellite ST-EMILION at ST-GEORGES. Consistent.

Magdelaine St-Em r ★★★ 89' 90' 94 95 96 98' 99 00 01 03 04 05 06 08 09'
10' 11 Leading côtes First Growth owned by J-P MOUEIX. Delicate, fine and
deceptively long-lived. Denser weight from 2008.

Malartic-Lagravière Pe-Lé r (w) ★★★ (r) 95 96 98 99 00' 01 02 03 04' 05' 06 08 09'
10' 11 (w) 99 00 01' 02 03 04' 05' 06 07 08 09' 10' 11 Léognan classed growth.

Rich, modern red wine since late 1990s; a little lush SAUV BL white. Belgian owner (since 1997) has revolutionized the property. ROLLAND advises. CH Gazin Rocquencourt (PESSAC-LÉOGNAN) new acquisition in 2006.

Malescasse H-Méd r ★★ 00 01 02 03 04 05 06 08 09 10 Renovated property nr MOULIS owned by Alcatel. Supple, inexpensive wines, accessible early. Second label: La Closerie de Malescasse.

Malescot-St-Exupéry Mar r ★★★ 95 96 98 99 00' 01 02 03 04 05' 06 07 08' 09' 10' 11 Third Growth returned to fine form in the 1990s. Now ripe, fragrant and finely structured. Ages well. MICHEL ROLLAND advises.

Malle, de Saut r w dr sw ★★★ (w sw) 89' 90' 94 95 96' 97' 98 99 01' 02 03' 05 06 07 09 10' 11 Beautiful 17th-century Preignac CH making v. fine, medium-bodied SAUTERNES; also M de Malle dry white and GRAVES Ch du Cardaillan.

Marbuzet St-Est r ★★ 98 99 00' 01 02 03 04 05' 06 Since 2007 integrated into COS-D'ESTOURNEL. Now a second label for certain markets.

Margaux, Château Mar r (w) ★★★★ 83' 85' 86' 88' 89' 90' 93 94 95' 96' 97 98' 99 00' 01' 02 03' 04' 05' 06' 07 08 09' 10' 11 First Growth; most seductive and fabulously perfumed wine of MARGAUX. Owned and run by Corinne Mentzelopoulos. Former PICHON-LALANDE winemaker new technical director from 2012. Pavillon Rouge (00' 01 02 03 04' 05' 06 08 09' 10') is second wine; a third wine shortly. *Pavillon Blanc* is best white (100% SAUV BL) of MÉDOC, but expensive (00' 01' 02 03 04' 05 06 07 08 09').

Marojallia Mar r ★★★ 99 00' 01 02 03 04 05' 06 07 08 09' 10 Micro-CH looking for big prices for big, rich, beefy, un-MARGAUX-like wines. VALANDRAUD owner consults. Upmarket B&B also. Second wine: CLOS Margalaine.

Marquis-d'Alesme Mar r ★★ 95 98 00 01 04 05 07 08 09' 10' Third Growth purchased by LABÉGORCE in 2006. Dropped "Becker" handle in 2009. Disappointing in recent yrs but improvement from 2007. To watch.

Marquis-de-Terme Mar r ★★→★★★ 89' 90' 95 96 98 99 00' 01 02 03 04 05' 06 07 08 09' 10' Fourth Growth with v'yd dispersed around AC. Better form since 2000. New manager in 2009 and richer style. Previously solid rather than elegant.

Lilian Barton has bought Ch Mauvesin in Moulis, 190 yrs after ancestor Hugh acquired Langoa-Barton.

Martinens Mar r ★★ 00 02 03 04 05 06 09 10 Cantenac estate. Light, supple.

Maucaillou Mou r ★★ 00' 01 02 03 04 05 06 08 09 10 11 Consistent property with gd standards. Clean, fresh, value wines. Second label: No 2 de Maucaillou.

Mazeyres Pom r ★★ 96' 98' 99 00 01 04 05' 06 08 09 10 Consistent, if not exciting lesser POMEROL on sandier soils. Alain Moueix, cousin of Christian of J-P MOUEIX, manages here. Biodynamic from 2012. *See* FONREQUE.

Meyney St-Est r ★★→★★★ 95 96 98 00 01 02 03 04 05' 06 08 09' 10' Large, riverside-slopes property next to MONTROSE. Rich, robust, well-structured wines. Same stable as GRAND-PUY-DUCASSE and RAYNE VIGNEAU (owned by a bank). Denis Dubourdieu consults. Second label: Prieur de Meyney.

Mission-Haut-Brion Blanc, la Pe-Lé r ★★★★ 85' 86 88 89' 90' 93 94 95 96' 98' 99 00' 01 02 03 04 05' 06 07 08 09' 10' 11 Neighbour and long-time rival to HAUT-BRION; since 1983, in same hands. Consistently grand-scale, full-blooded, long-maturing wine – more flamboyant than HAUT-BRION. LA TOUR HAUT-BRION v'yd integrated from 2006. Second label: La Chapelle de la Mission. White: previously LAVILLE-HAUT-BRION; renamed (2009) la Mission-Haut-Brion Blanc (09' 10' 11).

Monbousquet St-Em r (w) ★★★ 98 99 00' 01 02 03 04 05' 06 07 08 09' 10' 11 Substantial GRAND CRU CLASSÉ on sand and gravel plain revolutionized by new owner Gerard Pérse. Now concentrated, oaky, voluptuous wines. Rare *v.gd white* (AC B'x) from 1998. Same ownership as PAVIE and PAVIE-DECESSE.

Monbrison Mar r ★★→★★★ 89' 90 95 96' 98 99 00 01 02 04 05' 06 08 09' 10' Family-owned property at Arsac. Delicate, fragrant MARGAUX.

Mondotte, la St-Em r ★★★→★★★★ 96' 97 98' 99 00' 01 02 03 04' 05' 06 07 08 09' 10' 11 Intense, always firm, virile GARAGE wines from a plot on the limestone plateau. Same ownership as CANON-LA-GAFFELIÈRE, CLOS DE L'ORATOIRE.

Montrose St-Est r ★★★→★★★★ 88 89' 90' 93 94 95 96' 98 99 00' 01 02 03' 04' 05' 06 07 08 09' 10' 11 Second Growth famed for deep-coloured, forceful claret. Known as the LATOUR of ST-ESTÈPHE. Vintages 1979–85 (except 1982) were lighter. After 110 yrs in same family hands, change of ownership in 2006. Ex-HAUT-BRION director, Jean-Bernard Delmas, now managing. Environmentally conscious renovation. Second wine: La Dame de Montrose.

Moulin-à-Vent Mou r ★★ 98 00' 02 03 04 05' 06 09 10' Steady estate; reasonably regular quality. Supple, early drinking.

Moulin de la Rose St-Jul ★★ 00' 01' 02 03 04 05 06 08 09' 10 Tiny estate; high standards. Same ownership as Ségur de Cabanac in ST-ESTÈPHE.

Moulin du Cadet St-Em r p ★★ 96 98 00 01 03 05 09 10' Tiny GRAND CRU CLASSÉ v'yd on the limestone plateau, managed by Alain Moueix (*see also* MAZEYRES). Biodynamics practised. Robust wines but more depth and finesse since 2009.

Moulinet Pom r ★★ 98 00 01 04 05 06 08 09 10 One of POMEROL's bigger CHX. DERENONCOURT consultant from 2009. Lighter style. Gd value.

Moulin-Haut-Laroque r ★★ 04 05' 06 08 09' 10' Leading FRONSAC property in same family hands since the late 19th century. Makes structured wines that can age from MERLOT, CAB FR and 80-yr-old MALBEC.

Moulin Pey-Labrie r ★★ 98' 99 00' 01 02 03 04 05' 06 08 09' 10' 11 Leading CH in CANON-FRONSAC. Stylish wines, MERLOT-dominated with elegance and structure.

Moulin-St-Georges St-Em r ★★★ 98 99 00' 01 02 03 04 05' 06 08 09' 10' Stylish and rich wine. Classed-growth level. Same ownership as AUSONE.

The average vineyard holding in Bordeaux has increased from 6ha in 1990 to just over 14 today.

Mouton Rothschild Pau r (w) ★★★★ 82' 83' 85' 86' 88' 89' 90' 93' 94 95' 96 97 98' 99 00' 01' 02 03 04' 05' 06' 07 08' 09' 10' 11 The most exotic and voluptuous of the PAUILLAC first growths (80% CAB SAUV). Attains new heights from 2004. New cellar for 2012 harvest. The museum of wine artefacts reopens in 2013 after its renovation. Artists labels since 1945. White Aile d'Argent from 1991. Second wine: Le Petit Mouton from 1997. *See also* Opus One (California) and Almaviva (Chile).

Nairac Saut w sw ★★ 90' 95' 96 97' 98 99 01' 02 03' 04 05' 06 07 09' 10 11 Rich style of BARSAC; on top form since 2003. Second label: Esquisse de Nairac, equally rich but fresher in style.

Nenin Pom r ★★★ 95 96 98 99 00' 01 02 03 04 05 06 07 08 09' 10' 11 LÉOVILLE-LAS-CASES ownership since 1997. Massive investment. New cellars. 4ha of former Certan-Giraud added in 1999. On an upward swing. Built to age. 2009 and 2010 best yet. Gd-value second wine: Fugue de Nenin.

Olivier Pe-Lé r w ★★★ (r) 95 96 00 01 02 04' 05' 06 08 09' 10' 11 (w) 00 01 02 03' 04' 05' 06 07' 08 09 10' 11 Classed growth (majority red), surrounding a moated castle at Léognan. Underachiever being turned around. New investment and greater purity, expression and quality from 2002. Value at this level.

Ormes-de-Pez, les St-Est r ★★→★★★ 96 98 99 00' 01 02 03 04 05 06 07 08 09' 10' Outstanding ST-ESTÈPHE owned by LYNCH-BAGES. Dense, fleshy wines; need 5–6 yrs.

Ormes-Sorbet, les Méd r ★★ 98' 99 00' 01 02 03' 04 05 06 08 09' 10' Long-time leader in northern MÉDOC at Couquèques. Elegant, gently oaked wines that age. Consistently reliable. Second label: CH de Conques.

Palmer Mar r ★★★★ 83' 85 86' 88' 89 90 93 94 95 96' 98' 99 00 01' 02 03 04 05' 06' 07 08' 09' 10' 11 Neighbour of CH MARGAUX: a Third Growth on a par with the Super Seconds. Wine of power, delicacy and much MERLOT (40%). Dutch, British (SICHEL family) and French owners. £7 million investment in new cellars (2010–12). Second wine: *Alter Ego de Palmer*.

Pape-Clément Pe-Lé r (w) ★★★→★★★★ (r) 90' 94 95 96 98' 99 00' 01 02 03 04 05 06 07 08 09' 10' 11 (w) 00 01 02 03 04 05' 07 08 09 10' 11 Ancient PESSAC v'yd owned by Bernard Magrez; has a record of potent, scented, long-ageing if not typical reds. Plus tiny production of rich, exotic white. Ambitious new-wave direction, oak and potency from 2000 (grapes are hand-destemmed!). Also CH Poumey at Gradignan.

Parenchère, de r (w) ★★ 04 05 06 07 08 09' 10' Useful AC Ste-Foy B'X and AC BORDEAUX SUPÉRIEUR from large estate with handsome CH. CUVÉE Raphael best.

Patache d'Aux Méd r ★★ 00 02 03 04 05' 06 07 09 10 Northern MÉDOC property in Bégadan. Gd-value, reliable largely CAB SAUV wine. *See also* LIVERSAN.

Pavie St-Em r ★★★★ 90' 94 95 96 98 99 00' 01 02 03' 04 05' 06 07 08 09' 10' 11 Splendidly sited First Growth on the côtes. Great track record. Bought by owner of MONBOUSQUET, along with adjacent PAVIE-DECESSE. New-wave ST-EMILION: intense, oaky, strong, mid-Atlantic. New winery ready for 2013 harvest.

Pavie-Decesse St-Em r ★★ 98' 99 00' 01' 02 03 04 05' 06 07 08 09' 10' 11 Tiny classed growth (1,000 cases). Even more powerful and muscular than PAVIE.

Pavie-Macquin St-Em r ★★★ 89' 90' 94 95 96' 98' 99 00' 01 02 03 04 05' 06 07 08 09' 10' 11 Surprise promotion to PREMIER GRAND CRU CLASSÉ in 2006 classification. V'yd on the limestone plateau east of ST-EMILION. Astute management and winemaking by Nicolas Thienpont of PUYGUERAUD; DERENONCOURT consultant. Powerful, structured wines that need time in bottle.

Pedesclaux Pau r ★★ 98' 99 00 02 03 04 05 06 09 10' Underachieving Fifth Growth being revived and reorganized. New owner in 2009 (*see* LILIAN LADOUYS) and improvement. Supple wines with up to 50% MERLOT. Watch for change.

Petit-Village Pom r ★★★ 95 96 98' 99 00' 01 03 04 05 06 07 08 09' 10' 11 Top POMEROL opposite VIEUX-CH-CERTAN. Lagged until 2005. DERENONCOURT consulting. New cellar in 2007. Same owner (AXA Insurance) as PICHON-LONGUEVILLE since 1989. Powerful, plummy wine. Second wine: Le Jardin de Petit-Village.

Pétrus Pom r ★★★★ 78 79' 81 82' 83 85' 86 88' 89' 90 93' 94 95' 96 97 98' 99 00' 01 02 03 04' 05' 06 07 08 09' 10' 11 The (unofficial) First Growth of POMEROL: MERLOT solo *in excelsis*. V'yd on gravelly clay giving 2,500 cases of massively rich, concentrated wine, on allocation to the world's millionaires. Each vintage adds lustre. Olivier Berrouet winemaker since 2007. Jean-François MOUEIX owner. New cellar complex ready for 2012 harvest.

Peyrabon H-Méd r ★★ 00' 01 02 03 04 05 06 09' 10 Serious estate owned by négociant (Millésima). Also La Fleur-Peyrabon in PAUILLAC.

Pez, de St-Est r ★★★ 95' 96' 98' 99 00 03 04 05' 06 07 08 09' 10' Outstanding ST-ESTÈPHE owned by ROEDERER (1995). Same winemaking team as PICHON-LALANDE. Generous and reliable in style.

Phélan-Ségur St-Est r ★★★ 89' 90' 95 96' 98 99 00' 01 02 03 04 05' 06 07 08 09' 10' 11 Leading player in ST-ESTÈPHE; reputation solid since 1988; long, supple style. New MD, Véronique Dausse, from 2010. ROLLAND consultant since 2006.

Pibran Pau r ★★ 95 96 99 00' 01 03 04 05' 06 07 08 09' 10' Small property allied to PICHON-LONGUEVILLE. Classy wine with PAUILLAC drive.

Pichon-Longueville Pau (formerly **Baron de Pichon-Longueville**) r ★★★★ 86' 88' 89' 90' 93 94' 95 96 98 99 00' 01 02 03' 04 05' 06 07 08 09' 10' 11 Revitalized

Second Growth with powerful consistent PAUILLAC for long ageing. Owners AXA Insurance (1987). New barrel cellar (under an artificial lake) and visitor centre in 2008. Second label: Les Tourelles de Longueville (approachable).

Pichon-Longueville Comtesse de Lalande (Pichon Lalande) Pau r ★★★★ 82' 83 85' 86' 88' 89' 90' 94 95 96 98 99 00 01 02 03' 04 05' 06 07 08 09' 10' 11 Super-Second Growth neighbour to LATOUR. Always among the top performers; a long-lived, MERLOT-marked wine of fabulous breed, even in lesser yrs. ROEDERER owner since 2007. Sylvie Cazes (see LYNCH-BAGES) installed 2011 as new MD. Tendency in coming yrs to increase CAB SAUV. Second wine: Réserve de la Comtesse. Other property: CH BERNADOTTE.

Pin, le Pom r ★★★★ 85 86' 88 89 90' 94 95 96 97 98' 99 00 01' 02 04' 05' 06' 07 08 09' 10' 11 The original of the B'X cult mini-*crus* made in a cellar not much bigger than a GARAGE. Now a new (2011) modern winery. A mere 500 cases of 100% MERLOT, with same family behind it as VIEUX-CH-CERTAN. Almost as rich as its drinkers, but prices are ridiculous.

Spending the profits
Internationally famous architects and designers are having a field day in B'X, particularly on the Right Bank. Tops (with designer): CHEVAL BLANC (Christian de Portzamparc), LA DOMINIQUE (Jean Nouvel), FAUGÈRES (Mario Botta), SOUTARD (Fabien Pédalaborde) and PAVIE (Alberto Pinto). On the Left Bank, watch for developments at Margaux.

Pitray, de r ★★ 98' 00' 03 04 05 06 09' 10 Once the best known in CASTILLON, now overshadowed by leading lights. Earthy, but value and available.

Plince Pom r ★★ 98' 00' 01 04 05 06 08 09 10 Lighter, supple wines from sandy soils. Easy-drinking.

Pointe, la Pom r ★★→★★★ 98' 99 00' 01 04 05 06 07 08 09' 10' Large estate. New owner and investment (2007). ANGÉLUS owner consults. Distinct improvement from 2009. To watch.

Pontac-Monplaisir Pe-Lé r (w) ★★ 00 02 04 05' 06 07 08 09 10 Property in suburbs. Attractive white; supple, decent red. Value.

Pontet-Canet Pau r ★★★→★★★★ 88 89' 90 94' 95 96' 98 99 00' 01 02' 03 04' 05' 06' 07 08 09' 10' 11 Neighbour to MOUTON ROTHSCHILD. One of the most-improved MÉDOC estates in last ten yrs. V. PAUILLAC in style. Certified biodynamic from 2010. Price has soared. Second wine: Les Hauts de Pontet-Canet.

Potensac Méd r ★★ 95 96 98 99 00' 01 02 03 04' 05' 07 08 09' 10' 11 Well-known property of northern MÉDOC. Delon family of LEOVILLE-LAS-CASES; class shows. Firm, vigorous wines for long ageing. Second wine: Chapelle de Potensac.

Pouget Mar r ★★ 96 98' 00' 01 02 03 04 05' 06 07 08 09' 10' Obscure Fourth Growth attached to BOYD-CANTENAC. Old vines. Solid rather than elegant.

Poujeaux Mou r ★★★ 90' 94' 95' 96' 98 99 00' 01 03 04 05 06 08 09' 10' 11 Purchased by the owner of CLOS FOURTET in 2007. With CHASSE-SPLEEN the high point of MOULIS. DERENONCOURT consults. Full, robust wines that age. Second label: La Salle de Poujeaux.

Premier Grand Cru Classé St-Em *See* ST-EMILION classification box (p.108).

Prieuré-Lichine Mar r ★★★ 89' 90' 94' 95 96 98' 99 00' 01 02 03 04 05 06 07 08' 09' 10' Fourth Growth owned by a négociant; put on the map by Alexis Lichine. V'yds v. dispersed. Advised by STÉPHANE DERENONCOURT. Fragrant MARGAUX currently on gd form. Second wine: Confidences du Prieuré-Lichine. A gd white B'X, too.

Puygueraud r ★★ 98 99 00' 01' 02 03' 05' 06 08 09 10 Leading CH of this tiny FRANCS-CÔTES DE BORDEAUX AC. Oak-aged wines of surprising class. Gd-value Les

Charmes-Godard white, same owner. Special CUVÉE George with MALBEC (35%+) in blend. Same winemaker as PAVIE-MACQUIN and LARCIS-DUCASSE.

Rabaud-Promis Saut w sw ★★→★★★ 95 96 97' 98 99 01' 02 03' 04 05' 06 07 09' 10 11 Family-owned classed growth at Bommes. Discreet but generally v.gd.

Rahoul Grav r w ★★ (r) 00' 01 02 04 05 08 09' 10 V'yd at Portets; Supple, SÉM-dominated white (04' 05 07 08 09 10). Progress under DOURTHE management.

Ramage-la-Batisse H-Méd r ★★ 00' 02 03 04 05' 07 08 09 10 Reasonably consistent, widely distributed HAUT-MÉDOC at St-Sauveur, north of PAUILLAC. Second wine: CH Tourteran.

Rauzan-Gassies Mar r ★★★ 96' 98 99 00 01' 02 03 04 05' 07 08 09' 10' The Second Growth neighbour of RAUZAN-SÉGLA that has long lagged behind it and is now catching up. New generation making strides since 2001 (look at 09', 10).

Rauzan-Ségla Mar r ★★★★ 86' 88' 89' 90' 94' 95 96 98 99 00' 01 02 03 04' 05 06 07 08 09' 10' 11 A Second Growth long famous for its fragrance; owned by owners of Chanel (see CANON). On fine form. Karl Lagerfeld designed 2009 label to celebrate 350th anniversary. Second wine: Ségla.

Raymond-Lafon Saut w sw ★★★ 88 89' 90' 95 96' 97 98 99' 01' 02 03' 04 05' 06 07' 09' 10' SAUTERNES estate acquired by former YQUEM manager (1972); now run by his children. Rich, complex wines that age. First Growth quality.

Rayne Vigneau Saut w sw ★★★ 89 90' 95 96 97 98 99 01' 02 03 05' 07 09' 10' 11 Large classed growth at Bommes. €3m renovation underway. Denis Dubourdieu consults. Second label: Madame de Rayne.

Respide Médeville Grav r w ★★ (r) 00' 01 02 04 05' 06 08 09 10 (w) 00 01 02 04' 05' 07 08 09 10 One of the better GRAVES properties for both red and *white*. Same owner as GILETTE in SAUTERNES. Drink reds at around 4–6 yrs.

Reynon r w ★★ Leading CADILLAC-CÔTES DE BORDEAUX estate. Serious red (02 03 04' 05' 06 07 09' 10). Fragrant B'x white from SAUV BL 05' 06 07 08 09 10'. *See also* CLOS FLORIDÈNE. Owned by Dubourdieu family.

Reysson H-Méd r ★★ 00 02 03 04 05 06 08 09' 10' Renovated estate; mainly MERLOT; managed by négociant CVBG-DOURTHE (see BELGRAVE, LA GARDE). Rich, modern style.

Ricaud, de w (r) (dr) sw ★★ 97 99 01' 02 03' 05 07 09 10 Substantial LOUPIAC estate; producer of SAUTERNES-like, age-worthy wine just across the river. Red and dry white as well.

Rieussec Saut w sw ★★★★ 83' 85 86' 88' 89' 90' 95 96' 97' 98 99 01' 02 03' 04 05' 06 07 09' 10' 11 Worthy neighbour of YQUEM with v'yd in Fargues, bought in 1985 by the (LAFITE) Rothschilds. Vinified in oak (since 1996). Fabulously powerful, opulent wine. Also dry "R", now made in modern style – with less character. Second wine: Carmes de Rieussec.

Feeling flush? It's said that up to a third of Bordeaux chx could be for sale.

Ripeau St-Em r ★★ 98 00' 01 04 05' 06 08 09 10 Lesser classed growth on sandy soils nr CHEVAL BLANC. Lighter style. More consistent since 2004.

Rivière, de la r ★★ 98' 99 00' 01 02 03 04 05' 06 08 09' 10 The biggest and most impressive FRONSAC property, with a Wagnerian castle and cellars. Formerly big, tannic wines; now more refined. New owner in 2003, with consultant from LANGUEDOC, Claude Gros. Special CUVÉE: Aria.

Rochemorin, de Pe-Lé r w ★★→★★★ (r) 00' 01 02 04 05 06 08 09' 10' (w) 04 05 06 07 08 09 10 An important restoration at Martillac by André Lurton of LA LOUVIÈRE. It is a vast estate (with three-quarters red). SAUV BL-dominated white. A new state-of-the-art winery in 2004. The quality is fairly consistent and it is widely distributed.

Rol Valentin St-Em r ★★★ 00' 01' 02 03 04 05' 06 07 08 09' 10' Originally GARAGE-style and size, now bigger. Wines rich, modern but balanced. New owner 2010.

Rouget Pom r ★★ 95 96 98' 99 00' 01' 03 04 05' 06 07 08 09' 10' Attractive old estate on the northern edge of POMEROL. Burgundian owners (1992). ROLLAND consults. Now excellent; rich, unctuous wines. Gd value.

Royal St-Emilion St-Em Brand name of important, dynamic growers' co-op. See also GALIUS.

St-André-Corbin St-Em r ★★ 00' 01 03 04 05 08 09 10 Estate wth v'yd in MONTAGNE- and ST-GEORGES-ST-EMILION. Supple, MERLOT-dominated wine.

St-Georges St-Em r ★★ 96 98' 00' 01 03 04 05' 08 09 10 Noble 18th-century CH overlooking the ST-EMILION plateau from the hill to the north. V'yd represents 25% of ST-GEORGES AC. Gd wine sold direct to the public.

St-Pierre St-Jul r ★★★ 89 90' 95' 96' 98 99 00' 01' 02 03 04 05' 06 07 08 09' 10' 11 Once-understated Fourth Growth owned by the president of B'x football club. Stylish and consistent classic ST-JULIEN (since 2000). See GLORIA.

Sales, de Pom r ★★ 98' 00' 01' 04 05 06 08 09 10 Biggest v'yd of POMEROL on sandy/ gravel soils, attached to 16th-century CH. Lightish wine; never quite poetry. Try top vintages. Second label: Ch Chantalouette.

Sansonnet St-Em r ★★ 00' 01 02 03 04 05' 06 08 09' 10' 11 Small plateau estate. Ambitiously run in modern style (rich, dark and fat). New proprietor 2009. VALANDRAUD owner and ROLLAND associate consult.

Saransot-Dupré List r (w) ★★ 98' 00' 01 02 03 04 05 06 09' 10' Small property with firm, fleshy wines. Lots of MERLOT. Also one of LISTRAC's little band of whites (60% SÉM).

Sénéjac H-Méd r (w) ★★ 99 00 01 02 03 04 05' 06 08 09' 10' Property owned since 1999 by the same family as TALBOT. Well-balanced wines. V'yd run biodynamically by PONTET-CANET team since 2009.

Serre, la St-Em r ★★ 95 96 98' 99 00' 01 02 03 04 05 06 08 09' 10 11 Small classed growth on the limestone plateau. Fresh, stylish wines with plenty of fruit.

Sigalas-Rabaud Saut w sw ★★★ 86 88 89' 90' 95' 96' 97' 98 99 01' 02 03 04 05' 07' 09' 10' 11 The smaller part of the former Rabaud estate in Bommes; same winemaking team as LAFAURIE-PEYRAGUEY. V. fragrant and lovely. Top-ranking now. Second wine: Le Lieutenant de Sigalas.

Siran Mar r ★★-★★★ 95 96 98 99 00' 01 02 03 04 05 06 07 08 09' 10' 11 Owned by the Miailhe family since 1859; Edouard runs the show today. Neighbour of DAUZAC. The wines age well and have masses of flavour. Second wine: S de Siran.

Smith-Haut-Lafitte Pe-Lé r (p) (w) ★★★ (r) 90' 94 95 96 98 99 00' 01 02 03 04' 05' 06 07 08 09' 10' 11 (w) 98 99' 00 01 02 03 04 05 06 07' 08' 09 10' 11 Classed growth at Martillac. Regularly one of the stars of PESSAC-LÉOGNAN (since 1990s). But dizzy price for the 2010. Luxurious spa-hotel-restaurant also. White is full, ripe, sappy; red generous and now fine. Second label: Les Hauts de Smith. Also CAB SAUV-based Le Petit Haut Lafitte from 2007.

Sociando-Mallet H-Méd r ★★★ 89' 90' 94 95 96' 98' 99 00' 01' 02 03 04 05' 06 07 09' 10' Splendid, widely followed estate at St-Seurin. Independently-minded owner celebrated 40 vintages in 2009. Conservative, big-boned wines to lay down for yrs. Second wine: Demoiselle de Sociando. Also special CUVÉE Jean Gautreau.

Soudars H-Méd r ★★ 96' 98 99 00' 01 03 04 05 06 09 10' Sister to COUFRAN and VERDIGNAN. Relatively traditional and regular quality.

Sours, de r p w ★★ Valid reputation for B'x Rosé (DYA). 300,000 bottles annually Gd white and improving B'x red also.

Soutard St-Em r ★★★ 90′ 94 95 96 98′ 99 00′ 01 03 04 05 06 07 08 09 10 11 *Potentially excellent* classed growth on the limestone plateau. Now owned by same insurance group as LARMANDE and CADET-PIOLA. Massive investment; new cellars and visitor centre 2010. Finer style since 2007. Second label: Jardins de Soutard.

Suduiraut Saut w sw ★★★★ 85 86 88′ 89′ 90′ 95 96 97′ 98 99′ 01′ 02 03′ 04 05′ 06 07′ 09′ 10′ 11 One of the best classed-growth SAUTERNES: renovated CH and gardens by Le Nôtre. Owner AXA Insurance has achieved greater consistency and luscious quality. *See* PICHON-LONGUEVILLE. Dry wine "S" v. promising. New fresher, fruitier Sauternes Les Lions de Suduiraut from 2009.

Tailhas, du Pom r ★★ 96′ 98′ 99 00 01 04 05′ 08 09′ 10 Modest family-owned property on sandy-gravel soils nr FIGEAC. Agreeable, earlier drinking.

Taillefer Pom r ★★ 95′ 96 98′ 00′ 01′ 02 03 04 05′ 06 08 09′ 10 V'yd on the edge of POMEROL. Astutely managed by Catherine Moueix. Less power than top estates but gently harmonious. Gd value.

Talbot St-Jul r (w) ★★★ 89′ 90 94 95 96′ 98′ 99 00′ 01 02 03 04 05′ 08′ 09′ 10′ 11 Sizeable Fourth Growth, for many yrs younger sister to GRUAUD-LAROSE. Wine similarly attractive: rich, *consummately charming, reliable* (though wobbly in 2006–7). DERENONCOURT consults (from 2008). Second label: Connétable de Talbot. White: Caillou Blanc. SÉNÉJAC in same family ownership.

Tertre, du Mar r ★★★ 95 96′ 98′ 99 00′ 01 03 04′ 05′ 06 08 09′ 10′ Fifth Growth isolated south of MARGAUX. History of undervalued, fragrant (20% CAB FR) and fruity wines. Since 1997, same owner as CH GISCOURS. Former LATOUR winemaker. New techniques and massive investment have produced a concentrated, structured wine, really humming from 2003.

Tertre Daugay St-Em r ★★★ 96 98 99 00′ 01 04 05 06 07 09′ 10 Hilltop v'yd. Escaped declassification from GRAND CRU CLASSÉ in 2006. Improvement from 2000. Bought by Dillon family of HAUT-BRION in 2011. To watch.

Ch Tertre Daugay has been renamed Ch Quintus under new ownership.

Tertre-Rôteboeuf St-Em r ★★★★ 88′ 89′ 90′ 93 94 95 96 97 98′ 99 00′ 01 02 03′ 04 05′ 06′ 07 08 09′ 10′ 11 A cult star that has been making concentrated, dramatic, largely MERLOT-based wine since 1983. Fairly frightening prices. Also CÔTES DE BOURG property, Roc de Cambes, of ST-EMILION classed-growth quality.

Thieuley r p w ★★ E-2-M supplier of consistent-quality AC B'X (r w); fruity CLAIRET; oak-aged CUVÉE Francis Courselle (r w). Also owns CLOS Ste-Anne in CADILLAC-CÔTES DE BORDEAUX.

Tour-Blanche, la Saut (r) w sw ★★★ 85 86 88′ 89′ 90′ 95 96 97′ 98 99 01′ 02 03′ 04 05′ 06 07 09′ 10′ 11 Leading SAUTERNES classed growth. Back on form from 1988. SAUV BL and MUSCADELLE 20% of blend. Rich and powerful. Second wine: Les Charmilles de Tour-Blanche.

> **Why Bordeaux?**
> People ask whether B'X still justifies its own separate section of this international guide. The answer: it remains the motor of the fine-wine world, by far its biggest producer, stimulating debate, investment and collectors worldwide. Besides, there are few better drinks.

Tour-de-By, la Méd r ★★ 98 00 01 02 03 04 05′ 06 08 09 10 V.-well-run family estate in northern MÉDOC; sturdy but reliable wines with a fruity note. Usually gd value.

Tour-Carnet, la H-Méd r ★★ 95 96 98 99 00' 01 02 03 04 05' 06 08 09' 10' Fourth Growth with medieval moated fortress, owned by Bernard Magrez (*see* FOMBRAUGE, PAPE-CLÉMENT). Investment from 2000 has produced richer wines in more modern style. Second wine: Les Douves de CH La Tour Carnet. Also GARAGE Servitude Volontaire du Tour Carnet.

Tour Figeac, la St-Em r ★★ 95 96' 98' 99 00' 01' 02 04 05 06 07 08 09' 10' 11 Classed growth between FIGEAC and POMEROL. Biodynamic methods (DERENONCOURT and his wife consult). Full, fleshy and harmonious.

Tour Haut-Brion, la Pe-Lé r ★★★ 95 96' 98' 99 00' 01 02 03 04' 05' RIP from 2005 for this classed growth. The v'yd has now been integrated into that of LA MISSION-HAUT-BRION. Same owner.

Tour Haut-Caussan Méd r ★★ 00' 01 02 03 04 05' 06 08 09' 10' Well-run property at Blaignan. Reliable. Gd value. Interests in CORBIÈRES as well.

Tour-du-Haut-Moulin H-Méd r ★★ 96 98 00' 02 03 04 05' 06 08 09 10 Family-owned estate in Cussac; intense, consistent, wines to mature.

Tour de Mons, la Mar r ★★ 96' 98' 99 00 01 02 04 05' 06 08 09' 10 MARGAUX cru owned by a bank. A long dull patch then investment and improvement in the new millennium.

Tournefeuille r ★★ 00' 01' 02 03 04 05' 06 07 08 09 10' LALANDE DE POMEROL property overlooking Barbanne stream. Steady investment and improvement since 1998. Reliable.

Bye-bye petits châteaux?

In the best areas, at least. Many top properties have been increasing in size for the last decade or more, and petits CH with v'yds in prime areas have been happy to sell them land. These new vines probably don't go into the *grand vin* at their new addresses, but the boom in second and even third wines means these need supplying too. The bad news is that the second wine of Ch Posh costs more than Ch Humble ever did; the good news is that the vines have every possible care lavished on them. Good news if you're a vine, anyway.

Tour-du-Pas-St-Georges St-Em r ★★ 98 99 00' 01 03 04 05' 06 08 09' 10 ST-GEORGES-ST-EMILION estate owned by Pascal Delbeck (ex-BELAIR-MONANGE). Recent investment.

Tour du Pin, la St-Em r ★★ 96 98 00' 01 04 05 06 08 09' 10' 11 Formerly La Tour du Pin Figeac-Moueix but bought and renamed by CHEVAL BLANC in 2006. Unimpressive form previously, but new team turning things around attractive 2010.

Tour-St-Bonnet Méd r ★★ 98 99 00' 02 03 04 05 06 08 09' 10 Consistently well-made ample northern MÉDOC from St-Christoly. Gd value.

Tronquoy-Lalande St-Est r ★★ 98 99 00' 02 03 04 05 06 07 08 09' 10' 11 Same owners as MONTROSE from 2006. Lots of MERLOT and PETIT VERDOT. Definite progression. Second wine: Tronquoy de Ste-Anne. To watch.

Troplong-Mondot St-Em r ★★★ 89' 90' 94' 95 96' 98' 99 00' 01' 02 03 04 05' 06 07 08 09' 10 11 Premier GRAND CRU CLASSÉ from 2006. Well-sited v'yd on a high point of limestone plateau. *Wines of power and depth with increasing elegance.* MICHEL ROLLAND consults. Second wine: Mondot.

Trotanoy Pom r ★★★★ 88 89' 90' 93 94 95 96 98' 99 00' 01 02 03 04' 05' 06 07 08 09' 10' 11 A J-P MOUEIX property since 1953; at best a glorious, fleshy, structured, perfumed wine. Wobbled a bit in the 1980s, but back on top form since 1989. Can occasionally rival PÉTRUS.

Trottevieille St-Em r ★★★ 89' 90 94 95 96 98 99 00' 01 03' 04 05' 06 07 08 09' 10' 11 First Growth on the limestone plateau. Same owners as BATAILLEY and DOMAINE DE L'EGLISE have raised its game since 2000. Hail damage in 2009 so tiny crop. Denis Dubourdieu consults. Limited bottling of old, ungrafted CAB FR.

A bottle of 1811 Yquem sold for £75,000 – the most expensive white in the world.

Valandraud St-Em r ★★★★ 93 94 95' 96 98 99 00' 01' 02 03 04 05' 06 07 08 09' 10' 11 Unwitting instigator of the GARAGE movement. Originally super-concentrated; since 1998 greater complexity. V'yd now three plots; on average 15,000 bottles. Seeking classification in 2012. Virginie de Valandraud another selection. White Blanc de Valandraud from 2003.

Verdignan H-Méd r ★★ 98 99 00' 01 02 03 04 05 06 08 09 10 A substantial estate; sister to COUFRAN and SOUDARS. More CAB SAUV than Coufran. Gd value and ageing potential.

Vieille Cure, la Fronsac r ★★ 00' 01' 02 03 04 05' 06 08 09' 10' 11 Leading FRONSAC estate; US-owned. Same management as MOULIN-HAUT-LAROQUE. Gd value.

Vieux-Château-Certan Pom r ★★★★ 82' 83' 85 86' 88' 89 90' 94 95' 96' 98' 99 00' 01 02 04' 05' 06 07 08 09' 10' 11 Traditionally rated close to PÉTRUS in quality, but totally different in style (30% CAB FR and 10% CAB SAUV); elegance, harmony, even beauty. Old vines (average 40–50 yrs). 2010 utterly superb.

Vieux Château St-André St-Em r ★★ 00' 01 02 03 04 05 06 08 09' 10 Small v'yd in MONTAGNE-ST-EMILION owned by the former winemaker of PÉTRUS. Regular high quality.

Villegeorge, de H-Méd r ★★ 96' 98' 99 00' 02 03 04 05 06 08 09' 10 Property owned by Marie-Laure Lurton, sister of Henri at BRANE-CANTENAC. Classic MÉDOC style. Sister CHX Duplessis in MOULIS and La Tour de Bessan in MARGAUX.

Vray Croix de Gay Pom r ★★ 90 95 96 98' 00' 04 05' 06 08 09' 10' 11 Tiny v'yd in the best part of POMEROL. Improvements since 2005; impressive 2010. Sister to CH Siaurac in LALANDE DE POMEROL. DERENONCOURT consults.

Yon-Figeac St-Em r ★★ 98 00' 02 03 04 05 06 09 10' 11 Avoided relegation from GRAND CRU CLASSÉ in 2006. New owner from 2005; Dubourdieu consults. Lighter, supple style from sandy-gravel soils.

Yquem Saut w sw (dr) ★★★★ 79 80' 81' 83' 85 86' 88' 89' 90' 93 94 95' 96 97' 98 99' 00 01' 02 03' 04 05' 06' 07' 08 09' 10' 11 The world's most famous sweet wine estate. Strong, intense, luscious; kept 3 yrs in barrel. Most vintages improve for 15 yrs+; some live 100 yrs+ in transcendent splendour. Subtle changes under LVMH ownership: slightly more freshness, slightly less time in barrel. The management (same as CHEVAL BLANC) is forward-thinking, pushing prices sky-high. Also makes dry "Y" (pronounced *ygrec*).

Dry white revelation

B'x's dry white wines account for less than nine per cent of the annual production but the quality has become consistently better and better. From easy-drinking E-2-M or B'x Blanc to finer GRAVES and PESSAC-LÉOGNAN the wines have become cleaner, fresher and more expressive. Recent vintages have been favourable but growers that refrained from grubbing up their SAUV BL and SÉM in preference for red varieties have also invested in quality. And it seems to have paid off – the demand now exceeds the offer.

Italy

More heavily shaded areas are the
wine-growing regions.

Abbreviations used in the text:

Ab	Abruzzo	Sar	Sardinia
Ap	Apulia	Si	Sicily
Bas	Basilicata	T-AA	Trentino-Alto Adige
Cal	Calabria	Tus	Tuscany
Cam	Campania	Umb	Umbria
E-R	Emilia-Romagna	VdA	Valle d'Aosta
F-VG	Friuli-Venezia Giulia	Ven	Veneto
Lat	Latium		
Lig	Liguria		
Lom	Lombardy		
Mar	Marches		
Pie	Piedmont		

To grasp the profusion of what Italy has to offer the lover of good wine you should go to Vinitaly, the annual spring wine fair at Verona. The profusion, and the professionalism: 4,000 producers cover 24 acres with their stands. You could taste for days, meet hundreds of dedicated growers with the self-respect of real craftsmen, and show your palate a range of flavours you had no idea existed.

Italy used to be hit or miss. I used to say you needed a corkscrew and a sense of humour to explore her wine list. You didn't hesitate with Italian food; now the wine has caught up with it – raced ahead, in fact. Italians love complications, and they love showing off: wine gives them the opportunity of a lifetime to blend the two.

The food is still vital; you won't often see Italians drink wine except at a table. Regional accents in both are usually clear, thank goodness. But whereas good wine was limited to a few northern provinces and Tuscany in the middle, it is now the norm from the Alps to the toe of the boot – and very much so in Sicily. It is invidious to say so, but no New World chapter of this book contains as much exciting variety or novelty as Europe's oldest winemaking country.

Recent vintages

Amarone, Veneto & Friuli

2011 "Best year ever" for Amarone: perfectly healthy grapes; soil, well-watered in spring, passed through the August heatwave without problem. Whites balanced and concentrated. Some reds very tannic, with high alcohol.

2010 Cool year, good for lighter wines, though late rain caused problems for grapes in the process of *appassimento* (drying). Start drinking soon.

2009 Ideal drying conditions for passito: classic wines. Good for Prosecco,

Pinot Gr and other whites in the east. Drink Amarone from 2015 .
2008 Classic wines of high quality. Drink from 2016.
2007 Some excellent wines; selection needed.
2006 Outstanding; more Amarone made than ever before. Drink from 2012.
2005 Grape-drying technology saved Amarone and Recioto. Less successful for
    Soave and whites. Drink up.
2004 Classic: less concentrated, less rich than 2003. Drinking now and for the
    next ten years.

Campania & Basilicata

2011 Very dry and very hot. Wines concentrated and rich; high alcohol and tannin in reds. Whites better balanced.

2010 Whites lightish with good aromas; reds good average quality.

2009 Ripe, healthy, aromatic whites, and reds with substance and concentration. Keep classic Aglianico/Taurasi to drink from 2014.

2008 Classic year for Aglianico; good, too, for whites. Drink from 2013.

2007 Good to excellent quality. Drink from 2013.

2006 Rain and problems of rot in lower-lying zones, much sun and a long growing season in higher vineyards. Selection needed.

2005 Aglianico had weight, complexity and character – perhaps the finest wines of all Italy in 2005. Drink from 2012.

2004 Slow and uncertain ripening for Aglianico; has exceeded expectations. Drink now for ten years.

Marches & Abruzzo

2011 Fruit very healthy but in some cases overconcentrated, alcoholic and tannic (reds). Best should age well.

2010 Weather peaks and troughs good for aromas, but also rot, with vintage rain. A difficult year but some good results. Drink from 2013.

2009 Good to very good quality, especially whites. Drink from 2012 (Montepulciano d'Abruzzo/Conero).

2008 Some excellent wines. Drink from now for five years.

2007 Some top-quality reds. Drink from 2012.

2006 Better than 2004 and 2005, but not as good as 2003. Drink or miss.

2005 Good, ripe, structured wines for those who waited to pick. Drink now for three years.

2004 Better in Rosso Conero than Rosso Piceno in the Marches; best in Colline Teramane DOCG, Abruzzo. Drink now.

Piedmont

2011 Unusually hot from August to end of vintage, grapes healthy but tending to high alcohol with danger of overconcentration and loss of balance. Probably good average quality.

2010 Quality patchy, but patient growers made very good wines.

2009 Quality good to very good, especially for Nebbiolo. Drink Barolo/ Barbaresco from 2014 for ten years+.

2008 Some great Barberas; Nebbiolos good, balanced, not spectacular. Drink from 2012 for ten years.

2007 Good to excellent Barolo, Barbaresco, Barbera. Some classic wines. Drink from 2013 for ten years+.

2006 Excellent Nebbiolo and Barbera. The laying-down vintage of the decade. Drink from 2014 for 20 years.

2005 Uneven Barbera, Nebbiolo, some good wines. Drink now for five years+.

2004 High-quality Dolcetto, Barbera, Nebbiolo. Classic year for Barbaresco, Barolo. Drink from 2012 for 20 years.

Older fine vintages: 01 00 99 98 97 96 95 90 89 88. Vintages to keep: 01 99 96. Vintages to drink up: 03 00 97 90 88.

Tuscany

2011 Extreme August/September heat means quality is variable. Top Sangiovese was possible, but excess alcohol, bitter tannins are problems. Select carefully.

2010 Patchy. Brunello very successful.

2009 Quality very good at least. Drink Chianti/Brunello from 2014–16.

2008 Mixed results with points of excellence; not necessarily for long keeping. Drink from 2012/14 for five years.

2007 High-quality crop. Drink from 2013–15 for ten years.

2006 Probably greatest of last 20 vintages. Drink from 2012 for 20 years.

2005 Sangiovese at every quality level imaginable, from first-rate to diluted. Selection needed.

2004 Exceptional along the coast, in Montepulciano and in Montalcino. Some elegant wines throughout, beginning to drink. Drink from 2012 for 20 years.

Older fine vintages: 01 99 97 95 90. Vintages to keep: 01 99. Vintages to drink up: 03 00 97 95 90.

Aglianico del Vulture Bas DOC(G) r dr ★→★★★ 01' 04' 06' 07 08 09 (10) (11) DOC with minimum 1 yr ageing, DOCG SUPERIORE after 2 yrs, DOCG Superiore RISERVA after 5 yrs. Also, bizarrely, SPUMANTE. Recent law changes have produced confusion surrounding this potentially noble and historic red from the ancient AGLIANICO grape on the slopes of spent volcano Monte Vulture. Top: Basilisco, Elena Fucci, Macarico, Cantine Madonna delle Grazie, Cantine del Notaio, PATERNOSTER, Terre degli Svevi, d'Angelo. Perhaps the best-known, d'Angelo, following a family bust-up, is now known as DONATO D'ANGELO.

Agricoltori del Chianti Geografico ★★ 50-yr-old co-op grouping some 200 quality-minded growers in the south of CHIANTI CLASSICO. Technical skill makes an impressive range, incl Chianti Classico Contessa di Radda and Chianti Classico RISERVA Montegiachi, not forgetting the ever-drinkable basic Chianti Classico.

Alba Pie Major wine city of PIEDMONT, southeast of Turin, famous for truffles and chocolates, and home to Piedmont's, if not Italy's, most prestigious wines: BAROLO, BARBARESCO, NEBBIOLO D'ALBA, ROERO, BARBERA d'Alba and DOLCETTO d'Alba.

Albana di Romagna E-R DOCG w dr sw s/sw (sp) ★→★★★ DYA. Aka Romagna Albana. Italy's first white DOCG, justifiably for the sweet PASSITO version, less so for the unremarkable dry. Bertinoro is the commune with the best producers, incl Raffaella Alessandra Bissoni, Celli, Madonia Giovanna and *Fattoria Paradiso*. Outstanding ZERBINA makes perhaps the best sweet version in Scacco Matto.

Alcamo DOC r p w sp ★→★★ DYA (w) Name covering many styles and types from western SICILY; mostly minerally dry whites based on the indigenous CATARRATTO grape, once mainly a base for vermouth. Rapitalà is the best-known producer.

Allegrini Ven ★★★ World-famous maker of VALPOLICELLA; outstanding single-v'yd IGT wines (La Grola, Palazzo della Torre, La Poja), AMARONE, RECIOTO. Also joint owner of POGGIO al Tesoro in BOLGHERI and Poggio San Polo in MONTALCINO, TUSCANY (since 2009).

Altare, Elio Pie ★★★ Leading exponent of modern-style NEBBIOLO. A recent addition is BAROLO Cerretta from Serralunga, long-aged in bottle. Also La Morra crus Barolo Arborina, Barolo Brunate, LANGHE DOC Arborina (Nebbiolo), Larigi (BARBERA), Langhe Rosso La Villa.

Alto Adige T-AA DOC r p w dr sw sp ★★→★★★ The once-Austrian, largely German-speaking province of Bolzano, alias SÜDTIROL, has had phenomenal success with its mtn-fresh, minerally whites; less so with reds, except for the odd outstanding PINOT N or native LAGREIN. Boasts excellent co-ops and numerous private companies of real quality.

Ama, Castello di Tus ★★★ One of the best and most consistent modern CHIANTI CLASSICO estates, nr Gaiole. La Casuccia and Bellavista are top single-v'yd wines. Gd IGTS, CHARD and MERLOT (L'Apparita).

Amarone della Valpolicella Ven DOCG r ★★ →★★★★ 95 97 98 00 01 03' 04 06' 07 08 (09) (10) (11) Intense, strong red from air-dried VALPOLICELLA grapes; one of Italy's true classics, only recently recognized as DOCG, with appendage "CLASSICO" if from historic zone. Relatively dry version of the ancient RECIOTO DELLA VALPOLICELLA. (For producers, *see* box, p.153.) Older vintages are rare; they tend to dry out beyond 20 yrs.

Angelini, Tenimenti Tus Influential, privately financed group owning v'yds in TUSCANY's three classic zones: MONTALCINO (Val di Suga), MONTEPULCIANO (Trerose) and CHIANTI CLASSICO (San Leonino). Recently purchased FRIULIAN producer Puiatti and Veronese BERTANI.

Anselmi, Roberto Ven ★★★ Producer at Monteforte in SOAVE who, some yrs ago, abandoned the DOC rather than accept absurd new rules. Now sells wines under IGT brand names like Capitel Croce and Capitel Foscarino (dry) and I Capitelli PASSITO (sweet).

Antinori, Marchesi L & P Tus ★★ →★★★★ V. influential Florentine house owned by the Antinori family, led by Piero, one of Italian wine's postwar heroes. Famous for CHIANTI CLASSICO (Tenute Marchese Antinori and *Badia a Passignano*), Umbrian (*Castello della Sala*), PIEDMONT (PRUNOTTO) wines, but esp SUPER TUSCANS TIGNANELLO and SOLAIA. Also estates in Tuscan MAREMMA (Fattoria Aldobrandesca), MONTEPULCIANO (La Braccesca), MONTALCINO (Pian delle Vigne), BOLGHERI for Guado al Tasso, FRANCIACORTA for sparkling (*Montenisa*) and APULIA (Tormaresca).

Apulia Ap (Puglia). The heel of the Italian boot, historically a bulk producer, now interesting quality and value. Best DOC: BRINDISI, CASTEL DEL MONTE, MANDURIA (PRIMITIVO DI), SALICE SALENTINO. Top producers: AZIENDA MONACI, Botromagno, Candido, Cantele, Cantine Paradiso, Castel di Selva, Co-op Due Palme, Conti Zecca, Coppadoro, La Corte, Li Veli, D'Alfonso del Sordo, Michele Calò, RACEMI, RIVERA, Rubino, *Rosa del Golfo*, TAURINO, Tormaresca (ANTINORI), Valle dell'Asso, VALLONE.

Argiano Tus Avant-garde BRUNELLO estate where Hans Vinding-Diers also makes CAB/MERLOT/SYRAH blend Solengo and smooth 100% SANGIOVESE Suolo.

Argiano, Castello di Tus Aka *Sesti*. Astronomer Giuseppe Maria Sesti turns out classy biodynamic BRUNELLO and Bordeaux-influenced *Terra di Siena*. Not to be confused with neighbour called simply Argiano.

Argiolas, Antonio Sar ★★ →★★★ Top Sardinian producer using native grapes to make outstanding crus Turriga (★★★), Antonio Argiolas, Iselis Rosso and Iselis Bianco as well as well-crafted standards.

Ten top Barbarescos

Here are ten outstanding examples of BARBARESCO, worth hunting down, especially at this moment of depressed prices:
Cantina del Pino (Ovello); Castello di Neive (RISERVA Santo Stefano); Castello di Verduno (Rabajà); GAJA (Barbaresco); BRUNO GIACOSA (Asili RISERVA); Marchesi di Gresy (Camp Gros); Paitin (Vecchie Vigne); PRODUTTORI DEL BARBARESCO (Ovello); Rocca Albino (Brich Ronchi); BRUNO ROCCA (Rabajà).

Assisi DOC r p w ★→★★ DYA (w) Famous tourist city less known for its wines than its relics. A few decent whites, mainly from GRECHETTO. Sportoletti is the name to seek out.

Asti Pie DOCG w sw sp ★→★★★ NV Piedmontese MUSCAT sparkler, known in past as Asti SPUMANTE. Producers usually prefer low prices to high quality, making DOCG status questionable. *See* MOSCATO D'ASTI, BARBERA. Rare top producers: BERA, Cascina Fonda, CAUDRINA, Vignaioli di Santo Stefano.

> **Ten top Barberas**
>
> Most of the best BARBERAS are from the PIEDMONTESE DOCS of Barbera d'ASTI and Barbera d'ALBA, but there are occasional instances of excellence from elsewhere. Here are ten outstanding examples of Barberas from each DOC:
>
> **Barbera d'Alba** BOGLIETTI (Vigna dei Romani); CLERICO (Trevigne); PRUNOTTO (Pian Romualdo); Voerzio, Gianni (Ciabot della Luna); VOERZIO, ROBERTO (Pozzo dell'Annunziata).
>
> **Barbera d'Asti** BRAIDA (Bricco dell'Uccellone); COPPO (Pomorosso); Perrone (Mongovone); CS Vinchio Vaglio (Vigne Vecchie).
>
> **Langhe** ALTARE (Larigi).

Avignonesi Tus ★★★ Noble MONTEPULCIANO house, best-known for aged VIN SANTO and **Occhio di Pernice** (★★★★), also for VINO NOBILE from high-density, bush-trained v'yds planted according to the ancient *settone* system. RISERVA Grandi Annate is top red.

Azienda agricola/agraria An estate (large or small) making wine from own grapes.

Azienda Monaci Ap ★★→★★★ Was "Masseria Monaci". Estate of Severino Garofano, the enologist behind the continuing rise of quality wine in PUGLIA'S SALENTO. Characterful NEGROAMARO (Eloquenzia, I Censi), superb late-picked Le Braci, also Uva di Troia (Sine Pari) and AGLIANICO (Sine Die).

Badia a Coltibuono Tus ★★→★★★ Seasoned CHIANTI CLASSICO producer, making a comeback after yrs in doldrums. Top wine is 100% SANGIOVESE barrique-aged SUPER TUSCAN "Sangioveto".

Banfi (Castello or Villa) Tus ★→★★★ MONTALCINO CANTINA of major US importer of Italian wine. Huge plantings on lower-lying southern slopes at Montalcino, incl in-house-developed clones of SANGIOVESE; also CAB SAUV, MERLOT, SYRAH, PINOT N, CHARD, SAUV BL, PINOT GR. SUPER TUSCAN French-grape blends like Cum Laude and Summus tend to work better than somewhat overextracted BRUNELLOS.

Barbaresco Pie DOCG r ★★→★★★★ 97 99 01 04 06' 07 08' 09 (10) (11) Classic Piedmontese red, 100% NEBBIOLO; like BAROLO, boasting similar levels of complex aroma and flavour but with less power, more elegance. Minimum 2 yrs ageing, 1 in wood; at 4 yrs becomes RISERVA.

Barco Reale Tus DOC r ★★ 06 07 08 09 (10) DOC for junior wine of CARMIGNANO. *See* CAPEZZANA.

Bardolino Ven DOC(G) r p ★→★★ DYA Light, fresh, summery red from Europe's largest lake, GARDA. Bardolino SUPERIORE is DOCG with much lower yield than Bardolino DOC. The pale pink CHIARETTO is one of Italy's more interesting rosés. Gd producers incl: Cavalchina, Costadoro, Le Fraghe, *Guerrieri Rizzardi*, ZENATO, Zeni.

Barolo Pie DOCG r ★★★→★★★★ 95 96' 97 98 99' 01' 04' 05 06' 07' 08' (09') (10') (11) Italy's greatest red, 100% NEBBIOLO, from the village of the same name south of ALBA or any of ten others (or parts thereof). The best combine power and elegance, crisp tannins and floral scent. Must be 3 yrs old before release (5 for RISERVA), of which 2 in wood. *See* box, p.128 for top producers, divided between traditionalists (long maceration, large oak barrels) and modernists (shorter maceration, often aged in barrique). Barolo Chinato is an apéritif with quinine added.

Basciano Tus ★→★★ Producer of gd DOCG CHIANTI RUFINA and IGT wines.

Beato Bartolomeo da Breganze ★★ Well-run CO-OP in hills of Veneto, with one of the largest plantings of genuine PINOT GRIGIO. Also specializes in still, sparkling and sweet (TORCOLATO) wines of the indigenous Vespaiolo grape.

Bellavista Lom ★★★ FRANCIACORTA estate with convincing Champagne-style wines (Gran Cuvée Franciacorta is top). Also Extra Brut Vittorio Moretti and Satèn (a crémant-style sparkling).

Bera, Walter Pie ★★→★★★ A small Piedmontese estate producing top-quality MOSCATO wines (Moscato d'ASTI, Asti), also fine reds (BARBERA d'Asti, BARBARESCO, LANGHE NEBBIOLO).

Berlucchi, Guido Lom ★★ Italy's biggest producer of sparkling METODO CLASSICO.

Bersano Pie ★→★★ Historic house in Nizza Monferrato, with BARBERA D'ASTI Generala, BAROLO Badarina, most PIEDMONT DOC wines, incl BARBARESCO, MOSCATO D'ASTI, Asti.

Bertani Ven ★★→★★★ Long-established family-owned producer of VALPOLICELLA; 200ha in various parts of Verona province; two million bottles per annum. Boasts a library of every AMARONE vintage since 1959. Recently purchased by TENIMENTI ANGELINI.

Bianco di Custoza or Custoza Ven DOC w (sp) ★→★★ DYA Fresh, uncomplicated white from Lake GARDA, made from GARGANEGA, Cortese. Gd: Cavalchina, Le Tende, Le Vigne di San Pietro, Montresor, Zeni.

Bianco di Pitigliano DOC w ★→★★ DYA. Stunning medieval walled town, makes a less-than-stunning dry white from TREBBIANO and other grapes. CANTINA di Pitigliano makes a creditable version.

Biferno Mol DOC r p w ★→★★ (r) 06 07 08 09 10 (11) Gd to interesting wines from the easily forgotten region of Molise, sandwiched between Abruzzo and APULIA. Red based on MONTEPULCIANO, white on TREBBIANO. DI MAJO NORANTE (Ramitello) and Borgo di Colloredo (Gironia) are worth seeking out.

Biondi-Santi Tus ★★★★ Octogenarian Franco Biondi-Santi continues at his Greppo estate to make BRUNELLO DI MONTALCINO in a highly traditional manner, as did his father, Tancredi, and his grandfather, Ferruccio, aiming in best yrs at wines to last decades.

Ten top Barolos

Who makes the best BAROLO? These ten growers! All wines from vines in the central communes of Barolo, Castiglione Falletto, Monforte d'Alba and Serralunga:

Cavallotto (Bricco Boschis Vigna San Giuseppe); ALDO CONTERNO (Granbussia); GIACOMO CONTERNO (Monfortino); Bartolo MASCARELLO (Barolo); Giuseppe MASCARELLO (Monprivato); Massolino (Vigna Rionda); Giuseppe Rinaldi (Brunate-Le Coste); SANDRONE (Cannubi Boschis); PAOLO SCAVINO (Bric dël Fiasc); VIETTI (Lazzarito).

Bisol Ven Top brand of PROSECCO.

Boca Pie *See* GATTINARA.

Boglietti, Enzo Pie ★★★ Dynamic young producer of La Morra in BAROLO zone. Top modern-style Barolos (Arione, Case Nere) and outstanding BARBERA D'ALBA (Vigna dei Romani, Roscaleto).

Bolgheri Tus DOC r p w (sw) ★★→★★★★ Arty walled village on TUSCANY's Tyrrhenian coast, giving its name to an increasingly stylish, and expensive, group of SUPER TUSCANS based mainly on Bordeaux varieties with a bit of SYRAH and even the odd drop of SANGIOVESE, thrown in. The big names are here: SASSICAIA (original inspirer of the cult), ANTINORI (at Guado al Tasso), FRESCOBALDI (at ORNELLAIA), GAJA (at CA` MARCANDA), ALLEGRINI (at Poggio al Tesoro), Folonari (at Campo al Mare), plus the odd local in LE MACCHIOLE and MICHELE SATTA.

Bolla Ven ★★ Historic Verona firm for SOAVE, VALPOLICELLA, AMARONE, RECIOTO DELLA VALPOLICELLA, RECIOTO DI SOAVE. Today owned by powerful GRUPPO ITALIANO VINI.

Bonarda Lom DOC r ★★ 06 07 08 09 (10) Soft, fresh FRIZZANTE and still red from Lombardy's OLTREPÒ PAVESE, made from Croatina grape and not to be confused with Piedmontese Bonarda.

Looking for more information on grapes? Try the "Grapes" section on pp.16–26.

Borgo del Tiglio F-VG ★★★→★★★★ Nicola Manferrari is one of Italy's top white winemakers. His COLLIO FRIULANO RONCO della Chiesa and Studio di Bianco are especially impressive.

Boscarelli, Poderi Tus ★★★ Small estate with v.gd VINO NOBILE DI MONTEPULCIANO Nocio dei Boscarelli and SUPER TUSCAN blend Boscarelli.

Botte Large barrel, anything from 6–250hl, usually between 20–50, traditionally of Slavonian but increasingly of French oak. To traditionalists, the ideal vessel for ageing wines in which an excess of oak aromas is undesirable.

Brachetto d'Acqui/Acqui Pie DOCG r sw (sp) ★★ DYA. Sweet, sparkling red with enticing MUSCAT scent. Elevated DOCG status is disputed by some.

Braida Pie ★★★ The late Giacomo Bologna's estate; top BARBERA D'ASTI (Bricco dell'Uccellone, Bricco della Bigotta, Ai Suma).

Bramaterra Pie See GATTINARA.

Breganze Ven DOC r w sp ★→★★★ (r) DYA (w) 06 07 08 09 (10) (11) Major production area for PINOT GR, also gd Vespaiolo (white still and sparking, and sticky TORCOLATO); PINOT N, CAB. Main producers: MACULAN and BEATO BARTOLOMEO.

Brindisi Ap DOC r p ★★ (r) 06 07 08 09 (10) (11) (p) DYA. Smooth NEGROAMARO-based red with MONTEPULCIANO, esp from VALLONE, Due Palme, Rubino. ROSATO can be among Italy's best.

Brolio, Castello di Tus ★★→★★★ Historic estate, CHIANTI CLASSICO's largest, now thriving again under RICASOLI family after foreign-managed decline. V.gd Chianti Classico and IGT Casalferro.

Brunelli, Gianni Tus ★★★ Small-scale producer of elegant, refined BRUNELLO DI MONTALCINO. Not to be confused with others in MONTALCINO called Brunelli. Now run by Gianni's widow, Laura.

Brunello di Montalcino Tus DOCG r ★★★→★★★★ 90' 95 97 99' 00 01 04' 05 06' 07 (08') (09) (10') (11) Top wine of TUSCANY, dense but elegant with scent and structure, potentially v. long-lived. Min 4 yrs ageing, after 5 yrs RISERVA. Moves to allow small quantities of French grapes in this supposedly 100% varietal (SANGIOVESE) have been fought off, but vigilance is needed. See also ROSSO DI MONTALCINO.

Burlotto, Commendatore G B Pie ★★★ Fabio Alessandria turns out beautifully crafted and defined wines, esp BAROLO Cannubi and Monvigliero, the latter's grapes being crushed by foot.

Bussola, Tommaso Ven ★★★★ Leading producer of AMARONE, RECIOTO and RIPASSO in VALPOLICELLA. Excellent Amarone Vigneto Alto and Recioto TB.

Caberlot Tus Mellow, flavoury red from crossing of CAB FR and MERLOT claimed to be unique to the v'yds of Bettina Rogosky at her Il Carnasciale estate, nr Arezzo. Sold only in magnum.

Ca' dei Frati Lom ★★★ The best producer of DOC LUGANA, also v.gd dry white blend IGT Pratto, sweet Tre Filer and red IGT Ronchedone.

Ca' del Bosco Lom ★★★★ No 1 FRANCIACORTA estate owned by giant PINOT GR producer Santa Margherita, but still run by founder Maurizio Zanella. **Outstanding Classico-method fizz**, esp Annamaria Clementi (Italy's Dom Pérignon) and Dosage Zero; also excellent Bordeaux-style red Maurizio Zanella, burgundy-style PINOT N Pinero and CHARD.

Ca' Marcanda Tus ★★★ BOLGHERI estate created by GAJA (since 1996). Three wines in order of price (low to high): Promis, Magari and Ca' Marcanda – grapes are mainly international.

Ca' Viola Pie Play-on-words name of home estate of influential PIEDMONT-based consultant Beppe Caviola. Classy DOLCETTO and BARBERA-based wines.

Ca' Vit T-AA (Cantina Viticoltori) Group of co-ops nr Trento. Massive production, best being sparkling Graal.

Cafaggio, Villa Tus ★★★ V. reliable CHIANTI CLASSICO estate with excellent IGTS San Martino (SANGIOVESE) and Cortaccio (CAB SAUV).

Caiarossa Tus ★★★ Riparbella in the northern MAREMMA attracts serious winemakers by its combination of altitude and proximity to the sea. This international project – Dutch owner Jelgersma from Bordeaux, French winemaker Dominique Génot with Australian background – is making v. classy reds (Pergolaia, Caiarossa) plus v. tasty Caiarossa Bianco.

Caluso / Erbaluce di Caluso DOCG w ★★ DYA. Bright, minerally white from Erbaluce grape in northern PIEDMONT. Best: Orsolani, esp La Rustia and Favaro 13 Mesi.

Campania Cam The playground of the Romans; today a region of lively interest. Excellent native grapes – FALANGHINA, FIANO, GRECO, Coda di Volpe (w), plus AGLIANICO, Piedirosso (r); volcanic soils and cool v'yds on high slopes add up to gd potential being progressively realized. Most interesting wines tend to be varietal, but classic DOCGS incl Fiano d'Avellino, GRECO DI TUFO and TAURASI, with newer areas emerging such as Sannio (DOC) and Beneventano (IGT). Gd producers: Caggiano, Cantina del Taburno, Caputo, Colli di Lapio, D'Ambra, De Angelis, Benito Ferrara, *Feudi di San Gregorio*, GALARDI, LA GUARDIENSE, **Mastroberardino**, Molettieri, MONTEVETRANO, Mustilli, Terredora di Paolo, Trabucco and VILLA MATILDE.

The best of Brunello – top ten and the rest

Any of the below provides a satisfying BRUNELLO DI MONTALCINO, but we have put a star next to the ten we think best:

Pieri Agostina, Altesino, ARGIANO, ARGIANO (CASTELLO DI), Baricci, BIONDI-SANTI ★, Gianni BRUNELLI ★, Camigliano, La Campana, Campogiovanni, Canalicchio di Sopra, Canalicchio di Sotto, Caparzo, CASANOVA DI NERI, CASE BASSE ★, CASTELGIOCONDO, Cerbaiona ★, Ciacci Piccolomini, COL D'ORCIA, Collemattoni, Corte Pavone, Costanti, Eredi FULIGNI, Il Colle, Il Paradiso di Manfredi, La Fuga, La Gerla, Lambardi, LISINI ★, La Magia, La Mannella, Le Potazzine, Marroneto, Mastrojanni ★, Oliveto, SIRO PACENTI, Palazzo, Pertimali, Pieve di Santa Restituta, La Poderina, Pian dell'Orino ★, IL POGGIONE ★, POGGIO ANTICO, Poggio di Sotto ★, Salvioni-Cerbaiola ★, Uccelliera, Val di Suga, Valdicava.

Cantina A cellar, winery or even a wine bar.

Capezzana, Tenuta di Tus ★★★ Tuscan family estate west of Florence headed by nonagenarian Ugo Contini Bonacossi, still going strong. Gd BARCO REALE DOC, excellent CARMIGNANO (Villa di Capezzana, Villa di Trefiano). Also v.gd Bordeaux-style red, Ghiaie Della Furba and an exceptional VIN SANTO.

Capichera Sar ★★★ V.gd if high-priced producer of VERMENTINO DI GALLURA, esp VENDEMMIA *tardiva*. Excellent red Mantèghja from CARIGNANO grapes.

Cappellano Pie ★★★ The late Teobaldo Cappellano was one of the "characters" of BAROLO, devoting part of his v'yd in cru Gabutti to ungrafted NEBBIOLO vines (Pie Franco). Excellent Barolos in a highly traditional style; also "tonic" Barolo Chinato, invented by an ancestor.

Caprai Umb ★★★→★★★★ A large, experimentalist producer making v.-high-quality wines in Umbria's MONTEFALCO. Superb DOCG **Montefalco Sagrantino**, esp 25 Anni, v.gd DOC ROSSO DI MONTEFALCO.

Capri DOC r w ★ DYA (w) Mainly whites from the (in)famous island off Naples, based on FALANGHINA and GRECO; red based on Piedirosso. Try La Caprense.

Carema Pie DOC r ★★→★★★ 04' 06' 07 08 (09) (10) (11) Obscure, light and intense NEBBIOLO red from lower, if precipitous, Alpine slopes on Aosta border. Best: Luigi Ferrando (esp Etichetta Nera), Produttori Nebbiolo di Carema.

Carignano del Sulcis Sar DOC r p ★★→★★★ 06 07 08 09 (10) Mellow but intense red from SARDINIA's southwest. Best incl: *Terre Brune* and Rocca Rubia from SANTADI.

Carmignano Tus DOCG r ★★★ 97' 99 00 01 02 04 06 07 08 09 (10) (11) Fine Tuscan SANGIOVESE/international-grape blend effectively invented in 20th century by Ugo Contini Bonacossi of CAPEZZANA. Best: Ambra, CAPEZZANA, Farnete, Piaggia, Le Poggiarelle, Pratesi.

Carpenè-Malvolti Ven ★★ Historic and still important brand of PROSECCO and other sparkling wines at CONEGLIANO.

Cartizze Ven ★★ Famous, frequently too expensive and too sweet, DOC PROSECCO of supposedly best subzone of Valdobbiadene.

Casanova di Neri Tus ★★★ Modern BRUNELLO DI MONTALCINO, highly prized Cerretalto and Tenuta Nuova, plus Petradonice CAB SAUV and v.gd ROSSO DI MONTALCINO.

Case Basse Tus ★★★★ Eco-geek Gianfranco Soldera claims to make the definitive BRUNELLO; many lovers of the traditional style agree. V. expensive and rare.

Castel del Monte Ap DOC r p w ★→★★ (r) 06 07 08 09 10 (p w) DYA. Dry, fresh, increasingly serious wines of mid-APULIAN DOC. Gd Pietrabianca and excellent *Bocca di Lupo* from Tormaresca (ANTINORI). V.gd Le More from Santa Lucia. Interesting reds from Cocevola, Giancarlo Ceci. *See also* RIVERA, whose Il Falcone RISERVA is considered the iconic cru of the zone.

Castelgiocondo Tus ★★★ *See* FRESCOBALDI.

Castellare Tus ★★→★★★ CHIANTI CLASSICO producer. First-rate SANGIOVESE-based IGT I Sodi di San Niccoló and updated CHIANTI, esp RISERVA Vigna Poggiale. Also Poggio ai Merli (MERLOT) and Coniale (CAB SAUV).

Castell' in Villa Tus ★★★ Individual, traditionalist CHIANTI CLASSICO estate of excellence run by self-taught Princess Coralia Pignatelli.

Castelluccio E-R ★★→★★★ Quality SANGIOVESE varietals from Romagna: IGT RONCO dei Ciliegi and Ronco delle Ginestre. Massicone is an excellent Sangiovese/ CAB SAUV blend.

Caudrina Pie ★★★ Top MOSCATO D'ASTI: La Galeisa and Caudrina. Also one of few high-quality ASTI sparklers, La Selvatica.

Cavicchioli E-R ★→★★ Important producer of serious LAMBRUSCO and other sparkling wines: Lambrusco di Sorbara Vigna del Cristo is best.

Cerasuolo Ab DOC p ★ The ROSATO version of MONTEPULCIANO D'ABRUZZO. Worth trying.

Cerasuolo di Vittoria Si DOCG r ★★ 06 07 08 09 10 11 In southeast SICILY, a medium-bodied red from Frappato and NERO D'AVOLA grapes; try COS, PLANETA, Valle dell'Acate.

Ceretto Pie ★★→★★★ Leading producer of BARBARESCO (Bricco Asili), BAROLO (Bricco Rocche, Brunate, Prapò), LANGHE Rosso Monsordo and ARNEIS.

Cerro, Fattoria del Tus ★★★ Estate owned by insurance giants SAI, making v.gd DOCG VINO NOBILE DI MONTEPULCIANO (esp cru Antica Chiusina). Also owns La Poderina (BRUNELLO DI MONTALCINO), Colpetrone (MONTEFALCO SAGRANTINO) and the 1,000ha northern MAREMMA estate of Monterufoli.

Cesanese del Piglio or Piglio Lat DOCG r ★→★★ Medium-bodied red, gd for moderate ageing. Best: Petrucca e Vela, Terre del Cesanese. Cesanese di Olevano Romano and Cesanese di Affile are similar.

Chianti Tus DOCG r ★→★★★ For centuries the local wine of Florence and Siena: fresh, fruity, astringent and uncomplicated. The seven 20th-century-created subzones aim higher: RÚFINA (★★→★★★), Colli Fiorentini (★→★★★), Montespertoli can make CLASSICO-style RISERVAS. Montalbano, Colli Senesi, Aretini, Pisani are generally less serious.

Chianti Classico Tus DOCG r ★★→★★★★ 04 06 07 08 09 10 11 The historic CHIANTI zone was allowed to add Classico to its name when the Chianti area was extended to most of central TUSCANY in the early 20th century. Covering nine communes, the land is hilly and rocky with altitudes of 250–500 metres. Chianti Classico must consist of 80–100% SANGIOVESE, with an optional 20% of "other grapes" – usually CAB SAUV or MERLOT in "modern" versions, Canaiolo and increasingly Colorino if more traditional, which makes the same sense as adding SANGIOVESE to claret.

Chiaretto Ven Pale, light-blush-hued rosé (the word means "claret"), produced esp around Lake GARDA. *See* BARDOLINO, Riviera del Garda Bresciano.

Chiarlo, Michele Pie ★★→★★★ Gd PIEDMONT producer (BAROLOS Cerequio and Cannubi, BARBERA D'ASTI, LANGHE and MONFERRATO Rosso). Also BARBARESCO.

Ciabot Berton Pie ★★★ Small La Morra grower; classy BAROLOS at modest prices.

Ciliegiolo Tus Varietal wine of the TUSCAN coastal area MAREMMA, derived from the eponymous grape from which SANGIOVESE is probably derived. Try Rascioni e Cecconello, Sassotondo.

Cinque Terre Lig DOC w dr sw ★★ Dry whites from obscure grapes grown in steep, rocky tourist paradise on Riviera coast. Sweet version is called SCIACCHETRÀ.

Cirò Cal DOC r (p w) ★→★★★ Strong red from CALABRIA's main grape, Gaglioppo; or light, fruity white from GRECO (DYA). Best: Caparra, Ippolito, *Librandi* (Duca San Felice ★★★), San Francesco (Donna Madda, RONCO dei Quattroventi), Santa Venere.

Classico Term for wines from a restricted, usually historic and superior-quality area within the limits of a commercially expanded DOC. *See* CHIANTI CLASSICO, also METODO CLASSICO.

Clerico, Domenico Pie ★★★ Established modernist BAROLO producer, esp crus Percristina and Ciabot Mentin Ginestra. New is Barolo Aeroplan Servaj. Considered one of the best in Barolo, if not the best, by many Americans.

Coffele Ven ★★★ Grower with some of the finest v'yds in SOAVE CLASSICO, making steely, minerally wines of classic style. Try cru Cà Visco.

Col d'Orcia Tus ★★★ 3rd-largest and top-quality MONTALCINO estate owned by Francesco Marone Cinzano. Best wine: BRUNELLO RISERVA Poggio al Vento.

Colli Bolognesi E-R DOC r w ★★ DOC name for rarely seen varietal wines, excluding those from the otherwise ubiquitous SANGIOVESE and TREBBIANO grapes. Terre Rosse, the pioneer, now joined by Bonzara (★★→★★★) and others. *Colli* = hills.

Colli del Trasimeno Umb DOC r w ★→★★ (r) 06 07' 08 09 10 11 Lively white wines from nr Perugia, but gd reds as well. Best: Duca della Corgna, La Fiorita, Pieve del Vescovo, Poggio Bertaio.

Colli Euganei Ven DOC r w dr s/sw (sp) ★→★★ DYA. DOC southwest of Padua. Red, white and sparkling are pleasant, rarely better. Best producers: Ca' Lustra, La Montecchia, Vignalta.

Colli Orientali del Friuli F-VG DOC r w dr sw ★★→★★★★ Hills east of Udine. Zone similar to COLLIO but less experimental, more oriented towards reds and stickies. Top producers: Meroi, Miani, Moschioni, LIVIO FELLUGA, Rosa Bosco, RONCO del Gnemiz. Sweet wines from Verduzzo grapes (called Ramandolo if from around Nimis: Anna Berra, Giovanni Dri) or Picolit grapes (Ronchi di Cialla) can be amazing.

Colli Piacentini E-R DOC r p w ★→★★ DYA Traditional GUTTURNIO and Monterosso Val d'Arda, incl among 11 varieties, French and local, grown south of Piacenza. Gd fizzy MALVASIA. Most wines FRIZZANTE. Gd producers: Montesissa, Mossi, Romagnoli, Solenghi, La Stoppa, Torre Fornello, La Tosa.

Colline Novaresi Pie *See* GATTINARA.

Collio F-VG DOC r w ★★→★★★★ Important quality zone on border with Slovenia. Esp known for complex, sometimes deliberately oxidized whites, which may be vinified on skins in earthenware vessels/amphoras in ground. Some excellent, some shocking blends from various French, German and Slavic grapes. Numerous gd-to-excellent producers incl BORGO DEL TIGLIO, La Castellada, Castello di Spessa, MARCO FELLUGA, Fiegl, GRAVNER, Renato Keber, LIVON, Aldo Polencic, Primosic, Princic, Russiz SUPERIORE, *Schiopetto*, Tercic, Terpin, Venica & Venica, VILLA RUSSIZ, Zuani.

Who makes really good Chianti Classico?

CHIANTI CLASSICO is a seriously large zone with hundreds of producers, so picking out the best is tricky. The top ten get a ★.

AMA ★, ANTINORI, BADIA A COLTIBUONO ★, Bibbiano, Le Boncie, Il Borghetto, Bossi, BROLIO, Cacchiano, CAFAGGIO, Capannelle, Capraia, Carobbio, Casaloste, Casa Sola, CASTELLARE, CASTELL' IN VILLA, Le Cinciole, Collelungo, Le Corti, Mannucci Droandi, FELSINA ★, Le Filigare, FONTERUTOLI, FONTODI ★, ISOLE E OLENA ★, Lilliano, Il Molino di Grace, MONSANTO ★, Monte Bernardi, Monteraponi ★, NITTARDI, NOZZOLE, Palazzino, Paneretta, Petroio-Lenzi, Poggerino, Poggiolino, Poggiopiano, Poggio al Sole, QUERCIABELLA ★, RAMPOLLA, Riecine, Rocca di Castagnoli, Rocca di Montegrossi ★, RUFFINO, San Fabiano Calcinaia, SAN FELICE, SAN GIUSTO A RENTENNANO ★, Savignola Paolina, Selvole, Vecchie Terre di Montefili, Verrazzano, Vicchiomaggio, VIGNAMAGGIO, Villa La Rosa ★, Viticcio, VOLPAIA ★.

Colognole Tus ★★ Ex-Conti Spalletti estate making increasingly classy CHIANTI RUFINA and RISERVA del Don from spectacular sites on south-facing slopes of Monte Giovi.

Colterenzio CS / Schreckbichl T-AA ★★→★★★ Pioneering quality leader among ALTO ADIGE co-ops. Look for: Cornell line of selections; Lafoa CAB SAUV and SAUV BL; Cornelius red and white blends.

Conegliano Valdobbiadene Ven DOCG w sp ★→★★ DYA. Names for top PROSECCO: may be used separately or together.

Conterno, Aldo Pie ★★★→★★★★ Legendary grower of BAROLO at Monforte d'ALBA. V.gd CHARD Bussiadoro, BARBERA D'ALBA Conca Tre Pile. Best Barolos are made traditionally: Gran Bussia, Cicala, Colonello. LANGHE Favot is a modern barrique-aged version of NEBBIOLO.

Conterno, Giacomo Pie ★★★★ The iconic grower of super-traditional BAROLO at Monforte d'ALBA. Giacomo's grandson, Roberto, is now carrying on father Giovanni's work. The are two Barolos: Cascina Francia and *Monfortino*, long-macerated to age for yrs.

Conterno-Fantino Pie ★★★ Two families joined to produce excellent modern-style BAROLO Sori Ginestra and Vigna del Gris at Monforte d'ALBA. Also NEBBIOLO/BARBERA blend Monprà.

Conterno Paolo ★★→★★★ A family of NEBBIOLO and BARBERA growers since 1886, father Paolo with son and grandson continue with textbook cru BAROLOS Ginestra and Riva del Bric, plus a particularly fine LANGHE Nebbiolo Bric Ginestra.

Contesa Ab ★★→★★★ Consultant enologist Rocco Pasetti established his own v'yd at Collecorvino in the 1990s, and today makes gd MONTEPULCIANO D'ABRUZZO Vigna Corvino and Contesa. Fresh, intense *Cerasuolo*. A specialty is white Pecorino, a wine of complexity and character, which, unusually for Italy, ages well.

Contini, Attilio Sar ★☆★★★ Famous Sardinian producer of Sherry-like, *flor*-affected VERNACCIA DI ORISTANO. Best is vintage blend Antico Gregori.

Contucci Tus ★★→★★★ Millennial producer of traditional-style VINO NOBILE. His cellar at MONTEPULCIANO *vaut le détour*.

Copertino Ap DOC r (p) ★★★ 06 07 08 09 (10) (11) Smooth, savoury red made from NEGROAMARO, from the heel of Italy. AZIENDA MONACI and CS Copertino are gd producers.

Coppo Pie ★★→★★★ Top producers of BARBERA D'ASTI (Pomorosso and RISERVA della Famiglia). Also excellent CHARD Monteriolo and sparkling Riserva del Fondatore.

Cortese di Gavi Pie *See* GAVI. (Cortese is the grape.)

Cortona Tus Tuscan DOC contiguous to MONTEPULCIANO VINO NOBILE. Various red and white grapes; gd wines incl Avignonesi's Desiderio, a Bordeaux blend, and first-rate SYRAH from Luigi d'Alessandro, Il Castagno, *La Braccesca*.

CS (Cantina Sociale) Cooperative winery.

Cubi, Valentina Ven ★★→★★★ Valentina Cubi lends her name to this fine small estate, making AMARONE of individuality and breeding and VALPOLICELLA CLASSICO of charm and complexity. Her enologist is her husband, Giancarlo Vason, one of Italy's best wine chemists.

Looking for more information on grapes? Try the "Grapes" section on pp.16–26.

Curtefranca Lom DOC name for what used to be called Terre di Franciacorta (since 2008) – ie. still wines of FRANCIACORTA made from a mixture of mainly international grapes, usually playing second fiddle to DOCG Franciacorta sparklers.

Dal Forno, Romano Ven ★★★★ V. high-quality VALPOLICELLA, AMARONE and RECIOTO grower whose perfectionism is the more remarkable for the fact that his v'yds are outside the CLASSICO zone.

Dei ★★→★★★ Pianist Caterina Dei runs this aristocratic and elegant estate in MONTEPULCIANO, making VINO NOBILES with artistry and passion. Her *chef d'oeuvre* is Nobile di Montepulciano Bossona.

Di Majo Norante Mol ★★→★★★ Lone star of Molise, south of Abruzzo, with v.gd Biferno Rosso, Ramitello, Don Luigi Molise Rosso RISERVA and Molise AGLIANICO Contado, white blend FALANGHINA-GRECO Biblos and MOSCATO PASSITO Apianae.

DOC/DOCG Quality wine designation: *see* box, p.155.

Dogliani Pie DOCG r ★→★★★ 06 07 08 09 10 (11) One of three DOCG DOLCETTOS from PIEDMONT, the others being Diano d'ALBA and Ovada. Some versions for drinking young, others for moderate ageing. All subject to being trumped by mere DOC Dolcetto d'Alba. Gd producers: Marziano Abbona, Osvaldo Barbaris, Francesco Boschis, Chionetti, Einaudi, Pecchenino (Dogliani); Abrigo Fratelli, Alario, Bricco Maiolica, Renzo Castella, Poderi Sinaglio, Prandi (Diano d'Alba); Bondi, Carlotta e Rivarola, Gaggino (Ovada).

Donato d'Angelo Bas ★★★ Donato d'Angelo was previously known as Casa Vinicola d'Angelo. A wine bought under the old name risks not being made by this long-established wizard of AGLIANICO DEL VULTURE. A complex family dispute, but buyers need only remember to seek the whole name, "Donato d'Angelo".

Donnafugata Si r w ★★→★★★ Well-crafted Sicilian wines of Contessa Entellina DOC: top reds are Mille e Una Notte and Tancredi; top whites Chiaranda and Vigna di Gabri. Also v. fine MOSCATO PASSITO di PANTELLERIA Ben Rye.

Duca di Salaparuta Si ★★ Aka Vini Corvo. Once on the list of every trattoria in Christendom, the Corvo brand has given way to more upmarket wines like the reds Passo delle Mule and Lavico (and of course, old favourite Duca Enrico), plus whites Kados and Valguarnero.

Elba Tus r w (sp) ★→★★ DYA. The island's white, based on Ansonica and TREBBIANO, can be v. drinkable with fish. Dry reds are based on SANGIOVESE. Gd sweet white (MOSCATO) and red (*Aleatico Passito DOCG*). Gd producers: Acquabona, Sapereta.

Elena Walch T-AA ★★→★★★ After marrying producer Werner Walch, Elena turned from architecture to wine, making quintessential cru AA wines, such as GEWURZ Kastelaz and LAGREIN RISERVA Castel Ringberg.

Eloro Si DOC r p ★→★★ (r) 06 08 09 10 (11) Robust, satisfying reds (mainly) from the southeast corner of SICILY, based on NERO D'AVOLA, Frappato and Pignatello. Eloro Pachino is from a zone that makes structured reds. Cantina La Elorina is gd.

Enoteca Wine library; also wine shop or restaurant with extensive wine list. There is a national enoteca at the *fortezza* in Siena.

Esino Mar DOC r w ★→★★★ (r) 04 05 06 07 08 09 (10) (11) The alternative denomination of VERDICCHIO country, which allows 50% of other grapes to be added to Verdicchio for Bianco and 40% international grapes with SANGIOVESE/MONTEPULCIANO for Rosso. Top-quality red from MONTE SCHIAVO (Adeodato) and Belisario (Colferraio).

Est! Est!! Est!!! Lat DOC w dr s/sw ★ DYA. Unextraordinary white wine from Montefiascone, north of Rome. Trades on the improbable origin of its name. Best is FALESCO.

Etna Si DOC r p w ★★⌀★★★ (r) 04 05 06 07 08 09 (10) (11) Wine from volcanic slopes and often considerable altitude. Etna's v'yds went into steep decline in the 20th century, but new money has brought a flurry of planting and some excellent wines, rather in the style of burgundy, though based on NERELLO MASCALESE (r) and CARRICANTE (w). Gd producers: Benanti, Calcagno, Il Cantante, Cottanera, Terre Nere, *Passopisciaro*, Girolamo Russo, *Barone di Villagrande*, Nicosia.

Falchini Tus ★★→★★★ Producer of gd DOCG VERNACCIA DI SAN GIMIGNANO (Vigna a Solatio and oaked Ab Vinea Doni), plus a top Bordeaux blend Campora and a SANGIOVESE-based Paretaio. Recently deceased proprietor Riccardo Falchini was a champion of fine SAN GIMIGNANO. He is ably succeeded by his half-American children.

Falerno del Massico Cam ★★→★★★ DOC r w ★★ (r) 04 06 07 08 09 (10) (11) Falernum was the best-known wine of ancient times, probably sweet white. Today elegant red from AGLIANICO, fruity dry white from FALANGHINA. Best: VILLA MATILDE, Amore Perrotta, Felicia, Moio, Trabucco.

Falesco Lat ★★→★★★ Estate of Cotarella brothers, v.gd MERLOT Montiano and CAB SAUV Marciliano (both ★★★). Gd red IGT Vitiano and DOC EST! EST!! EST!!!

Fara Pie *See* GATTINARA.

Farnese Ab ★★ Gd-quality supplier of the Abruzzi's favourites, esp MONTEPULCIANO D'ABRUZZO, Colline Teramane, RISERVA Opis, Pecorino (w), Edizione (r).

Faro Si DOC r ★★★ 04' 06' 07' 08 09 (10) (11) Intense, elegant red from NERELLO MASCALESE and Nerello Cappuccio grown in the hills behind Messina. Palari, the major producer, administered the kiss of life when extinction seemed likely.

Fazi-Battaglia Mar ★★ Prolific producer of VERDICCHIO, best-known for amphora-bottle Titulus (2.5 million bottles). Also Massaccio, Le Moie, San Sisto. Owns Fassati (VINO NOBILE DI MONTEPULCIANO).

Felluga, Livio F-VG ★★★ Consistently fine COLLI ORIENTALI DEL FRIULI wines, esp blends Terre Alte and Illivio, also *Pinot Gr*, SAUV BL, FRIULANO, PICOLIT and MERLOT/REFOSCO blend Sossó.

Felluga, Marco F-VG ★★→★★★ The prolific brother of Livio owns a négociant house bearing his name, plus Russiz SUPERIORE in COLLIO DOC, Castello di Buttrio in COLLI ORIENTALI DOC. From Russiz Superiore come yardstick varietals FRIULANO, PINOT GRIGIO and SAUV BL.

Italy's lesser-known grapes
The appetite of Italian producers for reviving almost-extinct grape varieties is endless. Award yourself one glass of wine for each of these (all bottled, though usually blended) that you've heard of, two if you've tasted them: Pelaverga Piccolo, Foglia Tonda, Longanesi, Malbo Gentile, Pelara, Dindarella (all red); Drupeggio, Procanico, Ortrugo, Verdeca, Nascetta Bianca, Spergola, Dorona (white). The last is the easiest: grown in the Venetian lagoon (on an island, obviously) by Prosecco producer BISOL.

Felsina Tus ★★★ Giuseppe Mazzocolin has run this CHIANTI CLASSICO estate for 30 yrs: classic RISERVA Rancia and IGT Fontalloro, both 100% SANGIOVESE. Also gd CHARD, I Sistri and Castello di Farnetella, gd Chianti Colli Senesi.

Ferrari T-AA ★★→★★★ Trento-based maker of the best METODO CLASSICO wines outside of FRANCIACORTA. Giulio Ferrari is top cru, also gd are CHARD-based Brut RISERVA Lunelli and PINOT N-based Extra Brut Perle' Nero.

Feudi di San Gregorio Cam ★★→★★★ Much-hyped CAMPANIA producer, with DOCGS TAURASI Piano di Montevergine, FIANO di Avellino Pietracalda, GRECO DI TUFO Cutizzi. Also IGT reds Serpico (AGLIANICO), Patrimo (MERLOT), plus whites *Falanghina* and Campanaro.

Florio Si Historic quality producer of MARSALA. Best wine: Marsala Vergine Secco Baglio Florio. Best name: Terre Arse (burnt lands).

Folonari Tus Ambrogio Folonari and son Giovanni split off from brothers and cousins at RUFFINO to create their own house. They continue to make *Cabreo* (a CHARD and a SANGIOVESE/CAB SAUV), wines of NOZZOLE (incl top Cab Sauv Pareto), BRUNELLO DI MONTALCINO La Fuga, VINO NOBILE DI MONTEPULCIANO Gracciano Svetoni, plus wines from BOLGHERI, MONTECUCCO and COLLI ORIENTALI DEL FRIULI.

Fontana Candida Lat ★★ One of the biggest producers of FRASCATI. Single-v'yd Santa Teresa stands out. *See also* GRUPPO ITALIANO VINI.

Fontanafredda Pie ★★ →★★★ Large, much-improved producer of PIEDMONT wines on former royal estates, incl BAROLO Serralunga and Barolo crus Lazzarito Mirafiore and Vigna La Rosa. Excellent LANGHE NEBBIOLO Mirafiore. Plus ALBA DOCS and sparklers dry (Contessa Rosa Pas Dosè) and sweet (ASTI).

Fonterutoli Tus ★★★ Historic CHIANTI CLASSICO estate of the Mazzei family at Castellina with space-age new CANTINA. Notable are Castello di Fonterutoli (dark, oaky CHIANTI), IGT Siepi (SANGIOVESE/MERLOT). The family also owns Tenuta di Belguardo in MAREMMA, gd MORELLINO DI SCANSANO and IGT wines.

Fontodi Tus ★★★→★★★★ Giovanni Manetti runs this outstanding family estate at Panzano, making one of the absolute best straight CHIANTI CLASSICOS, RISERVA Vigna del Sorbo as well as a classic, pure-SANGIOVESE IGT Flaccianello, one of Italy's greatest wines. IGTs PINOT N and SYRAH Case Via are among the best of those varietals in TUSCANY.

Foradori T-AA ★★★ Elizabetta Foradori has, for 30 yrs, been one of the pioneering spirits of Italian viniculture, mainly via the great red variety of TRENTINO, TEROLDEGO. Currently she is experimenting with vinification in *anfora* (amphora) for reds like Morei and whites like Manzoni Bianco Fontanasanta. Peak of production remains Teroldego-based Granato.

Fossi, Enrico Tus ★★★ Enterprising Tuscan producer specializing in international varietals: MERLOT, CAB SAUV, SYRAH, PINOT N, GAMAY, MALBEC, SAUV BL, CHARD, RIES, PINOT BL and SANGIOVESE.

Franciacorta Lom DOCG w (p) sp ★★→★★★★★ Italy's major production zone for top-quality METODO CLASSICO sparkling. Best producers: Barone Pizzini, BELLAVISTA, CA'

DEL BOSCO, Castellino, Cavalleri, Gatti, Uberti, Villa. Also v.gd: Contadi Gastaldi, Monte Rossa, Il Mosnel, Ricci Curbastri. For still white and red, *see* CURTEFRANCA.

Frascati Lat DOC w dr sw s/sw (sp) ★→★★ DYA. Best-known wine of Roman hills: should be limpid, golden, tasting of whole grapes. Most is disappointingly neutral: look for Castel de Paolis, Conte Zandotti, Villa Simone, or Santa Teresa from FONTANA CANDIDA. The sweet version is known as Cannellino.

Freisa d'Asti Pie DOC r dr sw s/sw (sp) ★→★★★ Two distinct styles: frivolous, maybe FRIZZANTE, maybe sweetish; or serious, dry and tannic for ageing (so follow BAROLO vintages). Best of serious producers: Brezza, Cigliuti, CLERICO, ALDO CONTERNO, COPPO, Franco Martinetti, GIUSEPPE MASCARELLO, Parusso, Pecchenino, Pelissero, Sebaste, Trinchero, VAJRA, VOERZIO.

Frescobaldi Tus ★★→★★★★ Ancient noble family, leading CHIANTI RÙFINA pioneer at NIPOZZANO estate (look for **Montesodi** ★★★), also BRUNELLO from CASTELGIOCONDO estate in MONTALCINO. Sole owners of LUCE estate in MONTALCINO and ORNELLAIA in BOLGHERI. V'yds also in MAREMMA, Montespertoli and COLLIO.

Friulano F-VG ★→★★ Varietal wine of Friuli grape, which used to be called Tocai FRIULANO (aka Sauvignonasse or Sauvignon Vert), the "Tocai" part having disappeared due to pressure from Hungary. Fresh, pungent, subtly floral whites, best from COLLIO, ISONZO and COLLI ORIENTALI. Gd producers: BORGO DEL TIGLIO, LIVIO FELLUGA, LIS NERIS, Pierpaolo Pecorari, RONCO del Gelso, Ronco del Gnemiz, Russiz SUPERIORE, SCHIOPETTO, LE VIGNE DI ZAMÒ, VILLA RUSSIZ. The new name for ex-Tocai from Veneto, by the way, is "Tai".

Veneto, Emilia-Romagna, Apulia and Sicily (ie. the northeast and south) account for 60% of Italy's wine.

Friuli-Venezia Giulia F-VG The northeast region on the Slovenian border. Several DOCs , incl ISONZO, COLLIO and COLLI ORIENTALI. Gd reds, but considered the home of Italy's most adventurous and accomplished whites.

Frizzante Semi-sparkling, eg. MOSCATO D'ASTI and most PROSECCO.

Fuligni Tus ★★★ →★★★★ Outstanding producer of BRUNELLO and ROSSO DI MONTALCINO.

Gaja Pie ★★★★ Old family firm at BARBARESCO led by Angelo Gaja, highly audible apostle of Italian wine; daughter Gaja G following. High quality, even higher prices. BARBARESCO is the only PIEDMONTESE DOCG Gaja makes after down-classing his crus Sorì Tildin, Sorì San Lorenzo and Costa Russi as well as BAROLO Sperss to LANGHE DOC so that he could add a little BARBERA to his NEBBIOLO. Splendid CHARD (Gaia e Rey), CAB SAUV Darmagi. Acquisitions elsewhere in Italy: Marengo-Marenda estate (Barolo), commercial Gromis label; Pieve di Santa Restituta in MONTALCINO; CA' MARCANDA in BOLGHERI.

Galardi Cam ★★★ Producer of Terra di Lavoro, a highly touted blend of AGLIANICO and Piedirosso, in north CAMPANIA.

Gancia Pie Once-famous ASTI house also producing dry sparkling, today living mainly on past glory.

Garda Ven DOC r p w ★→★★ (r) 06 07 08 09 (10) (11) (w p) DYA. Catch-all DOC for early-drinking wines of various colours from provinces of Verona in Veneto, Brescia and Mantua in Lombardy. Gd producers are Cavalchina, Zeni.

Garofoli Mar ★★→★★★ The quality leader in the Marches region, specializing in VERDICCHIO (Podium, Macrina and Serra Fiorese) and ROSSO CONERO (Piancarda and Grosso Agontano).

Gattinara Pie DOCG r ★★→★★★ 99' 00 01' 04' 06 07' 08 (09) (10) (11) Best-known of a cluster of northern PIEDMONTESE DOC(G)s based on NEBBIOLO. Best producers: Travaglini, Antoniolo, Bianchi, Nervi, Torraccia del Piantavigna. Similar DOC(G)s of the zone: GHEMME, BOCA, BRAMATERRA, COLLINE NOVARESI, Costa della Sesia, FARA, LESSONA, SIZZANO; none of which, sadly, measure up to BAROLO/BARBARESCO at their best.

Gavi / Cortese di Gavi Pie DOCG w ★→★★★ DYA. At best, subtle dry white of Cortese grapes. Most comes from commune of Gavi, hence Gavi di Gavi. Best: Broglia, Cascina degli Ulivi, Castellari Bergaglio, Castello di Tassarolo, CHIARLO, La Giustiniana, Franco Martinetti, Podere Saulino, Toledana, Villa Sparina.

Ghemme Pie Pie DOCG *See* GATTINARA.

Giacosa, Bruno Pie ★★→★★★★ Considered Italy's greatest winemaker by some, this brooding genius suffered a stroke in 2006, but goes on crafting outstanding traditional-style BARBARESCOS (Asili, Santo Stefano) and BAROLOS (Falletto, Rocche di Falletto). Top wines (ie. RISERVAS) get famous red label. Also makes a range of fine reds (DOLCETTO, NEBBIOLO, BARBERA), whites (ARNEIS) and an amazing METODO CLASSICO Brut.

Grappa Pungent and potent spirit made from grape pomace (skins, etc., after pressing). Can be anything from disgusting to inspirational. What the French call "marc".

Grasso, Elio Pie ★★★→★★★★ Top BAROLO producer (crus Vigna Chiniera, Casa Maté); v.gd BARBERA D'ALBA Vigna Martina, DOLCETTO D'ALBA and CHARD Educato.

Grave del Friuli F-VG DOC r w ★→★★ (r) 06 07 08 09 10 11 Largest DOC of FRIULI-VENEZIA GIULIA, mostly on plains, giving important volumes of underwhelming wines. Exceptions from Borgo Magredo, Di Lenardo, Plozner, RONCO Cliona, San Simone, Villa Chiopris.

Gravner, Josko F-VG ★★★ Controversial COLLIO producer, believing in maceration on skins and long ageing in wood or amphora for whites. His wines are either loved for their complexity or loathed for their oxidation and phenolic profile. Expensive and hard to find.

Looking for more information on grapes? Try the "Grapes" section on pp.16–26.

Greco di Tufo Cam DOCG w (sp) ★★→★★★ DYA One of the best white wines of the south – fruity, slightly citric in flavour and at best age-worthy. V.gd examples from Caggiano, Caputo, Benito Ferrara, FEUDI DI SAN GREGORIO, LA GUARDIENSE, Macchialupa, *Mastroberardino* (Nova Serra and Vignadangelo), Vesevo, Villa Raiano.

Grevepesa Tus CHIANTI CLASSICO co-op – quality slowly rising.

Grignolino Pie DOC r ★ DYA lively light red of ASTI zone, for drinking young. Best: BRAIDA, Marchesi Incisa della Rocchetta. Also, G del Monferrato Casalese DOC (Accornero, Bricco Mondalino, La Tenaglia).

Gruppo Italiano Vini (GIV) Complex of co-ops and wineries, biggest v'yd holders in Italy. Estates incl Bigi, BOLLA, Ca'Bianca, Conti Serristori, FOLONARI, FONTANA CANDIDA, Lamberti, Macchiavelli, MELINI, Negri, Santi, Vignaioli di San Floriano. Has also expanded into south: SICILY and Basilicata.

Guardiense, la Cam ★★ Dynamic co-op, 1,000 grower-members, 2,000ha v'yd, turning out better-than-average whites and reds at lower-than-average prices under the technical direction of Riccardo Cotarella.

Guerrieri Rizzardi ★★ Long-established, noble producers of the wines of Verona, esp of Veronese GARDA. Gd BARDOLINO Classico Tacchetto, AMARONE Villa Rizzardi and ROSATO Rosa Rosae. Respectable SOAVE Classico Costeggiiola.

Gutturnio dei Colli Piacentini E-R DOC r dr ★→★★ DYA. BARBERA/BONARDA blend from the hills of Piacenza. Producers: Castelli del Duca, La Stoppa, La Tosa.

Haas, Franz T-AA ★★★ ALTO ADIGE producer, v.gd PINOT N, LAGREIN (Schweizer) and IGT blends, esp the white Manna.

Hofstätter T-AA ★★★ ALTO ADIGE producer of top PINOT N. Look for Barthenau Vigna Sant'Urbano, LAGREIN, CAB SAUV/PETIT VERDOT, GEWURZ.

Indicazione Geografica Tipica (IGT) *See* box, p.155.

Ischia Cam DOC (r) w ★→★★ DYA. The island off Naples, with its own grape varieties (eg. Forastera, Biancolella). Wines are sold mainly to tourists. Top producer is D'Ambra (Biancolella Frassitelli, Forastera Euposia). Also gd: Il Giardino Mediterraneo, Pietratorcia.

Isole e Olena Tus ★★★→★★★★ Top CHIANTI CLASSICO estate run by astute Paolo de Marchi, with superb red IGT Cepparello. V.gd VIN SANTO, CAB SAUV, CHARD, SYRAH. Also own Sperino in Lessona (*see* GATTINARA).

Isonzo F-VG DOC r w ★★★ Gravelly, well-aired plain of FRIULI Isonzo, a multi-DOC area covering many red and white varietals and blends. The stars are mostly white, scented and structured, such VIE DI ROMANS' Flors di Uis and LIS NERIS' Fiore de Campo. Also gd: Borgo Conventi, Pierpaolo Pecorari, RONCO del Gelso.

Jermann, Silvio F-VG ★★→★★★ Famous estate with v'yds in COLLIO and ISONZO. Top white blend Vintage Tunina, oak-aged blend Capo Martino and CHARD, ex-"Dreams".

Kante, Edi F-VG ★★→★★★ Leading light of FRIULI's Carso; fine DOC CHARD, SAUV BL, MALVASIA; gd red *Terrano*.

Lacrima di Morro d'Alba Mar DYA. Curiously named MUSCATTY light red from a small commune in the Marches, no connection with ALBA or La Morra in PIEDMONT. Gd producers: Mancinelli, MONTE SCHIAVO.

Lacryma (or Lacrima) Christi del Vesuvio Cam r p w dr (sw sp) ★→★★ DOC VESUVIO wines based on Coda di Volpe (w) and Piedirosso (r). Alas, despite the romantic name, Vesuvius comes nowhere nr Etna in the quality stakes. Caputo, De Angelis and MASTROBERARDINO produce uninspired wines.

Lageder, Alois T-AA ★★→★★★ Top ALTO ADIGE producer. The most exciting wines are single-v'yd varietals: *Sauv Bl Lehenhof*, PINOT GR Benefizium Porer, CHARD Löwengang, GEWÜRZ Am Sand, PINOT N Krafuss, LAGREIN Lindenberg, CAB SAUV Cor Römigberg. Also owns Cason Hirschprunn for v.gd IGT blends.

Lago di Corbara Umb r ★★ 06' 07' 08 09 (10) (11) Relatively recent DOC for quality reds of the ORVIETO area. Best from Barberani (Villa Monticelli) and Decugnano dei Barbi.

Lagrein Alto Adige T-AA DOC r p ★★→★★★ 04' 06' 07' 08 09 (10) (11) Plummy reds with bitter finish from the LAGREIN grape. Best growing zone is Gries, Bolzano suburb. Best producers incl: Colterenzio co-op, Gojer, Gries co-op, HAAS, HOFSTÄTTER, LAGEDER, Laimburg, Josephus Mayr, Thomas Mayr, MURI GRIES, NALS MARGREID, Niedermayr, Niedrist, St-Magdalena, TERLANO co-op, and TIEFENBRUNNER.

Laimburg, Cantina T-AA ★★→★★★ ALTO ADIGE's regional research institute also boasts a respected commercial branch making quality Alto Adige DOC varietals, esp GEWURZ Elyond and LAGREIN RISERVA Barbagol.

Lambruschi Lig ★★ Nothing to do with LAMBRUSCO, this is by a margin LIGURIA's most exciting VERMENTINO, Sartiocola, made by still-sprightly octogenarian Ottaviano Lambruschi from grapes grown on the rocky slopes of Ortonovo nr the TUSCAN border. Also a tasty Rosso Colli di Luni, Maniero.

Lambrusco E-R DOC (or not) r p w dr s/sw ★→★★ DYA. Once extremely popular fizzy red from nr Modena, mainly in industrial, semi-sweet, non-DOC version. Sometimes vinified blanc de noirs. Best is Secco, bottle-fermented or in tank. DOCS: L Grasparossa di Castelvetro, L Salamino di Santa Croce, L di Sorbara. Best: Bellei, Caprari, Casali, CAVICCHIOLI, Graziano, Lini Oreste, Medici Ermete (esp Concerto), Rinaldo Rinaldini, Venturini Baldini.

Langhe Pie The hills of central PIEDMONT, home of BAROLO, BARBARESCO, etc. DOC name for six Piedmontese varietals plus blends Bianco and Rosso. Those wishing to blend other grapes with their NEBBIOLO, such as GAJA, can do so at up to 15% as "Langhe Nebbiolo".

Le Potazzine Tus ★★★ The husband-and-wife team named their BRUNELLO and ROSSO DI MONTALCINO after their two little birds (two daughters) when they started at this lofty site just south of MONTALCINO in the 1990s. The wines, too, have grown in stature and today attract widespread admiration. All may be found at the family's tasty restaurant in the centre of Montalcino.

Le Pupille Tus ★★★ Top producer of MORELLINO DI SCANSANO, also excellent IGT blend Saffredi (CAB SAUV/MERLOT/SYRAH/Alicante).

Lessona Pie *See* GATTINARA.

Librandi Cal ★★★ Top Calabria producer pioneering research into Calabrian varieties. V.gd red CIRÒ (*Riserva Duca San Felice* is ★★★), IGT Gravello (CAB SAUV/Gaglioppo blend), Magno Megonio (r) from Magliocco grape and IGT Efeso (w) from Mantonico grape. Other local varieties in experimental phase.

Liguria Lig The Italian riviera is rocky, but viticulture is rewarding: most wines sell to sun-struck tourists at fat profits, so don't travel much. Main grapes: VERMENTINO (w) – best grape is LAMBRUSCHI – and DOLCETTO (r), but don't miss CINQUE TERRE's SCIACCHETRÀ or red PORNASSIO (ORMEASCO DI).

Lisini Tus ★★★→★★★★ Historic estate for some of the finest and longest-lasting BRUNELLO, esp RISERVA Ugolaia.

Lis Neris F-VG ★★★ Top ISONZO estate for gd whites, esp PINOT GR, CHARD (Jurosa), SAUV BL (Picol), FRIULANO (Fiore di Campo), plus blends Confini and Lis. Also v.gd Lis Neris Rosso (MERLOT/CAB SAUV) and sweet white Tal Luc (VERDUZZO/RIES).

Lison DOCG w ★ DYA. Veneto version of, and generally outclassed by, FRIULI's FRIULANO, both having lost right to use historic name Tocai.

Livon F-VG ★★→★★★ Substantial COLLIO producer, also some COLLI ORIENTALI wines like VERDUZZO. Expanded into the CHIANTI CLASSICO and MONTEFALCO DOCGS.

Loacker T-AA ★★→★★★ Biodynamic (and homeopathic) producer of ALTO ADIGE wines, installed in TUSCANY and making fine BRUNELLO and ROSSO DI MONTALCINO under the Corte Pavone label, plus gd MORELLINO DI SCANSANO Valdifalco.

Locorotondo Ap DOC w (sp) ★ DYA Thirst-quenching dry white from APULIA's Verdeca and Bianco d'Alessano varieties, much quaffed *in situ* by vacationing *trulli*-seekers; little sought back home.

Luce Tus ★★★ FRESCOBALDI is sole owner of this marketing exercise in hyperbole and high price, having bought out original partner Mondavi. The wine is a SANGIOVESE/MERLOT blend designed for Russian oligarchs.

Lugana DOC w (sp) ★→★★ DYA. Occasionally complex white of southern Lake GARDA, main grape TREBBIANO di Lugana (= VERDICCHIO, possibly). Dry and sappy. Best: CA' DEI FRATI, ZENATO, Zeni.

Lungarotti Umb ★★★ Leading producer of TORGIANO, with cellars, hotel and museum, nr Perugia. Star wine DOCG RISERVA *Rubesco*. Gd IGT Sangiorgio (SANGIOVESE/CAB SAUV), Aurente (CHARD), Giubilante. Gd MONTEFALCO SAGRANTINO.

Macchiole, le Tus ★★★ Eugenio Campolmi's widow, Cinzia, with the help of enologist Luca d'Attoma, continues his fine work with CAB FR (Paleo Rosso) and MERLOT (Messorio), as well as SYRAH (Scrio).

Maculan Ven ★★★ Excellent CAB SAUV (Fratta, Ferrata), CHARD (Ferrata), MERLOT (Marchesante) and TORCOLATO (esp RISERVA Acininobili).

Malenchini Tus ★★ Estate of long-standing Florentine family (from their balcony you can see the Duomo) making honest, simple CHIANTI and more complex Chianti Colli Fiorentini, plus SUPER TUSCAN Bruzzico.

Malvasia delle Lipari DOC w sw ★★★ Luscious sweet wine, from MALVASIA grape, from fascinating island off SICILIAN coast.

Mancini, Fattoria Mar ★★ Family estate on the sea nr Pesaro. *Remarkable Pinot N* (r w), fresh white Albanella and strange Ancellota red called Blu.

Manduria (Primitivo di) Ap DOC r s/sw ★★→★★★ PRIMITIVO's many producers incl Cantele, de Castris, Polvanera, RACEMI and CS Manduria.

Marchesi di Barolo Pie ★★ Historic, perhaps original BAROLO producer, in commune of Barolo, making crus Cannubi and Sarmassa, plus other ALBA wines.

Marchesi di Grésy, (Cisa Asinari) Pie ★★★ Consistent, sometimes inspired producer of traditional-style BARBARESCO (crus Gaiun and Camp Gros). Also v.gd SAUV BL, CHARD, MOSCATO D'ASTI, BARBERA D'ASTI.

Maremma Tus Fashionable coastal area of southern TUSCANY, esp province of Grosseto. DOCS incl MONTEREGIO, MORELLINO DI SCANSANO, PARRINA, Pitigliano, SOVANA (Grosseto). Lavish recent investment. Maremma Toscana IGT has recently given way to Maremma Toscana DOC.

Marsala Si DOC w sw SICILY's once-famous fortified wine (★→★★★), invented by Woodhouse Bros from Liverpool in 1773. In the 20th century it deteriorated to the level of cooking wine, and though such qualities no longer qualify for DOC status, the image remains low. Several versions from dry to very sweet, the best is bone-dry Marsala Vergine, potentially a highly valid apéritif if desperately unfashionable. *See also* VECCHIO SAMPERI.

Marzemino Trentino T-AA DOC r ★→★★★ 06 07 08 09 10 (11) Pleasant everyday red, fruity and slightly bitter. Esp from Bossi Fedrigotti, CA' VIT, De Tarczal, Gaierhof, Letrari, Longariva, Simoncelli, E Spagnolli, Vallarom.

Mascarello Pie The name of two top producers of BAROLO: Bartolo Mascarello (deceased), whose daughter, Maria Teresa, continues her father's highly traditional path. And Giuseppe Mascarello, of Monchiero, whose son, Mauro, makes superior, traditional-style Barolo from the great Monprivato v'yd in Castiglione Falletto. Beware other Mascarellos.

Masi Ven ★★→★★★★ Exponent/researcher of VALPOLICELLA, AMARONE, RECIOTO, SOAVE, etc., incl fine Rosso Veronese Campo Fiorin and Amarone-style wines from FRIULI and Argentina. V.gd barrel-aged red IGT *Toar*, from CORVINA and Oseleta grapes, also Osar (Oseleta). Top Amarones Mazzano and Campolongo di Torbe.

Massa, la Tus ★★★ Giampaolo Motta is a Bordeaux-lover making increasingly claret-like IGT wines with a TUSCAN accent (La Massa, Giorgio Primo), from CAB SAUV, MERLOT and SANGIOVESE, at his fine estate in Panzano in CHIANTI CLASSICO, which denomination he has abandoned.

Mastroberardino Cam ★★→★★★★ Historic producer of mountainous Avellino province in CAMPANIA, quality torch-bearer for Italy's south during dark yrs of mid-20th century. Top *Taurasi* (look for Historia Naturalis and Radici), also Fiano di Avellino. More Maiorum and GRECO DI TUFO Nova Serra.

Matura, Gruppo A group of agronomists and enologists headed by Alberto Antonini and Attilio Pagli, helping producers not only throughout TUSCANY but elsewhere in the country – and indeed, the world.

The Maremma: beside the seaside

Names to look for in the Maremma (for IGT**):** Ampeleia, Belguardo, La Carletta, Casina, Col di Bacche, Fattoria di Magliano, Lhosa, La Marietta, Marsiliana, Monteti, MORIS FARMS, Montebelli, LA PARRINA, Poderi di Ghiaccioforte, POGGIO Argentiera, Poggio Foco, Poggio al Lupo, Poggio Paoli, Poggio Verrano, Rascioni e Cecconello, Rocca di Frasinello, San Matteo, Sassotondo, La Selva, Solomaremma, Suveraia.

For MORELLINO DI SCANSANO**:** *Belguardo*, La Carletta, Fattoria di Magliano, *Mantellasi*, Masi di Mandorlaia, *Moris Farms*, Podere 414, Poderi di Ghiaccioforte, POGGIO Argentiera, Poggio al Lupo, Poggio Paoli, *Le Pupille*, Roccapesta, San Matteo, La Selva, Cantina di Scansano, Terre di Talamo and Vignaioli del Morellino di Scansano.

Melini Tus ★★ Major CHIANTI CLASSICO producer at Poggibonsi, part of GIV. Gd quality/ price, esp Chianti Classico Selvanella and RISERVAS La Selvanella, Masovecchio.

Metodo classico or tradizionale Italian for "Champagne method", as that phraseology is not permitted.

Mezzacorona T-AA ★✍★★ Massive TRENTINO co-op in the commune of Mezzocorona (spot the difference) with a wide range of gd technical wines, esp TEROLDEGO ROTALIANO Nos and METODO CLASSICO Rotari.

Monferrato Pie DOC r p w sw ★→★★ Hills between river Po and Apennines, bringing forth wines of mostly everyday-drinking style rather than of serious intent.

Monica di Sardegna Sar DOC r ★→★★ DYA. The mainstay of SARDINIA: light, dry red.

Monsanto Tus ★★★ Esteemed CHIANTI CLASSICO estate, esp for Il POGGIO RISERVA (first single-v'yd Chianti Classico), Chianti Classico Riserva and IGTS Fabrizio Bianchi (CHARD) and Nemo (CAB SAUV).

Montalcino Tus Small town in province of Siena, famous for concentrated, expensive BRUNELLO and more approachable, better-value ROSSO DI MONTALCINO.

Montecarlo Tus DOC r w ★★ (w) DYA. White, and increasingly red, wine area nr Lucca. Producers incl: Buonamico, Carmignani, Fattoria del Teso, La Torre, Montechiari.

The oldest bottle labelled Amarone – a wine style dating back to the Romans – dates from 1939.

Montecucco Tus SANGIOVESE-based TUSCAN DOC between Monte Amiata and Grosseto, increasingly trendy as MONTALCINO land prices ineluctably rise. As Montecucco Sangiovese it is DOCG. Look out for CASTELLO DI POTENTINO (Sacromonte, Piropo), also Begnardi, Ciacci Piccolomini, Colli Massari, Fattoria di Montecucco, Villa Patrizia. Much investment by the likes of FOLONARI, MASI, Pertimali, Riecine and Talenti.

Montefalco Sagrantino Umb DOCG r dr (sw) ★★★→★★★★ Super-tannic, powerful, long-lasting wines, till recently thought potentially great, today undergoing re-evaluation owing to difficulty of taming the phenolics without denaturing the wine. Traditional bittersweet PASSITO version may be better suited to the grape profile, though little market. Gd: Adanti, Antonelli, Paolo Bea, Benincasa, CAPRAI, Colpetrone, LUNGAROTTI, Tabarrini, Terre de' Trinci.

Montepulciano d'Abruzzo Ab DOC r p ★★→★★★ (r) 06 07 08 09 10 11 Gd-value, full-flavoured red and zesty, savoury pink (CERASUOLO) from grapes of this name grown in the Adriatic region east of Rome. Dominated by co-ops, gd ones incl Citra, Miglianico, Roxan, Tollo. There are also some excellent private producers, incl Cornacchia, Contesa, Illuminati, Marramiero, Masciarelli, Contucci Ponno, Pepe, La Valentina, VALENTINI, Zaccagnini. Not to be confused with TUSCAN town where VINO NOBILE DI MONTEPULCIANO comes from.

Monteregio Tus DOC nr Massa Marittima in MAREMMA, gd SANGIOVESE and CAB SAUV (r) and VERMENTINO (w) wines from MORIS FARMS, Tenuta del Fontino et al. Big-name investors (ANTINORI, BELLAVISTA, Eric de Rothschild of Château Lafite, ZONIN) have been attracted by the relatively low land prices, but the DOC has yet to establish itself market-wise.

Monte Schiavo Mar ★★→★★★ Switched-on, medium-size producer of VERDICCHIO and MONTEPULCIANO-based wines of various qualities, owned by world's largest manufacturer of olive-oil processing equipment, Pieralisi. V'yd holdings also in Abruzzo and APULIA.

Montescudaio Tus DOC r w ★★ Modest DOC between Pisa and Livorno; best are SANGIOVESE or Sangiovese/CAB SAUV blends. Try Merlini, Poggio Gagliardo, La Regola, Sorbaiano.

Montevertine Tus ★★★ Radda estate. Non-DOCG but classic CHIANTI-style wines. IGT *Le Pergole Torte* a fine, pioneering example of pure, long-ageing SANGIOVESE.

Montevetrano Cam ★★★ Iconic CAMPANIA AZIENDA, wine supervised by consultant Riccardo Cotarella. Superb IGT Montevetrano (CAB SAUV, MERLOT, AGLIANICO).

Morellino di Scansano Tus DOCG r ★→★★★ 06 07 08 09 10 (11) Recently, and somewhat mystifyingly, promoted SANGIOVESE-based red from the MAREMMA. Used to be relatively light and simple, now, regrettably, gaining weight and substance, perhaps to justify its lofty status. For producers, *see* box, p.141.

Moris Farms Tus ★★★ One of the first of the new-age producers of TUSCANY'S MAREMMA, with MONTEREGIO and *Morellino di Scansano* DOCS, plus VERMENTINO IGT. Top cru is the now iconic IGT Avvoltore, a rich SANGIOVESE/CAB SAUV/SYRAH blend. But try the basic Morellino.

Moscato d'Asti Pie DOCG w sw sp ★★→★★★ DYA Similar to DOCG ASTI, but usually better grapes; lower alcohol, sweeter, fruitier, often from small producers. Best DOCG MOSCATO: L'Armangia, BERA, BRAIDA, Ca'd'Gal, Cascina Fonda, Cascina Pian d'Oro, Caudrina, Il Falchetto, Forteto della Luja, *Marchesi di Grésy*, Icardi, Isolabella, Manfredi/Patrizi, Marino, La Morandina, Marco Negri, Elio Perrone, Rivetti, Saracco, Scagliola, VAJRA, Vietti, Vignaioli di Sante Stefano.

Murana, Salvatore Si ★★★ V.gd MOSCATO and PASSITO di PANTELLERIA.

Muri Gries T-AA ★★→★★★ This monastery, in the Bolzano suburb of Gries, is famous for LAGREIN, and is a traditional and still top producer of ALTO ADIGE DOC. Esp cru Abtei-Muri.

Nals Margreid T-AA ★★→★★★ Small but quality-oriented ALTO ADIGE co-op making mtn-fresh whites (esp PINOT BIANCO Sirmian).

Nebbiolo d'Alba Pie DOC r dr ★★→★★★ 06 07 08 09 10 (11) Two styles: full and complex, similar to BAROLO/BARBARESCO; and light, fruity and fragrant. Top examples of former from PIO CESARE, GIACOSA, G MASCARELLO, FONTANAFREDDA, PRUNOTTO, SANDRONE, VAJRA.

Negrar, Cantina Ven ★★→★★★ Aka CS Valpolicella. Under enologist Daniele Accordini, major producer of high-quality VALPOLICELLA, RIPASSO, AMARONE from grapes sourced in various parts of the CLASSICO zone. Look for the brand name Domini Veneti.

Nipozzano, Castello di Tus ★★★ FRESCOBALDI estate in RÚFINA east of Florence making excellent CHIANTI RUFINA RISERVAS Nipozzano and, esp, *Montesodi*.

Nittardi Tus ★★→★★★ Reliable source of high-quality, modern-style CHIANTI CLASSICO. Enologist Carlo Ferrini and German proprietor.

Nozzole Tus ★★→★★★ Famous estate owned by Ambrogio and Giovanni FOLONARI, in heart of CHIANTI CLASSICO, north of Greve. V.gd Chianti Classico Nozzole and excellent CAB SAUV Pareto.

Nuragus di Cagliari Sar DOC w ★★ DYA Lively, uncomplicated SARDINIAN wine from Nuragus grape.

Oasi degli Angeli Mar Benchmark all-MONTEPULCIANO wines from small producer in southern Marches; lush and mouthfilling.

Occhio di Pernice Tus A type of VIN SANTO made predominantly from black grapes, mainly SANGIOVESE. AVIGNONESI's is definitive. Also an obscure black variety found in RÚFINA and elsewhere.

Oddero Pie ★★→★★★ Traditionalist La Morra estate, gd to excellent BAROLO (Brunate, Villero) and BARBARESCO (Gallina) crus, plus other serious PIEDMONTESE wines.

Offida DOCG r w ★→★★ (w) DYA Recently upgraded from DOC, covering two characterful white grapes (PECORINO and Passerina) and one less interesting MONTEPULCIANO-based red. Gd: Aurora, Ciù Ciù, San Filippo, San Giovanni.

Oltrepò Pavese Lom DOC r w dr sw sp ★→★★★ Multi-DOC, incl numerous varietal and blended wines from Pavia province, mostly drunk in Milan. Sometimes v.gd PINOT N and SPUMANTE. Gd growers: Anteo, Barbacarlo, Casa Re, Castello di Cigognola, CS Casteggio, Le Fracce, Frecciarossa, Monsupello, Mazzolino, Ruiz de Cardenas, Travaglino, La Versa CO-op.

Ornellaia Tus ★★→★★★★ 01 04' 05 06' 07' 08 09 (10) (11) Famous estate nr BOLGHERI founded by Lodovico ANTINORI, who sold to FRESCOBALDI/Mondavi consortium, now owned solely by Frescobaldi. Top wines are of Bordeaux grapes and method: BOLGHERI DOC Ornellaia, IGT Masseto (MERLOT). Bolgheri DOC Le Serre Nuove and IGT Le Volte also gd.

Orvieto Umb DOC w dr sw s/sw ★→★★★ DYA The classic Umbrian white, from an ancient Etruscan capital. Wines comparable to Vouvray from tufaceous soil. *Secco* version is most popular today, *amabile* is more traditional. Sweet versions from noble rot (*muffa nobile*) grapes can be superb, eg. Barberani's Calcaia. Other gd producers: Bigi, Cardeto, CASTELLO DELLA SALA, Decugnano dei Barbi, La Carraia, Palazzone.

Pacenti, Siro Tus ★★★ Modern-style BRUNELLO and ROSSO DI MONTALCINO from a small, caring producer.

Pagadebit di Romagna E-R DOC w ★→★★★ DYA. So named because once, apparently, it "paid the bills". Must be 85% Bombino Bianco. Can be fresh and bright, rarely complex. Gd: Celli (Campi di Fratta), Campodelsole (San Pascasio).

Pantelleria Si Windswept, black- (volcanic) earth SICILIAN island off the Tunisian coast, noted for superb MOSCATO d'Alessandria stickies (and now tragic refugees). PASSITO versions are particularly dense/intense. Look for: Abraxas, Colosi, De Bartoli, DONNAFUGATA, MURANA.

Parrina, La Tus ★★ Large estate named after local DOC (plain "Parrina"), nr Argentario peninsula in southern MAREMMA making Parrina Bianco from a mix of grapes and Parrina Rosso from SANGIOVESE and French grapes.

Pasqua, Fratelli Ven ★→★★★ Massive producer and bottler of Verona wines: VALPOLICELLA, AMARONE, SOAVE. Also BARDOLINO, RECIOTO.

Passito Wine, often sweet, from grapes dried on trays under the sun (in the south), or indoors on trays, or hanging vertically (central and north); the process is called *appassimento*. Best-known: VIN SANTO (TUSCANY); VALPOLICELLA/SOAVE, AMARONE/RECIOTO (Veneto). *See also* MONTEFALCO, ORVIETO, TORCOLATO.

The best of Prosecco

PROSECCO (now just a wine, remember: no longer a grape) continues to boom in the market, but for how long? Prices have moved up sharply, which is nice for the growers, but even if there were something to celebrate with this Italian version of poor man's Champagne, a sharp downturn is predicted when the new v'yds, planted in their thousands of hectares following the law change, come on stream with their cheap and shoddy product. There remain gd few reliable producers, however, inc: Adami, Biancavigna, BISOL, Bortolin, Canevel, CARPENÈ-MALVOLTI, Case Bianche, Col Salice, Le Colture, Col Vetoraz, Nino Franco, Gregoletto, La Riva dei Frati, Ruggeri, Vignarosa, Zardetto.

Paternoster Bas ★★→★★★ Not a prayer but a producer of heavenly (well, pretty gd) AGLIANICO DEL VULTURE, esp Don Anselmo.

Pecorino Ab IGT Colli Pescaresi w ★★→★★★ Not a cheese but alluring dry white from a recently nr-extinct variety. Gd producers: Contesa, Franco Pasetti, FARNESE.

Piaggia Tus ★★★ Outstanding producer of CARMIGNANO RISERVA, Sasso and superb CAB FR POGGIO dei Colli, as well as of a couple of SANGIOVESE wines, Pietranera and Viti dell'Erta.

Piave Ven DOC r w ★→★★ (r) 06 07 08 09 10 (11) (w) DYA. Volume-producing DOC on plains northwest of Venice for red and white varietals. CAB SAUV, MERLOT, Raboso reds can all age. Gd: Loredan Gasparini, Molon, Villa Sandi.

Picolit F-VG DOCG w sw s/sw ★★→★★★ 04 05 06 07 08 09 (10). Somewhat mythical sweet white from COLLI ORIENTALI DEL FRIULI, might disappoint those who can a) find it and b) afford it. Gd from LIVIO FELLUGA, Meroi, Perusini, Specogna, VILLA RUSSIZ, Vinae dell'Abbazia.

Piedmont / Piemonte Pie With TUSCANY, the most important Italian region for top-quality wine. Turin is the capital, ASTI and ALBA the wine centres. No IGTS allowed; Piemonte DOC is lowest denomination, covering basic reds, whites, SPUMANTES and FRIZZANTES. Grapes incl: BARBERA, BONARDA, Brachetto, Cortese, DOLCETTO, GRIGNOLINO, CHARD, MOSCATO. *See also* BARBARESCO, BAROLO, GATTINARA, ROERO.

Pieropan Ven ★★★ The no 1 producer of SOAVE and the house that kept the quality flag flying when all others yielded to the pressures of cheap, volume production in the mid-20th century. Crus *La Rocca* and Calvarino are considered the best Soave can offer.

Pieve di Santa Restituta Pie ★★★ GAJA estate for a PIEDMONTESE interpretation of BRUNELLO DI MONTALCINO under names Sugarille and Rennina.

Pio Cesare Pie ★★→★★★ Long-established ALBA producer, offers BAROLO and BARBARESCO in both modern (barrique) and traditional (large-cask-aged) versions. Also the Alba range, incl whites (eg. GAVI). Particularly gd NEBBIOLO D'ALBA.

Planeta Si ★★→★★★★ Leading, still-trendy SICILIAN estate with 400ha v'yd in various parts of the island. Maroccoli SYRAH is notable, as is CERASUOLO DI VITTORIA, also a tasty Grecanico called Alastro.

Podere Small Tuscan farm, once part of a big estate.

Poggio Means "hill" in Tuscan dialect. "Poggione" means "big hill".

Poggio Antico Tus ★★★ Admirably consistent and sometimes inspired BRUNELLO DI MONTALCINO.

Poggione, Tenuta Il Tus ★★★ A marker for fine BRUNELLO, esp considering large volume; also v.gd ROSSO DI MONTALCINO. Administered for the Franceschi family by the excellent Fabrizio Bindocci.

Poggiopiano Tus ★★→★★★ Up-and-coming estate in San Casciano; polished CHIANTI CLASSICO and "Tradizione" using a blend of old and new techniques. Chiantis are pure SANGIOVESE, but SUPER TUSCAN Rosso di Sera incl up to 15% Colorino.

Pojer & Sandri T-AA ★★→★★★ Gd TRENTINO producer, red and white wines, SPUMANTE.

Poliziano Tus ★★★ MONTEPULCIANO estate. Federico Carletti makes superior VINO NOBILE (esp Asinone) and gd IGT Le Stanze (CAB SAUV/MERLOT).

Pomino Tus DOC r w ★★★ (r) 04 06 07 08 09 (10) (11) An appendage of RÚFINA, with fine red and white blends (esp Il Benefizio). Virtually a FRESCOBALDI exclusivity.

Pornassio/Ormeasco di Pornassio Lig DOC r ★ DYA. Insalubriously if suggestively titled light DOLCETTO-based red from LIGURIA. Fratelli Carli makes a gd one.

Potentino, Castello di Tus ★★ English eccentric Charlotte Horton takes on the might of what she calls "Mort-alcino" at this medieval redoubt on the slopes of Monte Amiata. V.gd SANGIOVESE *Sacromonte*; better PINOT N Piropo and Lyncurio (blush).

Prà Ven ★★★ Excellent SOAVE CLASSICO producer, esp cru Monte Grande and new Staforte, six mths in steel tanks on lees with mechanical *bâtonnage*. Now also producing a range of excellent VALPOLICELLA wines under the name Morandina.

Produttori del Barbaresco Pie ★★→★★★★ One of Italy's earliest co-ops, considered by some the best in the world. Aldo Vacca and his team make excellent traditional, straight BARBARESCO as well as crus Asili, Montefico, Montestefano, Ovello, Pora and Rio Sordo.

Prosecco Ven DOC(G) w sp ★→★★ DYA. Italy's default fizz. A recent change in the law, intended to protect the name, means "Prosecco" is no longer a grape but only a wine derived from the GLERA grape grown in specified DOC/DOCG zones (IGT no longer permitted) of the Veneto and FRIULI-VENEZIA GIULIA. May be still, sparkling or FRIZZANTE (usually the last). *See also* box, p.144.

Prunotto, Alfredo Pie ★★★→★★★★ Traditional ALBA company modernized by ANTINORI in 1990s, run by Piero's daughter Albiera. V.gd BARBARESCO (Bric Turot), BAROLO (Bussia), NEBBIOLO (Occhetti), BARBERA D'ALBA (Pian Romualdo), Barbera D'ASTI (Costamiole) and MONFERRATO Rosso (Mompertone, Barbera/SYRAH blend).

Puglia Ap *See* APULIA.

Querciabella Tus ★★★★ Top CHIANTI CLASSICO estate with IGT crus (SANGIOVESE/ CAB SAUV) Camartina and barrel-fermented CHARD/PINOT BL Batàr. Recent purchases in Radda and MAREMMA for more Chianti Classico and new Mongrana (Sangiovese, plus Cab Sauv and MERLOT). Palafreno, now 100% Merlot, is one of best of its type.

Quintarelli, Giuseppe Ven ★★★★ Arch-traditionalist, artisanal producer of sublime VALPOLICELLA, RECIOTO and AMARONE. Bepi died 2012; daughter and children are taking over, altering nothing.

Racemi Ap ★★ Various v'yds/wineries grouped under the Racemi name, run by enterprizing Gregory Perrucci. Based in MANDURIA, special PRIMITIVOS incl Dunico, Giravolta, Sinfarosa ZIN, Vigna del Feudo and Felline. Seek also obscure varietals Ottaviannello (= CINSAULT) Dedalo and Susumaniello Sum.

Rampolla, Castello dei Tus ★★★ CAB SAUV-loving estate in Panzano in CHIANTI CLASSICO, its top wines are the IGTS Sammarco and d'Alceo. International-style Chianti Classico.

Ratti, Renato ★★→★★★ Iconic BAROLO estate. Renato Ratti succeeded by son Pietro, aided by cousin Massimo Martinelli. Modern-style wines of abbreviated maceration but plenty of substance, esp Barolos Rocche dell'Annunziata and Conca.

Recioto della Valpolicella Ven DOCG r sw (sp) ★★★→★★★★ Recently – at last! – elevated to DOCG status, this most historic of all Italian wines (there is written testimony to it from the sixth century AD) is unique and potentially stunning with its sumptuous cherry-chocolate fruitiness.

Recioto di Soave Ven DOCG w sw (sp) ★★★→★★★★ 07 08 09 (10) (11) SOAVE made from selected half-dried grapes: sweet, fruity, slightly almondy; sweetness is cut by high acidity. Outstanding from ANSELMI, COFFELE, Gini, PIEROPAN, Tamellini, often v.gd from Ca' Rugate, PASQUA, PRÀ, Suavia, Trabuchi.

Refosco (dal Peduncolo Rosso) F-VG ★★ 07 08 09 10 (11) Dark, gutsy red of rustic style. Best from: COLLI ORIENTALI DOC, Moschioni, Le Vigne di Zamo, *Volpi Pasini* gd from LIVIO FELLUGA, Miani and from Dorigo, Ronchi di Manzano, Venica Ca' Bolani and Denis Montanara in Aquileia DOC.

Regaleali Si *See* TASCA D'ALMERITA.

Ribolla F-VG Colli Orientali del Friuli and Collio DOC w ★→★★ DYA. Acidic but characterful northeastern white. The best comes from COLLIO. Top estates: Il Carpino, La Castellada, Damijan, Fliegl, GRAVNER, Primosic Radikon, Tercic.

Ricasoli Tus Historic Tuscan family, 19th-century proposers of CHIANTI blend. The main branch occupies the medieval Castello di BROLIO. Related Ricasolis own Castello di Cacchiano and Rocca di Montegrossi.

Ripasso Ven *See* VALPOLICELLA RIPASSO.

Riserva Wine aged for a statutory period, usually in casks or barrels.

Rivera Ap ★★ Reliable winemakers at Andria in APULIA. ★★★ CASTEL DEL MONTE Il Falcone RISERVA (r). V.gd Nero di Troia-based Puer Apuliae.

Rivetti, Giorgio (La Spinetta) Pie ★★★ Fine MOSCATO D'ASTI, excellent BARBERA interesting IGT Pin, series of super-concentrated, oaky BARBARESCOS. Now owne

Top ten white varieties
When people think of Italian wine they tend to think of reds; whites used to be dull. No longer: all the following varitieties now make great wines for refreshment and eg. seafood. Ten to try (in geographical order) with one example of excellence for each:
PIEDMONT – ARNEIS (GIACOSA); ALTO ADIGE – TRAMINER (CS Tramin); Veneto – GARGANEGA (SOAVE PIEROPAN); FRIULI – FRIULANO (BORGO DEL TIGLIO); Marches – VERDICCHIO (Bucci); Umbria – GRECHETTO (Barberani); Abruzzo – PECORINO (Contesa); SARDINIA – VERMENTINO (CAPICHERA); CAMPANIA – FIANO (MASTROBERARDINO); SICILY – CARRICANTE (ETNA Bianco Benanti).

of v'yds both in the BAROLO and the CHIANTI Colli Pisane DOCGs. Early vintages of Barolo along lines of Barbaresco. Recently acquired the traditional SPUMANTE house, Contratto.

Rizzi Pie ★★→★★★ Father (Ernesto)-and-son (Enrico) team owning a substantial chunk of BARBARESCO v'yd in the commune of Treiso, making fine crus Nervo Fondetta, Boito and Pajore by traditional means (long maceration, ageing in large BOTTE).

Rocca, Bruno Pie ★★★ Admirable modern-style BARBARESCO (Rabajà) and other ALBA wines, also v. fine BARBERA D'ASTI.

Rocche dei Manzoni Pie ★★★ Modernist estate at Monforte D'ALBA. Oaky BAROLO (esp Vigna d'la Roul, Cappella di Santo Stefano, Big 'd Big), *Bricco Manzoni* (pioneer BARBERA/NEBBIOLO blend), Quatr Nas (LANGHE).

Roero Pie DOCG r ★★→★★★ 01 04 06' 07 08' 09 (10) (11) Potentially serious, occasionally BAROLO-level NEBBIOLOS from the LANGHE hills across the Tanaro from ALBA. Best: Almondo, Buganza, Ca' Rossa, Cascina Chicco, Correggia, Funtanin, Malvirà, Monchiero-Carbone, Morra, Pace, Pioiero, Taliano, Val di Prete. *See also* ARNEIS.

Roma Lat Brand-new DOC invented, doubtless, to exploit the fame of the Eternal City. Bianco contains a base of Lazio grapes (MALVASIA, Bellone, Bombino), Rosso is based on MONTEPULCIANO and Cesanese, but both are allowed a certain international input.

Ronco Term for a hillside v'yd in northeast Italy, esp FRIULI-VENEZIA GIULIA.

Rosato Rosé; also CHIARETTO, esp around Lake GARDA; and CERASUOLO, from Abruzzo; and Kretzer, from ALTO ADIGE.

Rosato del Salento Ap p ★★ DYA. From nr BRINDISI. Sturdy NEGROAMARO-based wine from a zone that has specialized in rosé. *See* COPERTINO, SALICE SALENTINO.

Rosso Conero Mar DOCG r ★★→★★★ 01' 04 06' 07 08 09 (11) Some of Italy's best MONTEPULCIANO (the grape, that is): GAROFOLI's Grosso Agontano, Moroder's Dorico, MONTE SCHIAVO's Adeodato, TERRE CORTESI MONCARO's Nerone and Vigneti del Parco, Le Terrazze's Sassi Neri and Visions of J. Also gd: Casato, FAZI-BATTAGLIA, Lanari, Leopardi Dittajuti, Malacari, Marchetti, Piantate Lunghe, Poggio Morelli, UMANI RONCHI.

Rosso di Montalcino Tus DOC r ★★→★★★ 06' 07' 08 09 (10) (11) DOC for earlier-maturing wines from BRUNELLO grapes, from younger or lesser v'yd sites. Recently an attempt by a few big producers to allow "international" grapes into the blend was defeated, but they'll try again.

Rosso di Montefalco Umb DOC r ★★→★★★ 04' 06 07 08 09 (10)(11) SANGIOVESE/SAGRANTINO blend, often with a splash of softening MERLOT. For producers, *see* MONTEFALCO SAGRANTINO.

Rosso di Montepulciano Tus DOC r ★★ 06 07 08 09 10 (11) Junior version of VINO NOBILE DI MONTEPULCIANO, growers similar. Seen much less than ROSSO DI

MONTALCINO, probably because of confusion with MONTEPULCIANO D'ABRUZZO, with which it has nothing in common.

Rosso Piceno Mar DOC r 06 07 08 09 10 (11) Gluggable MONTEPULCIANO/SANGIOVESE blend from southern half of Marches; SUPERIORE from restricted classic zone nr Ascoli, much improved in recent yrs and v.gd value. Best: Aurora, Boccadigabbia, Bucci, Fonte della Luna, Montecappone, MONTE SCHIAVO, Saladini Pilastri, TERRE CORTESI MONCARO, Velenosi Ercole, Villamagna.

Ruchè di Castagnole Monferrato Pie DOCG r ★★ DYA. Intense, quintessentially PIEDMONTESE pale red: sour-berry fruit, sharp acid, firm tannins. Calls for a bit of practice. Gd: Pierfrancesco Gatto.

Ruffino Tus ★→★★★ The venerable CHIANTI firm of Ruffino, in the hands of the FOLONARI family for 100 yrs, has graduated from plain Chianti. FOLONARIS (two branches) are busy acquiring new TUSCAN estates. At last count they were up to seven, of which three are in CHIANTI CLASSICO, incl Santedame (top wine Romitorio), one in MONTALCINO (Greppone Mazzi) and one in MONTEPULCIANO (Lodola Nuova). They also own Borgo Conventi in FRIULI.

Rúfina Tus ★★★ Important northern subregion of CHIANTI, east of Florence. Best wines: Basciano, CASTELLO DI NIPOZZANO (FRESCOBALDI), Castello del Trebbio, Colognole, Frascole, Lavacchio, SELVAPIANA, Tenuta Bossi, Travignoli. Villa di Vetrice/Grati does old vintages, sometimes aged 20 yrs+ in oak barrels or concrete vats.

Sala, Castello della Umb ★★→★★★ ANTINORI estate at ORVIETO. Top wine is the splendid *Cervaro della Sala*, oak-aged CHARD/GRECHETTO. Bramito del Cervo is a lesser but still v.gd white of the same grape mix. Muffato della Sala was a pioneering example of an Italian botrytis-influenced dessert wine. PINOT N also creditable.

Salento Ap The tip of Italy's heel – this flat peninsula, baking but breezy between two seas, boasting great expanses of old vines and older olive trees, has long been known for robust reds and ripe ROSATOS, based mainly on the NEGROAMARO grape. There are several DOCS, most superfluous, which is perhaps why IGT Salento is catching on.

Salice Salentino Ap DOC r ★★→★★★ 06 07 08 (10) (11) Best-known of SALENTO's many (too many) NEGROAMARO-based DOCS, made famous by long-established firms like Apollonio, Candido, Leone de Castris, TAURINO and VALLONE. RISERVA after 2 yrs.

San Felice Tus ★★→★★★ Important historic TUSCAN grower, owned by Gruppo Allianz. Fine CHIANTI CLASSICO and RISERVA POGGIO Rosso from its estate in Castelnuovo Berardenga. Vitiarium is an experimental v'yd for obscure varieties – the excellent Pugnitello (IGT from the eponymous grape) a first result. Other gd examples incl: IGT Vigorello (first SUPER TUSCAN, from 1968) and BRUNELLO DI MONTALCINO Campogiovanni.

San Gimignano Tus Tourist-overrun TUSCAN town famous for its towers and dry white VERNACCIA DI SAN GIMIGNANO DOCG, often overpriced and overvalued but occasionally convincing as a wine if not as a *vin de terroir*. Some gd SANGIOVESE-based reds under DOC San Gimignano. Producers incl: Cesani, FALCHINI, Guicciardini Strozza, Montenidoli, Mormoraia, Il Palagione, Panizzi, Podera del Paradiso, Pietrafitta, Pietrasereno, La Rampa di Fugnano.

San Giusto a Rentennano Tus ★★★→★★★★ Top CHIANTI CLASSICO estate owned by cousins of RICASOLI. Outstanding SANGIOVESE IGT Percarlo and sublime VIN SANTO (Vin San Giusto).

San Guido, Tenuta Tus *See* SASSICAIA.

San Leonardo T-AA ★★★ Top TRENTINO estate, run by Marchesi Guerrieri Gonzaga, consultant Carlo Ferrini. Main wine is Bordeaux blend *San Leonardo*, sometimes called the "SASSICAIA of the north". Also v. promising MERLOT Villa Gresti.

San Michele Appiano T-AA Top ALTO ADIGE co-op, esp for whites. Look for PINOT BIANCO Schulthauser and Sanct Valentin (★★★) selections: CHARD, PINOT GR, SAUV BL, CAB SAUV, PINOT N, GEWURZ.

San Severo Ap DOC r p w sp ★ Volume wines based on Bombino and TREBBIANO (w), MONTEPULCIANO and SANGIOVESE (r) generally as uninspiring as the flat landscape. D'Alfonso del Sordo tries hardest.

Sandrone, Luciano Pie ★★★ Exponent of modern-style ALBA wines with deep, concentrated BAROLO Cannubi Boschis and Le Vigne, DOLCETTO, BARBERA D'ALBA and NEBBIOLO D'ALBA.

Sangiovese di Romagna Mar DOC r ★★→★★★ Often well-made and v.gd value from La Berta, Berti, Calonga, Ca' Lunga, Cesari, Drei Donà, Paradiso, San Patrignano, Tre Monti, Trere (E-R DOC), Zerbina; IGT RONCO delle Ginestre, Ronco dei Ciliegi from CASTELLUCCIO.

Sannio Cam DOC r p w sp ★→★★★ (w) DYA. Wines of the Samnites of inland, upland CAMPANIA: various styles, from a mix of mainly Campanian varieties. LA GUARDIENSE is a notable producer.

Sant'Antimo Tus DOC r w sw ★★→★★★ Catch-all DOC for (almost) everything in MONTALCINO zone that isn't BRUNELLO DOCG or Rosso DOC. Sant'Antimo is a Romanesque abbey.

Santa Maddalena / St-Magdalener T-AA DOC r ★→★★ DYA. Appetizing light red from SCHIAVA grapes grown on v. steep slopes behind ALTO ADIGE capital Bolzano. Gd producers: CS St-Magdalena (Huck am Bach), Gojer, Josephus Mayr, Hans Rottensteiner (Premstallerhof), Heinrich Rottensteiner.

In the 1970s Italians drank c.120 litres of wine per head. Now it's a little over 40.

Santadi Sar ★★★ SARDINIA's, and one of Italy's, best co-ops, esp for CARIGNANO-based reds Terre Brune, Grotta Rossa and Rocca Rubia (all DOC CARIGNANO DEL SULCIS). Also whites *Vermentino Villa Solais* and Villa di Chiesa (VERMENTINO/CHARD).

Sardinia / Sardegna The Med's second-biggest island produces much decent and some v.gd wine, eg. Turriga from ARGIOLAS, Arbeskia and Dule from Gabbas, VERMENTINO of CAPICHERA, CANNONAU RISERVAS of Jerzu and Loi, Vermentino and Cannonau from Dettori and the amazing sherryish VERNACCIA of CONTINI. Best DOCS: Vermentino di Gallura (eg. Canayli from Cantina Gallura) and CARIGNANO DEL SULCIS (Terre Brune and Rocca Rubia from SANTADI).

Sartarelli Mar ★★★ One of top VERDICCHIO DEI CASTELLI DI JESI producers (Tralivio); outstanding, rare Verdicchio Vendemmia Tardiva (Contrada Balciana).

Sassicaia Tus r ★★★★ 85' 88' 90' 95' 97 98' 99 01' 04' 05 06 07' (08) (09) (10) (11) A CAB (SAUV and FR) made on First-Growth lines by Marchese Incisa della Rocchetta at TENUTA SAN GUIDO in BOLGHERI. More elegant than lush, made for age – and often bought for investment, but hugely influential in making Bolgheri and its SUPER TUSCANS world figures.

Satta, Michele Tus ★★★ Virtually the only BOLGHERI grower to succeed with 100% SANGIOVESE (Cavaliere) wines. Also makes BOLGHERI DOC red blends Piastraia and SUPERIORE I Castagni.

Scavino, Paolo Pie ★★★ Modernist BAROLO producer of Castiglione Falletto, esp crus Rocche dell'Annunziata, Bric del Fiasc, Cannubi and Carobric. Gd BARBERA LANGHE Corale.

Schiava Alto Adige T-AA DOC r ★ DYA. Traditional, light red popular in Teutonic markets from the most prevalent red grape of ALTO ADIGE, locally called VERNATSCH. Other Schiava DOCS incl Lago di Caldaro, SANTA MADDALENA, Colli di Bolzano.

Schiopetto, Mario F-VG ★★★→★★★★ Late legendary COLLIO pioneer with spacious modern winery. V.gd DOC SAUV BL, *Pinot Bl*, FRIULANO as well as IGT blend Blanc des Rosis, etc.

Sciacchetrà Lig *See* CINQUE TERRE.

Scolca, la Pie ★★ Famous GAVI estate for gd Gavi and SPUMANTE.

Sella & Mosca Sar ★★ Major SARDINIAN grower and merchant with v. pleasant white Torbato (esp Terre Bianche) and light, fruity VERMENTINO Cala Viola (DYA). Gd Alghero DOC Marchese di Villamarina (CAB SAUV) and Tanca Farrà (CANNONAU/ Cab Sauv). Also interesting Port-like Anghelu Ruju.

Selvapiana Tus ★★★ With possible exception of more famous NIPOZZANO estate of FRESCOBALDI, the no 1 CHIANTI RÚFINA estate. Best wines: RISERVA Bucerchiale and IGT Fornace, but even basic Chianti Rúfina is a treat. Also fine red POMINO, Petrognano.

Settesoli, CS Si ★→★★ Co-op with nearly 7,000ha, run by PLANETA family and giving SICILY a good name with reliable, gd-value varietals (*Nero d'Avola*, SYRAH, MERLOT, CAB SAUV, CHARD, Grecanico, VIOGNIER) and blends under the Mandrarossa label.

Sforzato / Sfursat Lom ★★★ Dried-grape NEBBIOLO; *speciality of Valtellina*.

Sicily The Mediterranean's largest island and modern source of *exciting original wines and value* using native grapes (NERO D'AVOLA, NERELLO MASCALESE, Frappato, INZOLIA, Grecanico, Grillo) and international varieties. Wisely, the IGT Sicilia is widely used, avoiding obscure DOCS. Look for Ceusi, Colosi, COS, De Bartoli, DONNAFUGATA, DUCA DI SALAPARUTA, Fazio, Firriato, Foraci, Gulfi-Ramada, Morgante, MURANA, Pellegrino, PLANETA, Rapitalà, Santa Anastasia, SETTESOLI, Spadafora, TASCA D'ALMERITA. *See also* ETNA.

Sizzano Pie *See* GATTINARA.

Assovini Sicilia
An association of 67 wine estates in the Mediterranean's largest island, accounting for 75% of DOCG, DOC or IGT production. In 2011 they produced 600,000 cases for a value of €200 million. Wines are from a mix of hot-, warm- and cool-climate conditions depending on exposure and altitude (sea level to 1,000 metres+ on Etna). Grape varieties are indigenous, Italian or international, with NERO D'AVOLA the principal red grape and SYRAH v. much at home (did it originate in eastern Sicily's Sira-cusa?)

Soave Ven DOC w (sw) ★→★★★ DYA. Famous, still underrated Veronese. From the CLASSICO zone can be intense, minerally, v. fine and quite long-lived. When labelled SUPERIORE is DOCG, but best Classico producers shun the "honour" and stick to DOC. Sweet RECIOTO can be superb. Best: Cantina del Castello, La Cappuccina, Ca' Rugate, Cecilia Beretta, COFFELE, Dama del Rovere, Fattori, Gini, GUERRIERI RIZZARDI, Inama, Montetondo, PIEROPAN, Portinari, PRÀ, Sartori, Suavia, Tamellini and TEDESCHI.

Solaia Tus r ★★★★ 85′ 90′ 95′ 97′ 99′ 01 04 06 07′ 08 (09) (10) (11) Potentially magnificent if somewhat massive CAB SAUV/SANGIOVESE blend by ANTINORI, made to the highest Bordeaux specs; needs yrs of laying down.

Sori Pie Term for a high south-, southeast-, or southwest-oriented site in PIEDMONT.

Sovana Tus MAREMMA DOC; reds with promise; inland nr Pitigliano. Look out for SANGIOVESE, Ciliegiolo from Tenuta Roccaccia, Pitigliano, Ripa, Sassotondo and MALBEC from ANTINORI.

Spumante Sparkling. What used to be called ASTI Spumante is now just Asti.

Südtirol T-AA The local name of German-speaking South Tyrol ALTO ADIGE.

Super Tuscan Tus From the 1970s TUSCAN wines underwent rapid improvement, often involving a dollop or more of Bordeaux grapes in the blend, plus barrique ageing, disqualifying them from DOC status. Those that had established themselves by the millennium held on. The rest are increasingly viewed as overpriced and irrelevant.

Superiore Wine with more ageing than normal DOC and 0.5–1% more alcohol. May indicate a restricted production zone, eg. ROSSO PICENO Superiore.

Tasca d'Almerita Si ★★★ A younger generation of Tasca d'Almeritas has taken over at this historic and still prestigious estate, which kept the flag of quality flying for SICILY in the dark yrs. High-altitude v'yds; balanced IGT wines under its old Regaleali label, CHARD and CAB SAUV gd, but the star, as ever, is NERO D'AVOLA-based *Rosso del Conte*.

Taurasi Cam DOCG r ★★★ 01 04 06 07 08 (09) (10) (11) CAMPANIA's historic and most-celebrated red, one of Italy's outstanding wines, though requiring bottle-age and a degree of understanding. RISERVA after 4 yrs. V.gd: Caggiano, Caputo, Colli di Lapio, FEUDI DI SAN GREGORIO, MASTROBERARDINO, Molettieri, Terredora di Paulo.

Taurino, Cosimo Ap ★★→★★★ Once top-rated producer of Salento, with NEGROAMARO-based Patriglione and Notarpanaro; slipped for a while but making a comeback with the same, plus SALICE SALENTINO RISERVA and Scaloti.

Tedeschi, Fratelli Ven ★★→★★★ Long-established producer of VALPOLICELLA, AMARONE, RECIOTO. Gd IGT Capitel San Rocco (r).

Tenuta An agricultural holding (*See* under name – eg. SAN GUIDO, TENUTA.)

Terlano T-AA w ★★→★★★ DYA. ALTO ADIGE Terlano DOC applies to one white blend and eight white varietals, esp PINOT BL and SAUV BL. Best: CS Terlano (Pinot Bl Vorberg, capable of remarkable ageing), LAGEDER, Niedermayr, Niedrist.

Teroldego Rotaliano T-AA DOC r p ★★→★★★ TRENTINO's best indigenous variety makes serious, full-flavoured wine on the flat Campo Rotaliano. *Foradori* is tops, also gd: Dorigati, Endrizzi, MEZZACORONA's RISERVA Nos, Zeni.

Terre Cortesi Moncaro Mar ★★★ Marches co-op; wines that compete with the best of the region at v. modest prices: gd VERDICCHIO DEI CASTELLI DI JESI (Le Vele), ROSSO CONERO, RISERVA (Nerone) and ROSSO PICENO SUPERIORE (Campo delle Mura).

Terre da Vino Pie ★→★★★ Association of 27 PIEDMONT producers with 4,500ha making most local DOCS. BARBERA specialists with Barbera D'ASTI La Luna e I Falò and Barbera D'ALBA Croere. Also gd: BAROLO Essenze, BARBARESCO La Casa in Collina.

Terre di Franciacorta Lom *See* CURTEFRANCA.

Terriccio, Castello del Tus ★★★ Large estate south of Livorno: excellent, v. expensive Bordeaux-style IGT Lupicaia, v.gd IGT Tassinaia. Impressive IGT Terriccio, an unusual blend of mainly Rhône grapes.

Tiefenbrunner T-AA ★★→★★★ Grower-négociant in quaint Teutonic castle (Turmhof) in south ALTO ADIGE. Christof T succeeds father Herbert (winemaker since 1943), making a wide range of mtn-fresh white and well-defined red varietals: French, Germanic and local, esp 1,000-metre-high *Feldmarschall* and Linticlarus range CHARD/LAGREIN/PINOT N.

Tignanello Tus r ★★★★ 99' 01' 04' 06' 07' 08 09 (10) (11) SANGIOVESE/CAB SAUV blend, barrique-aged, the wine that put SUPER TUSCANS on the map, created by ANTINORI's great enologist Giacomo Tachis in the early 1970s.

Torcolato Ven Sweet wine from BREGANZE in Veneto, made from Vespaiolo grapes laid on mats or hung up to dry for months, as nearby RECIOTO DI SOAVE. Best: MACULAN, CS BEATO BARTOLOMEO.

Torgiano Umb DOC r p w (sp) ★★ and **Torgiano, Rosso Riserva** DOCG r ★★→★★★ 97 99 00' 01' 04 06 07' 08 (09) (10) (11) Gd to excellent CHIANTI-style red from

Umbria, virtually an exclusivity of LUNGAROTTI, whose **Vigna Monticchio** Rubesco RISERVA is outstanding in vintages such as 1975, 1979, 1985; keeps many yrs.

Trebbiano d'Abruzzo Ab DOC w ★→★★★ DYA. Generally crisp, low-flavour wine, but much more when from VALENTINI of Pescara and Pepe of Teramo.

Trebbiano di Romagna E-R DOC w ★ DYA. Big-volume, low-price quaffing white; gd acidity, little complexity. Gd: ZERBINA's Dalbiere, Tre Monti's Vigna del Rio.

Trentino T-AA DOC r w dr sw ★→★★★ DOC for 20 wines, most named after grapes. Best: CHARD, PINOT BL, MARZEMINO, TEROLDEGO. Provincial capital is Trento.

Trinoro, Tenuta di Tus ★★★ Individualist TUSCAN red wine estate, pioneer in DOC Val d'Orcia between MONTEPULCIANO and MONTALCINO. Early vintages of Bordeaux blend Trinoro caused great excitement, then the price shot up. Le Cupole was Bordeaux grapes plus locals, now just CAB FR and MERLOT. Andrea Franchetti also has v'yds on Mt ETNA.

Tua Rita Tus ★★→★★★★ The first producer to establish Suvereto as the new BOLGHERI in the 1990s. Producer of possibly Italy's greatest MERLOT in Redigaffi, also outstanding Bordeaux blend **Giusto di Notri**. *See* VAL DI CORNIA.

Tuscany / Toscana The focal point of Italian wine's late 20th-century renaissance, with experimental wines such as the SUPER TUSCANS and modernized classics, CHIANTI, VINO NOBILE and BRUNELLO.

Umani Ronchi Mar ★★→★★★ Leading Marches producer, esp for VERDICCHIO (Casal di Serra, Plenio), ROSSO CONERO Cumaro, IGTS Le Busche (w), Pelago (r).

Vajra, G D Pie ★★★ Producer of immaculate BAROLO, BARBERA, DOLCETTO and FREISA in the red department as well as RIES in the white. Recently purchased Luigi Baudana estate in Serralunga.

Val di Cornia Tus DOC r p w ★★→★★★ 00 01' 04' 05 06' 07 08 (09) (10) (11) DOC south of BOLGHERI, province of Livorno. SANGIOVESE, CAB SAUV, MERLOT, SYRAH and MONTEPULCIANO. Look for: Ambrosini, Jacopo Banti, Bulichella, Gualdo del Re, Incontri, Montepeloso, Petra, Russo, San Michele, Tenuta Casa Dei, Terricciola, TUA RITA.

Valcalepio Lom DOC r w sw ★→★★ (w) DYA. Wines of the zone of Bergamo, where Po Valley meets last elevations of the Alps. Grapes largely international (CAB, MERLOT, PINOT BIANCO, CHARD), but mainly drunk locally.

Valdadige T-AA DOC r w dr s/sw ★ The name (in German: Etschtaler) for the simple wines of the valley of the Adige – from ALTO ADIGE through TRENTINO to northern Veneto.

Valentini, Edoardo Ab ★★★→★★★★ Son Francesco continues tradition of long-macerated, non-filtered, unfined, hand-bottled MONTEPULCIANO, CERASUOLO and TREBBIANO D'ABRUZZO. Quality unpredictable, potentially outstanding.

Looking for more information on grapes? Try the "Grapes" section on pp.16–26.

Valle d'Aosta VdA DOC r p w ★★ Regional DOC for some 25 Alpine wines, geographically or varietally named, incl Premetta, Fumin, Blanc de Morgex et de La Salle, Chambave, Nus Malvoisie, Arnad Montjovet, Torrette, Donnas and Enfer d'Arvier. Tiny production, wines rarely seen abroad.

Valle Isarco T-AA DOC w ★★ DYA. ALTO ADIGE DOC for seven Germanic varietal whites made along the Isarco (Eisack) River northeast of Bolzano. Gd GEWURZ, MÜLLER-T, RIES, SILVANER. Top producers: Abbazia di Novacella, Eisacktaler, Kuenhof.

Vallone, Agricole Ap ★★→★★★ Large-scale private grower in APULIA's SALENTO peninsula. Excellent, gd-value BRINDISI Rosso/ROSATO Vigna Flaminio, best-known for its AMARONE-like, semi-dried-grape wine Graticciaia. Vigna Castello is a classy addition to the range.

Valpolicella Ven DOC(G) r ★→★★★★ Complex denomination, incl everything from light quaffers with a certain fruity warmth through stronger SUPERIORES

ITALY

> **Tuscan coast**
> Recent yrs have seen a rush to plant in an area not historically noted
> for its fine (or indeed any) wines – the coast of TUSCANY, ie. the
> provinces of Pisa, Livorno and Grosseto. First it was French grapes
> such as the CAB brothers, MERLOT, SYRAH, PETIT VERDOT; now Italians like
> SANGIOVESE, Ciliegiolo and Alicante are in fashion. The best producers
> include: Argentiera, Belguardo (Mazzei), CAIAROSSA, CA' MARCANDA (GAJA),
> CASTELLO DEL TERRICCIO, Colle Massari, Guado al Tasso (ANTINORI), Gualdo
> del Re, LE MACCHIOLE, LE PUPILLE, Michele SATTA, Montepeloso, MORIS FARMS,
> ORNELLAIA (FRESCOBALDI), POGGIO al Tesoro (ALLEGRINI), Tenuta San Guido
> (SASSICAIA), TUA RITA.

(which may or may not be RIPASSOS) to AMARONES and RECIOTOS of ancient lineage.
Bitter-cherry is the common flavour characteristic of constituent CORVINA and
Corvinone (plus other) grapes. Best tend to come from CLASSICO subzone, but
there are excellent wines from outside. *See also* VALPOLICELLA RIPASSO.

Valpolicella Ripasso Ven DOC r ★★→★★★ 04 05 06 08 09 (10) (11) VALPOLICELLA
re-fermented on RECIOTO or AMARONE grape skins to make a complex, age-worthy
wine. Recently given own DOC after yrs of battle between main body of producers
and one who wanted exclusivity of the term. Gd to excellent: BUSSOLA, CANTINA
NEGRAR, Castellani, DAL FORNO, QUINTARELLI, ZENATO.

Valtellina Lom DOC r ★→★★★ DOC for tannic but elegant wines: mainly from
Chiavennasca (NEBBIOLO) in Alpine Sondrio province. V.gd SUPERIORE DOCG from
Grumello, Inferno, Sassella, Valgella v'yds. Best: Caven Camuna, Conti Sertoli-
Salis, Fay, Nera, Nino Negri, Plozza, Rainoldi, Triacca. *Sforzato DOCG* is the
most concentrated type of Valtellina, similar to AMARONE.

Vecchio Samperi Si ★★★ MARSALA Vergine-like wine from famous estate. Best is
barrel-aged Ventennale, blend of young and v.-old vintages. The sons of recently
deceased owner Marco de Bartoli also make top DOC MARSALAS and outstanding
PASSITO Bukkuram at their winery on PANTELLERIA.

Velletri DOC r w sp → (w) DYA. FRASCATI-style whites from Rome outskirts, featuring
MALVASIA and TREBBIANO. Interesting reds of SANGIOVESE, MONTEPULCIANO, Cesanese
and Bombino Nero. Cantina di Velletri is a competent producer.

Vendemmia Harvest or vintage.

Venegazzù Ven ★★★→★★★★ Iconic Bordeaux blend from east Veneto producer
Loredan Gasparini. Even more prestigious is the cru Capo di Stato (created for
the table of the president of Italy).

Verdicchio dei Castelli di Jesi Mar DOC w (sp) ★★→★★★ DYA. Versatile white from nr
Ancona, can be light and quaffable; sparkling; structured, complex and long-lived
(esp RISERVA DOCG, min 2 yrs old). Also CLASSICO. Best from: Accadia, Bonci-Vallerosa,
Brunori, Bucci, Casalfarneto, Cimarelli, Colonnara, Coroncino, FAZI-BATTAGLIA, Fonte
della Luna, GAROFOLI, Laila, Lucangeli Aymerich di Laconi, Mancinelli, Montecappone,
MONTE SCHIAVO, Santa Barbara, SARTARELLI, TERRE CORTESI MONCARO, UMANI RONCHI.

Verdicchio di Matelica Mar DOC w (sp) ★★→★★★ DYA. Similar to above, smaller,
less-known, longer lasting. RISERVA is likewise DOCG. Esp Barone Pizzini,
Belisario, Bisci, La Monacesca, Pagliano Tre, San Biagio.

Verduno Pie DOC r ★★ DYA. Pale red similar to GRIGNOLINO, from Pelaverga grape
grown only in BAROLO-zone commune of Verduno. Gd: Alessandria, Bel Colle,
BURLOTTO, CASTELLO DI VERDUNO.

Verduno, Castello di Pie ★★★ Husband/wife team Franco Bianco with v'yds in
Neive, and Gabriella BURLOTTO with v'yds in VERDUNO, make v.gd BARBARESCO
Rabajà and BAROLO Monvigliero with winemaker Mario Andrion.

Verduzzo F-VG DOC (Colli Orientali del Friuli) w dr sw s/sw ★★→★★★ Full-bodied white from local variety. Ramandolo (DOCG) is well-regarded subzone for sweet wine. Top examples: Dario Coos, Dorigo, Giovanni Dri, Meroi. Also gd: LIS NERIS sweet IGT Tal Luc.

Vermentino di Gallura Sar DOCG w ★★→★★★ DYA. *Best dry white of Sardinia*, from the northeast of the island, stronger and more intensely flavoured than VERMENTINO DI SARDEGNA. Esp from CAPICHERA, CS di Gallura, CS del Vermentino and Depperu.

Vermentino di Sardegna Lig DOC w ★★ DYA. One of Italy's most characterful whites, whether made light/dry or *robust*, grown throughout western LIGURIA, increasingly along TUSCAN coast and spreading inland to Umbria. In SARDINIA, grown island-wide. Gd producers: SANTADI, SELLA & MOSCA.

Vernaccia di Oristano Sar DOC w dr ★→★★★ 97' 00' 01 04 06 07 08 (09) (11) SARDINIAN *flor*-affected wine, similar to light Sherry, a touch bitter, full-bodied. SUPERIORE 15.5% alcohol, 3 yrs of age. Top: CONTINI.

Vernaccia di San Gimignano Tus *See* SAN GIMIGNANO.

Vesuvio *See* LACRYMA CHRISTI.

Vie di Romans F-VG ★★★→★★★★ Gianfranco Gallo has built up his father's ISONZO estate to top FRIULI status. Excellent ISONZO CHARD, PINOT GR Dessimis, SAUV BL Piere and Vieris (oaked), MALVASIA/RIES/FRIULANO blend called Flors di Uis.

Vietti Pie ★★★ Long-serving producer, at Castiglione Falletto, of characterful PIEDMONT wines, incl BARBARESCO Masseria, BARBERA D'ALBA Scarrone, Barbera d'ASTI la Crena. Mainly, *textbook Barolos*: Lazzarito, Rocche, Brunate, Villero.

Vigna (or vigneto) A single v'yd, generally indicating superior quality.

Vignalta Ven ★★ Top producer in COLLI EUGANEI, nr Padua (Veneto); v.gd Colli Euganei CAB SAUV RISERVA and MERLOT/Cab Sauv blend Gemola.

Vignamaggio Tus ★★→★★★ Historic, beautiful and v.gd CHIANTI CLASSICO estate, nr Greve. Leonardo da Vinci is said to have painted the Mona Lisa here.

Vigne di Zamò, le F-VG ★★★ First-class FRIULI estate. PINOT BL, FRIULANO, Pignolo, CAB SAUV, MERLOT and PICOLIT from v'yds in three areas of COLLI ORIENTALI DEL FRIULI DOC.

Villa Matilde Cam ★★★ Top CAMPANIA producer of FALERNO Rosso (Vigna Camarato) and Bianco (Caracci), PASSITO Eleusi.

Villa Russiz Lom ★★★ Historic estate for DOC COLLIO. V.gd SAUV BL and MERLOT (esp "de la Tour" selections), PINOT BL, PINOT GR, FRIULANO, CHARD. Director Gianni Menotti just retired; to watch.

Vin Santo / Vinsanto/ Vin(o) Santo DOC w sw s/sw ★★→★★★★ Sweet wine made from PASSITO grapes, usually TREBBIANO, MALVASIA and/or SANGIOVESE in TUSCANY ("Vin Santo"), Nosiola in TRENTINO ("Vino Santo"). Tuscan versions

---

Valpolicella: the best

VALPOLICELLA started with the Romans on the first foothills of the Alps above the Po Valley at Verona. It has never been better than today. AMARONE DELLA VALPOLICELLA and RECIOTO DELLA VALPOLICELLA have now been elevated to DOCG status, while Valpolicella RIPASSO has at last been recognized as an historic wine in its own right. The following producers make gd to great wine. The crème de la crème are indicated by ★: Accordini Stefano ★, Serego Alighieri, ALLEGRINI ★, Begali, BERTANI, BOLLA, Boscaini, Brigaldara, BRUNELLI, BUSSOLA ★, Ca' la Bianca, Campagnola, Ca' Rugate, Castellani, Corteforte, Corte Sant'Alda, CS Valpantena, Cantina Valpolicella, Valentina Cubi, DAL FORNO ★, GUERRIERI RIZZARDI, MASI, Mazzi ★, Nicolis, QUINTARELLI ★, Roccolo Grassi ★, Le Ragose, Le Salette, Speri ★, TEDESCHI ★, Tommasi, Venturini, VIVIANI ★, ZENATO, Zeni.

> What do the initials mean?
> **Denominazione di Origine Controllata (DOC)**
> Controlled Denomination of Origin, cf. AC in France.
> **Denominazione di Origine Controllata e Garantita (DOCG)**
> "G" = "Guaranteed". Italy's highest quality designation.
> **Indicazione Geografica Tipica (IGT)**
> "Geographic Indication of Type". Broader and more vague than DOC,
> cf. Vin de Pays in France.
> **Denominazione di Origine Protetta/Indicazione Geografica Protetta**
> **(DOP/IGP)**
> "P" = "Protected". The EU seems to want these designations to take over
> from DOC(G)/IGT in the long term, but for now you're much more
> likely to encounter DOC/G or IGT. Occasionally both.

can be extremely variable, anything from off-dry and Sherry-like to sweet and
v. rich. May spend three to ten unracked yrs in small barrels called *caratelli*.
AVIGNONESI's is legendary; plus CAPEZZANA, Corzano & Paterno, Fattoria del Cerro,
FELSINA, Frascole, ISOLE E OLENA, Rocca di Montegrossi, San Gervasio, SAN GIUSTO A
RENTENNANO, SELVAPIANA, Villa Sant'Anna, Villa di Vetrice. *See also* OCCHIO DI PERNICE.

Vino Nobile di Montepulciano Tus DOCG r ★★→★★★ OI' 04 06' 07' 08 09 (10)
(II) Historic SANGIOVESE (here called Prugnolo Gentile) from the town (as distinct
from Abruzzo's grape) MONTEPULCIANO, often tough with drying tannins, but
complex and long-lasting from best producers: AVIGNONESI, Bindella, BOSCARELLI,
La Braccesca, La Calonica, Canneto, Le Casalte, CONTUCCI, DEI, Fattoria del Cerro,
Gracciano della Seta, Gracciano Svetoni, Icario, Nottola, Palazzo Vecchio,
POLIZIANO, Romeo, Salcheto, Trerose, Valdipiatta, Villa Sant'Anna. RISERVA
after 3 yrs.

Vivaldi-Arunda T-AA ★★→★★★ Top ALTO ADIGE sparkling wines. Best: Extra Brut
RISERVA, Cuvée Marianna.

Viviani Ven ★★★ Claudio Viviani shows how modern a wine VALPOLICELLA, and
AMARONE, can be. V.gd CLASSICO SUPERIORE Campo Morar, better RECIOTO La
Mandrella, outstanding Amarone Casa dei Bepi and Tulipano Nero.

Voerzio, Roberto Pie ★★★→★★★★★ BAROLO modernist. Top, v. expensive, single-
v'yd: Brunate, Cerequio, Rocche dell'Annunziata-Torriglione, Sarmassa, Serra;
impressive BARBERA D'ALBA.

Volpaia, Castello di Tus ★★→★★★ V.gd CHIANTI CLASSICO estate at Radda. SUPER TUSCANS
Coltassala (SANGIOVESE/Mammolo), Balifico (Sangiovese/CAB SAUV).

Zenato Ven ★★ V. reliable, sometimes inspired for GARDA wines, also VALPOLICELLA,
SOAVE, AMARONE, LUGANA.

Zerbina, Fattoria E-R ★★★ Leader in Romagna; best sweet ALBANA DOCG (Scacco
Matto), v.gd SANGIOVESE (Pietramora); barrique-aged IGT Marzieno.

Zibibbo Si ★★ dr sw Sometimes the name of wine from PANTELLERIA made from
MUSCAT d'Alessandria, for which it is a synonym.

Zonin ★→★★ One of Italy's biggest private-estate owners, based at Gambellara in
Veneto, but also big in FRIULI, TUSCANY, APULIA, SICILY and elsewhere.

Zuani Lom ★★★ Small COLLIO estate owned by Patrizia, daughter of MARCO FELLUGA.
Superior white blend Zuani RISERVA (oaked) and Zuani Vigne (unoaked).

Germany

Abbreviations used in the text:

Bad   Baden
Frank   Franken
M-M   Mittelmosel
M Rh   Mittelrhein
M-S-R   Mosel-Saar-Ruwer
Na   Nahe
Pfz   Pfalz
Rhg   Rheingau
Rhh   Rheinhessen
Sachs   Sachsen
Würt   Württemberg

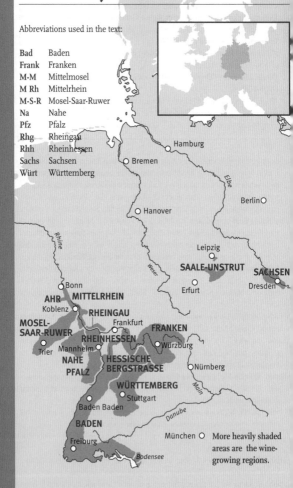

More heavily shaded areas are the wine-growing regions.

I never, these days, tell people I'm offering them German wine. Instead I just pour it and hand it to them and wait for the cries of pleasure. "Delicious," they invariably say. "What is it?" I tell them, and they're amazed. "But I thought...," they begin. It's time to think again.

Germany has spent the last 20 years refining what it already did better than anywhere else, which is to make wines of supreme elegance and complexity from the Riesling grape – sweet or dry. Germans today prefer it dry and full-bodied (I agree with them). You can drink Riesling young, old or anywhere in the middle; you can drink it with food or without; and you can get a superb wine for the price of a very middling Bordeaux. It is where people graduate when they have finally had enough of Sauvignon Blanc. And more and more people are discovering that no wine goes with a greater variety of food than German Riesling in all its range, from ethereal to sumptuous. As for value, only Sherry beats it – and they're giving Sherry away.

Germany is also now making some rather nifty Pinot Noir. But you might have to take a flight to Frankfurt to get it, because in spite of being the world's third-largest producer of the grape, with more planted than New Zealand and Australia put together, it exports only one per cent. But then, with what you're saving on Riesling, what's the price of an air fare?

Recent vintages

Mosel-Saar-Ruwer

Mosels (including Saar and Ruwer wines) are so attractive young that their keeping qualities are not often enough explored. But well-made Riesling wines of Kabinett class gain from at least five years in bottle and often much more: Spätlese from five to 20, and Auslese and Beerenauslese anything from ten to 30 years. As a rule, in poor years the Saar and Ruwer make sharp, lean wines, but in good years, which are increasingly common, they can surpass the whole world for elegance and thrilling, steely "breeding".

2011 Early spring, but cool summer. On August 26, a hailstorm with tennis-ball-sized hailstones hit the Middle Mosel. Dry and sunny September and October saved what was left. In the end, a brilliant vintage, particularly successful in the Saar and Ruwer, with sensational TBAs.

2010 A difficult vintage: many wines are either acidic or too heavily deacidified, but the successes are comparable to 1990. Some really good Spätlesen and Auslesen.

2009 Plenty of magnificent Spätlesen and Auslesen with perfect acidity. The dry wines have a rare balance of power and finesse. Keep the best in the cellar.

2008 Not a vintage for Auslesen, but Kabinetts and Spätlesen can be fine and elegant. Drink or keep.

2007 Good quality and good quantity, too. Now increasingly mature.

2006 Lots of botrytis, not only noble; quantities are low. Drink.

2005 Very high ripeness, but with far better acidity than, say, 2003. Exceptional, especially in the Saar. Drink or keep.

2004 A fine year to drink.

2003 Despite some sensational Trockenbeerenauslesen, considerable variation in quality. Not to keep.

2002 Succulent, lively Kabinett and Spätlese wines, now ready to drink.

2001 The best Mosel Ries since 1990. Saar and Ruwer less exciting but still perfect balance. Lots of Spätlesen and Auslesen to drink or keep.

2000 Dominated by QbA and Kabinett. Auslesen rarer – only the best are exciting.

1999 Excellent in Saar and Ruwer, lots of Auslesen; generally only good in the Mosel. Best can age further.

1997 Consistently fruity, elegant wines. Marvellous Auslesen in the Saar and Ruwer.

1996 Variable, fine Spätlesen, Auslesen from top sites. Many Eisweins.
Fine older vintages: 95 93 90 89 88 76 71 69 64 59 53 49 45 37 34 21.

Rheinhessen, Nahe, Pfalz, Rheingau

Even the best wines can be drunk with pleasure when young, but Spätlese and Auslese Ries gain enormously in character by keeping. Rheingau wines tend to be longest-lived, improving for 15 years or more, but best wines from the Nahe and Pfalz can last as long. Rheinhessen wines usually mature sooner, and dry Franken and Baden wines are generally best at three to six years.

2011 After May frost and a middling summer there was miraculously dry and sunny weather until late October. The wines are fruity, with harmonious acidity.

2010 For the first time in a decade, grapes had difficulty ripening. Uneven quality and a low crop (40% below average).

2009 Excellent wines, especially dry. Some acidification.

2008 Uneven quality. Late-harvest wines are good, in particular in the Rheingau. Very welcome: low alcohol levels.

2007 Dry wines are maturing faster than expected. Drink most.

2006 Top estates – small quantities of fair, middle-weight wines. Drink now.

2005 High ripeness levels, with excellent acidity and extract. A superb year. Drink or keep.

2004 Ripe, healthy grapes throughout the Rhine. A big crop; some dilution, though not at top estates.

2003 Rich wines; many lack acidity. Reds fared well, if alcohol levels were under control. Drink.

2002 Few challenge the best of 2001, but very good for both classic Kabinett/ Spätlese and for dry. Excellent Pinot N. Drink.

2001 More erratic than in the Mosel, but an exciting vintage for both dry and classic styles; excellent balance. Drink or keep.

2000 The farther south, the more harvest rain; Pfalz the worst. Drink.

1999 Quality average where yields high, but for top growers an excellent vintage of rich, aromatic wines with lots of charm to drink soon.

1998 Excellent: rich, balanced wines, many good Spätlesen and Auslesen with excellent ageing potential. Rain affected much of Baden and Franken. But a great Eiswein year.

1997 Excellent QbA: dry, classic styles. Little botrytis, so Auslesen rare.

1996 An excellent vintage, particularly in the Pfalz and the Rheingau, with many fine Spätlesen. Great Eiswein. Drink.

1995 Variable, but some excellent Spätlesen and Auslesen maturing well – like the 1990s. Weak in the Pfalz due to harvest rain.

Fine older vintages: 93 90 83 76 71 69 67 64 59 53 49 45 37 34 21.

German vintage notation

The vintage notes after entries in the German section are given in a different form from those elsewhere in the book. Two styles of vintage are indicated:

Bold type (eg. **99**) indicates classic, ripe vintages with a high proportion of SPÄTLESEN and AUSLESEN; or, in the case of red wines, gd phenolic ripeness and must weights.

Normal type (eg. 98) indicates a successful but not outstanding vintage. German white wines, esp RIES, have high acidity and keep well, and they display pure-fruit qualities because they are unoaked. Thus they can be drunk young for their intense fruitiness, or kept for a decade or two to develop more aromatic subtlety and finesse. This means there is no one ideal moment to drink them – which is why no vintages are specifically recommended for drinking now.

Achkarren Bad (r) w ★★→★★★ Village on the KAISERSTUHL, known esp for opulent GRAUBURGUNDER kept in balance by minerality. ERSTE LAGE v'yd: Schlossberg (volcanic soil). Best: DR. HEGER, Michel, SCHWARZER ADLER, St Remigius and co-op.

Adelmann, Weingut Graf Würt ★★→★★★ Estate based at the idyllic Schaubeck castle in WÜRTTEMBERG. Specialties are subtle red blends (notably Vignette), RIES (look for ERSTE LAGE Süßmund), and the rare Muskattrollinger.

Ahr ★★→★★★ 97 99 05 07 08 09 10 11 South of Bonn. Minerally, elegant SPÄTBURGUNDER and FRÜHBURGUNDER, previously renowned for their lightness. Recently more ripeness on the valley's slate soils: now wines regularly exceed 14% – unfortunately. Best producers: Adeneuer, Deutzerhof, KREUZBERG, MEYER-NÄKEL, Nelles, STODDEN.

Aldinger, Weingut Gerhard Würt ★★★ One of WÜRTTEMBERG's leading estates: dense LEMBERGER and SPÄTBURGUNDER, complex SAUV BL. Gd RIES, too.

Amtliche Prüfungsnummer (APNr) Official test number, on every label of a quality wine. Useful for discerning different lots of AUSLESE a producer has made from the same v'yd.

Ansgar Clüsserath, Weingut M-S-R ★★→★★★ Family estate led by young Eva Clüsserath (married to talented winemaker Philipp WITTMANN of RHEINHESSEN). Remarkably age-worthy, minerally dry RIES from Trittenheimer Apotheke.

Assmannshausen Rhg r ★→★★★ 93 96 97 98 99 01 02 04 05 07 08 09 10 11 Craggy RHEINGAU village known for its cassis-scented, *age-worthy Spätburgunders* from slate soils. ERSTE LAGE v'yd: Höllenberg. Growers incl: KESSELER, Robert König, WEINGUT KRONE and the state domain.

Auslese Wines from selective harvest of super-ripe bunches, in many yrs affected by noble rot (*Edelfäule*) and correspondingly unctuous in flavour. Dry Auslesen are often too alcoholic and clumsy for me.

Ayl M-S-R ★→★★★ 90 97 01 04 05 07 08 09 10 11 All Ayl v'yds are known since 1971 by the name of its historically best site: Kupp. Such are German wine laws. Growers incl: BISCHÖFLICHE WEINGÜTER, Lauer.

Bacharach M Rh (r) w ★→★★★ 97 01 02 04 05 07 08 09 10 11 Main wine town of MITTELRHEIN. Racy, austere RIES, some v. fine. Classified as ERSTE LAGE: Hahn, Posten, Wolfshöhle. Growers incl: Bastian, JOST, KAUER, RATZENBERGER.

Baden Bad 83 90 97 05 07 08 09 10 11 Huge southwest area of scattered v'yds best-known for the PINOTS, and pockets of RIES, usually dry. Best areas: KAISERSTUHL, ORTENAU. Pinot N now more balanced, graceful than of yore.

Badische Bergstrasse Bad Small district of north BADEN, surrounding the city of Heidelberg. Gd RIES and SPÄTBURGUNDER. Best producer: Seeger.

Bassermann-Jordan Pfz ★★★ 90 96 97 99 01 04 05 07 08 09 10 11 MITTELHAARDT estate, under new ownership since 2003, with 49ha of outstanding v'yds in DEIDESHEIM, FORST, RUPPERTSBERG, etc. Winemaker Ulrich Mell excels at producing majestic dry RIES and lavish sweet wines, too.

Becker, Friedrich Pfz ★★★ Renowned estate in the municipality of SCHWEIGEN (southern PFALZ), 18ha, specializing in refined, barrel-aged SPÄTBURGUNDER. Some of Becker's v'yds actually lie across the state border in Alsace.

Becker, J B Rhg ★★→★★★ 90 92 94 97 01 02 05 07 08 09 The best estate at WALLUF specializing in old-fashioned, cask-aged (and long-lived) dry RIES and SPÄTBURGUNDER. Excellent back list of Ries vintages back to the 1990s: Most of these (inexpensive) wines are in perfect shape.

Beerenauslese (BA) Luscious sweet wine from exceptionally ripe, individually selected berries concentrated by noble rot. Rare, expensive.

Bercher Bad ★★★ KAISERSTUHL estate; 25ha at Burkheim, consistently excellent GRAUBURGUNDER (try 2009 Feuerberg GROSSES GEWÄCHS and give it 5 yrs of age), CHARD, SPÄTBURGUNDER.

Bergdolt, Weingut Pfz ★★★ South of Neustadt in the PFALZ, this 24ha estate produces v. fine WEISSBURGUNDER (from the Mandelberg v'yd), as well as gd RIES and SPÄTBURGUNDER.

Bernkastel M-M ★→★★★★ 90 94 95 96 97 98 01 02 03 05 07 08 09 10 11 Senior wine town of the MITTELMOSEL; the epitome of RIES. ERSTE LAGE: Doctor, Lay. Top growers incl: Kerpen, LOOSEN, PAULY-BERGWEILER, PRÜM, Studert-Prüm, THANISCH (both estates), WEGELER. Don't confuse with Bernkastel (Bereich) – a wide area of deplorably dim quality, sold under the deceptive "Kurfürstlay" GROSSLAGE name.

Bischöfliche Weingüter M-S-R ★★ Famous though underperforming estate with cellars at TRIER, uniting cathedral's v'yds with those of three other charities, the Friedrich-Wilhelm-Gymnasium, the Bischöfliches Priesterseminar and the Bischöfliches Konvikt. Owns 130ha of top v'yds, esp in SAAR and RUWER. Under new management since 2010. To watch.

Looking for more information on grapes? Try the "Grapes" section on pp.16–26.

Bocksbeutel Inconvenient flask-shaped bottle used in FRANKEN and north BADEN.

Bodensee Bad Idyllic district of south BADEN, on Lake Constance. Dry RIES-like MÜLLER-T a specialty, and light but delicate SPÄTBURGUNDER. Top villages Meersburg, Hagnau. Lovely holiday wines.

Boppard M Rh ★→★★★ 90 97 01 04 05 07 08 09 10 11 Important wine town of MITTELRHEIN with best sites all in amphitheatre of vines called Bopparder Hamm (ERSTE LAGE). Growers incl: Toni Lorenz, Matthias Müller, August Perll WEINGART. Unbeatable *value* for money.

Brauneberg M-M ★★★★ 59 71 83 90 93 94 95 96 97 99 01 02 04 05 06 07 08 09 10 11 Top village nr BERNKASTEL; excellent full-flavoured RIES. ERSTE LAGE v'yds Juffer, Juffer-Sonnenuhr. Growers incl: F HAAG, W HAAG, Paulinshof, REICHSGRAF VON KESSELSTATT, RICHTER, SCHLOSS LIESER, THANISCH.

Breuer, Weingut Georg Rhg ★★★→★★★★ A family estate in RÜDESHEIM and RAUENTHAL, producing superb dry RIES. V. fine SEKT and SPÄTBURGUNDER as well Pioneering winemaker Bernhard Breuer died in 2004; his daughter Theresa maintains high quality.

Buhl, Reichsrat von Pfz ★★★ Historic PFALZ estate in DEIDESHEIM, FORST, RUPPERTSBERG Estate owned by businessman Achim Niederberger (also BASSERMANN-JORDAN DR. DEINHARD, VON WINNING). Newly organic, and striving for more refinement.

Bürgerspital zum Heiligen Geist Frank ★★→★★★ Ancient charitable estate Traditionally made whites (*Silvaner*, RIES) from outstanding sites in and around WÜRZBURG. Monopoly Stein-Harfe comprises the best parcels in the famous ERSTE LAGE Stein.

Bürklin-Wolf, Dr. Pfz ★★★→★★★★ Dynamic PFALZ family estate, known for age worthy, characterful RIES from FORST, DEIDESHEIM, RUPPERTSBERG, WACHENHEIM, inc many ERSTE LAGE sites. Full-bodied dry and off-dry wines. Now biodynamic.

Busch, Weingut Clemens M-S-R ★★→★★★ Family-run biodynamic property. Clemens Busch and his son Florian produce powerful, dry and elegant swee RIES from the steep Pündericher Marienburg in lower MOSEL. Best wines named for parcels with different slate soils: Fahrlay, Falkenlay, Rothenpfad, Raffes.

Castell'sches Fürstliches Domänenamt Frank ★→★★★ Historic princely estate Entry-level in a rather popular style, but single-v'yd SILVANER, RIES, RIESLANER dry and sweet, and the increasingly renowned SPÄTBURGUNDER are traditionally crafted. Superb monopoly v'yd *Casteller Schlossberg*.

Christmann Pfz ★★★ Estate in Gimmeldingen producing rich, dry RIES and SPÄTBURGUNDER from ERSTE LAGE v'yds, notably Königsbacher Idig. Biodynamic Steffen Christmann is president of the VDP.

Christoffel, J J M-M ★★→★★★ Tiny domain in ÜRZIG. Classic, elegant RIES. Since 2001, leased to Robert Eymael of MÖNCHHOF.

Clüsserath-Weiler, Weingut M-S-R ★★★ Helmut Clüsserath and his daughter Verena produce classic RIES from top TRITTENHEIMER Apotheke and the rare Fährfels v'yd. Steadily improving quality.

Crusius, Dr. Na ★★→★★★ Family estate at TRAISEN, NAHE. Vivid and age-worthy RIES from Bastei and Rotenfels of Traisen and SCHLOSSBÖCKELHEIM.

Deidesheim Pfz ★★→★★★★ 90 96 97 01 02 04 05 07 08 09 10 11 The largest top-quality village of the PFALZ. Rich, lively wines. ERSTE LAGE v'yds: Grainhübel, Hohenmorgen, Kalkofen, Kieselberg, Langenmorgen, Paradiesgarten. Top growers incl: BASSERMANN-JORDAN, Biffar, BUHL, BÜRKLIN-WOLF, CHRISTMANN, DEINHARD, MOSBACHER, VON WINNING.

Deinhard, Dr. Pfz ★★★ Fine estate owned by Achim Niederberger (*see* BASSERMANN-JORDAN and BUHL). Since 2008, a brand of the new VON WINNING estate, but continuing to produce PFALZ RIES of classical style.

Diel, Schlossgut Na ★★★→★★★★ Famous estate; omnipresent Armin Diel now being assisted by his daughter Caroline. The traditional *v'yd-designated Ries* is often exquisite. Also serious SEKT, and remarkable SPÄTBURGUNDER.

Dönnhoff, Weingut Hermann Na ★★★★ 90 94 95 96 97 98 99 01 02 03 04 05 07 08 09 10 11 Leading NAHE estate of admirable consistency. Experienced Helmut Dönnhoff continues to produce magnificent RIES at all quality levels. Dazzling EISWEIN from Oberhausen and outstanding GROSSES GEWÄCHS from NIEDERHAUSEN, Norheim and SCHLOSSBÖCKELHEIM. Even Dönnhoff's dry mid-price Tonschiefer label is a wine of real class.

Duijn, Jacob Bad ★★→★★★ Former sommelier/merchant, now a grower of spicy, tannic SPÄTBURGUNDER from steeply sloping granite v'yds in the Bühler Valley, ORTENAU.

Durbach Bad ★★→★★★ 05 07 08 09 10 11 Village of which Plauelrain is ERSTE LAGE. Top growers incl: Graf Metternich, LAIBLE, H Männle, Schloss Staufenberg. Klingelberger (RIES) is the outstanding variety.

Egon Müller zu Scharzhof M-S-R ★★★★ 59 71 76 83 85 88 89 90 93 94 95 96 97 98 99 01 02 03 04 05 06 07 08 09 10 11 Legendary SAAR estate at WILTINGEN, v'yds rising steeply behind the Müllers' manor house. Its rich and racy SCHARZHOFBERGer RIES in AUSLESEN vintages is among the world's greatest wines: sublime, honeyed, immortal. *Kabinetts* seem feather-light but keep 5 yrs+. Old vines (in some parcels ungrafted) and low-tech winemaking are the key.

Einzellage Individual v'yd site. Never to be confused with GROSSLAGE.

Eiswein Made from frozen grapes with the ice (ie. water content) discarded, producing v. concentrated wine in flavour, acidity and sugar – of BA ripeness or more. Alcohol content can be as low as 5.5%. V. expensive. Outstanding Eiswein vintages: 1998, 2002, 2004, 2008.

Ellwanger, Weingut Würt ★★→★★★ Jürgen Ellwanger pioneered oak-aged reds in WÜRTTEMBERG. Today aided by his sons, who continue to turn out sappy but structured LEMBERGER, SPÄTBURGUNDER, ZWEIGELT.

Emrich-Schönleber Na ★★★→★★★★ In village of Monzingen; known for classical, precise, reliable RIES. Werner Schönleber has knack for dry, botrytized sweet wines.

Erden M-M ★★★ 88 89 90 93 95 96 97 98 99 01 02 03 04 05 07 08 09 10 11 Village adjoining ÜRZIG: noble, full-flavoured, vigorous wine – more herbal and mineral than the wines of nearby BERNKASTEL and WEHLEN but usually long-living. Classified as ERSTE LAGE: Prälat, Treppchen. Growers incl: J J CHRISTOFFEL, LOOSEN, Meulenhof, MÖNCHHOF, Schmitges, WEINS-PRÜM.

Erste Lage V'yd site of exceptional quality, classified by the top wine-growers' association VERBAND DEUTSCHER PRÄDIKATSWEINGÜTER (VDP). On labels, Erste Lage

> **Beware of Bereich and Grosslage**
> *Bereich* means district within an *Anbaugebiet* (region). *Bereich* on a label should be treated as a red light. The wine is a blend from arbitrary sites within that district. Do not buy. The same holds for wines with a GROSSLAGE name, though these are more difficult to identify. Who could guess if "Forster Mariengarten" is an EINZELLAGE or a GROSSLAGE?

sites are marked with a grape logo with a "1" next to it. A producer's best dry wine from an Erste Lage site is called GROSSES GEWÄCHS or ERSTES GEWÄCHS. Off-dry or sweet wines from Erste Lage v'yds display the logo, but are not called Grosses or Erstes Gewächs. From vintage 2012, there will be a second designation besides Erste Lage: GROSSE LAGE (comparable to Burgundy's Grand Cru).

Erstes Gewächs "First growth". Only for RHEINGAU v'yds, but VDP-members intend to give up ERSTES GEWÄCHS in favour of GROSSES GEWÄCHS. *See* ERSTE LAGE.

Erzeugerabfüllung Bottled by the producer. Incl the guarantee that only the producer's own grapes have been processed. May be used by co-ops also. GUTSABFÜLLUNG is stricter and applies only to estates.

Escherndorf Frank ★★ →★★★ 97 01 04 05 07 08 09 10 11 Important wine village, with steep ERSTE LAGE Lump. Best for SILVANER and RIES. Growers incl: Michael Fröhlich, JULIUSSPITAL, H SAUER, R SAUER, Egon Schäffer.

Feinherb Imprecisely defined traditional term for wines with around 10–20g of sugar per litre. Favoured by some as a more flexible alternative to HALBTROCKEN.

Forst Pfz ★★ →★★★★ 90 96 97 01 04 05 07 08 09 10 11 Outstanding MITTELHAARDT village. Richly fragrant, full-bodied yet subtle. ERSTE LAGE v'yds: Jesuitengarten, Kirchenstück, Freundstück, Pechstein, Ungeheuer. Top growers: Acham-Magin, BASSERMANN-JORDAN, BÜRKLIN-WOLF, DR. DEINHARD/VON WINNING, MOSBACHER, WOLF.

Franken 90 97 01 04 05 07 08 09 10 11 (Franconia) Region of distinctive dry wines, esp *Silvaner*, mostly bottled in round-bellied flasks (BOCKSBEUTEL). The centre is WÜRZBURG. *Bereich* names: MAINDREIECK, MAINVIERECK, STEIGERWALD. Top villages: Klingenberg, RANDERSACKER, IPHOFEN, ESCHERNDORF.

Franzen, Weingut Reinhold M-S-R ★ →★★ From Europe's steepest v'yd, Bremmer Calmont, the Franzen family makes reliable, sometimes exciting dry RIES and EISWEIN. Owner Ulrich Franzen died 2010 in a terrible work accident.

Fuder Traditional RIES cask with sizes from 500–1,500 litres, depending on the region. Unlike a barrique, a *Fuder* is used for many years. Traditionalists use the cask for fermentation, giving individuality to each *Fuder's* wine.

Fürst, Weingut Rudolf Frank ★★★ →★★★★ Family estate in Bürgstadt. Paul Fürst now joined by son Sebastian. Outstanding quality: Burgundian SPÄTBURGUNDER (arguably Germany's finest), dense and silky FRÜHBURGUNDER, full-flavoured RIES, classical SILVANER, oak-aged WEISSBURGUNDER.

Gallais, Le M-S-R The second estate of EGON MÜLLER ZU SCHARZHOF, comprising v'yds apart from the SCHARZHOFBERG, above all the 4ha-monopoly Braune Kupp of WILTINGEN. Soil is schist with more clay than in Scharzhofberg: wines fatter, less refined, but still v. gd; AUSLESEN (eg. Gold Cap 2009) even exceptional.

Graach M-M w ★★★ →★★★★ 88 89 90 93 94 95 96 97 98 99 01 04 05 07 08 09 10 11 Small village between BERNKASTEL and WEHLEN. ERSTE LAGE v'yds: Domprobst, Himmelreich, Josephshof. Top growers: Kees-Kieren, von KESSELSTATT, LOOSEN, M MOLITOR, J J PRÜM, S A PRÜM, SCHAEFER, SELBACH-OSTER, WEINS-PRÜM. Regrettably, all threatened by planned new Autobahn.

Grans-Fassian M-S-R ★★★ 97 01 02 05 07 08 09 10 11 Fine MOSEL estate. Steely, elegant, age-worthy RIES from TRITTENHEIM, PIESPORT, LEIWEN, Drohn. EISWEIN specialty.

Grosser Ring M-S-R Group of top (VDP) MOSEL-SAAR-RUWER estates, whose annual Sept auction at Trier sets world-record prices.

Grosses Gewächs "Great/top growth". The top dry wine from a VDP-classified ERSTE LAGE (until 2012) or GROSSE LAGE (since 2012) – *see* ERSTES GEWÄCHS.

Grosslage A collection of secondary v'yds with supposedly similar character – but no indication of quality. Not to be confused with GROSSE LAGE.

Grosse Lage V'yd of Grand Cru quality, classified in 2012 according to VDP. Meant to replace ERSTE LAGE for v. best v'yd sites. Erste Lage designation will be kept, however, for v.gd v'yds (comparable to Burgundy's Premier Cru).

Gunderloch Rhh ★★★→★★★★ 90 96 97 99 01 04 05 07 08 09 10 11 At this NACKENHEIM estate Fritz Hasselbach makes some of the finest RIES on the entire Rhine, esp at AUSLESE level and above. Also owns Balbach estate in NIERSTEIN.

Gutsabfüllung Estate-bottled, and made from own grapes.

Haag, Weingut Fritz M-S-R ★★★★ 88 89 90 94 95 96 97 98 99 01 02 04 05 06 07 08 09 10 11 BRAUNEBERG's top estate; veteran Wilhelm Haag now joined by son Oliver. MOSEL RIES of crystalline purity for long ageing. Haag's other son, Thomas, runs SCHLOSS LIESER estate.

Haag, Weingut Willi M-S-R ★★ BRAUNEBERG estate, led by Marcus Haag. Old-style RIES, remarkably gd in 2010: aromatic Juffer KABINETT and rich, but balanced Juffer-Sonnenuhr AUSLESE.

Haart, Reinhold M-S-R ★★★→★★★★ Best estate in PIESPORT and Wintrich. Refined, aromatic wines capable of long ageing. Minerally and *racy copybook Mosel Ries*.

Halbtrocken Medium-dry (literally "semi-dry"), with 9–18g of unfermented sugar per litre. Halbtrocken on a label is a bit of a sales-killer. FEINHERB sounds better.

Hattenheim Rhg w ★★→★★★★ 97 01 04 05 07 08 09 10 11 Town famous for ERSTE LAGEN STEINBERG, Mannberg, Nussbrunnen, Wisselbrunnen. Estates incl: Barth, Knyphausen, Lang, LANGWERTH VON SIMMERN, Ress, SCHLOSS SCHÖNBORN, STAATSWEINGUT. The *Brunnen* (well) v'yds lie on solid rock (that collects rain like a basin) – a gd protection against drought.

The first harvest of Spätlese wine was in 1775 at Schloss Johannisberg.

Heger, Dr. Bad ★★★→★★★★ 97 99 05 07 08 09 10 11 Estate in KAISERSTUHL producing mineral whites from v. steep slopes in ACHKARREN and IHRINGEN (esp GRAUBURGUNDER, WEISSBURGUNDER, RIES, SILVANER). Recently more SPÄTBURGUNDER, with a refined parcel selection Häusleboden. Wines from rented v'yds under Weinhaus Joachim Heger label.

Hessische Bergstrasse (r) w ★★→★★★★ 90 97 01 05 08 09 10 11 Germany's smallest wine region, north of Heidelberg. Pleasant RIES from STAATSWEINGÜTer, Simon-Bürkle, Stadt Bensheim.

Heyl zu Herrnsheim Rhh ★★ Historic NIERSTEIN estate, bought in 2006 by Detlev Meyer. Biodynamic. Now part of ST-ANTONY estate, same owners. GROSSES GEWÄCHS from monopoly site Brudersberg can be excellent, but overall quality is uneven.

Heymann-Löwenstein M-S-R ★★★ Family-run estate at WINNINGEN nr Koblenz, specializing in spontaneously fermented, terroir-minded RIES, dry and sweet, from picturesque terraces in the steep Uhlen and Röttgen v'yds.

Hochgewächs Designation, in use since 1987, for a RIES Qualitätswein that obeys stricter requirements than plain QBA (+10 degrees OECHSLE). Although intended to apply for all regions, scarcely used outside the MOSEL Valley.

Hochheim Rhg w ★★→★★★★ 90 93 95 96 97 98 01 04 05 07 08 09 10 11 Town east of main RHEINGAU area, once thought of as best on Rhine. Rich, earthy RIES from ERSTE LAGE v'yds: Domdechaney, Hölle, Kirchenstück. Growers: Himmel, Königin-Victoriaberg, *Künstler*, SCHLOSS SCHÖNBORN, STAATSWEINGUT, Werner.

Hock Traditional English term for Rhine wine, derived from HOCHHEIM.

Hoensbroech, Weingut Reichsgraf zu Bad ★★ Top KRAICHGAU estate. Look for dry WEISSBURGUNDER from Michelfelder Himmelberg, a v'yd on calcareous loess soils.

Hövel, Weingut von M-S-R ★★→★★★ Fine SAAR estate at Oberemmel (Hütte is a 4.8ha monopoly) and in SCHARZHOFBERG, known for subtle SPÄTLESEN and Auslesen. Eberhard von Kunow has now handed over to his son Maximilian.

Huber, Bernhard Bad ★★★ Leading estate in Breisgau, with powerful long-lived SPÄTBURGUNDER (esp *Alte Reben*, Bombacher Sommerhalde, Wildenstein) and burgundy-style CHARD (Hecklinger Schlossberg).

Ihringen Bad ★→★★★ 97 99 01 05 07 08 09 10 11 Village in KAISERSTUHL. Best-known for SPÄTBURGUNDER and GRAUBURGUNDER from volcanic soils on steep Winklerberg. Stupidly the law permits wines from the loess plateau to be sold under the same name. Top growers: DR. HEGER, Konstanzer, Pix, Stigler.

Iphofen Frank ★★→★★★ 90 97 01 05 06 07 08 09 10 11 Village in STEIGERWALD area of FRANKEN, renowned for RIES, SILVANER, RIESLANER. First Class v'yds: Julius-Echter-Berg, Kronsberg. Growers: JULIUSSPITAL, RUCK, WIRSCHING, Weltner, Zehntkeller.

Jahrgang Year – as in "vintage".

Johannisberg Rhg w ★★→★★★★ 89 90 93 95 96 97 99 01 04 05 07 08 09 10 11 Classic RHEINGAU village for superlative long-lived RIES. ERSTE LAGE v'yds: Hölle, Klaus, SCHLOSS JOHANNISBERG. GROSSLAGE (avoid!): Erntebringer. Top growers incl: JOHANNISHOF, PRINZ VON HESSEN, SCHLOSS JOHANNISBERG.

Johannishof-Eser Rhg ★★→★★★ JOHANNISBERG family estate. Johannes Eser produces intense RIES in a modern style, more fruity than minerally.

Johner, Karl-Heinz Bad ★★→★★★ Estate at Bischoffingen, long-known for New World-style SPÄTBURGUNDER and oak-aged WEISSBURGUNDER, CHARD, GRAUBURGUNDER. Linked to Johner estate in Wairarapa, New Zealand.

Josephshöfer M-S-R ERSTE LAGE v'yd at GRAACH, the sole property of KESSELSTATT. Harmonious, berry-flavoured RIES, both dry and sweet. Like its neighbours, soon to be overshadowed by new Autobahn bridge.

Number of German wine-growers today: 48,000 – down from 76,600 in 1989.

Jost, Toni M Rh ★★★ Leading estate, mainly RIES, in BACHARACH (sharply mineral-toned wines). Since 2009, the excellent ERSTE LAGE Hahn is a monopoly of Jost's. He also runs a second estate at WALLUF in the RHEINGAU.

Juliusspital Frank ★★★ Ancient WÜRZBURG charity with top v'yds. Look for *dry Silvaners* (they age well), RIES and top blend BT.

Kabinett See "Germany's quality levels" box opposite.

Kaiserstuhl Bad Outstanding district with notably warm climate and volcanic soil. Villages incl: ACHKARREN, Burkheim, IHRINGEN, Jechtingen, Oberrotweil. Renowned for PINOTS (r w) and some surprising RIES and MUSCAT.

Kanzem M-S-R ★★★ 90 93 94 95 96 97 99 01 04 05 07 08 09 10 11 SAAR village, neighbour of WILTINGEN. ERSTE LAGE v'yd: Altenberg. Growers incl: BISCHÖFLICHE WEINGÜTER, Vereinigte Hospitien, VON OTHEGRAVEN.

Karlsmühle M-S-R ★★★ Estate with two Lorenzhöfer monopoly sites making classic RUWER RIES. Consistently excellent quality.

Karthäuserhof M-S-R ★★★★ 90 93 95 97 99 01 04 05 07 08 09 10 11 Outstanding RUWER estate at Eitelsbach; monopoly v'yd Karthäuserhofberg. Easily recognized as bottles have neck label only. Polished TROCKEN wines, magnificent AUSLESEN.

Kasel M-S-R ★★→★★★ 90 99 01 05 07 08 09 10 11 Stunning flowery and well-ageing Ruwer Valley RIES. ERSTE LAGE v'yds: Kehrnagel, Nies'chen. Top growers incl: Beulwitz, BISCHÖFLICHE WEINGÜTER, KARLSMÜHLE, REICHSGRAF VON KESSELSTATT.

Kauer, Randolf M Rh ★★→★★★ Family estate at BACHARACH. Crystalline, aromatic RIES is organic. Randolf Kauer is professor of organic viticulture at Geisenheim.

Keller, Weingut Rhh ★★→★★★★ Superlative, powerful GROSSES GEWÄCHS RIES from Dalsheimer Hubacker and expensive RIES blend from an undisclosed single-v'yd plot called G-Max. Astonishing TBA and SPÄTBURGUNDER.

Germany's quality levels

The official range of qualities and styles in ascending order is:

1 **Wein:** formerly known as Tafelwein. Light wine of no specified character, mostly sweetish.

2 **ggA:** *geschützte geographische Angabe*, formerly known as LANDWEIN. Dryish Wein with some regional style. Mostly a label to avoid, but some thoughtful estates use the LANDWEIN, or "ggA" designation in order to bypass constraints of state authorities.

3 **gU:** *geschützte Ursprungsbezeichnung*, or Protected Designation of Origin. Replacing Qualitätswein.

4 **Qualitätswein:** dry or sweetish wine with sugar added before fermentation to increase its strength, but tested for quality and with distinct local and grape character. Don't despair.

5 **KABINETT:** dry or dryish natural (unsugared) wine of distinct personality and distinguishing lightness. Can occasionally be sublime.

6 **SPÄTLESE:** stronger, often sweeter than KABINETT. Full-bodied. Today many top Spätlesen are TROCKEN or completely dry.

7 **AUSLESE:** sweeter, can be stronger than SPÄTLESE, often with honey-like flavours, intense and long-lived. Occasionally dry and weighty wines.

8 **BEERENAUSLESE (BA):** v. sweet, can be strong, intense. Can be superb.

9 **EISWEIN:** from naturally frozen grapes of BA or TBA quality: concentrated, sharpish and v. sweet. Some examples are extreme and unharmonious.

10 **TROCKENBEERENAUSLESE (TBA):** intensely sweet and aromatic; alcohol slight. Extraordinary and everlasting.

Kesseler, Weingut August Rhg ★★★ Estate making fine SPÄTBURGUNDER from ASSMANNSHAUSEN and RÜDESHEIM. V.gd classic-style RIES (Rüdesheim and LORCH).

Kiedrich Rhg w ★★→★★★★ Village linked inseparably to the WEIL estate; top v'yd Gräfenberg. Other growers (eg. HESSEN, Knyphausen) own only small plots here.

Kloster Eberbach Rhg Glorious 12th-century Cistercian abbey in HATTENHEIM, starred in the film *The Name of the Rose*. Now the label of the STAATSWEINGÜTER with a string of great v'yds in ASSMANNSHAUSEN, RÜDESHEIM, RAUENTHAL, etc. Coasting for yrs, now up for it with a brand-new winery.

Knebel, Weingut M-S-R ★★★ WINNINGEN is the top wine village of the lower MOSEL. Knebel shows how its sites can produce remarkable RIES in all styles.

Knipser, Weingut Pfz ★★★→★★★★ Brothers Werner and Volker specialize in barrique-aged SPÄTBURGUNDER and other reds such as ST-LAURENT, SYRAH and Cuvée X (a Bordeaux blend). Dry RIES can be exceptional.

Koehler-Ruprecht Pfz ★★→★★★★★ 97 99 01 02 05 07 08 09 10 11 Outstanding Kallstadt grower. Bernd Philippi's winemaking is entirely traditional, v.long-lived, dry RIES from Kallstadter Saumagen. Barrel-aged SPÄTBURGUNDER equally gd.

Kraichgau Bad Small district southeast of Heidelberg. Top growers incl: Burg Ravensburg/Heitlinger, HOENSBROECH, Hummel.

Kreuzberg, Weingut Ahr ★★★ Ludwig Kreuzberg has recently made a name for minerally, not overly alcoholic, distinctly cool-climate SPÄTBURGUNDER from steep sites in the AHR Valley at Dernau, Ahrweiler and Bad Neuenahr.

Krone, Weingut Rhg ★★→★★★ 97 99 02 05 06 07 08 09 Estate in ASSMANNSHAUSEN with some of the best and oldest v'yds in the ERSTE LAGE Höllenberg. Famous for richly perfumed, age-able SPÄTBURGUNDER. Now run by WEGELER.

Kruger-Rumpf, Weingut Na ★★→★★★ Most important estate in Münster, with charming but not superficial RIES.

Kuhn, Philipp Pfz ★★★ Reliable producer in Laumersheim. Dry RIES rich and harmonious, barrel-aged SPÄTBURGUNDER combines succulence, power, complexity.

Kühn, Weingut Peter Jakob Rhg ★★★ Excellent estate in OESTRICH. Kühn's obsessive v'yd management (now biodynamic) and individualistic methods in the cellar (long macerations) bring about nonconformist but exciting RIES.

Künstler, Franz Rhg ★★★ 90 97 01 05 07 08 09 10 11 Uncompromising Gunter Künstler produces superb dry RIES at HOCHHEIM (esp ERSTE LAGE v'yds Hölle, Kirchenstück) and Kostheim (calcareous Erste Lage Weiß Erd); also excellent AUSLESE and firm SPÄTBURGUNDER.

Laible, Weingut Andreas Bad ★★★ DURBACH estate; limpid, often crystalline dry RIES from Plauelrain v'yd as well as SCHEUREBE and GEWÜRZ. Andreas Sr now joined by son Andreas Jr. Younger brother Alexander founded an estate of his own – with wines that deserve to be followed.

Landwein Now "ggA". *See* "Germany's quality levels" box on p.165.

Langwerth von Simmern, Weingut Rhg ★★→★★★ Famous Eltville estate, traditional winemaking. Top v'yds: Baiken, Mannberg (monopoly), MARCOBRUNN. Now back on form and still improving. Stunning 2009 Marcobrunn ERSTES GEWÄCHS.

Lauer, Weingut Peter M-S-R ★★→★★★ The village of AYL lacked conscientious growers in the early 2000s Florian Lauer began exploring its subtleties with a range of v.gd parcel selections.

Leitz, Josef Rhg ★★★ Fine RÜDESHEIM family estate for rich but elegant dry and sweet RIES. Since 1999, Johannes Leitz has multiplied his production from 5–41ha, and continues to go from strength to strength.

Leiwen M-M ★★→★★★ 97 99 01 02 04 05 07 08 09 10 11 ERSTE LAGE: Laurentiuslay Village neighbouring TRITTENHEIM. GRANS-FASSIAN, CARL LOEWEN, Rosch, SANKT URBANS-HOF have put these once-overlooked v'yds firmly on the map.

Liebfrauenstift-Kirchenstück Rhh A walled v'yd in city of Worms producing flowery RIES renowned for its harmony. Producers: Gutzler, Schembs. Not to be confused with Liebfraumilch, which is a cheap and tasteless imitation.

Loewen, Carl M-S-R ★★→★★★ Enterprising grower of LEIWEN on MOSEL making ravishing AUSLESE from ERSTE LAGE Laurentiuslay site, and from Thörnicher Ritsch, a v'yd he rescued from obscurity.

Loosen, Weingut Dr. M-M ★★→★★★★ 90 93 95 96 97 01 02 04 05 07 08 09 10 1 MITTELMOSEL at its best: complex, old-vines RIES from BERNKASTEL, ERDEN, GRAACH, ÜRZIG, WEHLEN. Reliable Dr. L Ries from bought-in grapes. Restless Ernie Looser also leases WOLF in the PFALZ (since 1996). Joint-venture Ries from Washington State with Chateau Ste Michelle, and recently, new PINOT N project in Oregon.

Lorch Rhg ★→★★★ 97 01 05 07 08 09 10 11 Village in the extreme west of the RHEINGAU. Now re-discovered for its minerally, austere RIES and SPÄTBURGUNDER. Best: Chat Sauvage, Fricke, Johanninger, von Kanitz, KESSELER.

Löwenstein, Fürst Frank, Rhg ★★★ Top estate: tangy, savoury SILVANER and minera RIES from historic Homburger Kallmuth – v. dramatic slope with 12km of stone walls in the v'yd. Also owns RHEINGAU estate in Hallgarten. In 2010 Prince Car Friedrich Löwenstein died in a car crash; his widow has taken over.

Lützkendorf, Weingut Sa-Un ★→★★ Leading estate in the region. Best are usually the elegant, bone-dry SILVANER and WEISSBURGUNDER.

Maindreieck Frank District name for central FRANKEN, incl WÜRZBURG.

Mainviereck Frank District name for western FRANKEN. Best-known are the SPÄTBURGUNDER v'yds of Bürgstadt and Klingenberg.

Marcobrunn Rhg Historic v'yd in Erbach; potentially one of Germany's v. best Contemporary wines scarcely match this v'yd's past fame.

Markgräflerland Bad District south of Freiburg. Typical GUTEDEL wine can be refreshing when drunk v. young.

Maximin Grünhaus M-S-R w ★★★★ 88 89 90 93 95 96 97 98 99 01 05 07 08 09 10 11 Supreme RUWER estate at Mertesdorf, known for RIES of delicacy and longevity, both dry and sweet. Owner Dr. Carl von Schubert is now joined by his daughter Anna Helene.

Meyer-Näkel, Weingut Ahr ★★★→★★★★ Father-daughter team Werner and Meike Näkel make fine SPÄTBURGUNDER in Dernau, Walporzheim and Bad Neuenahr that exemplify modern, oak-aged (but nevertheless minerally) AHR Valley reds.

Mittelhaardt Pfz The north-central and best part of the PFALZ, incl DEIDESHEIM, FORST, RUPPERTSBERG, WACHENHEIM; largely planted with RIES.

Mittelmosel M-M The central and best part of the MOSEL, incl BERNKASTEL, PIESPORT, WEHLEN, etc. Its top sites are (or should be) entirely RIES.

Mittelrhein M Rh Northern and dramatically scenic Rhine area popular with tourists. BACHARACH and BOPPARD are the most important villages. Delicate yet steely RIES, underrated and underpriced. Many gd sites lie fallow.

Molitor, Markus M-M ★★★ With outstanding v'yds through MOSEL and SAAR, Molitor is a major player. Magisterial sweet RIES, acclaimed (if earthy) SPÄTBURGUNDER.

Mönchhof, Weingut M-M ★★ From his manor house hotel in ÜRZIG, Robert Eymael makes fruity, stylish RIES from ÜRZIG and ERDEN. Erdener Prälat usually best. Also leases J J CHRISTOFFEL estate.

Mosbacher, Weingut Pfz ★★★ Some of best GROSSES GEWÄCHS RIES of FORST. Wines are traditionally aged in big oak casks.

Mosselland, Winzergenossenschaft M-S-R Huge MOSEL-SAAR-RUWER co-op at BERNKASTEL. After mergers with co-ops in the NAHE and PFALZ, now 3,290 members, with a collective 2,400ha. Little is above average.

Mosel-Saar-Ruwer Region between Trier and Koblenz; incl MITTELMOSEL, RUWER, SAAR; 60% RIES. From 2007, wines from the three regions can be labelled just Mosel.

Müller-Catoir, Weingut Pfz ★★→★★★ 90 93 96 97 98 99 01 07 08 09 10 11 Retired director Hans Günter Schwarz pioneered non-interventionist winemaking; his successors are struggling to catch up with the estate's previous fame.

Nackenheim Rhh ★→★★★★ 90 97 01 05 06 07 08 09 10 11 NIERSTEIN neighbour, also with top Rhine terroir (red shale); similar best wines (esp ERSTE LAGE Rothenberg). Top growers: GUNDERLOCH, Kühling-Gillot.

Nahe Na 01 05 07 08 09 10 11 Tributary of the Rhine and a high-quality region making balanced, fresh, clean (and often inexpensive) RIES, at its best with MOSEL-like minerality and PFALZ-like fruit. EISWEIN a growing specialty.

Neckar Würt The river with many of WÜRTTEMBERG's finest v'yds, mainly between Stuttgart and Heilbronn.

Neipperg, Graf von Würt ★★→★★★ Noble estate in Schwaigern: elegant dry RIES, robust LEMBERGER. Specialty: MUSKATELLER up to BA quality. Count Stephan von Neipperg makes wine at Château Canon la Gaffelière in Bordeaux and elsewhere.

Niederhausen Na ★★→★★★★ 90 97 99 01 02 04 05 07 08 09 10 11 Neighbour of SCHLOSSBÖCKELHEIM. Graceful, powerful RIES. ERSTE LAGE v'yds: Hermannsberg, Hermannshöhle. Growers: CRUSIUS, DÖNNHOFF, Gut Hermannsberg, Mathern.

Nierstein Rhh ★→★★★★ 90 97 01 04 05 07 08 09 10 11 526ha. Famous but treacherous village name. Beware GROSSLAGE Gutes Domtal: a supermarket deception. Superb ERSTE LAGE v'yds: Brudersberg, Hipping, Oelberg, Orbel, Pettenthal. Ripe, aromatic, rich wines, dry and sweet. Try Gehring, Guntrum, HEYL ZU HERRNSHEIM, Kühling-Gillot, Manz, ST-ANTONY, Strub.

Obermosel (Bereich) M-S-R District name for the upper MOSEL above TRIER. Wines from the Elbling grape, generally uninspiring unless v. young.

Ockfen M-S-R ★★→★★★★ 90 93 95 97 01 04 05 07 08 09 10 11 The village that brings about sturdy, intense SAAR RIES from ERSTE LAGE v'yd Bockstein. Growers incl: OTHEGRAVEN, SANKT URBANS-HOF, WAGNER, ZILLIKEN.

> #### Historical charities
>
> As in Burgundy, hospital foundations were important wine producers in medieval and renaissance Germany. The most famous among those still active are the Vereinigte Hospitien at TRIER (in its contemporary form founded in 1805, but the predecessors are much older), as well as the two WÜRZBURG charities, JULIUSSPITAL (1576) and BÜRGERSPITAL (1316). Less known, but even older, are three charities in BADEN: the St. Andreas-Stiftung at Offenburg (1500), the Stiftungsweingut Freiburg (1297), and the Spitalkellerei Konstanz (1225). All of these continue to make wine – and keep on financing hospitals, retirement homes and other social facilities.

Oechsle Scale for sugar content of grape juice.

Oestrich Rhg w ★★→★★★ 90 97 01 02 04 05 07 08 09 10 11 Big village; variable, but some splendid RIES. ERSTE LAGE v'yds: Doosberg, Lenchen. Top growers incl: August Eser, PETER JAKOB KÜHN, Querbach, SPREITZER, WEGELER.

Oppenheim Rhh ★→★★★ 90 97 01 05 07 08 09 10 11 Town south of NIERSTEIN; spectacular 13th-century church. ERSTE LAGE Kreuz and Sackträger. Growers incl: Heyden, Kühling-Gillot, Manz. The younger generation is starting to realize the full potential of these sites.

Ortenau Bad District around and south of Baden-Baden. Gd Klingelberger (RIES) and SPÄTBURGUNDER, mainly from granite soils. Top villages incl: DURBACH, Neuweier, Waldulm.

Palatinate Pfz English for PFALZ.

Pauly-Bergweiler, Dr. M-M ★★→★★★ Fine BERNKASTEL estate; v'yds in most villages of the MITTELMOSEL. Formerly renowned second label, Peter Nicolay, has disappeared from both domestic and some export markets (eg. the UK).

Pfalz 90 97 01 05 07 08 09 10 11 Usually balmy region bordering Alsace in the south, and RHEINHESSEN to the north. The MITTELHAARDT area is the source of full-bodied, mostly dry RIES. Southerly SÜDLICHE WEINSTRASSE is better suited to PINOT (r w) varieties.

Piesport M-M w ★→★★★★ 90 97 01 02 03 04 05 07 08 09 10 11 Tiny village with famous vine amphitheatre: at best glorious, rich, aromatic RIES. ERSTE LAGE v'yds: Goldtröpfchen, Domherr. GROSSLAGE: Michelsberg (mainly MÜLLER-T; avoid). Esp gd are GRANS-FASSIAN, Joh Haart, R HAART, Kurt Hain, KESSELSTATT, SANKT URBANS-HOF.

Prädikat Special attributes or qualities. *See* QMP.

Prinz von Hessen Rhg ★★★→★★★★ Glorious wines of vibrancy and precision from this historic JOHANNISBERG estate.

Prüm, J J M-S-R ★★★★ 71 76 83 88 89 90 94 95 96 97 98 99 01 02 03 04 05 06 07 08 09 10 11 Legendary WEHLEN estate; also GRAACH and BERNKASTEL. Delicate but long-lived wines with astonishing finesse and distinctive character. Long lees ageing: hard to taste when young, but they reward patience. Dr. Manfred Prüm now joined by daughter Katharina.

Prüm, S A M-S-R ★★→★★★ 90 97 01 05 07 08 09 10 11 If WEHLEN neighbour J J PRÜM is resolutely traditional, Raimond Prüm works in a more popular style. Sound if sometimes inconsistent wines from WEHLEN and GRAACH.

Qualitätswein bestimmter Anbaugebiete (QbA) Middle quality of German wine, with sugar added before fermentation (as in French *chaptalization*), but controlled as to areas, grapes, etc. Its new name: gU (*see* p.170) is little improvement.

Qualitätswein mit Prädikat (QmP) Top category, for all wines ripe enough not to need sugaring (KABINETT to TBA).

Randersacker Frank ★★→★★★ 01 05 07 08 09 10 11 Leading village south of WÜRZBURG for distinctive dry wine, esp SILVANER. ERSTE LAGE v'yds: Pfülben, Sonnenstuhl, Teufelskeller. Top growers: BÜRGERSPITAL, JULIUSSPITAL, STAATLICHER HOFKELLER, SCHMITT'S KINDER, Störrlein, Trockene Schmitts.

Ratzenberger M Rh ★★→★★★ Estate making racy dry and off-dry RIES in BACHARACH; best from ERSTE LAGE v'yds: Posten and Steeger St-Jost. Gd SEKT, too.

Rauenthal Rhg ★★→★★★★ 97 01 02 04 05 07 08 09 10 11 Supreme (sometimes underrated) village on inland slopes: spicy, complex RIES. ERSTE LAGE v'yds: Baiken, Gehrn, Nonnenberg, Rothenberg, Wülfen. Top growers: BREUER, KLOSTER EBERBACH, LANGWERTH VON SIMMERN.

How to drink mature Mosel Riesling Auslesen? With game.

Rebholz, Ökonomierat Pfz ★★★→★★★★ 97 01 04 05 07 08 09 10 11 Top SÜDLICHE WEINSTRASSE estate known for bone-dry and long-lived wines (MUSKATELLER, GEWÜRZ, burgundian-style CHARD and SPÄTBURGUNDER). Outstanding RIES GROSSES GEWÄCHS from the Kastanienbusch v'yd (red shale) and from the Ganshorn parcel at Siebeldingen (red sandstone).

Reichsgraf von Kesselstatt, M-S-R ★★★→★★★★ The largest privately owned Mosel estate: 650 yrs old. Run for two decades by the quality-obsessed Annegret Reh-Gartner. Consistently high-quality, eg. JOSEPHSHÖFER, PIESPORTER Goldtröpfchen, KASELer Nies'chen and SCHARZHOFBERGer. Village-level wines ie. Graacher and Wiltinger are unbeatable value.

Restsüsse Unfermented grape sugar remaining in (or in cheap wines added to) wine to give it sweetness. Range: 3g per litre in a TROCKEN wine to 300 in a TBA.

Rheingau 90 96 97 99 01 04 05 07 08 09 10 11 Best v'yd region of Rhine, mainly west of Wiesbaden. Classic, substantial RIES, yet now eclipsed by brilliance elsewhere and hampered by some underperforming, if grand, estates. Controversially, one-third of region is classified (since 2000) as ERSTES GEWÄCHS, subject to regulations that differ from the VDP's for GROSSES GEWÄCHS.

Rheinhessen 05 07 08 09 10 11 Germany's largest region, between Mainz and Worms. Much dross, but incl top RIES from NACKENHEIM, NIERSTEIN, OPPENHEIM, etc. Remarkable spurt in quality in formerly unknown areas, from growers such as KELLER and WITTMANN in the south and WAGNER-STEMPEL in the west.

Richter, Weingut Max Ferd M-M ★★→★★★ Reliable MITTELMOSEL estate at Mülheim. Esp gd RIES KABINETT and SPÄTLESEN – full and aromatic. Wines from purchased grapes carry a slightly different label.

Ruck, Weingut Johann Frank ★★→★★★ Reliable and spicy SILVANER and RIES from IPHOFEN in FRANKEN's STEIGERWALD district. Traditional in style.

Rüdesheim Rhg w ★★→★★★★ 90 97 01 04 05 07 08 09 10 11 Rhine resort with outstanding ERSTE LAGE v'yds; the four best (Roseneck, Rottland, Schlossberg, Kaisersteinfels) are called Rüdesheimer Berg. Full-bodied wines, fine-flavoured, often remarkable in off-yrs. Best growers: BREUER, Chat Sauvage, Corvers-Kauter, JOHANNISHOF, KESSELER, LEITZ, Ress, SCHLOSS SCHÖNBORN, Staatsweingüter.

Ruppertsberg Pfz ★★→★★★ 90 97 01 05 07 08 09 10 11 Southern village of MITTELHAARDT. Classic PFALZ RIES from ERSTE LAGE sites Gaisböhl, Reiterpfad, Spiess. Growers incl: BASSERMANN-JORDAN, Biffar, BUHL, BÜRKLIN-WOLF, CHRISTMANN, DR. DEINHARD/VON WINNING.

Ruwer M-S-R 90 97 01 03 04 05 07 08 09 10 11 Tributary of MOSEL nr TRIER. V.-fine, delicate but highly aromatic and remarkably long-lived RIES both sweet and dry. A string of warm summers has helped ripeness. Best growers: Beulwitz, KARLSMÜHLE, KARTHÄUSERHOF, KESSELSTATT, MAXIMIN GRÜNHAUS.

Saale-Unstrut Sa-Un 03 05 07 08 09 10 11 Climatically challenging region around confluence of these two rivers at Naumburg, nr Leipzig. Terraced v'yds of

WEISSBURGUNDER, SILVANER, GEWÜRZ, RIES, SPÄTBURGUNDER have Cistercian origins. Quality leaders: Böhme, Born, Gussek, Kloster Pforta, LÜTZKENDORF, Pawis.

Saar M-S-R 90 93 94 95 96 97 99 01 02 04 05 07 08 09 10 11 Hill-lined tributary of the MOSEL, south of RUWER. Climate colder than MITTELMOSEL: v'yds are 50–100 metres higher. The most brilliant, austere, steely RIES of all. Villages incl: AYL, KANZEM, OCKFEN, SAARBURG, Serrig, WILTINGEN (SCHARZHOFBERG). Many fine estates here, most at the top of their game.

Saarburg M-S-R Small town in the SAAR Valley, Rausch v'yd is one of the best of the region. Best growers: WAGNER, ZILLIKEN.

Sachsen 03 05 07 08 09 10 11 Region in the Elbe Valley around Dresden and Meissen, making characterful dry whites from grapes such as WEISSBURGUNDER, GRAUBURGUNDER, TRAMINER, RIES. Best growers incl: Vincenz Richter, SCHLOSS PROSCHWITZ, Schloss Wackerbarth, Martin Schwarz, Zimmerling.

Salm, Prinz zu Na, Rhh Owner of Schloss Wallhausen in NAHE and Villa Sachsen in RHEINHESSEN. The RIES wines at Schloss Wallhausen (organic) have made gd progress recently, with recommendable mid-price labels Vom Roten Schiefer and Grünschiefer.

Salwey, Weingut Bad ★★★ Leading estate at Oberrotweil, top KAISERSTUHL sites. Early in 2011 Wolf-Dietrich Salwey died in a road accident; son Konrad continues to keep quality levels high. Best wines: golden-coloured Henkenberg, Eichberg GRAUBURGUNDERS and Kirchberg SPÄTBURGUNDER Rappen (fermented with stems).

Sankt Urbans-Hof M-S-R ★★★→★★★★ New star based in LEIWEN, PIESPORT, OCKFEN. Limpid RIES of impeccable purity and raciness (eg. refined 2010 AUSLESEN from Piesport and Ockfen).

Sauer, Horst Frank ★★★→★★★★ The finest exponent of ESCHERNDORF's top v'yd Lump. Racy, straightforward dry SILVANER and RIES, and sensational TBA.

Sauer, Rainer Frank ★★★ Rising family estate at ESCHERNDORF (see HORST SAUER), specializing in complex, dry SILVANER, from elegant, minerally KABINETT to creamy, full-bodied SPÄTLESEN.

Schaefer, Willi M-S-R ★★★ The finest grower of GRAACH (but only 4ha). Classic, pure MOSEL RIES, rewarding at all quality levels. Late August 2011 affected by hailstorm; luckily Sept and Oct weather was dry enough to limit the damage.

Schäfer-Fröhlich, Weingut Na ★★★ Increasingly brilliant RIES, dry and nobly sweet, from this estate in Bockenau, NAHE. Superb 2010 *Grosses Gewächs* Felseneck, and breathtaking EISWEIN.

Scharzhofberg M-S-R ★★★★ 71 83 88 89 90 93 94 95 96 97 99 01 04 05 07 08 09 10 11 Superlative SAAR v'yd: a rare coincidence of microclimate, soil and human intelligence brings about the perfection of RIES – best as AUSLESEN. Top estates: BISCHÖFLICHE WEINGÜTER, EGON MÜLLER, von HÖVEL, VON KESSELSTATT, VAN VOLXEM.

Schloss Johannisberg Rhg w ★★→★★★ 90 97 01 02 04 05 07 08 09 10 11 Famous RHEINGAU estate, 100% RIES, owned by Henkell (Oetker group). Improved v'yd management under new director, Christian Witte, starts to pay off.

Schloss Lieser M-M ★★★ Thomas Haag, from FRITZ HAAG estate, makes pure, racy

---

New EU terminology

Germany's part in the new EU classification involves, firstly, abolishing the term Tafelwein in favour of plain Wein and secondly changing LANDWEIN to "ggA": *geschützte geographische Angabe* or "Protected Geographical Indication". Qualitätswein and QUALITÄTSWEIN MIT PRÄDIKAT will be replaced by gU: *geschützte Ursprungsbezeichnung*, or Protected Designation of Origin. The existing terms – SPÄTLESE, AUSLESE and so on (see box: GERMANY'S QUALITY LEVELS, p.165) – will be tacked on to gU where appropriate; the rules for these styles won't change.

RIES from underrated Niederberg Helden v'yd in LIESER, as well as from best sites in BRAUNEBERG. Brilliant 2010 Juffer-Sonnenuhr SPÄTLESE.

Schloss Neuweier Bad ★★★ Leading producer of dry RIES from volcanic soils nr Baden-Baden.

Schloss Proschwitz Sachs ★★ A resurrected princely estate at Meissen in SACHSEN, leading former East Germany in quality; esp with dry WEISSBURGUNDER and GRAUBURGUNDER. A great success.

Schloss Reinhartshausen Rhg ★★→★★★ Famous estate in Erbach, HATTENHEIM, KIEDRICH, etc. Originally property of Prussian royal family, now in private hands.

Schloss Saarstein, Weingut M-S-R ★→★★★ 90 97 01 05 07 08 09 10 11 Steep but chilly v'yds in Serrig need warm yrs to succeed but can deliver steely, minerally and long-lived AUSLESE and EISWEIN.

Schloss Schönborn Frank, Rhg ★★→★★★ HATTENHEIM estate: full-flavoured wines, variable, but excellent at their best. The Schönborn family also owns Schloss Hallburg in FRANKEN.

Schloss Vaux Rhg ★★→★★★ Superior SEKT manufacturer, specalizing in bottle-fermented RIES and SPÄTBURGUNDER from top RHEINGAU sites (eg. STEINBERG). No owned v'yds, but gd sources for base wine (mainly from VDP members).

Schloss Vollrads Rhg ★★ One of the greatest historic RHEINGAU estates, now owned by a bank. RIES in a popular and accessible style, sometimes disappointing.

Schlossböckelheim Na w ★★→★★★★ 90 97 01 02 04 05 07 08 09 10 11 Village with top NAHE v'yds, incl ERSTE LAGE Felsenberg, Kupfergrube. Wines firm yet delicate, age well. Top growers: CRUSIUS, DÖNNHOFF, Gut Hermannsberg, SCHÄFER-FRÖHLICH.

Schmitt's Kinder Frank ★★→★★★ Uncompromising TROCKEN wines made from RANDERSACKER's best v'yds. Textbook FRANKEN SILVANER and RIES. Gd barrel-aged SPÄTBURGUNDER and sweet RIESLANER, too.

Schnaitmann, Weingut Würt ★★★ New WÜRTTEMBERG star with complex, barrel-aged reds, such as SPÄTBURGUNDER and LEMBERGER. GROSSES GEWÄCHS are outstanding, but entry-level wines are also v.gd.

Frozen Eiswein grapes may need pressing for 24 hrs before juice appears.

Schneider, Cornelia and Reinhold Bad ★★→★★★ Family estate in Endingen, KAISERSTUHL. Age-worthy SPÄTBURGUNDER; old-fashioned, opulent RULÄNDER.

Schoppenwein Café (or bar) wine, ie. wine by the glass.

Schwarzer Adler, Weingut Bad ★★→★★★ Fritz Keller runs a one-star-restaurant and makes top dry GRAU-, WEISS-, and SPÄTBURGUNDER at Oberbergen, KAISERSTUHL. Now engaged in producing wine for a discount chain.

Schwegler, Albrecht Würt ★★★ Small estate known for gd, unusual red blends, such as Granat (MERLOT, ZWEIGELT, LEMBERGER and others). Worth looking for.

Schweigen ★★ Southern PFALZ village. Best growers: FRIEDRICH BECKER, Bernhart, Jülg.

Sekt German sparkling wine v. variable in quality. Bottle fermentation is not mandatory. Estates that are sekt specialists incl: Raumland, Schembs, SCHLOSS VAUX, Wilhelmshof, von Orthegraven.

Selbach-Oster M-M ★★★ Scrupulous ZELTINGEN estate among MITTELMOSEL leaders. Also makes wine from purchased grapes: estate bottlings are best.

Sonnenuhr M-S-R Sundial. Name of several v'yds ERSTE LAGE sites at WEHLEN and ZELTINGEN soon to be overshadowed by new Autobahn bridge.

Spätlese Late-harvest. One better (riper, with more substance and usually more sweetness) than KABINETT. Gd examples age at least 7 yrs, often longer. TROCKEN Spätlesen, often similar in style to GROSSES GEWÄCHS, can be v. fine with food.

Spreitzer, Weingut Rhg ★★★ Andreas and Bernd Spreitzer produce RIES, mainly in OESTRICH. Deliciously racy wines, vinified with patience and aged in FUDER. Charta Ries 2010, slightly off-dry, is a bargain.

GERMANY

St-Antony, Weingut Rhh ★★ NIERSTEIN estate with exceptional v'yds. Quality was uneven, new owner (see HEYL ZU HERRNSHEIM) seems to be turning things around.

Staatlicher Hofkeller Frank ★★ The Bavarian state domain. 120ha of the finest FRANKEN v'yds, with spectacular cellars under the great baroque Residenz at WÜRZBURG. Quality sound but rarely exciting.

Staatsweingut / Staatliche Weinbaudomäne The state wine estates or domains. Some have been privatized in recent yrs.

Steigerwald Frank District in eastern FRANKEN. V'yds lie at considerable altitude but bring powerful SILVANER and RIES. Look for: CASTELL, RUCK, Weltner, WIRSCHING.

Steinberg Rhg ★★★ 90 97 01 04 05 07 08 09 10 11 Famous HATTENHEIM walled RIES v'yd, a German Clos de Vougeot, planted by Cistercian monks 700 yrs ago. Now a monopoly of KLOSTER EBERBACH. Premium label "aus dem Cabinetkeller" is gd, but pricey.

Looking for more information on grapes? Try the "Grapes" section on pp.16–26.

Steinwein Frank Wine from WÜRZBURG's best v'yd, Stein. Goethe's favourite, too.

Stodden, Weingut Jean Ahr ★★★ Burgundy enthusiast Gerhard Stodden crafts richly oaky AHR SPÄTBURGUNDER. First-rate since 1999, but v. pricey.

Südliche Weinstrasse Pfz District name for south PFALZ. Quality has improved tremendously in past 25 yrs. Best growers incl: BECKER, Leiner, Münzberg, REBHOLZ, Siegrist, WEHRHEIM.

Tauberfranken Underrated district of northeast BADEN: FRANKEN-style wines from limestone soils: bone-dry, distinctly cool-climate in style. Best grower is Schlör.

Thanisch, Weingut Dr. M-M ★★→★★★ BERNKASTEL estate, incl part of the Doctor v'yd. This famous estate was divided in the 1980s, but the two confusingly share the same name: Erben Müller-Burggraef identifies one; Erben Thanisch the other. Similar in quality but the latter sometimes has the edge.

Traisen Na ★★★ 90 97 01 05 07 08 09 10 11 Small village, incl ERSTE LAGE v'yds Bastei and Rotenfels. RIES of concentration and class from volcanic soils. Top growers incl: CRUSIUS, von Racknitz.

Trier M-S-R Great wine city of Roman origin, on MOSEL, between RUWER and SAAR. Large charitable estates have cellars here among splendid Roman remains.

Trittenheim M-M ★★→★★★ 90 97 01 02 04 05 07 08 09 10 11 Attractive south MITTELMOSEL light wines. However, only best plots in ERSTE LAGE v'yd Apotheke deserve that classification. Growers incl: ANSGAR CLÜSSERATH, Ernst Clüsserath, CLÜSSERATH-WEILER, GRANS-FASSIAN, Milz.

Trocken Dry. Trocken wines have a max 9g unfermented sugar per litre. Quality has increased dramatically since the 1980s. Most dependable in PFALZ and all points south.

Trockenbeerenauslese (TBA) Sweetest, most expensive category of German wine, extremely rare, with concentrated honey flavour. Made from selected shrivelled grapes affected by noble rot (botrytis). Half-bottles a gd idea.

Ürzig M-M ★★★★ 71 83 90 93 94 95 96 97 01 02 04 05 07 08 09 10 11 Village on red sandstone and red slate, famous for firm, full, spicy wine unlike other MOSELS. ERSTE LAGE v'yd: Würzgarten. Growers incl: Berres, Erbes, CHRISTOFFEL, LOOSEN, MÖNCHHOF, PAULY-BERGWEILER, WEINS-PRÜM. Threatened by an unneeded Autobahn bridge 160 metres high.

Van Volxem, Weingut M-S-R ★★→★★★ Estate revived by brewery heir Roman Niewodniczanski (since 1999). V. low yields from top sites (SCHARZHOFBERG, KANZEM Altenberg) result in ultra-ripe dry and off-dry RIES. Atypical but impressive.

Verband Deutscher Prädikatsweingüter (VDP) Pace-making association of premium growers. Look for its eagle insignia on wine labels, and for the ERSTE LAGE logo on wines from classified v'yds. President: Steffen CHRISTMANN.

Vollenweider, Weingut M-S-R ★★★ Daniel Vollenweider from Switzerland has revived the Wolfer Goldgrube v'yd nr Traben-Trarbach (since 2000). *Excellent Ries*, but v. small quantities.

von Othegraven, Weingut M-S-R ★★→★★★ 01 05 07 08 09 10 11 Since 2010, this fine KANZEM (SAAR) estate with its superb ERSTE LAGE Altenberg is led by TV star Günther Jauch, who is a member of the von Othegraven family. The estate also owns parcels in OCKFEN (Bockstein) and, newly, in the forgotten Herrenberg of Wawern.

Wachenheim Pfz ★★★ 97 01 04 05 07 08 09 10 11 Village with, according to VDP, no ERSTE LAGE v'yds. Top growers: Biffar, BÜRKLIN-WOLF, Odinstal, Karl Schäfer, WOLF.

Wagner, Dr. M-S-R ★★ Estate with v'yds in OCKFEN and SAARSTEIN, best-known for steely, dry RIES. However, FEINHERB and sweet wines are often preferable.

Wagner-Stempel, Weingut Rhh ★★★ Estate, 50% RIES, in RHEINHESSEN nr NAHE border in obscure Siefersheim. Recent yrs have provided excellent wines, both GROSSES GEWÄCHS and nobly sweet.

Walluf Rhg ★★★ 90 92 94 96 97 99 01 02 04 05 07 08 09 10 11 Neighbour of Eltville. Underrated wines. ERSTE LAGE Walkenberg. Growers: J B BECKER, JOST.

Wegeler M-M, Rhg ★★→★★★ Important family estates in OESTRICH and BERNKASTEL plus a stake in the famous KRONE estate of ASSMANNSHAUSEN. Wines of high quality in gd quantity; even the "Geheimrat J" brand maintains v. high standards.

Wehlen M-M ★★★→★★★★ 90 93 94 95 96 97 98 01 02 03 04 05 07 08 09 10 11 BERNKASTEL neighbour with equally fine, somewhat richer wine and almost no weak vintages lately. ERSTE LAGE: SONNENUHR. Top growers: Kerpen, LOOSEN, MOLITOR, J J PRÜM, S A PRÜM, REICHSGRAF VON KESSELSTATT, RICHTER, Studert-Prüm, SELBACH-OSTER, WEGELER, WEINS-PRÜM. V'yds soon to be overshadowed by Autobahn bridge.

Wehrheim, Weingut Dr. Pfz ★★★ Top family estate of SÜDLICHE WEINSTRASSE. Full, v. dry and firm, mineral core, eg. ERSTE LAGE Kastanienbusch RIES, SPÄTBURGUNDER.

Weil, Weingut Robert Rhg ★★★→★★★★ 17 37 49 59 75 90 97 01 02 04 05 07 08 09 10 11 Outstanding estate in KIEDRICH owned by Suntory of Japan. Superb EISWEIN, TBA, BA; entry-level wines more variable. Three ERSTE LAGEN: Gräfenberg, Turmberg and, newly, Klosterberg.

Weingart, Weingut M Rh ★★★ Outstanding estate at Spay, v'yds in BOPPARD. Refined, minerally RIES, superb value, both dry and sweet.

Weingut Wine estate.

Organic – what does it mean?
Depends who you ask. The EU norm for organic viticulture permits, for example, 8kg copper per year and ha. (Copper is a heavy metal but necessary, as copper sulphate, for controlling disease.) German associations Ecovin, Bioland and Naturland limit copper to 3kg per year and ha, as does biodynamic Demeter. And where the EU permits the use of meat- and bonemeal as fertilizer, these organizations will have none of it. But only Demeter insists on picking by hand; all others permit machine-picking.

Weins-Prüm, Dr. ★★★ Small estate in WEHLEN. Superb MITTELMOSEL v'yds. Scrupulous winemaking from owner Bert Selbach, who favours a taut, minerally style.

Weissherbst Pale-pink wine, sometimes botrytis-affected and occasionally even BA made from a single variety, often SPÄTBURGUNDER. Worth trying.

Wiltingen M-S-R ★★→★★★★ 90 97 01 04 05 07 08 09 10 11 Heartland of the SAAR. Famous SCHARZHOFBERG crowns a series of ERSTE LAGE v'yds (Braune Kupp, Kupp, Braunfels, Gottesfuss). But even Wiltinger village RIES is rich and aromatic –

far beyond the ordinary. Top growers: BISCHÖFLICHE WEINGÜTER, Le Galais, EGON MÜLLER, REICHSGRAF VON KESSELSTATT, SANKT URBANS-HOF, VAN VOLXEM.

Winning, von Pfz New DEIDESHEIM estate, incl former DR. DEINHARD. The von Winning label is used for top wines from Dr. Deinhard v'yds. First vintage 2008: *Ries of great purity* and terroir expression, slightly influenced by 10–20% oak fermentation. A label to watch.

Record-breaking 2011s

TBA are sweet, OK? The min must weight is 150° OECHSLE. In 2011, several came in at 250–270° Oechsle. GUNDERLOCH picked one at over 300° Oechsle, and he wasn't the only one. The 2011 vintage is set to be a great sweet wine yr of the quality of 1971, 1959, 1945, 1921 and 1911.

Winningen M-S-R w ★★ →★★★ Lower MOSEL town nr Koblenz; excellent dry RIES and TBA. ERSTE LAGE v'yds: Röttgen, Uhlen. Top growers: HEYMANN-LÖWENSTEIN, KNEBEL, Kröber, Richard Richter.

Wirsching, Hans Frank ★★★ Estate in IPHOFEN, FRANKEN. Dry RIES and *Silvaner*, powerful and long-lived. ERSTE LAGE v'yds: Julius-Echter-Berg, Kronsberg.

Wittmann, Weingut Rhh ★★★ Philipp Wittmann has propelled this organic estate to the top ranks (since 1999). Crystal-clear, minerally, dry RIES from QBA to GROSSES GEWÄCHS and magnificent TBA.

Wöhrwag, Weingut Würt ★★ →★★★ Just outside Stuttgart, this estate produces succulent reds, but above all elegant, dry RIES and brilliant EISWEIN.

Wolf, J L Pfz ★★ →★★★ WACHENHEIM estate, leased by Ernst LOOSEN of BERNKASTEL. Dry PFALZ RIES (esp Forster Pechstein), with a MOSEL-like finesse. Sound and consistent rather than dazzling.

Württemberg 05 07 08 09 10 11 Southern region, little-known outside Germany. Ambitions now rising, esp concentrated, fruit-driven reds (LEMBERGER, Samtrot, SPÄTBURGUNDER). Experiments, incl SAUV BL and dark new crossings bred by Weinsberg research station. RIES (mostly TROCKEN) tends to be rustic, although those from the high-altitude Remstal area close to Stuttgart can have refinement.

Würzburg Frank ★★ →★★★★ 97 01 03 04 05 08 09 10 11 Great baroque city on the Main, centre of FRANKEN wine: fine, full-bodied, dry RIES and esp SILVANER. ERSTE LAGE v'yds: Innere Leiste, Stein, Stein-Harfe. Growers incl: BÜRGERSPITAL, JULIUSSPITAL, STAATLICHER HOFKELLER, Weingut am Stein.

Zehnthof, Weingut Frank ★★ SILVANER and Pinot varieties, typically cask-fermented, from Luckert family in Sulzfeld.

Zell M-S-R w ★ →★★★ 97 01 05 07 08 09 10 11 Best-known lower MOSEL village, esp for awful GROSSLAGE: Schwarze Katz (Black Cat). RIES on steep slate gives aromatic wines. Top grower is Kallfelz.

Zeltingen M-M ★★ →★★★★ 90 93 95 96 97 98 99 01 02 04 05 06 07 08 09 10 11 Top but sometimes underrated MOSEL village nr WEHLEN. Lively, crisp RIES. ERSTE LAGE v'yd: SONNENUHR. Top growers: M MOLITOR, J J PRÜM, SELBACH-OSTER.

Ziereisen, Weingut Bad ★★★ 03 04 05 07 08 09 10 11 Carpenter Hans-Peter Ziereisen turned winemaker. Full palette from BADEN: minerally GUTEDEL, dry PINOTS (w). Best are SPÄTBURGUNDERS from small v'yd plots with dialect names: Schulen, Tschuppen, Rhini. V.gd old-vine selections Jaspis (GRAU- and Spätburgunder).

Zilliken, Forstmeister Geltz M-S-R ★★★ →★★★★ 93 94 95 96 97 01 02 04 05 07 08 09 10 11 Former estate of Prussian royal forester at SAARBURG and OCKFEN, SAAR. Produces intensely minerally *Ries from Saarburg Rausch* and OCKFEN Bockstein, incl superb AUSLESE and EISWEIN with excellent ageing potential.

Luxembourg

It doesn't hurt to think of Luxembourg as a halfway house between Germany and France – in wine terms, at least. Its Rieslings seem half-German, half-French: old-school Alsace Riesling on the nose, with the lightness and the sweet-and-sour notes of an off-dry Nahe on the palate. The 1,270ha of vines along the *Moselle Luxembourgeoise* are, however, a particular mix. There's more Rivaner (Müller-Thurgau, 27%), Auxerrois (14%) and Pinot Gris (14%) than Riesling (12%). The soil is a patchwork of Trias soils: deep Keuper, red sandstone and shell limestone.

Auxerrois is Luxembourg's specialty. Good examples (Bechelsberg from Stronck-Pinnel, or Schumacher-Lethal) show a complex spiciness, with a rounder palate than its relative, Pinot Blanc. But poor Auxerrois is just sweetish and lean. Pinot Gris usually has more extract and more depth.

The wine law doesn't differentiate between dry and off-dry. Most whites have strong acidity and some sweetness. There's a lot of sparkling wine, too. Crémant de Luxembourg can be anything from refined to rustic, cheaper versions typically tasting extra-dry even if labelled brut. *The best can be very good value* – look for Heritage Brut from Gales, St Pierre et Paul Brut from Stronck-Pinnel, Riesling Brut from Legill, Montmollin Brut from Duhr Frères, Brut Vintage from Clos de Rochers, Brut Vintage from Bernard-Massard or Brut Tradition from Sunnen-Hoffmann.

Best growers incl: Alice Hartmann at Wormeldange (Crémant Grande Cuvée, very good Riesling La Chapelle and Les Terrasses); Aly Duhr at Ahn (Machtum Pinot Gris Fût 9, Riesling Nussbaum and barrel-aged Chardonnay Monsalvat) and Gales at Remich (Wellenstein Kurschels Riesling, Wellenstein Foulschette Pinot Gris).

There are two organic producers: Sunnen-Hoffmann at Remerschen (well-structured Riesling from Remerschen and Wintrange) and Krier-Welbes at Ellange (in conversion, salty Riesling from Remerschen Hiischeberg Sélection and dense Pinot Gris from Bech-Kleinmacher Naumberg).

Producers at ★★→★★★: Château de Schengen (Pinot Gris), Cep d'Or (good Pinots, white and red), Clos de Rochers (Riesling from Grevenmacher and Ahn, intense Riesling Vin de Glace), Duhr Frères/ Clos Mon Vieux Moulin (good Gewurztraminer Fût 13, very good Pinot N Fût 2 and lovely Riesling Äiswäin (aka Icewine), Schumacher-Knepper (Wintringer Felsberg Riesling Fût 35) and Stronck-Pinnel (very good Riesling Sélection, Hëtt and Deifert – with almost Saar-like flavours – and excellent Pinot Blanc Sélection).

Young and ambitious producers set out to join the top class: Fränk Kayl, Schmit-Fohl, Château Pauqué and Paul Legill. Other good producers incl: Mathis Bastian, Charles Decker, Gloden & Fils, Domaine Mathes, Schlink-Hoffeld, Caves St-Martin. Domaines Vinsmoselle is a union of co-ops, with wines that are made mostly in a more commercial style. Good premium label: François Valentiny.

Spain & Portugal

Abbreviations used in the text:

Alel	Alella	P Vas	País Vasco
Alen	Alentejo	Pen	Penedès
Alg	Algarve	Pri	Priorat
Alic	Alicante	Rib del D	Ribera
Ara	Aragón		del Duero
Bair	Bairrada	Rio	Rioja
Bei Int	Beiras Interior	R Ala	Rioja Alavesa
Bier	Bierzo	R Alt	Rioja Alta
Bul	Bullas	RB	Rioja Baja
Cád	Cádiz	Set	Setúbal
Can	Canaries	Som	Somontano
C-La M	Castilla-	Tej	Tejo
	La Mancha	U-R	Utiel-Requena
C y L	Castilla y León	V'cia	Valencia
Cat	Catalunya		
Cos del S	Costers del Segre		
Dou	Douro		
Emp	Empordà-Ampurdán		
Gal	Galicia		
La M	La Mancha		
Lis	Lisboa		
Mad	Madrid, Vinos de		
Mall	Mallorca		
Min	Minho		
Mont-M	Montilla-Moriles		
Mur	Murcia		
Nav	Navarra		

Whether Spain is a serious challenger to Italy at the moment is a good subject for debate. On the Italian side are a multitude of different grapes, each in its cultural corner, strung out along the hugely varied Italian boot. Italy wins for variety of styles and flavours, for food (despite Spain's super-chefs) and for overall charm. Spain scores for the consistency of its product: fewer surprises and generally lower prices.

The Spanish wine picture is changing fast. No longer are the most famous regions necessarily the most exciting; but equally, the panacea adopted by some emerging regions to tame rustic tannins or add value – the excessive use of new oak – is looking dated. The best of Spain is focusing on balance. Even Priorat is less fearsomely chunky than in the past. Tempranillo is more popular than ever, and winemakers are relishing the depth of old (centenarian) plantings of Garnacha. Spain's greatest reds today come from Priorat, Ribera del Duero and Jumilla as well as Rioja, but never forget that Spain's greatest wines are Sherries.

Portugal will have to dig deeper than ever to front out the current economic crisis, but it has a fabulous selling point in its scarcely explored native vines, varieties reared for its Atlantic climate, and in the climate itself. The tannic balance of Bordeaux comes naturally to Portugal. What's more, its best winemakers are spreading their wings and visiting

More heavily shaded areas are the wine-growing regions.

their talents on other regions. Many of Portugal's best wines are blends, although there is pressure to copy the global trend for mono-varietal wines, singling out a handful of native grapes for international stardom. The hot favourites are red Touriga Nacional and white Alvarinho. But there's resistance; in Bairrada the grubbing-up of the excellent variety Baga has prompted producers to form Baga Friends to promote it. Expect tannins, more or less intelligently handled, and remember the best reds need time. There is real class in some unexpected places.

SPAIN

Recent vintages

Rioja

2011 A long, hot summer with healthy grapes, but lower yields and more concentrated fruit than 2010.

2010 Officially an *excelente* vintage. For growers it was disastrous as the economic crisis meant low prices. One for buyers.

2009 Despite the hot summer a repeat of 2003 was avoided. Some very good results, with Riojas Alta and Baja faring best.

2008 The best are fresh and aromatic, a little lower in alcohol.

2007 A difficult vintage; most wines are ready to drink with bright, fresh fruit.

2006 Wines to drink now; fragrant when young, not built to last.

2005 Another stand-out vintage of the decade, with wines to drink or keep. Some prefer 2004; others 2005. Try them both.

2004 Outstanding vintage, with wines in balance retaining vibrant young fruit.

2003 Very hot summer spoiled freshness of much fruit. In general, drink up.

2002 In contrast with 2001, wines are showing poorly and will not keep.

2001 This remains an exceptional year. Many Gran Reservas are slipping into a silky maturity.

Aalto Rib del D r ★★★→★★★★ 04' 05 06 07 08 Founded 1996, with tip-top pedigree. Mariano García, ex-VEGA SICILIA, and partner from CONSEJO REGULADOR aim to make best TINTO FINO (TEMPRANILLO) in region. PS is dense; built to last. Family wineries are MAURO, Maurodos.

Abadía Retuerta C y L r ★★→★★★ 04 05 06 07 08 09 Next door to RIBERA DEL DUERO; famed for ripe, modern style, international varieties, influential winemakers and grand hotel in historic former monastery. Gd-value Rívola; spicier Selección Especial; 100% TEMPRANILLO Pago Negralada; sumptuous SYRAH Pago la Garduña.

Albet i Noya Cat r p w sp ★★→★★★ Pioneer and leader in organics. Wide portfolio with gd CAVA.

Alicante Alic r w sw ★→★★★ The Levant is coming to life. All around the coastal fleshpots, and in the desert interior, new generations are reviving family v'yds. Ths is red wine country led by ENRIQUE MENDOZA, Bernabé Navarro, ARTADI's El Sequé, Sierra Salinas. Don't miss outstanding sweet MOSCATELS, esp GUTIÉRREZ DE LA VEGA; historic sweet MONASTRELL FONDILLÓN.

Alión Rib del D ★★★★ 03 04' 05' 06 07 The more modern cousin, not the poor relation, of VEGA SICILIA. 100% TINTO FINO, Nevers oak, with dense black fruit.

Álvaro Palacios Pri r ★★→★★★★ The man who had the confidence to charge sky-high prices for PRIORAT and so put the region on the map. Camins del Priorat (09) is v.gd value, floral, introduction to Priorat's charms. Les Terrasses is bigger, spicier (07); FINCA DOFÍ (06) has a dark undertone of CAB SAUV, SYRAH, MERLOT, CARIÑENA. Super-pricey L'Ermita (04) is powerful and dense from low-yielding GARNACHA. Also see his influence in BIERZO, RIOJA.

Ameztoi P Vas w ★★ Leading producer of briskly spritzy DYA CHACOLÍ, just outside San Sebastián.

Artadi Alic, Nav, R Ala r ★★★ 04' 05 06 07 Outstanding modern RIOJAS: taut, powerful single-v'yd El Pisón needs 8–10 yrs; as does spicy, smoky Pagos Viejos. V.gd, equally modern El Sequé (r) ALICANTE, and Artazuri (r, DYA p) NAVARRA.

Baigorri R Ala r w ★★★ 04' 05' 06 07' 08 Wines as glamorous as the architecture, both statement of modern RIOJA. Emphatic style, black fruits, bold tannins, upbeat oak. Garage (*see* France) wins the prizes. RESERVA more approachable.

Barón de Ley RB r p w ★→★★ Modern wines made in one-time Benedictine monastery. V.gd 7 VIÑAS, red blend of seven varieties, and DYA ROSADO.

Báscula, La Alic, Rib del D, Rio r w sw ★★ A young brand offering wines in fashionable regions, eg. ALICANTE, JUMILLA, RIBERA DEL DUERO, RIOJA, Terra Alta, Yecla. Made by South African winemaker Bruce Jack and British MW Ed Adams.

Benjamin Romeo Rio r w ★★→★★★★ Formerly of ARTADI, Romeo is a new-wave star, with precise expression of bush vines. Gd white blend, Predicador; rich, *top white Que Bonito Cacareaba*, well-priced DYA red, also called Predicador. Flagship red Contador, "super second" La Cueva del Contador. V. concentrated parcel, La VIÑA de Andrés Romeo.

Berberana Rio r w p ★ Popular, juicy RIOJAS, part of BODEGAS UNIDAS group, which also incl MARQUÉS DE MONISTROL CAVA, workmanlike Marqués de la Concordia, MARQUÉS DE GRIÑÓN RIOJAS and Durius RIBERA DEL DUERO. GRAN RESERVA VIÑA Alarde 03 is finely spicy.

Beronia Rio r w p ★★ 04 05 06 07 08 09 A transformation. Owner GONZÁLEZ BYASS invested in oak and winemaking. Result: confidently revived red; gd ROSADO.

Bierzo Bier r w ★→★★★ Slate soils, a crunchy *Pinot-like red – Mencía* – and ethereal white GODELLO have brought young winemakers buzzing. Best: Dominio de Tares, DESCENDIENTES DE J PALACIOS, Gancedo, Luna Berberide, Peique, Pittacum. Also: Castro Ventosa of influential winemaker Raúl Pérez – his top wine: Ultreia St Jacques 08 (r).

Binissalem Mall r w p ★★ Best-known MALLORCA DO northeast of Palma. Two-thirds red, mainly tannic Mantonegro grape. Biniagual, Binigrau, Macià Batle.

Bodega A cellar; a wine shop; a business making, blending and/or shipping wine.

Borsao Ara r ★★ Leader of GARNACHA revival in CAMPO DE BORJA, with wines superior to former rustic profile of DO. Tres Picos is top wine.

Briones R Alt Small RIOJAN hilltop town nr HARO, peppered with underground cellars. Producers incl FINCA ALLENDE, Miguel Merino. Worth a detour to the DINASTÍA VIVANCO wine musuem.

Bullas Mur r w p ★→★★ High (400–800 metres), dry in an excessively Mediterranean climate. Just 14 producers. Best: BODEGAS Monastrell, with dense, rich Chaveo.

Calatayud Ara r w p ★→★★★ Rapidly improving DO rediscovering its old-vine GARNACHA; sometimes blended with SYRAH. Best: BODEGAS Ateca (*see* JUAN GIL), El Escocés Volante (Scots MW Norrel Robertson), esp El Puño, El Jalón, Lobban (El Gordito Garnacha by Scots winemaker Pamela Geddes), Virgén de la Sierra (Cruz de Piedra).

Spain has twice the vineyard acreage of France but makes less wine.

Campo de Borja Ara r w p ★→★★★ Prices creeping up but still spot-on source of good-value DYA juicy GARNACHA and TEMPRANILLO, eg. BODEGAS Aragonesas, BORSAO. Top wine Alto Moncayo's Aquilón.

Campo Viejo r w p ★→★★ RIOJA's biggest brand. Gd-value RESERVA and GRAN RESERVA. Top-of-the-range Dominio. Also CAVA producer.

Canary Islands (Islas Canarias) r p w ★→★★★ V'yds not visited by phylloxera; original wines. No less than nine DOS. Best bet are the dessert MALVASÍAS and MOSCATELS. But local dry wines from white LISTÁN and Marmajuelo, black Negramoll and Vijariego should be tried.

Capçanes, Celler de Cat r w p sw ★→★★★ One of Spain's top co-ops. Great-value, expressive wines from MONTSANT. Also a kosher specialist.

Cariñena Ara r w p ★→★★★ The one DO that is also the name of a grape variety. Solid, not exciting, but gd value; BODEGAS Añadas and Victoria are reliable.

Castaño Mur r w p sw ★→★★ Putting YECLA on the map with v fine MONASTRELL, from value Espinal to excellent Casa Cisca. Delicious sweet red DULCE.

Castell del Remei Cos del S r p w ★★→★★★★ Picturesque restored 18th-century estate. Gd white blends: gd-value vanilla and red-cherry Gotim Bru 07 TEMPRANILLO/ MERLOT/CAB SAUV blend; elegant, spicy 1780; powerful Oda.

Castilla y León r p w ★→★★★ Province is an exciting source of authentic local wines, revived varieties (some elegant, some rustic) and great value. Unfamiliar DOS well worth discovering incl Arribes (esp La Setera), BIERZO, CIGALES, Tierra de León, Tierra del Vino de Zamora, plus quality region Valles de Benavente. Red grapes incl MENCÍA, Juan García, Prieto Picudo, TINTA DEL PAÍS; whites Doña Blanca. Gd, deeply coloured ROSADO.

Castillo Perelada Emp, Pri r p w sp ★→★★★ Glamorous project with large estate, hotel, summer concerts and rapidly improving wines. Gd CAVAS esp Gran

Claustro; modern reds, incl Ex Ex MONASTRELL, FINCA Garbet SYRAH. Rare 12-yr-old, solera-aged GARNATXA de l'Empordà. Exceptional Casa Gran del Siurana, Gran Cruor (06), SYRAH blend from PRIORAT.

Catalunya r p w sp Still less than a decade old (2004) this vast DO covers the whole of Catalonia: seashore, mtn and in-between. Contains some of Spain's top names incl, TORRES and much else besides.

Cava Spain's traditional-method sparkling is getting better. Most is made in PENEDÈS – in or around San Sadurní d'Anoia – but the term applies to a number of other regions, incl RIOJA. Market leaders are FREIXENET and CODORNÍU. Try Agustí Torelló, Castell Sant Antoni, CASTILLO PERELADA, GRAMONA, PARXET, Raimat, Recaredo (biodynamic), Sumarroca. CHARD and PINOT were invading blends, but now much research into improving quality of traditional XAREL-LO grape.

Cérvoles Cos del S r w sw ★★→★★★ High mountainous estate just north of PRIORAT making concentrated reds from CAB SAUV/TEMPRANILLO/GARNACHA and powerful, creamy, lemon-tinged, barrel-fermented Blanc; also succulent sweet red.

Chacolí / Txakoli P Vas (r) (p) w ★→★★★ DYA The Basque wine. V'yds face the chilly winds of the Cantabrian sea, hence the aromatic, often thrilling crunchiness of the *pétillant* whites, locally poured into tumblers from a height. Top names: Ameztoi, Txomin Etxaniz.

Chivite Nav r p w sw ★★→★★★★ Historic NAVARRA BODEGA. Many gd wines, some stars. Popular DYA range Gran Feudo, esp ROSADO and Sobre Lias (*sur lie*). Excellent *Colección 125* range, incl serious CHARD 07, delicate botrytis MOSCATEL. Young PAGO wine of beautiful Arínzano estate finding its feet. In RIOJA owns VIÑA Salceda (v.gd Conde de la Salceda), in RUEDA *Baluarte* (superb DYA VERDEJO).

Cigales C y L r p (w) ★→★★★ Lying between RIBERA DEL DUERO and TORO, tiny Cigales fights to make itself heard. Yet there is real potential beyond commercial DYA reds for serious old-vine TEMPRANILLO. Voluptuous César Príncipe; more restrained Traslanzas and Valdelosfrailes.

Cillar de Silos Rib del D r p ★★ Dense, structured, smoky reds from the talented Aragón family.

Clos d'Agon Cat r w ★★★ Blue-chip project. Peter Sisseck of PINGUS made first vintage, still consults. Fresh, spicy, herbal VIOGNIER/ROUSSANNE/MARSANNE white and delicious, modern, deeply flavoured CAB SAUV/SYRAH/MERLOT/CAB FR Clos d'Agón Negre as well as less-seen Clos Valmaña.

Clos Mogador Pri r ★★★→★★★★ 03 04 05 06 07 08 In a region now filled with big names, René Barbier has been a quiet godfather to the younger generations of winemakers. Clos Mogador still commands respect and the '05 was the first to receive the new, high *Vi de Finca Qualificada* classification. Exceptionally interesting is his spicy, fragrant, honeyed Clos Nelin (09) white blend.

Spain now even makes its own Icewine – with a little help from a freezer!

Codorníu Cos del S, Pen, Pri, Rib del D, Rio r p w sp ★→★★★★ One of the two largest CAVA firms, owned by the Raventós family, rivals to FREIXENET, favouring non-indigenous varieties, esp CHARD. Best: gd vintage, Reina Maria Cristina, v. dry Non Plus Ultra and PINOT N. Now new winemaking team leads research into local varieties, plus revives other members of group. Extensive v'yds of Raimat in COSTERS DEL SEGRE yielding quality, Legaris in RIBERA DEL DUERO improving; though formerly slumbering Bilbaínas in RIOJA still work in progress. *See also* SCALA DEI.

Conca de Barberà Cat r p w Small Catalan DO once purely a feeder of quality fruit to large enterprises, now has some excellent wineries, incl the biodynamic Escoda-Sanahuja. Top TORRES Grans Muralles and Milmanda both produced in this DO.

Condado de Haza Rib del D r ★★★ 05 06 07 08 Pure TINTO FINO aged in American oak. Second wine of Alejandro Fernández's PESQUERA and unfairly overlooked.

Consejo Regulador Organization that controls a DO, each DO has its own. Quality as inconsistent as the wines they represent: some bureaucratic, others enterprising.

Contino R Ala r (p) w ★★★★ 01 04 05' 06 07' Jesus Madrazo focuses on his single v'yd (RIOJA's first) with consistent success. His GRACIANO is a perfect expression of this difficult variety; top wine is VIÑA del Olivo. Ripe, nutty, textured white (09); trials of ROSADO look promising. *See* CUNE.

Costers del Segre Cat r p w sp ★★→★★★ Geographically divided DO with excellent producers, incl mountainous Castell d'Encus (run by TORRES MD Raul Bobet, experimenting with medieval fermenters carved out of rock), CASTELL DEL REMEI, CÉRVOLES, coastal Raimat, TOMÁS CUSINÉ.

> ### Varying the diet
> The ubiquitous TEMPRANILLO sails under different flags of convenience according to where you are in Spain: TINTO FINO, Tinta de Toro, CENCIBEL... they're all listed on pp.16–26. GARNACHA has fewer synonyms but is also widely spread. But Spain has been discovering a raft of other grapes. MENCÍA, Bobal, GRACIANO, Caino, Lado, Juan García, Manto Negro, Maturana, Doña Blanca, Albillo, Samsó.... There are around 100 different grapes being grown in Spain now, if you incl foreign invaders, adding nuance and complexity.

Crianza Refers to the ageing of wine. New or unaged wine is *sin* (without) Crianza or JOVEN. In general Crianzas must be at least 2 yrs old (with six mths–1 yr in oak) and must not be released before the 3rd yr. *See* RESERVA.

CVNE R Alt r p w ★→★★★★ Pronounced *"coo-nee"*, the once-traditional Compañía Vitivinícola del Norte de España (1879), now on the up. Barrel-fermented Blanco (09) is revived and refreshed. Reliable, fruity RESERVA 06; brambly Imperial Reserva 07; delicate, savoury VIÑA Real GRAN RESERVA 01. CONTINO is a member of the group but operates independently.

Cusiné, Tomás Cos del S r w ★★→★★★ One of Spain's most innovative winemakers, originally behind CASTELL DEL REMEI and CÉRVOLES. Individual, modern wines, incl TEMPRANILLO blend Vilosell, and original ten-variety white blend Auzells.

Denominación de Origen (DO), Denominación de Origen Protegida (DOP) Changes to EU legislation are showing only slowly on back labels. In Spain the former Denominación de Origen (DO) and DO Calificada are now grouped as DOP along with the single-estate PAGO denomination. The lesser category of VCPRD is becoming VCIG (*Vinos de Calidad de Indicación Geográfica*). Got that?

Dinastía Vivanco R Alt r w ★★ Major family-run commercial BODEGA in BRIONES, with some interesting varietal wines. *Wine museum is worth the detour*.

Dominio de Valdepusa C-La M r w ★★→★★★ 04 05 06 07 08 Carlos Falcó, MARQUÉS DE GRIÑÓN, is a determined innovator. At family estate nr Toledo he has been a confident rule-breaker since 1970s, pioneering SYRAH, PETIT VERDOT, drip irrigation, soil science, working with top consultants. Ultimately recognized as a PAGO. Wines are savoury and v. concentrated. Top wine is dense Emeritus blend 04. Makes wine in VINOS DE MADRID DO at El Rincón.

Dulce Sweet.

Empordà-Ampurdán Cat r p w ★→★★ Small, fashionable DO nr French border, a centre of creativity. Best wineries: CASTILLO PERELADA, Celler Marti Fabra, Pere Guardiola. Quirky, young Espelt grows 17 varieties: try GARNACHA/CARIGNAN Sauló.

Enate Som r p w ★★→★★★ Established SOMONTANO name, known for artistic labels, DYA GEWURZ and barrel-fermented CHARD, gd modern SYRAH, but also round, satisfyingly balanced CAB/MERLOT Especial RESERVA 01 02 05.

Enrique Mendoza Alic r w sw ★★ Pepe Mendoza is a key figure in the resurgence of DO and of MONASTRELL grape. Wines as expressive and individual as the man. Vibrant Tremenda **08**, dense, rustic Estrecho **06**. Also honeyed, sweet MOSCATEL.

Espumoso Sparkling wine, but not made according to the traditional method, unlike CAVA. Usually cheaper.

Finca Farm or estate (eg. FINCA ALLENDE).

Finca Allende R Alt r w ★★★ **04' 05** A leader in the "high expression" movement in BRIONES, Miguel Ángel de Gregorio focuses on single-v'yd TEMPRANILLO. *Tinto is floral, spicy*; single-v'yd Calvario is bold and balanced; Aurus is sumptuous. V. fine, oak-influenced Martires RIOJA Blanco **08**. Also FINCA Coronado, LA MANCHA.

Finca Sandoval C-La M r ★★→★★★ Wine-writer Victor de la Serna is serious about making wine, too: with his FINCA Sandoval (SYRAH/MONASTRELL/Bobal) he champions two indigenous varieties. Second wine, Salia (Syrah/GARNACHA/Bobal) simpler but half the price.

Chardonnay has finally made it into a Rioja blend: Faustino V Blanco.

Fondillón Alic sw ★→★★★ Once-fabled sweet red from MONASTRELL, aged to survive sea voyages. Now matured in oak for min 10 yrs; some soleras (*see* Sherry) of great age. Small production by eg. GUTIÉRREZ DE LA VEGA, Primitivo Quiles.

Freixenet Pen p w sp ★→★★★ Huge CAVA firm owned by Ferrer family. Rival of similarly enormous CODORNÍU. Best-known for frosted, black-bottled Cordón Negro and standard Carta Nevada. New top Cava Elyssia is a real step up; refreshed by CHARD and PINOT N. Also controls Castellblanch, Conde de Caralt, Segura Viudas and Bordeaux négociant Yvon Mau.

Galicia (r) w Rainy northwestern corner of Spain producing some of Spain's best whites (*see* RÍAS BAIXAS, MONTERREI, Ribeira Sacra, RIBEIRO, VALDEORRAS).

Gramona Pen r w sw sp ★★→★★★ Star CAVA cellar; fifth generation makes impressive long-aged CAVAS, incl Imperial GRAN RESERVA, III Lustros **04**, Argent **07**. Extensive research and experimental plantings also give rise to gd XAREL-LO-dominated Celler Batle, sweet wines, incl Icewines and impressive CHARD/SAUV BL Gra a Gra Blanco DULCE.

Gran Reserva *See* RESERVA.

Gutiérrez de la Vega Alic r w sw ★→★★★ Small estate of opera-loving former general. Produces reds but focuses on fragrant, honeyed Casta Diva range of sweet MOSCATELS. Also keeps up FONDILLÓN tradition.

Hacienda Monasterio Rib del D r ★★ **04 05 06 07** Cult winemaker Peter Sisseck's involvement ensures a high profile for TINTO FINO/CAB/MERLOT blends. Reputation is deserved with reliable *tinto*, approachable CRIANZA and elegantly round, complex RESERVA.

Haro R Alt The heart of the RIOJA Alta, with the great names of Rioja clustered in and around the old transport hub of the railway station. Visit LÓPEZ DE HEREDIA, MUGA, LA RIOJA ALTA, as well as modern RODA.

Huerta de Albalá Cád r ★★→★★★ V. ambitious young (2006) Andalusian estate in foothills of Sierra de Grazalema, blending SYRAH, MERLOT, CAB SAUV and rare, local Tintilla de Rota. Dark, figgy 15% Tintilla blend DYA Barbazul, gd serious Taberner **07**.

Inurrieta Nav r p w ★★→★★★ Stylish modern estate; one to watch. Gd French-oaked Norte CAB/MERLOT, lively DYA Mediodía ROSADO. Top wine: Altos de Inurrieta. Promising production of GRACIANO, trials of varieties not yet permitted by DO.

Jaro Rib del D r ★★→★★★ A great site for v'yds: between HACIENDA MONASTERIO and PESQUERA. Founded 2000 by member of the Osborne (Sherry) family. Gd-value Sembro, intense, minerally Chafandín, seriously expensive Sed de Caná.

Jorge Ordoñez US-based importer of top Spanish wines. Investor in v'yds, influential in building reputation of New Spain in the USA, esp "forgotten" regions: eg. CALATAYUD, MÁLAGA, RUEDA.

José Pariente w ★★ Victoria Pariente makes crisp DYA VERDEJO of shining clarity in tiny RUEDA winery named after her father.

Joven Young, unoaked wine, increasingly popular as quality improves, esp reds from RIOJA Alavesa with some Beaujolais-style carbonic maceration. *See* CRIANZA.

Juan Gil Mur r ★★→★★★ Fourth-generation family business relaunched in 2002 with mission to make the best in JUMILLA. Gd young MONASTRELLS; dense, powerful top wines Clio and El Nido. Family group also incl modern wines in rising DOS, incl Shaya (RUEDA), Can Blau (MONTSANT).

Jumilla Mur r (p) (w) ★→★★★ Part of the new Spain. Arid v'yds in mtns north of Murcia; old MONASTRELL vines being rediscovered by ambitious winemakers. TEMPRANILLO, MERLOT, CAB, SYRAH, PETIT VERDOT also important. Top producer: JUAN GIL with El Nido. Also follow: Agapito Rico, Casa Castillo, CASTAÑO with Casa Cisca, Carchelo, Luzón, Valle del Carche.

Juvé & Camps Pen w sp ★★★ Consistently gd family firm for top-quality CAVA from free-run juice. RESERVA de la Familia is the stalwart, with top-end GRAN RESERVA and Milesimé CHARD GRAN RESERVA.

La Mancha C-La M r p w ★→★★ Spain's largest, least impressive wine region, south of Madrid, now slowly moving. Best: PESQUERA's El Vínculo, MARTÍNEZ BUJANDA's FINCA Antigua, Volver.

León, Jean Pen r w ★★★ 04 05 06 07 Small firm; TORRES-owned since 1995. Gd, oaky CHARDS, expressive MERLOT and high-priced super-cuvée Zemis.

López de Heredia R Alt r p w sw ★★→★★★★ Remarkable "château" by HARO station. Wines just as remarkable. Vast old oak vats dominate winery; style all about long-bottle-aged, unfiltered wine. Cubillo 05 is younger range with GARNACHA; darker Bosconia; delicate, ripe *Tondonia 64, 70, 88, 89, 91, 01*. Whites have extensive barrel and bottle age: fascinating Gravonia 00, Tondonia GRAN RESERVA 87 91 93. Parchment-like Gran Reserva ROSADO 00.

Luis Cañas R Ala r w ★→★★★ Widely awarded family business giving honest quality from JOVEN to garage-style wines. Gd Selección de la Familia RESERVA 04, ultra-concentrated Hiru 3 Racimos 04. Also BODEGAS Amaren: modern, concentrated.

Madrid, Vinos de Madr r p w ★→★★ Historically Madrid's GARNACHA vines provided the capital's bar wines. Today old, often abandoned vines are part of a new wave of quality. Go-ahead names incl Bernabeleva: interesting burgundian white, top GARNACHA VIÑA Bonita. Also Marañones, Gosálbez-Ortí, run by a former Iberia pilot, Jeromín, Divo, Viñedos de San Martín (part of ENATE group) and El Regajal.

Málaga Once-famous DO now all but vanished in the face of rocketing real-estate values. TELMO RODRIGUEZ revived the moribund MOSCATEL industry with subtle, sweet *Molino Real*. Exceptional No 3 Old Vines Moscatel 06 from JORGE ORDOÑEZ's portfolio of sweet wines. Young producer Bentomiz, with promising sweet Moscatel, also reds, incl local Romé variety.

Mallorca r w ★→★★★ 05 06 07 08 09 10 Formerly tourist wines, now much improved; serious, fashionable in Barcelona. Family cellars remain, new investment brings innovation: eg. 4 Kilos. Plenty of interest in Anima Negra, tiny Sa Vinya de Can Servera, Hereus de Ribas, *Son Bordils, C'an Vidalet*. Also Biniagual. Reds blend traditional varieties (Mantonegro, Callet, Fogoneu) plus CAB, SYRAH, MERLOT. Whites (esp CHARD) improving fast. Two DOS: BINISSALEM, PLÁ I LLEVANT.

Marqués de Cáceres R Alt r p w ★→★★★ 01 04 05 06 07 08 09 Revered as original pioneer of fine French winemaking techniques in RIOJA. Faded glory at present. Gaudium is modern style; GRAN RESERVA the classic.

Marqués de Griñón R Alt RIOJA brand owned by BERBERANA. No longer any connection with the Marqués – *see* DOMINIO DE VALDEPUSA.

Marqués de Monistrol, Bodegas Pen r p sw sp ★→★★ Old BODEGA now owned by BODEGAS UNIDAS. Gd, reliable CAVA; but once-lively, modern PENEDÈS reds no longer so lively.

Marqués de Murrieta R Alt r p w ★★★ →★★★★ One of RIOJA's great names, most famous for magnificent Castillo de Ygay GRAN RESERVA. RESERVA Especial also outstanding. Best-value is dense, flavoursome Reserva. Convincingly modern Dalmau a surprise. *Capellania* is complex, textured white, one of Rioja's best.

Marqués de Riscal R Ala r (p) w ★★★ 01 04 05 06 07 08 09 Frank Gehry's titanium-roofed hotel sits uneasily by the traditional BODEGA. Wines also contrast modern and classic. Powerful Barón de Chirel RESERVA impresses more than traditional. A pioneer in RUEDA (since 1972) making vibrant DYA SAUV BL, VERDEJO.

Martínez Bujanda, Familia C-La M, Rio r p w ★→★★ Commercially astute business with a number of wineries, also makes private-label wines. Most attractive are *Finca Valpiedra*, charming single estate in RIOJA; FINCA Antigua in LA MANCHA.

Mas d'en Gil Pri r w ★★→★★★ Excitingly mineral Coma Blanca is one of PRIORAT's top whites; v.gd Coma Vella (r).

Mas Martinet Pri r ★★★→★★★★ 04 05 06 07 Boutique PRIORAT pioneer, producer of excellent Clos Martinet. Second wine: Martinet Bru 07. Now run by 2nd generation, incl influential winemaker Sara Pérez.

Mauro C y L r ★★★ 04 05 06 07 08 No need for DO in this new-wave BODEGA in Tudela del Duero. Pedigree of Mariano García of AALTO and formerly VEGA SICILIA says it all. Best is the pricey, Old-World-meets-New VENDIMIA Seleccionada, though top cuvée is powerful Terreus (04). Sister winery: Maurodos in TORO.

Méntrida C-La M r p ★→★★ Part of the New Spain. Former co-op country south of Madrid, now being put on the map by Arrayan, Canopy, and the influential Daniel Jiménez-Landi (Piélago 06, Sotorrondero 06).

Miguel Torres Cat, Pri, Rio r p w sw ★★→★★★★ Spain's most consistent producer. Consistently innovative – from low-alcohol Natureo to pioneering environmental management. Consistent quality from commercial to single-v'yd: ever-reliable DYA CATALUNYA VIÑA Sol and grapey Viña Esmeralda and PENEDÈS SAUV BL/ Parellada *Fransola*. Best reds: fine Penedès CABERNET Mas la Plana; balanced old-style RESERVA Real. CONCA DE BARBERÁ duo (*Milmanda*, one of Spain's finest CHARDS, *Grans Muralles* blend of local varieties) is stunning, and JEAN LEÓN has v.gd offerings, too. The range continues to expand with workmanlike offerings from RIBERA DEL DUERO (Celeste) and RIOJA (Ibéricos), gd PRIORAT (Salmos). Next generation Miguel and Mireia playing ever-larger part in company.

Monterrei Gal w ★→★★★ DYA Small but growing DO in Ourense, south-central GALICIA, making full-flavoured aromatic whites from Treixadura, GODELLO and Doña Blanca. Shows there is more to GALICIA than ALBARIÑO. Best is Gargalo.

Montilla-Moriles Mont-M w sw ★→★★★ Close to Córdoba, this is the home of succulent sun-dried PX grapes. Makes treacly black wines, but also fresher, more honeyed versions. Top names: TORO ALBALÁ, Alvear, Pérez Barquero. Also dry Fino-styles. Many PX grapes go to Jerez, which needs more.

Montsant Cat r (p) w ★→★★★ 04 05 06 07 08 09 Tucked in around PRIORAT Montsant echoes its neighbour's wines at lower prices. Fine GARNACHA BLANCA esp from Acústic. CARIÑENA and GARNACHA deliver dense, balsamic, minerally reds: Celler de Capçanes, Celler el Masroig, Can Blau, Étim, Joan d'Anguera Mas Perinet and Portal del Montsant (partner to gd Portal del Priorat) all offer impressive, individual wines.

Muga R Alt r p w (sp) ★★★→★★★★ Classic name in HARO, producing RIOJA's most aromatic and balanced reds. Gd barrel-fermented DYA VIURA reminiscent of burgundy; gd dry ROSADO; reds finely crafted and delicate. Best are wonderfully fragrant GRAN RESERVA Prado Enea (98 01); warm, full and long-lasting *Torre*

Muga (01 05 06); expressive and complex Aro and dense, rich, structured, full-flavoured Selección Especial (05).

Mustiguillo V'cia r ★★★ This decade-old BODEGA prefers to sit outside the DO and make its own rules, with scrupulous v'yd and cellar work. Shows the potential of local Bobal grape, blending in CAB SAUV, TEMPRANILLO. Junior, juicy Mestizaje, Cedar and cassis FINCA Terrerazo. Top wine: Quincha Corral aims to 100% Bobal.

Navarra r p (w) ★★→★★★ 01 04 05 06 07 08 09 10 Always in RIOJA's shadow. Freedom to use international varieties can work against it, confusing its real identity. Gd DYA ROSADO. Up-and-coming names incl: Pago de Larrainzar and confident, youthful Tandem. Best producers: Alzaña, ARTADI's Artazu, JULIÁN CHIVITE, INURRIETA, Nekeas, OCHOA, OTAZU, Pago de Cirsus, Señorío de Sarría with v.gd Rosado.

Nido, El r ★★★ Glamorous new star in the unpromising region of JUMILLA, with hitherto unfavoured MONASTRELL grapes. From serious, successful JUAN GIL stable results are impressive. Second wine, Clio, is 70% MONASTRELL, 30% CAB SAUV; dense, perfumed El Nido is the reverse proportions.

Ochoa Nav r p w sw sp ★→★★ Ochoa father made significant technical contribution to growth of NAVARRA. Ochoa children now working to return family BODEGA to its former glory. V.gd ROSADO; fine, sweet MOSCATEL; fun, sweet, Asti-like sparkling.

Otazu Nav r ★★★ NAVARRA estate awarded PAGO status in 2009, with a TEMPRANILLO/MERLOT/CAB SAUV blend.

Rioja's whites are returning to favour in all styles: from fresh to seriously aged.

Pago, Vinos de *Pago* denotes v'yd. In Spain legal status makes it roughly equivalent to French Grand Cru. But criticisms persist of lack of objective quality and differing traditions of *pagos* so far. Obvious absentees incl L'Ermita, PINGUS, Calvario (FINCA ALLENDE), CONTINO's VIÑA del Olivo and TORRES properties.

Pago de Carraovejas Rib del D r res ★★★ 01 04 05 06 07 V.gd Tinto CRIANZA; despite name no mere Crianza in quality. Top wine: v.gd Cuesta de las Liebres.

Palacio de Fefiñanes w ★★★★ DYA The most ethereal of ALBARIÑOS. Standard cuvée one of the finest. Two superior styles: creamy but light-of-touch barrel-fermented 1583 (yr winery was founded) and a super-fragrant, pricey, lees-aged, mandarin-orange-scented III.

Palacios, Descendientes de J Bier r ★★★ Young biodynamic producer Ricardo Pérez, nephew of ÁLVARO PALACIOS, draws out the floral character of the difficult MENCÍA grape. Fine young *Petalos* 09, plus serious Villa de Corullón and Las Lamas, grown on schist soils.

Palacios Remondo RB r w ★★→★★★ ÁLVARO PALACIOS, prince of PRIORAT, has revved up his family RIOJA winery (founded 1945); good news for Rioja Baja. Complex oaked-white Plácet (08) suggests citrus, peach and fennel. Reds: super-fruity, unoaked La VENDIMIA; organic, smoky, red-fruity La Montesa; big, mulberry-flavoured, GARNACHA-dominated Propiedad.

Parxet p w sp ★★→★★★ DYA Small CAVA producer valiantly competing with real-estate agents from Barcelona. Zesty styles incl Cuvée 21, excellent Brut Nature, fragrant Titiana PINOT N and expensive dessert version Cuvée Dessert. Best-known for refreshing, off-dry PANSÀ BLANCA and still white Marqués de Alella. Concentrated Tionio its outpost in RIBERA DEL DUERO.

Pazo de Señorans Gal w ★★★ DYA Exceptionally fragrant ALBARIÑOS from a benchmark BODEGA in RÍAS BAIXAS. V. fine Selección de Añada.

Penedès Cat r w sp ★→★★★★ Demarcated region w. of Barcelona, best-known for CAVA. Identity rather confused, esp since recent arrival of extensive CATALUNYA DO. Best: ALBET I NOYA, Can Rafols dels Caus (makers of barrel-fermented curiosity El Rocallis, from Italian Incrozio Manzoni variety), GRAMONA, JEAN LEÓN, TORRES.

Pesquera Rib del D r ★★★★ Veteran Alejandro Fernández built the global reputation of his wines and of RIBERA DEL DUERO, from his family v'yd opposite VEGA SICILIA. Using less oak-ageing than his neighbour, he makes satisfying CRIANZA and RESERVA, and excellent, mature Janus for those who can afford the price tag. Also at CONDADO DE HAZA. Dehesa La Granja (Zamora), El Vinculo (LA MANCHA).

Pingus, Dominio de Rib del D r ★★★★ 04 05 06 07 08 09 Dane Peter Sisseck's star continues to shine. Production of deluxe biodynamic Pingus (his childhood name) remains tiny. V. fine *Flor de Pingus* comes from rented v'yds, while Amelia is a single-barrel named after his wife.

Plá i Llevant Mall r w ★→★★★ 11 wineries comprise this tiny, lively island DO. Aromatic whites and intense, spicy reds. Best: Toni Gelabert, Jaime Mesquida, Miguel Oliver and Vins Can Majoral.

Priorat / Priorato Cat r w ★★→★★★★ 01 04 05 06 07 08 09 Isolated enclave, named after old monastery, renowned for *llicorella* (slate) soils, terraced v'yds. Rescued by René Barbier of CLOS MOGADOR, ÁLVARO PALACIOS and others. They remain consistently v.gd, showing characteristic minerally purity. Others piled in, but the resulting heavy oak and pricing is fortunately calming down. Palacios has driven the introduction of "village" DOS within Priorat. Other top names: Cims de Porrera, Clos Erasmus, Clos de l'Obac, Clos Nelin, Clos i Terrasses, MAS MARTINET, SCALA DEI, Val-Llach. Newer arrivals: Ferrer-Bobet, TORRES, Dits del Terra (project of South African Eben Sadie).

Looking for more information on grapes? Try the "Grapes" section on pp.16–26.

Rafael Palacios Gal w ★★★ Small estate producing exceptional wine from old GODELLO vines in the Bibei Valley. Rafael – ÁLVARO PALACIOS' younger brother, as quiet as his sibling is extrovert – is devoted to whites. Two distinct styles, both DYA: As Sortes is intense, toasty, citrus and white-peachy with v.gd acidity, a fine expression of GODELLO; oak-aged Louro do Bolo.

Remelluri, La Granja Nuestra Señora R Ala r w ★★→★★★ Glorious mountainous estate. TELMO RODRIGUEZ has returned to his family property where he created the intriguing DYA white made from six different varieties. Coming back to form.

Reserva Increasingly producers prefer simply to ignore the regulations. However – rare in the wine world – RESERVA has actual meaning in Spain. Red Reserva must spend at least 1 yr in cask and 2 yrs in bottle; GRAN RESERVAS, 2 yrs in cask and 3 yrs in bottle. With the crisis in Spain there are gd prices to be found for unsold Gran Reservas.

Rías Baixas Gal (r) w ★★→★★★★ Atlantic DO producing DYA whites, the darling of Madrid's diners, with prices to match. With crisis, prices are cooling and exports increasing. Founded on ALBARIÑO grown in five subzones: Val do Salnés, O Rosal, Condado do Tea, Soutomaior, Ribera do Ulla. The best are outstanding: Adegas Galegas, As Laxas, Castro Baroña, Castro Celta, Fillaboa, Coto de Xiabre, Gerardo Méndez, VIÑA Nora, Martin Codax, PALACIO DE FEFIÑANES, Pazo de Barrantes, PAZO DE SENORANS, Quinta do Lobelle, Santiago Ruíz, Terras Gauda, La Val, Valdamor, Zarate. Growing interest in longer lees-ageing and barrel-ageing.

Ribeiro Gal (r) w ★→★★★ DYA GALICIAN DO in western Ourense. Whites are relatively low in alcohol and acidity, made from Treixadura, TORRONTÉS, GODELLO, LOUREIRO, Lado. Top producers: VIÑA MEÍN, Lagar do Merens. Also specialty sweet-wine style Tostado.

Ribera del Duero Rib del D r p ★→★★★★ 04 05 06 07 08 09 Glamorous and pricey but still uneven is the verdict. The DO that houses VEGA SICILIA, HACIENDA MONASTERIO, PESQUERA and PINGUS has to be serious, but with 250 BODEGAS consistency is hard to find. Other top names: AALTO, ALIÓN, Astrales, CILLAR DE SILOS, CONDADO DE HAZA, Pago de los Capellanes, PAGO DE CARRAOVEJAS, Pérez Pascuas.

See also VDT ABADÍA RETUERTA and MAURO. Others to look for: Bohórquez, Dehesa de los Canónigos, O Fournier, Protos, Sastre, Tinio (*see* PARXET) and Vallebueno.

Rioja r p w ★→★★★★ Rioja has it all. International fame (supported by strong marketing), beautiful countryside, wines charming young and at 40 yrs. The region is cut three ways. Alavesa (part of the Basque country) offers fruity, Beaujolais-style winemaking for juicy JOVENS. Alta is the traditional home of Rioja and its great names. Warmer, lower Rioja Baja is gaining recognition by the efforts of eg. PALACIOS REMONDO. Styles come in three also: a revival in quality in the Jovens, an emphasis on serious RESERVAS with gd clean oak, and ultra-modern "high-expression" producers, with shiny wineries to match, who follow their own rules. Just a few BODEGAS, notably LA RIOJA ALTA, MUGA, LÓPEZ DE HEREDIA, continue to make delicate, aromatic, old-fashioned wines. Whites are looking up, with serious burgundy-style oak treatment and much-improved v'yd work.

Rioja Alta, La r ★★→★★★★ One of the great traditional RIOJAS with lovely RESERVAS and two outstanding GRAN RESERVAS. Alberdi is light, pretty and cedary; Ardanza is riper, a touch spicier but still elegant, boosted by GARNACHA; excellent, tangy, vanilla-edged Gran Reserva 904 (**95 97**) and fine, multi-layered Gran Reserva 890 (**95 97**), aged 6 yrs in oak. Also owns RÍAS BAIXAS Lagar de Cervera.

Roda R Rioj r ★★★★ 04' 05' 06 07 08 Modern BODEGA nr the station in HARO. Serious RESERVA reds from low-yield TEMPRANILLO, backed by study on clones. Just three wines: Roda, Roda I and Cirsión. Seek out outstanding Dauro olive oils from the same owners.

Rueda C y L w ★★→★★★ DO south of Valladolid with Spain's response to SAUV BL: zesty VERDEJO. Mostly DYA whites. "Rueda Verdejo" is 100% indigenous Verdejo. "Rueda" is blended with eg. Sauv Bl, VIURA. Barrel-fermented versions remain fashionable though less appealing. Best: Alvarez y Diez, Baluarte (*see* CHIVITE), *Belondrade*, François Lurton, MARQUÉS DE RISCAL, Naia, Ossian, JOSÉ PARIENTE, Palacio de Bornos, Javier Sanz, SITIOS DE BODEGA, Unzu, Veracruz, Vinos de Nieva, Vinos Sanz.

Scala Dei r ★★★★ V'yds of the "stairway to heaven" cling to slopes that tower over the old monastery. One of PRIORAT's classics, now carefully tended by part-owner CODORNÍU. Cartoixa (06) is a powerful CAB SAUV/GARNACHA with exceptional PRIORAT freshness. Negre is the most accessible; Prior Garnacha-dominated.

Sierra Cantabria Rioj r ★★★ Long-established in RIOJA (1870), the Eguren family rose to fame recently and rapidly. Now known for their first-rate Riojas, here and at their Vinedos de Pagans estate. Other properties incl Teso la Monja in TORO.

Sitios de Bodega C y L w ★★ 5th-generation winemaker Ricardo Sanz and siblings left father Antonio Sanz's Palacio de Bornos to set up their own winery in 2005. Excellent DYA RUEDA whites (Con Class, Palacio de Ménade). Also has other projects to work with MENCÍA and TEMPRANILLO.

Terroir is the new focus in Rioja, but Consejo won't allow village name on the label.

Somontano r p w ★★→★★★ Cool-climate DO in Pyrenean foothills east of Zaragoza has failed so far to fulfil hopes. Its freedom to use international varieties has also been its problem. Opt for MERLOT, GEWURZ, or CHARD. Best producers: ENATE, VIÑAS DEL VERO (with its top property Secastilla) owned by GONZÁLEZ BYASS (*see* Sherry); interesting arrivals incl the space-age BODEGAS Irius and Laus.

Tares, Dominio de Bier r w ★★★ MENCÍA is a tough grape, but dark, spicy *Bembibre* and *Cepas Viejas* prove what can be achieved. Sister winery VDT Dominio dos Tares makes a range of wines from the interesting black Prieto Picudo variety: simple Estay, more muscular Leione and big, spicy Cumal.

Telmo Rodríguez, Compañía de Vinos r w sw ★★→★★★ Telmo Rodríguez made his name, and many fine wines, by finding ancient v'yds. Now sources and makes a wide range of excellent DO wines from all over, incl MÁLAGA (*Molina Real* MOSCATELS), RIOJA (Lanzaga and Matallana), RUEDA (Basa), TORO (Dehesa Gago, Gago and Pago la Jara) and *Valdeorras* (DYA Gaba do Xil GODELLO). Now returning to REMELLURI in Rioja – look for rise in quality.

Toro C y L r ★→★★★★ Small, fashionable DO west of Valladolid starting to make wines that live up to its high profile. The local Tinta de Toro (TEMPRANILLO) is still often rustic and overalcoholic but some now boldly expressive. Try Maurodos (*see* AALTO), with fresh, black-fruit-scented Prima and glorious old-vine San Román, as well as VEGA SICILIA-owned Pintia. Glamour comes with Numanthia, Teso la Monja. Also recommended: Domaine Magrez Espagne, Elias Mora, Estancia Piedra, Pago la Jara from TELMO RODRÍGUEZ, QUINTA de la Quietud, Sobreño.

The evolution of oak

Spain is gradually learning to rein back on oak. In hot regions with alarmingly rustic tannins it was at first seen as a way of smoothing out those tannins (it makes the chains of molecules longer, and they feel softer in the mouth). But winemaking has evolved, the vines have got older, and the growers are moving towards greater balance; the result is that you no longer need a knife and fork to tackle even a glass of PRIORAT.

Toro Albalá Mont-M ★★→★★★ Antonio Sánchez is known for his eccentric wine museum and his remarkable old PXS. The Don PX is made from sun-dried grapes, barrique-aged for a minimum of 25 yrs. Black, with flavours of molasses, treacle, figs, it ages indefinitely. Current vintage is 1979, yet the 1910 was only recently released. Look out for un-aged amber-coloured DYA DULCE de Pasas, tasting of liquid raisins and apricots.

Txomin Etxaniz P Vas w ★★ Producer of zesty DYA CHACOLÍ, also offering different styles, incl riper, late-harvest version.

Unidas, Bodegas Umbrella organization controlling MARQUÉS DE MONISTROL and the BERBERANA brand, as well as workmanlike RIOJA Marqués de la Concordia and Durius from RIBERA DEL DUERO. Controls MARQUÉS DE GRIÑÓN Rioja brand.

Utiel-Requena U-R r p (w) ★→★★ Satellite region of VALENCIA forging its own identity with the excellent Bobal grape variety. However, it is hampered by its size (more than 40,000ha), which makes it primarily a feeder for the industrial requirements of nearby Valencia. New projects appearing, eg. Alvares Nölting. Pablo Ossorio of Murviedro (*see* Valencia) is behind ambitious Hispano-Suizas project. Makes Bassus PINOT N; Tantum Ergo CAVA, though an award-winner in Spain, is less impressive. Visit Vicente Gandía for lively wine museum of decorated barrels.

Valbuena Rib del D r ★★★ 99 00 01 02 03 04 05 VEGA SICILIA junior sold when just 5 yrs old. Best at about 10 yrs; some prefer it to its elder brother.

Valdeorras Gal r w ★→★★★ GALICIAN DO in northwest Ourense fighting off its co-op-inspired image by virtue of its DYA GODELLO. Best: Godeval, RAFAEL PALACIOS, A Tapada and TELMO RODRÍGUEZ.

Valdepeñas C-La M r (w) ★→★★ Large DO nr Andalucían border. Gd-value lookalike RIOJA reds, made primarily from CENCIBEL (TEMPRANILLO) grape. One producer shines: Félix Solís; *Viña Albali* brand offers real value.

Valduero Rib del D, Rio, C y L r w ★★ RIBERA DEL DUERO family business. V.gd RESERVA 05, gd 6 Años 04, ripe, modern, concentrated Una Cepa 07. Outposts in RIOJA, CASTILLA Y LEÓN. Also TORO (Arbucala 06: bold, dense).

Valencia V'cia r p w sw ★→★★ Big exporter of table wine. Primary source of budget, fortified, sweet MOSCATEL. Most reliable producer: Murviedro. Growing interest in inland, higher-altitude old-vines and minimal intervention in winemaking: eg. *garagiste* Rafael Cambra.

Vega Sicilia Rib del D r ★★★★ Spain's "first growth", though surprisingly not from the prestige zone of RIOJA. The only Spanish wine to have real value in the secondary auction market. Winemaking is distinguished by meticulous care and long maturation. Wines are deep in colour, with a cedarwood nose, intense and complex, finishing long; and long-lived. Youthful VALBUENA (05 06) – Tinto Fino with a little MALBEC, MERLOT – released with min 5 yrs in oak. Controlled, elegant flagship Único (98 00 02) is aged for 6 yrs in oak before bottling; RESERVA Especial spends up to 10 yrs in barrel, then declared as NV. Both wines have some CAB SAUV and Merlot. *See also* ALIÓN. Owns Pintia (TORO) and Oremus TOKÁJI (Hungary).

Vendimia Vintage.

Viña Literally, a v'yd.

Viña Meín Rib w ★★ Small estate in a gradually emerging GALICIAN DO, making two DYA exceptional whites of same name: one steel- and one barrel-fermented; both from some seven local varieties.

Viñas del Vero Som r p w ★★→★★★ Amid the mixed bag of varieties and wines in SOMONTANO, VIÑAS del Vero offers promise after its purchase by GONZÁLEZ BYASS (*see* Sherry). Its top wines are dense, modern cheerleaders for GARNACHA, with other varieties blended in. Second wines: La Miranda de Secastilla and v.gd Secastilla. Blecua is highly concentrated, made in best years.

Vino de la Tierra (VDT) Table wine usually of superior quality made in a demarcated region without DO. Covers immense geographical possibilities; category incl many prestigious producers, non-DO by choice to be freer of inflexible regulation and use the varieties they want.

Yecla Mur r (p) w ★→★★ Something stirs in Yecla. Only 11 producers, but a real focus on reviving MONASTRELL, esp CASTAÑO.

PORTUGAL

Recent vintages

2011 Widespread mildew reduced crops but fruit quality was excellent and the wines balanced, especially in Vinho Verde and Lisboa.

2010 Good quality and quantity all round. Bairrada had another excellent year. In Alentejo, may have been too hot.

2009 A good year overall. Bairrada and Lisboa excellent. Heat spikes in the Douro, Tejo and Alentejo resulted in some big wines with high alcohol.

2008 Almost uniformly excellent; Bairrada and Alentejo particularly. Good fruit intensity, balance and aroma.

2007 Aromatic whites and well-balanced reds with round tannins.

2006 Forward reds with soft, ripe fruit and whites with less acidity than usual.

2005 Powerful reds; the Douro's finely balanced reds shine.

2004 A cool summer but glorious September and October. Well-balanced reds.

Adega A cellar or winery.

Afros Vin r w sp ★★★ Dynamic and biodynamic (Portugal's first certified), crafting intense LOUREIRO and Vinhão (r) VINHO VERDE. Silenus is new oaked Vinhão; rosé on the cards.

Alenquer Lis r w ★★→★★★ 06 07 08 09' 10 11 Sheltered DOC making gd reds, now whites, just north of Lisbon. SYRAH pioneer MONTE D'OIRO leads the field; neighbour QUINTA do Convento makes a promising Syrah, too.

Alentejo Alen r (w) ★→★★★ 03 04' 05 06 07' 08' 09 10 11 Huge, southerly DOC divided into subregions with own DOCS: Borba, Redondo, Reguengos, PORTALEGRE, Evora, Granja-Amareleja, Vidigueira and Moura. VR name Alentejano preferred by many top estates. Dry climate makes rich, ripe reds: key varieties incl. SYRAH, Alicante Bouschet and recently PETIT VERDOT. Gd whites from Antão Vaz, blended with ARINTO, VERDELHO and Roupeiro. Established players CARTUXA, ESPORÃO, HERDADE DE MOUCHÃO, MOURO, JOÃO PORTUGAL RAMOS and Zambujeiro have potency and style. Of the new guard, HERDADE DA MALHADINHA NOVA, dos Grous and Dona Maria impress. Names to watch incl. HERDADE SÃO MIGUEL and do Rocim, Monte da Ravasqueira, Terrenus, Tiago Cabaço and QUINTA do Centro. Best co-ops: Borba, Redondo, Reguengos.

Algarve Alg r p w sp ★→★★ Southern coast VINHO REGIONAL; DOCS incl Lagos, Tavira, Lagoa, Portimão. Crooner Cliff Richard's ADEGA do Cantor and QUINTA do Morgado lead a shift from quaffers to quality. Names to watch: Monte da Casteleja and Quinta do Frances.

Aliança, Caves Bair r p w sp ★★→★★★ Large firm with four estates in BAIRRADA, incl QUINTA das Baceladas making gd reds and classic-method sparkling. Also interests in BEIRA INTERIOR (Casa d'Aguiar), ALENTEJO (Quinta da Terrugem), DÃO (Quinta da Garrida) and the DOURO (Quatro Ventos).

Ameal, Quinta do Vin w sw sp ★★★ DYA Leading LOUREIRO VINHO VERDE made by ANSELMO MENDES. Age-worthy, oaked Escolha; Special Late-Harvest; ARINTO ESPUMANTE.

Aveleda, Quinta da Vin r p w ★→★★ DYA Beautiful estate owned by four generations of the Guedes family. Consultancy of Denis Dubourdieu ensures standards, whether from estate fruit or widely sourced for *Casal García*, VINHO VERDE's biggest-selling brand. Also gd (if not esp inspiring) Charamba (DOURO), Follies (Vinho Verde, BAIRRADA) and AVA (table wine).

Azevedo, Quinta do Vin w ★★ DYA SOGRAPE's throughly modern estate-grown LOUREIRO-led VINHO VERDE is now available under screwcap.

Bacalhoa, Quinta da Set r w ★★★★ 02 03 04 05 06 07 08' 09 Once owned by the royal family, now by BACALHOA VINHOS, this National Monument estate nr SETÚBAL gives its name to Portugal's best CAB SAUV, planted in 1979. Fleshier Palaçio de Bacalhoa has more MERLOT. Gd white Bordeaux blend with ALVARINHO.

Looking for more information on grapes? Try the "Grapes" section on pp.16–26.

Bacalhoa Vinhos Alen, Lis, Set r p w sw sp ★★→★★★ Like BACALHOA, owned by millionaire José Berardo's Group (plus holdings in CAVES ALIANÇA, SOGRAPE, HENRIQUES & HENRIQUES). Worth visiting for the art collection as well as its accomplished range of wines: Berardo Reserva Familiar, Dupla, JP, Serras de Azeitão, Só, Catarina, Cova da Ursa (PENÍNSULA DE SETÚBAL), Loridos (Estremadura) and QUINTA do Carmo, TINTO DA ANFORA (ALENTEJO). V.gd SETÚBAL MOSCATEL.

Bágeiras, Quinta das Bair r w sp ★★★→★★★★ (GARRAFEIRA r) 01' 03 04' 05' Stunning Garrafeira, red (BAGA) and white are traditionally crafted and built to age, as is Reserva red. Fine *zero dosage* sparkling.

Bairrada Bair r p w sp ★→★★★★ 00 01 03' 04 05' 06 07 08' 09' 10' 11 Atlantic-influenced DOC. Traditional strengths: sparkling wines; austere, age-worthy reds made from BAGA. Permitting other grapes has improved approachability, but endangered Baga plantings. Top Baga specialists: CAVES SÃO JOÃO, LUÍS PATO, QUINTA de Foz de Arouce, Sidónia de Sousa, QUINTA DAS BÁGEIRAS. Leading modernists: CAMPOLARGO, Quinta do Encontro. Watch: FILIPA PATO, Quinta da Vacariça.

Barca Velha Dou r ★★★★ 82 83 85 91' 95' 99 00 Portugal's most famous red, created in 1952 by FERREIRA. Made only in exceptional yrs in v. limited quantities. Intense, complex, with a deep bouquet, it forged the DOURO's reputation for stellar wines. Distinguished, traditional style (aged several yrs before release). Second wine: *Reserva Ferreirinha*.

Beira Atlântico ★→★★★★ New VINHO REGIONAL covering solely the westernmost part of former Vinho Regional Beiras, in and around the BAIRRADA DOC.

Beira Interior ★ Large DOC between DÃO and Spanish border. Huge potential from old, high v'yds of mostly Dão red varieties or Siria for whites. QUINTAS DO CARDO and DOS CURRAIS impress.

Branco White.

Filipa Pato's fortified Baga sounds newfangled, but it revives a Bairrada tradition.

Brito e Cunha, João Dou r w ★★→★★★ 04 05 07 08' 09 Young gun Brito e Cunha makes intense, elegant reds from QUINTA de San José, esp Reserva. More widely sourced Azéo, esp Reserva (r w) also v.gd. New: Grande Reserva (r) and elegant Vintage Port.

Bucelas Lis w ★★ DYA Tiny DOC north of Lisbon focused on ARINTO whites (known as "Lisbon Hock" in 19th-century England). QUINTAS DA ROMEIRA and da Murta make tangy, racy wines.

Bussaco r w ★★★ (r) 83 00' 01 04 05' 06' unique wines made by ancient methods at and exclusively for the extravagant Bussaco Palace Hotel, once a royal hunting lodge. V. age-worthy wines blend BAIRRADA BAGA and DÃO TOURIGA NACIONAL (r) and Dão Encruzado (w) with MARIA GOMES and Bical from Bairrada.

Cabriz, Quinta de Dão r p w ★★→★★★ 03 04 05 06 07 08 Owned by DÃO SUL; modern, fruity, fresh, characterful wines, with gd typicity. Flagship Four C v.gd.

Campolargo Bair r w sp ★→★★★ 06 07 08 09 10' Large estate, eclectic plantings, innovative reds of native and Bordeaux varieties, and PINOT N. Gd DÃO (r) made at SAES. New single-parcel 100% CERCEAL (w) v.gd.

Carcavelos Lis br sw ★★★ Minute, practically defunct DOC west of Lisbon, now better known for surfing. Hen's-teeth sweet apéritif or dessert wines average 19% alcohol and resemble honeyed MADEIRA.

Cardo, Quinta do Bei In ★★★ One of estates of Companhia das Quintas. Cool site; one of Portugal's most elegant TOURIGA NACIONALS, also perfumed red blends and a racy white from the Síria grape.

Carmo, Quinta do Alen r w p ★★→★★★ 03 04' 05 06 07' 50 ha once co-owned by Rothschilds (Lafite), now 100% BACALHÔA VINHOS. Fresh white and polished reds with CAB SAUV have Bordeaux restraint. Second wine: Dom Martinho.

Cartuxa, Adega da Alen r w sp ★★→★★★★ Moved from 17th-century cellars to brand new winery in 2007 to increase quantity and quality. Good trad-style flagship Pêra Manca (w r) (95 97 98 01 03 05' 07) Also second wine Cartuxa Reserva. Flashier Scala Coeli is from non-local grapes. EA reds are value for money.

Carvalhais, Quinta dos Dão r p w sp ★★→★★★ (r) 01 03 04 05 06 07 SOGRAPE's principal DÃO brand: single-estate wines, incl flagship Unico and v.gd Encruzado (w). Volume Duque de Viseu is from estate and bought-in grapes.

Casal Branco, Quinta de Tej r w ★★→★★★ Large family estate. Solid entry-level wines, blend incl local grapes CASTELÃO and FERNÃO PIRES. Gd-value flagship Falcoaria range, incl Reserva red (03 04' 05' 07) from old-vine local varieties.

Chocapalha, Quinta de Lis r p w ★★→★★★ (r) 04 05 06 07' 08' Modern estate. TOURIGA NACIONAL and TINTA RORIZ underpin rich reds, incl new flagship CH by Chocapalha Touriga Nacional 2008. CAB SAUV is sinewy. Gd unoaked SAUV BL, ARINTO, Arinto-blend and fine oaked CHARD/native white blend.

Chryseia Dou r ★★★→★★★★ 04 05' 06 07 08' 09 Bordeaux's Bruno Prats and SYMINGTON FAMILY ESTATES partnership is now based at QUINTA de Roriz. Since 2009, greater density and minerality in this rich, elegant red, mostly TOURIGA NACIONAL and Franca. Quinta de Roriz and Prazo de Roriz made here, too. Second wine *Post Scriptum* (06 07 08 09).

Churchill Estates Dou r w p ★★ 04 05 06 07 08 09' Fast-expanding range now incl a white. Peppery, grippy, floral reds incl Reserva, Grande Reserva, single-variet TOURIGA NACIONAL (and ROSADO) and estate QUINTA da Gricha.

Colares Lis r w ★★ Tiny DOC west of Lisbon. Ungrafted Ramisco vines on th beach give tannic reds and old-school MALVASIA whites. Biggest producer: ADEG Regional de Colares (co-op). Newcomers Fundação Oriente and Stanley H make more contemporary styles.

Crasto, Quinta do Dou r w ★★→★★★★ (r) 02 03' 04 05' 06 07' 08 09' Site high above the DOURO yields exceptionally concentrated, old-vine, single-v'yd blend Vinha da Ponte (00' 01 03 04 07') and María Theresa (00' 03' 05' 06 07 09'' also (great-value) Reserva. Crasto Superior and gd entry-level Crasto and Flo de Crasto are from young Douro Superior v'yd. Occasional varietals (TOURIG NACIONAL, TINTA RORIZ), eg. in 2009. Gd Port, too.

Currais, Quinta dos Bei In ★★→★★★ Family estate in the warm, rugged south o DOC BEIRA INTERIOR. Consistently impressive red blends, esp powerful Reserv (02 03' 07') and exciting mineral white from Síria and Fonte-Cal grapes.

Dão Dão r w p sp ★★→★★★★ 01 02 03' 04 05 06 07' 08' 09 Historic DOC in centra Portugal. New VINHO REGIONAL: Terras do Dão. Rustic co-ops once dominate but new producers now make structured, elegantly fruity, perfumed reds an textured whites from DÃO SUL and QUINTAS MAIAS, PELLADA, ROQUES, SAES. Rising stars: Julia Kemper, Vinha Paz and QUINTAS do Mondego, da Falorca, do Corujã (the latter just leased by the winemakers of POEIRA, WINE & SOUL, VALE MEÃO).

Dão Sul Dão r w ★★→★★★★ Impressive range with international appeal, inc QUINTA CABRIZ, CASA DE SANTAR and Quinta dos Grilos (DÃO), Sá de Baixo and da Tecedeiras (DOURO), do Encontro (BAIRRADA), do Gradil (LISBOA) and Herdad Monte da Cal (ALENTEJO). Quirky collaborations incl Homenagen (with LUÍS PATO' Dourat (Douro TOURIGA NACIONAL/Spanish GARNACHA) and Pião (Dão Touriga Nacional/Italian NEBBIOLO). Latest venture is VINHO VERDE, with QUINTA de Lourosa

Denominacão de Origem Controlada (DOC) Demarcated wine region controlled b a regional commission. *See also* VINHO REGIONAL.

Doce (vinho) Sweet (wine).

Douro Dou r p w sw ★★→★★★★ 01 02 03' 04' 05' 06 07' 08' 09' Home of Port, bu table wine (r and now w), now has a firm grip. Perfume, fruit and minerals typif its best reds. Top whites are textured and complex. Both can have freshness and balance. Look for BARCA VELHA, CRASTO, DUAS QUINTAS, NIEPOORT, PASSADOURO POEIRA, VALE DONA MARIA, VALE MEÃO, VALLADO, WINE & SOUL. Watch: JOÃO BRITO E CUNHA Conceito, Maritávora and QUINTAS DO NOVAL and de Tourais. VR is Duriense.

You want a source of juicy, appetizing, good-value red? Try the Alentejo.

Duas Quintas Douro Dou r w ★★★ (r) 02 03' 04 05 06 07' 08 09' Port shippe Ramos Pinto's concentrated reds incl. v.gd Reserva, Collection and outstanding Especial. New fruity, complex Reserva white.

Duorum Dou r w ★★→★★★ Joint project of JOÃO PORTUGAL RAMOS and José Maria Soares Franco, who oversaw BARCA VELHA for 27 years. Castelo Melhor is new 250ha v'yd in DOURO Superior for modern, fruit-led table wines, "Tons" (incl new white), Colheita and Reserva, sourced from old, elevated v'yds. V.gd Vintage Port

Esporão, Herdade do Alen r w sw ★★→★★★ 04 05 06 07' 08' 09 Big estate making high-quality modern wines. Monte Velho, Alandra, Vinha da Defesa brands showcase ripe fruit. Quatro Castas, single-varietal range, Esporão Reservas Private Selection (r w) and GARRAFEIRA offer increasing depth and complexity

Private Selection White is a delicious blend of SÉM, MARSANNE, ROUSSANNE. New DOURO estate QUINTA das Murças shows great promise.

Espumante Sparkling. Best wines: BAIRRADA, DOURO (Vértice) and now VINHO VERDE.

Falua Tej r p w JOÃO PORTUGAL RAMOS' new venture. Well-made export brands: entry-level Monte de Serra followed by Tagus Creek, incl Reserva, blends grapes native/international. Tâmara and Conde de Vimioso (v.gd Reserva) are gd traditional.

Feital, do Quinta Vin w ★★★ 07' 08' 09 Young GALICIAN winemaker Marcial Dorado makes characterful VINHO VERDE: powerful and textured. Auratus, a blend of ALVARINHO and Trajadura, is also v.gd.

Ferreira Dou r w ★→★★★★ SOGRAPE-owned Port shipper making gd to v.gd DOURO wines under Casa Ferreirinha labels: Esteva, Vinha Grande, QUINTA de Leda, Reserva Especial Ferreirinha and BARCA VELHA.

Fonseca, José Maria da Lis r p w dr sw sp ★★→★★★ Historic family-owned estate, pioneer of SETÚBAL fortified MOSCATEL: exciting back catalogue used to great effect in Apoteca, 20-yr-old Alambre and 20-yr-old Roxo. Volume branded wines LANCERS and PERIQUITA remain popular. Once cutting-edge brands like Vinya, Privada Domingos Soares Franco, FSF, Domini/Domini Plus (DOURO), Hexagon and José de Sousa (ALENTEJO) look a tad dated.

Gaivosa, Quinta de Dou r w ★★★ 03 04 05' 06 07 08' 09 Characterful range incl old-school Branco da Gaivosa, concentrated old-vine reds (v.gd TOURIGA NACIONAL) and blends from different terroirs, incl Abandonado, QUINTA das Caldas, Vinha de Lordelo, Reserva Pessoal, Vale da Raposa. Expanding Port range.

Garrafeira Label term: merchant's "private Res", aged for min 2 yrs in cask and 1 in bottle, often longer. Once most Portuguese merchants' reds were called this.

Lagoalva, Quinta da Tej r p w ★★ 06 07 08 09 Young winemaker Diego Campilho has dragged his family's estate into the 21st century. Easy, fresh wines from native and international (esp CHARD, SAUV BL, SYRAH) brim with fruit; oak can be over-done. Gd single-varietal Alfrocheiro. Hobby label extends range into ALENTEJO.

Lancers p w sp ★ Semi-sweet (semi-sparkling) ROSADO, widely shipped to the USA by JOSÉ MARIA DA FONSECA. Rosé Free is alcohol-free.

Lavradores de Feitoria Dou r w ★★→★★★ Collaboration of 18 producers with unusual strength in whites, esp SAUV BL and v.gd new white Meruge (100% Viosinho). Also v.gd single-v'yd red: QUINTA da Costa das Aguaneiras. X Edição Special 2006 (Tinta Cão) stylishly marks 10 yrs in the market. Principal labels: Meruge, Três Bagos.

Lisboa Lis VR on west coast, formerly called Estremadura. DOCS: ALENQUER, Arruda, BUCELAS, CARCAVELOS, COLARES, Encostas d'Aire, Obidos, Torres Vedras. Wines can be pedestrian but CHOCAPALHA and esp MONTE D'OIRO reveal potential. Watch: QUINTAS de SANT'ANA, do Convento, do Pinto (esp for whites).

Madeira Mad r w ★→★★ Famous for fortified, Portugal's Atlantic island also makes table wine of modest pretensions. (Terras Madeirenses VR and Madeirense DOC). Best is probably made by Rui Reguinga and Francisco Albuquerque (of Blandy's), Primeira Paixão VERDELHO.

Maias, Quinta das Dão ★★→★★★ (r) 03 04 05' 06 07' 08' 09' (w) DYA Sister of QUINTA DOS ROQUES. Benchmark Jaen and DÃO's only VERDELHO; Flor das Maias (2005; 2007) is showy TOURIGA NACIONAL-dominated blend.

Malhadinha Nova, Herdade da Alen r p w sw ★★★ 04 05 06 07 08' 09 The Soares family's Midas touch applies to both wines and country house hotel. V.gd entry level da Peceguina (blends and varietal) through to rich, spicy flagship Marias da Malhadinha. Muscular Malhadinha Tinto gives plenty of bang for buck.

Mateus Rosé p (w) sp ★ The world's bestselling, medium-dry, lightly carbonated rosé table wine from SOGRAPE; and Portugal's biggest vinous export. A double-edged sword for a country still carving out its reputation for table wine.

PORTUGAL

Mendes, Anselmo Vin w sw sp ★★→★★★★ Acclaimed winemaker; his ALVARINHO focused range incl Contacto, Muros Antigos, Muros de Melgaço and top-notch oak-aged Curtimenta and single-v'yd Parcela Única. Gd LOUREIRO, too. Consults widely, incl at QUINTAS AMEAL, GAIVOSA and dos Frades.

Messias Bair r w ★→★★★ Large BAIRRADA-based firm; interests in DOURO (incl Port). Old-school reds best.

Minho Vin River between north Portugal and Spain, also VR. A number of leading VINHO VERDE producers prefer to use VR Minho.

Monte d'Oiro, Quinta do Lis r w ★★★→★★★★ (Res) 03 04' 05 06' 07 08' Thanks to Chapoutier's (see France) consultancy and vine cuttings, Portugal's best SYRAH incl Lybra, Reserva and Homenagem Antonio Carqueja. New Syrah 24 2007 is from 60-yr-old Hermitage vines. V.gd VIOGNIER (Madrigal), blended with MARSANNE and ARINTO in new Lybra white. Ex-Aequo Syrah/TOURIGA NACIONAL (06' 07') is collaboration between Bento & Chapoutier.

Moscatel do Douro Little-known DOC centred around high Favaios region producing surprisingly fresh, fortified MOSCATEL Galego (MUSCAT À PETIT GRAINS) to rival those of SÉTUBAL. Leading producers: ADEGA Cooperativa Favaios, PORTAL, NIEPOORT.

Mouchão, Herdade de Alen r w ★★★→★★★★★ 99 00 01 03' 05' 06 Leading traditional estate. Intense, fragrant, sensual wines realize full potential of the Alicante Bouschet grape. *Flagship Tonel 3–4*, exceptional yrs only, has great complexity and persistence. Ponte das Canas is a contemporary blend of Alicante Bouschet with TOURIGA NACIONAL and Franca, and SHIRAZ; Dom Rafael is value.

Mouro, Quinta do Alen r ★★★ 98 99 00 04' 05' 06' 07 Imposingly concentrated reds, mostly ALENTEJO grapes, but also TOURIGA NACIONAL and CAB SAUV. Flagship Mouro Gold in exceptional yrs (99 00 02 05 06'). Gd second wine: Casa dos Zagalos. Modern, forward Vinha do Mouro gd value.

Murganheira, Caves ★ Largest producer of ESPUMANTE. Gd vintage Bruto is PINOT N. Owns RAPOSEIRA.

Will the trickle of screwcaps become a flood? Surely high treason in cork country.

Niepoort Dou r p w ★★★→★★★★ Family Port shipper; plus many exceptional wines: Tiara (w); Vertente (r); Redoma (r p w, incl w Res) 03 04' 05' 06' 07' 08' 09', Robustus (r) 04 05 07'; Batuta (r) 03 04 05' 07 08' 09'; Charme (r) 04 05' 06 07' 08 09. Experimental Projectos range incl: DOURO RIES (!), SAUV BL, PINOT N. Collaborates widely, with eg. PELLADA, SOALHEIRO (Niepoort Docil, LOUREIRO VINHO VERDE), also Spain's Equipo Navazos, Telmo Rodriguez, Raul Perez-Ultreia. Ladredo is own Spanish stunner (Ribeira Sacra).

Noval, Quinta do Dou r ★★★ AXA-owned. Made first super-premium unfortified reds in 2004: Quinta do Noval and gd-value Cedro. Innovative SYRAH blend Cedro; Syrah does well on the DOURO, viz. new 100% Syrah called Labrador – after the winemaker's dog.

Palmela Set r w ★→★★★ CASTELÃO-focused DOC (see PEGOS CLAROS). Can be long-lived.

Passadouro, Quinta do Dou r w ★★★ Winemaker Dieter Bohrmann, who shifted the estate towards table wines, recently died. Winemaker, WINE & SOUL's Jorge Serôdio Borges, runs the QUINTA with Bohrmann's family. Superbly concentrated old-vine Reserva (03 04' 05' 06 07' 08 09') and estate wine. Gd whites, too. Entry label, Passa, v.gd value.

Pato, Filipa Beir Int r w sp ★★★ It's all change for LUÍS PATO's dynamic daughter, now 100% focused on BAIRRADA. New range shows best of tradition and terroir, incl three sparkling wines, FP (r w), stunning Nossa Calcario Bical and Nossa Calcario BAGA. Seemingly innovative fortified Saga de Baga in fact revives a tradition.

Pato, Luís Bair r w sw sp ★★→★★★★ 95' 97 99 00 01' 03' 04 05' 06 07 08' Fine *seriously age-worthy, single-v'yd Baga*: Vinhas Barrio, Pan, Barrosa and flagship

QUINTA do Ribeirinho Pé Franco (ungrafted vines). Also v.gd are elegant *Vinhas Velhas* (now in Burgundy bottle) and Quinta do Ribeirinho 1st Choice (a BAGA/TOURIGA NACIONAL blend). João Pato, early-drinking Touriga Nacional, now joined by single-v'yd Touriga from Vinha Formal. Equal flair with whites (Vinhas Formal, Velhas). More straightforward are sparkling wines (incl InFormal sealed under crown cap), sweet Abafado range and BAGA Rebel (fermented on Bical skins). In honour of grandson Fernão, Pato's latest wine is a red FERNÃO PIRES fermented on Baga skins.

Pegões, Adega de Set r p w sw sp ★→★★★ Portugal's most dynamic co-op, in up-and-coming PENÍNSULA DE SETÚBAL. Gd range from top to bottom, incl varietals and blends of natives and internationals. Stella label and new low-alcohol Nico white offer gd, clean fruit. V.gd Colheita Seleccionada (r w) exceptional value.

Pegos Claros Set r ★★ 04 05' 07 08' Owned by Companhia das Quintas. Flamboyantly fruity benchmark PALMELA Castelão. Foot-trodden and aged min 3 yrs before release. GARRAFEIRA top yrs only.

Pellada, Quinta de Dão r p w ★★→★★★ 04 05' 06 07' 08 Owned with SAES by leading DÃO light, Álvaro de Castro. Intense, not dense reds, incl flagship Pape (TOURIGA NACIONAL from Passarela v'yd with Pellada BAGA) and Carrocel (100% Touriga). Primus is old-vine, textured white. A rosé has a dash of CAB SAUV.

Península de Setúbal Set VR (formerly Terras do Sado). Established producers incl ADEGA DE PEGÕES, BACALHOA VINHOS and Casa Ermelinda Freitas clustered around sandy plains of Sado Estuary. Up-and-coming names fanning out further west and south: Herdades da Comporta and Portocarro, Mala Tojo, Soberanas, QUINTAS de Catralvos and Alcube.

Periquita Nickname for the CASTELÃO grape and successful brand name and trademark of JOSÉ MARIA DA FONSECA. Periquita Classico is original 100% Castelão; red, RESERVA (and rosé and white) feature other varieties.

Peso, Herdade do Alen ★→★★★ SOGRAPE-owned estate in Vidigueira, southern ALENTEJO. V. well-made wines from native varieties, incl intense, shapely flagship Ícone and v.gd Callabriga Reserva.

Poeira, Quinta do Dou r w ★★★ 03' 04' 05' 06 07' 08' 09' QUINTA DE LA ROSA's elegant flagship red from cool, north-facing slopes. Classy second wines Pó de Poeira (r w). CS is a young-vine CAB SAUV and DOURO-variety blend.

Portal, Quinta do Dou r p w sw ★★★ 01 03 04 05' 06 07 08 09 Known for oaky modern reds, incl Grande Reserva and flagship Auru. New high plantings focus on whites. V.gd sweet wine and fortified MOSCATEL do DOURO.

Portalegre Alen r p w ★→★★★ Northernmost ALENTEJO subregion (DOC). Elevated v'yds on granite and schist and double the rainfall account for fresh, structured wines. Gd co-op, but names to watch are Altas QUINTAS (consultant Paulo Laureano of Herdade de Mouchão),Terrenus, owner/consultant Rui Reguinga) and Quinta do Centro, joint-venture with English writer Richard Mayson.

Quinta Estate (*see* under name, eg. PORTAL, Quinta Do)

Ramos, João Portugal Alen r w DYA Leading modernist's estate. Fruit-forward but elegant ALENTEJO range incl Loios, Vila Santa, top-notch QUINTA da Viçosa and Marquês de Borba, esp Reserva (04 05 07 08). New Ramos Reserva (r) is v.gd value. Traditional approach for imposing wines from related QUINTA de Foz de Arouce, BEIRA ATLANTICO.

Raposeira Dou w sp ★★ Well-known fizz with native varieties and CHARD made by classic method.

Real Companhia Velha Dou r p w sw ★★→★★★ r 03 04 05 06 07 08 09 Company founded in 1756 to promote and control the Port trade – trades as ROYAL OPORTO. Now pioneer of dedicated table wine v'yds with range of QUINTA de Cidro single-variety wines, incl CHARD, ALVARINHO, GEWURZ and gd TOURIGA NACIONAL.

PORTUGAL

Evel Grande Reserva, Quinta dos Aciprestes and Porca de Murça are blends Grantom and sweet Granjó are from SÉM. Also Quinta de Ventozelo and new Delaforce (*see* Port) wines.

Romeira, Quinta da w ★★→★★★ Leading BUCELAS estate of Companhia das Quintas has a modern take on "Lisbon Hock." ARINTO-based, honeyed, ripe, citrus-streaked wines, best are minerally, too, and give ALVARINHO a run for its money. Prova Regia Arinto is VR from LISBOA. DOC wines are (just off-dry) Regia Premium and v.gd, oaked Morgado Sta Catherina Reserva.

Roques, Quinta dos Dão r w sp ★★★ (r) 03' 04 05 06 07' 08' 09 V.gd, age-worthy reds, esp Reserva and flagship GARRAFEIRA (2008 to follow 2003). Benchmark, modern Encruzado and varietal TOURIGA NACIONAL, TINTA RORIZ, Tinta Cão and Alfrocheiro Preto. Gd value, entry-level Correio label.

Roriz, Quinta de Dou r ★★★ Historic estate bought by Symington Family Estates in 2009. Though home to Prats & Symington's CHRYSEIA table wine project, still making gd Ports: 99 00' 01 02 03' 04 05 06 07.

Rosa, Quinta de la Dou r p w ★★★ 05' 06 07' 08' 09' Rich but elegant reds, esp Reserva. Bright, juicy DouROSA entry level. QUINTA das Bandeiras Passagem from the warmer DOURO Superior is spicier. Gd whites, incl Passagem.

Rosado Rosé; there is life beyond MATEUS ROSÉ; new breed of textured, sophisticated rosés, incl: NIEPOORT, QUINTA DE PELLADA, CHURCHILL.

Saes, Quinta de Dão r w ★★★ 01 02 03 04 05 06' 07' 08' Alvaro Castro's other v'yd (*see* QUINTA DE PELLADA); equally fine wines, incl v.gd Reserva Branco and Dado/ Doda (*see* NIEPOORT).

Sant'Ana, Quinta de ★★→★★★ An English-owned estate at Mafra. RIES and PINOT N v. promising.

Santar, Casa de Dão r w ★★★ 03 04 05' 08' Old estate making comeback under DÃO SUL leadership. Poised reds: new Nature from biodynamic v'yd; Encruzado whites reward burgundian approach.

São João, Caves Bair r w sp ★★→★★★ (r sp) 97 00 01 03 05 06 Small, traditional firm for v.gd, old-fashioned wines. Reds are bottle-aged, pre-release and v. age-worthy. BAIRRADA: *Frei João*, Poço do Lobo. DÃO: Porta dos Cavaleiros.

São Miguel, Herdade de Alen r p w ★★→★★★ Dynamic operation making smart wines with consultant Luís Duarte (also of MALHADINHA and MOURO). Entry-level Ciconia, incl Reserva and firmer Montinho gd value. São Miguel labels denote serious and well-defined estate wines, esp the Reserva and Dos Descobridores range. The Private Collection is showier. Same team behind impressive new Herdade da Pimenta.

Looking for more information on grapes? Try the "Grapes" section on pp.16–26.

Seco Dry.

Setúbal (r) (w) br (dr) sw ★★★ Tiny DOC south of the river Tagus. Fortified dessert wines – mainly MOSCATEL – incl rare red Moscatel Roxo. Main producers incl: BACALHOA VINHOS, JOSÉ MARIA DA FONSECA. Watch: António Saramago, Horácio dos Reis Simões.

Soalheiro, Quinta de Vinho Verde w sp ★★★ 02' 03 06 07' 08' 09 10 Concentrated ALVARINHO from warm Melgaço v'yd. Even basic VINHO VERDE is age-worthy. Also barrel-fermented Reserva and, with Dirk NIEPOORT's advice, stunning old-vine Primeiras Vinhas and off-dry Dócil, also the new name of Niepoort's LOUREIRO (formerly Girosol).

Sogrape Vinho Verde ★→★★★★ Portugal's biggest player produces both MATEUS ROSÉ and BARCA VELHA – jewels in the crown for contrasting reasons. Portfolio encompasses VINHO VERDE (AZEVEDO, Gazela, Morgadio da Torre), DÃO (CARVALHAIS), ALENTEJO (HERDADE DO PESO – best of all) and DOURO (BARCA VELHA, also Ferreira,

Sandeman and Offley Port). Approachable multiregional brands incl Grão Vasco, Pena de Pato, Callabriga.

Symington Family Estates Dou r w ★★→★★★★ Port shipper producing serious table wines since 2000, incl CHRYSEIA with Bruno Prats, RORIZ, QUINTA do Vesúvio and Pombal do Vesúvio. Well-made Altano brand incl organic red and 100% TOURIGA NACIONAL Quinta do Ataíde Reserva (replaces Reserva) hails from three Vilariça valley v'yds in DOURO Superior, all certified organic.

Tejo r w The DOC and VR of the area around the river Tagus. Fertile engine-room of gd-value wines from native vines is now raising its game with TOURIGA NACIONAL, TINTA RORIZ, CAB SAUV, SYRAH, PINOT N, CHARD and SAUV BL on poorer soils. Leading lights: QUINTA DA LAGOALVA, Pinhal da Torre and FALUA. Rising star: VALE D'ALGARES, Rui Reguinga (Tributo). Subregions: Almeirim, Cartaxo, Coruche, Chamusca, Tomar and Santarem.

Terras da Beira ★→★★ New VR covering solely the easternmost part of former VR Beiras, in and around the BEIRA INTERIOR DOC.

Terras do Dão New VINHO REGIONAL covering the mid-section (around the DÃO) of now superseded VINHO REGIONAL Beiras.

Tinto Red.

Tinto da Anfora Alen r ★★ 04 05' 06 07 08 Reliable red from BACALHOA VINHOS. Richer Grande Escolha.

Trás-os-Montes Tras High inland DOC with subregions Chaves, Valpaços, Planalto Mirandês. VR Transmontano.

Vale d'Algares Tej r p w sw ★★→★★★ No-expense-spared project. Whites already impressive, incl new sweet style; reds improving with vine age. New D Tinto and D Branco and gd VIOGNIER are ambitiously priced. Viognier is blended with ALVARINHO for 2nd-tier Selection White. Guarda Rios is the junior brand. A name to watch.

Vale Dona Maria, Quinta do Dou r p w ★★★→★★★★ 02 03' 04' 05' 06 07' 08' 09' Cristiano van Zeller makes *v.gd plush yet elegant reds*, incl CV, Casa de Casal de Loivos and new single-parcel Vinha do Rio. VZ white worthy companion to reds. Gd-value Van Zellers range from bought-in fruit.

Vale Meão, Quinta do Dou r ★★★→★★★★ 03 04' 05 06 07' 08 09 Once the source of BARCA VELHA. Fine big wines from high percentage of TOURIGA NACIONAL and warm, easterly location. V.gd second wine: Meandro. Fruit from new v'yd at 350 metres on-stream from 2009.

Vallado Dou r p w ★★★ (r) 03' 04 05' 06 07 08' 09' Expanding family estate at Regua. Red blends and varietal Sousão and TOURIGA NACIONAL show increased elegance. V.gd Reserva (now with 30% Touriga Nacional) and flagship old-vine red Adelaide (05 07 08' 09'). New: gd, dry Touriga Nacional ROSADO and Adelaide Vintage Port.

Vinho Regional (VR) Has the same status as French Vin de Pays. More leeway for experimentation than DOC.

Vinho Verde r w sp ★→★★★ DOC between river DOURO and north frontier, for fresh "green wines". Large brands like Casal García usually varietal blend with added carbon dioxide – DYA. Best are single-QUINTA with natural spritz, if any, esp ALVARINHO from Monção and Melgaço (eg. ANSELMO MENDES, QUINTA DE SOALHEIRO, do Reguengo, de Melgaço, DO FEITAL) and LOUREIRO from Lima (eg. QUINTA DO AMEAL or AFROS). Red Vinhão grape is an acquired taste worth a try (eg. AFROS).

Wine & Soul Dou r w (r Pintas) 04' 05' 06 07' 08' 09' (w Guru) 07 08' 09' 10' Increasingly shapely wines (and Port) from winemaking couple Sandra Tavares and Jorge Serôdio Borges. Second wine: Pintas Character (r). Maiden flagship, single-v'yd, old-vine QUINTA da Manoella 2009 is immensely concentrated.

Port, Sherry & Madeira

Fortified producers are handling the economic situation in different ways. Sherry producers are finding that there's a growing, and greedy, market for old and rare wines – or perhaps just rare and unusual wines (eg. González Byass' En Rama Fino: bottled without filtration and designed for quick and appreciative drinking). Meanwhile Port producers find the *beneficio*, the quota they're given for Port production, cut in response to shrinking overall sales – and so the list of Douro table-wine producers gets ever longer. New names in the Douro tend to make table wine and Vintage Port: both sell well, both sell quickly, and there's no need to hold years and years of stock (unlike the finest, oldest Sherries that rely on ancient soleras). And Madeira? Nothing can beat Madeira for longevity. You can, if you hunt, find wines from when Marie Antoinette was on the throne of France. They might cost you an arm and a leg, but not a head.

Recent Port vintages

Port vintages are "declared" when the wine is outstanding and meets the shippers' highest standards. In good but not quite classic years most shippers now use the names of their quintas (estates) for single-quinta wines of great character but needing less ageing in bottle. The vintages to drink now are 1966, 1970, 1977, 1980, 1983, 1985, 1987, 1992, 1994

2011 Very good, perhaps great. A general declaration? Watch this space.

2010 Single-quinta year. Hot, dry but higher yields than 2009.

2009 Controversial year. Declared by Fladgate, but not Symington's or Sogrape. Stars: Taylor, Niepoort, Fonseca, Warre.

2008 Single-quinta year. Low-yielding, powerful wines. Stars: Noval, Vesuvio, Taylor Terra Feita, Passadouro.

2007 Classic year, widely declared. Deep-coloured, rich but well-balanced wines. Taylor and Vesuvio are stars.

2006 A difficult year; only a handful of single-quinta wines. Stars: Vesuvio, Roriz, Barros Quinta Galeira.

2005 Single-quinta year. Stars: Niepoort, Taylor de Vargellas, Dow da Senhora da Ribeira – iron fist in velvet glove.

2004 Single-quinta year. Stars: Pintas, Taylor de Vargellas Vinha Velha, Quinta de la Rosa – balanced, elegant wines.

2003 Classic vintage year. Hot, dry summer. Powerfully ripe, concentrated wines, universally declared. Drink from 2015/2020.

2001 Single-quinta year. Stars: Noval Nacional, Fonseca do Panascal, do Vale Meão – wet year; relatively forward wines.

2000 Classic year. A very fine vintage, universally declared. Rich, well-balanced wines for the long term. Drink from 2018.

1999 Single-quinta year. Stars: Vesuvio, Taylor de Terra Feita, do Infantado – smallest vintage for decades; powerful.

1998 Single-quinta year. Stars: Dow da Senhora da Ribeira, Graham dos Malvedos, Cockburn dos Canais – bullish, firm wines.

Almacenista Small producer, typically a source of individual, complex Sherries. In Sherry's heyday boosted major producers' stocks. Now scarcer; showcased by Lustau. Can be superb, eg. Vides Palo Cortado; toasted, walnutty Cuevas Jurado Manzanilla.

Álvaro Domecq ★★→★★★★ DOMECQ has been one of Sherry's great families. After corporate shake-up, scion Álvaro Domecq launched his own brand based on SOLERAS of Pilar Aranda, said to be the oldest bodega in JEREZ. In 2007, joined boutique wine group Inveravante. Excellent 1730 series, incl Palo Cortado, Oloroso. Gd Fino La Janda. Also one of the best Sherry vinegars.

Alvear Mont-M ★★→★★★★ Largest MONTILLA producer; v.gd Fino-like apéritif, esp Fino CB. Leader in v. sweet, raisined wines. Silky, supple SOLERA 1927.

Andresen ★★→★★★ Family-owned. Gd 20-yr-old TAWNY; grand old COLHEITAS (1910' 68' 75 80' 91' 97); WHITE PORT with age indication (10-yr-old, 20-yr-old, 40-yr-old).

Barbadillo ★→★★★★ The former bishop's palace dominating SANLÚCAR is appropriate for such a significant producer. Makes a locally popular, budget white from PALOMINO but also some of Sanlúcar's finest Sherries. Reliquia range is costly but outstanding, esp Amontillado and the tangy, buttery Palo Cortado. Solear Manzanilla is a local favourite at *feria*. Also Príncipe Amontillado; the spicy, peppery Obispo Gascón Palo Cortado; the buttery, mahogany Cuco Dry Oloroso; Manzanilla EN RAMA, with seasonal *sacas*.

Barbeito ★★→★★★★ Ricardo Freitas is as dynamic as his Madeiras are racy. No added caramel makes finely-honed 20-yr-old, 30-yr-old MALVASIA and VERDELHO/BUAL blend; citrus COLHEITAS (Single Harvest, Single Cask). Doesn't have aged stock of other shippers, stylish FRASQUEIRAS (SERCIAL 1978', BOAL 1978).

Barros Almeida ★→★★★ Sogevinus-owned house with several brands (incl Feist, Feuerheerd and KOPKE): wood-aged Ports. Best: v.gd 20-yr-old TAWNY, COLHEITAS (57' 78') and WHITE PORTS, incl Very Old Dry White and 1935 Colheita.

Barros e Sousa ★★★ 3rd-generation producer. Tiny output of 100% hand-bottled CANTEIRO-aged Madeira. Rare vintages (Terrantez 1979, VERDELHO 1983), Bastardo Old Res, gd 10-yr-old and unusual 5-yr-old Listrao blend. No export.

Blandy ★★→★★★★ Fittingly, in its bicentenary year, the Blandy family resumed control of The MADEIRA WINE COMPANY, owner of its famous brand. Short ferments make rich house style. Vast lodges house a visitors' centre and rich pickings for fine old vintages (eg. BUAL 1920', 1968', MALMSEY 1985, VERDELHO 1952, SERCIAL 1966'). V.gd COLHEITAS (Malmsey 1992, 2001, Bual 1991, Single Harvest 1977). Alvada is an innnovative, moreish blend of BUAL and MALVASIA.

Borges, HM ★→★★★ Family company; v.gd 10-yr-olds, fruit-forward COLHEITAS (SERCIAL 1995, MALMSEY 1998) and vintages, esp Sercial 1977, 1979, BUAL 1977.

Bual (or Boal) Classic Madeira grape: tangy, smoky, sweet wines; not as rich as MALMSEY. Perfect with cheese and lighter desserts.

Burmester ★→★★★ Small Sogevinus-owned house; fruity Gilbert's G-Porto label and much more sophisticated 20- and 40-yr-old TAWNY and COLHEITAS (55' 89) and age-dated WHITE PORTS, incl fine 40-yr-old; vintage improving (07').

Butt 600-litre barrel of long-matured American oak used for Sherry. Filled 5/6 full, allows space for FLOR to grow.

Caballero Developed by genial giant Luis Caballero into drinks group with highest-quality Sherries – LUSTAU – plus Viña Herminia RIOJA; wineries in RUEDA, RIBERA DEL DUERO; leading spirits brands.

Cálem ★→★★★ Sogevinus-owned house. Velhotes main brand. V.gd COLHEITAS (89 00); VINTAGE PORTS returning to form (03' 05 07). New ROSÉ PORT has braille label.

Canteiro Method of naturally cask-ageing the finest Madeira in warm, humid lodges (warehouses). Creates subtler, more complex wines than ESTUFAGEM.

Chiclana Zone of production of MOSCATEL grapes for JEREZ.

Churchill ★★★ Founded by John GRAHAM (1981). V.gd VINTAGE PORT (82 85 91 94 97 00 03 07), esp single-QUINTA da Gricha (00 01 03' 04 05' 06 07 09') and LBV benefit from TOURIGAS NACIONAL and Franca. Benchmark WHITE PORT, incl 10-yr-old. Gd age-dated TAWNY in 50cl bottles. Best enjoyed in Churchill's own new Port glass.

PORT, SHERRY & MADEIRA

Cockburn ★★→★★★ Historic shipper bought by SYMINGTON FAMILY ESTATES in 2010 sees its QUINTA do Tua appropriated for GRAHAM and repackaged. Popular Special RESERVE Ruby. Dry house style for VINTAGE PORTS (63 67 70 75 83' 91 94 97 00 03' 07'). V.gd TOURIGA NACIONAL-dominated single-quinta: dos Canais (01' 05' 06 07' 08 09').

Colheita Vintage-dated Port or Madeira of a single yr, cask-aged at least 7 yrs for Port and 5 yrs for Madeira. Bottling date shown on the label.

Cossart Gordon Mad Top-quality label of the MADEIRA WINE COMPANY; higher, cooler v'yds and longer ferment produces drier style than BLANDY. Best-known for the Good Company brand. Also 5-yr-old RESERVES, COLHEITAS (SERCIAL 1991, *Bual 1995, 1997*, MALVASIA 1996, 1998, Harvest 1999), old vintages (1977 Terrantez, 1908, 1961 BUAL).

Croft ★★→★★★ Acquired by FLADGATE (2001). Foot-treading much-improved VINTAGE PORT (63' 66 70 75 77 82 85 91 94 00 03' 07 09). Quinta da Roêda is lighter. Popular: Indulgence, Triple Crown and Distinction. Pink is pioneering ROSÉ PORT.

Croft Jer Now owned by GONZÁLEZ BYASS. Makes sweetish, dull Croft Original.

Crusted Port, usually blend of several vintages, bottled young and aged so it throws a deposit, or "crust"; needs decanting.

Looking for more information on grapes? Try the "Grapes" section on pp.16–26.

Delaforce ★★→★★★ Port shipper owned by REAL COMPANHIA VELHA; also making table wines since 2010. FLADGATE still produces the Ports. Curious and Ancient 20-yr-old TAWNY and *Colheitas* (64 79 88) *are jewels*; VINTAGE PORTS improved (63 66 70' 75 77 82 85 92' 94 00 03). Single-QUINTA: da Corte.

Delgado Zuleta ★★ Historic (1774) SANLÚCAR firm. La Goya is a light Manzanilla. Top new range is Monteagudo. Rare Amontillado Viejo has bold, steely appeal. Las Señoras is aged sweet Oloroso.

Dios Baco ★→★★ Family-owned JEREZ bodega. V.gd Imperial VORS Palo Cortado.

Domecq One of the historic names in Sherry. Outstanding VORS wines now sold under Osborne label; La Ina, Botaina, Rio Viejo, Viña 25 SOLERAS went to LUSTAU.

Douro Rising in Spain as the Duero, the river Douro flows through Port country, lending its name to the region and its table wines. It is divided into the Cima Corgo and Douro Superior, home of the best Ports, and the Baixo Corgo.

Dow ★★★→★★★★ Brand name of Port house Silva & Cosens. Belongs to SYMINGTON FAMILY ESTATES. Traditionally drier style, though two fine single-QUINTAS show terroir differences: Bomfim (firm), da Senhora da Ribeira (opulent). V.gd range, incl CRUSTED, 20- and 30-yr-old TAWNY and vintage (63 66 70 72 75 77 80 83 85' 91 94 97 00' 03 07').

Drake & Friends ★★→★★★ New Sherry business following EQUIPO NAVAZOS model of buying and bottling fine Sherries, incl EN RAMA Fino. Sources incl MAESTRO SIERRA.

Emilio Hidalgo ★★★→★★★★ Exceptional small bodega with classic wines. Following tradition though not today's custom, all wines (except PX) start by spending time under FLOR. Excellent La Panesa single-v'yd Fino, v.gd Santa Ana PX 1861.

En rama Sherry bottled from the butt without filtration or cold stabilization. More flavoursome but less stable, hence unpopular with some retailers. Back in fashion with GONZÁLEZ BYASS launch of Tio Pepe EN RAMA. The *saca* or withdrawal is when the FLOR is most abundant, in spring and autumn. Keep in fridge, drink up quickly.

Equipo Navazos ★★★★ Collection of unique Sherries created by a group (*equipo*) of specialists who source and bottle individual butts from SOLERAS in top bodegas. Numbering of Sherries starts at 1, eg. Bota (butt) no 1; La Bota de Amontillado NPI no 5; La Bota de Palo Cortado no 21; impressive Cream, La Bota no 21. Now making table wine with Dirk NIEPOORT.

Estévez, Grupo Energetic family business; extensive quality brands in JEREZ and SANLÚCAR, incl LA GUITA, Gil Luque, MARQUÉS DEL REAL TESORO, Valdespino.

Estufagem Bulk process of slowly heating, then cooling, cheaper Madeiras to attain characteristic scorched-earth tang; less subtle than CANTEIRO process, though shift to lower temperatures has improved freshness.

Fernando de Castilla ★★→★★★ Small bodega with v. fine Sherries and brandies. Excellent Antique Oloroso and PX, outstanding Antique Amontillado and Palo Cortado. All qualify as age-dated, though bodega avoids the system. Lower priced Classic range.

Ferreira ★★→★★★ Historic Port house owned by SOGRAPE. Esp renowned for spicy, wood-aged styles: 10- and 20-yr-old TAWNY, QUINTA do Porto and *Duque de Bragança*. Gd RESERVE (Don Antónia). Early-maturing vintages: 66 70 75 77 78 80 82 83 85 87 90 91 94 95' 97 00 03 07'.

Fladgate Independent family-owned partnership and owner of leading Port houses TAYLOR, FONSECA, CROFT. In 2010 opened luxury hotel The Yeatman, which, within a year, boasted Oporto's first Michelin-starred restaurant.

Flor Spanish word for "flower": refers to the layer of *Saccharomyces* yeasts that live on top of Fino/Manzanilla Sherry in a butt 5/6 full and block oxygen (process known as "biological ageing"). Traditional Amontillados and a few Olorosos begin as Finos before the *flor* dies naturally or with addition of fortifying spirit. *Flor* grows a thicker layer nearer the coast at EL PUERTO DE SANTA MARÍA and SANLÚCAR, hence lighter character of Sherry there.

Fonseca Guimaraens ★★★→★★★★ FLADGATE's Technical director David Guimaraens continues his family's distinguished Port-making tradition. V.gd Bin 27 and organic Terra Prima RESERVE and sumptuous yet structured vintages: Fonseca 63' 66' 70 75 77' 80 83 85' 92 94' 97 00' 03' 07 09. Impressive, earlier-maturing Fonseca Guimaraens and single-QUINTA Panascal when no classic declaration.

Frasqueira "Vintage" Madeira from a single yr, bottled after at least 20 yrs in wood. Date of bottling compulsory; longer in cask, the more concentrated and complex.

Garvey ★→★★ One of the great old names of JEREZ, now with an uncertain future. The bodega, and the others in the same group (Soto, Teresa Rivero, VALDIVIA, Zoilo RUIZ-MATEOS in Jerez) owned by the Ruiz-Mateos family, were sold nr the end of 2011 to a private equity fund. Garvey's treasures incl San Patricio Fino, *Tío Guillermo* Amontillado, the age-dated 1780 line.

González Byass ★★★→★★★★ Despite Jerez's corporate upheavals GB (founded 1845) remains a family business, renewing itself with enthusiasm. One of the best Finos: *Tío Pepe*. From same SOLERA now comes an EN RAMA. Newest launch: fascinating Palmas range: three aged Finos (6-, 8-, 10-yrs-old) plus rare 40-yr-old Amontillado. Also v. fine: Viña AB, Matúsalem Oloroso, Apóstoles Palo Cortado, outstanding, ultra-rich Noë PX. Extensive interests in brandy; table wines, incl BERONIA (RIOJA), VIÑAS DEL VERO (SOMONTANO). Also owns CROFT JEREZ.

Gould Campbell ★★ Port shipper belonging to SYMINGTON FAMILY ESTATES. Gd-value, full-bodied VINTAGE PORTS (70 77' 80 83 85' 91 94 97 00 03' 07).

Gracia Hermanos Mont-M ★ Bodega within same group as PÉREZ BARQUERO and Compañia Vinícola del Sur making gd-quality MONTILLAS. Esp Tauromaquia Amontillado and PX.

Graham ★★★→★★★★ Prestigious SYMINGTON FAMILY ESTATES-owned Port house. V.gd range from Six Grapes RESERVE RUBY, LBV and TAWNY (Res) to excellent yr-aged Tawnies, rare COLHEITAS (1961') and rich, sweet, but age-worthy single-QUINTA vintage (dos Malvedos) and VINTAGE PORTS (63 66 70' 75 77' 80 83' 85' 91' 94' 97 00' 03' 07').

Gran Cruz ★ The single biggest Port brand, owned by La Martiniquaise. Light, low-price TAWNY, also ROSÉ PORT. New multimedia visitor centre in Oporto.

Guita, La ★→★★★ *Esp fine Manzanilla*. Owned by GRUPO ESTÉVEZ.

Gutiérrez Colosía ★→★★★ Former ALMACENISTA on Guadalete River, EL PUERTO DE SANTA MARÍA, one of few bodegas remaining in the town. Excellent old Palo Cortado.

Harvey's ★→★★★ Major producer now owned by Beam Global. Famed for Bristol Cream (medium-sweet), once an icon. Most VORS wines show briskness in old age, but the 30-yr-old PX is exceptional – aromatic and spicy.

Henriques & Henriques ★★→★★★★ Madeira shipper uniquely with own v'yds (11ha). Breezy extra-dry apéritif Monte Seco; rich, well-structured wines, incl outstanding 10- and 15-yr-olds, 20-yr-old MALVASIA and Terrantez, "Single Harvest" COLHEITAS, vintage and SOLERA wines (VERDELHO 1934, Terrantez 1954, Malvasia 1954, BUAL 1980, Century Malmsey-Solera 1900). Experimenting with new oak.

Herederos de Argüeso ★→★★★ One of SANLÚCAR's top Manzanilla producers with v.gd San León, exceptional, dense and salty *San León Reserva* and youthful Las Medallas; also impressively lively VORS Amontillado Viejo.

Hidalgo La Gitana ★★★ Old (1792) family firm fronted by indefatigable Javier Hidalgo, with popular Manzanilla La Gitana. New EN RAMA La Gitana is brilliantly expressive. Intense, savoury single-v'yd aged *Pastrana Manzanilla Pasada* is in impressive contrast to most Manzanillas. Also fine Oloroso, lovely Palo Cortado and treacly PX, v.gd VORS range, incl Faraon Oloroso.

Jerez de la Frontera Centre of Sherry industry, between Cádiz and Seville. "Sherry" is a corruption of the ancient name, pronounced *her-éth*. In French, Xérès.

Justino ★→★★★ Largest Madeira shipper, wholly owned by La Martiniquaise. Gd 10-yr-old, TINTA NEGRA COLHEITA (1996, 1999), Terrantez Old Res NV and Vintage. CANTEIRO-aged Tinta Negra from certified organic grapes in the works. Also makes Madeira under the Broadbent label, incl v.gd Terrantez 1978.

Kopke ★→★★★ The oldest Port house (1638), owned by BARROS ALMEIDA. Drawing on aged stocks, wood-aged styles excel, esp COLHEITAS (37', 38', 66 80' 87 89), 40-yr-old TAWNY and 30-yr-old WHITE PORT. VINTAGE PORTS (incl single-QUINTA Quinta São Luiz) mostly early-maturing but some v.gd (83 85 87 89 91 94 97 00 03 04 05' 07). ROSÉ PORT, too.

Krohn ★→★★★ Family-owned Port shipper. Gd 20- and 30-yr-old TAWNY, excellent COLHEITAS (61' 66' 67' 78 82 83' 87' 91 2000). VINTAGE PORTS on the up (07' 09), incl single-QUINTA do Retiro Novo. New ROSÉ PORT.

Late Bottled Vintage (LBV) Robustly fruity Port from a single year kept in wood for twice as long as VINTAGE PORT (around 5 yrs) and much less powerful and complex than Vintage. Volume commercial styles broachable on release and do not need decanting, unlike unfiltered versions from CHURCHILL, FERREIRA, NIEPOORT, QUINTA do Nova, QUINTA DO NOVAL, SMITH WOODHOUSE, WARRE.

Leacock Volume label of MADEIRA WINE COMPANY; sweet, rich house style. Main brand is St John. Older vintages: 1927, 1963 SERCIAL, 1914 BUAL and 1808, 1860 SOLERA.

Los Infantes Orleans Borbon ★★ Small bodega with links to the Spanish royal family. Freshly yeasty Manzanilla Torrebreva.

Lustau ★★★→★★★★ Bodega famous for wide *range of excellent individual wines* under *capataz* (winemaker) Manuel Lozano. Pioneered the identifying and shipping of ALMACENISTA Sherries. Lozano has recently restored La Ina Fino to its former glory. Other v.gd Sherries incl Botaina Amontillado, East India SOLERA, MOSCATEL Emilín, VORS Oloroso and PX, Oloroso 97.

Madeira Wine Company An association of all 26 British Madeira companies. Originally formed in 1913 by just two firms, it accounts for over 50% of bottled Madeira exports. BLANDY family resumes reins after a brief (c.20 yr) but innovative interlude being run in partnership with SYMINGTON FAMILY ESTATES. Principal brands: Blandy, COSSART GORDON, LEACOCK, Miles, each retains individual house style. Blandy, Cossart Gordon lead the pack. All except basic wines CANTEIRO-aged.

Sherry styles

Manzanilla Fashionably pale, dry Sherry: fresh green-apple character; a popular, unchallenging introduction to the flavours of Sherry. Matured (though not necessarily grown) in the humid, maritime conditions of SANLÚCAR DE BARRAMEDA where the FLOR grows more thickly, and the wine is said to acquire a salty tang. Drink cold from a newly opened bottle. Do not keep. Eg. HEREDEROS DE ARGÜESO, San León RESERVA.

Manzanilla Pasada Manzanilla aged longer than most; v. dry, complex. Eg. HIDALGO LA GITANA's single-v'yd Manzanilla Pasada Pastrana.

Fino Dry; weightier than Manzanilla; 3 yrs age min (as Manzanilla). Eg. GONZÁLEZ BYASS Tio Pepe. Serve as Manzanilla. Don't keep.

Amontillado A fino in which the layer of protective yeast FLOR has died, allowing the wine to oxidize, creating more complexity. Naturally dry. Eg. Valdespino Tio Diego. Commercial styles may be sweetened.

Oloroso Not aged under FLOR. Heavier, less brilliant when young, matures to nutty intensity. Naturally dry. May be sweetened with PX and sold as *dulce*. Eg. LUSTAU Los Arcos (dry), Old East India (sweet). Keeps well.

Palo Cortado V. fashionable. Traditionally a wine that had lost its FLOR – between Amontillado and Oloroso. Today often blended to create the style. Difficult to identify with certainty, though some suggest it has a keynote "lactic" or "bitter butter" note. Dry, rich, complex: worth looking for. Eg. BARBADILLO Reliquía, FERNANDO DE CASTILLA Antique.

Cream Blend sweetened with grape must, PX, and/or MOSCATEL for an inexpensive, medium-sweet style. Unashamedly commercial. Eg. HARVEY's Bristol Cream, CROFT Pale Cream. EQUIPO NAVAZOS La Bota No. 21 is outstanding exception.

Pedro Ximénez (PX) Raisined, sweet, dark, from partly sun-dried PX grapes (grapes mainly from MONTILLA; wine made in JEREZ DO). Concentrated, unctuous, decadent, bargain. Sip with ice-cream. Overall, world's sweetest wine. Eg. Rey Fernando de Castilla Antique, EMILIO HIDALGO Santa Ana 1861, Valdespino Toneles.

Moscatel Aromatic, around half sugar of PX. Eg. Lustau Emilín. Unlike PX not required to be fortified. Now permitted to be called "JEREZ".

VOS/VORS Age-dated sherries: some of the treasures of the JEREZ bodegas. Exceptional quality and maturity at relatively low prices. Wines assessed by carbon dating to be more than 20 yrs old are called VOS (Very Old Sherry/Vinum Optimum Signatum); those over 30 yrs old are VORS (Very Old Rare Sherry/Vinum Optimum Rare Signatum). Also 12-yr-old and 15-yr-old egs. Applies only to Amontillado, Oloroso, Palo Cortado, PX. Eg. VOS Hidalgo Jerez Cortado Wellington. Some VORS wines can be bitter or attenuated and maybe softened with PX – occasionally producers can be over-generous with the PX.

Añada "Vintage" Sherry with a declared vintage. Runs counter to tradition of vintage-blended SOLERA. Formerly private bottlings now winning public accolades. Eg. Lustau Sweet Oloroso Añada 1997.

Maestro Sierra ★→★★★ Owned by JEREZ's grandest dame Pilar Plá Pechovierto, widow of a direct descendant of the ALMACENISTA founder (1832). Gd Fino and 12- and 15-yr-old Amontillado and Oloroso.

Malmsey (Malvasia Candida) The sweetest and richest of traditional Madeira grape varieties; dark-amber and honeyed, yet with Madeira's unique sharp tang, perfect match for rich fruit and chocolate puddings.

Marqués del Real Tesoro ★★ Fine Tio Mateo fino. Part of GRUPO ESTÉVEZ.

Martinez Gassiot ★★ Port firm now owned by SYMINGTON FAMILY ESTATES, known esp for rich and pungent Directors 20-yr-old TAWNY. Gd-value, age-worthy VINTAGE in drier, traditional style: 63 67 70 75 82 85 87 91 94 97 00 03 07.

Montecristo Mont-M Brand of popular MONTILLAS by Compañía Vinícola del Sur.

Montilla-Moriles ★→★★★ Andalucian DO nr Córdoba. Once known simply for its cheaper versions of fino Sherry styles, now known for the quality of its sun-dried super-sweet PX grapes, some with long ageing in SOLERA. Still great value. Top producers: ALVEAR, GRACIA HERMANOS, PÉREZ BARQUERO, BODEGAS TORO ALBALÁ.

Niepoort ★★★→★★★★ Small family-run Port house, VINTAGE (66 70' 75 77 78 80 82 83 87 91 92 94 97 00' 03 05' 07 09'), incl unique *garrafeira* (aged in demijohns), Broadbent, new single-v'yd Bioma (formerly "Pisca", Secundum is earlier drinking. Exceptional TAWNY and COLHEITAS. Benchmark Dry White, also 10-yr-old WHITE. New CRUSTED Port bottled in 2007.

Noval, Quinta do ★★★ →★★★★ Elegant yet structured VINTAGE PORT (63' 66 67 70 75 7 82 85 87 91 94' 95 97' 00' 03' 04 07' 08'), esp intense, slow-maturing Nacional from 2.5ha of ungrafted vines often made outside classic declared yrs. Second vintage label: Silval. V.gd age-dated TAWNY, COLHEITAS; single-estate unfiltered LBV. Early-drinking Noval Black RESERVE and table wines from younger v'yds.

Offley ★→★★ Fresh, modern labels signpost SOGRAPE's fruit-driven brand. Gd TAWNY Ports (incl volume label Duke of Oporto and 10-yr, 20-yr, 30-yr), also Boa Vista VINTAGE. Apéritif/cocktail styles incl Cachuca RESERVE WHITE PORT and ROSÉ PORT.

Osborne Jer ★★ →★★★★ Historic bodega dominating EL PUERTO DE SANTA MARIA. Also makes table wines in Rioja, Rueda, Ribera del Duero. Fino quinta a classic; fino Amontillado SOLERA AOS; gd-value Bailén Oloroso.

Paternina, Federico ★★ →★★★ Owned by the RIOJA producer. Based on the cellars of Díez Hermanos together with three VORS wines, the excellent and unique *Fino Imperial*, Victoria Regina Oloroso and Vieja SOLERA PX.

Pereira d'Oliveira Vinhos ★★★ Family-owned; stars of the show are characterful, intense vintages (labelled RESERVA), bottled on demand from cask (1937 1971 SERCIAL, 1966 VERDELHO, 1912' 1978' BUAL). 15-yr-old wines upwards CANTEIRO-aged Fine, traditional COLHEITAS (Boal 1988, MALVASIA 1987, Terrantez 1988).

Pérez Barquero Mont-M ★★ →★★★ A leader in revival of MONTILLA PX. Fine Gran Barquero Fino, Amontillado, Oloroso; v.gd La Cañada PX.

Poças ★★ →★★★ Portuguese-owned fourth-generation Port house known esp for its TAWNY, COLHEITAS (67' 86' 91' 00). Gd LBV; recent VINTAGES (97 00' 03 04 05' 07 09). Also ROSÉ PORT.

Puerto de Santa María, El The former port of Sherry, one of the three towns forming the "Sherry Triangle". Production now in serious decline; remaining bodegas incl former ALMACENISTA GUTIÉRREZ COLOSÍA, OSBORNE and TERRY. Puerto's finos are considered lighter than those of JEREZ, not as "salty" as SANLÚCAR.

Quarles Harris ★★ One of the oldest Port houses (since 1680) owned by SYMINGTON FAMILY ESTATES. Mellow, well-balanced VINTAGES, often v.gd value: 63 66 70 75 77 80 83 85 91 94 97 00' 03 07.

Quevedo ★ →★★ New Port brand courting a 30-something audience via social media and forward styles of WHITE, RUBY, VINTAGE (07', 08) and ROSÉ. Made 20-yr-old TAWNY for re-launched Villar d'Allen brand.

Quinta Portuguese for "estate", traditionally denoted VINTAGE PORTS from shippers' single v'yds; declared in gd, not exceptional yrs, but growers increasingly making single-QUINTA Port in top yrs. Rising stars: Duorum, da Gaivosa, Passadouro, Romaneira, Tedo, Whytingham's Vale Meão, Wine & Soul's Pintas.

Ramos Pinto ★★★ Dynamic house owned by Champagne Roederer; gd wines, too. Outstanding single-QUINTA (de Ervamoira – v.gd 09) and TAWNY, incl de Ervamoira (10-yr-old), do Bom Retiro (20-yr-old) and 30-yr-old. Rich, sweet, generally early-maturing vintages.

Reserve/Reserva Better than basic premium Ports, bottled without a vintage date or age indication. Mostly RUBY; some TAWNY and WHITE PORT. New: QUINTA do Crasto (*see* Portugal chapter) Finest Res.

Rosa, Quinta de la ★★★ V.gd, elegant, dryish single-QUINTA Port 94 95 00 03' 04 05' 07' 09', TAWNY, LBV and COLHEITA (table wines, too) from the Bergqvist family.

Rosé Port Growing category. Officially recognized in 2009, prompted by CROFT's pioneering "Pink". Serve chilled, on ice or in a cocktail.

Royal Oporto ★→★★ REAL COMPANHIA VELHA's main Port brand (also owns QUINTA de Ventozelo and DELAFORCE). Gd TAWNY (spends average 5 yrs in wood), COLHEITAS and VINTAGE PORTS. Also ROSÉ PORT.

Rozès ★→★★★ Port shipper owned by Champagne house Vranken. Three new DOURO Superior QUINTAS (Grifo, Anibal, Canameira) account for improved Terras do Grifo VINTAGE. ROSÉ PORT and exciting late-harvest sweet wine, too.

Ruby Youngest, cheapest Port style: simple, sweet, red; best is labelled RESERVE.

Ruiz-Mateos Family business in JEREZ with chequered story. Bodegas of the holding company Rumasa were expropriated by the government in 1983. Nueva ("new") Rumasa relaunched with interests incl GARVEY. Rumasa collapse led to sale of Garvey group (2011). Future of SOLERAS not clear at the time of writing.

Vintage Port is delicious young, within 3–4 years of the vintage. Or at 10 years+.

Sánchez Romate ★★→★★★ Family firm in JEREZ since 1781. Best-known in Spanish-speaking world, esp for brandy Cardenal Mendoza. V. fine, nutty Amontillado NPU, excellent VORS amontillado and Oloroso La Sacristía de Romate, unctuous Sacristía PX.

Sandeman Jer ★→★★ Some fine wines, incl Royal Esmeralda VOS Amontillado, *Royal Ambrosante* VOS Oloroso and PX.

Sandeman ★★→★★★★ SOGRAPE Port brand; aged stocks to produce v.gd aged TAWNY, esp 20-yr-old. New QUINTA do Seixo winery has improved VINTAGE since 2007 (63 66 70 75 77 94 97 00 03 07'). Second label: fruity Vau Vintage (97' 99 00 03).

Sanlúcar de Barrameda Magellan sailed from here. So did Columbus. Bodega town at mouth of the river Guadalquivír. Seaside air encourages FLOR growth, is said to give the wines a salty character. Analytically unproven but evident, esp in older wines such as HIDALGO's Manzanilla Pasada Pastrana.

Santa Eufemia, Quinta de ★★★ Portuguese-owned, 4th-generation Port house. V.gd 10-, 20- and 30-yr-old TAWNY and WHITE PORTS.

Sercial Both the wine and the grape: driest of all Madeiras. Supreme apéritif or try with smoked-salmon canapés. *See* Grapes chapter.

Silva, C da ★★→★★★ Port shipper. Sophisticated new range incl Dalva Golden White COLHEITA WHITE PORTS (1952' 1963) and chef collaboration Miguel Castro e Silva (a new dry White) and Rui Paula (1967 Colheita).

Smith Woodhouse ★★★ Small Port firm founded in 1784, now owned by SYMINGTON FAMILY ESTATES. Gd unfiltered LBV; some v. fine VINTAGES: 63 66 70 75 77' 80 83 85 91 94 97 00' 03 07. Occasional single-estate wines from QUINTA da Madelena.

Solera System for ageing Sherry and, less commonly now, Madeira. Consists of topping up progressively more mature BUTTS with slightly younger wine of same sort from previous stage, or *criadera*. The object is maintaining vigour of FLOR, also gives consistency. Min age for a Fino or Manzanilla is 3 rs in solera.

Symington Family Estates ★★→★★★★ Fifth-generation forward-looking family-run Port shippers, latterly farmers; now DOURO's largest v'yd owner (26 QUINTAS over

PORT, SHERRY & MADEIRA

2,300 acres). In 2011 reduced MADEIRA WINE COMPANY shareholding to focus on Port and Douro table wine brands incl: COCKBURN, DOW, GOULD CAMPBELL, GRAHAM, MARTINEZ GASSIOT, QUARLES HARRIS, QUINTA DE RORIZ, SMITH WOODHOUSE, VÉSUVIO and WARRE Altano and Chryseia.

Tawny Wood-aged Port style (hence tawny colour), though many basic Tawnies are little more than attenuated RUBY. Best are wines with an indication of age: 10-, 20-, 30-, 40-yr-old or RESERVE.

Taylor, Fladgate & Yeatman (Taylor's) ★★→★★★★ Fladgate's jewel in the crown. Imposing, long-lived VINTAGE PORTS (66 70 75 77' 80 83 85 92' 94 97 00' 03' 07' 09'). V.gd range, incl RESERVE, LBV and aged TAWNY. QUINTAS Vargellas and Terra Feita produce impressive single-Quinta Vintage Port, esp rare Vargellas Vinha Velha (95 97 00 04 07' 09') from 70+-yr-old vines. Limited-edition Scion is a bottling of two recently discovered pipes of pre-phylloxera 1850s Tawny Port (Winston Churchill apparently had a third).

Terry ★→★★ Bodega dominating entrance to EL PUERTO DE SANTA MARÍA.

Toro Albalá Mont-M One of the top MONTILLA producers; v. fine Don PX.

Tradición ★★→★★★ Small, serious bodega making only VOS and VORS wines (ie. no fino) from an art-filled cellar in JEREZ's old town.

Valdespino Jer ★★→★★★★ Famous Jerez bodega producing Inocente Fino from the esteemed Macharnudo v'yd. Terrific dry Amontillados, Tio Diego and *Coliseo* vibrant SOLERA 1842 Oloroso VOS; remarkable Toneles MOSCATEL.

Valdivia ★★→★★★ Former home of RUIZ-MATEOS family, acquired by GARVEY group (2008), but with uncertain future given recent sale of group. V.gd 15-yr-old Sacromonte Amontillado, gd oloroso.

Vale D Maria, Quinta do ★★★ Gd-value, elegant, forward single-QUINTA VINTAGE PORT (01 02 03 05 07 09') and unfiltered LBV.

Verdelho Style and grape of medium-dry Madeira; pungent but without the austerity of SERCIAL. Gd apéritif or pair with pâté. Increasingly popular for table wines.

Vesúvio, Quinta do ★★★★ With NOVAL, a single-QUINTA Port on par with best VINTAGE PORT (91 92 94 95' 96' 97 98 99 00' 01 03' 04 05' 06 07' 08' 09). Only SYMINGTON FAMILY ESTATES Port still foot-trodden by people (not robotically). Limited-edition Capela Vintage Port made in 2007, as were the first table wines.

Vila Nova de Gaia City across the river DOURO from Oporto. Traditionally home to the major Port shippers' lodges, but increasingly Port is aged up the Douro in air-conditioned lodges.

Vintage Port Classic vintages: best wines declared in exceptional yrs by shippers between 1 Jan and 30 Sept in the second yr after vintage. Bottled without filtration after 2 yrs in wood, wine matures v. slowly in bottle throwing a crust or deposit (always decant). Modern vintages broachable earlier but best will last 50 yrs+. Single-QUINTA Vintage Ports also drinking earlier; best can last 30 yrs+.

Warre ★★★→★★★★ Oldest of British Port shippers (1670); owned by SYMINGTON FAMILY ESTATES since 1905. V.gd, rich, age-worthy VINTAGE (63 66 70' 75 77' 80' 83 85 91 94 97 00' 03 07' 09'), Single-QUINTA (da Cavadinha) and unfiltered LBV. Consistently gd, fruity RESERVE, vintage character (Warrior), also 10- and 20-yr old TAWNY Otima. Special 2009' Vintage Port marks the 200th anniversary of Wellington's victory in the Peninsular War.

White Port Port from white grapes. Styles range from dry to sweet (*lagrima*) mostly off-dry and blend of yrs. Apéritif straight or drunk long with tonic and fresh mint. Also rare COLHEITAS eg. C DA SILVA's Dalva Golden White and, since 2006, new serious age-dated category (10-, 20-, 30-, or 40-yr-old).

Williams & Humbert ★→★★★★ Traditional Sherry bodega. Once a famous name now much involved in making private-label wines. Bestsellers: Dry Sack, Winter's Tale Amontillados. V.gd old wines incl *Dos Cortados PC*.

Switzerland

Abbreviations used in the text:

Aar	Aargau
Ber	Bern
Gris	Grisons
Neu	Neuchâtel
Schaff	Schaffhausen
Thur	Thurgau
Tic	Ticino
Val	Valais
Vd	Vaud
Zür	Zürich

S witzerland doesn't play by Euro-rules, or indeed by any rules except its own. Even its wine bottles are a different size. Export is not its priority, but go there and you will be amazed by the qualty and originality of its wines. Skiers may glug Fendant, but the Swiss are keener on their unique indigenous grapes with herbal, mineral, stone-fruit characters – and their rapidly improving reds. Pinot Noir is now mainstream, nearly one-third of the vineyard. The Valais makes good, potent standard wines; Vaud lighter and subtler interpretations of, above all, Chasselas. Swiss wine is for those who collect original tastes and don't demand blockbusters. With the current worldwide interest in old, indigenous grape varieties, Switzerland's moment should have arrived.

Recent vintages

2011 Very good vintage, from a unusually long, warm autumn.
2010 A classic vintage. Very elegant; lower quantity than 2009.
2009 One of the best of recent years.
2008 Difficult year with lots of rain. Quality OK, but not tops.
2007 Reds are less opulent than 2006. Whites are superb.
2006 Very promising; being compared to 2005.

Aigle Vd r w ★★→★★★ Well-known for elegant CHASSELAS and supple PINOT N.

AOC Still v. unclear system. Every wine canton defines its own rules. There are cantonal, regional and local AOC rules.

Auvernier Neu r p w ★★→★★★ Old wine village on Lake NEUCHÂTEL. Try Caves du Château d'Auvernier.

Bachtobel, Schlossgut Thur ★★★→★★★★ 08' 09' 10' 11' Johannes Meier is the eighth generation of this family estate. V.gd PINOT N, RIES and SAUV BL.

Badoux, Henri Vd w ★★ Big producer of commercial wines. Try CHASSELAS AIGLE les Murailles (classic lizard label), YVORNE Petit Vignoble and new range Lettre de Noblesse with a MALBEC and CAB blend from ST-SAPHORIN.

Bern Capital and French- and German-speaking canton. Best wine villages: L Neuveville, Ligerz, Schafis, Schernelz and Twann. CHASSELAS, PINOT N, MÜLLER-T.

Bielersee Ber r p w ★→★★ 09' 10 11 Wine region on northern and western shore of the Bielersee (dry, light CHASSELAS, PINOT N, MÜLLER-T, CHARD, PINOT GR, SAUV BL, MALBEC, ZWEIGELT). Best producers: Johanniterkeller, Domaine du Signolet Schernelz Village.

Bovard, Louis Vd w ★★★★ Classical interpretation of CHASSELAS; can last here more than ten yrs. V.gd DÉZALEY Médinette. Family business for ten generations. Try also SAUV BL Ribex.

Bündner Herrschaft Gris r p w ★★★→★★★★ 08 09' 10 11' Best German-Swiss win region. Top villages: Fläsch, Jenins, Maienfeld, Malans, Zizers. BLAUBURGUNDE S'land's best; ripens well due to warm *Föhn* wind; cask-aged v.gd. Also CHARD, MÜLLER THURGAU, Completer. Best: CICERO WEINBAU ★★, Weingut Weingut Davaz ★★, Domain Donatsch ★★, WEINGUT GEORG FROMM ★★★, GANTENBEIN ★★★★, Familie Christian & Ursula Marugg ★★, Winebau Manfred Meier ★★, Weingut Annatina Pelizzati ★★, Wegelin Scadenagut ★★, Schloss Salenegg ★★, Weinbau von Tscharner ★★.

Looking for more information on grapes? Try the "Grapes" section on pp.16–26.

Chablais Vd r w ★★→★★★★ Wine region at the upper end of Lake GENEVA, incl villages AIGLE, Bex, Ollon, Villeneuve, YVORNE, all known for CHASSELAS.

Chanton, Josef-Marie and Mario Val ★★★ *Terrific Valais spécialités*: Eyholzer Rote Gwäss, HEIDA, Himbertscha, Lafnetscha, Plantscher, Resi. Josef-Marie Chanton is the Indiana Jones of Swiss indigenous grape varieties. Try sweet HEIDA.

Chappaz Val ★★★ Marie-Thérèse Chappaz of FULLY is the queen of sweet wine Outstanding Petite ARVINE and MARSANNE Blanche GRAIN NOBLE CONFIDENCIEL Small production.

Château Maison Blanche Vd w ★★ Best in the area; a single CHASSELAS.

Cicero Weinbau Gris r w ★★ Zizers (Grisons). Wonderful PINOT N (esp De Mattmann) and SAUV BL. Try RIES x SYLVANER Alte Reben, from v. old vines.

Côte, la Vd r p w ★→★★★ Largest VAUD AOC between LAUSANNE and Nyon. The white are traditional in style with finesse; the fruity reds are harmonious. Esp from MONT-SUR-ROLLE, Vinzel, Luins, FÉCHY, MORGES. Try Château de Luins, Bolle DOMAINE LA COLOMBE.

Cruchon, Henri Vd r w ★★★ Biodynamic producer. Wonderful CHASSELAS, SAUV BL Gamaret and GAMAY.

Dézaley Vd (r) w ★★→★★★★ Celebrated LAVAUX v'yd on slopes above Lake GENEVA Potent CHASSELAS develops, esp after ageing. Try La Baronnie du Dézaley (12 producers), Domaine Blondel, LOUIS BOVARD, Chaudet Vins, *Fonjallaz*. Try them at Georges Wenger's restaurant in Le Noirmont: vintages dating back to 1974.

Dôle Val r ★★→★★★★ Traditional red blend: mostly PINOT N plus some GAMAY, perhaps with some other VALAIS reds: full, supple, often v.gd. Traditional style is light more recent style heavier, using expressive grapes like Diolinoir, Garamet SYRAH. Lightly pink Dôle Blanche is pressed straight after harvest. Try SIMON MAYE ET FILS, provins valais, Gérald Besse, ANNE-CATHERINE & DENIS MERCIER.

Domaine la Colombe Vd w ★★★★ Family company; one of the best producers of fresh, elegant, minerally CHASSELAS; also try Rés PINOT GR.

Epesses Vd (r) w ★→★★★★ 10' 11 LAVAUX AOC: supple, full-bodied whites. Luc Masse Vins, Domaine Blaise Duboux, Fonjallaz.

Féchy Vd ★→★★ Famous appellation of LA CÔTE, esp elegant whites. DYA. Try Domaine du Martheray, DOMAINE LA COLOMBE, Domaine du Saugey.

Federweisser / Weissherbst German-Swiss fresh white/rosé from BLAUBURGUNDER.

Fendant Val w ★→★★★ VALAIS appellation for CHASSELAS. The ideal wine for Swiss cheese dishes such as fondue or raclette. Try PROVINS, Les Fils de Charles Favre, MAURICE ZUFFEREY, ADRIAN & DIEGO MATHIER NOUVEAU SALQUENEN, Domaine des Muses, JEAN-RENÉ GERMANIER, Cave Mabillard-Fuchs, SIMON MAYE & FILS.

Flétri / Mi-flétri Late-harvested grapes for sweet/slightly sweet wine.

Fontannaz, André Val w ★★★ Cave La Madeleine. Nobody understands the AMIGNE de Vétroz grape better.

Fribourg Smallest French-Swiss wine canton (115ha, nr Jura). Try Cru de l'Hôpital, Cave de la Tour.

Fromm, Georg Weingut ★★★ 08 09' 10 (11) Malans grower Georg Fromm sold his 2nd estate in New Zealand and focuses on outstanding BLAUBURGUNDER and CHARD.

Fully Val r w Village nr Martigny: excellent ERMITAGE and GAMAY. Best producer: Marie-Thérèse CHAPPAZ; try Grain Noble wines ★★→★★★ 09' 10 (11).

Gantenbein, Daniel & Martha Gris 07 08 09' 10' (11) ★★★★ Most famous growers in Switzerland, based in Fläsch. Top PINOT N from DRC clones (see France), RIES with clones from Loosen (see Germany). Strong in export. Some CHARD.

Geneva Capital, and French-Swiss canton; 4rd-largest wine region. Key areas: Mandement, Entre Arve et Rhône, Entre Arve et Lac. Mostly CHASSELAS, GAMAY. Also Gamaret, CHARD, PINOT N, SAUV BL and gd ALIGOTÉ. Best: JEAN-MICHEL NOVELLE ★★★; interesting: Domaines des Charmes, Domaine Dugerdil, Domaine Les Hutins, Grand'Cour, Stéphane Gros ★★.

Germanier, Jean-René Val Top Vétroz estate. Cayas (SYRAH) ★★★ 07 08' (09') (10); Mitis (sweet AMIGNE) ★★★ 06 07 08' 09' (10). Pure CORNALIN 07' 08 09' and PINOT N Clos du Four ★★★. New single-terroir 10' CHASSELAS Clos de la Malettaz.

Glacier, Vin du (Gletscherwein) Val Fabled oxidized, wooded white from rare Rèze grape of Val d'Anniviers. Almost impossible to find on sale. Keep looking. If you love Sherry, this is a must.

Grain Noble ConfidenCiel Val Quality label for top Swiss sweet wines. Try Domaine du Mont d'Or, Cave La Liaudisaz, Domaine Thierry Constantin, Domaine Cornulus.

Grisons (Graubünden) Mtn canton, mainly German-Swiss (BÜNDNER HERRSCHAFT, Churer Rheintal; esp BLAUBURGUNDER), part south of Alps (Misox, esp MERLOT). PINOT N king, CHARD v.gd, also MÜLLER-T. Best: GANTENBEIN, FROMM, CICERO WEINBAU, Weinbau von Tscharner, IRENE GRÜNENFELDER, Obrecht Weingut zur Sonne, Weingut Bovel.

Grünenfelder, Irene Gris r ★★★ Weingut Eichholz, Jenins. Only four wines but they're outstanding.

Huber, Daniel Tic r ★★★ 08 09' 10 (11) MERLOT Montagna Magica is superb.

Junge Schweiz Aar, Gris, Schaff, Zür Dynamic group of young growers. There are 21 members, incl Susi Wehrli, Carina Kunz, Nadine und Stefan Saxer, Andreas Schwarz, Roger Schwarzenbach.

Lausanne Vd Capital of VAUD. No longer with v'yds in town area, but long-time owner of classics: Abbaye de Mont, Château Rochefort (LA CÔTE); Clos des Moines, Clos des Abbayes, Domaine de Burignon (LAVAUX).

Lavaux Vd (r) w ★→★★★★ Now a UNESCO world heritage site: v'yd terraces stretch 30km along the south-facing north shore of Lake GENEVA from Château de Chillon to the eastern outskirts of LAUSANNE. Main grape is CHASSELAS. Wines named for the villages: Lutry, ST-SAPHORIN, Ollon, EPESSES, DÉZALEY, Montreux and more. *Terravin* is an annual award for top wines

Mathier, Adrian & Diego Noveau Salquenen Val r w ★★★★ Top wine estate in Salgesch/Valais. Try PINOT N, wide range of spécialités.

Mauler Neu sp ★★→★★★ Old family business focused on *méthode traditionnelle* sparkling from NEUCHÂTEL, esp Cuvée Louis-Edouard Mauler.

Maye, Simon et Fils Val r w ★★★ Interesting FENDANT, Païen, PINOT N, SYRAH.

Mercier, Anne-Catherine & Denis Val ★★★ 08 09' 10 (11) Growers in SIERRE, with outstanding CORNALIN and SYRAH.

Mont-sur-Rolle Vd (r) w ★★ DYA Important appellation within LA CÔTE. CHASSELAS is king. Try Clos des Cordelières, Domaines de Autecour, de Haute-Cour, du Coteau, Châteaux de Châtagneréaz, de Mont.

Morges Vd r p w ★→★★ DYA Large AOC with 39 communes: CHASSELAS, fruity reds. Try Château de Vufflens.

Neuchâtel Neu City and canton; 591ha from Lake Neuchâtel to BIELERSEE. CHASSELAS: fragrant, lively (*sur lie*, sparkling). Gd OEIL DE PERDRIX, PINOT GR, CHARD. Try: Châteaux d'Auvernier, Souaillon; Chantal Ritter, Jacques Tatasciore.

Non Filtré Neu Spécialité available from January from NEUCHÂTEL, from unfiltered CHASSELAS. First Swiss Wine of the new vintage. Try Christian Rossel.

Novelle, Jean-Michel Gen ★★★ 09' 10 11 GENEVA-based, Domaine le Grande Clos. V.gd SAUV BL, PETIT MANSENG, GAMAY, MERLOT, SYRAH. V. limited.

Oeil de Perdrix Neu PINOT N rosé. DYA, esp NEUCHÂTEL's; name can be used anywhere. Try Château d'Auvernier, Cru de l'Hôpital. The name refers to the colour of a partridge's eye.

Paccot, Raymond Vd ★★★ 09' 10' 11' FÉCHY. DOMAINE LA COLOMBE. Look here for excellent CHASSELAS, esp Le Brez. Biodynamic.

Provins Valais Val Biggest winery (co-op) in Switzerland, making 10% of total. Outstanding for Maître de Chais and Crus des Domaines labels, interesting Les Titans range. Chief winemaker Madeleine Gay big on the preservation of indigenous grapes.

Rahm, Weinkellerei Schaff r w ★★ Big, innovative commercial producer in Hallau. Try Selection Pierre.

Rouvinez Vins Val r w ★★★ Important producer. Try Château Lichten, CORNALIN from Montibeux, La Trémaille. Also owns Caves Orsat.

Salgesch Val Important German-speaking village. Try ADRIAN & DIEGO MATHIER NOUVEAU SALQUENEN, Cave du Rhodan, Vins des Chevaliers, Grego Kuonen – Caveau de Salquenen, Albert Mathier et Fils, Cave Biber.

Salvagnin Vd r ★→★★ 10 11 GAMAY and/or PINOT N appellation. Spécialité from VAUD.

Schaffhausen German-Swiss canton/town on the Rhine with the famous Falls. BLAUBURGUNDER, also MÜLLER-T and spécialités. Best: Baumann Weingut, Bad Osterfingen, WeinStamm ★★.

Schenk Vd Europe-wide wine giant, founded 1893 and based in Rolle. Owns firms in France (Burgundy and Bordeaux), Germany, Italy, Spain. Best address for classic-style Swiss wines. Founder of the Clos, Domaines & Châteaux (association of Swiss noble wines).

Schwarzenbach Weinbau Zür w ★★★ Family producer on the lake. Dry, crisp whites, Räuschling, KERNER, MÜLLER-T.

Sierre Val r w ★★→★★★ Sunny resort known for FENDANT, PINOT N, ERMITAGE, MALVOISIE. V.gd DÔLE. Visit Château de Villa – raclette restaurant, wine museum and vinotheque with largest VALAIS wine collection. Top names: Imesch Vins, ANNE-CATHERINE ET DENIS MERCIER, Domaine des Muses, ROUVINEZ VINS, MAURICE ZUFFEREY.

Sion Val r w ★★→★★★ Capital/wine centre of VALAIS. Esp FENDANT de Sion. Top: Charles Bonvin Fils, Les Fils de Charles Favre, Robert Gilliard, Giroud Vins, PROVINS VALAIS.

St-Saphorin Vd (r) w ★★→★★★ 10 11' Famous LAVAUX AOC for fine light whites. Try Château de Glérolles, Domaine Bovy.

Sternen, Weingut zum Aar r ★★★ Producer of an interesting interpretation of PINOT N – try Kloster Sion Pinot N. Owner Andreas Meier also runs a vine nursery and a restaurant.

Ticino Italian-speaking southern Switzerland (with Misox), growing mainly MERLOT (gd from mountainous Sopraceneri region) and spécialités. Try CAB SAUV (oaked Bordeaux style), SAUV BL, SÉM, CHARD, MERLOT (p w). Best producers: Agriloro, Guido Brivio, Chiodi Ascona, Gialdi, DANIEL HUBER, Tenuta Montalbano, Werner Stucky, Tamborini Carlo Eredi, Tenuta Castello di Morcote, Tenuta San Giorgio, LUIGI ZANINI, CHRISTIAN ZÜNDEL. All ★★→★★★ 08 09' 10 11.

Valais (Wallis) Rhône Valley from German-speaking upper Valais to French lower Valais. Largest, most varied and exciting wine canton (30% of total) and the biggest of the six wine regions. Wide range: 47 grape varieties, plus many spécialités; FLÉTRI/MI-FLÉTRI wines. Here CHASSELAS is called FENDANT.

Vaud (Waadt) French Switzerland's 2nd-largest wine canton and wine region; stronghold of CHABLAIS, LA CÔTE, LAVAUX, Bonvillars, Côtes de l'Orbe, Vully. CHASSELAS is main grape. Most wines here are named after the terroirs they come from.

Vessaz, Christian Fribourg Cru de l'Hopital, Morges. Dynamic wine-grower. Wonderful CHASSELAS. New top cuvée Premier (Gamaret/MALBEC/MERLOT).

Visperterminen Val (r) w ★★→★★★ Upper VALAIS v'yds, esp for HEIDA grape. One of the highest v'yds in Europe (at 1,000+ metres; called Riben). See it by taking train to Zermatt or Saas Fee. Try CHANTON, St Jodern Kellerei.

Volg Weinkellereien Zür r w ★★→★★★ Co-op that focuses on local terroirs and spécialités. Try MÜLLER-T, Completer, PINOT N.

Yvorne Vd (r) w ★★ 10 11' Top CHABLAIS AOC for strong, fragrant wines. Try CHÂTEAU MAISON BLANCHE.

Zanini, Luigi Tic ★★→★★★★ 08 09' 10 11 Top producer with focus on MERLOT. Best: Castello Luigi, Vinattieri Ticinesi. For some the red Castello Luigi is the best in Switzerland. Bordeaux-lover Zanini built his house in Besazio to look like a Bordeaux château.

Zufferey, Maurice Val r ★★★ 09' 10' (11) Try SYRAH, HUMAGNE Rouge, CORNALIN.

Zündel, Christian Tic ★★★ 08 09' 10' (11) A grower to remember for top TICINO MERLOT. Also CHARD.

Zürich Capital of largest canton. BLAUBURGUNDER mostly; also MÜLLER-T, Räuschling, KERNER. Try Ladolt, SCHWARZENBACH, Schipf, Zweifel Weine.

Spécialités and others

These are rare, indigenous grape varieties, incl (w) AMIGNE, ARVINE, Completer, Himbertscha, HUMAGNE, Lafnetscha, Rèze and (r) CORNALIN, HEIDA, Humagne Rouge. Switzerland also has a few (v. few) Gouais vines – an ancestor of PINOT N and others. Gamaret and Garanoir are modern crossings of GAMAY. Diolinoir is another modern crossing of gd-quality. Rauschling is white, found in medieval Germany and modern Switzerland.

Austria

Abbreviations used in the text:

Burgen	Burgenland
Carn	Carnuntum
Kamp	Kamptal
Krems	Kremstal
Low A	Lower Austria
M Burg	Mittelburgenland
N'see	Neusiedlersee-Hügelland
S/W/SE Sty	Styria
Therm	Thermenregion
Trais	Traisental
Wach	Wachau
Wag	Wagram
Wein	Weinviertel

Austria, after years of excitement about the potential of international wine styles – based of course on Cabernet Sauvignon and the rest – is busy rediscovering its cool-climate roots. And its indigenous vines: Grüner Veltliner and Riesling for whites, Blaufränkisch, St Laurent and Zweigelt for reds, as well as more niche vines like Bouvier, Furmint, Gelber Muskateller, Rotgipfler and Zierfandler, are what are attracting attention now. Regional character is what everybody wants: wines of precision and balance that have a sense of place. Austria has become a thoroughly grown-up wine country.

Recent vintages

2011 One of the finest vintages in living memory. An unusually warm spring was followed by largely indifferent, rainy months, but in September the sun came out. Picking began up to two weeks early, with grapes in perfect health.

2010 Hand-picking and meticulous work were imperative, yields down by as much as 55%. A small number of surprisingly fine wines.

2009 Uneven, with some outstanding whites (Lower Austria, Styria) and reds (Neusiedlersee, Middle Burgenland).

2008 The coolest year since 2004. There were some outstanding results. Not to be discounted.

2007 Good in Styria and in Burgenland for Blaufränkisch, Zweigelt and Pinot N. Excellent yields in Vienna, better Grüner Veltliner than Ries.

2006 A great year.

Achs, Paul N'see r (w) ★★★ 03 07 09 11 Outstanding GOLS producer, esp red PANNOBILE blends, Ungerberg and elegant PINOT N.

Allram Kamp w ★ Reliable KAMPTAL estate, esp for RIES and GRÜNER VELTLINER.

Alphart Therm ★ Traditional, reliable estate, good PINOT N and esp ROTGIPFLER.

Alzinger Wach w ★★★★ 03 05 06 07 08 09 11 Top estate: highly expressive RIES and GRÜNER VELTLINER, esp from Steinertal v'yd.

Angerer Kamp w Highly idiosyncratic estate, v. interesting GRÜNER VELTLINER Loam and Eichenstaude.

Aumann Therm r w Modern, ambitious producer, interesting ST-LAURENT.

Ausbruch PRÄDIKAT wine with sugar levels between Beerenauslese and Trockenbeerenauslese. Traditionally produced in RUST.

Ausg'steckt ("Hung out") HEURIGEN are not open all yr; when they are, a green bush is hung above their doors.

Bayer r w ★★ Négociant producing polished, reliable reds, BLAUFRÄNKISCH the base.

Beck, Judith N'see r w ★★ Rising and accomplished biodynamic winemaker. Well-crafted reds, esp gd PINOT N and *St-Laurent*.

Biodynamism Now firmly rooted in Austria, incl producers such as P ACHS, J BECK, Fritsch, Geyerhof, GRAF HARDEGG, HIRSCH, F LOIMER, Meinklang, Sepp & Maria Muster, NIKOLAIHOF, B OTT, J NITTNAUS, PITTNAUER, F WENINGER.

Brandl, Günter Kamp w ★★→★★★ 03 05 06 09 Consistently *fine Kamptal estate*, known esp for RIES and GRÜNER VELTLINER Novemberlese.

Braunstein, Birgit N'see r w ★ Gd N'SEE-HÜGELLAND estate: cuvée Oxhoft.

Bründlmayer, Willi Kamp r w sw sp ★★★★ 02 03 05 06 07 08 09 11 Outstanding Langenlois-KAMPTAL estate. World-class RIES and GRÜNER VELTLINER, esp Ries Heiligenstein Alte Reben and GV Käferberg. Also Austria's best sparkling *méthode traditionelle*.

Burgenland Province and wine region in the east bordering Hungary. Warm climate, esp around shallow LAKE NEUSIEDL. Ideal conditions for reds and esp botrytis wines nr N'SEE. Four areas: MITTELBURGENLAND, N'see, N'SEE-HÜGELLAND and SÜDBURGENLAND.

The current fashion for Grüner Veltliner started in restaurants: it's perfect with food.

Buschenschank A wine tavern, often a HEURIGE country cousin.

Carnuntum r w Dynamic region southeast of VIENNA now showing gd reds, often on ST-LAURENT base. Best: Glatzer, Grassl, G Markowitsch, MUHR-VAN DER NIEPOORT, Netzl, PITTNAUER, Wiederstein.

Christ r w Reliable VIENNA producer, particularly for GEMISCHTER SATZ.

Deutschkreutz M Burg r (w) MITTELBURGENLAND red-wine area, esp for BLAUFRÄNKISCH.

Districtus Austriae Controllatus (DAC) Austria's appellation system, introduced in 2003. Similar to France's AOP, and rapidly gaining acceptance. Current DACs: KAMPTAL, KREMSTAL, LEITHABERG, MITTELBURGENLAND, TRAISENTAL, WEINVIERTEL.

Donabaum, Johann Wach w ★★ Small grower, well-balanced RIES, GRÜNER VELTLINER, esp Ries Offenberg.

Draxler M Burg BLAUFRÄNKISCH specialist in MITTELBURGENLAND, making appealingly focused wines.

Ehmoser Wag w ★ Small individualist producer, gd GRÜNER VELTLINER Aurum.

Erste Lage First Growth in new v'yd classification. Used in Lower Austria, along the Danube.

Esterhazy ★ Princely house at Eisenstadt (BURGENLAND) back in the business with a new winery and promising wines, esp BLAUFRÄNKISCH.

Federspiel Wach The medium level of the VINEA WACHAU categories, roughly corresponding to Kabinett. Elegant, dry wines, less overpowering than the higher SMARAGD category.

Feiler-Artinger N'see r w sw ★★★★ 95 02 03 04 05 06 07 08 09 Outstanding RUST estate with top AUSBRUCH dessert wines *often v.gd value* for money and red blends. Beautiful baroque house, too.

Forstreiter Krems w ★ Consistent producer, particularly gd RIES.

Gager M Burg r Reliable estate; gd BLAUFRÄNKISCH and cuvée Quattro.

Gemischter Satz Blend of (mostly white) grape varieties planted in same v'yd and vinified together. Traditional method that spreads risk; back in fashion in VIENNA and the WEINVIERTEL and yielding gd results: Christ, WIENINGER.

Gesellmann M Burg r w ★★ Reliable producer focusing on BLAUFRÄNKISCH and red cuvées: Opus Eximium.

Geyerhof Krems ★★ One of Austria's pioneers of organic viticulture, Ilse Mayer's KREMSTAL estate produces fine RIES and GRÜNER VELTLINER.

Giefing N'see r sw ★ Small and individualist RUST producer, esp cuvée Cardinal, BLAUFRÄNKISCH Res.

Gols N'see r w dr sw Dynamic wine commune on north shore of LAKE NEUSIEDL in BURGENLAND. Top producers: P ACHS, J BECK, GSELLMANN, G HEINRICH, A & H Nittnaus, PITTNAUER, C PREISINGER, Renner, STIEGELMAR.

Graf Hardegg Wein r w Large WEINVIERTEL estate. VIOGNIER, SYRAH, PINOT N and RIES.

Gritsch Wach w ★ Consistently interesting producer, esp fine Gelber MUSKATELLER.

Gross S Sty w ★★★ 03 06 07 08 09 11 Perfectionist south STYRIAN producer. Esp CHARD, SAUV BL and his own favourite, PINOT BL.

Grüner Veltliner is good at all price levels; Austrian Riesling, by contrast, tends to be pricey.

Gsellmann, Hans N'see r w sw ★ Formerly Gsellmann & Gsellmann, in GOLS, esp well-made reds and dry whites.

Gumpoldskirchen Therm r w dr sw Famous HEURIGE village south of VIENNA, centre of THERMENREGION. Signature white varieties: ZIERFANDLER and ROTGIPFLER. Best producers: Biegler, Spaetrot Gebeshuber, ZIERER.

Heinrich, Gernot N'see r w dr sw ★★★★ 06 07 08 09 11 Accomplished GOLS estate, member of the PANNOBILE group. Outstanding single-v'yd red wines: Salzberg.

Heinrich, J M Burg r w dr sw ★★★ 03 05 06 08 09 11 Leading MITTELBURGENLAND producer. V.gd BLAUFRÄNKISCH Goldberg Res. Succulent cuvée Cupido.

Heurige Wine of the most recent harvest, called "new wine" for one yr.

Heurigen are wine taverns in which growers-cum-patrons serve their own wine with simple local food – a Viennese institution.

Hiedler Kamp w sw ★★★ 06 09 11 Excellent grower; concentrated, expressive wines. V.gd RIES Maximum.

Hirsch Kamp w ★★★ 03 05 06 09 11 Searching organic grower. Esp fine Heiligenstein, Lamm and Gaisberg v'yds. Also Austria's screwcap pioneer.

Hirtzberger, Franz Wach w ★★★★ 03 05 06 07 08 09 11 Top producer at SPITZ AN DER DONAU. *Highly expressive, minerally Ries* and GRÜNER VELTLINER, esp from the Honivogl and Singerriedel v'yds.

Högl Wach ★ w sw Individualist grower; often fine RIES and GRÜNER VELTLINER.

Holzapfel Wach w Small, often fine grower, esp RIES Vorderseiber.

Horitschon MITTELBURGENLAND region for reds: IBY, F WENINGER.

Igler M Burg ★ r Consistent grower, esp Ab Ericio, Vulcano.

Illmitz N'see (r) w dr sw SEEWINKEL region famous for Beerenauslesen and Trocken-beerenauslesen. Best: Angerhof, Martin Haider KRACHER, Helmut Lang, OPITZ.

Jäger w WACHAU producer, gd RIES and GRÜNER VELTLINER, but esp Gelber MUSKATELLER.

Jamek, Josef Wach w ★ Traditional estate with restaurant. Not typical WACHAU style: often some residual sugar.

Johanneshof Reinisch Therm r w sw Large, consistent estate; esp gd whites.

ɹrtschitsch / Sonnhof Kamp w (r) dr (sw) ★★ Large, highly respected KAMPTAL estate: reliable whites (RIES, GRÜNER VELTLINER, CHARD).

Kamptal Low A r w Wine region along river Kamp north of WACHAU. Top v'yds: Heiligenstein, Käferberg, Lanum. Best: ANGERER, G BRANDL, W BRÜNDLMAYER, Ehn, Eichinger, HIEDLER, HIRSCH, JURTSCHITSCH, F LOIMER, G RABL, SCHLOSS GOBELSBURG, STEININGER. Kamptal is now DAC (from 2008) for GRÜNER VELTLINER and RIES.

Kattus Vienna Producer of traditional sekt in VIENNA.

Kerschbaum M Burg r ★★★ 03 05 06 07 08 09 11 BLAUFRÄNKISCH specialist, individual and often fascinating wines.

Klassifizierte Lage Second Growth or Classified Growth in the new v'yd classification system used in the regions along the river Danube. *See also* ERSTE LAGE.

Klosterneuburg Wag r w Main wine town of Donauland. Rich in tradition, with a wine college founded in 1860. Best: Stift Klosterneuburg, Zimmermann.

KMW Abbreviation for Klosterneuburger Mostwaage ("must level"), the unit used in Austria to measure the sugar content in grape juice.

Knoll, Emmerich Wach ★★★★ 01 03 05 06 07 08 09 11 Outstanding traditional estate in Loiben. *Delicate, fragrant Ries, complex Grüner Veltliner*, part from Loibenberg, Schütt.

Kollwentz-Römerhof Burgen r w dr (sw) ★★★★ 05 06 07 08 09 11 Outstanding producer nr Eisenstadt: SAUV BL, CHARD and Eiswein. Also renowned for *fine reds: Steinzeiler.*

Kracher N'see w dr (r sw) ★★★★ 95 01 02 03 04 05 06 07 08 09 Top-class ILLMITZ producer specializing in botrytized PRÄDIKATS (dessert); barrique-aged (Nouvelle Vague), others in steel (Zwischen den Seen); gd reds.

Kremstal Krems w (r) Wine region esp for GRÜNER VELTLINER and RIES. Top: Buchegger, Malat, S MOSER, NIGL, SALOMON-UNDHOF, Stagård, WEINGUT STADT KREMS.

Krug Therm r w sw Well-made, international-style wines, esp full-bodied PINOT GR and red cuvées.

Krutzler S Burg r ★★★★ 03 06 07 08 09 11 Outstanding south BURGENLAND producer of outstanding BLAUFRÄNKISCH, esp Perwolff.

Lackner-Tinnacher SE Sty ★ Fine SÜD-OSTSTEIERMARK estate known for fragrant MORILLON and MUSKATELLER.

Leberl N'see r w sw ★ Traditional N'SEE-HÜGELLAND estate, gd red cuvée Peccatum and Trockenbeerenauslese.

Leithaberg N'see V'yd hill on the northern shore of LAKE NEUSIEDL; also a lively group of producers successfully redefining the regional terroir-based style. Now a DAC.

Loimer, Fred Kamp w ★★★→★★★★ Thoughtful and biodynamic producer, 50% GRÜNER VELTLINER; also RIES, CHARD, PINOT GR, v.gd PINOT N.

Mantlerhof Krems w ★★ Grower with a well-considered, traditional approach. Gd ROTER VELTLINER.

Mayer am Pfarrplatz Vienna w ★ Producer and HEURIGE, recent markedly better, esp GEMISCHTER SATZ Nussberg.

Minkowitsch Wein w Traditional WEINVIERTEL producer, interesting GEWÜRZ.

Austria's "cool" grapes

In 50 yrs' time Vienna may be as warm as Montpellier in France is today. That's bad news for RIES and other "cool" grape varieties, and for Eiswein such as those picked in the glacial February of 2012. Hold on to your hats, though: there may be meaty Austrian 2061 SYRAH, TEMPRANILLO and ZIN. Some experimental "hot variety" v'yds have been planted already.

Mittelburgenland r dr (w sw) Wine region on Hungarian border concentratin on BLAUFRÄNKISCH (also DAC) and increasingly fine. Producers: BAYER, GAGER GESELLMANN, J HEINRICH, Iby, IGLER, KERSCHBAUM, Wellanschitz, F WENINGER.

Moric M Burg r ★★★★ 03 05 06 09 11 Outstanding benchmark BLAUFRÄNKISCH made by Roland VELICH from old vines in villages of Lutzmannsburg an Neckenmarkt, vinified according to site. A beacon.

Moser, Lenz Krems r w Austria's largest producer, based in Krems.

Moser, Sepp Krems r w sw Grower of consistent RIES, GRÜNER VELTLINER.

Muhr-van der Niepoort Carn r w ★★ Rising winery. And yes, Niepoort as in Port Well-judged reds, esp BLAUFRÄNKISCH Spitzerberg.

Müller, Domaine W St r w sw Eccentric but often fine producer with international outlook, esp SAUV BL and CHARD.

Neumayer Trais w ★★★ Top estate; powerful, focused, dry GRÜNER VELTLINER and RIES

Neumeister SE Sty w ★★★ 03 05 06 09 11 Modernist, meticulous producer, es fine SAUV BL and CHARD.

Neusiedlersee r w dr sw Wine region north and east of NEUSIEDLERSEE. Best: P ACHS J BECK, G HEINRICH, KRACHER, J NITTNAUS, J & R PÖCKL, STIEGELMAR, J UMATHUM, VELICH.

Neusiedlersee (Lake Neusiedl) Burgen V. shallow BURGENLAND lake on Hungaria border. Warmth and autumn mists encourage botrytis. See next entry.

Neusiedlersee-Hügelland r w dr sw Wine region west of LAKE NEUSIEDL base around Oggau, RUST and Mörbisch on the lake shores, Eisenstadt in the Leith foothills. Best incl: B BRAUNSTEIN, FEILER-ARTINGER, Kloster am Spitz, KOLLWENTZ RÖMERHOF, PRIELER, Schandl, H SCHRÖCK, Schuller, Sommer, E TRIEBAUMER, WENZEL.

Niederösterreich (Lower Austria) Northeastern region with 58% of Austria's v'yds CARNUNTUM, Donauland, KAMPTAL, KREMSTAL, THERMENREGION, TRAISENTAL, WACHA and WEINVIERTEL.

Nigl Krems w ★★★★ 05 06 07 08 09 11 The best in KREMSTAL, making sophisticated dry whites with remarkable mineral character from Senftenberg v'yd.

Nikolaihof Wach w ★★★★ 03 05 06 07 08 09 11 Impeccable estate, pioneered BIODYNAMISM in Austria. Outstanding RIES from Steiner Hund v'yd, often grea ageing potential.

The Neusiedlersee is 36km long but nowhere more than two metres deep.

Nittnaus, John N'see r w sw ★★★ 03 05 06 09 11 Organic winemaker. Esp elegan and age-worthy reds: Comondor.

Opitz N'see Eccentric but publicity-savvy producer of mainly sweet wines in ILLMITZ Esp STROHWEIN.

Ott, Bernhard Low A w ★★→★★★ GRÜNER VELTLINER specialist from Donauland. Fass 4; also Der Ott and Rosenberg. Also wine vinified in large amphorae, eccentric but fascinating.

Pannobile N'see Association of youngish and ambitious N'SEE growers centred on GOLS and aiming to create great wine with regional character. Current members: P ACHS, J BECK, HANS GSELLMANN, G HEINRICH, Leitner, J NITTNAUS, PITTNAUER, C PREISINGER, Renner.

Pfaffl Wein r w ★★★ 05 06 07 08 09 11 Estate nr VIENNA, in Stetten. Known for dry GRÜNER VELTLINER and RIES.

Pichler-Krutzler Wach w r ★★ A recent arrival on the scene, a marriage of two famous names. Fine, balanced wines esp from the Wunderburg v'yds. Also reds, grown in SÜDBURGENLAND.

Pichler, Franz Xaver Wach w ★★★★ 05 06 07 08 09 11 Iconic producer. Intense and *iconic Ries*, GRÜNER VELTLINER (esp Kellerberg).

Pichler, Rudi Wach w ★★★→★★★★ 03 05 06 09 11 Outstanding, individualist producer of powerful, expressive RIES and GRÜNER VELTLINER.

Pittnauer, Gerhard N'see r w ★★★ Striving N'SEE producer, one of Austria's finest for ST-LAURENT wines.

Pöckl, Josef & René N'see r (sw) ★★★ 03 06 09 11 Fine estate, esp for reds: Admiral, Rêve de Jeunesse and Rosso e Nero.

Polz, Erich & Walter S Sty w ★★★ 03 05 06 07 08 09 V.gd large (Weinstrasse) growers, esp Hochgrassnitzberg: SAUV BL, CHARD, GRAUBURGUNDER, WEISSBURGUNDER.

Prädikat, Prädikatswein German-inspired system of classifying wine by the sugar content of the juice, from Spätlese upwards (Spätlese, Auslese, Eiswein, STROHWEIN, Beerenauslese, AUSBRUCH and Trockenbeerenauslese). Now widely thought outdated in Austria. *See* Germany.

Prager, Franz Wach w ★★★★ 01 03 05 06 07 08 09 11 Top-quality dry whites, run by Toni Bodenstein. RIES and GRÜNER VELTLINER of impeccable elegance and mineral structure: Wachstum Bodenstein.

Preisinger, Claus N'see r ★ Ambitious young winemaker with stylish reds, esp PINOT N and cuvée Paradigma.

Prieler N'see w r ★★★ Consistently fine producer. Esp gd BLAUFRÄNKISCH Goldberg.

Proidl, Erwin Krems ★★ Highly individual grower making interesting, age-worthy RIES and GRÜNER VELTLINER.

Looking for more information on grapes? Try the "Grapes" section on pp.16–26.

Rabl, Günter Kamp w r sw ★ Consistent grower long overshadowed by more-famous colleagues. V.gd GRÜNER VELTLINER.

Ried Austrian term for v'yd.

Rust N'see r w d sw Historic town on the shores of LAKE NEUSIEDL, beautiful 17th-century houses testifying to centuries of wine, esp of Ruster AUSBRUCH. Top: FEILER-ARTINGER, Giefing, Schandl, H SCHRÖCK, E TRIEBAUMER, WENZEL.

Sabathi, E S Sty w ★ Youthful and highly professional estate, esp SAUV BL Merveilleux.

Salomon-Undhof Krems w ★★★ Dynamic and fine producer: RIES, WEISSBURGUNDER, TRAMINER. Berthold Salomon also makes wine in Australia.

Sattler, Willi S Sty w ★★★★ 03 05 06 07 08 09 11 Top grower. Esp for SAUV BL, MORILLON, often v. steep v'yds.

Schiefer S Burg ★★★ *Garagiste* Uwe Schiefer has quickly reached the top with his deep, powerful BLAUFRÄNKISCH, esp from Szapary and Reihburg v'yds.

Schilcher W St Rosé from indigenous Blauer Wildbacher grapes (sharp, dry, high acidity). A local taste, or at least an acquired one. Specialty of west STYRIA. Try: Klug, Lukas, Reiterer, Strohmeier.

Schloss Gobelsburg Kamp w r ★★★★ 01 03 05 06 07 08 09 11 Renowned estate run by Michael Moosbrugger. Excellent dry RIES and GRÜNER VELTLINER, and fine PINOT N.

Schloss Halbturn N'see r w sw ★★★ 06 09 11 Publicity-shy estate representing a considered, international interpretation of Austrian varieties and terroir. Esp cuvée Imperial, also PINOT N.

Schlumberger Vienna Largest sparkling-wine maker in Austria. Also on the Loire.

Schmelz Wach w ★★★ Fine, often underestimated producer, esp outstanding RIES Dürnsteiner Freiheit.

Schneider Therm Consistent producer, esp succulent ST-LAURENT and gd PINOT N.

Schröck, Heidi N'see r w sw ★★★ Wines of great purity and focus from a thoughtful RUST grower. V.gd AUSBRUCH. Also v.gd dry FURMINT. *See* Hungary.

Schuster N'see r w ★→★★ N'SEE-HÜGELLAND estate. Son Hannes makes fine ST-LAURENT.

Schwarz N'see r sw Small, classy producer specializing in ZWEIGELT and STROHWEIN.

Seewinkel N'see ("Lake corner") Name given to part of N'SEE, incl Apetlon, ILLMITZ and Podersdorf. Ideal conditions for botrytis.

Smaragd Wach Highest category of VINEA WACHAU, similar to dry Spätlese, often complex and powerful.

> **Red revival**
> Austria's reds are benefiting both from climate change and from a focus on more elegant styles. They're settling into a cool-climate pattern, expressive and fine rather than overwhelmingly powerful. BLAUFRÄNKISCH and ST-LAURENT are tops for complexity and moreishness.

Spätrot-Rotgipfler Therm Typical blend of THERMENREGION. Aromatic and weighty wines, often with orange-peel aromas. *See* Grapes pp.16–26.

Spitz an der Donau Wach w Cool area, esp Singerriedel v'yd. Top growers incl: J DONABAUM, F HIRTZBERGER, HÖGL, Lagler.

Stadlmann Therm r w sw ★★ Producer specializing in opulent ZIERFANDLER-ROTGIPFLER wines.

Steinfeder Wach VINEA WACHAU category for light, fragrant, dry wines.

Steininger Kamp r w sp ★★ Grower with outstanding single-varietal sparkling; plus still, too.

Stiegelmar (Juris-Stiegelmar) N'see r w dr sw ★★ Well-regarded GOLS grower. CHARD, SAUV BL. Reds: ST-LAURENT.

Strohwein Sweet wine made from grapes air-dried on straw matting.

Styria (Steiermark) Southernmost wine region of Austria. Some gd dry whites, esp SAUV BL and CHARD, called MORILLON locally. Also fragrant MUSKATELLER. Incl SÜDSTEIERMARK, SÜD-OSTSTEIERMARK and WESTSTEIERMARK (South, Southeast and West Styria).

Südburgenland S Burg r w Small wine region. V.gd BLAUFRÄNKISCH. Best: KRUTZLER, SCHIEFER and Wachter-Wiesler.

Süd-Oststeiermark SE Sty (r) w STYRIAN region with excellent v'yds. Best: NEUMEISTER, WINKLER-HERMADEN.

Südsteiermark S Sty w Best STYRIA region; popular whites (MORILLON, MUSKATELLER, WELSCHRIESLING and SAUV BL). Best: GROSS, Jaunegg, LACKNER-TINNACHER, E & W POLZ, Potzinger Sabathi, W SATTLER, Skoff, M TEMENT, Wohlmuth.

Tegernseerhof Wach w ★ Grower of v. interesting RIES and GRÜNER VELTLINER.

Tement, Manfred S Sty w ★★★★ 03 05 06 07 08 09 11 Renowned estate with esp fine SAUV BL and MORILLON from Zieregg site. International-style wines and modern reds.

Thermenregion Therm r w dr sw Region of hot springs. Indigenous grapes (eg. ZIERFANDLER, ROTGIPFLER), historically one of the most important regions for reds (esp ST-LAURENT) from Baden, GUMPOLDSKIRCHEN, Tattendorf, Traiskirchen areas. Producers: Alphart, Biegler, Fischer, JOHANNESHOF REINISCH, Schafler, Spätrot-Gebelshuber, STADLMANN, ZIERER.

Traisental 700ha, just south of Krems on Danube. Dry whites can be similar to WACHAU in style, not usually in quality. Top producers: Huber, NEUMAYER.

Triebaumer, Ernst N'see r (w) dr sw ★★★★ 03 05 06 07 08 09 11 Outstanding RUST producer; BLAUFRÄNKISCH (incl legendary Mariental), CAB SAUV/MERLOT blend. V.gd AUSBRUCH.

Uhudler S Burg Local south BURGENLAND specialty. Wine made directly from American rootstocks, with a foxy, strawberry taste.

Umathum, Josef N'see r w dr sw ★★★ V.gd, thoughtful producer. V.gd reds, incl PINOT N, ST-LAURENT; gd whites.

Velich N'see w sw ★★★★ A searching, intellectual producer. Excellent burgundian-style, barrel-aged Tiglat CHARD (03 06 09 11). Some of the top sweet wines in SEEWINKEL.

Veyder-Malberg Wach w ★ A 2008 start-up, cultivating some of WACHAU's most labour-intensive v'yds and producing wines of great purity and finesse.

Vienna (r) w Wine region in the suburbs. Mostly simple wines, served to tourists in HEURIGEN. Quality producers on the rise incl: Christ, MAYER AM PFARRPLATZ, F WIENINGER, Zahel.

Vinea Wachau WACHAU appellation started by winemakers in 1983 with three categories of dry wine: STEINFEDER, FEDERSPIEL and the powerful SMARAGD.

Wachau w World-renowned Danube region and home to some of Austria's best wines. Top producers: Alzinger, J DONABAUM, Freie Weingärtner Wachau, F HIRTZBERGER, HÖGL, J JAMEK, E KNOLL, Lagler, NIKOLAIHOF, FX PICHLER, R PICHLER, F PRAGER, Schmelz, WESS.

Wachau, Domäne Wach w (r) ★★★ 06 07 08 09 11 Important growers' co-op in Dürnstein, top wines ever better. V.gd GRÜNER VELTLINER and RIES.

Wagram w (r) Region west of VIENNA, inc KLOSTERNEUBURG. Mainly whites, esp GRÜNER VELTLINER. Best: EHMOSER, Fritsch, Stift Klosterneuburg, Leth, B OTT, Wimmer-Czerny, R Zimmermann.

Weingut Stadt Krems Krems ★★ Co-op capably steered by Fritz Miesbauer, esp RIES and GRÜNER VELTLINER. Miesbauer also vinifies for Stift Göttweig.

Weinviertel ("Wine Quarter") (r) w Largest Austrian wine region, between the Danube and the Czech border. Largely simple wines but increasingly striving for quality and regional character. Refreshing whites, esp Poysdorf and Retz. Best producers: Bauer, J Diem, GRAF HARDEGG, Gruber, PFAFFL, Schwarzböck, Weinrieder, Zull.

Weninger, Franz M Burg r (w) ★★★ 03 05 06 09 11 Top (Horitschon) estate, with *fine reds, esp Blaufränkisch*, Dürrau and MERLOT.

Looking for more information on grapes? Try the "Grapes" section on pp.16–26.

Wenzel N'see r w sw ★★★ V.gd AUSBRUCH. Junior Michael makes ambitious and increasingly fine reds. Father Robert pioneered the FURMINT revival in RUST.

Wess Wach w ★ Gd winemaker of bought-in grapes, some from famous v'yds.

Weststeiermark W St p Small wine region specializing in SCHILCHER. Best: Klug, Lukas, DOMAINE MÜLLER, Reiterer, Strohmeier.

Wieder M Burg Exponent of the BLAUFRÄNKISCH renaissance, well-structured wines.

Wiederstein Carn One of the young generation of CARNUNTUM winemakers, Birgit Wiederstein makes understated but appealingly focused reds.

Wien See VIENNA.

Wieninger, Fritz Vienna r w ★★★ 06 07 08 09 11 Leading grower with HEURIGE: CHARD, BLAUER BURGUNDER, esp gd GEMISCHTER SATZ.

Winkler-Hermaden SE Sty r w sw ★★★ Outstanding and individual producer, gd TRAMINER and MORILLON, also one of the region's few v.gd reds, the ZWEIGELT-based Olivin.

Winzer Krems Large KREMSTAL co-op with 1,300 growers.

Zierer Therm r w Producer of esp fine ROTGIPFLER.

AUSTRIA

England & Wales

Every year brings good news for English (and Welsh) wines these days. The awards keep rolling in, internationally, too: overwhelmingly for sparkling wines. At last the high street seems to have got the message. England and Wales now have more vineyards than Luxembourg. However, for all the encouraging news, vintage 2011 will go down as very difficult, with widespread *millerandage* (undeveloped berries) on Pinot Noir halving the crop in some vineyards. Sugar levels were at an all-time high, though, so there should be some good wines, and even perhaps some good reds.

Astley Worcester ★★ The wines from this estate continue to win medals. Veritas **09** and Severn Vale **10** v.gd.

Biddenden Kent ★ Established in 1969 so one of the UK's oldest v'yds. Zesty Bacchus **09** and spicy Ortega **09** worth trying. Also makes v.gd cider and apple juice.

Breaky Bottom E Sussex ★★ Planted in 1974; now only making sparkling, using SEYVAL BL, PINOT N and CHARD. Cuvée Francine **07** and Chard-based Cuvée Princess Colonna **08** best sparklers to date.

Camel Valley Cornwall ★★★ Lindo *père et fils*, Bob and Sam, continue to create great wines and win lots of prizes. Darnibole Bacchus **09**, PINOT N Rosé **10** and Anniversary **09** excellent.

Chapel Down Kent ★★★ Still (just) the UK's largest producer. New winemaker from 2010 vintage. *NV Brut* still excellent value. NV Rosé Brut, fruity **09** Trinity Red and **10** Flint Dry worth trying.

Coates & Seely Hants Sparkling newcomer with high standards. NV Rosé and Blanc de Blancs showing v. well.

Davenport E & W Sussex, Kent ★★ Organic. Limney Horsmonden Dry White **10** and Limney Blanc de Blancs **07** worth trying.

Denbies Surrey ★★ Wines getting better with veteran winemaker John Worontschak now in charge. Still wines better than sparkling. Rosé NV and Bacchus **09** well worth trying.

Gusbourne Kent ★ Large new sparkling producer. Blanc de Blancs **07** excellent.

Hush Heath Estate Kent ★★ Balfour Brut Rosé **08 09** are excellent. Also try the v.gd apple juice.

Nyetimber W Sussex ★★★★ Best wines are currently Blanc de Blancs **03**, Classic Cuvée **06** and Rosé **07** – all quite classy Champagne lookalikes.

Plumpton College E Sussex ★★ The UK's only wine college now starting to make interesting wines. The Dean NV Blush sparkling excellent and Sutherland's Block PINOT N **10** still red both worth trying.

*Ridge*View E Sussex ★★★★ Great quality, consistency and gd value keep this winery at the top of the UK producers. Grosvenor Magnum Blanc de Blancs **00** and Grosvenor Blanc de Blancs **09** exceptional quality. Fitzrovia **09** and new Victoria Rosé **09** best rosés to date.

Sharpham Devon ★★ Gd range of wines (and also cheese). V.gd **09** Rosé. Estate Selection **10** and Bacchus **10** also worth trying. Watch for *Pinot N*.

Stanlake Park Berks ★★ Large range of wines of above-average quality. Fruity Pinot Blush and soft Madeleine **10** both worth trying.

Three Choirs Gloucestershire ★★ A large range of gd-value wines, plus v.gd hotel and restaurant. Gd range of **10** wines incl Bacchus, Siegerrebe and Willow Brook blend.

Central & Southeast Europe

More heavily shaded areas are the wine-growing regions.

Abbeviations used in the text:

Bal	Balaton	N Croa	North Croatia
Cri & Mar	Crisana & Maramures	N Hun	North Hungary
		N/S Pann	North/South Pannonia
Dalm	Dalmatia	Pod	Podravje
Dob	Dobrogea	Pos	Posavje
Mold	Moldova	Prim	Primorje
Mun	Muntenia & Oltenia Hills	Tok	Tokaj

HUNGARY

Hungary is at last starting to gain greater recognition for the thrilling quality of its best wines. Tourism to Budapest helps to spread the word, and the country has a growing wine and food culture; Hungary now has its first Michelin stars. The sweet wines of Tokaj are showing the qualities that first made them famous several centuries ago, and boutique hotels are being built there, too, to lure travellers. But there are terrific dry whites as well, and reds, from native grape varieties all over the country. The 2010 vintage was a wash out for most regions, but 2009 and 2011 look very good everywhere.

Alana-Tokaj Tok ★★ Promising producer with great v'yds. Also owns NAG wines in Mátra. Gd MUSCAT, FURMINT and ASZÚ.

Árvay Tok ★★ Revived family winery (since 2009) after Janos Árvay split with SAUSKA and returned to his roots. Gd v'yd sites and track record as winemaker so one to watch. Appealing Sárgamuskotály.

Aszú Tok Botrytis-affected and shrivelled grapes, and the resulting sweet wine from TOKAJ. The wine is graded in sweetness, from 3 PUTTONYOS up to 6.

Aszú Essencia Tok Historically 2nd-sweetest TOKAJI quality (7 PUTTONYOS+), but not used since 2010 vintage.

Badacsony Bal w dr sw ★★→★★★ Extinct volcano on north shore of Lake BALATON. Rich, flavoursome whites; esp well-made RIES and SZÜRKEBARÁT. Look for *Szeremley* (esp KÉKNYELŰ), Villa Tolnay and Laposa.

Balaton Region and Central Europe's largest freshwater lake. BADACSONY, Balatonfüred-Csopak (Feind, Figula, Jasdi), Balatonmelléke (DR. BUSSAY), SOMLÓ to the north. BALATONBOGLÁR to the south.

Balatonboglár Bal wr dr ★★→★★★ Wine district, also progressive winery owned by TÖRLEY, south of Lake BALATON. Top producers: GARAMVÁRI, KONYÁRI, Légli. Budjosó improving.

Bor is Hungarian for "wine": *vörös* is red; *fehér* is white; *édes* is sweet, *száraz* is dry and *minőségi* is quality.

Barta Tok ★★★ New firm, owns highest v'yd in TOKAJ, making wines since 2009. Dry FURMINT Válogatás 09 impressive. Also v.gd sweet Furmint-Muskotály.

Beres Tok w sw dr 06 07 08 ★★ Dramatic new winery. Good ASZÚ wines and dry Lőcse FURMINT.

Bikavér N Hun r ★→★★★ 06' 07 08 09 Literally "Bull's Blood". Being revived as flagship blended red. Protected origin status in SZEKSZÁRD and EGER. Min three varieties; usually KÉKFRANKOS and sometimes KADARKA. Res is min of four varieties and restricted yield. Best producers for Egri Bikavér: Bolyki, Demeter, Grof Buttler, Kaló Imre, Pók Tamás, ST ANDREA, Thummerer.

Bock, József S Pann r dr ★→★★★ 00 03 05' 06' 07' 08 Leading family winemaker in VILLÁNY. Noted for hearty reds. Best: CAB FR Selection, Capella Cuvée, SYRAH.

Bodrogkeresztúr Village in TOKAJ region. Gd producers: DERESZLA, Füleky, PATRICIUS, Tokaji Nobilis, Puklus. Lapis v'yd notable.

Bussay, Dr. Bal w dr ★★ 06 07 08 09 Doctor/winemaker in Balatonmelléke. Intense TRAMINI, PINOT GR, OLASZRIZLING. Also v.gd Kerkaborum wines with HEIMANN.

Csányi S Pann r ★→★★ Major investment in VILLÁNY. Chateau Teleki range is best, esp velvety CAB FR 07.

Degenfeld, Gróf Tok w dr sw ★★★ 00 03 05 06 07 08 Large TOKAJ estate with luxury hotel. Sweet wines better than dry. Try 6 PUTTONYOS, Fortissimo, Andante FURMINT.

Demeter Zoltán Tok w sw ★★★→★★★★ 07' 08' 09 Superb dry and ASZÚ wines from own grand cru v'yds, esp Veres and Lapis FURMINTS and stunning Szerelmi HÁRSLEVELŰ. Don't confuse with Demeter (also gd) in EGER.

Dereszla Tok w dr sw ★★★ 03 05 06 07 08 09 d'Aulan family from Champagne owners. V.gd ASZÚ, *flor*-matured dry SZAMORODNI. Superb dry Kabar, MUSCAT Res.

Disznókő Tok w dr sw ★★→★★★ 99' 00' 03' 05 06 07' 08' Important TOKAJ estate, owned by French company AXA. Fine expressive ASZÚ and gd-value late-harvest.

Dobogó Tok ★★★→★★★★ 05' 06 07' 08 09 Superb small TOKAJ estate. V.gd ASZÚ and late-harvest Mylitta, wonderful Mylitta Álma (modern take on ASZÚ ESZENCIA), thrilling dry FURMINT and new Szerelmi Dulő. PINOT N since 07.

Dulő Named v'yd; single site.

Duna Region comprising three separate districts of the Great Plain, merged to improve reputation. Districts: Hajós-Baja (Sümegi), Csongrád (Somodi), Kunság (Frittmann is quality step up: gd Cserszegi Fűszeres, EZERJÓ and KÉKFRANKOS.

Eger N Hun r w dr ★→★★★ Best-known red region of north. BIKAVÉR is most famous, but CAB FR, PINOT N, SYRAH increasingly important. Whites: LEÁNYKA, OLASZRIZLING, CHARD, PINOT BL. Top producers: Bolyki, Gróf Buttler (under new ownership), Demeter, TIBOR GÁL, Kaló Imre, KOVÁCS NIMRÓD winery, ST ANDREA, Thummerer.

Essencia / Eszencia Tok ★★★★ 93 96 99 00 03 06 (09) Heart of TOKAJI: thick and syrupy, luscious, aromatic juice that trickles from ASZÚ grapes. Alcohol around 2–3%; sugar can be over 800g/l. Wines are reputed to have miraculous medicinal properties.

Etyek-Buda N Pann Dynamic region noted for expressive crisp whites, esp CHARD, SAUV BL, PINOT GR. V. promising for PINOT N. Leading producers: Etyeki Kúria (v.gd Pinot N, Sauv Bl), Nyakas (fresh whites under Budai label), György-Villa (TÖRLEY), Haraszthy-Vallejo.

Garamvári Bal r w dr sp ★★ Family-owned v'yd and St Donatus winery. Also owns *Chateau Vincent*, Hungary's top bottle-fermented fizz. Good DYA IRSAI OLIVÉR and Sinai Hill CAB SAUV.

Gere, Attila S Pann r ★★★→★★★★ 00 03' 04 06' 07' 08 Family winemaker in VILLÁNY making some of country's best reds, esp rich Solus MERLOT, intense Kopar Cuvée and top Attila selections. CAB SAUV Barrique is gd value and ages well.

Heimann S Pann r ★★→★★★ 06 07 08 Impressive family winery in SZEKSZÁRD. Best wines: Franciscus, Barbar blend and Baranya KÉKFRANKOS. Also partner in stylish U&I KÉKFRANKOS (with Heumann from VILLÁNY).

Hétszőlő Tok w dr sw ★★ Noble first-growth TOKAJ estate bought in 09 by Michel Rebier, owner of Château Cos d'Estournel (Bordeaux).

Hilltop Winery N Pann r w dr ★→★★ Export-focused winery in Neszmély makes meticulous and gd-value varietal wines, incl Woodcutters White from Cserszegi Fűszeres. Premium range best, esp PINOT GR.

Homonna Tok w dr ★★★ 07 08 09 Maverick winemaker with deserved reputation for fine, elegant FURMINT, esp Hatari v'yd.

Királyudvar Tok w dr sw ★★★→★★★★ 03' 05 06' 07 08 TOKAJ winery in old royal cellars at Tarcal, owned by Anthony Hwang (*see also* Vouvray). Wines incl dry and late-harvest FURMINT, Cuvée Ilona (early-bottled ASZÚ), stunning Cuvée Patricia and superb 6 PUTTONYOS Lapis Aszú.

Konyári Bal r w dr ★★→★★★ 06 07 08 09 Father and son making high-quality estate wines at BALATONBOGLÁR, esp drinkable DYA rosé, consistent Loliense (r w) and excellent Szárhegy (w), Sessio (r) and top Pava blend. Also Ikon winery for better-value varietals.

Kovács Nimród N Hun w r dr ★★ 06 07 08 Winery in EGER. Battonage CHARD impresses, also gd Rhapsody red blend.

Kreinbacher Bal w dr ★★ 07 08 09 Established 2002, organic methods since 2008; focus on local grapes, esp blends. Long-lived whites: Öreg Tőkék 07 and Somlói Cuvée 07 impress.

Mád Tok Old trading town in centre of TOKAJ region with top v'yds and circle of Mád producers. Growers incl: ALANA-TOKAJ, BARTA, OROSZ GABOR, DEMETER ZOLTÁN, ROYAL TOKAJI, SZEPSY, Tokaj Classic.

Malatinszky S Pann r w dr ★★★ 06' 07 08 09 Immaculate winery, excellent unfiltered Kúria CAB FR, CAB SAUV, supple Pinot Bleu, fine CHARD. Single-v'yd red blend Kövesföld and appealing Serena white.

Mátra N Hun (r) w ★→★★ District in Mátra foothills. Reliable PINOT GR, CHARD, Muskotály, SAUV BL. Better producers incl drummer-turned-winemaker Gábor Karner, NAG (*see* ALANA-TOKAJ), Szőke Mátyás, Borpalota (Fríz label) and co-op Szölöskert (Nagyréde and Spice Trail labels).

Maurus Winery N Pann w dr ★★ 06 07 08 (09) Young winemaker Ákos Kamocsay Jr is waking up sleepy MÓR. EZERJÓ, CHARD, RIES, TRAMINI show promise.

Mézes-Mály One of TOKAJ's best crus, in Tarcal. Gd single-v'yd ROYAL TOKAJI, Balassa.

Mór N Pann w ★→★★ Region noted for fresh, crisp EZERJÓ. Also RIES, CHARD, TRAMINI. Look for MAURUS.

Oremus Tok w dr sw ★★→★★★★ 99' 00' 02 03' 05 06' 07 08 Ancient TOKAJ v'yd of founding Rakóczi family. The name is used by Spain's Vega Sicilia for its winery: first-rate ASZÚ and v.gd dry FURMINT Mandolás.

Orosz Gábor Tok w dr sw ★★→★★★ 03 05 06 07 08 09 TOKAJ producer: try dry single-v'yd FURMINT and HÁRSLEVELŰ, plus excellent ASZÚ. Bodvin is cheaper second label.

HUNGARY

Pajzos-Megyer Tok w dr sw ★★→★★★ 93 99 00 03' 05 06' 07 08 Jointly managed TOKAJ properties. Megyer is typically lighter from cooler north of region, gd for dry FURMINT; appealing dry and sweet MUSCAT. Pajzos is richer sweet wines only.

Pannonhalma N Pann r w dr ★★ 08 09 Region in north. 800-year-old Pannonhalma Abbey winery and v'yds. Expressive whites, esp RIES, TRAMINI, SAUV BL; fine PINOT N and classy Hemina.

Patricius Tok w dr sw ★★★ 00' 02 03' 05 06' 07 08 Quality TOKAJ estate (2000). V.gd dry FURMINT and 6 PUTTONYOS ASZÚ. Superb ASZÚ ESZENCIA Czigany 08.

Pécs S Pann w (r) ★→★★ District around the city of Pécs. Known for whites, incl local CIRFANDL. Ebner PINOT N impresses.

Pendits Winery Tok w sw dr ★★→★★★ 00 03 05 06 07 08 Organic estate worked by horses, run by Márta Wille-Baumkauff and sons. Luscious ASZÚ ESZENCIA, attractive Szello Cuvée and pretty Dry MUSCAT.

Puttonyos Measure of sweetness in TOKAJI ASZÚ. Nowadays 3 puttonyos = 60g of sugar per litre, 4 = 90g, 5 = 120g, 6 = 150g. Traditionally a *puttony* was a 25kg measure (a bucket or hod) of shrivelled grapes. The number added per barrel (136 litres) of dry base wine or must determined the final sweetness of the wine.

Royal Tokaji Wine Co Tok ★★★ →★★★★ 96 99 00 03 05 06 07 08 09 Pioneer foreign joint-venture at MÁD that led renaissance of TOKAJ (I am a co-founder). Mainly first- or second-growth v'yds. Single-v'yd bottlings: esp Betsek, MÉZES-MÁLY, Szent Tamás, Nyulászó. Also well-made dry FURMINT and v.gd-value late-harvest Áts Cuvée. New winery opened 2010.

Sauska ★★→★★★★ 06 07 08 09 (10) Immaculate winery in VILLÁNY. Beautifully balanced KADARKA, KÉKFRANKOS, CAB FR and impressive red blends, esp Cuvée 7 and Cuvée 5. Also Sauska-Tokaj in old casino in TOKAJ (formerly Árvay) with focus on v.gd dry whites, esp Cuvée 111 and 113 and FURMINT Birsalmás.

Cabernet Franc is set to be Hungary's red star. Will it be as good as the Loire?

Somló Bal w ★★→★★★ 06 07 08 (09) Dramatic basalt pillars overlook sloping v'yds on extinct volcano, famous for mineral-rich, age-worthy whites: Juhfark ("sheep's tail"), OLASZRIZLING, FURMINT and HÁRSLEVELŰ. Region of small producers making long-lived, barrel-fermented wines, esp Fekete, Györgykovács Imre, Hollóvár and Spiegelberg. TORNAI and KREINBACHER are also v.gd, larger, more accessible.

Sopron N Pann r ★★→★★★ District on Austrian border overlooking Lake Fertő. KÉKFRANKOS most important, plus CAB SAUV, SYRAH, PINOT N. Top is biodynamic *Weninger*, also try the v. characterful wines of Ráspi (esp Electus ZWEIGELT).

St Andrea N Hun r w dr ★★★ 05 06' 07 08 09 Top name in EGER, leading way in modern, high-quality BIKAVÉR (Merengő, Hangács, Áldás). Excellent white blends: Napbor, Örökké, organic Boldogságos, plus v.gd HÁRSLEVELŰ and PINOT N.

Szamorodni Tok Literally "as it was born"; describes TOKAJI not sorted in the v'yd. Dry or sweet (Édes), depending on proportion of ASZÚ grapes present. Sweet style can offer ASZÚ character at less cost. The best dry versions are *flor*-aged; try TINON, Dereszia or Karádi-Berger.

Szekszárd S Pann r ★★→★★★ Southern district making ripe, rich KÉKFRANKOS, CAB SAUV, CAB FR and MERLOT. Also KADARKA being revived and BIKAVÉR. Look for: Dúzsi, Domaine Gróf Zichy, HEIMANN, Mészáros, Sebestyén, Szent Gaál, TAKLER.

Szepsy, István Tok w dr sw ★★★★ 99' 00' 02 03' 05 06 07 08 Brilliant producer of long-ageing TOKAJI ASZÚ in MÁD. Excellent single-v'yd dry wines, esp Urbán, Szent Tamás and Király HÁRSLEVELŰ 05 06' 07' 08, and sweet SZAMORODNI from 03 06 08. Same family name as the man who created the ASZÚ method in 17th century.

Szeremley, Huba Bal w dr sw ★★ 05 06 07 08 09 Pioneer in BADACSONY. Intense, mineral RIES, *Szürkebarát* (aka PINOT GR), Kéknyelű, and appealing sweet Zeus.

Takler S Pann ★★ 06 07 08 09 Significant family producer in SZEKSZÁRD, making

> **Districtus Hungaricus Controllatus (DHC)**
> Term adopted for wines with specific protected designation of origin (PDO). Symbol is a local crocus and DHC on label.

super-ripe, supple reds. Best: Res selections of CAB FR, KÉKFRANKOS, SYRAH and BIKAVÉR. Super-cuvée Regnum well regarded locally and in USA.

Tibor Gál N Hun r w dr ★ Winery in EGER founded by the late Tibor Gál, famed as winemaker at ORNELLAIA, Tuscany. Son (also Tibor) has bought new cellars and is working hard to improve the wines.

Tinon, Samuel Tok ★★→★★★ 00 01 04 r dr sw Frenchman from Bordeaux, in TOKAJ since 1991. Distinctive and v.gd Tokaji ASZÚ with v. long maceration and barrel-ageing. Also superb *flor*-aged *Szamorodni*.

Tokaj / Tokaji w dr sw ★★→★★★★★ Tokaj is the town; Tokaji is the wine. *See* ASZÚ, ESSENCIA, FURMINT, PUTTONYOS, SZAMORODNI. Also dry table wine of increasingly exciting quality.

Tokaj Trading House Tok State-owned TOKAJ company, buying grapes from over 2,000 small growers plus own vines, incl the fine Szarvas v'yd. Also called Kereskedőház, or Crown Estates. Quality is underperforming.

Tolna S Pann Largest estate is Antinori-owned Tűzkő at Bátaapáti. Gd TRAMINI, CHARD and blended red Talentum.

Törley r w dr sp ★→★★ Innovative large company. Consistent international varietals (PINOT GR, CHARD, PINOT N, rosé), also local varieties IRSAI OLIVÉR, Zenit and Zefir. Major fizz producer (esp *Törley* and Hungaria labels) and v.gd classical method, esp François Rosé Brut and President Brut. Chapel Hill is well-made, gd-value brand, and György-Villa for top selections.

Tornai Bal w dr ★★→★★★ 06 07 08 09 Family-owned producer in Somló, making gd, complex, intense dry whites, esp Top Selection range (Juhfark, HÁRSLEVELŰ, OLASZRIZLING and FURMINT).

Villány S Pann Southern wine region, Hungary's best red zone. Local KÉKFRANKOS and PORTUGIESER are ripe and fruity, plus more serious Bordeaux varieties (esp CAB FR) and blends. Recent appearance of gd SYRAH and PINOT N in cooler spots. High-quality producers: *Bock*, CSÁNYI, ATTILA GERE, Tamás Gere, Heumann, *Malatinszky*, SAUSKA, Tiffán, WENINGER-GERE, *Vylyan*, Wunderlich.

Vylyan S Pann r dr ★★→★★★ 06' 07 08 (09) Run by the dynamic Monika Debreczeni. Burgundian consultant's influence shows in stylish PINOT N. Also try CAB FR. *Duennium Cuvée* (Cab Fr, CAB SAUV, MERLOT, ZWEIGELT) is flagship red.

Weninger N Hun r ★★→★★★ 04 06 07 08 09 Benchmark winery in SOPRON run by Austrian Franz Weninger Jr. Biodynamic since 2006. Single-v'yd *Spern Steiner* KÉKFRANKOS one of the best in the country. SYRAH, PINOT N and red Frettner blend also impressive.

Weninger-Gere S Pann r ★★★ 03' 04' 06' 07' 08 Joint-venture between Austrian Franz Weninger Sr and ATTILA GERE. CAB FR Selection excellent, supple PINOT N, gd-value Cuvée Phoenix and fresh Rosé.

BULGARIA

The challenge for Bulgaria now, with its long-standing reputation for producing international grape varieties at low prices, is to make something distinctively Bulgarian. Partly it's a question of growing the right vine in the right place; partly a question of careful harvesting. Producers are upping their game, undoubtedly. The 2011 vintage was deemed good, despite a cooler-than-average summer.

Assenovgrad Thrace r ★→★★ Longstanding specialist in local MAVRUD and RUBIN.

Bessa Valley Thrace r ★★★ Stephan von Neipperg (of Canon la Gaffelière, Bordeaux) and K-H Hauptmann's winery nr Pazardjik. Enira and Enira Res 07. The only quality Bulgarian wine readily available in the UK.

Blueridge Thrace r w ★→★★ Large DOMAINE BOYAR winery. Gd everyday CHARD, CAB SAUV.

Borovitsa Danube r w ★★ One of a small number of old v'yds, distinctive terroir close to Danube. Dux 03, Dux 06. Les Amis CHARD 08, PINOT N 09 worth trying.

Castra Rubra Thrace r ★★ New winery of TELISH in south. Michel Rolland (Bordeaux) advises young team. Try the Via Diagonalis 08, Pendar 08 and Castra Rubra 08.

Chateau de Val Danube r ★★ Small producer of distinctive quality wines: Grand Claret 09. Cuvée Trophy 10.

Damianitsa Thrace r (w) ★★ Winery specializing in MELNIK. Uniqato single varieties RUBIN and Melnik 08, Kometa No Man's Land MERLOT/CAB SAUV 08. Consistent.

Domaine Boyar Big exporter, own v'yds and wineries. Award-winning Ars Longa and Quantum wines. CAB SAUV Res 08, Solitaire CAB FR 08.

Dragomir Thrace r (w) ★★ Promising winery nr Plovdiv. CAB SAUV/MERLOT brands such as Karizma 08 and Rezerva 08.

Katarzyna Thrace r w ★★★ Quality reds and whites from this winery bordering Greece and Turkey. Encore SYRAH 08 is excellent; also recommended: Question Mark 07 (a stylish CAB SAUV/MERLOT), Halla Merlot 10, Twins Cab Sauv 10.

Khan Krum Danube w ★ Gd whites, esp CHARD and TRAMINER.

Korten Thrace r ★★ Boutique cellar of DOMAINE BOYAR; quality and traditional-style wines. Look out for Cluster, Solitaire and Royal Res ranges.

Leventa Danube (r) w ★★ Small new winery in Russe, particularly gd whites, esp SAUV BL 10 and TRAMINER 10, Also MERLOT Grand Selection 08 and CAB SAUV Grand Selection 08.

Logodaj Thrace r w ★→★★ Blagoevgrad winery. MERLOT 10, Nobile RUBIN 07, Hypnose Res 07.

Malkata Zvezhda Thrace r w ★ Promising winery aims for limited production, high quality. Enigma range, esp MERLOT and blended Experience, both recommended.

Midalidare Estate Thrace r w ★→★★ New boutique winery making an impression with red and white. Try SYRAH Grand Vintage 09, Eric Moro SAUV BL/SÉM 10.

Minkov Brothers Thrace r w ★★ Smooth, elegant reds and fresh whites in the Cycle range: single varietals and blends of two grapes (bicycles) or three (tricycles).

Miroglio, Edoardo Thrace r w ★★ Italian investor. Own v'yds at Elenovo. MERLOT 09, PINOT N 07, and *Bulgaria's best fizz*, Miroglio Brut Metodo Classico 07.

Pomorie Thrace (Black Sea Gold) (r) w ★ Golden Rhythm and Premium ranges 10.

Slaviantsi Thrace (r) w ★→★★ Gd whites and some promising reds. Try Leva: CHARD, MUSCAT and DIMIAT 10, Res CHARD 09.

Sliven, Vini Thrace r (w) ★ Everyday MERLOT, MISKET and CHARD.

Targovishte (r) w ★→★★ Winery in the east, gd for CHARD, SAUV BL, MUSCAT and TRAMINER and some promising new reds.

Telish Danube r (w) ★★ Innovative winery in north. Gd value and quality. Nimbus SYRAH Premium 09, CAB SAUV and MERLOT 09.

Todoroff Thrace r (w) ★→★★ High-profile winery. Boutique MAVRUD 09. CAB SAUV Todoroff Teres 05.

Valley Vintners *See* BOROVITSA

Varna Wine Cellar Danube (r) w ★→★★ Some excellent fresh young whites, incl: TRAMINER 11, RIES, Varnenski MISKET 11.

Villa Lyubimets Thrace r w ★→★★ V'yds in increasingly popular area for wineries, the southeast. MERLOT Premium Res 06. Villa Hissar, sister white label, made award-winning +359 Metaphor 09.

Yambol Thrace r (w) ★ Winery in Thracian plain, specializing in CAB SAUV, MERLOT.

SLOVENIA

This tiny and beautiful nation has celebrated 20 years of independence and is gaining global recognition for thrilling wines and fantastic terroirs. The green movement is strong: organic and natural wines (see France chapter; here natural whites are often big, skin-macerated and amber in colour) remain a trend but fresher, lighter and more conventional whites are gaining ground. The chill wind of the eurozone crisis is discouraging ambitious pricing at the top end; we should soon be seeing better value emerging.

Batič Prim ★★ 06 07 08 09 Organic, natural wine-grower in VIPAVA. Try Rosé, PINELA and Zaria.

Bjana Prim ★★ Gd traditional-method sparklers from BRDA, esp Brut Rosé and Cuvée Prestige 05.

Blažič Prim ★★★ 06 07 08 09 BRDA producer making superb REBULA, aromatic SAUVIGNONASSE and complex white blend Blaž Belo in top yrs.

Brda (Goriška) Prim Exciting top-quality district in PRIMORJE and home to many leading wineries, incl: Bjana, BLAŽIČ, EDI SIMČIČ, Erzetič, JAKONČIČ, Kabaj, Klinec, KRISTANČIČ, MOVIA, Prinčič, SIMČIČ, ŠČUREK, VINSKA KLET GORIŠKA BRDA, ZANUT.

Burja Prim ★★→★★★ 09 new venture in VIPAVA from Primož Lavrenčič (also involved with SUTOR), focusing on local varieties Zelen and MALVAZIJA. Also delicious PINOT N 09'.

Slovenians are big wine-drinkers, officially consuming 38.4 litres each every year.

Čotar Prim ★★ 99 03 04 05 07 08 Natural wine pioneer in KRAS. Long-lived, distinctive wines, esp Vitovska (w), MALVAZIJA, SAUV BL. Reds need long ageing. Try: TERAN, Terra Rossa, CAB SAUV.

Čurin-Prapotnik (PRA-VinO) Pod ★★★★ 99' 04' 05' 06' 07 Pioneer of private wine production in 1970s. World-class sweet wines (drier styles disappoint), incl fantastic Icewine (*ledeno vino*) from frozen grapes, and botrytis wines from ŠIPON, LAŠKI RIZLING, CHARD). Brand is PRA-VinO.

Cviček Pos Traditional low-alcohol, sharp, light red blend of POSAVJE, based on Žametovka. Try Bajnof.

Dveri-Pax Pod ★★ 07 08 09 10 Excellent winery nr Maribor. Basic range is crisp, v.gd-value whites, esp SAUV BL, ŠIPON, RIES. Admund range is single v'yd selections: try Šipon Ilovci, Sauv Bl Vagyen, Ries "M", MODRI PINOT. Also superb sweet wines, esp rare Šipon 09 straw wine.

Edi Simčič Prim ★★★→★★★★ 04 05 06 07 08 Leading BRDA producer, bucking trend for maceration. Excellent SIVI PINOT, REBULA, white blend Triton Lex. Superb Kozana single-v'yd CHARD 05' 07', red blend Duet Lex and v. expensive top-class Kolos 04.

Guerila Prim ★★ 09 10 Organic producer in VIPAVA making benchmark local PINELA and Zelen.

Istria Aka Slovenska Istra. Coastal zone extending into Croatia. Mediterranean climate. Known for REFOŠK and MALVAZIJA. Best producers: Bordon (E.Vin rosé, Malvazija), Korenika & Moškon (PINOT GR, Kortinca red), Rojac (Renero, Stari d'Or), Pucer z Vrha (Malvazija), SANTOMAS.

Jakončič Prim ★★★ 07 08 09 10 V.gd BRDA producer with elegant whites and reds, esp Bela Carolina REBULA/CHARD blend and Rdeča (r) Carolina.

Joannes Pod ★★ 06' 07' 08 09 10 Nr Maribor. RIES is focus; gd CHARD, MODRI PINOT.

Kogl Pod ★★★ Small hilltop winery nr Ormož, dating back to 16th century. Finely crafted elegant whites incl Quartet blends and varietal Mea Culpa (try AUXERROIS 09, late-harvest CHARD 08).

Kras Prim Small, famous district on Terra Rossa soil in PRIMORJE. Best-known f TERAN but also whites, esp MALVAZIJA. Look for ČOTAR, Lisjak Boris, Renčel.

Kristančič Dusan Prim ★★ 08 09 BRDA producer straddling Italian border. Try Pa CHARD and Rdeče red blend.

Kupljen Pod ★★ 07 08 09 Consistent dry wine pioneer nr Jeruzalem known f RENSKI RIZLING, SAUV BL, SIVI PINOT, CHARD, PINOT N. Wines age well.

Ljutomer Ormož Pod ★→★★★ Famous and improving wine subdistrict in PODRAV known for crisp, delicate whites and top botrytis. *See* ČURIN-PRAPOTNIK, P&F, KO Krainz, KUPLJEN, VERUS.

Marof Pod ★★→★★★ 07 08' 09' 10 Exciting new winery in Prekmurje raising t image of the district. DYA classic range: v.gd LAŠKI RIZLING Bodonci, RENSKI RIZLIN barrel-fermented Breg CHARD, SAUV BL; single-v'yd Cru Chard and BLAUFRÄNKISCH

Mlečnik Prim ★★★ 05 06 In VIPAVA, making natural, macerated, oak-aged whites

Movia Prim ★★★→★★★★ 02 03 04 05 06 07 09 High-profile biodynamic wine run by charismatic Aleš Kristančič. Winemaking is extreme with v. long o ageing, but excellent results, esp Veliko Belo (w) and Veliko Rdeče (r). V.g MODRI PINOT, while macerated Lunar (REBULA) and long-aged sparkling Puro a distinctive, and split opinion.

P&F Pod ★★ 09 10 Former Jeruzalem Ormož co-op now renamed P&F (Puklav & Friends). 600ha v'yds + 600 ha under contract, nr dramatic hilltop town Jeruzalem. Now v.gd value, *consistent crisp, aromatic whites*. Try Gomila FURMIN SAUV BL, PINOT GR and great-value blend Terrace.

Penina Quality sparkling wine made by either *charmat* or traditional method. Lo for RADGONSKE GORICE (biggest), Istenič, BJANA, Medot, MOVIA.

Podravje Region in the northeast. Much-improved quality, esp crisp, dry white better value than west. A few light reds from PINOT N and MODRA FRANKINJA.

Posavje Wine region in the southeast. Most successful wine styles are sweet, es PRUS, Šturm and sparkling from Istenič (reliable Miha NV, best Blanc de Blan 03 and PINOT N 06 Gourmet rosé).

Primorje Region in the southwest from Slovenian ISTRA to BRDA. Aka Primorska.

Prus ★ Small family producer making stunning ★★★★ sweet wines, esp c Icewines from Rumeni MUŠKAT and TRAMINER; amazing aged botrytis SAUV BL 01

Ptujska Klet Pod ★★→★★★ 08 09 10 V.gd crisp, modern whites, esp Pullus SAU BL, RIES, Ranfol. Excellent "G" wines (esp Sauv Bl and Sladko) and lovely RENS RIZLING TBA (*see* Germany, p.165) 08'.

Radgonske Gorice Pod ★ Wine zone and name of co-op producing bestsellin Slovenian sparkler Srebrna (silver) PENINA, classic-method Zlata (golden) PENIN and popular demi-sec black label TRAMINEC.

Santomas Prim ★★★ 05 06 07 08 09 In ISTRIA with French consultant. Some of th country's best *Refošk* and REFOŠK-CAB SAUV blends with long ageing potential, es Antonius, Grande Cuvée. Mezzoforte is v.gd value, Casme Ré rosé tasty.

Šćurek Prim ★★→★★★ 06 07 08 09 10 Gd consistent BRDA producer. DYA varietie BELI PINOT, CHARD and REBULA. The best wines focus on local grapes, esp Sta Brajda (r w).

Simčič, Marjan Prim ★★★★ 03 04 06 07 08 09 Excellent BRDA producer. White esp SIVI PINOT, SAUVIGNONASSE, REBULA, CHARD and SAUV BL Selekcija impress and ag

---

Macerated whites

A strong trend in PRIMORJE in the last few yrs, linked with the natural wine movement (*see* France). Whites undergo long maceration on skins (like reds) for days or even weeks, usually at higher temperatures. The result is big, structured and potentially long-lived wines, best with food.

well. Teodor Belo (w) and MERLOT-based Teodor Rdeče (r) are superb. MODRI PINOT is elegant. Excellent Opoka single-v'yd range, esp notable Sauv Bl 07. Sweet Leonardo is great.

ooking for more information on grapes? Try the "Grapes" section on pp.16–26.

tajerska Slovenija Pod Important wine district since 2006 that encompasses practically whole PODRAVJE region.

teyer Pod ★★ 07 08 09 10 TRAMINER specialist in RADGONSKE GORICE: all styles from sparkling to excellent sweet Vaneja. New SAUV BL is v. drinkable.

Sutor Prim ★★★ 06 07 08 Excellent producer from VIPAVA. Superb CHARD 08 is one of country's best, as is thrilling white Burja blend 08. Also v.gd MALVAZIJA and red Burja 07.

Tilia Prim ★★→★★★ 07 08 09 10 Husband-and-wife team in VIPAVA produce lovely, elegant PINOT N (esp 06' 08'), gd macerated REBULA Grace, plus appetizing SIVI PINOT, SAUV BL and local Zelen.

Valdhuber Pod ★★→★★★ 08 09 10 First to do dry whites in PODRAVJE. Notable SAUV BL and gd LAŠKI RIZLING.

Verus Pod ★★★ 07' 08' 09' 10 Young team continue to impress with fine, focused whites, esp v.gd FURMINT, crisp SAUV BL and zesty RIES.

Vinakoper Prim ★★ Large company with own v'yds in ISTRIA. Gd-value Capris line (DYA MALVAZIJA and REFOŠK 08) and premium Capo d'Istria CAB SAUV 04 06.

Vinska Klet Goriška Brda Prim ★→★★★ 06 07 08 09 10 Modernized major winery in BRDA. Usually v.gd value for DYA whites, esp Quercus SIVI PINOT, PINOT BL. Bagueri is higher-quality line, and top selection A+ red and white both gd.

Vipava Prim Valley noted for cool breezes in PRIMORJE, recently source of some of Slovenia's best wines. Producers: BATIČ, BURJA, GUERILA, Štokelj, MLEČNIK, SUTOR, TILIA. Also try better Lanthieri range from co-op Vipava 1894.

Zanut Prim ★★ From BRDA. Expressive SAUV BL 09, single-v'yd MERLOT Brjač 03 06, Augustus CAB SAUV 06.

Zlati Grič Pod ★★ New investment nr Maribor. 75ha, New Zealand winemaker.

CROATIA

Croatia is is due to join the EU in July 2013, which will mean a big shake-up for the wine industry. It will lose favourable trading terms with other parts of former Yugoslavia, and imports will get easier, so suddenly its wines (that are never exactly cheap, especially big brands from the coastal zones) will have tough competition. What will stand Croatia in good stead is its wealth of great terroirs and indigenous grapes, and tourism. Over six million visitors per year, and growing, makes for a lot of wine ambassadors when they get home.

Agrokor ★→★★ 07 08 09 10 Major group with over 30% of Croatian wine market and six wineries, incl Agrolaguna, Belje, Istravino, Iločki Podrumi and Mladina. Best wines from Belje: v.gd Belje MERLOT, Goldberg GRAŠEVINA and CHARD, also Iločki: Graševina and TRAMINAC Icewine.

Badel 1862 Dalm ★→★★ 06 07 08 09 One of biggest producers, surprisingly gd. Best: Ivan Dolac (PZ Svirče), DINGAČ (PZ Vinarija Dingač). Duravar range is reliable and v.gd for sweet wines, esp GRAŠEVINA.

Bodren N Croa ★★→★★★ 07 08 09 Small producer, superb sweet wines in otherwise unregarded area, incl Château Bezanec CHARD, SIVI PINOT, RIES. Superb Icewine.

Bolfan N Croa w dr ★★ 09 10 New producer nr Zagreb with 20ha. Fresh, appetizing wines, incl gd PINOT N rosé, PINOT GR, RIES and SAUV BL.

Cattunar Ist r w dr ★★ 09 10 One of ISTRIA's largest private producers. MALVAZIJA, esp late-harvest Collina, is v.gd.

Coronica Ist ★★ Notable ISTRIAN winery, esp MALVAZIJA. Gran TERAN 07 is benchmark for this tricky grape.

Dalmatia Rocky coastal zone and islands. Warm Mediterranean climate gives weighty, full-bodied wines.

Dingač Dalm 05′ 06 07 08 1st quality designation in 1961, now PDO, on Pelješac peninsula in southern DALMATIA. Noted for robust, full-bodied reds from PLAVAC MALI. Look for: Bura-Mrgudić, Kiridžija, Lučić, Matuško, Madirazza, SAINTS HILLS Vinarija Dingač.

Enjingi, Ivan N Croa ★★ 03 06 Producer of v.gd sweet botrytis and dry whites, esp GRAŠEVINA and Venje.

Vrhunsko vino is premium-quality wine, *kvalitetno vino* is quality wine, *stolno vino* is table wine; *suho* is dry.

Gracin, Leo Dalm ★★ Academic, owner/winemaker at Suha Punta (excellent Babić 08); consultant to Jako Vino on Brač island (POŠIP, PLAVAC MALI worth trying).

Grgić Dalm ★★→★★★ Legendary Napa Valley producer returned to his roots to make PLAVAC MALI and rich POŠIP on Pelješac Peninsula.

Hvar Dalm Beautiful island in mid-Dalmatia: PLAVAC MALI, incl Ivan Dolac designation. Producers of note: Carić, Plančić, ZLATAN OTOK, PZ Svirče, TOMIĆ (Bastijana winery).

Istria North Adriatic peninsula. MALVAZIJA is the main grape. Gd also for CAB SAUV, MERLOT and TERAN. Look for Benvenuti (Malvazija), CATTUNAR, Clai (Sveti Jakov), CORONICA, Cossetto (Malvazija Rustica, Mozaik), Degrassi (MUSCAT, Terre Bianche), Gerzinić (Teran), Kozlović (Santa Lucia), MATOŠEVIĆ, Radovan (Malvazija, Teran, Cab Sauv), ROXANICH, SAINTS HILLS, TRAPAN.

Korta Katarina Dalm ★★★ 06 07 08 New-generation small producer with modern take on traditional styles. POŠIP is excellent, PLAVAC MALI v.gd, esp Reuben's Res.

Krauthaker, Vlado N Croa ★★★ 06 07 08 09 Top producer from KUTJEVO, esp CHARD, Rosenberg, dry GRAŠEVINA Mitrovac and sweet Izborna Berba. Increasingly impressive reds, esp SYRAH and PINOT N.

Kutjevo N Croa Name shared by a town in SLAVONIJA, heartland of GRAŠEVINA, and ★★→★★★ Kutjevo Cellars. Look for Traminac, Graševina and De Gotho CHARD and Berba 08.

Matošević Ist ★★→★★★ 08 09 10 Pioneering producer and head of Istrian producers' association. Benchmark MALVAZIJA in several styles. Also v.gd Grimalda red, esp 08 and white.

Pošip Dalm Best DALMATIAN white, mostly on island of Korčula.

Postup Dalm Famous v'yd designation northwest of DINGAČ. Medium- to full-bodied red from PLAVAC MALI. Donja Banda, Miličić, Mrgudić Marija, Vinarija Dingač are noted.

Prošek Dalm Passito-style dessert wine from DALMATIA, made from dried local grapes Bogdanuša, Maraština, Prč. Look for Hectorovich from TOMIĆ.

Grape varieties

Croatia has a wealth of indigenous grapes, incl red Babić (best is GRACIN 08), Borgonja (a clone of GAMAY), Bogdanuša (from HVAR), Debit (try Bibich Lučica), Gegić (try Boškinac), Grk (try GRGIĆ), Maraština (Sladić is gd) and Zelenac (aka Austria's ROTGIPFLER, try KRAUTHAKER). Almost extinct Crljenak turns out to be ZIN and parent of PLAVAC MALI, while Štajerska Belina is parent of CHARD.

Roxanich Ist ★★→★★★ 06 07 New organic producer making powerful intriguing whites (MALVAZIJA Antica); impressive, complex reds, esp TERAN Ré, Superistrian Cuvée, MERLOT.

Saints Hills Ist ★★→★★★ 08 09 10 New high-profile producer since 2008 with Michel Rolland consulting. V.gd Nevina MALVAZIJA/CHARD. DINGAČ 08 already promising. Fun St Heels rosé.

Istrian Malvazija + small acacia-wood barrels = magic.

Slavonija N Croa Subregion in North, historically for whites but gd reds now, esp PINOT N. Look out for Adzić, Bartolović, Belje, ENJINGI, Galić, KRAUTHAKER, KUTJEVO, Mihalj, Zdjelarević. Also famous for growing oak.

Tomič Dalm ★★→★★★ r dr sw 05 06 07 08 Owner of Bastijana winery on island of HVAR. V.gd barrique PLAVAC MALI and PROŠEK Hectorovich from dried grapes.

Trapan, Bruno Ist ★★→★★★ 08 09 10 Rising star, making some of Croatia's best MALVAZIJA, incl aged Uroboros and fresh Ponente. Pioneer with SYRAH in ISTRIA. Stylish CAB SAUV, too.

Zlatan Otok Dalm ★★→★★★ 05 06 07 08 09 10 Much admired for huge reds, esp Zlatan PLAVAC Grand Cru. V'yd investments now showing in better-balanced wines: Zlatan Ostatak Bure 08, Plavac 09 and POŠIP 10

Zlatan Plavac Dalm Grand cru designation for PLAVAC MALI. Usually v. high alcohol.

BOSNIA & HERZEGOVINA, SERBIA, MONTENEGRO, MACEDONIA (FYROM)

We're right in the Balkans here, so you'd expect something a bit – well, Balkan. Modern winemaking is smoothing things out somewhat, but Bosnia & Herzegovina has its plummy red Blatina grape and grapey white Žilavka (try Hercegovina Produkt for both) plus characterful, ripe Vranac (try Vinarija Vukoje and Tvrdoš Monastery).

Serbia's WOW winery is forward-looking (esp SAUV BL, PINOT GR, CHARD Barrique), Radovanvić (CAB Res) and Aleksandrović also impress; try whites Trijumf, Harizma, Trijumf Barik and PINOT N-based Trijumf Noir.

Montenegro's vineyards are confined to the coastal zone and around Lake Skadar: 13 Jul Plantaže is the (still state-owned) major producer but consistent (try Procorde Vranac), also look out for first private winery Milenko Sjekloća (decent Vranac). In FYROM, rows still rumble on with Greece about use of the name Republic of Macedonia, affecting some exports to Germany, and as wine contributes around one-fifth of GDP, anything affecting exports is a concern.

Within Macedonia, there's an increasing focus on quality: improving wineries incl Cekorov, Château Kamnik, Dalvina, Fonko, Negotino (belongs to Slovenia's P&F), Pivka, Popov, Popova Kula, Skovin and Tikveš (one of Europe's largest, and much improved recently with Slovenian consultancy).

CZECH REPUBLIC & SLOVAK REPUBLIC

Czech Republic

Czech wines – coming from the two wine regions of Bohemia and Moravia – are good at winning medals in international competitions, although high demand at home means that prices are far too high and there is no need to export. Per-capita consumption has risen, while generous EU subsidies mean wineries continue to invest on a grand scale. The German system of must-weight levels (*see* Germany) has given rise to a fashion for semi-sweet and sweet offerings that may please the public but have little other intrinsic value. New VOC designation – the first step in focusing on place as opposed to variet on the label – began in Znojmo, and now incl other regions (Mikulov, Modré Hory, with Pálava VOC in the offing).

Bohemia A small region, making wines similar to neighbouring Saxony: light, pleasant enough. Best in Elbe Valley north of Prague, esp Mělník (Bettina Lobkowicz, Vilém Kraus III), Žernoseky, Roudnice. Also Karlštejn, Otmíče to the west, Kutná Hora and Kuks to the east and small-vineyard renewal around Prague itself (Salabka, Gröbovka, Svatováclavská, Modřanská). Also kosher wines from Chrámce near Most in the northwest. Two giants, Bohemia Sekt and Soare, dominate sparkling-wine production.

Moravia By far the larger region. Many small, progressive producers: Stapleton Springer, Springer Family Winery and Jedlička & Novák (all Bořetice), Dobrá Vinice (Nový Šaldorf), Krásná Hora (Starý Poddvorov), Sonberk (Pouzdřany), Gotberg (Popice), Volařík (Mikulov), plus large producers with top ranges such as Vinselekt Michlovský (Rakvice), Znovín (Znojmo), Habánské Sklepy (Velké Bílovice) and Radomil Baloun (Velké Pavlovice).

The final Czech 2011s were picked at -13°c in Feb 2012 for Icewine.

Slovak Republic

Still has much in common with the Czech Republic, including similar languages and a similar approach to winemaking, dating from Austro-Hungarian days. Six wine regions are spread across the central mountainous plateau and along the southern and eastern borders: Southern, Central and Eastern Slovakia, Lesser Carpathia, Nitra and Tokaj. This last is a small district adjoining its larger Hungarian neighbour. Best producers include: Mrva-Stanko of Trnava, Víno Matyšák, Milan Pavelka and Roman Janoušek, all from Pezinok, Karpatská Perla (Šenkvice), Masaryk (Skalica), Fedor Malík & Sons (Modra), Víno Nitra (Nitra) and JJ Ostrožovič of Velká Tŕňa, the most notable of Slovakia's handful of Tokaj producers. Also some wealthy newcomers, such as Château Belá in Mužla (with German Egon Müller's involvement) and Elesko in Modra, a spanking new investment boasting a "wine park" and a gallery featuring Andy Warhol originals, with Kiwi winemaker Nigel Davies.

ROMANIA

Membership of the EU has directed colossal amounts of cash Romania's way, and signs informing people that this project or that is being funded by the EU are everywhere. But the economic crisis is being felt here, too, and the vineyard area has fallen, while domestic consumption has dropped around 20%. Romania is still a net importer of wine, and while the smaller and mid-sized wineries are making better wine than ever, the big five that dominate still have a long way to go.

Banat Smallest wine region in west. *See* CRAMELE RECAŞ. Also location of new Italian estate, Petro Vaselo.

Budureasca Mun ★ Large estate, mostly replanted (formerly Carpathian winery). Decent commercial wines. Brit Stephen Donnelly consults.

Carl Reh Mun ★★→★★★ 06 07 08 09 10 Large German-owned winery in Oprisor (southwest). Val Duna and River Route are gd export ranges, esp PINOT GR. V.gd reds in Crama Oprisor range, esp La Cetate SHIRAZ, Caloian, Crama Oprisor CAB SAUV and Smerenie. Top red blend: Fragmentarium.

Cotnari Mold Region in northeast, famous for over 500 yrs for botrytized wines, Romania's curtsey to Tokaj. Now mostly medium to sweet GRASĂ, FETEASCĂ ALBĂ, TĂMÂIOASĂ and dry Frâncuşă. Also ★ Cotnari Winery, with 1,200ha. Collection wines can be long-lived.

Merlot, Romania's most widely planted red grape, probably arrived early 18th century.

Crama Girboiu Mold New winery (founded 2005) with 200ha in Vrancea.

Cramele Recaş Banat r w dr ★★→★★★ 06 07 08 09 10 British/Romanian firm continuing to invest in BANAT region. Quality better than ever, esp Sole CHARD, FETEASCĂ REGALA, Solo Quinta white, La Putere reds. Also value modern varietals under First Cape Discovery, Wolfhouse, V, Castle Rock, Terra Dacica labels. V.gd super-premium Cuvée Uberland red blend 07.

Crişana and Maramures Region to northwest. Wine Princess, Nachbil based here.

Davino Winery Mun ★★★ 06 07' 08 09 10 One of Romania's best, with 68ha in DEALU MARE. V.gd Dom Ceptura (r w). Alba Valahica and Purpura Valahica highly recommended. Flamboyant red blend is excellent and new Rezerva red 07 sets new quality standards for Romania.

Dealu Mare Mun (Dealul Mare) "The Big Hill". Important area in southeast Carpathian foothills. Some of Romania's best reds; location of promising new boutiques: Lacerta (try Cuvée IX red and Cuvée X white), Rotenberg (MERLOT, esp Notorius), Crama Basilescu (Merlot and FETEASCĂ NEAGRĂ).

Dobrogea Black Sea region. Incl DOC regions of MURFATLAR, Badabag, Sarica Niculitel. Historically famous for sweet, late-harvest CHARD and now for full-bodied reds.

Domeniile Ostrov Dob ★ €20m investment with 1,200ha in DOBROGEA since 2008. Decent commercial CAB SAUV.

Domeniile Sahateni Mun ★→★★ 70 ha estate in DEALU MARE. Nomad (New World style), Artisan (local varieties: try TĂMÂIOASĂ ROMÂNEASCĂ) and Anima for top wines (esp MERLOT 08).

Domeniul Coroanei Segarcea Mun ★★ 08 09 10 Historic royal estate resurrected by former cardiologist. Look for dry, aromatic whites, incl SAUV BL, TĂMÂIOASĂ (also appealing rare rosé, semi-sweet version). Also gd CAB SAUV 08, PINOT N 09.

Drăgăşani Mun Dynamic region south of Carpathians. PRINCE STIRBEY has led renaissance, followed recently by Avincis and Ecoterra. Gd for aromatic, crisp whites, esp local Crâmposie Selectionată and unique local reds: Novac, Negru de Drăgăşani. International varieties also do well.

Halewood Romania Mun ★→★★ British-owned company with new quality focus since 09. Best wines: Hyperion FETEASCĂ NEAGRĂ, CAB SAUV, PINOT N. Also v.gd: La Catina Pinot N, Scurta VIOGNIER and TĂMÂIOASĂ, Adrian SHIRAZ. La Umbra is new brand from 2010.

Jidvei Expensively modernized winery; 2,100ha; mostly replanted; in subregion of same name in TRANSYLVANIA. 14% of domestic market; sound whites at best.

Moldova (Moldavia) Largest wine region northeast of Carpathians. Borders Republic of Moldova. DOC areas: Bohotin, COTNARI, Huşi, Iaşi, Odobeşti, Coteşti, Nicoreşti.

Romania's second language is French, and its wine culture stems from France.

Muntenia & Oltenia Hills Major wine region in south covering DOC areas of DEALU MARE, Dealurile Olteniei, DRĂGĂŞANI, Pietroasa, Sâmbureşti, Stefaneşti, Vanju Mare.

Murfatlar Dob DOC area in DOBROGEA nr Black Sea. Subregions: Cernavoda, Megidia.

Murfatlar Winery Dob ★→★★ Dominates domestic market (28% share). Variable quality; best: Trei Hectare (FETEASCĂ NEAGRĂ, CAB SAUV, CHARD) and M1 limited-edition SYRAH. Nederburg (see South Africa) winemaker Razvan Macici consults from 2011.

Prince Ştirbey Mun w r dr sw ★★→★★★ 08 09 10 Pioneering estate in DRĂGĂŞANI restituted to Austrian-Romanian noble family. V.gd whites, esp local Crâmpoşie Selectionată, FETEASCĂ REGALĂ Genius Loci 07, sweet TĂMĂIOASĂ ROMÂNEASCĂ. Has successfully revived local reds, esp v.gd Novac and Negru de Drăgăşani.

Senator Mold ★ Newcomer based in Odobeşti with 900 ha in MOLDOVA, BANAT and Danube Delta. Try Private Collection red 2008.

SERVE Mun w dr ★★→★★★ 06' 07' 08 09 10 DEALU MARE winery founded by late Count Guy de Poix of Corsica, now run by his widow. Vinul Cavalerului whites gd, Terra Romana range excellent, esp *Cuvée Charlotte* and Cuvée Amaury white.

Transylvania Cool mtn plateau in centre of Romania. Mostly whites with gd acidity from FETEASCĂ ALBA and REGALĂ, MUSCAT, TRAMINER, Italian RIES. Promising PINOT N.

Vinarte Winery Mun ★★→★★★ 06' 07' 08 09 10 Italian investment, three estates: Villa Zorilor in DEALU MARE, Castel Bolovanu in DRĂGĂŞANI, Terase Danubiane in Vanju Mare. Best: Soare CAB SAUV, Prince Matei MERLOT and new white blend of TĂMĂIOASĂ ROMÂNEASCĂ/SAUV BL.

Vincon Vrancea Winery Mold r w dr sw ★ One of Romania's largest producers with 2,150ha in Vrancea, plus DOBROGEA and DEALU MARE.

Vinia Mold r w dr sw ★ One of Romania's largest wineries at Iaşi. Major producer of COTNARI wines.

Vitis Metamorfosis Mun r w ★★ 07 09 High-profile joint venture between Italy's Antinori family and British-owned Halewood. First release is 07 Cantus Primus CAB SAUV. V.gd second label Vitis Metamorfosis 09 white blend and MERLOT 09.

DOC
Denumire de Origine Controlată is the Romanian term for AOP (*see* France). Sub-categories incl DOC-CMD for wines harvested at full maturity, DOC-CT for late-harvest and DOC-CIB for noble-harvest. *Vin cu indicaţie geografică* is the term for IGP.

WineRo Dob r ★★ New premium estate in DOBROGEA owned by Stephan von Niepperg of Canon la Gaffelière (*see* Bordeaux), with Dr. Hauptmann and Marc Dworkin. The same team owns/runs Bulgaria's Bessa Valley. First release is appealing, juicy Alira MERLOT 09. To watch.

Looking for more information on grapes? Try the "Grapes" section on pp.16–26.

MALTA

Malta's v'yds cannot hope to supply the island's entire consumption – the place isn't big enough, and tourism tends to take precedence when it comes to land use. Plus much of the wine on sale here is made locally from grapes imported from Italy. Real Maltese wine is subject to *Demoninazzjoni ta' Origini Kontrollata* (DOK) rules that are in line with EU practices. The traditional, indigenous grapes are Girgentina (w) and Gellewza (r), but many international grapes are also grown. Antinori-backed Meridiana is in the lead, producing excellent Maltese Isis and Mistral CHARDS, Astarte VERMENTINO, Melquart CAB SAUV/MERLOT, Nexus Merlot, **outstanding Bel Syrah** and premium Celsius Cab Sauv Res from island vines. Volume producers of note are Delicata, Marsovin and Camilleri.

Greece

G reece's image has been somewhat bruised over the last couple of years, but the wine sector remains one of the most vibrant parts of the Greek economy. The numbers speak for themselves, with exports increasing steadily since 2008. And with good reason: Greece has unique grape varieties and some inimitable flavours. Abbreviations: Aegean Islands (Aeg), Attica (Att), Central Greece (C Gr), Cephalonia (Ceph), Ionian Islands (Ion), Macedonia (Mac), Northern Greece (N Gr), Peloponnese (Pelop), Thessaloniki (Thess).

Aivalis Pelop ★★★ Boutique NEMEA producer of dark wines. Top (and pricey) wine is "4", from 120-yr-old+ vines. Monopati is less-ambitious Nemea.

Alpha Estate Mac ★★★ Impressive estate in cool-climate Amindeo. Excellent MERLOT/SYRAH/XINOMAVRO blend, pungent SAUV BL, exotic MALAGOUSIA, unfiltered New-World-style Xinomavro from old, ungrafted vines. Top wine Alpha 1 demands ageing.

Antonopoulos Pelop ★★★ PATRAS-based winery, with top-class MANTINIA, crisp Adoli Ghis (w), burgundian Anax CHARD and CAB-based Nea Dris (stunning 04 and 06). Top wine: violet-scented Vertzami/CAB FR.

Argatia ★★★ Small KTIMA, just outside NAOUSSA, for tiny quantities of XINOMAVRO in a modern vein.

Argyros Aeg ★★★ Top SANTORINI producer; exemplary VINSANTO aged 20 yrs in cask (★★★★). Exciting KTIMA (w) that ages for a decade, oak-aged Vareli (w) and fragrant (dry) Aidani. Try the rare MAVROTRAGANO (r).

Avantis C Gr ★★★ Boutique Evia winery Evia with v'yds in Boetia. Dense SYRAH, Aghios Chronos Syrah/VIOGNIER; pungent SAUV BL; rich MALAGOUSIA; interesting Oneiropagida value range. Top: Rhône-like single-v'yd Collection Syrah 03 04 05 06 07.

Biblia Chora Mac ★★★ Matches top quality and huge commercial success. Pungent SAUV BL/ASSYRTIKO. Ovilos CS and Areti AGHIORGHITIKO are stunning. Ovilos (w) could rival top white Bordeaux. Easily.

Boutari, J & Son ★→★★★ Producer with several wineries around Greece. Excellent-value wines, esp *Grande Reserve Naoussa* that can age for decades. V. popular MOSCHOFILERO. Top SANTORINI Kalisti Res, Skalani (r) from CRETE and Flliria (r) from GOUMENISSA.

Cair Aeg Large co-op winery in RHODES specializing in sparkling (the 96 rosé is the *best sparkling* ever made in Greece) but Pathos still range (r w) is v.gd value.

Cambas, Andrew ★ Large-volume brand owned by BOUTARI.

Carras, Domaine ★→★★ Estate at Sithonia, Halkidiki; own OPAP (Côtes de Meliton; but *see* box, p.236). Chateau Carras 01 02 03 04 05 and MALAGOUSIA. Getting back to form since 2010.

Cava Legal term for cask-aged still white and red non-appellation wines, eg. Cava Amethystos KOSTAS LAZARIDI, Cava HATZIMIHALI.

Cephalonia Important island with three appellations: ROBOLA (w), MUSCAT (w sw) and MAVRODAPHNE (r sw), which can incl grapes from south Ithaki.

Crete An exciting region, with young producers taking a closer, fresher look at tradition. To watch.

Dougos Thess ★★→★★★ OPAP (*see* box, p.236) in Olympus area. Exciting range, esp Opsimo (r) and Acacia (w). RAPSANI shows the way.

Driopi Pelop ★★★ Venture of TSELEPOS in NEMEA. Serious (esp single-v'yd KTIMA), high-octane style. Tavel-like Driopi rosé.

Economou Crete ★★★ One of great artisans of Greece; brilliant yet esoteric Sitia (r).

> **Greek appellations**
> Changing in line with other EU countries. The quality appellations of OPAP and OPE are now fused together into POP (or PDO) category. Regional wines, known as TO, will now be PGE (or PGI). The base category of table wine (EO) will be phased out. But expect old terms to persist on labels for some time.

Emery Aeg ★→★★ Historic RHODES producer, specializing in local varieties. Brands Villaré (w), Grand Rosé. V.gd-value Athiri. Sweet Efreni MUSCAT.

Feggites Mac ★★ Winery in Drama, from talented ex-winemaker of NICO LAZARIDI. Interesting range, top Deka (r w).

Gaia Pelop ★★★ Top-quality NEMEA- and SANTORINI-based producer. Fun Notios range. New-World-like AGHIORGHITIKO. Thought-provoking, top-class, dry white Thalassitis SANTORINI and revolutionary *wild-ferment* ASSYRTIKO. Top wine: Gaia Estate (99 00 01 03 04 05 06 07). Anatolikos sweet NEMEA, dazzling "S" red (Aghiorghitiko with a touch of SYRAH).

Gentilini Ion ★★→★★★ Exciting Cephalonia whites, incl *v.gd Robola*. V.gd dry MAVRODAPHNE (r), serious SYRAH and benchmark Selection ROBOLA.

Georgakopoulos C Gr ★★ Full-throttle, New-World-style reds, Blanc de Noir CAB SAUV and rich, unoaked CHARD. Some funky sweet styles.

Gerovassiliou Mac ★★★ Perfectionist miniature estate nr Salonika. Benchmark ASSYRTIKO/MALAGOUSIA, smooth SYRAH/MERLOT blend, top Malagousia. Complex Avaton (r) 03 04 05 06 from rare indigenous varieties and Syrah (01 02 03 04 05). For many, the quality leader.

Goumenissa Mac (OPAP) ★→★★ XINOMAVRO and Negoska oaked red, lighter than NAOUSSA. Esp Aidarinis (single v'yd is ★★★), BOUTARI (esp Filiria), Tatsis.

Greek Wine Cellars New company name for KOURTAKIS.

Hatzidakis Aeg ★★★ Low-tech, high-class producer, redefining SANTORINI appellation, esp with cuvées No. 15 and 17. Stunning range, bordering on the experimental. Nihteri and Pyrgos bottlings could age for decades. Collio meets Aegean Sea.

Hatzimichalis C Gr ★→★★ Large estate in Atalanti. Huge range. Greek, French grapes, many bottlings labelled after v'yds. Top red: Kapnias CAB SAUV, top white: Veriki.

Helios Pelop New umbrella name for Semeli, Nassiakos and Orinos Helios wines. Stunning Nassiakos MANTINIA, complex NEMEA Grande Res.

Karydas Mac ★★★ Small estate, great v'yd (NAOUSSA); classic XINOMAVRO of great breed.

Katogi-Strofilia ★★→★★★ V'yds and wineries in Attica, Peloponnese, east Epirus. Katogi was the first premium Greek wine. Top wines: KTIMA Averoff and Rossiu di Munte range.

Katsaros Thess ★★★ Small winery on Mt Olympus. KTIMA red, a CAB SAUV/MERLOT, has staying power. Esoteric CHARD. Broad-shouldered Merlot.

Kir-Yanni ★★→★★★ V'yds in NAOUSSA and Amindeo. Vibrant Samaropetra (w); characterful Tesseris Limnes (w); complex and age-worthy Dyo Elies (r). Benchmark Ramnista turning towards more supple approach, making way for XINOMAVRO/SYRAH Diaporos.

Kourtakis, D ★★ Huge, reliable merchant trading as GREEK WINE CELLARS: *mild Retsina*.

Ktima Estate, domaine.

Lazaridi, Nico ★★→★★★ Wineries in Drama, Kavala and Mykonos. Gd Château Nico Lazaridi (r p w). Top wines Magiko Vouno white (oaky SAUV BL) and red (CAB SAUV) enjoy cult status in Greece.

Lazaridis, Kostas ★★★ V'yds, wineries in Drama and Attika (sold under the Oenotria Land label). Popular Amethystos label. Top wine: amazing CAVA Amethystos CAB SAUV (97 98 99 00 01 02 03 04). Michel Rolland (Bordeaux) consults.

Limnos Aeg Island making mainly dessert wines, from delicious, lemony MUSCAT of Alexandria but also some refreshing dry white. Best producer: Hatzigeorgiou.

Lyrarakis Aeg ★★→★★★ V.gd producer from Heraklio. Whites from the rare Plyto and Dafni varieties (single v'yd versions are extraordinary). Deep and complex SYRAH/Kotsifali.

Magel N Gr ★★ Up-and-coming KTIMA in uncharted territory, in Kastoria, west Macedonia. Dressed-to-kill, rich, dense wines, mainly from Bordeaux varieties.

Manoussakis Crete ★★★ Impressive estate with Rhône-inspired blends. Delectable range under Nostos brand, led by age-worthy ROUSSANNE and SYRAH.

Mantinia Pelop (OPAP) w High altitude, cool region. Fresh, crisp, utterly charming, sometimes sparkling *Moschofilero*. More German than Greek in style.

Matsa, Château Att ★★→★★★ Historic and prestigious small estate, now owned by BOUTARI but still run by Roxani Matsa. MALAGOUSIA is leading example of the variety.

Mavrodaphne Variety and usually sweet wine, meaning "Black laurel". Cask-aged Port-style/Recioto-like, concentrated, fortifieds. Specialty of PATRAS, north Peloponnese but also found in CEPHALONIA. Dry versions (eg. ANTONOPOULOS) show great promise.

Mediterra Crete ★★ Gd producer from PEZA. Herbaceous Xerolithia (w), spicy Mirabelo (r). oaky Nobile (w) to age. V.gd-value Silenius range.

Mercouri Pelop ★★★ One of the most beautiful family estates in Europe. V.gd KTIMA (r), delicious RODITIS, age-worthy CAVA. Classy REFOSCO (r), stunning sweet Belvedere MALVASIA and leathery, dry MAVRODAPHNE.

Mezzo Aeg Sweet wine made in SANTORINI from sun-dried grapes – lighter, less sweet than VINSANTO.

Looking for more information on grapes? Try the "Grapes" section on pp.16–26.

Mitravelas Pelop ★★→★★★ Outstanding producer in NEMEA, promising great things from AGHIORGHITIKO.

Moraitis Aeg ★★ Small, quality producer on the island of Paros. V.gd smoky (w) Monemvasia, (r) earthy and complex Paros Res.

Naoussa Mac (OPAP) High-quality region for XINOMAVRO. Best examples are on a par with Italy's Barolo and Barbaresco, and can sometimes age even longer.

Nemea Pelop (OPAP) Source of dark, spicy AGHIORGHITIKO wines. Huge potential for quality here. High Nemea merits its own appellation. Koutsi is frontrunner for cru status (*see* GAIA, HELIOS, DRIOPI).

Nemeion Pelop ★★★ A KTIMA in NEMEA, high prices (esp Igemon red), with wines to match. Owned by Vassiliou, an Attica producer.

Oenoforos Pelop ★★→★★★ V.gd producer with fantastic high v'yds. Extremely elegant RODITIS Asprolithi. Also delicate Lagorthi (w), nutty CHARD (magnum only), and delicate Mikros Vorias (r w). Ianos is prestige range.

Papaïoannou Pelop ★★★ If NEMEA were Burgundy, Papaïoannou would be Jayer. Classy reds (incl PETIT VERDOT); flavourful whites. A wonderful flight of NEMEAS: KTIMA Papaioannou, Palea Klimata (old vines), Microklima (a micro-single v'yd) and top-end Terroir (a super-strict, 200%-new-oaked selection).

Patras Pelop White OPAP based on RODITIS from v. diverse terroir: some great parts, some less so. Also home of both OPE MAVRODAPHNE and Rio-Patras sweet MUSCAT.

Pavlidis Mac ★★★ Ambitious estate at Drama. Gd ASSYRTIKO/SAUV BL. Emphasis on varietals, incl classy Assyrtiko, SYRAH and TEMPRANILLO. KTIMA (r) recently switched from Bordeaux blend to AGHIORGHITIKO/Syrah in a masterful move. This really is top-ranking stuff.

Peza Appellation nr Heraklio. Vilana (w), Mandilaria/Kotsifali (r). Underperforming.

Pyrgakis Pelop ★★→★★★ Highly experimental KTIMA capitalizing on the highest parts of NEMEA. Esp new PETIT VERDOT and 24 CHARD.

Rapsani ★★★ Historic OPAP from Mt Olympus. Introduced in the 1990s by TSANTALIS, but new producers, such as Liappis and DOUGOS, are moving in.

Retsina Specialty white with Aleppo pine resin added. Modern, high-quality versions, like The Tear of the Pine from Kehris, are stunning.

Rhodes Aeg Easternmost island and OPAP for red and white. Home to lemony, elegant Athiri whites. Top wines: CAIR (co-op) Rodos 2400 and EMERY's Villare. Also sparkling.

Samos Aeg (OPE) Island nr Turkey famed for sweet golden MUSCAT. Esp (fortified) Anthemis and (sun-dried) Nectar. Rare old bottlings can be ★★★★ without the price tag, such as the hard-to-find Nectar 75.

Santo Aeg ★★→★★★ Important co-op of SANTORINI. Vibrant portfolio with dazzling Grande Res and full VINSANTOS.

Santorini Aeg Volcanic island north of CRETE and OPAP for white, dry and sweet. Luscious VINSANTO and MEZZO, minerally, bone-dry white from ASSYRTIKO. Oaked examples can also be amazing. Top producers: ARGYROS, GAIA, HATZIDAKIS, SANTO, SIGALAS. Try ageing everything. Possibly the cheapest ★★★★ whites around.

Sigalas Aeg ★★★ Top SANTORINI estate, makes fine oaked Vareli. Stylish VINSANTO. Also breathtaking MOURVÈDRE-like MAVROTRAGANO (try the 08). Keep all wines at least a decade.

Retsina still accounts for 10% of Greek wine – think of it as Greece's Fino Sherry.

Skouras Pelop ★★★ Innovative estate, eg. screwcaps on CHARD Dum Vinum Sperum. Interesting Synoro (CAB FR-dominated). Top wines: Grande Cuvée NEMEA, Megas Oenos and solera-aged Labyrinth. V. stylish Fleva SYRAH.

Spiropoulos Pelop ★★ Organic producer in MANTINIA and NEMEA. Oaky red Porfyros (AGHIORGHITIKO, CAB SAUV, MERLOT). Sparkling Odi Panos has potential. Firm, single-v'yd Astala Mantinia.

Tetramythos Pelop ★★ Promising winery exploring cool v'yds. Suffered in the summer fires of 2007, but now back on form. Excellent MALAGOUSIA, RODITIS and Mavro Kalavritino.

Tsantalis ★→★★★ Producer in Macedonia, Thrace and other areas. Gd Metoxi (r), RAPSANI Res and Grande Res, gd-value organic CAB SAUV, excellent Avaton and cult Kormilitsa. Major exporter.

Tselepos Pelop ★★★ Top-quality MANTINIA producer. Greece's best GEWURZ and best MERLOT (Kokkinomylos). Others: oaky CHARD, v.gd spark Amalia, single-v'yd Avlotopi CAB SAUV. *See also* DRIOPI.

Vinsanto Aeg Sun-dried sweet ASSYRTIKO and Aidani from SANTORINI. Deserves long ageing, in oak and bottle. The best are ★★★★ and practically indestructible. *See also* MEZZO.

Voyatzi, Ktima Mac ★★ Small estate nr Kozani. Classy XINOMAVRO, startling CAB FR sold as Tsapournakos.

Zafeirakis Thess ★★→★★★ Small KTIMA in Tyrnavos, uncharted territory for quality wine. Fastidious winemaker. Limniona red, a v. promising and rare variety. MALAGOUSIA is sublime.

Zitsa N Gr Mountainous Epirus OPAP. Delicate Debina white, still or sparkling. Best from Glinavos.

Eastern Mediterranean & North Africa

EASTERN MEDITERRANEAN

This is an intriguing region: wine culture began here, and now a new quality revolution is well under way. Israeli wines are not only for kosher shops; Lebanese, Cypriot or Turkish wines are not only for expat communities or ethnic restaurants. Israel and Lebanon are already well ahead in quality, and there are encouraging signs in Cyprus and Turkey.

Cyprus

Things are improving in Cyprus, at least vinously. There is investment in and, crucially, subsidies for, grubbing up poorer vineyards, green harvesting and simply better winemaking. But the vineyard area is falling, and is dominated by (unexciting) local grapes Mavro and Xynisteri. Competition comes from imports; not much is exported. But at least the different sides of industry have started to work together. Lemesos, Pafos, Larnaca and Lefkosia have regional wine status (PGI). PDOs cover Commandaria, Laona-Akamas, Pitsilia, Vouni-Panayias/Ambelitis and Wine Villages of Lemesos.

Ayia Mavri ★★ 08 09 10 Lovely sweet MUSCATS from semi-dried Muscat of Alexandria.

Commandaria Legendary sweet, deliberately oxidized wine made from sun-dried XYNISTERI and MAVRO, grown in 14 villages in the Troodos Mtns. The poet Hesiod mentioned it in 800BC. At its best, rich, complex and long-lived. Try St John (KEO), St Nicolas (ETKO), or the 100% Xynisteri St Barnabas from SODAP.

ETKO r w ★→★★ 09 10 Now focusing on higher quality from its Olympus winery, esp SHIRAZ and CHARD/SÉM. Produces St Nicholas COMMANDARIA.

Hadjiantonas ★★ 08 09 10 Spotless small winery owned by pilot, making v.gd CHARD, XYNISTERI, Rosé and SHIRAZ.

KEO ★ 08 09 10 Large drinks distributor, with shrinking wine production. Stick to estate wines from Keo Mallia, esp Rosé, XYNISTERI and Heritage MARATHEFTIKO. St John is ★★ COMMANDARIA brand.

Kyperounda r w dr ★★ →★★★ 08 09 10 Probably Europe's highest v'yd at 1,450 metres. White Petritis from barrel-aged XYNISTERI is island's best. V.gd CHARD, CAB SAUV, SHIRAZ and excellent-value Andessitis red.

Makkas ★ New winery in Pafos region since 07 aiming to become quality leader. CHARD, MARATHEFTIKO showing promise.

SODAP r w dr ★★ 08 09 10 Largest producer and grower-owned co-op. Quality transformed since move to state-of-art winery at Stroumbi village in hills, esp consistent and v.gd-value DYA whites and rosé. Look for Island Vines, Mtn Vines and Kamanterena labels.

Tsiakkas r w dr ★★ Banker-turned-winemaker with help from VLASSIDES. Makes v.gd fresh, zesty whites, esp SAUV BL, XYNISTERI and CHARD.

Vasa ★★ 06' 07' 08 09 10 Immaculate pioneering estate winery. Excellent MARATHEFTIKO. V.gd CHARD and Agyrides red blend. VLASSIDES consults.

Vasilikon, K&K ★→★★ 09 10 One of the biggest small wineries owned by Kyriakides brothers. Always reliable XYNISTERI and decent red Ayios Onoufrios.

Vlassides ★★→★★★ 06' 07' 08 09 10 Sophocles Vlassides uses his UC Davis training to make some of the island's best wines in his tiny village winery. SHIRAZ Res shows thrilling potential of Cyprus. V.gd XYNISTERI, CAB SAUV, MARATHEFTIKO.

Zambartas ★★·★★★ 08 09 10 Father and Australian-trained son run new winery making exciting CAB FRANC/LEFKADA rosé, v.gd SHIRAZ/Lefkada red, 100% MARATHEFTIKO and attractive XYNISTERI.

> **Pambos Argyrides**
> Cyprus wine has recently mourned the loss of one of its leading figures, Pambos Argyrides. A pioneer in estate winemaking and quality standards, and all-round nice guy. Founder of VASA winery.

The world's oldest winery (4100BC has been discovered in Armenia.

Israel

Israeli wine has been transformed in the last 20 years by producers who have imported wine expertise to go with their existing technological and agricultural prowess. Israel is a hot and humid country, but the higher-altitude vineyards of the Upper Galilee, Golan Heights and Judean Hills provide a longer, cooler growing season. Reds, from Cabernet Sauvignon, Shiraz, old-vine Carignan and Petite Sirah, are particularly worth tasting.

Abbreviations: Galilee (Gal), Golan (Gol), Judean Hills (Jud), Lower Galilee (L Gal), Negev (Neg), Samson (Sam), Shomron (Shom); Upper Galilee (Up Gal).

Agur Jud r ★→★★ A characterful boutique winery. Look for the well-integrated Kessem Bordeaux blend.

Amphorae Gal r w ★→★★ Beautiful winery; Michel Rolland (Bordeaux) consulting.

Avidan Jud r (w) ★→★★ The interesting Prio blend is gently spicy and leathery.

Barkan-Segal Gal, Sam r w ★→★★ Owned by Israel's largest brewery. V.gd Barkan PINOTAGE and Segal Argaman (Israeli vine). Barkan Altitude and Assemblage reds are gd. The two brands, Barkan and Segal, are marketed separately.

Binyamina Gal, Sam r w ★→★★ Traditional winery, with heavy investments by new owner. Aromatic semi-sweet and sweet GEWURZ. Cave is the best red.

Carmel Up Gal, Shom r w sp ★★·★★★ Founded in 1882 by a (Lafite) Rothschild. Strong v'yd presence in Up Gal. Elegant Limited Edition (03 04' 05 07' 08). Award-winning Kayoumi v'yd SHIRAZ. Characterful old-vine CARIGNAN and PETITE SIRAH. Complex Mediterranean-style blend. Luscious GEWURZ dessert.

Château Golan Gol r (w) ★★·★★★ Pioneer of Mediterranean varieties. Geshem (r w) are blends to follow. Flavourful SYRAH. Eliad is Bordeaux blend.

Chillag Gal r ★★ Labels Primo, Solo and Vivo show owner's Italian leanings.

Clos de Gat Jud r w ★★★ Classy estate with big, blowsy wines. The spicy, powerful Sycra SYRAH (04' 06 07) and buttery CHARD are superb. Chanson (r w) gd value.

Dalton Up Gal r w ★★ Well-run winery owned by family with English roots. Wild-yeast VIOGNIER. Flagship is rich Matatia. Spicy, concentrated PETITE SIRAH.

Domaine du Castel Jud r w ★★★★ Family estate in Jerusalem Mtns, owned by perfectionist, Francophile Eli Ben Zaken. Characterful, supple Grand Vin (04' 05 06' 07 08' 09). Second label, Petit Castel, is great value, esp 08. Also gd CHARD.

Ella Valley Jud r w ★→★★ Gd, lean CHARD. Aromatic CAB FR. Intense blend, "E".

Flam Jud r (w) ★★·★★★ Owned by sons of ex-CARMEL winemaker. Fine CAB SAUV, earthy, herbal SYRAH/Cab. Classico gd value. Crisp, fragrant rosé.

Galilee Quality region in north, esp higher-altitude Up Gal.

Galil Mtn Up Gal r w ★★ Firm Yiron blend. Fruity PINOT N. Owned by YARDEN.

Golan Heights Leading wine area: volcanic plateau, altitude up to 1,200 metres.

Judean Hills Mountainous region on the way to Jerusalem.

Kosher Means "pure". Needed for Jews observing dietary laws. Not all Israeli wineries are kosher, but the best happen to be, so quality is not affected.

Lewinsohn Gal rw ★★ Quality *garagiste* in a garage. Gd CHARD.

Margalit Gal r ★★★ Father and son making elegant wines, in particular Bordeaux blend Enigma (06 07' 08 09), and *Special Reserve*.

Negev Desert region in the south of the country.

Pelter Gol r w (sp) ★★→★★★ Tight, well-made reds. Trio gd value. V.gd CAB FR.

Recanati Gal r w ★★→★★★ Superb Special Res, complex CARIGNAN. Elegant wines.

Samson Region incl the Judean plain and foothills, southeast of Tel Aviv.

Saslove Up Gal r (w) ★★ Father-and-daughter team. Reds showing an avalanche of fruit and spice. Converting to organic.

Sea Horse Jud r (w) ★→★★ Idiosyncratic *garagiste*, producing exotic blends from unusual varieties.

Shomron Region with the most v'yds, which are concentrated around Mt Carmel and Zichron Ya'acov.

Tabor L Gal r w sp ★→★★ Growing fast. Aromatic SAUV BL. New PETITE SIRAH.

Teperberg Jud, Sam r w →★★ Efrat reborn. Israel's largest family-owned winery. MALBEC and Meritage are fruity, juicy reds.

Tishbi Jud, Shom r w sp ★→★★ Family of veteran grape-growers. Deep Bordeaux blend from Sde Boker in desert, best yet.

Tulip Gal r (w) ★★ Winery workers are people with special needs. Spicy, full-bodied SYRAH. Fragrant White Tulip and White Franc blush.

Tzora Jud r w ★★→★★★ Terroir-led winery, talented winemaker. Misty Hills and Shoresh deep reds with ageing potential.

Vitkin Jud r w ★★ Small winery specializing in rarer varieties. V.gd CARIGNAN and PETITE SIRAH.

Yarden Gol r w sp ★★★ Large winery, six million bottles. Pioneer of quality revolution. Yarden label best. CAB SAUV always gd. Well-balanced Odem V'yd CHARD. Rare Bordeaux blend Katzrin (96 00' 03 04' 07) and heralded Rom (06' 07) are flagships. Oustanding Blanc de Blancs sparkling and Heights Wine dessert.

Yatir Jud, Neg r (w) ★★★→★★★★ Rich, velvety, concentrated Yatir Forest (02 03' 04 05' 06 07 08') outstanding. Edgy SHIRAZ, mouthfilling CAB SAUV and powerful PETIT VERDOT. Fragrant VIOGNIER. Owned by CARMEL.

Lebanon

There's a flood of new wineries here, and vines appearing in areas other than the traditional Bekaa Valley. Reds are a fusion of French expertise and Middle Eastern spice – very good at best.

Chateau Belle-Vue r ★★ Le Chateau and La Renaissance are top-notch reds.

Château Ka r w ★→★★ Great-value CAB SAUV/MERLOT/SYRAH blend.

Chateau Kefraya r w ★★→★★★ Spicy *Comte de M* (06 07 08) from CAB SAUV and SYRAH. Easy-drinking Les Bretèches. Plush Vissi d'Arte from CHARD and VIOGNIER.

Chateau Ksara r w ★★→★★★ Founded 1857 by Jesuits. Excellent-value wines. Mouthfilling Res du Couvent. Top-of-range Troisième Millénaire (05 06 07). Silky Le Souverain of interest – from CAB SAUV and Arinarnoa.

Château Marsyas r (w) ★★ Promising and powerful red from impressive newcomer.

Château Musar r w ★★★ Next generation taking over. Long-lasting CAB SAUV/CINSAULT/CARIGNAN r (96' 99 00' 02 03 04). Legendary to some, overrated to others, but unique. Hochar red more approachable. Oaky white from the indigenous Obaideh and Merwah grapes.

Clos St-Thomas r w ★★ Gd-quality, deep, silky red wines. Les Emirs great-value.

Domaine de Baal r (w) ★★ Quality red from CAB SAUV, MERLOT, SYRAH. Organic v'yd.

Domaine des Tourelles r w ★→★★ Old winery reborn. Elegant Marquis des Beys.

Domaine Wardy r w ★→★★ New-World-style Private Selection. Crisp, fresh whites.

IXSIR r w ★★ Ambitious newcomer. V.gd white from VIOGNIER, SAUV, CHARD.

Karam r w ★→★★ Promising boutique winery, Jezzine (south). Cloud 9 gd value.

Massaya r w ★★ Silver Selection red is a complex Rhône-style blend showing sun and spice. Classic series is gd value. Now has the highest v'yd in the country (1,600–1,700 metres) and Lebanon's first VERMENTINO.

Turkey

There's huge potential here, and indigenous vines of real interest: look for the classic blend of Öküzgözü and Boğazkere, or the juicy, spicy Kalecik Karasi. Turkey is keen to sell abroad and is making huge efforts; worth trying for some unusual and very good flavours.

Büyülübag r (w) ★★ One of the new small, quality wineries. Gd CAB SAUV.

Corvus r w ★★→★★★ Boutique winery on Bozcaada island. Corpus is powerful.

Doluca r w ★→★★ Large winery. Karma label blends local and classic varieties.

Kavaklidere r w sp ★→★★★ Largest winery in Turkey. Specialist in local varieties. Best are plummy Pendore ÖKÜZGÖZÜ and complex, sweet Tatl Sert NARINCE.

Kayra r w ★→★★ Reincarnation of state enterprise Tekel. Californian winemaker. V.gd Imperial SHIRAZ and CAB SAUV.

Likya r w ★ Gd. CAB SAUV/BOĞAZKERE blend, Mediterranean winery.

Sarafin r w ★→★★ Gd CAB SAUV and SAUV BL. Brand owned by DOLUCA.

Sevilen r w ★ FUMÉ BLANC with great acidity. Deep SYRAH.

Turasan r w ★ Winery situated in volcanic rock of Cappodocia.

NORTH AFRICA

The Arab Spring has had little effect on wineries. Democracy may reinforce Tunisia's traditional liberal attitude to wine but religious strictures could make things more difficult. There is progress and great potential in Tunisia and Morocco.

Castel Frères Mor r p ★ Owner of Sahari, Meknes, Boulaoune facilities. Gd-value brands like Bonassia, El Baraka, Halana, Larroque, Mayole.

Celliers de Meknès, Les Mor r p w ★→★★ Dominates Moroccan market. Modern facility Chateau Roslane. Gd-value Riad Jamil CARIGNAN, fresh CHARD.

Ceptunes Tun r w ★ Gd wines, esp Jour et Nuit from classic varieties.

Domaine Atlas Tun r w ★ Austrian-Tunisian joint venture. Gd CARIGNAN and SYRAH.

Domaine Neferis Tun r p w ★→★★ Calastrasi joint venture. Selian CARIGNAN best.

Kurubis Tun r w sp ★ Producer of traditional-method sparkling wine.

Les Deux Domaines Mor r ★★ Depardieu-Bernard Magrez (Bordeaux) joint venture. Magrez Kahina and Depardieu Lumière powerful SYRAH/GRENACHE blends.

Thalvin Mor r p w ★→★★ Gd white. Spicy Tandem (★★★) SYRAH with Alain Graillot from France's Rhône Valley.

Val d'Argan Mor r p ★ Organic v'yds nr Essaouira on west coast.

Vignerons de Carthage Tun r p w ★ Best from UCCV co-op: Clipea CHARD, Kelibia dry MUSCAT and Magon Magnus red. Encouraging foreign partners.

Vins d'Algerie Alg r ★ OCNC marketing company. Top blend: Cuvée du President. Wines named after regions: Mascara, Medea and Tlemcen.

Volubilia Mor r p w ★★ Promising new joint venture. Excellent Vin Gris.

"No nation is drunken where wine is cheap." *Thomas Jefferson*

Asia & Old Russian Empire

ASIA

China is a vinous contradiction. Most of the world's wine producers are desperately trying to gain access to the Chinese market, but wine imports are still modest at 12% of sales. Only around 8% of the population drinks wine, but this still ranks China as the world's seventh-largest wine-drinking country. What China is actually doing is planting its own v'yds, and already makes 80 million cases of mostly red. It is set to become the world's largest winemaker within 50 yrs. The main areas are in Shandong and Ningxia Hui, with the largest producer, Chang Yu, controlling over 40,000ha (and making gd Icewine). International investment comes from Pernod Ricard (France), Domaine Helan Mountain and Torres (Spain), and others; Bordeaux's Château Lafite has a joint venture in Shandong. Champagne's Moët & Chandon has also signed up to a joint venture, with Ningxia Nongken. Gd domestic producers incl Grace V'yds and Silver Heights; Catai and Huadong are also gd.

India With just 60,000ha of wine vines, this is a small industry. Wine consumption is v. low (around 0.1 litres per head), little is exported. But there is desire by a number of winemakers to create gd popular wines. They are from mainly Nashik, nr Mumbai, and Karnataka, nr Goa. There are approx 60 wine producers in India, the majority are found in the state of Maharashtra. The biggest handicap is that around half the v'yds are planted with Sultana, which can never compete with the CHARD, SAUV BL, CHENIN BL, CAB SAUV, PINOT N, MERLOT planted by producers such as Chateau Indage, Grover V'yds, Sula V'yds.

Want to try Japanese wine? Look for one from the Koshu grape.

Japan has been making wine since 1875, but the rest of the world has been largely unaware of it. Over the past few yrs, small parcels of Japanese wine have found their way to the UK and now North America. Within Japan, supermarkets and top-end department stores are devoting more space to wine, with wine magazines and books also becoming more popular, although the majority of wine sold in Japan is inexpensive. Sales to young women seem to be a driver. It is a wonder that Japan can produce wine at all, with its combination of summer rain, high humidity and soils that are too fertile yet quite strongly acidic. The best areas are still in the horticultural prefectures of Yamanashi and Hokkaido, with pockets in Nagano and nr Kobe. White Koshu (a *vinifera* variety native to Japan) makes the most distinctive Japanese wine, and is often promoted abroad; most others are from hybrids such as Muscat Bailey A, Black Queen and Yama Sauvignon. There are plantings of CHARD and MERLOT, but the rules that allow up to 95% imported wine to be blended with local wine and labelled as "Wine of Japan" make it difficult to assess quality. What is significant is the number of Japanese winemakers studying in the West. There have been improvements in recent yrs. Bordeaux winemakers Denis Dubourdieu and Bernard Magrez have invested. Large corporations such as Mercian, Sapporo and Suntory still dominate the market, but the real interest, among the country's 250 wineries, lies in boutique family-owned enterprises such as Takahata Wines and Grace.

Looking for more information on grapes? Try the "Grapes" section on pp.16–26.

OLD RUSSIAN EMPIRE

Most ex-Soviet vineyards are around the Black Sea, and were planted to supply the USSR with huge volumes of cheap wine. They've had to adjust their focus since, and they're increasingly attracting international interest, but consistency is a problem. Some wineries have hired international consultants, and modern wines can be found in all countries: Armenia has a promising new project underway. Indigenous varieties from a new wave of small producers are the way forward, and Russian producers are eyeing the 2014 Winter Olympics in Sochi as an opportunity to present their wines to the world.

Russia will stop using the term *Shampanskoye* for fizz. No timetable, though.

Georgia A unique viticultural heritage is a trump card. Georgia has been making wine for over 7,000 yrs; clay vats *(kwevris)* for fermenting wine constitute part of its national identity, even if modern production methods are widely used. There are around 500 indigenous grape varieties, although red SAPERAVI (intense, structured) and white RKATSITELI (lively, refreshing) cover most of the v'yd. There are five defined areas, with 70% produced in Kakheti (southeast). Producers incl: Tbilvino, Telavi Wine Cellar, Teliani Veli, Shumi, Askaneli, Château Mukhrani. Foreign investors have developed, among others, GWS, Vinoterra, Pheasant's Tears and Schuchmann. In small producers, look for Chandrebi, Glakhuna, Khetsuriani, Metekhi.

Moldova What Moldova needs is some new impetus, and exemption from excise and duty, due in 2012, might help. The potential is there, but quality is patchy. There are four geographic areas, and European grapes are widely grown, with gd results for CHARD, SAUV BL, PINOT GR, MERLOT, CAB SAUV. Historic red blends Roşu de Purcari (Cab Sauv, Merlot, MALBEC) and Negru de Purcari (Cab Sauv, Rara Neagră, SAPERAVI) are revived by Vinăria Purcari. Quality leaders: Acorex Wine Holding, Vinăria Bostavan, Château Vartely, Dionysos Mereni, DK Intertrade, Lion Gri, Cricova (sparkling).

Gorbachev tore up half of Russia's v'yds to combat alcoholism. The result? Vodka sales rose.

Russia There are a lot of v'yds in the southwest, but fewer than half are for wine. The Krasnodar region is the largest producer, focusing on European varieties: ALIGOTÉ is particularly promising, also big improvements with CHARD, SAUV BL, MERLOT, PINOT N. Premium ranges are offered by Château le Grand Vostock (Cuvée Karsov, Chêne Royal), Fanagoria (Cru Lermont), Myskhako (Grand Reserve), Kuban Vino (Château Tamagne). Vinodelnya Vedernikoff in the Rostov region successfully experiments with local white Sibirkovy, red Krasnostop and Tsimliansky. Quality sparkling wines are revived by Abrau-Durso (Premium and Imperial), Tsimlianskiye Vina (esp original red sweet Tsimlianskoye). Rising small producers: Gai-Kodzor, Villa Victoria.

Ukraine Wine is grown around the Black Sea and on the border with Hungary. Natural conditions are favourable, but most wines are simple, semi-sweet reds made to suit local tastes. Odessa makes the most, but Crimea has greater quality potential. Traditionally the best Ukrainian wines were modelled on Sherry, Port, Madeira and Champagne. Historic producers Massandra, Koktebel, Magarach and Solnechnaya Dolina have gd fortifieds. Try Novy Svet and Artyomovsk Winery for traditional-method sparkling, Inkerman and Odessavinprom for dry wines. Names to watch: Veles (Kolonist), Guliev Wines. New association of independent winemakers is introducing gd small-volume wines.

United States

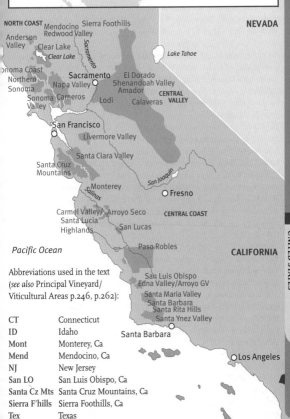

NORTH COAST

Mendocino
Anderson Redwood Valley
Valley
Clear Lake
Clear Lake

onoma Coast
Northern
Sonoma
Sonoma Carneros
Valley

Sierra Foothills

NEVADA

Lake Tahoe

Sacramento

El Dorado
Shenandoah Valley
Amador
CENTRAL
VALLEY
Lodi Calaveras

Napa Valley

San Francisco

Livermore Valley

Santa Clara Valley

Santa Cruz
Mountains

Monterey

San Joaquin

Fresno

Carmel Valley/ Arroyo Seco
Santa Lucia
Highlands San Lucas

CENTRAL COAST

Pacific Ocean

Paso Robles

CALIFORNIA

Abbreviations used in the text
(*see also* Principal Vineyard/
Viticultural Areas p.246, p.262):

San Luis Obispo
Edna Valley/Arroyo GV
Santa Maria Valley
Santa Barbara
Santa Rita Hills
Santa Ynez Valley

Santa Barbara

Los Angeles

CT	Connecticut
ID	Idaho
Mont	Monterey, Ca
Mend	Mendocino, Ca
NJ	New Jersey
San LO	San Luis Obispo, Ca
Santa Cz Mts	Santa Cruz Mountains, Ca
Sierra F'hills	Sierra Foothills, Ca
Tex	Texas
VA	Virginia
Y Car	Yamhill-Carlton, Or

CALIFORNIA

With around 3,500 wineries, California is the fourth-largest wine producer in the world. Almost 90 per cent of all wine made in North America is made in the state. A few years ago there were dire warnings that a corporate takeover of California wine was inevitable. There were fears that global giants like Constellation would dumb it all down. There is certainly room for debate about the impact of corporate ownership, but growth of small-scale artisan producers is reassuring. California wine is not about to be terminally globalized. Families are strong, and several generations are often involved – and proud of it. Many small producers, family or not (eg. Selene in Napa or M2 Wines in Lodi) bring an intellectual and emotional commitment to their wines, as well as an internet marketing savvy, that enables them to compete with the global players. American drinkers are learning and understanding more too – eg. that balance is better than brute force.

Principal vineyard areas

There are hundreds of American Viticultural Areas (AVAs) in California, some key, some insignificant. Below are the key AVAs mentioned here. *See also* box, p.270.

Alexander Valley (Alex V) Sonoma. Warm region in upper RRV. Gd Sauv Bl nr river; Cab Sauv, Zin on hillsides.

Anderson Valley (And V) Mendocino. Cool Pacific fog and winds follow Navarro River inland; gd Ries, Gewurz, Pinot N; v.gd Zin on benchlands above river.

Arroyo Seco Monterey. Warm AVA; gd Cab Sauv, Chard.

Calistoga (Cal) Napa. New AVA in northern end of Napa Valley. Red territory.

Carneros (Car) Napa, Sonoma. Cool AVA at north tip of San Francisco Bay. Gd Pinot N, Chard; Merlot on warmer sites. V.gd sparkling wine.

Dry Creek Valley (Dry CV) Sonoma. Outstanding Zin, gd Sauv Bl; gd Cab Sauv and Zin on hillsides above valley floor.

Edna Valley (Edna V) San Luis Obispo. Cool Pacific winds; v.gd.minerally Chard.

Howell Mtn Napa. Classic Napa Cab Sauv from steep hillside v'yds.

Livermore Valley (Liv V) Alameda. Historic district mostly swallowed by suburbs but regaining some standing with new-wave Cab Sauv and Chard.

Mt Veeder Napa. High mtn v'yds for gd Chard, Cab Sauv.

Napa Valley (Napa V) Napa. Cab Sauv, Merlot, Cab Fr. Look to sub-AVAs for meaningful, terroir-based wines. Note Napa V is an area within Napa.

Oakville (Oak) Napa. Prime Cab Sauv territory.

Paso Robles (P Rob) San Luis Obispo. Excellent Zin, Rhône varietals; gd Cab Sauv.

Red Hills Lake County. Promising for Cab Sauv, Zin on cooler hillsides.

Redwood Valley Mendocino. Warmer inland region; gd Zin, Cab Sauv, Sauv Bl.

Russian River Valley (RRV) Sonoma. Cool Pacific fog lingers; Pinot N, Chard, gd Zin on benchland.

Rutherford (Ruth) Napa. Outstanding Cab Sauv, esp on hillside v'yds.

St Helena Napa. Lovely balanced Cab Sauv; v.gd Sauv Bl.

Santa Lucia Highlands (Santa LH) Monterey. Higher elevation with gd Pinot N, Syrah, Rhônes.

Santa Maria Valley (Santa MV) Santa Barbara. Coastal cool; gd Pinot N, Chard and Viognier.

Sta Rita Hills (Santa RH) Santa Barbara. Excellent Pinot N; for legal reasons calls itself Sta rather than Santa.

Santa Ynez (Santa Y) Santa Barbara. Rhônes, Chard, Sauv Bl the best bet.

Sonoma Coast (Son Coast) Sonoma. V. cool climate; edgy Pinot N.

Sonoma Valley (Son V) Sonoma. Gd Chard, v.gd Zin; excellent Cab Sauv from Sonoma Mountain (Son Mtn) sub-AVA. Note Sonoma V is an area within Sonoma.

Spring Mtn Napa. Terrific Cab Sauv; v.gd Sauv Bl.

Stags Leap District (Stags L) Napa. Classic Cab Sauv; v.gd Merlot.

Recent vintages

Because of the diversity and size of the California wine-growing regions it is almost impossible to make an off-the-peg vintage report for the state. Keeping that in mind, the following assessments can be useful in a general way.

2011 Another difficult year with a below-average crop. Similar weather to 2010 except for a burst of heat during harvest, which helped to bring sugar up to balance acidity. Those who picked later reported very good quality, especially for Cab Sauv and Pinot N.

2010 A very difficult year, cool and wet. Picking of some reds continued into November. But some outstanding bottlings, especially Rhône varieties and Zin.

2009 A superb growing season, moderate temperatures. Both reds and whites show good balance and ageing potential.

2008 Uneven quality. Acid levels are low and in some areas the grapes may not have reached full ripeness.

2007 Rain; results were mixed, especially for Cab Sauv on the North Coast.

2006 Looking good, especially Pinot N and Chard. Cab Sauv improving with age. Overall, above average.

2005 Cab Sauv especially good early on but fading fast.

2004 Some of the early promise has faded. Wines for short-term consumption.

2003 A difficult year all around. Overall: spotty.

2002 The growing season was cool, and quality superior.

2001 Excellent Cab Sauv. Drink in the next year or two.

Abreu Vineyards Napa V ★★★ 05 07 09 Supple but powerful CAB SAUV: balanced for early drinking, ageing potential, too.

Acacia Car ★★★ (PINOT N) Pioneer in Carneros CHARD and Pinot N, better each vintage. Look for single-v'yd bottlings and esp the superb VIOGNIER.

Alante St Helena ★★★ Low-production, outstanding CAB SAUV from a single v'yd. Gd structure with layered finish; capable of long ageing. Too gd to be cult candidate.

Alban Vineyards Edna V ★★→★★★ Got into the Rhône game early and has stayed ahead of the pack. Top wines are VIOGNIER, GRENACHE.

Alma Rosa Sta RH ★★★ Richard Sanford pioneered PINOT N on Central Coast. He now has his own organic v'yds and the wine is better than ever. Also a temping PINOT GR and delicious Vin Gris from PINOT N.

Altamura Vineyards Napa V ★★★ 00 01 02 03 04 05 06 08 09 Splendid CAB SAUV; depth of flavour and structure to age. Also a gd SANGIOVESE.

Amador Foothills Winery Sierra F'hills ★★→★★★ Top ZIN and a bright, zingy SAUV BL. Katie's Côte (Rhône varieties) is a winner.

AmBeth Estate P Rob ★★★ Outstanding Rhône varieties, dry-farmed biodynamic v'yds. Look esp for Priscus, a blend of GRENACHE BLANC, VIOGNIER, ROUSSANNE and MARSANNE; Majestes, a red Rhône blend.

Ancient Oaks Cellars Son ★★→★★★ Delicious estate PINOT N backed by a brilliant CHARD from Sonoma County grapes.

Andrew Murray Santa B ★★★ It's Rhônes around the clock here and the hits keep coming. The SYRAH is a favourite but don't overlook the VIOGNIER and ROUSSANNE.

Antica Napa V ★★★ Elegant CAB SAUV, with a hint of an Italian accent from Piero Antinori's (*see* Italy) Napa outpost on Atlas Peak. CHARD also v.gd.

Araujo Napa V ★★★★ 01 02 03 04 05 06 08 09 Long-lasting cult CAB SAUV from historic *Eisele v'yd*.

Au Bon Climat Santa B ★★★ For decades Jim Clendenen has followed his muse and made outstanding wines, esp toasty CHARD, flavourful PINOT N, light-hearted PINOT BL. Vita Nova label for Bordeaux varieties, Podere Olivos for Italianates. *See* QUPÉ.

San Francisco still has its first known restaurant, Tadich, founded in 1849.

August Ridge P Rob ★★ A specialist in Italian varieties, incl v.gd DOLCETTO and SANGIOVESE and Jovial, a silky Super-Tuscan-style blend.

Babcock Vineyards Santa Y ★★★ The Grand Cuvée PINOT N, is brilliant. Also v.gd CHARD and SAUV BL from cool-climate v'yds.

Barnett Vineyards Napa V ★★★ Uses grapes from several v'yds for a range of v.gd to outstanding wines. Carneros CHARD is a creamy treat, as is the spicy Tina Maria PINOT N from the RRV. Also look for the Spring Mtn MERLOT, estate-grown from steeply terraced vines.

Beaulieu Vineyard Napa V ★★ →★★★ 05 07 09 The Georges de Latour Private Res CAB SAUV can still hold up its head, but the glory days of Beaulieu seem to be over. Budget wines under the Beaulieu Coast label are acceptable.

Benziger Family Winery Son V ★★★ Leaders in the biodynamic movement in California. The estate wines are esp gd. Look for CAB SAUV, MERLOT and SAUV BL.

Beringer Blass Napa ★ →★★★ (CAB SAUV) 01 02 05 07 09 10 A St Helena classic now owned by Foster's. Single-v'yd Cab Sauv Reserves can be over the top, but otherwise worthy of ageing. Velvety, powerful Howell Mtn MERLOT one of best. Look for Founder's Estate bargain bottlings. Also owns CHÂTEAU ST JEAN, ETUDE, Meridian, ST CLEMENT, STAGS' LEAP WINERY and Taz, a brawny ★★ PINOT from Santa B.

Bernardus Mont ★★ →★★★ 07 08 The Marinus Bordeaux red blend is superb; gd for early drinking but will age 10–15 yrs. V.gd SAUV BL; CHARD a step down but still first rate.

Bodegas Paso Robles P Rob ★★ →★★★ A delicious glass of Spain on the Central Coast. Spanish varieties only, incl Donna Blanca, a charming blend of GARNACHA BLANCA and MALVASIA Bianca. Vaca Negra, a blend of TEMPRANILLO and MOURVÈDRE, is a tempting elbow-bender.

Boeger Central V ★★ →★★★ Wines are not only gd value but just plain gd to drink. Best is the ZIN but also look for MERLOT and BARBERA.

Bogle Vineyards Central V ★ →★★ Attractive line of consistently gd and affordable wines. Look esp for Old-Vine ZIN.

Bokisch Lodi ★★ →★★★ Bokisch family brings Spain to Lodi. Estate wines incl v.gd GARNACHA, TEMPRANILLO and ALBARIÑO. All show gd varietal character.

Bonny Doon ★★★ →★★★★ A few years ago Randall Grahm sold his mass-market budget brands to concentrate on single-v'yd biodynamic wines, with v.gd results. Flagship *Le Cigare Volant* moved into ★★★★ territory. Italian line Ca'Del Solo better than ever, esp SANGIOVESE and DOLCETTO. Now trialling vines grown from seed as part of his quest to reflect terroir.

Bonterra *See* FETZER.

Bourassa Napa V ★★★ →★★★★ 06 Symphony, one of Napa's best CAB SAUVS, is made from cool v'yds in the south of the valley. Also a v.gd CAB FR. Veteran Napa hand Garry Galleron is winemaker.

Bronco Wine Company Founded by Fred Franzia, nephew of Ernest GALLO. Franzia uses low-cost Central Valley grapes for his famous Charles Shaw Two-Buck Chuck. Other labels incl: Napa Creek and Napa Ridge. Quality is not the point: Franzia is selling wine as a popular beverage.

Buehler Napa ★★★ 05 07 09 10 Classic Napa CAB SAUV in a pleasing brambly style with gd structure. Also look for an outstanding ZIN from Napa grapes and a v.gd CHARD from RRV fruit.

Buena Vista Car ★★★ Sonoma's oldest winery continues to produce v.gd CHARD and PINOT N from estate grapes.

Burgess Cellars Napa V ★★★ (CAB SAUV) 03 05 07 09 10 Powerful and age-worthy Cab Sauv from Howell Mtn grapes.

Cade Howell Mtn ★★★ From the PlumpJack stable, the CAB SAUV is a sleek and elegant front runner – typical herbaceous Howell Mtn style.

Cafaro Cellars Napa V ★★★ Always reliable, sometimes outstanding CAB SAUV. Recent MERLOTS have been excellent. A winery to study and follow.

Cain Cellars Napa V, ★★★ 03 05 07 09 10 Cain Five, a supple blend of the five Bordeaux reds from Spring Mtn grapes is consistently gd.

Cakebread Napa V ★★★→★★★★ 01 02 03 05 06 07 09 10 A gold standard for Napa CAB SAUV shows great balance and harmony. Also gd SAUV BL.

Calera ★★★★ 07 08 09 10 Josh Jensen fell in love with PINOT N while at Oxford. He makes three supple, fine Pinots named after v'yd blocks in the dry hills of San Benito, inland from Monterey: Reed, Seleck, Jensen; also intense VIOGNIER.

Carter Cellars Napa V ★★★ It's all about CAB SAUV here with an esp gd Hossfeld V'yds Red Blend: delicious layering of flavour; powerful finish stops well short of jammy.

Cass P Rob ★★→★★★ They just keep coming! Yet another Central Coast specialist in Rhône varieties getting it right. SYRAH is superb with deep chocolate/coffee tones and a long finish.

Caymus Napa V ★★★→★★★★★ 00 01 05 06 07 09 10 Special Selection CAB SAUV is a Napa icon, consistently one of California's most formidable: rich, intense, slow to mature. The regular Napa bottling is no slouch. Gd CHARD from Mer Soleil brand in Monterey, incl an unoaked Chard called Silver.

Ceja Vineyards Napa ★★→★★★ An immigrant success story, Ceja was established and is owned by Mexican former v'yd workers. CAB SAUV and Carneros CHARD tops.

Cesar Toxqui Cellars Mend ★★★ Toxqui came north from Mexico when he was 16, and landed his first job at FETZER. He makes a tiny amount of PINOT N from organic v'yds in Lake and Mendocino counties. Superb: well-worth the search.

Chalone Mont ★★★ High above the Salinas Valley in Monterey, this historic mtn estate is not resting on its laurels. There is a v.gd flinty CHARD and a rich and palate-pleasing PINOT N.

Chappellet Napa V ★★★ 03 05 06 07 08 09 10 Serious age-worthy CAB SAUV, *esp Signature label*. Pleasing CHARD; gd CAB FR, MERLOT. Dry CHENIN BL is one of the best.

Charles Krug Napa V ★★→★★★ Historically important winery is on the comeback trail following investment in new equipment. SAUV BL is excellent, as is the sleek, elegant CAB SAUV.

Château Montelena Napa V ★★★→★★★★ (CHARD) 08 09 10 (CAB SAUV) 01 03 05 06 07 09 10 Veteran classic winery. Supple Cab Sauv drinks well young but goes many years; v.gd Chard also a keeper.

Château St Jean ★★→★★★ Sonoma standout has gone through many changes since Richard Arrowood days, but still makes v.gd SAUV BL and CHARD. A red blend, Cinq Cépages, made from five Bordeaux red varieties, rises to ★★★★ on occasion.

Chimney Rock Stags L ★★★ (CAB SAUV) 01 03 05 07 09 10 V.gd, understated Cab Sauv from Stags L grapes is delicious and age-worthy.

Christopher Creek Son ★★→★★★ Delicous VIOGNIER from estate grapes: outstanding apéritif. Brambly CAB SAUV also v.gd, estate PETITE SIRAH is brooding, concentrated.

Claiborne & Churchill Santa B ★★★ The focus here is on Alsace-style whites, with a consistently top-rated RIES, v.gd PINOT GR and GEWURZ.

Clark-Clauden Napa V ★★★→★★★★ Balanced and elegant CAB SAUV with focused fruit and lasting wraparound flavours. V.gd SAUV BL. Much **underrated** producer.

Clayhouse P Rob ★★ →★★★ Old-vine PETITE SIRAH restores faith in variety: lovely black cherry, chocolate and black pepper, and a long, balanced finish. More, please.

Cliff Lede Stags L ★★★ Balanced, elegant CAB SAUV from Stags L AVA is built to age.

Clos du Bois Son ★★→★★★ Briarcrest CAB SAUV and Calcaire CHARD can be v.gd. Rest of line-up is quaffable everyday wines. No problem there.

Clos du Val Napa V ★★★ Consistently elegant CAB SAUVs, much underrated. *Chard is a delight* and a SÉM/SAUV BL blend called Ariadne is a charmer.

Cobb Wines Son Coast ★★★ PINOT N and CHARD are gd examples of cool-climate wines: crisp acidity and restrained fruit.

Conn Creek Napa V ★★★ 01 03 05 06 07 09 10 Elegant CAB SAUV with gd structure, sourced from several Napa V v'yds. A gd candidate for the cellar.

Constellation ★→★★★ Owns wineries in California, NY, Washington State, Canada, Chile, Australia and NZ. Produces 90+ million cases a year, the world's largest wine company. Once a bottom-feeder, now going for the top, incl ROBERT MONDAVI, FRANCISCAN V'YD, Estancia, Mt Veeder, RAVENSWOOD, Simi, among others.

Corison Napa V ★★★★ 95 96 97 99 00 01 02 05 06 07 09 10 Cathy Corison is a national treasure. While many in Napa V follow the $iren call of powerhouse wines for big scores, small satisfaction, Corison continues to make flavoursome, *age-worthy Cab Sauv.*

Cuvaison Napa V ★★★ (CAB SAUV) 01 02 05 07 09 Long-term, reliable producer of v.gd CHARD and SYRAH from Carneros v'yds and a most impressive CAB SAUV from Mt Veeder.

Darioush Napa V ★★★ 06 07 09 Napa CAB SAUV with a decided Bordeaux tilt. The Signature Cab Sauv has depth and power, a silky, luscious centre and long finish. MERLOT can be v.gd, VIOGNIER from Oak Knoll AVA is an unexpected treat.

Dashe Cellars Dry CV ★★★ All about Dry CV ZIN, with several single-v'yd bottlings. The wines are classic Dry Creek: balanced, layered with black raspberry, clove and black pepper. Should improve over 5–10 yrs.

David Bruce Santa Cz Mts ★★★ Legendary mtn estate is still on top of the game with powerful, long-lasting CHARD and superb PINOT N.

Davis Bynum Son ★★★ Bynum pioneered often superb single-v'yd PINOT N in RRV. CHARD is lean and minerally with a silky mouthfeel. Winery now owned by Rodney Strong V'yds.

Dehlinger Son ★★★★ (PINOT N) 06 07 08 09 10 Outstanding Pinot N from estate RRV v'yd. Also gd CHARD and SYRAH.

Delicato Vineyards ★→★★ Central Valley jug producer moving upscale with purchase of Monterey v'yds and several new bottlings from Lodi grapes. V.gd quality at bargain prices.

Diamond Creek Napa V ★★★★ 95 99 00 01 03 06 07 09 10 Austere, stunning cult CABS from hilly v'yd nr Calistoga, go by names of v'yd blocks: Gravelly Meadow, Volcanic Hill, Red Block Terrace. Wines age beautifully. One of Napa's jewels.

Thinking pink

With rosé sales soaring in the USA, more producers are beginning to take the pink stuff seriously. At this point, imports dominate the market, but a number of producers are making a strong case for California and Pacific Northwest rosé. Barnard Griffin, BONNY DOON, DONKEY & GOAT, Edmunds St John, L'UVAGGIO and STEPHEN ROSS all make outstanding examples.

Domaine Carneros Car ★★★ Vintage Blanc de Blancs La Rêve is one of the state's top bubblies. Also impressive still PINOT N, CHARD. Owned by Champagne Taittinger.

Domaine Chandon Napa V ★★→★★★ V.gd Rosé sparkler and a NV Res called Etoile are worth a glass or three. Outpost of Moët & Chandon (Champagne).

Dominus Estate Napa V ★★★★ 97 99 01 02 05 06 07 08 09 10 Red Bordeaux blend is simply beautiful, slow to open but repays cellar time with layers of deep flavours. Owned by Christian Moueix (Bordeaux).

Donkey & Goat ★★★ One of the trendy "urban wineries" that have sprung up in the San Francisco Bay Area. Wines hard to find but worth a search, esp two bottlings of SYRAH: El Dorado in the Sierra F'hills, and old vines in Mendocino.

Dry Creek Vineyard Dry CV ★★→★★★ Clones of old-vine ZIN; remarkably impressive wines. SAUV (FUMÉ) BL set standard for California for decades and is still v.gd. Pleasing CHENIN BL.

Duckhorn Vineyards Napa V ★★★→★★★★ Known for dark, tannic, plummy-ripe single-v'yd MERLOTS (esp Three Palms) and CAB SAUV-based blend Howell Mtn. Also Golden Eye PINOT N, made in a robust style. Also makes ZIN/Cab Sauv blend in Paraduxx, a second Napa V winery.

Dunn Vineyards Howell Mtn ★★★★ 91 95 97 99 01 03 06 07 09 10 Randy Dunn makes superb and *intense Cab Sauv* from Howell Mtn that ages magnificently; milder bottlings from valley floor. One of few Napa V winemakers to resist the stampede to jammy, lush wines to curry critics' favour.

Dutton-Goldfield Son ★★★→★★★★ Incredibly gd PINOT N and CHARD, from coastal v'yds, from winemaker-grower duo who pay attention to terroir. Wines are modern California classics.

Eagles Trace Napa V ★★★ 04 05 07 09 10 The red Bordeaux blend from Conn Valley estate v'yds has depth and exceptional power without going over the top. Latitude 38 bottling is a splendid homage to Bordeaux.

Eberle San LO ★★→★★★ Long-time winemaker Gary Eberle offers a solid CAB SAUV and a range of Rhône styles, most in a muscular but balanced style; look esp for Steinback v'yd SYRAH. Also gd VIOGNIER.

Edna Valley Vineyard Edna V ★★★ Lovely SAUV BL for openers, then crisp, (tropical) fruity CHARD. Finish with impressive SYRAH.

Elke Vineyards And V ★★→★★★ One of several new producers in this cool spot, Mary Elke makes an elegant and silky PINOT N in the Diamond series, and a beginner's wine with forward fruit under the Mary Elke label.

Elyse Vineyards Napa V ★★★ 05 08 09 10 Small lots of single-v'yd CAB SAUV; bright fruit with layered flavours and excellent ageing potential, esp Tietjen and Morisoli. V.gd old-vine ZIN, also from Morisoli. Jacob Franklin brand features gd Rhône blends.

Envy Cellars Napa V ★★★→★★★★ Napa superstar winemaker Nils Venge, focused on PETITE SIRAH. A stunning Vaca Mtn bottling, dark fruit balanced with peppery spice. A second bottling from Nord V'yd is v.gd, with a lighter hand on the fruit.

Etude Napa *See* BERINGER BLASS.

Far Niente Napa V ★★★ (CAB SAUV) 00 01 03 05 07 09 Full-bodied and rich Cab Sauv and CHARD from estate grapes. Opulence is the goal; can go over the top.

Fetzer Vineyards Mend ★★→★★★ A leader in organic/sustainable viticulture, Fetzer has produced consistent-value wines from least-expensive range (Sundial, Valley Oaks) to brilliant Res wines. Also owns BONTERRA v'yds (all organic grapes) where ROUSSANNE and MARSANNE are stars.

Ficklin Vineyards Madera ★★★ Lush, delicious Port-style dessert wines made from classic Portuguese varieties.

Firestone Santa Y ★★ A pleasing off-dry RIES for starters, followed by first-rate SAUV BL. Discovery series features off-the-beaten track wines, incl an esp tasty MOSCATO.

Flora Springs Wine Co Napa V ★★★ Two Meritage wines made from hillside v'yds, red Trilogy and white Soliloquy, are always on the A-list. Regular bottlings of CAB SAUV and MERLOT are gd to v.gd.

Flowers Vineyard & Winery Son ★★★ Flowers has won well-deserved praise for intense coastal PINOT N and CHARD.

Foppiano Son ★★→★★★ One of the grand old families. You can count on the ZIN every time, but look esp for PETITE SIRAH, better known as "petty sir" among the California rearguard. Also an appealing CAB SAUV.

Climate change could make 50% of Napa too hot for Cabernet in 30 years.

Forman Vineyard Napa V ★★★★ 00 01 03 05 07 09 Terrific CAB SAUV and intense CHARD from hillside v'yds are outstanding and age-worthy.

Franciscan Vineyard Napa V ★★★ Quality has been maintained under CONSTELLATION ownership, esp. top-of-the-line red Magnificat and the Cuvée Sauvage CHARD. Gd budget wines under Estancia label.

Freeman RRV ★★★ Freeman has developed a cult following with outstanding cool-climate PINOT N (Akiko's Cuvée from Son Coast) and RRV Pinot N.

Freemark Abbey Napa V ★★★→★★★★ *Stylish* CAB SAUV worthy of cellar time from this often-underrated classic producer. Look esp for single-v'yd Sycamore and Bosche bottlings.

Freestone Son Coast ★★★ CHARD and PINOT N from vines only a few miles from the Pacific show intense fruit (esp Chard). Owned by Joseph Phelps, producer of top Napa CAB SAUV.

Frog's Leap Ruth ★★★ 01 02 03 05 07 09 10 Small winery, as charming as its name (and T-shirts). Lean, *minerally Sauv Bl*, toasty CHARD, spicy ZIN. Supple and delicious MERLOT, CAB SAUV. Converting to organic and biodynamic; recent wines more depth and intensity. Not a coincidence.

Gallo, E & J ★→★★ California's biggest winery is an easy target for wine snobs, but in the long view Gallo has done more to open up the American palate to wine than any other winery. Its 1960s Hearty Burgundy was groundbreaking. Gallo still does the basic commodity wines, but has also created an imposing line of regional varieties, such as Anapauma, Marcellina, Turning Leaf and more, all wines of modest quality, perhaps, but predictable and affordable.

Gallo Sonoma Son ★★→★★★ Coastal outpost of Central Valley giant sources grapes from several Sonoma v'yds. CAB SAUV can be v.gd, esp the single-v'yd. CHARD also better than average. A gd PINOT GR under the McMurray label.

Gary Farrell Son ★★★ Highly regarded PINOT N and CHARD from the Russian River. Also look for ZIN and a v.gd SAUV BL. Encounter, a red Bordeaux blend, is also v.gd.

Gloria Ferrer Car ★★★ Built by Spain's Freixenet for sparkling wine, now producing spicy CHARD and bright, silky PINOT N and other varietals, all from Carneros fruit. Bubbly has developed a sweet tooth.

Grace Family Vineyard Napa V ★★★★ 01 03 05 06 07 09 10 Stunning CAB SAUV shaped for long ageing. One of the few cult wines that might actually be worth the price.

Grgich Hills Cellars Napa V ★★★ An historic name; minerally SAUV (FUME) BL, supple CHARD even capable of ageing. Balanced and elegant CAB SAUV, ripe ZIN from Sonoma grapes.

Groth Vineyards Napa V ★★★ 97 99 00 01 05 06 07 09 10 Estate CAB SAUV has big, wraparound flavours made for ageing.

Gustafson Family Estates Dry CV ★★→★★★ A terrific SYRAH and tempting PETITE SIRAH lead the way but watch for the ZIN and don't overlook the SAUV BL.

Hall Napa V ★★★ A stunning Diamond Mtn District CAB SAUV ★★★★ and a v.gd St Helena Bergfeld Cab Sauv. Minerally SAUV BL is delicious.

Handley Cellars And V ★★★ Mila Handley makes excellent CHARD, GEWURZ and PINOT N from And V v'yds. V.gd SAUV BL and Chard from Dry CV; a small amount of intense sparkling wine as well as excellent family's Dry CV v'yds.

Hanna Winery Son ★★★ A Sonoma classic with an outstanding SAUV BL and a reliable (often v.gd) CAB SAUV.

Hanzell Son ★★★★ (CHARD) 07 08 09 10 (PINOT N) 05 07 08 09 10 The 1950s pioneer. Small producer of outstanding and site-specific Chard *and Pinot N* from estate vines. Always gd; quality level has risen sharply in the past few yrs. Deserves to be ranked with the best of California.

Harlan Estate Napa V ★★★★ 06 07 09 10 Concentrated, sleek cult CAB SAUV from perfectionist estate commanding luxury prices. Harlan owns Meadowood Club.

HdV Wines Car ★★★ Fine, complex *Chard* with a mineral edge from grower Larry Hyde's v'yd in conjunction with Aubert de Villaine of DRC (France).

Heitz Cellar Napa V ★★★ 01 03 05 07 09 History-making, deeply flavoured, minty CAB SAUV from Martha's V'yd. Bella Oaks and newer Trailside V'yd rival but can't match Martha. Some feel quality has slipped in recent vintages.

Heller Estate Mont ★★ *Gd organic Cab Sauv* and a charming CHENIN BL.

Hess Collection, The Napa V ★★→★★★ CAB SAUV from Mt Veeder estate v'yd hits a new quality level; recent addition of Lake County SAUV BL is v.gd. CHARD crisp and bright; Hess Select label v.gd value.

Hobbs, Paul ★★★ RRV PINOT N is lush and silky; CHARD (also from RRV) is creamy with a gd bit of oak. Napa V CAB SAUV is supple, with hints of bitter chocolate and gd structure.

Howell at the Moon Howell Mtn ★★★ 06 07 Behind the painful pun is a terrific bottle of CAB SAUV: brambly fruit within an elegant structure. Cab Sauv is all they do and they do it right.

Inglenook Oak *See* NIEBAUM COPPOLA.

Iron Horse Vineyards Son ★★★ The bubbly is first rate, as is the tempting (another glass, please) CHARD from RRV v'yds. A bright and delicious CAB SAUV is made from Alex V grapes.

Ironstone Sierra F'hills ★→★★ A destination winery with an eye on the tourist trade, true, but also v.gd old-vine ZIN from Lodi and a delicious elbow-bender CAB FR from estate vines.

Jessie's Grove Lodi ★★★ Long-time grower checks in with a complex old-vine ZIN.

Jordan Alex V ★★★★ (CAB SAUV) 98 99 00 01 02 05 07 09 10 Rob Davis makes consistently balanced and elegant wines from Alex V estate. The Cab Sauv is an homage to Bordeaux – and it lasts. Minerally and delicious CHARD is ditto to Burgundy. Davis is our choice for winemaker of the yr.

Joseph Phelps Napa V ★★★★ (Insignia) 97 99 00 01 03 05 06 07 08 09 10 A true Napa "first growth". Phelps CAB SAUVS, esp Insignia and Backus, are always nr the top, capable of long ageing.

Joseph Swan Son ★★★ Long-time RRV producer of intense ZIN and classy PINOT N, capable of ageing in the 10-yr range.

Juslyn Spring Mtn ★★→★★★★ 05 07 Difficult to find but worth the effort, the CAB SAUV is an iconic Spring Mtn red. Also look for Perry's Blend, made from red Bordeaux varieties.

J Vineyards Son ★★★ Judy Jordan left the family winery several years ago and established her own RRV winery. The creamy, rich Brut sparkling wine is always one of state's best. Also look for v.gd PINOTS N and GR.

Kendall-Jackson ★★→★★★ Legendary market-driven CHARD and CAB SAUV. Even more noteworthy for developing a diversity of wineries under the umbrella of Artisans & Estates (*see* STONESTREET).

Kenefick Ranch Napa V ★→★★★ A gd portfolio from a new producer in the new

> **White Rhône rising**
> As West Coast wine-growers expand and deepen their knowledge of
> Rhône varieties, GRENACHE BLANC is attracting more attention. Early
> on, most considered it simply as a blending wine, but it could be
> California's new secret weapon. Gd example is ZACA MESA's, with zesty
> layers of flavour. Other gd choices: BONNY DOON, PRESTON, TABLAS CREEK.

Calistoga AVA. Pickett Road Red is a supple Bordeaux blend based on MERLOT.
Pickett Road White blend – VIOGNIER and GRENACHE BLANC – is also v.gd.

Kent Rasmussen Winery Car ★★★ Hard to choose between the mineral and
lingering CHARD and the delicious rounded fruit of the PINOT N. Ramsay is an
alternative label for small production lots.

Kenwood Vineyards Son ★★→★★★ (Jack London CAB SAUV) 01 03 05 07 08 09
Consistently gd quality at fair prices. The Jack London Cab Sauv is high point.
Several v.gd bottlings of ZIN and a gulpable, delicious SAUV BL round out the line.

Kistler Vineyards RRV ★★★ There's been a dramatic change of direction here, with
a welcome move away from the powerful, oaky CHARD to a more subtle version.
PINOT N is also showing more restraint.

Konsgaard Napa ★★★★ Judge V'yd CHARD may be the best Chard in California, with
intense minerality and great power. The rocky v'yd gives just one ton of grapes
per acre. Napa V Chard, from Carneros grapes, is also splendid.

Korbel ★ Largest US producer of classic-method fizz with focus on fruit flavours.
Recently added an organic bottling. Take along on your next picnic.

Krupp Brothers Napa V ★★★ 05 06 07 09 10 Bold Veraison CAB SAUV: concentrated
richness that never loses its balance. Should age well. Also gd CHARD.

Kunde Estate Son V ★★★ The family has grown grapes in Sonoma for decades. The
wines reflect their experience, incl understated CHARD and silky MERLOT. Try the
fruity VIOGNIER or the fruit-forward SAUV BL.

Lamborn Howell Mtn ★★★ One more intense CAB SAUV from Howell Mtn grapes.
Big, juicy ZIN is also popular.

Landmark Son V ★★→★★★ CHARD from the Bien Nacido V'yd in the Santa MV has
deep fruit flavours edged with lemon zest and dried fruit. Look also for Detour
PINOT N from Son Coast grapes.

Lane Tanner Santa B ★★★ Owner-winemaker makes v. personal and superb single-
v'yd PINOT N from Santa Barbara v'yds, reflecting terroir with quiet elegance.

Lang & Reed Napa V ★★★ Bright Loire-style CAB FR makes you wonder why more
California winemakers don't take the variety seriously.

La Rochelle ★★→★★★ PINOT N specialist; wines from cool-climate v'yds in California
and Oregon. Look esp for Son Coast bottling from Four Sisters V'yd; opens with
pretty red-cherry fruit and finishes with yummy dark-spice notes.

Laurel Glen Son V ★★★★ 01 03 05 06 09 10 Patrick Campbell made some of
California's best CAB SAUV, supple, balanced and age-worthy, for more than 30 yrs
from a steep v'yd on Son Mtn. He sold up in 2011; fans hope the new owners
won't change a thing.

Lohr, J ★★→★★★ Excellent CAB SAUV and a series of Meritage red wines are first rate,
made chiefly from Paso Robles fruit. Cypress is gd budget line.

Long Meadow Napa V ★★★ Now a destination winery in Napa; doesn't seem to have
hurt the wines. Supple and age-worthy CAB SAUV improves every vintage. Lively
Graves-style SAUV BL is brilliant. V'yd is organically farmed.

Longoria Santa B, Ca ★★★ Veteran Rick Longoria consistently crafts balanced and
supple Sta RH CHARD; also v.gd ALBARIÑO and TEMPRANILLO. They speak Spanish
with a New World accent.

Louis M Martini Napa ★★★ Napa treasure; has made a brilliant comeback since 2002 Gallo buy-out. Gallo took a hands-off approach, giving Mike Martini the tools and letting him work with the great CAB SAUV and ZIN v'yds the family had owned for decades. Marvellous wines once again. Look esp for Cab Sauv from Monte Rosso and Alex V.

Lucas Lodi ★★→★★★ The ZINS go to the head of the class, for sure, but the Lucas family also has a way with CHARD.

L'Uvaggio ★★→★★★ Former ROBERT MONDAVI winemaker Jim Moore specializes in Italian varieties. Outstanding BARBERA leads way; also look for VERMENTINO from Lodi and splendid rosé reminiscent of northern Spain. Can't go wrong here.

M2 Wines Lodi ★★→★★★ Lodi old-vine ZIN gets top marks. Lani's V'yd, a northern-Rhône lookalike from the Sierra F'hills, is terrific.

McIntire Vineyards Santa LH ★★→★★★ McIntire family, long-time growers, now make their own wines and do a fine job. PINOT N offers rich cherry fruit backed by gd acidity. Brilliant, Burgundian-style CHARD: deep minerality and long finish.

MacPhail Son ★★★ Intense and tightly wound PINOT N from Son Coast and And V. Silky and luscious rounded flavours.

Marimar Torres Estate RRV ★★★ (CHARD) 07 08 09 10 (PINOT N) 03 05 06 07 08 09 Several bottlings of Chard and Pinot N from Don Miguel estate v'yd in Green Valley. Chard is complex, sometimes rather edgy, with gd ageing potential. Acero Don Miguel Chard is unoaked, *a lovely expression of Chard fruit*. Pinot N from Doña Margarita v'yd, nr the ocean, is intense and surprisingly rich for young vines. V'yds now farmed organically and moving towards biodynamics.

Looking for more information on grapes? Try the "Grapes" section on pp.16–26.

Masut Mend ★★★ Jacob and Ben Fetzer, third generation of the respected family, made an awesome debut with a 2009 PINOT N, gentle yet assertive fruit backed by a solid tannic structure. Keep an eye on the kids.

Mayacamas Vineyards Mt Veeder ★★★ Pioneer Napa boutique with rich CHARD and firm (but no longer steel-hard) *Cab Sauv, capable of long ageing*. Also a gd SAUV BL.

Merry Edwards RRV ★★★→★★★★ PINOT N doesn't get much better than this salute to Burgundy with a bit of California. The wines are rounded, layered with flavour and edged with dark spice. As a bonus there is a lovely SAUV BL.

Merryvale Napa V ★★★ Remarkable MERLOT, supple and balanced. CAB SAUV and SAUV BL also v.gd.

Milano Mend ★★★ Artisan producer of ZIN, CAB SAUV, worth seeking out. Hopland Cuvée, unusual blend of Cab Sauv and PINOT N, is remarkably gd.

Miner Family Vineyards Oak ★★★ Powerful CAB SAUV-based reds with gd ageing potential. Look esp for the Icon bottling, a blend of Bordeaux varieties. The family also owns OAKVILLE RANCH.

Miraflores Sierra F'hills ★★ SYRAH from El Dorado County v'yds is v.gd, with bright, engaging fruit and gd balance. VIOGNIER is also gd with excellent varietal *typicité*.

Miura ★★→★★★ Master Sommelier Emmanuel Kemiji makes several wines from v'yds on the Central Coast and Napa, and in Spain. (Miura is a breed of fighting bull.) Best bet is Antiqv2s, PINOT N from Santa LH. Also look for Cuvée Kemiji, a CAB SAUV-based blend.

Morgan Santa LH ★★★ Top-end single-v'yd PINOT NS and CHARDS. Esp fine, unoaked Chard Metallico. Estate Double L v'yd farmed organically. New Rhônish entry Côtes du Crows is charming.

Moshin Vineyards RRV ★★→★★★★ Creamy, rich CHARD is the go-to wine here. SAUV BL and PINOT N are also worth a look.

Mumm Napa Valley Napa V ★★★ Stylish bubbly, esp *delicious Blanc de Noirs* and a rich, complex DVX single-v'yd fizz to age a few yrs in the bottle.

Nalle Son ★★★ Doug Nalle makes lovely ZINS from Dry CV fruit; juicy and delicious young, matures gracefully.

Napa Wine Company Napa V ★★★ Largest organic grape-grower in Napa V with 600+ acres. Most is sold to other producers. Also operates a custom-crush facility for several small premium producers, incl some of the cults. Temescal CAB SAUV is its own wine and v.gd indeed: concentrated but supple on the palate with gd fruit and acidity.

PS I Love You has its own meaning in California: PS = Petite Sirah.

Navarro Vineyards And V ★★★ RIES and GEWURZ from this cool-climate pioneer are outstanding. But the star turn is PINOT N, made in two styles: an estate-bottled homage to Burgundy from And V grapes, and a brisk and juicy bottling from bought-in grapes.

Newton Vineyards Spring Mtn ★★★→★★★★ (Icon) 03 05 06 07 09 10 Beautiful English-founded estate with three tiers of wines: Icon, a Bordeaux blend; The Puzzle, site-specific bottlings of CAB SAUV, MERLOT and CHARD, and the fruit-forward Red Label. Supple and elegant expressions of mtn v'yds. Gd ageing potential.

Nickel & Nickel ★★★ Specialist in exceptional terroir-driven single-v'yd CAB SAUV from Napa V and Sonoma. Line-up changes with each vintage but always something to treasure.

Niebaum-Coppola Estate Ruth ★★★→★★★★ (Rubicon) Baby of "Godfather" Francis Ford Coppola. In 2011 he acquired the historic name of INGLENOOK, as well as the house and land. Bordeaux blend Rubicon is the star, can be jammy; new Château Margaux (Bordeaux) winemaker should find more elegance. Edizione Pennino is delightfully old-fashioned ZIN. Lovely Blancaneaux (white blend). Coppola also owns CHÂTEAU SOUVERAIN and continues to expand production.

Niven Family Estates Edna V ★★→★★★ The Niven stable incl five San Luis Obispo wineries. Baileyana Firepeak Cuvée CHARD is in the classic tropical-fruit style of the Central Coast. Trenza Blanco, a blend of ALBARIÑO and GRENACHE BLANC, is excellent.

Novy Family ★★ Owns several v'yds in California and Oregon. RRV VIOGNIER esp outstanding; ripe pear fruit and rounded flavours. Sister label Siduri, for single-v'yd PINOT N, can be v.gd.

Oakville Ranch Oak ★★★ Sometimes overlooked jewel, this estate on the Silverado Trail (owned by MINER FAMILY) makes consistently gd CAB SAUV and a creamy CHARD.

Ojai Santa B ★★★ A v.gd range of Rhône varieties is offered by former AU BON CLIMAT partner Adam Tolmach. Look esp for the SYRAH.

Opus One Oak ★★★★ 05 07 09 Mondavi-Rothschild creation in the heart of Napa has made glorious wines; sometimes not quite. Excellent current form.

Pahlmeyer Napa V ★★★ Supple MERLOTS are a treat; CAB SAUV can be v.gd, if sometimes a tad too tannic.

Parducci Mend ★★→★★★★ Reliable, gd-value wines from historic winery. Recent vintages have raised the bar. True Grit PETITE SIRAH is a brilliant new example of why this orphan variety is getting new respect and attention in California.

Patel Napa V ★★★ 07 08 09 10 Limited production of CAB SAUV and a MERLOT-dominated Bordeaux blend can be hard to find but worth the search. The Cab is esp gd, with layers of flavours and a long finish. Gd ageing potential.

Patianna Vineyards RRV ★★★ Patty Fetzer makes incredibly gd SAUV BL from biodynamioc v'yds in Son County. SYRAH almost matches it.

Paul Dolan Mend ★★★ Long-time organic and biodynamic leader Paul Dolan offers outstanding ZIN, SYRAH, CAB SAUV, CHARD and SAUV BL from North Coast v'yds.

Pedroncelli Son ★★ Old hand in Dry CV producing bright, elbow-bending ZIN, CAB SAUV and a solid CHARD.

Peltier Station Lodi ★★→★★★ Growers for 50 yrs+, the Schatz family's own wines are gd to outstanding. Look esp for the refreshing VIOGNIER and a yummy ZIN.

Periano Lodi ★★ Start with the brilliant VIOGNIER, but save room for the fruity BARBERA and a lovely CHARD, all gd examples of new-wave Lodi, bright and user-friendly.

Peter Michael Winery Son ★★★★ Two CHARDS on offer: a powerful and complex Howell Mtn, can be stunning; and a more supple Alex V bottling. Tight CAB SAUV.

Philip Togni Vineyards Spring Mtn ★★★→★★★★ 00 01 03 05 07 09 10 Veteran winemaker makes v. *fine, long-lasting Cab Sauv* from Spring Mtn.

Pine Ridge Napa V ★★★ Tannic and concentrated CAB SAUVS, from several Napa V v'yds, have a loyal following. The just off-dry CHENIN BL is a treat.

Preston Dry CV ★★★ Lou Preston is a demanding terroirist, making Dry CV icons, such as ZIN and fruity, marvellous BARBERA. New are Rhône varieties and an esp gd GRENACHE BLANC.

Quady Winery Central V ★★→★★★ Imaginative Madera MUSCAT dessert wines incl famed orangey Essensia, rose-petal-flavoured Elysium and Moscato d'Asti-like Electra. A recent addition, Vya Vermouth, is an excellent apéritif.

Quintessa Napa V ★★★ Red blend from this biodynamic mid-valley estate shows supple balance and fruit in an homage-to-Bordeaux style. Can age.

Quivira Dry CV ★★★ A v.gd range of Rhône varieties from this biodynamic estate, but it is, after all, in Dry CV and the delicious ZIN steals the show.

Latest wine fad among rap and hip-hop stars? Moscato, of all things.

Qupé Santa B ★★★ A remarkable range of wines, esp a brilliant *Marsanne*. A glass or two of PINOT BL or SYRAH would also be welcome.

Radio-Coteau Son ★★★ La Neblina PINOT N from Son Coast is terrific, with gd structure and rounded fruit. SYRAH also v.gd.

Rafanelli, A Son ★★★ ZIN specialist makes intense wines with bright, brambly fruit characteristic of Dry CV ZIN. It will age, but it's so delightful young, why bother?

Ramey Wine Cellars RRV ★★★ V.gd single-v'yd CAB SAUV from Napa V, and rich and complex CHARD from cooler v'yds, esp the Hudson V'yd Napa V-Carneros. Don't pass on the intense and complex Son Coast SYRAH.

Ravenswood ★→★★ Once the shining star of California ZIN, the lustre has dimmed under CONSTELLATION ownership. Still, the single-v'yd bottlings are worth a look.

Raymond Vineyards and Cellar Napa V ★★★ 01 03 05 07 09 10 CAB SAUV is the story here and it is well told. The wines are balanced, understated but capable of long-term ageing, esp the Generations blend.

Ridge Santa Cz Mts ★★★★ (CAB SAUV) 99 00 01 03 05 07 08 09 10 It's difficult to state how important Ridge founder Paul Draper has been to modern California wine. Supple and harmonious estate *Montebello Cab Sauv* is superb. Also outstanding single-v'yd ZIN from Sonoma, Napa V, Sierra F'hills and P Rob. Most Zin has gd ageing potential. And don't overlook *outstanding Chard* from wild-yeast fermentation. Keep up the gd work, Paul.

Robert Mondavi ★→★★★ Top are Napa V Res, followed by Napa V appellation series (eg. Carneros CHARD, Oakville CAB SAUV, etc.), with Napa V bottlings at the base. Various Central Coast wines and Robert Mondavi-Woodbridge from Lodi are gd-value brands. Robert Mondavi is owned by CONSTELLATION.

Rochioli Vineyards & Winery Son ★★★ Look for Special Cuvée PINOT N, a brilliant and complex wine from top long-time RRV grower. Also v.gd SAUV BL.

Roederer Estate And V ★★★★ The house style here tends to restraint, showing supple elegance, esp in luxury cuvée L'Ermitage. Overall, one of the top three sparklers in California and hands-down the best rosé. Owned by Champagne Roederer.

Rosenblum Cellars ★★→★★★ Above-average range of ZIN and Rhône varieties from v'yds scattered throughout the state. Line-up changes with the vintage.

Rusack Santa B ★★→★★★ The story here is gd-quality wines at gd-value prices. Excellent SAUV BL, SYRAH and GRENACHE. CHARD steals the show with fruit, structure and finish.

Saddleback Cellars Napa V ★★★→★★★★ 01 05 06 07 08 10 Owner-winemaker Nils Venge is a legend in Napa V. Lush ZIN and long-lived CAB SAUV. In some vintages he makes a super SAUV BL.

St Clement Napa V ★★★ 99 00 01 03 05 06 07 09 10 (CAB SAUV) Oroppas, a Cab Sauv-based blend, is outstanding. MERLOT and CHARD can be v.gd.

St Francis Son ★★★ 00 01 03 05 06 07 09 10 The Wild Oak V'yd CHARD has a distinct Burgundian accent and is super. Also a rich, concentrated CAB SAUV. Old-vine ZIN is textbook stuff.

Saintsbury Car ★★★ Intense PINOT N is denser than most in Carneros and will age. A more light-hearted version is bottled as Garnet. There is also a nicely balanced and full-flavoured CHARD.

Santa Cruz Mountain Vineyard Santa Cz Mts ★★→★★★ Wines of strong varietal character from estate grapes, incl v.gd PINOT N and exceptional CAB SAUV – big, concentrated and age-worthy.

Sattui, V ★★ King of direct-only sales (ie. winery door or mail order). Wines made in a rustic, drink-now style. Reds are best, esp CAB SAUV, ZIN.

Sbragia Dry CV ★★★ Ed Sbragia, long-time winemaker at BERINGER BLASS, now has his own winery and a splendid selection of single-v'yd CAB SAUV and MERLOT. Classic California character, concentrated but not over-the-top. Also a v.gd SAUV BL from estate vines.

Scenic Root N Coast ★★→★★★ Jonathan and Susan Pey make small lots of wine from cool North Coast v'yds. Textbook CHARD from Napa-Carneros and Yountville is a classic – a touch of butter, balanced and long. CAB from Oakville is v.gd. Coastal PINOT N always a winner.

Schramsberg Napa V ★★★→★★★★ J Schram, the creamy and utterly delicious luxury cuvée, has been called California's Krug. Blanc de Noirs is outstanding, as is Brut, while Res is rich and intense. Second label Mirabelle is v. agreeable. Plus v.gd CAB SAUV, J Davies, from mtn estate vines. Schramsberg stands test of time.

Screaming Eagle Napa V ★★★★ Small lots of cult CAB SAUV at luxury prices for those who like and can afford that kind of thing.

Seasmoke Santa RH ★★★ All about PINOT N and CHARD: Ten Pinot leads the way; brooding, intense, silky, luscious. Character Chard is elegant, balanced, long.

Seghesio Son ★★★ Respected family winery with a double focus: Italian varieties and ZIN. *The Zins are superb*, drinkable when young, taking on depth with age. The Italians are a cut above most California efforts in that line, esp BARBERA and SANGIOVESE.

Selene Napa V ★★★→★★★★ Check out state-of-the-art Napa CAB SAUV with Mia Klein at Selene. Klein makes small lots of Bordeaux varietals and they are superb. The Dead Fred V'yd Cab Sauv is top dog, sometimes facing a challenge from the Hyde V'yd SAUV BL. Also try a glass of the Chester V'yd Red Blend. There's even a rosé – hurrah!

Sequana Son ★★→★★★ PINOT N-only venture of veterans Tom Selfridge and James MacPhail (who also has his own label). Three wines, two from RRV and one from Santa LH in Monterey. All have silky complexity and intensity.

Sequoia Grove Napa V ★★★ If you are looking to stock a cellar, the Estate CAB SAUV would be a gd place to begin. It is intense, concentrated but balanced and built to last. CHARD is also v.gd.

Shafer Vineyards Napa V ★★★→★★★★ (CAB SAUV) 02 03 05 07 09 10 (MERLOT) 07 08 09 10 Top-rated veteran for potent, deep, smooth Cab Sauv (esp Hillside Select) and Merlot, which will age several yrs.

Signorello Napa V ★★★ Padrone is top of the line: a rich and concentrated CAB SAUV, The Fuse Cab Sauv also v.gd. CHARD is full-bodied and oaky. SYRAH and a series of Carneros PINOT N worth a look. Overall, Signorello seems to get better with each vintage.

Silverado Vineyards Stags L ★★★ Supple and lean CAB SAUV is almost always on target, as is the minerally CHARD.

Silver Oak ★★★ Separate wineries in Napa V and Alex V make CAB SAUV only. Napa V wines can be super-concentrated but they have a loyal following. Alex V wines are a bit more supple.

Sinskey Vineyards Car ★★★ The CHARD has the typical delicious flavours of Carneros plus enough acidity to give it bite; the PINOT N has bright fruit that fairly dances on the palate.

Smith-Madrone Spring Mtn ★★★ California is not noted for its RIES, but Ries from dry-farmed mtn v'yds can hold its own anywhere. It's made in an off-dry style with brilliant floral minerality.

Sodaro Estate Napa V ★★★ Veterans Bill and Dawnine Dyer are consultants at this newish Italian family winery, so don't look for cult-wine knockoffs here. Nothing old-fashioned about these elegant and balanced wines. Look esp for the CAB SAUV-based Felicity.

Somerston Napa V ★★★ Priest Ranch CAB SAUV is outstanding, with gd structure and layers of flavour. SYRAH is rich and full-bodied.

Sonoma-Cutrer Vineyards Son ★★ → ★★★ CHARD is the long-running story here, made mostly from cooler-climate grapes. It has an edgy bite, flinty and almost chewy. Capable of ageing.

Whither Napa Cab?

The pendulum might be swinging away from overextracted CABS. These jammy wines, often with alcohol of more than 15 degrees, are being shunned by younger, knowledgeable sommeliers who want balanced wines to complement food, not "wine cocktails". A shortlist of Napa classics would incl: CLOS DU VAL, CORISON, FROG'S LEAP, LOUIS M MARTINI, SPOTTSWOODE, TREFETHEN and newcomer TOR WINES.

Spottswoode St Helena ★★★★ 97 99 00 01 03 05 06 07 09 10 Add to the shortlist of California "first growths". The *outstanding Cab Sauv* is irresistible, but try to keep it. Brilliant SAUV BL is a bonus.

Spring Mountain Vineyard Spring Mtn ★★★ CAB SAUV with concentration and depth is capable of ageing. SAUV BL also outstanding.

Staglin Family Vineyard Napa V ★★★ 03 05 07 09 10 An elegant CAB SAUV from Rutherford Bench v'yd has gd ageing potential.

Stag's Leap Wine Cellars Stags L ★★★ 99 00 01 03 05 07 09 10 Celebrated for silky, seductive CAB SAUVS (SLV, Fay, top-of-line Cask 23) and MERLOTS. Gd CHARD is often overlooked. Holds the line for balance and harmony against the local blockbusters. Now owned by partnership of Piero Antinori (Italy) and CHATEAU STE MICHELLE in Washington State.

Stags' Leap Winery Napa *See* BERINGER BLASS.

Stama Lodi ★ → ★★ Grape-growers for five generations, starting in Greece. Friendly wines, incl a remarkably gd old-vine ZIN from Lodi and a v.gd estate CAB SAUV.

Stephen Ross Edna V ★★★ A rising star for PINOT N and CHARD, with a nod to SYRAH and ZIN. Burgundian approach adds complexity and interest.

Stephen's Cellar ★★ Gd to v.gd CHARD and PINOT N, plus a delicious PINOT GR from Central Coast fruit. Look esp for the McBride V'yd Chard, lively and lingering.

CALIFORNIA

Sterling Napa V ★★→★★★ Showpiece 1960s winery, a solid producer of v.gd CHARD and CAB SAUV, usually understated.

Steven Kent ★★★ 06 07 09 When Gallo bought Mirassou, Steve M set out to revive CAB SAUV in historic Livermore. His remarkable single-v'yd bottlings are hard to find but worth the search.

Stonestreet Son ★★★ One of the stars of Jess Jackson's Artisans & Estates stable. Alex V CAB SAUV is brawny but balanced with layers of flavours. CHARD can get too buttery but worth a look.

Stony Hill Napa V ★★★★ (CHARD) 91 95 97 99 00 01 03 05 06 07 09 Legendary producer of minerally Chard made in a graceful and supple "homage to Chablis" style. Long-lived.

St-Supéry Napa ★★→★★★ Start with the lovely SAUV BL; there are few better. MERLOT has unusual power. CAB SAUV is v.gd, as is red Meritage. Owned by Skalli of France.

Sutter Home ★→★★★ Will probably never live down White ZIN, though new Signature Series and Trinchero Family Estates may help, esp a v.gd CAB SAUV from Chicken Ranch V'yd.

Swanson Oak ★★★ Alexis CAB SAUV is lean and supple with excellent fruit and a balanced finish. Also gd SANGIOVESE, one of the few in California.

Tablas Creek P Rob ★★★ Holy ground for Rhônistas. V'yd based on cuttings from Châteauneuf, as a joint venture between Château de Beaucastel (France) and importer Robert Hass. Côtes de Tablas Red and White are amazingly gd, as is the Tablas Creek Esprit.

Talbott, R Mont ★★★ A Burgundian approach to CHARD from single-v'yds in Monterey. Look esp for Sleepy Hollow from Santa LH.

Terry Hoage P Rob ★★→★★★ Former footballer Terry Hoage is passionate about Rhône varieties. The wines are quite gd and incl 5 Blocks, a red blend, and The Gap, an outstanding white.

Thacher P Rob ★★→★★★ Outstanding ZIN and SYRAH plus a brilliant Central Coast red GSM (GRENACHE, Syrah, MOURVÈDRE).

Thomas Fogarty Santa Cz Mts ★★→★★★ Age-worthy CHARD is rich and complex; gd PINOT N from estate vines. Spicy and intense GEWURZ.

Thomas George RRV ★★→★★★ Small producer of single-v'yd wines, mostly from RRV. Cresta Ridge PINOT N offers bright fruit and spice; Eagle Ridge Pinot N is darker. Also gd VIOGNIER.

Tor Wines Napa V ★★★ Napa veteran Tor Kenward on his own with outstanding CAB SAUV from the famed To Kalon v'yd. Rich, intense wine to age. Also a v.gd SYRAH called Rock and outstanding CHARD.

Treana P Rob ★★ Only two wines: Treana Red, based on CAB SAUV, and Treana White, a blend of VIOGNIER and MARSANNE. You can't go wrong with either.

Trefethen Family Vineyards Napa V ★★★ Off-dry RIES is one of the best in the state. CAB SAUV on an upward curve in recent vintages. CHARD can be excellent and will even improve in the cellar for a few yrs.

Looking for more information on grapes? Try the "Grapes" section on pp.16–26.

Tres Sabores Ruth ★★★ In the heart of CAB SAUV territory, Tres Sabores is making a name for its ZIN, dry-farmed on organic hillside v'yds. It's a beauty. Sleek and powerful with terrific long-lasting fruit and a rounded finish. CAB SAUV is also worth a look.

Tricycle Wine Company Lake ★★ New producer has captured Lake County's CAB SAUV style with a supple and balanced wine from the Red Hills AVA.

Trinchero Napa V ★★→★★★ This long-time Napa producer is trying to ugrade its image with a series of CAB SAUVS from Napa vines. Look esp for Chicken Ranch V'yd bottling.

Truchard Car ★★★ Carneros veteran has branched out with brilliant bottlings of TEMPRANILLO and ROUSSANNE. Also tangy, lemony CHARD and flavourful MERLOT. CAB SAUV and SYRAH also v.gd.

Turnbull Napa V ★★★ 06 07 09 Turnbull CAB SAUV is often overlooked but is a Napa classic, powerful yet supple and balanced. The Res bottling should be cellared for at least a decade.

Valley of the Moon Son ★→★★ Textbook example of gd-value quaffs. PINOT BL and ZIN can reach ★★ level.

Viader Estate Napa V ★★★★ 99 00 01 03 05 06 07 08 09 10 Long-lived and powerful blend of CAB SAUV and CAB FR from this Howell Mtn hillside estate; classic Napa V mtn red. Also look for new occasional small-lot bottlings, incl SYRAH and TEMPRANILLO.

Merlot grape prices rise in 2011, Pinot Noir falls: *Sideways* effect reversed.

Villa Ragazzi Napa V ★★★ Only SANGIOVESE and not much of that, but perhaps the best Sangiovese in California – dark and intense with rich fruit, miles from the usual thin versions. Shows what the grape can do on a rocky hillside, given proper care.

Vina Robles San LO ★★→★★★ Estate producing gd CAB SAUV and SAUV BL, but everyday Red and White have bright fruit and pleasing acidity. The white is a blend of VERMENTINO, VIOGNIER, VERDELHO and a drop of Sauv Bl – priced at around $15, it's a real bargain.

Volker Eisele Family Estate Napa V ★★★ 00 01 03 05 07 09 10 Makes a supple and luscious blend of CAB SAUV and CAB FR from the little-known Chiles Valley AVA. Also spicy SAUV BL.

Wente Vineyards Mont ★★→★★★ There is an obvious effort to raise the quality standard at this historic winery. New CHARD bottlings in particular are more complex. Also v.gd *Livermore Sauv Bl* and SÉM.

Williams Selyem Son ★★★ Intense, smoky RRV PINOT N, esp Rochioli V'yds and Allen V'yd. Now reaching to Son Coast, Mendocino for grapes. Cultish favourite can sometimes turn jammy and overconcentrated.

Willowbrook Son ★★★ The focus here is on stylish PINOT N with bright fruit and long flavours.

Wilson Vineyards Son ★★→★★★ ZIN from Dry CV is outstanding. Also v. impressive Res Zin: rich and brambly.

Wine Group, The Central V The Wine Group is now the 3rd-largest producer of wine in the world, by volume, after E & J GALLO and CONSTELLATION. It offers mostly bargain wines, such as Glen Ellen and Almaden, as well as bag-in-box bargains such as Franzia. The wine is drinkable, for the most part, and certainly helps balance out grape supply and demand in California and around the world.

Wrath Vineyards Mont ★★→★★★ Several v'yd bottlings of CHARD and PINOT N and a powerful SYRAH. Also a graceful SAUV BL. The Pinot N looks to Burgundy.

Zaca Mesa Santa B ★★→★★★ The new focus on estate Rhône varieties here is showing gd results. The Black Bear Block SYRAH is one of the best in the state; also look for Z Three, a delicious blend of Syrah and GRENACHE, and check out the ROUSSANNE.

Zahtila Vineyards Napa ★★★ Elegant, inviting CAB SAUV and intense ZIN. A winery to watch.

CALIFORNIA

THE PACIFIC NORTHWEST

While California wine is both old and new – hence really no news to anybody – the wines of Oregon and Washington are still scarcely known outside their home country. Who knows, for example, that while Oregon has climate and countryside that would pass for northern Europe, the Yakima Valley in Washington is, strictly speaking, desert? The advantage of a semi-arid zone, given water (and the Columbia River has lots of that) is that you can irrigate precisely when and when you want. No fungus, few pests, hot days, cool nights; it may not be pretty, but it makes for killer grapes.

Of course there are variants of soil and situation, and it is these (call them "terroirs") that are spurring an excited wave of new plantings and brilliant wines – more European in style than most of California's, with a lighter touch. Oregon made its reputation with Pinot Noir, Washington, curiously, with Riesling; but both have gone far beyond stereotyping. They are trying everything – and so should we.

Principal viticultural areas

Applegate Valley (App V) Oregon. Warm region in south; gd Cab Sauv, Syrah.
Columbia Valley (Col V) Washington. A huge AVA incl much of southern and central Washington; Cab Sauv, Ries, Syrah, Chard, Cab Fr and more. Incl the important sub-AVAs of Horse Heaven Hills, Red Mtn, Walla Walla (Walla) and Yakima Valley (Yak V).
Umpqua Valley (Um V) Oregon. Warmer region but with cooling Pacific winds. Promising plantings of Tempranillo; Cab Sauv.
Willamette Valley (Will V) Oregon. This is Pinot N central. Several sub-AVAs have been established as Oregon growers make serious efforts to sort out terroir. Also gd Ries, Pinot Gr and Chard.

Recent vintages

Any general discussion of vintages is difficult because of the wide variation in climate over the area and the jumble of microclimates in small regions.
2011 Classic Oregon Pinot N and superb Washington Bordeaux varieties from a cool year.
2010 Very difficult for both Oregon and Washington. Those who picked carefully may produce wines with good acidity.
2009 Hot, with the red wines in particular showing good fruit.
2008 In Oregon the Pinot N looked especially promising. In Washington and Idaho the grapes were in near-perfect condition.
2007 Not an easy vintage, but those who paid attention will get it right.
2006 Incredible quality across the board in Oregon. Washington and Idaho were similar.
2005 Excellent, if the winery paid attention. Oregon Pinot N, Washington Cab Sauv and Merlot could be exceptional.

Oregon

Abacela Vineyards Um V ★★★ Unusual varietal line-up for Oregon: v.gd TEMPRANILLO and DOLCETTO. Also gd CAB FR and SYRAH.
Adelsheim Vineyard Y-Car ★★★→★★★★ 05 06 07 09 10 PINOT N remains the go-to wine from this Oregon pioneer, but the Dijon-clone CHARD is also excellent. V.gd RIES and fine PINOTS GR and BL.

Alexana Will V ★★★ Winemaker Lynn Penner-Ash focuses on edgy PINOT N, which is made with a firm hand; the wines are supple with gd acidity. Also try the engaging PINOT GR.

Amity Will V ★★→★★★ The RIES is marvellous, plus there is an exceptional PINOT BL. The PINOT N is often ★★★.

Andrew Rich (Tabula Rasa) Will V ★★→★★★ A supple PINOT N, outstanding SYRAH.

Antica Terra Will V ★★→★★★ Four partners, incl ex-California winemaker Maggie Harrison (Sine Qua Non), are making v.gd PINOT N with deep, rich flavours in a kind of California-meets-Oregon mode.

Archery Summit Will V ★★★ Bold and powerful PINOT N is not typical of Oregon but has a loyal following.

Argyle Y-Car ★★→★★★ V.gd RIES and v. fine PINOT N lead the way; also *bargain bubbly*. Winery founded by Aussie superstar winemaker Brian Croser.

Arterberry ★★★ Veteran PINOT N specialist has a winner with Maresh from Dundee Hills; supple, flavoury and complex.

Beaux Frères Y-Car ★★★ PINOT N has more concentration than most Oregon offerings. Part-owned by critic Robert Parker.

Bergstorm Estate Will V ★★★ Consistently one of Oregon's top PINOT NS as well as a bright PINOT GR. The estate Pinot N, certified biodynamic, is an intense wine with gd mouthfeel and a long finish. CHARD also gd.

Bethel Heights Will V ★★→★★★ *Outstanding Chard* and estate PINOT N.

Brandborg Cellars Um V ★★→★★★ The SYRAH from estate grapes is v.gd. Also an appealing PINOT GR and a stylish PINOT N.

Brick House Y-Car ★★★ Dark and powerful estate PINOT N has its fans. Estate Select is a leaner version.

Chehalem Y-Car ★★→★★★ Estate CHARD gd for a few years in the cellar; also an early-drinking no-oak Chard; v.gd RIES, PINOT GR.

Cooper Mtn Will V ★★★★ Complex PINOT N and a rich, intense CHARD. Res Pinot N is capable of some bottle-age. Certified biodynamic.

Latest Oregon treatment for mildew: powdered milk whey. Smells like a latte...

Domaine Drouhin Will V ★★★→★★★★ 05 06 07 08 09 10 Daughter-house to Drouhin of Beaune (France). Silky PINOT N one of the best in the state. CHARD also v.gd and elegant, improving with each vintage.

Domaine Serene Will V ★★★→★★★★ Consistently one of top PINOT N not just in Oregon but elsewhere as well. Single-v'yd bottlings with Burgundian approach, bottled unfiltered.

Erath Vineyards Y-Car ★★★→★★★★ After more than 40 yrs of making PINOT N you know they are doing it right. Also gd CHARD and an age-worthy RIES.

Et-Fille Y-Car ★★★ This father-daughter team makes small lots of PINOT N and VIOGNIER. The Kalita V'yd Pinot N is a show-stopper; bright, raspberry, spicy. Viognier is also v.gd.

Evening Land Will V ★★★ Highlight here is Seven Springs CHARD: powerful, lemon-peel accents, focused.

Evesham Wood Will V ★★★ PINOT N on a steady upward curve; dry GEWURZ is a lovely glass. Farmed organically.

Eyrie Vineyards Will V ★★★ David Lett planted the first PINOT N vines in the Will V in 1965 and has been at or nr the top ever since. Also v.gd PINOT GR and excellent CHARD, both rich yet crisp.

Henry Estate Um V ★★★ Gd CAB SAUV and fine MERLOT from this warmer corner of Oregon. Dry GEWURZ is a treat.

Ken Wright Cellars Y-Car ★★★ Excellent and highly regarded producer. V'yd select PINOT N and CHARD.

King Estate Will V ★★★ First-rate CHARD and PINOT N from organic v'yds. Quality seems to rise each vintage.

Lachini Vineyards Will V ★★★ Outstanding PINOT N and PINOT GR from biodynamic v'yds in Will V. Also a gd RIES and attractive ALBARIÑO. A fine CAB SAUV from the Red Mtn AVA in Washington.

Lemelson Vineyards Will V ★★★ Terroir-driven PINOT N from seven v'yds, all farmed organically. Any given yr there are up to 12 bottlings. In general, gd minerality and acidity; early-drinking, but also gd with cellaring.

Patricia Green Cellars Y-Car ★★★→★★★★ This estate produces several bottlings of single-v'yd PINOT N that vary from light and almost Beaujolais-like to bold and more concentrated – all gd.

Penner-Ash Y-Car ★★★ REX HILL winemaker Lynn Penner-Ash and her husband are making intense, rich PINOT N from up to six v'yds in a bolder style than many in Oregon. Also v.gd VIOGNIER.

2011: umbrellas not sunshades

The harvest of 2011 was brutal in The Pacific Northwest. First, there wasn't much of it: summer was cool and rain (even in Washington's normally dry areas) meant that an untold number of tons of grapes was left on the vine. But when grapes did ripen (thanks to a warm late Sept) they did so at lower sugar levels, which meant (hooray!) less alcohol plus gd acidity. So we're looking at classic wines. Where would we be without cold and rain?

Ponzi Vineyards Will V ★★★→★★★★ 03 05 06 Long-established with consistently *outstanding Pinot N* and v.gd PINOT GR and CHARD.

Rex Hill Will V ★★★→★★★★ Res bottlings of round and full-flavoured PINOT N, PINOT GR and CHARD consistently hit ★★★★. Regular bottlings from select v'yds also worth a look.

Roxy Ann ★★ South Oregon producer of an excellent and true-to-varietal VIOGNIER and a silky PINOT GR. Claret red blend is a pleasing quaff.

Sineann ★★→★★★ Stylish wines of great intensity: terrific old-vine ZIN and astonishingly gd MERLOT from Horse Heaven Hills in Washington.

Sokol Blosser Will V ★★★→★★★★ One of Oregon's top wineries offering balanced and harmonious PINOT N in classic Oregon style; superb CHARD. SYRAH is a treat.

Soter Y-Car ★★★ *Mineral Springs V'yd Pinot N*, made by Tony Soter (ex-ETUDE from California), is balanced and harmonious with a long, lyrical finish.

Stoller Estate ★★★ The SV Estate PINOT N is a balanced and elegant wine, with supple fruit; JV Estate Pinot N is riper with softer tannins. There is also a gd CHARD made from estate grapes.

Torii Mor Y-Car ★★★ V.gd single-v'yd PINOT N bottlings and superior PINOT GR.

Van Duzer Winery Will V ★★→★★★★ PINOT N with gd acidity and minerality from cool hillside v'yds. Also a delicious PINOT GR.

Willakenzie Estate Y-Car ★★★ There are always gd wines to be found here, made in small lots with a changing line-up each vintage. Outstanding PINOT N and v.gd PINOT GR and PINOT BL as well as rare bottlings of PINOT MEUNIER and GAMAY Noir.

Willamette Valley Vineyards Will V ★★→★★★★ CHARD is looking better than ever, with bright and focused fruit; also gd PINOT N and a tempting RIES.

Looking for more information on grapes? Try the "Grapes" section on pp.16–26

Washington & Idaho

Amavi Cellars Walla ★★★ CAB SAUV with intense varietal *typicité*; also a v.gd SYRAH.

Andrew Will ★★★ 00 01 02 05 07 08 08 09 10 Small lots of single-v'yd Bordeaux varieties with tremendous ageing potential, elegant and balanced.

Badger Mountain Col V ★★→★★★ Washington's first organic v'yd, making gd CAB SAUV and excellent CHARD with no added sulphites.

Barnard Griffin Col V ★★→★★★ Excellent MERLOT: gd structure and balance. Barrel-fermented CHARD is a winner. V.gd SAUV BL and SYRAH, plus a delicious VIOGNIER and a fine Rosé.

Betz Yak V ★★★→★★★★ The Rhône inspires for Bob Betz, especially SYRAH, where Betz sets the standard for Washington. Most yrs there are three bottlings, Serenne (approachable), Côte Rousse and La Côte Patriarche (both to age).

Brian Carter Cellars ★★→★★★ Top dog here is Byzance, a Rhône blend, but don't overlook the SANGIOVESE-based Tuttorosso.

Buty Walla ★★★ Outstanding Bordeaux blends, esp the Champoux V'yd Horse Heaven Hills bottling: lovely fruit and a long, elegant finish.

Cadence Red Mtn ★★★ This Bordeaux-style specialist offers several bottlings, and one of best is the Ciel du Cheval v'yd, with dark, brooding fruit and a silky, spicy finish.

Cayuse Walla ★★→★★★ V'yds are now biodynamic. V.gd Bordeaux blend and an outstanding SYRAH.

Charles Smith Wines Walla Ex-rock-band-manager Smith has gained a cult following for jammy, concentrated SYRAH and blends. Also under the K-Wine label. Get it? K-Syrah.

Chateau Ste Michelle ★★→★★★★ Washington's largest winery; also owns COLUMBIA CREST, Northstar (top MERLOT) and SNOQUALMIE, among others. Major v'yd holdings, first-rate equipment and skilled winemakers keep wide range of varieties in front ranks. V.gd v'yd-designated CAB SAUV, MERLOT and CHARD. Links with Loosen (Germany) and Antinori (Italy).

Chinook Wines Yak V ★★★ Outstanding CAB FR backed by v.gd MERLOT and CAB SAUV.

Columbia Crest Col V ★★→★★★ The one that started it all. CAB SAUV, MERLOT, SYRAH and SAUV BL are gd-value favourites. Grand Estate wines a move up in quality, esp red blend Amitage.

Columbia Winery Wash ★★★ Marvellous *Syrah*, sleek and powerful.

Côte Bonneville Yak V ★★★ V'yd on steep basalt wins medals for deep, sleek CAB blends, esp Carriage House.

DeLille Cellars ★★★→★★★★ 00 01 02 03 05 07 08 09 Powerful, balanced Bordeaux blends often rise to ★★★★. Line-up changes with the vintage. Also v.gd SYRAH.

Dunham Cellars Walla ★★→★★★ CAB SAUV should age for up to a decade. Also look for a superb SYRAH and a v.gd CHARD.

Glen Fiona Walla ★★→★★★ Rhône meets Walla: everyone wins. The SYRAH/CINSAULT/ Counoise cuvée is brilliant.

Gramercy Cellars Walla ★★★ Master Sommelier-turned-winemaker Greg Harrington is crafting outstanding Rhône styles, esp SYRAH/GRENACHE-based blend, Third Man, v. pleasing. Watch this winery.

Hedges Cellars Yak V ★★★→★★★★ Hedge family is consistently turning out winning Bordeaux-style reds. FUMÉ is delicious, popular CHARD/SAUV BL blend.

Hogue Cellars, The Yak V ★→★★ Wines are a gd quaff at a gd price. Fair enough. Look esp for RIES, CHARD.

Hyatt Vineyards Yak V ★★→★★★ V.gd MERLOT is always worth a glass. Roza Ridge is the flagship label. Look esp for MALBEC and SYRAH.

Januik Col V ★★★ Super CAB SAUV built to last by Mike Januik, former head winemaker at CHATEAU STE MICHELLE; also a v.gd MERLOT.

Kiona Vineyards Yak V ★★→★★★ Pioneer in Red Mtn AVA producing top-rated CAB SAUV, excellent RIES and CHENIN BL. Rare bottling of LEMBERGER gd.

Latah Creek ★★→★★★ Outstanding MERLOT, a must-drink if you want iconic Washington Merlot. Also pleasing CHARD and SANGIOVESE.

L'Ecole No 41 Walla ★★★→★★★★ (MERLOT) 04 05 06 07 09 10 Bold and high-profile reds that manage to stay in balance. CAB SAUV and Merlot are the star turns and both will age for at least a decade.

Leonetti Walla ★★★→★★★★ CAB SAUV and terrific MERLOT in a bold, in-your-face style but never over the top. Sleek with layers of dark fruit and structure for ageing.

Red Mountain's balancing act
Red Mtn AVA, Washington's smallest, is where you go if you want CAB SAUV with exceptional balance of fruit, acidity and tannin. HEDGES and KIONA are located here; others taking grapes from Red Mtn incl: ANDREW WILL, Barnard Griffin, DELILLE CELLARS, L'ECOLE NO 41, QUILCEDA CREEK and WOODWARD CANYON.

Long Shadows Col V ★★★→★★★★ Allen Shoup's brilliant plan to unite international winemakers and Washington grapes gains strength each year. Seven wines now; you can't go wrong with any. Look esp for *Poet's Leap Ries* by Armin Diel (Germany); Feather CAB SAUV by Randy Dunn (California); glorious SYRAH Sequel by John Duval (Australia).

McCrea ★★★ Rhônista making small lots of excellent VIOGNIER, SYRAH and GRENACHE, plus rare varietal bottling of Counoise.

Nota Bene Cellars ★★→★★★ Outstanding red wines sourced in Red Mtn AVA and other top Washington v'yds. Wines are built to last. Worth seeking out.

Owen Roe ★★→★★★ V.gd CHARD and RIES from Yakima Valley v'yds; Bordeaux-style reds from Columbia Valley are excellent.

Pacific Rim ★★→★★★ Randall Grahm first made Pacific Rim RIES at his California winery BONNY DOON in 1992; it was a hit, and he built a winery in Washington in 2006. Several Ries; both dry and sweet are super. Also *gd single-v'yd Ries*. Don't overlook CHENIN BL.

Pend d'Oreille ID★★→★★★ Outstanding VIOGNIER and v.gd MERLOT are the opening act for the star turn, a lovely fruit-forward CHARD with bright acidity.

Quilceda Creek ★★★→★★★★ 01 03 04 05 07 09 10 Elegant and beautifully balanced *Cab Sauv from Columbia Valley* is drinkable young but will age a decade or more.

Sandhill Winery Col V ★★★ CAB SAUV and MERLOT, made with grapes from Red Mtn AVA, are improving each vintage. Also a v.gd PINOT GR.

Sawtooth Cellars ID★★→★★★ A taste of Rhône in Idaho featuring a fine SYRAH, excellent VIOGNIER and ROUSSANNE. CAB SAUV also v.gd.

Sineann *See* same entry in Oregon section.

Snoqualmie Vineyards Col V ★★→★★★ Innovative producer of v.gd CAB SAUV and MERLOT. Recent introduction of Naked Wines (no oak) from organic v'yds has been a hit. Look esp for luscious Naked RIES.

Ste Chapelle ID★★ Gd-value CHARD, CAB SAUV, MERLOT and SYRAH in a pleasant drink-me-now style. V.gd dry RIES and GEWURZ, and gd bubbly.

Woodward Canyon Walla ★★★→★★★★ (CAB SAUV) 01 02 03 04 05 06 07 09 10 The gold standard for *Washington Cab Sauv* and MERLOT for more than three decades. Also excellent CHARD.

NORTHEAST, SOUTHEAST & CENTRAL

The urge to ferment grapes has hit susceptible individuals in almost every state of the Union. Few wineries in most are yet of interest beyond their neighbourhoods, but New York has been at it longest and has progressed furthest. Oeno-tourism is a strong factor, especially in the Finger Lakes. NY now has around 300 wineries and Virginia (growing strongly) around 200. Pennsylvania, New Jersey, Michigan, Missouri... they're all at it. The hot, humid summers and cold winters aren't easy, and results are generally leaner than West Coast, but this is a space to watch.

Recent vintages

In 2011 torrential rain and cool temperatures hit shortly after harvest began. New York's Hudson Valley was devastated by Hurricane Irene and Tropical Storm Lee; in parts of Virginia it rained 33 out of 35 days in August and September. Nevertheless, 2011 looks promising for certain areas where the grapes came in with good quality. 2010 was much easier: hot and dry, an ideal vintage in most places.

Alba NJ ★ Unique microclimate for gd PINOT N and CAB FR, and excellent RIES.

Anthony Road Finger L, NY ★★★★ 09 10 11 One of the best producers in the east with exceptional RIES, fine PINOT GR, CAB FR/LEMBERGER, late-harvest Vignoles.

Barboursville VA ★★ 08 09 10 11 Pioneering property, founded 1976, and one of best wineries in the East. Owned by Italy's ZONIN family. Outstanding Italian varieties, incl BARBERA and NEBBIOLO, plus succulent Bordeaux-style blend, excellent CAB FR, and *Malvasia*. Elegant inn and Tuscan-style restaurant.

Bedell Long I, NY ★★ 09 10 11 One of LONG ISLAND's first serious estates; outstanding varietal wines, incl CHARD, GEWURZ and CAB FR, plus toothsome blends. Sophisticated tasting room, gardens, etc.

Boxwood NJ ★★ 08 09 10 11 Elegant estate notable for three Bordeaux-style blends, plus two dry rosés.

Breaux VA ★ 09 10 11 Hilltop v'yd an hour from Washington DC. Gd CHARD, MERLOT.

Chamard CT★ 09 10 11 Established winery with CHARD, PINOT N and CAB FR.

Channing Daughters Long I, NY ★★★ 09 10 11 South Fork estate with v.gd Tocai FRIULANO, PINOT BIANCO, PINOT GRIGIO, MUSCAT Ottonel; also MERLOT, DORNFELDER, CABS FR and SAUV.

Chateau LaFayette Reneau Finger L, NY ★★ 08 09 10 11 V.gd CABS, MERLOT, CHARD and RIES. Inn with scenic lake views.

Chrysalis V ★★ 09 10 11 Outstanding VIOGNIER and Norton; v.gd PETIT MANSENG, ALBARIÑO, TANNAT and PETIT VERDOT.

Connecticut This small state has more than 30 wineries, incl pioneering CHAMARD.

Debonné Vineyards L Erie ★ 10 11 Largest OHIO estate winery produces *vinifera*, incl CHARD, CAB FR and RIES, also SEYVAL, VIDAL and other hybrids.

Ferrante Winery Harpersfield Historic OHIO producer (founded 1937), with CHARD, PINOT GRIGIO, GEWURZ, RIES, native Catawba, Icewine.

Finger Lakes Scenic region in upstate NY; over 113 wineries around the three major lakes. Source of most of the state's wines. Among top wineries are ANTHONY ROAD, Bloomer Creek, CHATEAU LAFAYETTE RENEAU, DR. KONSTANTIN FRANK, FOX RUN, Heart and Hands, HERMANN J. WIEMER, HERON HILL, KING FERRY, Lakewood, LAMOREAUX LANDING, Ravines, RED NEWT, Red Tail Ridge, STANDING STONE, Swedish Hill.

Firelands L Erie ★ 10 11 Founded 1880. V.gd GEWURZ and Icewine, also PINOT GRIGIO, CHARD, CAB FR and CAB SAUV. Some vines grown on Lake Erie islands.

Fox Run Finger L, NY ★ 09 10 11 Notable winery, café overlooking Lake Seneca. Fine RIES, CHARD, GEWURZ, PINOT N.

Frank, Dr Konstantin (Vinifera Wine Cellars) Finger L, NY ★★★ 07 08 09 10 11 Historic FINGER LAKES estate remains a leader in the East; *excellent Ries*, GEWURZ; gd CHARD, GRÜNER VELTLINER and RKATSITELI. Plus fine Château Frank sparkling.

Georgia Now over 12 wineries. Look for: Three Sisters (Dahlonega), Habersham V'yds and Chateau Elan (Braselton) that features southern splendour with v'yds, wine and a resort.

Glen Manor Vineyards VA ★ 09 10 11 Produces gd flinty SAUV BL and age-worthy Bordeaux varietal blends.

Hamptons, The (aka South Fork) Long I, NY Enchanting New York AVA with three wineries: CHANNING DAUGHTERS, Duckwalk and WOLFER ESTATE.

Hermann J Wiemer Finger L, NY ★→★★★ 08 09 10 11 Established 1976; one of first estates in the east to plant *vinifera*. Superior RIES, CHARD, GEWURZ, also v.gd sparkling wine and late-harvest Ries.

Heron Hill Finger L, NY ★ 10 11 Estate and informal café with views of Keuka Lake. Notable RIES and dessert wines.

Hillsborough VA ★ One of VIRGINIA'S most promising young wineries, with fine ROUSSANNE, PETIT MANSENG, TANNAT, Fer Servadou, and CAB SAUV.

Horton VA ★ 10 11 Early Virginia visionary (first vintage 1991). Gd VIOGNIER, Norton.

Hudson River Region NY State's first AVA. Straddles the Hudson 90 minutes' drive north of Manhattan. Along with neighbouring Catskills region now has 38 wineries.

Jefferson VA ★ 09 10 Minutes away from Thos Jefferson's Monticello estate. Fine PINOT GR, VIOGNIER, Bordeaux blend, also gd CHARD and MERLOT.

Donald Trump's now a winery owner. He bought bankrupt Kluge Estate, Virginia.

Keswick VA ★★ 10 11 V.gd VIOGNIER and TOURIGA.

King Family Vineyards VA ★ 09 10 11 Toothsome Meritage, fine PETIT VERDOT, luscious VIOGNIER/PETIT MANSENG dessert wine.

King Ferry Finger L, NY ★ 09 10 11 V. fine RIES, CHARD, Meritage. Exceptional dessert wines, incl late-harvest Vignoles and RIES.

Lake Erie Tri-state AVA that incl portions of NEW YORK, PENNSYLVANIA and OHIO. Important grape-growing area; v'yds along the lake shore mainly Concord grapes, mostly for juice and jelly. *Vinifera* plantings increasing.

Lamoureaux Landing Finger L, NY ★★★ 08 09 10 11 Handsome winery with superb lake views. Some of *New York's best Chard*; excellent RIES, GEWURZ CAB FR.

Lenz Long I, NY ★★ 09 10 11 One of top producers in NORTH FORK AVA. Excellent Brut sparkling wine, CHARD, GEWURZ, CABS and MERLOT.

Linden VA ★★★ 09 10 11 60 miles west of Washington DC. One of region's first (since 1981) and best estates with superb SAUV BL, also CAB FR, PETIT VERDOT, Bordeaux-style red blends from high-altitude v'yds.

Long Island NY On the doorstep of NYC. Three AVAs: LONG ISLAND, NORTH FORK and THE HAMPTONS), all *vinifera*. First winery est. 1973, more than 60 today, mostly on NORTH FORK. Top estates: Grapes of Roth, Jamesport, Rafael, Sherwood House. Also Bouké, Clovis Point, Comtesse Thérèse, Martha Clara, Raphael, Roanoke, Sherwood House, Shinn Estate and Sparkling Pointe.

Maryland Some 50 wineries; top new estates are Black Ankle, Serpent Ridge, Sugarloaf and Bordeleau, all producing impressive *vinifera* wines. Venerable Elk Run and Woodhall continue to turn out gd wines.

Massachusetts Mostly cool-climate grapes: RIES, CHARD, PINOT GR. Westport Rivers noted for sparkling.

Michael Shaps/Virginia Wineworks VA ★★ 08 09 10 11 Some of the best VIOGNIER in the east. Also complex CHARD, notable PETIT VERDOT, CAB FR, MERLOT and fine Meritage, plus Raisin d'Être made with dried Petit Verdot and Cab Fr.

Michigan Impressive RIES, GEWURZ and PINOT GR; v.gd CAB FR and blends. Best: Bel Lago, Black Star, Bowers Harbor, Brys, Chateau Grand Traverse, Fenn Valley, Peninsula Cellars (esp dry Gewurz), Tabor Hill and L Mawby (outstanding sparkling). Up-and-coming: Chateau Chantal, Chateau Fontaine, Circa Estate, 45 North, Lawton Ridge, Left Foot Charley, Longview, 2 Lads. Two-thirds of the vines are *vinifera*.

Millbrook Hudson R, NY ★ 10 11 Hudson Valley estate with new RIES v'yd. Decent CHARD, MERLOT, CAB FR.

Missouri The University of Missouri has a new experimental winery to test techniques and grape varieties in local conditions. Best so far: SEYVAL BLANC, VIDAL, Vignoles (sweet and dry versions) and Chambourcin. Stone Hill in Hermann produces v.gd Chardonel (a frost-hardy hybrid of Seyval Bl and CHARD), Norton and gd Seyval Blanc and Vidal Blanc. Hermannhof is also drawing notice for Vignoles, Chardonel and Norton. Also notable: St James for Vignoles, Seyval, Norton; Mount Pleasant in Augusta for rich, Port-style and Norton; Adam Puchta for Port-style wines and Norton, Vignoles, Vidal Blanc; Augusta Winery for Chambourcin, Chardonel, Icewine; Les Bourgeois: gd SYRAH, Norton, Chardonel, Montelle, v.gd Cynthiana and Chambourcin.

New Jersey The state is suddenly teeming with wineries. Leading estates are ALBA (outstanding dry GEWURZ, RIES, CHARD, SYRAH, CABS FR and SAUV), and UNIONVILLE (Chard, PINOT GRIGIO, PINOT N).

New York Dynamic wine-producing state with a more diverse landscape than any other in the East. Regions: FINGER LAKES, LONG ISLAND, HUDSON RIVER and Catskills, Central New York, LAKE ERIE, Niagara Escarpment, Greater Adirondacks, Lake Ontario, Lake Champlain, Thousand Islands, New York City.

North Carolina This southern state now has 106 wineries, incl Biltmore, Childress, Duplin (for Muscadine), Hanover Park, Iron Gate, Laurel Gray, McRitchie, Old North State, RagApple, RayLen, Raffaldini, Rockhouse, Shelton. Top varieties: CHARD, VIOGNIER, CAB FR and native Muscadine.

North Fork Long I, NY Popular getaway destination for Manhattanites. Top estates incl: BEDELL, Jamesport, Lieb, LENZ, PALMER, PAUMANOK, PELLEGRINI, PINDAR, Raphael.

Ohio 157 wineries, five AVAs. Some exceptional PINOT GR, RIES, PINOT N, Icewine. Top producers: DEBONNÉ, FERRANTE, FIRELANDS, Harmony Hill, Harpersfield, Henke, Kinkead Ridge, Paper Moon, St Joseph and Valley V'yds.

Palmer Long I, NY ★ 10 11 Founded 1986. Gd CHARD, PINOT BL, CAB FR, MERLOT.

Paumanok Long I, NY ★★ 09 10 11 Family-run NORTH FORK estate, founded 1982. Quality RIES, CHARD, MERLOT, CABS, and PETIT VERDOT. Exceptional CHENIN BL.

Pellegrini Long I, NY ★★ 08 09 10 Beautifully designed winery, gd PETIT VERDOT, CHARD and CAB FR.

Pennsylvania Top estates: Blair (burgundy-styled PINOT N, CHARD), Allegro (Chard and MERLOT), Pinnacle Ridge (sparkling, Bordeaux-style red blend, Chambourcin), Galen Glen (RIES, VELTLINER, CAB FR), Manatawny Creek (Cab Fr, CAB SAUV, Bordeaux-style blend), Waltz (Chard, Cabs) and LAKE ERIE's Mazza (VIDAL Icewine).

Pollack VA ★★ 09 10 11 Superior VIRGINIA winery (founded 2003) with outstanding CHARD, PINOT GR, PETIT VERDOT, CAB FR, CAB SAUV, MERLOT, Meritage, VIOGNIER.

RDV VA ★★ 08 09 Fledgling estate (opened 2011) already turning out exceptional, complex and velvety Bordeaux blends.

Red Newt Finger L, NY ★★ 09 10 11 One of the FINGER LAKES' best, with superb RIES, outstanding CHARD, GEWURZ, CAB FR, MERLOT and Bordeaux-inspired blend. Fine bistro features regional food.

Sakonnet Rhode I ★ 10 11 Venerable estate with gd CHARD, VIDAL Blanc and sparkling.

Sheldrake Point Finger L, NY ★★ 09 10 11 Beautifully situated winery, bistro on shore of Lake Cayuga. Outstanding RIES, GEWURZ, CAB FR, CAB SAUV. Gd PINOT GR.

American Viticultural Areas
Federal regulations on appellation of origin in the USA were established in 1977, rather late in the day and confusing, too. There are two categories. First is a straightforward political AVA, which incl an entire state, ie. California, Washington, Oregon and so on. Individual counties can also be used, such as Santa Barbara or Sonoma. When the county designation is used, all grapes must come from that county. The second category is a geographical designation, such as Napa Valley or Willamette Valley within the state. These AVAs are supposed to be based on similarity of soils, weather, etc. In practice, they tend to be inclusive rather than exclusive. Within these AVAs there can be further sub-appellations. For example, the Napa Valley AVA contains Rutherford, Stags Leap District and others. When these geographical designations are used, all grapes must come from that region. A producer who has met the regulatory standards can choose a political listing, such as Napa, or a geographical listing, such as Napa Valley.

Standing Stone Finger L, NY ★ 09 10 11 V.gd RIES, GEWURZ, CHARD and CAB SAUV.

Unionville Vineyards NJ ★ Notable CHARD, RIES; fine Bordeaux-style red.

Veritas VA ★ 09 10 Fine producer with stylish Brut sparkling, SAUV BL, CHARD, CAB FR and PETIT MANSENG.

Villa Appalaccia VA ★ 09 10 In the scenic Blue Ridge Mts, turns out wines with a taste of Italy, incl PRIMITIVO, SANGIOVESE, PINOT GR and a MALVASIA Bianca blend.

Virginia The fastest-growing wine-producing state in the east. Overall quality has skyrocketed and just keeps getting better. Several wines of real style and elegance; esp gd VIOGNIER.

Wisconsin Best is Wollersheim, specializing in variations of Maréchel Foch. Prairie Fumé (SEYVAL BL) is a commercial success.

Wölffer Estate Long I, NY ★★ 08 09 Fine CHARD, vibrant Rosé and gd MERLOT from talented German-born winemaker.

THE SOUTHWEST

Thanks to both a love of wine and the growth of agro-tourism, there are now more than 500 wineries in the southwest corner of the USA. Each state is surprisingly varied in climate and growing conditions: there are cool, high plains and hot, dry lowlands. Wine festivals, wine clubs and almost constant wine-trail promotions are also helping draw in aficionados. Texas is the largest. With over 250 wineries, it's the fifth-largest producer in the USA. Colorado has over 100 wineries, all rapidly learning which grapes to plant where. Arizona's 50+ wineries (already) can take advantage of the huge terroir differences between the north and south of the state. New Mexico, too, ranges from cool north to desert south. Their wineries are using a full range of European grapes, but look out especially for Dolcetto and Tempranillo. Oklahoma's wineries are using *vinifera* as well as hybrid and native American grapes.

Arizona Alcantara V'yds: gd SAUV BL, MOURVÈDRE. Cadeuceus Cellars: ★ owned by Tool-man Maynard James Keenan with top reds Sancha and Nagual de la Paciencia. Callaghan V'yds: ★★ one of Arizona's best wineries, esp red blends Padres and Caitlin's. Cimarron: label of Dick ERATH of Oregon producing red blend Rojo del Sol. Dos Cabezas: ★ look for red blends Campo and Aguileon. Keeling Schaefer V'yds: gd GRENACHE, SYRAH. Lightning Ridge: ★ MONTEPULCIANO ideally suited to Arizona terroir, and v.gd red blend Resonance. Page Springs: Rhône-style white and red wines, but also check out anything with PETITE SIRAH. Pillsbury Wine Company: filmmaker Sam Pillsbury finds success with his Arizona wines and catchy labels: Roan Red, WildChild White, WildChild Red worth seeking out. Soniota: a pioneer of Arizona wines with gd SYRAH, COLOMBARD, CAB SAUV.

Becker Vineyards Tex r w ★★→★★★ Superb (and large!) collection of interesting wines. Esp Newsom CAB SAUV, VIOGNIER, Res MALBEC, Clementine.

Brennan Vineyards Tex r w Excellent VIOGNIER, v.gd CAB SAUV and SYRAH.

Colorado Alfred Eames Cellars: gd PINOT N and SYRAH. Bookcliff: gd PETITE SIRAH and Syrah. Boulder Creek: v.gd RIES, Rosé, Syrah. Canyon Wind: v.gd PETIT VERDOT and Bordeaux blends. Garfield Estates: v.gd SAUV BL, CAB FR, Syrah. Graystone: specializes in Port-styles, all v.gd with rich aftertaste. Grande River: Sauv Bl, VIOGNIER, Petit verdot, MALBEC. Guy Drew: ★★ excellent GEWURZ, CHARD, Syrah, Metate. Jack Rabbit Hill: biodynamic and organic, Ries, M&N. Stoney Mesa/ Ptarmigan: Ries, Gewurz, MERLOT, Cab Sauv. Reeder Mesa: gd Cab Fr, Syrah, Land's End Red blend. Two Rivers: ★ excellent Ries, v.gd Chard, Syrah. Winery at Holy Cross: ★ excellent Cabs Sauv and Fr.

Duchman Tex r w ★★★ Winery has rocketed to among the best in Texas with nr-perfect VERMENTINO and DOLCETTO.

Haak Winery Tex r w ★ Gd MALBEC, dry Blanc du Bois; one of best "Madeira" copies.

Texas' oldest winery, Val Verde, opened its doors in 1883.

Inwood Estates Tex ★★★ Exceptional TEMPRANILLO and v.gd PALOMINO/CHARD blend.

Llano Estacado Tex r w ★★ One of Texas's earliest and largest wineries. V.gd Viviana (w) and Viviano (r), Newsom TEMPRANILLO, PINOT GRIGIO, Port-style.

Lone Oak Tex r w In Burleson. V.gd TEMPRANILLO, gd MERLOT.

McPherson Cellars Tex ★★ Owner Kim McPherson was first big award-winner in Texas. Delicious Rosé of SYRAH, Res SANGIOVESE and Res ROUSSANNE.

Messina Hof Wine Cellars Tex r w ★ Excellent RIES, esp late-harvest. V.gd Papa Paolo Port-style wines.

Nevada Tahoe Ridge, previously Churchill V'yds: Gd Res ZIN, PETITE SIRAH. Pahrump Valley: quite a showplace, with restaurant. Gd Symphony, Zin.

New Mexico Black Mesa: ★★ Coyote, PETITE SIRAH, Woodnymph RIES. Casa Abril V'yds: MALBEC, ZIN, TEMPRANILLO. *Gruet:* ★★★ excellent sparkling wines, esp Blanc de Noirs, also excellent CHARD, PINOT N. Matheson Winery: Chard, CAB SAUV, sweet Doce. Don Quixote: enterprising boutique winery and craft distillery nr Los Alamos. Wines under Manhattan Project label worth watching. Intriguing grappa and Blue Corn Vodka. Wines of San Juan: gd Cab Sauv and white blend Pale Morning Dun. Luna Rossa: ★ v.gd MONTEPULCIANO, Cab Sauv.

Oklahoma Chapel Creek: gd Traminett, Norton. Greenfield V'yd: gd MERLOT, SAUV BL. Stone Bluff Cellars: gd Vignoles, Cynthiana, Chardonel. Oak Hills Winery: v.gd SEYVAL BL, Traminette. The Range V'yd: gd Traminette and MUSCAT Blanc.

Pedernales Cellars r p w ★ GARNACHA Dry Rosé great for a hot Texas afternoon. MERLOT is the best buy on the list.

Peregrine Hill / Ste Genevieve Tex r w Peregrine Hill has gd CHARD and PINOT N. Ste Genevieve is, by far, the largest winery in Texas.

Spicewood Vineyards r w p ★ Exceptional Sancerre-like SAUV BL and v.gd SÉM.

Val Verde Tex r w Fourth-generation tradition. V.gd Port-style, gd CHARD, PINOT GRIGIO.

William Chris Wines r w ★ In tiny Hye, this winery is already picked as one of the state's hot new wineries. Red blends Emotion and Enchante are both winners.

Canada

You may be amazed to learn Canada now boasts over 500 wineries from coast to coast. Equally surprising is that Icewine makes up only a tiny proportion of total wine prodcution. Most of the wine is fresh, modern, food-friendly red and white that is beginning to reflect its origins. Chardonnay, Riesling, Pinot Noir and Cabernet Franc are at the forefront of Ontario's two major subregions, Niagara Peninsula and Prince Edward County. Far to the west, British Columbia's Okanagan and Similkameen Valleys and select sites along the east coast of Vancouver Island, are making equally noteworthy wines, led by Pinot Gris, Merlot, Syrah and an array of aromatic white blends. From the Atlantic coast, Nova Scotia continues to hone impressive sparkling wines.

Ontario

Ontario has four appellations of origin, all adjacent to Lakes Ontario and Erie: Niagara Peninsula, Lake Erie North Shore, Pelee Island and Prince Edward County. Within Niagara Peninsula the vineyards are further sub-divided into ten growing areas.

13th Street ★★★ 07 (10) New owner and winemaker, Jean-Pierre Colas, will add SAUV BL and PINOT N to an impressive line-up of small-batch GAMAY, CHARD, RIES and sparkling wine.

Cave Spring ★★★ 09 10 (11) Ontario's oldest functioning winery building turns out benchmark RIES, especially CSV and Estate labels, elegant, old-vines CHARD, exceptional late-harvest wines and Icewines.

Château des Charmes ★★ The Bosc family farms 114ha in Niagara-on-the-Lake. Excellent RIES from bone-dry to Icewine. Equuleus, from the Paul Bosc Estate V'yd, is a standout Bordeaux-style red.

Colaneri Estate Winery ★★ 09 10 (11) Winemaker Andrej Lipinski is using a mix of *appassimento*, *ripasso* and *recioto* methods on PINOT GR, GEWURZ, CAB SAUV, VIDAL and a standout Visone SYRAH.

Creekside ★★★ 07 (10) Broad range of Bordeaux red blends, CHARD, SYRAH and excellent SAUV BL. A new series of organic, single-barrel lots labelled Undercurrent is making waves.

Flat Rock ★★ 09 10 (11) Crisp, modern, cool-climate wines. Consistently excellent RIES, PINOT N and CHARD. Single-block Nadja's Ries is a standout.

Henry of Pelham ★★ 09 10 (11) Family-run, Niagara-centric; CHARD and RIES; Bordeaux-style reds, unique Baco Noir and Ries Icewine. Top labels tagged: Speck Family Res (SFR).

Inniskillin ★★ 09 10 (11) The pioneer Icewine house. Now a new era under winemaker Bruce Nicholson. The focus is on delicious RIES, PINOT GR, PINOT N and CAB FR and specialty Ries and VIDAL Icewine.

Looking for more information on grapes? Try the "Grapes" section on pp.16–26.

Jackson-Triggs ★★ 09 10 (11) State-of-art winery in Niagara-on-the-Lake. Delaine V'yd and Grand Res whites lead pack: promising CHARD, PINOT N, SYRAH releases.

Le Clos Jordanne ★★★ 08 09 10 (11) A Franco-Canadian joint venture making benchmark Niagara PINOT N and CHARD from organic v'yds.

Malivoire ★★→★★★ 07 09 (10) Small, innovative, gravity-flow winery producing v.gd organically grown PINOT N, CHARD, GAMAY and GEWURZ.

Ravine Vineyard ★★★ A new 14ha v'yd set over ancient Niagara River watercourse making v.gd Res CHARD and MERLOT.

Stratus ★★★ 07 (10) High-tech, LEED-certified (ie. green) winery, flagship white and red blends; MALBEC and SYRAH improving under consultant Paul Hobbs.

Tawse ★★★ 08 09 10 (11) Outstanding CHARD, RIES; high-quality PINOT N, CAB FR, MERLOT; v'yds certified organic and biodynamic.

Thirty Bench Wine Makers ★★ 09 10 (11) Impressive single-lot estate v'yds from 27ha site in Beamsville Bench appellation; top old-vine RIES, CAB FR; MERLOT, PINOT N.

Vineland ★★★ 07 09 (10) Beautiful country estate with first-class restaurant. Fine RIES, Icewine and Bordeaux-style reds.

British Columbia

BC has identified five appellations of origin: Okanagan Valley, Similkameen Valley, Fraser Valley, Vancouver Island and the Gulf Islands.

Blue Mountain ★★★ 07 08 09 10 Respected producer of sparkling wine, and high-quality, age-worthy PINOT N, GAMAY, CHARD, PINOT GR. Outstanding Res Pinot N.

Burrowing Owl ★★ 08 09 10 Picture-perfect estate making excellent CAB FR, PINOT GR and SYRAH; acclaimed boutique hotel and restaurant.

CedarCreek ★★ 09 10 Terrific aromatic RIES, GEWURZ, Ehrenfelser, classic northwest MERLOT; plus top-end Platinum CHARD, SYRAH, PINOT N and a delicious MALBEC.

Church and State Wines ★★ 09 10 (11) Lush, New World-style reds and whites from Okanagan Valley and Vancouver Island v'yds. Top red is Quintessential blend; also well-made SYRAH and VIOGNIER.

Hester Creek ★★ 09 10 (11) A new state-of-the-art winery, six-suite guest villa and restaurant welcome visitors. Electric TREBBIANO from 40-yr-old vines; aromatic PINOT GR, PINOT BL and CAB FR.

Jackson-Triggs Okanagan ★★ 09 10 Popular, easy-drinking style with gd SHIRAZ, Meritage and outstanding RIES Icewine. Impressive Rhône-style SunRock Shiraz.

Mission Hill ★★★ 08 09 10 Architecturally stunning. Acclaimed CHARD, SYRAH and Legacy Series: Perpetua, Oculus, Quatrain and Compendium. Award-winning al fresco dining.

Nk'Mip Cellars ★★ 09 10 Part of $25m Aboriginal resort and spa. Well-made PINOT BL, RIES, PINOT N; top picks Qwam Qwmt Pinot N and SYRAH. The Desert Cultural Centre is a must-visit.

Osoyoos Larose ★★★ 07 08 09 10 Benchmark, single-v'yd, age-worthy Bordeaux blend by Groupe Taillan and Vincor Canada. Second label is Pétales d'Osoyoos.

Painted Rock ★★★ Steep-sloped 24ha Skaha Bench, v.gd SYRAH, CHARD, red blend.

Pentâge Winery ★★ 10 (11) A 5,000-case Skaha Bench producer with a low-yielding 10ha site producing fine VIOGNIER and PINOT GR, plus ROUSSANNE, MARSANNE and VIOGNIER-style Rhône wine.

Quails' Gate ★★ 08 09 10 Family-owned estate making terroir-based PINOT N and CHARD, aromatic RIES, CHENIN BL, with cult-like following for its Old Vines Foch.

Road 13 ★★★ 09 The Luckhurst family revamped the former "Golden Mile" winery, launching popular Honest John blends and top-tier Jackpot CHARD, SYRAH and old-vine CHENIN BL.

Red Rooster ★★ 10 (11) Clean, fresh, aromatic, balanced wines are the signature of this Naramata Bench producer. Look for refreshing CHARD, PINOT GR, RIES; supple SYRAH and red blends.

Tantalus ★★★ 08 09 10 LEED-certified (green) facility complements one of the oldest (1927) continuously producing v'yds. Non-interventionist PINOT N and RIES are the story. Res Ries is v.gd.

South America

Abbreviations
used in the text:

Aco	Aconcagua
Bío	Bío-Bío
Cach	Cachapoal
Casa	Casablanca
Cata	Catamar
Col	Colchagua
Cur	Curicó
Elq	Elqui
Ley	Leyda
Lim	Limarí
Mai	Maipo
Mau	Maule
Men	Mendoza
Pat	Patagonia
Rap	Rapel
Sal	Salta
San A	San Antonio
San J	San Juan
Sant	Santiago

Recent vintages

Vintages do differ but not as much as in Europe. Whites, apart from some of the tauter Chardonnays, are at their best within two years of vintage, reds within three years. The most ambitious reds (Chilean Cabernet-based wines and Syrah, Argentine Cabernets and Malbecs) can last for a decade or more but whether they improve beyond their fifth year is debatable (although the top 2010 and 2011 Chilean reds have great potential). Also, recent improvements mean that wines from a lesser vintage today outperform those from earlier, more favourable years.

CHILE

Which is better, is the regular question: Chile or Argentina? Frankly, if you are simply looking for your daily infuriator at a good price, there is nothing between them. You might prefer the earthier notes of a standard red Chilean, or find the fleshier Malbec of Argentina more to your liking. Chile does a wider range of grapes better – especially the whites; Argentina does perhaps more original tastes. At the top level, where both can be pretty ambitious about price, there is not a grape-skin between them. What is more important is that both have been refining their offerings, getting better in leaps and bounds.

In general, the further south you go in Chile, the cooler it becomes. But even more important in determining flavours are altitude and proximity to the sea. This has now been enshrined in law, with the familiar valleys now being officially divided into three zones: Costa (coastal), Entre Cordilleras (between mountain ranges) and Andes (Andean foothills). Still with terroir in mind, subzones within existing regions are flexing their muscles, among them Lo Abarca in San Antonio, Quebrada Seca in Limarí and Los Morros in Maipo, while new regions continue to be pioneered, among them Futrono 350km south of Bío-Bío. Don't be surprised to see further expansion in the south in places where there is enough rainfall without irrigation: a succession of dry winters in more established regions means that water is becoming an issue.

Aconcagua Traditionally a warm region for sturdy reds, but coastal v'yds now impressing with whites and PINOT N.

Almaviva Mai ★★★ Expensive but classy claret-style red; joint venture: CONCHA Y TORO and Baron Philippe de Rothschild (whose Escudo Rojo red blend is also v.gd).

Altaïr Rap ★★→★★★ Complex, earthy, CAB SAUV/CARMENÈRE; Pascal Chatonnet of Bordeaux consults. Second wine: Sideral, earlier-drinking. Part of the VSPT group.

Anakena Cach, Col, Ley ★→★★ Solid range. Flagship wines under ONA label incl punchy SYRAH, single-v'yd bottlings; Res CHARD gd. Look for VIOGNIER, ONA PINOT N.

Antiyal Mai ★★→★★★ Biodynamic specialist making fine, complex red blend from CARMENÈRE, CAB SAUV, SYRAH. Second wine is Kuyen, also gd varietal Carmenère.

Apaltagua Rap ★★→★★★ CARMENÈRE specialist drawing on old-vine fruit from Apalta (Colchagua). Grial is rich, herbal flagship wine. Second label is Tutunjian.

Aquitania, Viña Mai ★★→★★★ Chilean/French joint venture involving Paul Pontallier and Bruno Prats (Bordeaux), making v.gd Lazuli CAB SAUV and Sol de Sol CHARD (from Malleco).

Arboleda, Viña Aco, Casa, Ley ★★→★★★ Part of the ERRÁZURIZ/CALITERRA stable, with whites from Leyda, CASABLANCA and reds from ACONCAGUA, incl excellent varietal CARMENÈRE. MARSANNE/VIOGNIER/ROUSSANNE peachy but refined.

Aristos Cach, Mai ★★→★★★ Terroir-specialist Pedro Parra and two French wine-makers make intriguing Duquesa CHARD and two classy CABS (Duque and Barón) with a SYRAH/PETITE SIRAH bubbling under. Some fruit sourced from CALYPTRA.

Bío-Bío Promising southern region, cool enough for gd whites and PINOT N.

Botalcura Cur ★★★ French winemaker Philippe Debrus makes v.gd Grand Res CAB FR and red blend Cayao; promising NEBBIOLO, too.

Caliboro Mai ★★ Winery under the same ownership as Col d'Orcia estate in Montalcino (see Italy), making refined CAB SAUV-based blend Erasmo.

Caliterra Casa, Col, Cur, Ley ★→★★ Sister winery of ERRÁZURIZ. CHARD and SAUV BL improving, reds becoming less one-dimensional, esp Tributo range and flagship red Cenit. Bio-Sur is organic range.

Calyptra Cach ★★→★★★ Frenchman François Massoc (also part of ARISTOS team) makes v.gd Zahir CAB SAUV, decent SAUV BL and CHARD from 900-metre-altitude v'yd in eastern Cachapoal.

Carmen, Viña Casa, Col, Elq, Mai ★★→★★★ Organic pioneer; same ownership as SANTA RITA. Ripe, fresh CASABLANCA CHARD Special Res; top late-harvest SÉM. Reds even better, esp PETITE SIRAH and Gold Res CAB SAUV.

Casablanca Casa Cool-climate region between Santiago and coast. Little water: drip irrigation essential. Top-class CHARD, SAUV BL; promising MERLOT, PINOT N.

Casa Marín San A ★★★ Dynamic white specialist, v.gd GEWURZ and superb SAUV BL. SYRAH and PINOT N promising..

Casas del Bosque Cach, Casa ★→★★★ Elegant range, incl juicy SAUV BL, svelte PINOT N, peppery SYRAH Res and refined Cachapoal CAB SAUV.

Casa Silva Col ★★ Colchagua estate, with v'yds in the coastal zone of Paredones (v.gd SAUV BL). Solid range topped by silky, complex Altura red, smoky Microterroir CARMENÈRE and Quinta Generación Red and White. Also commendable Doña Dominga range. New wine (2012) from Lake Ranco – v. far south and v. cool.

Clos des Fous Cach, Casa, South Regions ★★ New venture drawing fruit from Alto Cachapoal, Alto MAIPO and Traiguen (south of Bío-Bío). *See* ARISTOS, CALYPTRA.

Clos Ouvert Mau ★★ New winery; natural winemaking using old-vine fruit. Range incl Loncomilla (CARMENÈRE), Huaso (País) and red blend Otono.

Concha y Toro ★→★★★ Mammoth, quality-minded operation. Best: subtle Amelia CHARD (CASABLANCA); *grippy Don Melchor* CAB SAUV; new SYRAH Gravas del MAIPO; Terrunyo; Winemaker Lot single-v'yd range; and complex Carmin de Peumo (CARMENÈRE). Marqués de Casa Concha, Trio, Explorer, Casillero del Diablo offer v.gd value (classy LIMARÍ fizz). Gran Reserva Serie Riberas range features wines from v'yds close to different rivers. Owns Fairtrade producer Viña Los Robles and Palo Alto. *See also* ALMAVIVA, CONO SUR, MAYCAS DEL LIMARÍ, TRIVENTO (Argentina).

Cono Sur Casa, Col, Bío ★★→★★★ V.gd PINOT N, headed by Ocio. Other top releases appear as 20 Barrels selection; new innovations called Visión (BÍO-BÍO RIES is superb). Also *dense, fruity* CAB SAUV, delicious VIOGNIER, rose-petal GEWÜRZ, impressive SYRAH. Second label: Isla Negra; owned by CONCHA Y TORO. New v'yd planted at 1,200 metres, lots of different grapes: MOURVÈDRE, CARIGNAN and others.

Cousiño Macul Mai ★★ Historic Santiago winery. Reliable Antiguas Res CAB SAUV; zesty Sauvignon Gris; top-of-the-range blend Lota is gd rather than great. Cab Sauv Rosé v. refreshing.

Looking for more information on grapes? Try the "Grapes" section on pp.16–26.

De Martino Cach, Elq, Mai, Mau ★★→★★★ Subtle winemaking (top reds now see no new oak), best-known for CARMENÈRE, but also impressing with CAB SAUV Gran Familia, single v'yd old-vine MAULE wines and Legado range, esp Choapa SYRAH and LIMARÍ CHARD. Have highest v'yd in Chile in Elqui called Altos los Torres: first release a Syrah/PETIT VERDOT blend.

Dos Andes ★→★★ Major company, formerly VC Family Estates, with v'yds in various regions, incl BÍO-BÍO. Brands incl Gracia de Chile, Porta, Agustinos (gd, peppery Grand Res MALBEC) and Veranda, formerly a joint venture with Boisset of Burgundy, and now making v.gd PINOT N – Millerandage is top cuvée.

Edwards, Luís Felipe Col, Ley ★★ Decent Colchagua reds, with new LFE900 range (esp MALBEC) from v'yds at 900 metres, and Leyda wines (citrussy Gran Reserva CHARD, tangy Marea de Leyda SAUV BL, lush Marea de Leyda PINOT N).

Elqui Northern regions cooled by sea breezes, v'yd altitudes range from 350–2,200 metres (Chile's highest), suitable for several varieties.

Emiliana Casa, Rap, Bío ★→★★★ Organic/biodynamic specialist involving Alvaro Espinoza (*see* ANTIYAL, GEO WINES). Complex, SYRAH-heavy "G" and Coyam show almost Mediterranean-style wildness; cheaper Adobe and Novas ranges v.gd for affordable complexity.

Errázuriz Aco, Casa ★→★★★ Complex *Wild Ferment* CHARD; brooding La Cumbre SYRAH; complex Don Maximiano CAB SAUV; fragrant KAI CARMENÈRE. Promising new Coastal ACONCAGUA wines. *See also* ARBOLEDA, CALITERRA, SEÑA, VIÑEDO CHADWICK.

Falernia, Viña Elq ★★ ELQUI pioneer making Rhône-like SYRAH, fragrant CARMENÈRE (incl an dried-grape version) and tangy SAUV BL; also complex red blend Number One. Labels incl: Alta Tierra and Mayu.

Fournier, Bodegas O Ley, Mau ★★→★★★ Sister venture of same-name Argentine winery, v'gd Leyda SAUV BL and MAULE red blends: Centauri and Alfa Centauri.

Garcés Silva, Viña San A ★★→★★★ An exciting bodega; gd, full-bodied SAUV BL, commendable PINOT N and CHARD, Amayna.

Geo Wines Ley, Mai, Bío ★→★★ Umbrella under which Alvaro Espinoza makes wines for several wineries. Look for earthy Chono San Lorenzo MAIPO red blend, Ventolera Leyda PINOT N and tangy Quintay BÍO-BÍO RIES.

Hacienda Araucano Casa, Rap ★★→★★★ François Lurton's Chilean enterprise. Complex Gran Araucano SAUV BL (CASABLANCA), refined CARMENÈRE/CAB SAUV Clos de Lolol, heady Alka Carmenère.

Haras de Pirque Mai ★★→★★★ Estate in Pirque. Smoky SAUV BL, stylish CHARD, dense CAB SAUV/MERLOT. Top wines solid, smoky red Albis (Cab Sauv/CARMENÈRE) is made with ANTINORI (*see* Italy) and refined Elegance Cab Sauv-based blend.

Kingston Casa ★★ Exciting newcomer specializing in SYRAH, PINOT N and SAUV BL.

Lapostolle Cach, Casa, Col ★★→★★★★ Impressive French-owned estate; v'yds farmed biodynamically. SÉM best of increasingly elegant whites; Cuvée Alexandre MERLOT and SYRAH, CARMENÈRE-based Clos Apalta the pick of the fine reds.

Leyda, Viña San A ★★→★★★ Excellent portfolio incl elegant CHARD (Lot 5 Wild Yeasts is the pick), lush PINOT N (esp Lot 21 cuvée and lively rosé), tangy Garuma SAUV BL, firm, spicy Canelo SYRAH. Under same ownership as TABALÍ.

Limarí Northerly but cool region, thanks to Pacific influence; good for SYRAH, SAUV BL and esp CHARD, thanks to limestone in many v'yds.

Loma Larga Casa ★★→★★★ V. classy range, with SAUV BL, PINOT N, CAB FR and SYRAH all impressive. Second label: Lomas del Valle.

Maipo Mai Famous wine region close to Santiago. Chile's best CAB SAUVS often come from higher eastern subregions, such as Pirque and Puente Alto.

Matetic San A ★★★ Decent PINOT N and CHARD from exciting winery. Stars are fragrant, *zesty* SAUV BL and spicy, berry EQ SYRAH. Second label: Corralillo.

Maule Southernmost region in Valle Central. Claro, Loncomilla, Tutuven Valleys. CARIGNAN from Cauquenes currently in vogue.

Maycas del Limarí Lim ★★ Concha y Toro offshoot; SAUV BL, CHARD, PINOT N and SYRAH have full flavours with elegance. Quebrada Seca Chard taut, minerally flagship.

Montes Casa, Col, Cur, Ley ★★→★★★★ Highlights of a wide first-class range: Alpha CAB SAUV, Bordeaux-blend Montes Alpha M, *Folly* SYRAH from Apalta and intense Purple Angel CARMENÈRE. Also decent SAUV BL and PINOT N from both Leyda and Zapallar. Experiments with high-density plantings in Marchihue and Southern Rhône-inspired blend (GRENACHE/CARIGNAN/MOURVÈDRE) in Apalta.

MontGras Col, Ley, Mai ★★→★★★ Fine limited-edition wines, incl SYRAH, ZIN. High-class flagships Ninquén CAB SAUV and Antu Ninquén SYRAH. Gd-value organic Soleus, gentle but fine Intriga (MAIPO) Cab Sauv; excellent Amaral (Leyda) whites.

Morandé Casa, Mai ★★ Gd-value selection plus Edición Limitada range, incl a spicy SYRAH/CAB SAUV, inky MALBEC, smoky CARIGNAN, marmaladey Golden Harvest SAUV BL; top wine is Cab Sauv-based House of Morandé.

Neyen Rap ★★★ Apalta project for Patrick Valette of St-Emilion; intense, old-vine CARMENÈRE/CAB SAUV blend. Now owned by VERAMONTE.

Odfjell Mai, Mau ★→★★★ Red specialist with v.gd CARMENÈRE, CARIGNAN (from MAULE) and Aliara blend; other ranges Orzada and entry-level Armador.

Pargua, Viña Mai ★★ Refined reds from winemaker at QUEBRADA DE MACUL. Pargua is CARMENÈRE/CAB SAUV/CAB FR blend, Anka Pargua II mostly Cab Fr/Cab Sauv/MERLOT.

Pérez Cruz, Viña Mai ★★★ MAIPO winery with Alvaro Espinoza (ANTIYAL) in charge. Fresh, spicy SYRAH, aromatic CÔT, stylish Quelen, Liguai red blends.

Polkura Col ★★ A SYRAH specialist making rich but restrained wine in the Marchihue district.

Principal, El ★→★★★ Fleshy yet grown-up CAB/CARMENÈRE blends from high-altitude v'yd: Calicanto, Memorias, El Principal.

Quebrada de Macul, Viña Mai ★★→★★★ Ambitious winery making gd CHARD and v.gd Domus Aurea CAB SAUV; sister Cabs Stella Aurea and Peñalolen also tasty.

CHILE

Rapel Quality region divided into Colchagua and Cachapoal Valleys. Best for hearty reds, esp CARMENÈRE, SYRAH, but watch for cooler coastal subregions Marchihue and Paradones.

San Antonio Coastal region west of Santiago benefiting from sea breezes; best for whites, SYRAH and PINOT N. Leyda is a subzone.

San Pedro Cur ★→★★★ Massive Curicó-based producer. 35 South (35 Sur) for affordable varietals; Castillo de Molina a step up. Best are 1865 Limited Edition reds, Kankana del Elqui SYRAH and elegant Cabo de Hornos. Under same ownership as ALTAÏR, VIÑA MAR, Missiones de Rengo, Santa Helena, TARAPACÁ.

Santa Alicia Mai ★→★★★ Red specialist. Best wines: firm but juicy Millantu CAB SAUV-based flagship wine, and lithe but structured Anke Blend I (CAB FR/PETIT VERDOT).

Santa Carolina, Viña Sant ★★→★★★ Extensive range from several regions, highlights incl: Specialties range (SAN ANTONIO SAUV BL, LIMARÍ CHARD, MAULE CARIGNAN, MAIPO SYRAH), VSC CAB SAUV/Syrah/PETIT VERDOT blends and Syrah and CARMENÈRE at all levels. New Herencia (Carmenère) from Peumo excellent but pricey.

Santa Ema Cach, Ley, Mai ★→★★ Gd-value range from a MAIPO winery, working with grapes from several regions. Top wines: two Peumo (Cachapoal) reds, CARMENÈRE-based Rivalta and CAB-based Catalina; next tier Amplus also impressive.

Santa Mónica Rap ★→★★ Rancagua (RAPEL) winery; the best label is Tierra del Sol. RIES, SÉM and MERLOT under Santa Mónica label also gd.

Santa Rita Mai ★★→★★★★ Long-established MAIPO winery, now working with Aussie Brian Croser. Best: *Casa Real* CAB SAUV; but Pehuén (CARMENÈRE), Triple C (Cab Sauv/CAB FR/Carmenère) and Floresta range nearly as gd. Part of a group that incl CARMEN, Terra Andina, Nativa and DOÑA PAULA (Argentina).

"Chilensis" (Via Wines brand) is very rude in Cantonese: HK sales have soared.

Seña Aco ★★★★ Established with ROBERT MONDAVI, but now wholly owned by the Chadwick family of ERRÁZURIZ, this blend of Bordeaux grapes from a hillside v'yd in ACONCAGUA holds its own against the world's best in comparative tastings.

Tabalí ★★→★★★ Refined cooler-climate wines, often influenced by limestone soils. Single v'yd Payen SYRAH, Caliza SAUV BL, Talinay CHARD and PINOT N top the range. Also wines under the Encantado and Los Molles labels.

Tarapacá, Viña Casa, Ley, Mai ★★ Improving historic winery, part of VSPT group. Top wines: Tara Pakay (CAB SAUV/SYRAH), Etiqueta Negra Gra Reserva (Cab Sauv).

TerraMater Rap ★→★★ Wines from several regions, incl v.gd Altum CAB SAUV, cola-like SANGIOVESE and lively ZIN/SHIRAZ.

Terra Noble Mau ★→★★ Talca winery specializing in grassy SAUV BL and light, peppery MERLOT. Range now incl v.gd, spicy CARMENÈRE Gran Res.

Torres, Miguel Cur ★★→★★★ Fresh whites and gd reds, esp sturdy *Manso de Velasco* single-v'yd CAB SAUV and CARIÑENA-based Cordillera. Conde de Superunda is rare top cuvée, also organic range Tormenta, a rare sparkling País and pioneering plantings in the Empedrado zone of MAULE. *See also* Spain.

Undurraga Casa, Ley, Lim, Mai ★→★★★ Revitalized MAIPO estate. Best wines: Altazor (CAB SAUV-based), LIMARÍ SYRAH and SAUV BL from Leyda and CASABLANCA under the TH (Terroir Hunter) label; also lively Brut Royal CHARD/PINOT N sparkler and peachy Late Harvest SÉM. Now experimenting with egg-shaped fermenters.

Valdivieso Cur, San A ★→★★★ Major producer impressing in recent yrs, with Res and single-v'yd range from top terroirs around Chile (*Leyda Chard* esp gd), NV red blend Caballo Loco and wonderfully spicy CARIGNAN-based Éclat.

Vascos, Los Rap ★→★★★ Lafite-Rothschild venture now improving its Bordeaux wannabe reds. Top: Le Dix and Grande Rés.

Ventisquero, Viña Casa, Col ★→★★★ Ambitious winery; labels incl Chilano and Yali; top wines are two Apalta reds: rich but fragrant Pangea SYRAH and CARMENÈRE/

Syrah blend Vertice. Promising Herú CASABLANCA PINOT N. Also have Chile's most northerly v'yds in Huasco for Ramirana SAUV BL. Increasingly exciting.

Veramonte Casa, Col ★★ Ripe but elegant reds from Colchagua (Primus blend is the pick); fresher styles from CASABLANCA: Ritual PINOT N, Reserva SAUV BL best.

Villard Casa, Mai ★★ Sophisticated wines made by French-born Thierry Villard. Gd MAIPO reds, esp heady MERLOT, Equis CAB SAUV and CASABLANCA whites.

Viñedo Chadwick Mai ★★★ Stylish CAB SAUV improving with each vintage from v'yd owned by Eduardo Chadwick, chairman of ERRÁZURIZ.

Viu Manent Col ★→★★ Emerging Colchagua winery. Fragrant MALBEC-based Viu I and CARMENÈRE-based El Incidente top range; Secreto Malbec and VIOGNIER also v.gd. Late-harvest SÉM top-notch.

Von Siebenthal Aco ★★→★★★ Swiss-owned boutique winery. V.gd Carabantes SYRAH, elegant Montelig blend, fine-boned Toknar PETIT VERDOT and concentrated but v. pricey CARMENÈRE-based Tatay de Cristóbal.

VSPT Important wine group that owns ALTAÏR, Viña Mar, Missiones de Rengo, SAN PEDRO and Santa Helena.

ARGENTINA

With wine having been declared the national drink, the inaugural World Malbec Day (April 17) a success, and enthusiasm for their wines (especially Malbec) growing in the USA, many Argentine producers are smiling. Too many of their wines, however, put intensity before elegance; those looking for aroma and freshness should seek out wines from cooler spots such as Tupungato in Mendoza or Neuquen and Río Negro in Patagonia. Whites still lag behind reds, but enthusiasm for the offbeat, aromatic Torrontés is growing.

Achaval Ferrer Men ★★★ Super-concentrated Altamira, Bella Vista and Mirador single-v'yd MALBECS and Quimera Malbec/CAB/MERLOT blends. Even the "basic" Malbec shames most competitors.

Aleanna Men ★★ Project for CATENA winemaker Alejandro Vigil and Adrianna Catena making gd El Enemigo range and top red CAB FR/PETIT VERDOT/MALBEC blend Gran Enemigo.

Alpamanta Men ★★ Organic Luján de Cuyo winery with Chilean Alvaro Espinoza (ANTIYAL) as winemaker. Top wine Reserva MALBEC, also gd entry-level range Natal.

Alta Vista Men ★→★★★ Excellent dense, spicy *Alto* (MALBEC/CAB) and trio of single-v'yd Malbecs: Alizarine, Serenade (Luján de Cuyo) and Temis (Uco Valley). Fresh, zesty TORRONTÉS. Sister winery Navarrita: fine Winemaker's Selection Malbec.

Altocedro Men ★★→★★★ Lightly-oaked MALBEC, TEMPRANILLO are trump cards for this La Consulta (Valle de Uco) winery; the two are blended for top wine Desnudos.

Altos las Hormigas Men ★★→★★★ Elegant MALBECS based on old Valle de Uco vines. Top wine: Vista Flores Single V'yd. Impressive smoky Colonia las Liebres BONARDA.

Antucura Men ★★→★★★ Valle de Uco bodega with beautifully balanced, spicy CAB SAUV/MERLOT blend. Second label: Calvulcura.

Argento Men ★→★★★ CATENA offshoot making gd commercial wine under Libertad, Malambo and Argento labels.

Atamisque Men ★→★★★ Based in Tupungato and impressing with tangy, fresh reds, esp MALBEC/MERLOT/CAB SAUV Assemblage. Serbal and Catalpa are lower tiers in v.gd range.

Belasco De Baquedano Men ★★ Four bottlings of old-vine Agrelo MALBEC: Swinto and Ar Guentota are best, plus rare late-harvest Antracita. Winemaker is Bertrand Bourdil, ex-Mouton-Rothschild (Bordeaux).

Benegas Men ★★→★★★ Top-notch CAB FR and Meritage under the Benegas Lynch label, also fleshy but fresh Libertad SYRAH and MALBEC.

Bressia Men ★★→★★★ Tiny winery; classy MALBEC-dominated Profundo from Agrelo, Conjuro Malbec from Tupungato and solid, meaty Monteagrelo SYRAH.

Canale, Bodegas Humberto Rio N ★→★★ Known for SAUV BL and PINOT N (Marcus is top wine), but MERLOT and MALBEC (esp Black River label) are better.

Catena Zapata, Bodega Men ★★→★★★★ Consistently gd range rises from Alamos through Catena and Catena Alta (*v.gd Chard*) to flagship Nicolas Catena Zapata and Malbec Argentino, plus Adrianna and Nicasia single-v'yd MALBECS. Also joint venture with the Rothschilds of Lafite: seriously classy *Caro* and younger Amancaya; *see* ARGENTO/LUCA/TIKAL/TAHUAN/ALMA NEGRA.

Chacra Río Negro ★★★ *Superb Pinot N* from bodega owned by Piero Incisa della Rocchetta of Sassicaia (*see* Italy), top cuvée Treinta y Dos from 1932 vines; also v.gd Mainqué MERLOT. Wines made by the team at NOEMIA.

Chakana Men ★★ Agrelo winery to watch for joyful MALBEC, CAB SAUV, SYRAH, BONARDA. Top Malbec Ayni.

Chandon, Bodegas Men ★→★★ Makers of Baron B and M Chandon sparkling under Moët et Chandon supervision; promising PINOT N/CHARD blend. *See* TERRAZAS DE LOS ANDES.

Clos de los Siete Men ★★ Reliable, plump Vistaflores (Valle de Uco) blend of MERLOT, MALBEC, SYRAH and CAB SAUV, with Michel Rolland overseeing winemaking (*see* DIAMANDES, MONTEVIEJO, VAL DE FLORES).

Cobos, Viña Men ★★→★★★★ Ultra-rich, ultra-ripe (too ripe?) reds from Californian Paul Hobbs, best from Marchiori v'yd. Bramare and Felino are 2nd and 3rd tiers. Also look for Marchiori & Barraud wines from two of the Cobos winemakers.

Colomé, Bodega Sal ★★→★★★ Bodega in remote Calchaquí Valley owned by California's Hess Collection. Pure, intense, biodynamic MALBEC-based reds, lively TORRONTÉS, smoky TANNAT. Former second label Amalaya now operates as a separate winery in Cafayate.

Del Río Elorza Pat ★★ New RÍO NEGRO estate with Alberto Antonini (*see* ALTOS LAS HORMIGAS) as consultant, impressing with PINOT N, MALBEC under the Verum label.

The world's highest vineyard is in the Salta province in Argentina, at 3,015 metres.

DiamAndes Men Part of the Clos de los Siete project, owned by the Bonnie family of Château Malartic-Lagravière (Bordeaux), making solid, meaty Gran Reserva (MALBEC/CAB SAUV).

Dominio del Plata Men ★→★★★ Dynamic Susana Balbo; v.gd wines (incl excellent TORRONTÉS) under the Crios, Susana Balbo, BenMarco, Zohar, Anubis, Bodini labels. Nosotros is bold MALBEC/CAB SAUV flagship. BenMarco Expresivo also v.gd.

Doña Paula Men ★→★★ Luján de Cuyo estate; SANTA RITA (*see* Chile) owned. Elegant, structured MALBEC; modern, fleshy CAB SAUV; tangy Los Cardos SAUV BL; exotic Naked Grape VIOGNIER; experiments with VERDELHO, TOURIGA NACIONAL and Ancellotta.

Etchart Sal ★★→★★★ Reds, topped by plummy Cafayate CAB SAUV. TORRONTÉS also one of the best, with intriguing late-harvest Tardío.

Fabre Montmayou Men, Río Negro ★★ French-owned operation, aka Domaine Vistalba; v'yds in Luján de Cuyo (MENDOZA) and RÍO NEGRO (sometimes labelled Infinitus); reds with a French accent esp gd. Second label: Phebus; also gd-value Viñalba wines on some export markets.

Finca Decero Men ★★→★★★ Lush yet elegant reds, incl fine Amano MALBEC/CAB SAUV blend and lush PETIT VERDOT, from the Remolinos v'yd in Agrelo.

Fin del Mundo, Bodega del ★★ NEUQUÉN pioneer: MALBEC a specialty; top wine Special Blend is MERLOT/Malbec/CAB SAUV.

Flichman, Finca Men ★★ Owned by Sogrape (*see* Portugal), impressing with SYRAH.

Best: Dedicado blend (mostly CAB SAUV/Syrah). Paisaje de Tupungato (Bordeaux blend), Paisaje de Barrancas (Syrah-based). Gd Extra Brut CHARD/MALBEC sparkler.

Fournier, O Men ★→★★★ Spanish-owned Valle de Uco bodega. Urban Uco v.gd entry-level range; then come B Crux, Alfa Crux (both fine TEMPRANILLO/MERLOT/MALBEC blends) and top wine O Fournier CAB SAUV/SYRAH blend. *See* Chile.

Goulart Men ★★ Luján de Cuyo MALBEC specialist: Grand Vin is intense flagship, Marshall Malbec also gd.

Kaikén Men ★★→★★★ Owned by MONTES (*see* Chile); user-friendly range, new Mai MALBEC followed by Ultra CAB SAUV and Malbec, and Corte blend.

Krontiras Men ★★→★★★ Greek-owned biodynamic MALBEC specialist with v'yds in Maipú and Luján de Cuyo: wines labelled Dona Silvina.

La Anita, Finca Men ★★→★★★ MENDOZA estate making high-class reds, esp SYRAH, MALBEC and Varúa MERLOT. Intriguing whites, incl SÉM and FRIULANO.

Lagar Carmelo Patti, El Men ★★ Tiny bodega making intense MALBEC, CAB SAUV and blend Gran Assemblage.

La Riojana ★→★★ Currently the world's largest Fairtrade wine producer. *Raza Ltd Edition* MALBEC is top wine, but quality and value at all levels.

Las Moras, Finca San J ★→★★ Chunky TANNAT, chewy MALBEC Reserva, solid Gran SHIRAZ and plump, fragrant Malbec/BONARDA blend Mora Negra.

Luca / Tikal / Tahuan / Alma Negra Men ★★→★★★ Classy boutique wineries owned by Nicolas CATENA's children Laura (Luca) and Ernesto (Tikal/Tahuan/Alma Negra, the last making a sparkling MALBEC). Winemaker Luis Reginato also makes excellent La Posta del Viñatero range.

Luigi Bosca Men ★★→★★★ Wise range now topped by muscly Icono (MALBEC/CAB SAUV). Finca Los Nobles Malbec/PETIT VERDOT and Cab Sauv/Bouchet (aka CAB FR) also v.gd, as are the Gala blends, esp Cab Fr-based Gala IV. Finca La Linda gd entry level. *See* VIÑA ALICIA.

Lurton, Bodegas François Men ★→★★★ Juicy Piedra Negra MALBEC, complex, earthy Chacayes (Malbec) head range; Flor de TORRONTÉS more serious than most. Sweet but fresh Pasitea Torrontés/PINOT GRIGIO, slightly oaky white blend Corte Friulano.

Manos Negras Men, Pat, San J ★→★★ Two ex-CATENA employees making wines in several parts of Argentina, and now Chile. Altamira MALBEC top wine. TeHo and ZaHa are related labels, also based on Altamira fruit.

Masi Tupungato Men ★★→★★★ Owned by Masi of Valpolicella (*see* Italy). Passo Doble is fine *ripasso*-style MALBEC/CORVINA/MERLOT blend; Corbec is even better Amarone lookalike (Corvina/Malbec).

Mendel Men ★★★ Former TERRAZAS DE LOS ANDES winemaker Roberta de la Mota makes plummy MALBEC, incl super Finca Remota from Altamira v'yd, and graceful Unus blend. Decent SÉM, too.

Mendoza Most important province for wine (over 70% of plantings). Best subregions: Agrelo, Valle de Uco (incl Tupungato), Luján de Cuyo, Maipú.

Michel Torino Sal ★★ Rapidly improving organic Cafayate enterprise; Don David MALBEC, CAB SAUV and SYRAH v.gd. Altimus is rather oaky flagship.

Montesco Men ★★ A blend of MALBEC, BONARDA and CAB from SOPHENIA winemaker Matías Michelini. Also Agua de Roca SAUV BL from Gualtallary region.

Monteviejo Men ★★→★★★★ One of the v'yds of CLOS DE LOS SIETE, now with top-class range of reds headed by wonderfully textured Monteviejo blend (MALBEC/MERLOT/CAB SAUV/SYRAH); Lindaflor Malbec also v.gd.

Neuquén Patagonian region to watch: huge developments since 2000, although salinity proving a problem.

Nieto Senetiner, Bodegas Men ★★ Luján de Cuyo-based bodega. Quality rises from tasty *entry-level Santa Isabel* through Reserva to top-of-range Cadus reds.

Noemía ★★★→★★★★ Old-vine MALBEC from Hans Vinding-Diers and Noemí Cinzano of Montalcino. Second labels: J Alberto, A Lisa. Also MALBEC Rosé and CAB SAUV/MERLOT blend "2". *See* CHACRA.

Norton, Bodega Men ★→★★★ Gd whites; v.gd reds, esp MALBEC (Privada v.gd), Malbec/MERLOT/CAB SAUV blends Privada and Perdriel, Malbec-based Gernot Langes icon and Finca La Colonia range incl SANGIOVESE and BARBERA.

Peñaflor Men ★→★★★ Argentina's biggest wine company. Labels incl Andean V'yds and finer TRAPICHE, FINCA LAS MORAS, Santa Ana and MICHEL TORINO.

Piatelli Sal ★→★★ Tangy Cafayate TORRONTÉS and decent MENDOZA reds topped by the gamey Grande Res range.

Poesia Men ★★→★★★ Exciting Luján de Cuyo outfit; same owner as Clos l'Eglise (Bordeaux); stylish Poesia (CAB SAUV/MALBEC), chunkier but fine Clos des Andes (Malbec) and juicy Pasodoble Malbec/SYRAH/Cab Sauv blend.

Porvenir de los Andes, El Sal ★★ Cafayate estate with classy Laborum reds, incl fine, smoky TANNAT. Amauta blends also gd. Also Camino del Inca label for US-only Tannat-based Quipu, MALBEC and TORRONTES.

Pulenta Estate Men ★★→★★★ Luján de Cuyo winery. Gd SAUV BL and v.gd reds. Best: Gran Corte (CAB SAUV/MALBEC/MERLOT/PETIT VERDOT), CAB FR and Malbec.

Raffy Men ★★ French enterprise making two lightly oaked versions of Tupungato MALBEC, Terroir and Rés.

Renacer Men ★★→★★★ An old-vine MALBEC specialist. Flagship Renacer (mostly Malbec), but most interesting is Enamore – Amarone-style red made with help from ALLEGRINI (*see* Italy).

Riglos Men ★★ Intense, powerful, oak-infused reds from Tupungato fruit.

Río Negro Patagonia's oldest wine region. Gd PINOT N and MALBEC in the right hands.

Rosso, Diego Men ★★ Project of one of the partners in ACHAVAL-FERRER; small amounts of high-class wine, incl gd PINOT N from Uco Valley.

Ruca Malen Men ★★→★★★ Promising red specialist with v'yds in Luján de Cuyo and Uco Valley. Top range is Kinien, tender, floral MALBEC and svelte, aromatic Don Raúl blend. New PETIT VERDOT rich and smoky.

Salentein, Bodegas Men ★★ Highlights: Primus PINOT N, MALBEC; Numina (Malbec/MERLOT). Portillo gd, cheaper; also Bodegas Callia in SAN JUAN, SHIRAZ focus.

Salta Northerly province with some of the world's highest v'yds, esp in Calchaquí Valley. Subregion Cafayate renowned for TORRONTÉS.

Looking for more information on grapes? Try the "Grapes" section on pp.16–26.

San Juan Second-largest wine region, majoring in full-bodied SHIRAZ and TANNAT.

San Pedro de Yacochuya Sal ★★★ Cafayate collaboration between Michel Rolland (*see* France) and the ETCHART family. Ripe but fragrant TORRONTÉS; dense, earthy MALBEC; and powerful, stunning Yacochuya Malbec from oldest vines.

Schroeder, Familia Neuq ★★ V.gd Saurus Select range, incl sappy SAUV BL, earthy MERLOT and fragrant MALBEC. Top wine Familia Schroeder PINOT N/Malbec.

Sophenia, Finca Men ★★ Tupungato bodega. Advice from Michel Rolland (*see* France). MALBEC and CAB SAUV shine; gd Altosur entry-level range; top Synthesis.

Tapiz Men ★★ Luján de Cuyo-based bodega; punchy SAUV BL, v'gd red range topped by serious Black Tears MALBEC and Reserva Selección de Barricas (CAB SAUV/Malbec/MERLOT). Sister label Zolo.

Terrazas de los Andes Men ★★→★★★ Three ranges: entry-level Terrazas (juicy CAB SAUV is star), mid-price Reserva and top-of-the-tree Afincado, incl v.gd Tardio PETIT MANSENG. Joint venture with Cheval Blanc (Bordeaux) making superb *Cheval des Andes* blend.

Toso, Pascual Men ★★→★★★ Californian Paul Hobbs heads a team making gd-value, tasty range, incl ripe but finely structured Magdalena Toso (mostly MALBEC) and Malbec/CAB SAUV single-v'yd Finca Pedregal.

Trapiche Men ★★→★★★ Old name, big firm with increasingly classy range. Incl a trio of single-v'yd MALBECS: Manos Malbec shines out; red blend Iscay is gd but pricey. Better-value: Oak Cask, Fond de Cave, Briquel (gd CAB FR) and Medalla labels.

Trivento Men ★→★★ Owned by CONCHA Y TORO of Chile. Eolo MALBEC is pricey flagship, otherwise a gd-value range, with VIOGNIER standing out; also under Otra Vida label.

Val de Flores Men ★★★ Michel Rolland's own estate in the CLOS DE LOS SIETE enterprise for compelling yet elegant (and biodynamic) old-vine MALBEC.

Viejo Isaias Men ★→★★ Promising range from Rodrigo Manuel Romero, incl v.gd BONARDA, MALBEC, SYRAH and a late-harvest TORRONTES.

Viña 1924 de Angeles Men ★★→★★★ Luján de Cuyo winery whose forte is old-vine MALBEC. Top wine Gran Malbec.

Viña Alicia ★★ Sister winery to LUIGI BOSCA. Interesting range incl NEBBIOLO, PETIT VERDOT (Cuarzo) and blend of RIES, ALBARIÑO and SAVAGNIN called Tiara.

Weinert, Bodegas Men ★→★★ Potentially fine reds, esp Cavas de Weinert blend (CAB SAUV/MERLOT/MALBEC), occasionally spoiled by too long in old oak. Also owns Argentina's most southerly v'yd in Chubut.

Zuccardi, Familia Men ★→★★ A dynamic estate; gd-value Santa Julia range, better Q label (impressive MALBEC, MERLOT, TEMPRANILLO), spicy Emma Zuccardi BONARDA and deep yet elegant Zeta (Malbec/Tempranillo). Gd fortified Malamado (r w).

OTHER SOUTH AMERICAN WINES

Bolivia The province of Tarija on the border with Argentina is the heart of Bolivia's tiny wine industry. With the heat tempered by altitude, SYRAH, CAB and MALBEC are being produced with some success. Pick of the wineries are La Concepción, Kohlberg, Magnus, Aranjuez, Campos de Solana, Casa Real and Casa Grande.

Brazil Is it the humidity that gives many of Brazil's wines a more "European" feel than you'll find elsewhere in South America? Certainly the number of wineries is growing, with Vale dos Vinhedos in the southern province of Rio Grande do Sul being home to many of the best. Reds so far lead the way, with MERLOT, TANNAT and – thanks to a strong northern Italian influence – TEROLDEGO and NEBBIOLO performing well. Sparkling wines are also popular, with most being in the Prosecco mould, although there are also some v.gd traditional-method cuvées. Pick of the producers are Salton, Lidio Carraro, Pizzato, Domaine Cândido, Amadeu (for the Geisse sparklers), Casa Valduga and the pioneering Miolo. Look out, too, for the Rio Sol wines produced close to the equator, where harvesting takes place all year round.

Peru Viña Tacama is the only winery of note, with the Quantum PETIT VERDOT, Gran Vino Blanco, CAB SAUV and *classic-method sparkling* standing out. Chincha, Moquegua and Tacha are all regions that are making progress, but phylloxera is a serious problem.

Uruguay TANNAT is the Uruguayan USP, and one of the wine experiences you should not miss. The style is fleshier than in Madiran, but still tannic, and it's often blended with MERLOT and CAB SAUV, and even VIOGNIER (a grape that also performs well solo). Pisano wines are stylish and fine. Juanicó is equally impressive, with flagship red blend Preludio and JV with France's Bernard Magrez to produce Gran Casa Magrez de Uruguay. Bouza is focused, elegant. Others: Ariano, Bruzzone & Sciutto, Carrau/Castel Pujol, Casa Filguera, Castillo Viejo, De Lucca, Los Cerros de San Juan, Dante Irurtia, Marichal, Pizzorno, Stagnari and Traversa.

Australia

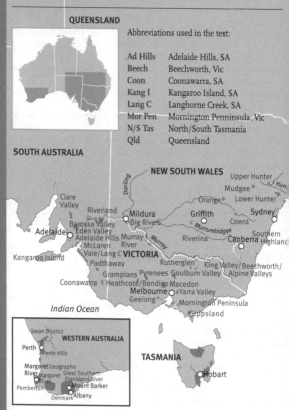

QUEENSLAND

Abbreviations used in the text:

Ad Hills	Adelaide Hills, SA
Beech	Beechworth, Vic
Coon	Coonawarra, SA
Kang I	Kangaroo Island, SA
Lang C	Langhorne Creek, SA
Mor Pen	Mornington Penninsula, Vic
N/S Tas	North/South Tasmania
Qld	Queensland

SOUTH AUSTRALIA

NEW SOUTH WALES

Upper Hunter
Mudgee
Orange · Lower Hunter
Hun.
Darling
Clare Valley
Riverland
Mildura
Big Rivers
Griffith
Cowra
Sydney
Barossa Valley
Adelaide
Eden Valley
Adelaide Hills
Murray River
Murrumbidgee
Riverina
Canberra
Southern Highland
McLaren Vale/Lang C
VICTORIA
Kangaroo Island
Padthaway
Rutherglen
King Valley/Beechworth/
Alpine Valleys
Coonawarra
Grampians Pyrenees Goulburn Valley
Heathcote/Bendigo Macedon
Melbourne
Yarra Valley
Indian Ocean
Geelong
Mornington Peninsula
Gippsland

TASMANIA

Swan District
WESTERN AUSTRALIA
Swan
Perth
Perth Hills
Margaret Geographe
River Margaret
River Frankland River
Pemberton Great Southern
Mount Barker
Denmark Albany
Hobart

The theme of today in Australia is whether or not size matters. For a long time it has been a wine nation obsessed with its growing size – in number of individual producers, in amount of wine made, in the amount of penetration into the UK and US markets – but thanks to an inflated domestic currency and all manner of competitive and climatic pressures, in recent years it has been forced to pull in its horns and rethink. The producers of boring industrial fodder for supermarkets may not agree, but it's a process that has been overwhelmingly positive.

Hand-made, single-site, low-volume wines are increasingly where Australian wine is either at, or is headed. It is also where it started. Old-vine Shiraz and Chardonnay, Cabernet and Riesling (and Semillon) are Australia's classics, but Grenache and Pinot Noir, with Sangiovese and Tempranillo in the wings, have found ideal homes, too, in Australia's extraordinary range of geology and geography. Be prepared to pay sensible prices and Australia will amaze you yet.

Recent vintages

New South Wales (NSW)

2011 Escaped flood problems of further south, but it was still a cold, damp year.

2010 Regular heavy rain made for a tricky year in most districts. Lighter reds, good whites.

2009 Excellent vintage all over, although reds better than whites. Both rain and heat caused some damage, but Mudgee, Cowra, Hilltops and the Canberra District very good.

2008 Good whites; torrential rain then destroyed virtually all Hunter reds. Canberra reds outstanding.

2007 Full flavour across white and red wines. Peak Hunter red vintage.

2006 A burst of extreme heat around Christmas in some regions did no real damage. Time kind to reds.

Victoria (Vic)

2011 Wet; disease pressure in vineyards. Generally better for whites than reds. Producers pulled hair out. Central Victorian regions likely to do best.

2010 Normal transmission was resumed. Temperate vintage with no great alarms or surprises. Whites and reds should be good/excellent from most districts.

2009 Bush fire (and resultant smoke taint). Extreme heat and drought. Yarra Valley worst affected. Beechworth, Grampians, King Valley, Pyrenees, Mornington Peninsula and Sunbury reds of good, concentrated quality.

2008 Reds excellent in Grampians, Mornington Peninsula, Yarra Valley.

2007 Frost and bush-fire smoke-taint hit some regions hard.

2006 A charmed year.

South Australia (SA)

2011 Some call it a shocking year; others say it's one of the greats. Cool, wet, troublesome – if you did well, you were either lucky or extremely vigilant.

2010 Excellent year. Clare and Eden Valley Ries both very good. Shiraz from all major districts best since 2005. Coonawarra Cab Sauv on song.

2009 Hot. Dire predictions for whites but Clare and Eden Ries look very good. Adelaide Hills good whites and reds. Coonawarra reds excellent. McLaren Vale and Barossa Valley generally good for Shiraz.

2008 Excellent wines picked prior to March heatwave, non-fortified "Ports" for those picked after. Very high alcohols. Coonawarra produced Cab of note.

2007 A dry, warm vintage favoured red wines across the board. Good at best.

2006 A great Cab year; for other reds those picked before Easter rains did best.

Western Australia (WA)

2011 Warm, dry, early vintage. Particularly good Cab. Delicate whites less successful. WA's great run of vintages continues.

2010 Reds generally better than whites. Some were caught by late rains but, in general, a very good vintage.

2009 Especially good for Margaret River (r w) and Pemberton (w). Margaret River so often experiences polar-opposite conditions to the regions of the eastern states; here so again.

2008 The best for many years across all regions and all varieties.

2007 A warm, quick-fire vintage made white quality variable; fine reds.

2006 Opposite to Eastern Australia: cool, wet and late – searing whites, highly dubious reds.

Accolade Wines *See* CONSTELLATION.

Adelaide Hills SA Best SAUV BL region: cool 450-metre sites in Mt Lofty ranges.

Alkoomi Mt Barker, WA r w ★★ (RIES) 01 02' 04 05' 07' 08 09 10 (CAB SAUV) 01' 02' 04 05' 07 08 A veteran of 35 yrs making fine Ries and long-lived reds. Less prominent of late.

All Saints Rutherglen, Vic r w br ★★ Historic producer making great fortifieds. Wooded MARSANNE, CHARD and Pierre CAB blend v.gd table wines.

Alpine Valleys Vic Geographically and varietally similar to KING VALLEY. Best: Mayford.

Angove's SA r w (br) ★ Long-established MURRAY VALLEY family business. Excellent-value (r w) varietals. New organic offerings. Super-premium reds less successful.

Annie's Lane Clare V, SA r w ★★ Part of TWE. Consistently gd, boldly flavoured wines. Flagship Copper Trail excellent, esp RIES and SHIRAZ.

Arrivo Ad Hills, SA r Long-maceration NEBBIOLO. Dry, sophisticated and sexy rosé. Minute quantities.

Ashton Hills Ad Hills, SA r w (sp) ★★★ Long-lived RIES and compelling PINOT N made by Stephen George from 25-yr-old v'yds.

Bailey's NE Vic r w br ★★★ Rich SHIRAZ and magnificent dessert MUSCAT (★★★★) and TOPAQUE. Part of TWE. V'yds now grown organically. PETIT VERDOT a gd addition. Run of tough vintages.

Balgownie Estate r w ★★ Old name for fine CAB, rejuvenated, with v. well-balanced wines, esp Cab Sauv, now with separate YARRA VALLEY arm.

Balnaves of Coonawarra SA r w ★★★ Grape-grower since 1975; winery since 1996. V.gd CHARD; excellent supple, medium-bodied SHIRAZ, MERLOT. Full-bodied Tally CAB SAUV flagship.

Bannockburn Vic r w ★★★ (CHARD) 00 02' 03 04 05' 06' 08' (Pinot N) 02' 03' 04' 05' 06 07 08 Intense, complex Chard and PINOT N. Funkified SAUV BL the estate's rising star. Winemaker Michael "Gloverboy" Glover is a whizz.

Banrock Station Riverland, SA r w ★ Almost 1,600ha property on Murray River, 243ha v'yd, owned by ACCOLADE. Impressive budget wines.

Barossa Valley SA Australia's most important winery (but not v'yd) region. Local specialties: v. old-vine SHIRAZ, MOURVÈDRE, CAB SAUV and GRENACHE.

Bass Phillip Gippsland, Vic r ★★★ (PINOT N) 99' 02' 04 06' 07' 09 Tiny amounts of stylish, sought-after Pinot N in three quality grades. Quality can be erratic (to say the least), but recent vintages top-notch. CHARD improving (09 Premium v.gd).

Bay of Fires N Tas r w sp ★★ Pipers River outpost of ACCOLADE empire. Stylish table wines and Arras super-cuvée sparkler. Complex PINOT N.

Beechworth Vic Cool-climate, inland, undulating region in lee of Victorian Alps. CASTAGNA, GIACONDA, Sorrenberg, Savaterre best-known. SHIRAZ, CHARD best.

Bellarmine Wines Pemberton, WA (r) w ★★ German Schumacher family is long-distance owner of this 20ha v'yd: (*inter alia*) startling Mosel-like RIES at various sweetness/alcohol levels, at lowish prices.

Bendigo Central Victorian region with dozens of small v'yds. Some v.gd quality: BALGOWNIE ESTATE, Sutton Grange, Pondalowie, Bress, Harcourt Valley V'yds, Turner's Crossing, Water Wheel.

Best's Grampians, Vic r w ★★→★★★★ (SHIRAZ) 97' 01' 03' 04' 05' 06 08 09 Conservative old family winery; *v.gd mid-weight reds*. Thomson Family Shiraz from 120-yr-old vines is superb. Recent form excellent.

Bindi Macedon, Vic r w ★★★→★★★★ (PINOT N) 04' 06' 08' 10 Ultra-fastidious, terroir-driven maker of outstanding, long-lived Pinot N and CHARD.

Blue Pyrenees Pyrenees, Vic r w sp ★ 180ha of mature v'yds; better utilized than before across a broad range of wines. CAB SAUV quality resurgent.

Boireann Granite Belt Qld r ★★→★★★ Consistently the best producer of red wines in Queensland (in tiny quantities). SHIRAZ/VIOGNIER stand out.

Brand's of Coonawarra Coon, SA r w ★★ 91' **94** 96 98' 02' 03 05' Owned by MCWILLIAM'S. Custodian of 100-yr-old vines, but quality has struggled of late.

Bremerton Lang C, SA r w ★★ Red wines with silky-soft mouthfeel and mounds of flavour. Has thrived since sisters Lucy and Rebecca Willson – who are definitely doing it for themselves – took over the family winery.

Brokenwood Hunter V, NSW r w ★★★ (ILR Res SEM) 03' 05' **06'** (Graveyard SHIRAZ) 93' 97' 98' 00' 02' 03' 05' 07' **09'** and Cricket Pitch Sem/SAUV BL fuel sales. One of the great Hunter names.

The Limestone Coast is a great place for crayfish (especially at Robe).

Brookland Valley Margaret R, WA r w ★★★ Superbly sited winery doing exciting things, esp SAUV BL and CAB SAUV. Owned by ACCOLADE.

Brown Brothers King V, Vic r w br dr sw sp ★→★★★ (Noble Ries) 99' 00 02' 04 05 Old family firm with new ideas. Wide range of delicate varietal wines, many from cool mtn districts. CAB SAUV blend is best red. Extensive GLERA (as in Prosecco) plantings. Recently bought extensive Tasmanian PINOT N v'yds. Known mostly for its sweet commercial lines.

Buller Rutherglen, Vic br ★★★ Rated for superb Rare Liqueur MUSCAT and the newly minted name TOPAQUE.

By Farr / Farr Rising Vic r w ★★★★ Father Gary and son Nick's own, after departure from BANNOCKBURN. CHARD and PINOT N can be minor masterpieces. Nick mostly in charge of winemaking now. Quality soaring.

Calabria Estate Riverina, NSW r w ★ Thriving family producer of tasty bargains, esp Private Bin SHIRAZ/Durif. Creative, charismatic Bill C is in charge.

Campbells Rutherglen, Vic r (w) br ★★ Elegant, smooth, ripe reds (esp Bobbie Burns SHIRAZ); Merchant Prince Rare MUSCAT and Isabella Rare TOPAQUE (★★★★).

Canberra District NSW Both quality and quantity on increase; altitude-dependent, site selection important. CLONAKILLA best-known: thoroughly ascendant.

Capel Vale Geographe, WA r w ★★→★★★ 165-ha estate. V'yds across four regions and 13 varieties make every post a winner.

Cape Mentelle Margaret R, WA r w ★★★ Has hit a vein of rich gd form. Robust CAB SAUV gd, CHARD even better; also ZIN and v. popular SAUV BL/SEM. SHIRAZ on the rise. Owned by LVMH Veuve Clicquot (*see* France).

Capercaillie Hunter V, NSW r w ★★→★★★ Hasn't skipped a beat since the sudden death of co-owner Alasdair Sutherland in 2007. Supplements local grapes with purchases from elsewhere, incl MCLAREN VALE, WRATTONBULLY, etc.

Capital Wines Canberra, NSW r w ★★★ The estate's Kyeema v'yd has a history of growing some of the region's best. SHIRAZ (table and sparkling), RIES stand-outs.

Carlei Estate Yarra V, Vic r w ★★ Winemaker Sergio Carlei sources PINOT N and CHARD from cool regions to make characterful wines. Largely biodynamic.

Casella Riverina, NSW r w ★ The (YELLOW TAIL) phenomenon incl multimillion-case sales in the USA. Like Fanta: soft, sweet. High Aussie dollar a lingering threat.

Castagna Beech, Vic r ★★★★ (SYRAH) 01' 02' **04'** 05' 06 08 Julian Castagna, as much chef as winemaker, is deserved leader of the Oz biodynamic brigade. SHIRAZ/ VIOGNIER and SANGIOVESE/Shiraz blends excellent. Rosé among Oz best.

Chalkers Crossing Hilltops, NSW r w ★★ Cool-climate wines made by French-trained Celine Rousseau; esp SHIRAZ. Alcohol levels v. high of late.

Chambers Rosewood NE Vic (r) (w) br ★★→★★★ Viewed with MORRIS as the greatest maker of sticky TOPAQUE and MUSCAT. Less-successful table wines.

Chapel Hill McLaren V, SA r Mojo returned in 2005. Range since has expanded successfully. SHIRAZ and CAB lead the way, but TEMPRANILLO and GRENACHE both v.gd.

Charles Melton Barossa V, SA r w (sp) ★★★ Tiny winery with bold, luscious reds, esp Nine Popes, an old-vine GRENACHE/SHIRAZ blend. Shiraz continues to shine.

Clarendon Hills McLaren V, SA r ★★ Full-monty reds (high alcohol, intense fruit) made with grapes grown on the hills above MCLAREN VALE.

Clare Valley SA Small, picturesque, high-quality area 145km north of Adelaide. Best for RIES; also gumleaf-scented SHIRAZ and CAB SAUV.

Clonakilla Canberra, NSW r w ★★★★ (SHIRAZ) 01' 03' 05' 06' 07' 08 09 10 *Deserved leader of the Shiraz/Viognier brigade*. RIES and other wines also v.gd. Might well be Australia's best auction performer.

Coldstream Hills Yarra V, Vic r w (sp) ★★★ (CHARD) 02' 03 04' 05' 06' 07' 08' (PINOT N) 92' 96' 02' 04' 06' Established in 1985 by wine critic James Halliday. Delicious Pinot N to drink young, and *Res to age*. V.gd Chard (esp Res). Part of TWE.

Collector Wines Canberra, NSW r ★★★ (Res SHIRAZ) 06' 07' 08' 09' Alex McKay (ex-Constellation) is a local star. His Res Shiraz shows layers of spicy, perfumed, complex flavour.

Constellation Wines Australia (CWA) Name for all wines/wineries previously under HARDYS brand. Now under new ownership and renamed Accolade Wines.

Coonawarra SA Southernmost v'yds of state: home to some of Australia's best (value and quality) CAB SAUV; successful CHARD, RIES, SHIRAZ.

Coriole McLaren V, SA r w ★★→★★★ (Lloyd Res SHIRAZ) 91' 96' 98' 02' 04' 06' To watch, esp for SANGIOVESE and old-vine Shiraz Lloyd Res. Interesting white made with FIANO.

Craiglee Macedon, Vic r w ★★★ (SHIRAZ) 96' 97' 98' 00' 02' 04' 05 06' 08 Re-creation of famous 19th-century estate. Fragrant, peppery Shiraz, and CHARD. Low-key Aussie gem.

Crawford River Heathcote, Vic r w ★★★ John Thomson consistently produces some of Australia's best RIES from this ultra-cool region.

Cullen Wines Margaret R, WA r w ★★★★ (CHARD) 00' 02' 04' 05' 07 08' 09 (CAB SAUV/MERLOT) 94' 95' 98' 04' 05' 07' 09' Vanya Cullen makes substantial but subtle SEM/SAUV BL, bold Chard and outstanding Cab/Merlot.

Cumulus Orange, NSW r w ★★ By far the largest v'yd owner and producer in Orange. Variable quality.

Curly Flat Macedon, Vic r w ★★★ (PINOT N) 03' 05' 06' 08' Robust but perfumed Pinot N (esp impressive). Full-flavoured CHARD. Both eminently age-worthy.

Dalwhinnie Pyrenees, Vic r w ★★★ (CHARD) 04' 05' 06' 08 (SHIRAZ) 99' 00 02 04' 05' 06' 07 08 Rich Chard, CAB SAUV and Shiraz. Best PYRENEES producer.

d'Arenberg McLaren V, SA r w (br) (sw) (sp) ★★→★★★ Sumptuous SHIRAZ and GRENACHE, lots of varieties and wacky labels (incl The Cenosilicaphobic Cat SAGRANTINO). Regional stalwart.

Deakin Estate Vic r w ★ Makes large volumes of high-value varietal table wines. V. low-alcohol MOSCATO. Spicy SHIRAZ.

De Bortoli Griffith, NSW; Yarra V, Vic r w (br) dr sw ★★★ (Noble SEM) Both irrigation-area winery and leading YARRA producer. Excellent PINOT N, SHIRAZ, CHARD, SAUV BL and v.gd sweet, botrytized, Sauternes-style Noble Sem.

Devil's Lair Margaret R, WA r w ★★ Opulent CHARD and CAB SAUV/MERLOT. Fifth Leg is popular second label. Ex-Penfolds winemaker Oliver Crawford starting to place his stamp. Part of TWE.

Domaine A S Tas r w ★★★ Swiss owners/winemakers Peter and Ruth Althaus are perfectionists; v.gd SAUV BL (FUMÉ BLANC). Polarizing (but exceptional) style of cool-climate CAB SAUV.

Domaine Chandon Yarra V, Vic (r) (w) sp ★★ Gd sparkling wine, grapes from cooler wine regions. Owned by Moët & Chandon (*see* France). Well-known in UK as Green Point.

Eden Road r w ★★★ New producer making wines from Hilltops, TUMBARUMBA, CANBERRA DISTRICT regions. V.gd SHIRAZ, CHARD and CAB SAUV. Major award-winner.

Eden Valley SA Hilly region home to HENSCHKE, Torzi Matthews, Radford and PEWSEY VALE; RIES and SHIRAZ of v. high quality.

Elderton Barossa V, SA r w (br) (sp) ★★ Old vines; rich, oaked CAB SAUV and SHIRAZ. Trialling organics/biodynamics.

Eldridge Estate Mor Pen, Vic ★★★ Winemaker David Lloyd is a fastidious experimenter. PINOT N, GAMAY and CHARD worth the fuss.

Epis r w ★★★ (PINOT N) Alec Epis is an ex-professional (Aussie Rules) footballer, but he grows a mighty grape. Long-lived Pinot N; elegant CHARD.

Evans & Tate Margaret R, WA r w ★★→★★★ Owned by MCWILLIAM'S since 2007. Commendable quality, esp Res SHIRAZ and Res CHARD.

Faber Vineyards Swan V, WA r ★★ John Griffiths is a (young-looking) veteran of West Australian wine and a guru of the winemaking west. His home estate makes concentrated SHIRAZ of perception-altering quality.

Ferngrove Vineyards Gt Southern, WA r w ★★ Cattle farmer Murray Burton's 223ha wine venture. V.gd RIES, MALBEC, CAB SAUV.

Flametree Margaret R, WA r w ★★ Exceptional CAB SAUV; spicy and seductive SHIRAZ. New winemaker Cliff Royle (ex-Voyager) sure to add polish.

Fletcher Pyrenees, Vic r Tiny production (less than 100 dozen per wine). NEBBIOLO-focused (incl a sparkling version). New face of Australian wine.

Fosters Wine Estates (FWE) *See* TWE.

Fraser Gallop Estate Margaret R, WA r w New breed of Margaret River; concentrated CAB SAUV and CHARD of note.

Freycinet Tas r w (sp) ★★★ (PINOT N) 96' 00' 02' 05' 06' 07' 08' 09' An east coast winery producing dense Pinot N and gd CHARD. Radenti sparkling perhaps challenges both.

Frogmore Creek Tas r w ★★★ One of the few Australian producers to move from organic/biodynamic back to conventional farming. Wine is excellent, regardless. Off-dry RIES, age-worthy CHARD, undergrowthy PINOT N.

Geelong Vic Region west of Melbourne. Excellent performer since re-establishment in the mid-1960s. V. cool, dry climate. Names to note incl: BANNOCKBURN, BY FARR, Curlewis, LETHBRIDGE, Bellarine Estate and SCOTCHMANS HILL.

Gemtree Vineyards McLaren V, SA r w (w) ★★→★★★ Top-class SHIRAZ alongside TEMPRANILLO and other exotica, linked by quality. Largely biodynamic.

Geoff Merrill McLaren V, SA r w ★★ Ebullient maker of Geoff Merrill and Mt Hurtle brands. TAHBILK owns 50%. Wine report mixed.

Geoff Weaver Ad Hills, SA r w ★★ An 8ha estate at Lenswood. V. fine SAUV BL, CHARD, RIES and CAB SAUV/MERLOT blend.

Giaconda Beech, Vic r w ★★★★ (CHARD) 96' 00' 02' 04' 05' 06' 08' (SHIRAZ) 02' 04' 06' 08' In the mid-1980s Rick Kinzbrunner did that rare thing: walked up a steep, stony hill and came down a champion wine producer. Ranks beside LEEUWIN ESTATE as Australia's best Chard. Shiraz the new star. NEBBIOLO of promise.

Glaetzer-Dixon Tas r w ★★ The GLAETZER clan is famous in Australia for cuddly, warm-climate SHIRAZ. Then Nick Glaetzer set up shop in cool TASMANIA and hit the jackpot with Euro-style RIES, Rhôney Shiraz and meaty PINOT N.

Glaetzer Wines Barossa V, SA r ★★★ Hyper-rich, unfiltered, v. ripe old-vine SHIRAZ led by iconic Amon-Ra. V.gd examples of high-octane style.

Goulburn Valley Vic Old region in temperate mid-Victoria. Full-bodied savoury table wines. MARSANNE, CAB SAUV, SHIRAZ the pick, TAHBILK and MITCHELTON are the mainstay wineries.

Grampians Vic Temperate region in northwest Vic previously known as Great Western. High-quality SHIRAZ and sparkling Shiraz.

Granite Belt QLD High-altitude, (relatively) cool region just north of Queensland/NSW border. Spicy SHIRAZ and rich SEM.

Grant Burge Barossa V, SA r w (br) (sw) (sp) ★★ Smooth reds and whites from the best grapes of Burge's large v'yd holdings.

Great Southern WA Remote, cool area. Albany, Denmark, Frankland River, Mount Barker and Porongurup are official subregions. First-class RIES and SHIRAZ.

Greenstone Vineyard Heathcote, Vic r ★★★ Partnership between David Gleave MW (London), Alberto Antonini (Italy) and Australian viticulturist Mark Walpole: v.gd SHIRAZ, gd SANGIOVESE.

Grosset Clare V, SA r w ★★★→★★★★ (RIES) 00' 02' 03 06' 07' 10' 11' (Gaia) 90' 91' 96' 98' 99 02' 04' 05' 06 09 Fastidious winemaker. Foremost Australian Ries, lovely CHARD, PINOT N and v.gd Gaia CAB SAUV/MERLOT.

Hanging Rock Macedon, Vic r w sp ★→★★★ (Heathcote SHIRAZ) 00' 01' 02' 04' 06' Has successfully moved upmarket with sparkling Macedon and Heathcote Shiraz; bread and butter comes from contract winemaking.

Harcourt Valley Vineyards Bendigo, Vic ★★ r Was "steady as she goes" for yrs, but following a family tragedy has sprung thoroughly to life. Dense, syrupy, seductive SHIRAZ, MALBEC, CAB SAUV.

Hardys r w (sw) sp ★★★→★★★★ (Eileen CHARD) 01' 02' 04' 05 06' 08' 09' (Eileen SHIRAZ) 70' 96' 98' 02' 04' 06' Historic company now part of ACCOLADE. Blends wines from several areas. Best are Eileen Hardy Shiraz and Chard. New Eileen Hardy PINOT N.

Looking for more information on grapes? Try the "Grapes" section on pp.16–26.

Heathcote Vic The 500-million-yr-old, blood-red Cambrian soil has great potential to produce high-quality reds, esp SHIRAZ.

Heggies Eden V, SA r w dr (sw) ★★ V'yd at 500 metres owned by S Smith & Sons, like PEWSEY VALE with v.gd RIES and VIOGNIER. *Chard is still the in-the-know tip.*

Henschke Eden V, SA r w ★★★★ (SHIRAZ) 58' 84' 86' 90' 91' 96' 98' 01 02' 04' 06' (CAB SAUV) 86' 88 90' 96' 98 99' 02' 04' 06' Pre-eminent 120-yr-old family business known for delectable Hill of Grace (Shiraz), v.gd Cab Sauv and red blends, gd whites and some scary prices.

Hewitson SE Aus r (w) ★★★ (*Old Garden Mourvèdre*) 98' 99' 02' 05' 06' 09' Dean Hewitson sources parcels off v. old vines. SHIRAZ and varietal release from "oldest MOURVÈDRE vines on the planet".

Hollick Coon, SA r w (sp) ★★ Gd CAB SAUV, SHIRAZ, MERLOT. Lively restaurant with v'yd views.

Hope Estate Lower Hunter V, NSW ★★ Snapped up Rothbury Estate Winery from TWE; also owns Virgin Hills and Western Austalia v'yds.

Houghton Swan V, WA r w ★★→★★★ The most famous old winery of Western Australia, but now part of ACCOLADE. Soft, ripe Supreme is top-selling, age-worthy white; *a national classic.* V.gd CAB SAUV, VERDELHO, SHIRAZ, etc. sourced from MARGARET RIVER and GREAT SOUTHERN. Doesn't seem to have had much love of late.

Howard Park WA r w ★★★ (RIES) 97' 99' 02' 04 05' 07' 08' 09' (CAB SAUV) 88' 94' 96' 99' 01' 05' 07' 09 (CHARD) 01' 02' 04 05' 07' 08' Scented Ries, Chard; spicy Cab Sauv. Second label: MadFish is excellent value.

Hunter Valley Great name in NSW. Broad, soft, earthy SHIRAZ and gentle SEM that can live for 30 yrs. Terroir-driven styles abound.

Islander Estate, The Kang I, SA r w ★★ Interesting development by Jacques Lurton (Bordeaux). GRENACHE, MALBEC, CAB SAUV/SHIRAZ/VIOGNIER all gd.

Jacob's Creek (Orlando) Barossa V, SA r w (br) (sw) (sp) ★→★★★ A pioneering wine company, now owned by Pernod Ricard. Almost totally focused on various tiers of Jacob's Creek wines, covering all varieties and prices. Premium St Hugo range expanding.

Jasper Hill Heathcote, Vic r w ★★★ (SHIRAZ) 85' 96' 97' 98' 99' 02' 04' 06' 08' 09'

Emily's Paddock Shiraz/CAB FR blend and Georgia's Paddock Shiraz from dry-land estate are intense, long-lived and much admired. Biodynamic.

Jim Barry Clare V, SA r w ★★→★★★ Some great v'yds provide gd RIES, McCrae Wood SHIRAZ and richly robed and oaked The Armagh Shiraz.

John Duval Wines Barossa V, SA r ★★★ John Duval – former chief red-winemaker for PENFOLDS (and Grange) – makes *delicious Rhôney reds* that are supple and smooth, yet amply structured.

Kaesler Barossa V, SA r (w) ★★→★★★ Old Bastard SHIRAZ outranks Old-Vine Shiraz. Wine in the glass generally gd, too (heroic style), but alcohol levels often intrude.

Katnook Estate Coon, SA r w (sw) (sp) ★★★ (Odyssey CAB SAUV) 91' 92' 94' 96' 97' 98' 00 01' 02' 05' 08' Excellent pricey icons *Odyssey* and Prodigy SHIRAZ. Cannily oaked. Standard 2009 Cab Sauv v.gd.

Keith Tulloch Hunter V, NSW r w ★★ Ex-Rothbury winemaker fastidiously crafting elegant yet complex SEM, SHIRAZ, etc.

Kilikanoon Clare V, SA r w ★★→★★★ RIES and SHIRAZ excellent performers in recent yrs. Luscious, beautifully made reds in general. In 2007 bought SEPPELTSFIELD.

King Valley Vic Altitude between 155–860 metres has massive impact on varieties and styles. Around 30 brands headed by BROWN BROTHERS, Dal Zotto, Chrismont and PIZZINI.

Kingston Estate SE Aus ★→★★ Kaleidoscopic array of varietal wines from all over the place, consistency and value (often) providing the glue.

Knappstein Wines Clare V, SA r w ★ Reliable RIES, CAB SAUV/MERLOT, SHIRAZ and Cab Sauv. Owned by LION NATHAN. Modest performance in recent yrs.

Kooyong Mor Pen, Vic ★★★ PINOT N and CHARD of power and structure, PINOT GR of charm. Single-v'yd wines. Winemaker Sandro Moselle has made this estate one of Australia's finest.

Lake Breeze Lang C, SA r (w) ★★ Long-term grape-growers turned winemakers, producing succulently smooth SHIRAZ and CAB SAUV.

Lake's Folly Hunter V, NSW r w ★★★ (CHARD) 97' 99' 00' 01' 04' 05' 07' (CAB SAUV) 69' 89' 93 97' 98' 03' 05' 07' Founded by Max Lake, pioneer of HUNTER VALLEY Cab Sauv. New owners since 2000. Chard often better than Cab Sauv blend.

Langmeil Barossa V, SA r w ★★ Owns oldest block of SHIRAZ (planted in 1843) in world plus other old v'yds, making opulent Shiraz. Oak use could be classier.

Larry Cherubino Wines Frankland R, WA r w ★★★ Ex-HARDYS wunderkind winemaker now putting runs on the board under his own name. Intense SAUV BL, *spicy Shiraz* and curranty CAB SAUV. Crisp Wallflower RIES. Spicy, specific, thoughtful styles.

Lazy Ballerina McLaren V, SA r ★★ Run by young viticulturist James Hook, who calls his winery newsletter *Wine Fight Club*. Rich, tannic, textured SHIRAZ.

Leasingham Clare V, SA r w ★★ Once-important brand with v.gd RIES, SHIRAZ, CAB SAUV and Cab Sauv/MALBEC blend. Husk of its former self: brand-owned by ACCOLADE; v'yds and winery sold off.

Leeuwin Estate Margaret R, WA r w ★★★★ (CHARD) 85' 87' 92' 97' 99' 01' 02' 04' 05' 06 07' 08' Leading Western Australia estate. Superb, age-worthy Art Series Chard. SAUV BL and *Ries* also gd. CAB SAUV fast improving.

Leo Buring Barossa V, SA w ★★★ 79' 84' 91' 94 98 02' 04 05' 06' 08 Part of TWE. Now exclusively RIES; Leonay top label, *ages superbly*. Screwcapped.

Lethbridge Vic r w ★★★ Stylish, small-run producer of CHARD, SHIRAZ, PINOT N. Reputation grows annually.

Limestone Coast Zone SA Important zone, incl Bordertown, COONAWARRA, Mt Benson, Mt Gambier, PADTHAWAY, Robe, WRATTONBULLY.

Lindeman's r w ★→★★★ One of the oldest firms, now owned by TWE. Low-price Bin range now its main focus, a far cry from former glory. Lindeman's COONAWARRA Trio reds unexciting.

Lion Nathan New Zealand brewery; owns KNAPPSTEIN, MITCHELTON, PETALUMA, ST HALLETT, Smithbrook, STONIER and TATACHILLA.

Macedon and Sunbury Vic Adjacent regions, Macedon higher elevation, Sunbury nr Melbourne airport. BINDI, CURLY FLAT, CRAIGLEE, EPIS, Granite Hills, HANGING ROCK.

Main Ridge Estate Mor Pen, Vic r w ★★★ Rich, age-worthy CHARD, PINOT N. Peninsula pioneer Nat White boasts that the region has now made all of its mistakes "because I made them all".

Majella Coon, SA r (w) ★★★ Rising to the top of COONAWARRA cream. SHIRAZ and CAB SAUV often as gd as the super-premium Malleea Cab Sauv/Shiraz.

Margaret River WA Temperate coastal area south of Perth, with superbly elegant wines. Australia's most vibrant tourist wine (and surfing) region. Powerful CHARD, structured CAB SAUV.

Mayford NE Vic r w ★★ Tiny v'yd in a hidden valley that it has all to itself. Star producer of the Alpine Valleys region. SHIRAZ, CHARD, exciting TEMPRANILLO.

McLaren Vale SA Historic region on southern outskirts of Adelaide. Big, alcoholic, flavoursome reds have great appeal in the USA, but CORIOLE, CHAPEL HILL, WIRRA WIRRA, GEMTREE and growing number of others show elegance as well as flavour.

McWilliam's SE Aus r w (br) (sw) ★★→★★★ Family-owned and thriving. Elizabeth SEM the darling of Sydney (though quality wavering), cheaper Hanwood blends outstanding value in many parts of the world. *Lovedale Sem* so consistent and age-worthy that vintages irrelevant. O'Shea SHIRAZ excellent.

Australia didn't have Chardonnay until the mid-20th century. Neither did California.

Meerea Park Hunter V, NSW r w Brothers Garth and Rhys Eather have taken 20 yrs to be an overnight success. Bright-flavoured SEM, CHARD, SHIRAZ.

Mike Press Wines Ad Hills, SA r w ★★ Tiny production, high value. SHIRAZ, CAB SAUV, CHARD, SAUV BL. Has fast become a crowd favourite among those who can get hold of its goodies.

Mitchelton Goulburn V, Vic r w (sw) ★★ Reliable producer of RIES, SHIRAZ, CAB SAUV at several price points, plus specialty made of *Marsanne* and ROUSSANNE.

Mitolo r ★★★ One of best "virtual wineries" (ie. contract v'yds, wineries, winemaker), paying top dollar for high-quality SHIRAZ and CAB SAUV; Ben GLAETZER winemaker. Heroic but (often) irresistible wines.

Moorilla Estate Tas r w (sp) ★★ Nr Hobart on Derwent River. V.gd RIES, CHARD; PINOT N gd. Superb restaurant and you-have-to-see-it-to-believe-it art gallery.

Moorooduc Estate Mor Pen, Vic r w ★★★ Stylish and sophisticated (wild yeast, etc.) producer of top-flight CHARD and PINOT N. Influential.

Moppity Vineyards Hilltops, NSW r w ★★ Making a name for its Res SHIRAZ/VIOGNIER (Hilltops) and CHARD (TUMBARUMBA). Aspirational.

Mornington Peninsula Vic Exciting, cool coastal area 40km south of Melbourne; 1,000ha. Scores of quality boutique wineries. Brilliant tourist destination.

Morris NE Vic (r) (w) br ★★→★★★★ Old winery at RUTHERGLEN for some of Australia's greatest dessert MUSCATS and Tokays/TOPAQUES.

Moss Wood Margaret R, WA r w ★★★★ (CAB SAUV) 80' 85 90' 91' 04' 05' 07' 08' Makes MARGARET RIVER'S most opulent wines from its 11.7ha. SEM, CHARD, super-smooth *Cab Sauv*. Overt oak, dense fruit.

Mount Horrocks Clare V, SA r w ★★→★★★★ Fine, dry RIES and sweet Cordon Cut Ries; CHARD best in region. Reliable quality.

Mount Langi Ghiran Grampians, Vic r w ★★★★ (SHIRAZ) 89' 93' 96' 05' 06' 08' 09' Rich, peppery, *Rhône-like Shiraz*, one of Australia's best cool-climate versions. V.gd sparkling Shiraz, too. Sister of YERING STATION. Winemaker Dan Buckle recently departed; a blow.

Mount Mary Yarra V, Vic w ★★★★ (PINOT N) 97' 99 00' 02' 05' 06' (Quintet) 84' 86'

88' 90' 92' 96' 98' 02' 04' 06 The late Dr John Middleton made tiny amounts of suave CHARD, vivid Pinot N and (best of all) CAB SAUV blend. All age impeccably. Jury still out on modern era.

Mudgee NSW A long-established region northwest of Sydney. Making big reds, surprisingly fine SEM and full CHARD. Struggling to gain traction. Return of Robert Oatley a lifeline.

Murray Valley SA Vast irrigated v'yds. Now at the centre of the drought/climate-change firestorm.

Ngeringa Ad Hills, SA r w ★★ Excellent, perfumed, biodynamic PINOT N. Family history in the cosmetics industry. Rhône SHIRAZ charting well, too.

Ninth Island Tas *See* PIPERS BROOK.

O'Leary Walker Wines Clare V, SA r w ★★★ Two whiz-kids have midlife crisis and leave Beringer Blass to do their own thing – v. well. Low profile, excellent quality.

Orange NSW Cool-climate, high-elevation region: lively MERLOT and SHIRAZ (when ripe) but excellent SAUV BL and CHARD.

Padthaway SA Large area developed as overspill of COONAWARRA. Cool climate; gd CHARD and excellent SHIRAZ (Orlando). Salinity an issue.

Pannell, SC McLaren V, SA r ★★★ Ex-HARDYS chief winemaker Steve Pannell now with his own label. V.gd SHIRAZ and (esp) GRENACHE-based wines. NEBBIOLO rising. Pulled out some beautiful wines of late.

Paringa Estate Mor Pen, Vic r w ★★★★ Maker of spectacular CHARD, PINOT N, SHIRAZ, winning innumerable trophies.

Paxton McLaren V, SA r ★★ Significant v'yd holder. Largely organic/biodynamic. Ripe but elegant SHIRAZ and GRENACHE. Hugely influential – by its deeds – in Australia's biodynamic movement.

Pemberton WA Region between MARGARET RIVER, GREAT SOUTHERN; initial enthusiasm for PINOT N replaced by RIES, CHARD, MERLOT, SHIRAZ.

Penfolds Originally Adelaide, now everywhere r w (br) (sp) ★★→★★★★ (Grange) 52' 53' 55' 60' 62' 63' 66' 71' 76' 78' 83' 86' 90' 94' 96' 98' 99' 02' 04' 05' 06' (CAB SAUV Bin 707) 64' 66' 76' 86' 90' 91' 96' 98' 02' 04' 06' 07' Consistently Australia's best warm-climate red-wine company. Grange (was called Hermitage) deservedly ★★★★. Yattarna CHARD and Bin Chard nr comparable quality to reds. St Henri SHIRAZ champion of understatement.

Penley Estate Coon, SA r w ★★ Rich, textured, fruit-and-oak CAB SAUV; SHIRAZ/ Cab Sauv blend; CHARD. Persistently high levels of alcohol threaten to mar the estate's reputation.

Perth Hills WA Fledgling area 30km east of Perth, with a larger number of growers on mild hillside sites. Millbrook and Western Range best.

Petaluma Ad Hills, SA r w sp ★★★ (RIES) 04' 05' 06' (CHARD) 01' 03' 04' 05 06' (CAB SAUV COONAWARRA) 79' 90' 91 98' 99' 04' 05' 06' '08 Created by industry leader Brian Croser. Reds richer from 1988 on. Fell prey to LION NATHAN in 2002; has lost some of its prominence since.

Peter Lehmann Wines Barossa V, SA r w (br) (sw) (sp) ★★★ Defender of BAROSSA V faith; fought off Allied-Domecq by marriage with Swiss Hess group. Consistently well-priced wines made in substantial quantities. Try Stonewell SHIRAZ and outstanding Res Bin SEM and RIES with 5 yrs' age. 30-yr anniversary in 2012.

Pewsey Vale Ad Hills, SA w ★★★→★★★★ Glorious RIES, esp The Contours, released under screwcap with 5 yrs' bottle-age.

Piano Piano Beech, Vic r w New producer working a v'yd in the next paddock along from GIACONDA. Fine but powerful barrel-fermented CHARD.

Pierro Margaret R, WA r w ★★★ (CHARD) 96' 99' 00' 01' 02' 03 05' 06' 07' 08' 09' Producer of expensive, tangy SEM/SAUV BL and barrel-fermented Chard.

Pipers Brook Tas r w sp ★★ (RIES) 99' 00' 01' 02' 04' 06' 07' 09' (CHARD) 00' 02' 05'

07' 08' Cool-area pioneer; gd Ries, *restrained Chard and sparkling* from Tamar Valley. Second label: Ninth Island. Owned by Belgian Kreglinger family.

Pirramimma McLaren V, SA r w ★★ Century-old family business with large v'yds moving with the times; snappy new packaging, the wines not forgotten.

Pizzini King V, Vic r ★★★ (NEBBIOLO) **98'** 02' 05' 06' Leads the charge towards Italian varieties in Australia. Nebbiolo, SANGIOVESE and blends. Vintages have been difficult of late.

Plantagenet Mt Barker, WA r w (sp) ★★ The region's elder statesman: wide range of varieties, esp rich CHARD, SHIRAZ and vibrant, potent CAB SAUV.

Primo Estate SA r w dr (sw) ★★★ Joe Grilli's many successes incl v.gd MCLAREN VALE cherry, spicy SHIRAZ/SANGIOVESE, tangy COLOMBARD and potent Joseph CAB SAUV/MERLOT.

Punch Yarra V, Vic r w ★★★ The Lance family ran and established Diamond Valley for decades but when they sold it, they retained the close-planted PINOT N v'yd. It grows detailed, decisive, age-worthy wines.

Pyrenees Central Victoria region producing rich, often minty reds. DALWHINNIE, TALTARNI, Blue Pyrenees, Mt Avoca, FLETCHER and Dog Rock wineries all ascendant.

Richmond Grove Barossa V, SA r w ★ Gd RIES at bargain prices; not much else. Owned by Orlando Wyndham but faceless.

Riverina NSW Large-volume irrigated zone centred on Griffith.

Robert Oatley Wines Mudgee, NSW r w ★ Robert Oatley created ROSEMOUNT ESTATE. Ambition burns anew. Quality slowly improving. Single-v'yd SHIRAZ v.gd.

Rockford Barossa V, SA r w sp ★★→★★★★ Small producer from old, low-yielding v'yds; reds best, also iconic sparkling Black SHIRAZ.

Rosemount Estate r w A major presence in production terms, but a shadow of its former self quality-wise.

Ruggabellus Barossa V, SA r w ★★★ New outfit causing a stir. Funkier, more savoury version of the BAROSSA. Old oak, minimal sulphur, wild yeast, whole bunches/ stems. Blends of GRENACHE, SHIRAZ, MATARO, CINSAULT and others.

Rutherglen and Glenrowan Vic Two of four regions in the northeast Vic zone, justly famous for sturdy reds and magnificent fortified dessert wines.

Saltram Barossa V, SA r w ★★ Mamre Brook (SHIRAZ, CAB SAUV, CHARD) and No 1 Shiraz are leaders. TWE owned.

Samuel's Gorge McLaren V, SA r ★★ Justin McNamee has hair like Sideshow Bob (*The Simpsons*) but is making SHIRAZ and TEMPRANILLO of character and place.

Sandalford Swan V, WA r w (br) ★★ Fine old winery with contrasting styles of red and white single-grape wines from SWAN VALLEY and MARGARET RIVER regions.

Savaterre Beech, Vic r w ★★★ (PINOT N) 02' **04'** 06' 08' Tough run of seasons but a v.gd producer of CHARD and Pinot N. Close-planted.

Scotchmans Hill Vic ★★ r w Makes significant quantities of cool-climate PINOT N, CHARD and spicy SHIRAZ.

Seppelt Grampians, Vic r w br (sw) sp ★★★ (St Peter's SHIRAZ) **71' 85 86' 91' 96' 97'** 99' 04' 05' 06 08' Historic name now owned by TWE. An impressive array of region-specific RIES, CHARD, Shiraz.

Seppeltsfield Barossa V, SA National Trust Heritage Winery bought by KILIKANOON in 2007. Fortified wine stocks back to 1878.

Setanta Wines Ad Hills, SA r w ★★★ The Sullivan family, first-generation Australians originally from Ireland, makes wonderful RIES, CHARD, SAUV BL, SHIRAZ, CAB SAUV, with Irish mythology labels of striking design.

Sevenhill Clare V, SA r w (br) ★ Owned by the Jesuitical Manresa Society since 1851. Consistently gd SHIRAZ; RIES.

Seville Estate Yarra V, Vic r w ★★★ (SHIRAZ) **94 97' 99'** 02' 04' 05' 06' 08' Excellent CHARD, Shiraz, PINOT N. Bit of a buzz about this place of late.

Shadowfax Vic r w ★★ →★★★ Stylish winery, part of Werribee Park; also hotel based on 1880s mansion. V.gd CHARD, PINOT N, SHIRAZ.

Shaw & Smith Ad Hills, SA (r) w ★★★ Founded by Martin Shaw and Australia's first MW, Michael Hill-Smith. Crisp, harmonious SAUV BL; complex, barrel-fermented M3 CHARD; and, surpassing them both, SHIRAZ.

Shelmerdine Vineyards Heathcote, Vic r w ★★ V. elegant wines from estate in the YARRA VALLEY and HEATHCOTE.

South Burnett Qld's second region: 15 wineries and more births (and some deaths) imminent, symptomatic of southeast corner of the state.

South Coast NSW Zone Incl Shoalhaven Coast and Southern Highlands.

Southcorp Former Australian giant; now part of TWE. Owns LINDEMAN'S, PENFOLDS, ROSEMOUNT ESTATE, Seaview, SEPPELT, WYNNS and many others.

Southern NSW Zone Incl CANBERRA, Gundagai, Hilltops, TUMBARUMBA.

Spinifex Barossa V, SA r ★★★ Small, high-quality producer of complex SHIRAZ and GRENACHE blends. Nothing over-the-top. Wonderful producer.

Stanton & Killeen Rutherglen, Vic r br ★★★ The untimely death of Chris Killeen in 2007 was a major blow to this fine producer of fortified and dry red wines but his children carry on – in gd style, too.

Stefano Lubiana S Tas r w sp ★★★ Beautiful v'yds on the banks of the Derwent River 20 minutes from Hobart. V.gd PINOT N, sparkling, MERLOT and CHARD.

Stella Bella Margaret R, WA r w ★★★ Some humdinger wines here. Try CAB SAUV, SEM/SAUV BL, CHARD, SHIRAZ, SANGIOVESE/Cab Sauv. Highly individual.

St Hallett Barossa V, SA r w ★★★ (Old Block) 86' 90' 91' 98 99' 01' 02' 05' 06' 08' Old Block SHIRAZ the star, rest of range is smooth, stylish. LION NATHAN-owned.

Stoney Rise Tas r w ★★★ In another life Joe Holyman was wicket-keeper for the Tasmanian cricket team; he holds the first-class record for the most number of catches on debut. His PINOT N and CHARD now catch Tassie's cool rays; Joe keeps the wines taut and tidy. Age-worthy.

Shiraz tops – in Tasmania?
The Jimmy Watson Trophy is Australia's most famous wine award. It was won in 2011 by, of all things, a Tasmanian SHIRAZ. TASMANIA has an inglorious history of hard, unripe, green Shiraz. Or so many thought, until the 2010 GLAETZER-DIXON Shiraz stole the show. It's a ripper of a wine: spicy, ripe, characterful. Is it a freak, or an early sign of a climate-changed world?

Stonier Wines Mor Pen, Vic r w ★★ (CHARD) 02 03' 04' 05' 06' 07' (PINOT N) 00' 02' 04' 05 06' 07' 08' 09' Consistently gd; Res notable for elegance. LION NATHAN-owned.

Sunbury Vic *See* MACEDON AND SUNBURY.

Swan Valley WA Located 20 minutes north of Perth. Birthplace of wine in the west. Hot climate makes strong, low-acid wines; being rejuvenated for wine tourism. FABER V'YDS leading the quality way.

Tahbilk Goulburn V, Vic r w ★★★ (MARSANNE) 74' 82' 92' 97' 99' 01' 03' 05' 06' 07' 08' (SHIRAZ) 68' 71' 76' 86 98' 02' 04' 05 06' Historic family estate: long-ageing reds, also RIES and some of Australia's best *Marsanne*. Res CAB SAUV outstanding; value for money ditto. Rare 1860 Vines Shiraz, too.

Taltarni Pyrenees, Vic r w sp ★★★ SHIRAZ and CAB SAUV in best shape for yrs. Long-haul wines but jack-hammer no longer required to remove the tannin from your gums. Clover Hill repaying the faith.

Tamar Ridge N Tas r w (sp) ★★ 230+ha of vines make this a major player in TASMANIA. Acquired in 2010 by BROWN BROTHERS. Gd PINOT N.

AUSTRALIA

Tapanappa SA r ★★★ WRATTONBULLY collaboration between Brian Croser, Bollinger and J-M Cazes of Pauillac. CAB SAUV blend, SHIRAZ, MERLOT. Surprising *Pinot N* from Fleurieu Peninsula.

TarraWarra Yarra V, Vic r w ★★★ (CHARD) 02' 04' 05' 06' 08' 09' (PINOT N) 00' 01 02' 04' 05' 06' Has moved from hefty and idiosyncratic to elegant, mainstream Chard and Pinot N. Res far better than standard.

Tasmania Production continues to surge but still small. Outstanding sparkling PINOT N, RIES in cool climate, CHARD, SAUV BL, PINOT GR v.gd cool-climate styles, all in great demand.

Tatachilla McLaren V, SA r w ★★ Significant production of whites and gd reds. Acquired by LION NATHAN in 2002. Off the boil.

Taylors Wines Clare V, SA r w ★★ Large-scale production led by RIES, SHIRAZ, CAB SAUV. Exports under Wakefield Wines brand (trademark issues with Taylor's Port) with success.

Ten Minutes by Tractor Mor Pen, Vic r w ★★★ Amusing name, smart packaging; this estate is rapidly growing under owner Martin Spedding. SAUV BL, CHARD, PINOT N all v.gd.

Teusner Barossa V, SA r ★★★ Old vines, clever winemaking, pure fruit flavours. Leads a BAROSSA VALLEY trend towards "more wood, no gd". All about the grapes.

Topaque Vic Iconic Rutherglen sticky Tokay gains new name to placate the Magyars.

Torbreck Barossa V, SA r (w) ★★★ The most stylish of the cult wineries beloved of the USA. Focus on old-vine Rhône varieties led by SHIRAZ. Rich, sweet, high alcohol – a sip goes a long way.

Torzi Matthews Eden V, SA r ★★ Rich, stylish SHIRAZ. Lower-priced wines often as gd. Torzi Schist Rock Shiraz difficult to say, politely, after a glass or two.

Treasury Wine Estates (TWE) Aussie wine behemoth. New name of the merged Beringer Blass and SOUTHCORP wine groups. Dozens of brands in Australia that come and go like mushrooms after rain.

Trentham Estate Vic (r) w ★★ 60,000 cases of family-grown and -made, sensibly priced wines from "boutique" winery on Murray River.

Tumbarumba Cool-climate NSW region nestled in Australian Alps. Sites between 500–800 metres above sea level. CHARD the star. Mandatory to add "cha-cha-cha" after saying "Tumbarumba".

Turkey Flat Barossa V, SA r p ★★★ Top producer of bright-coloured rosé, GRENACHE and SHIRAZ from core of 150-yr-old v'yd. Controlled alcohol and oak. New single-v'yd wines.

Two Hands Barossa V, SA r ★★ Cult winery with gd SHIRAZ from PADTHAWAY, MCLAREN VALE, Langhorne Creek, BAROSSA VALLEY and HEATHCOTE stuffed full of alcohol, rich fruit and the kitchen sink.

Tyrrell's Hunter V, NSW r w ★★★★ (SEM) 99' 00' 01' 05' 07' 08' 09' 10' 11' (Vat 47 CHARD) 00' 02' 04' 05' 07' 09' 10' Australia's greatest maker of SEM, Vat 1 now joined with a series of individual v'yd or subregional wines. *Vat 47*, Australia's first Chard, continues to defy the climatic odds. Outstanding old-vine 4 Acres SHIRAZ and Vat 9 Shiraz. The real deal.

Vasse Felix Margaret R, WA r w ★★★ (CAB SAUV) 97' 98' 99' 01 04' 07' 08' 09' With CULLEN, pioneer of MARGARET RIVER. Elegant Cab Sauv for mid-weight balance. Generally resurgent. CHARD on rapid rise. Winemaker Virginia Willcock has the place singing.

Voyager Estate Margaret R, WA r w ★★★ 35,000 cases of estate-grown, powerful, rich SEM, SAUV BL, CHARD, CAB SAUV/MERLOT. Terrific quality. Hard to fault.

Wendouree Clare V, SA r ★★★ Treasured, iconic maker (tiny quantities) of powerful and concentrated reds, based on SHIRAZ, CAB SAUV, MOURVÈDRE, MALBEC. Immensely long-lived. Recently moved to screwcap. Buy for the next generation.

West Cape Howe Denmark, WA r w ★★ The minnow that swallowed the whale in 2009 when it purchased 7,700-tonne Goundrey winery and 237ha of estate v'yds. V.gd SHIRAZ and CAB SAUV blends.

Willow Creek Mor Pen, Vic r w ★★★ Gd gear. Impressive producer of CHARD and PINOT N in particular. Ex-STONIER winemaker Geraldine McFaul in charge.

Wirra Wirra McLaren V, SA r w (sw) (sp) ★★★ (RSW SHIRAZ) 98' 99' 02' 04' 05' 06' 07' 09' (CAB SAUV) 97' 98' 01' 02' 04' 05' 06' 09' High-quality wines in flashy new livery. RSW Shiraz has edged in front of Cab Sauv; both superb. The Angelus Cab Sauv now Dead Ringer in export markets.

Wolf Blass Barossa V, SA r w (br) (sw) (sp) ★★ (Black Label CAB SAUV blend) 90' 91' 96' 98' 02' 04' 05 06' 07' Owned by TWE. Not the noisy player it once was.

Woodlands Margaret R, WA r (w) ★★★ 7ha of 30-yr-old+ CAB SAUV, among the top v'yds in the region; plus younger but still v.gd plantings of other Bordeaux reds. Flying.

Wrattonbully SA Important grape-growing region in LIMESTONE COAST ZONE for 30 yrs; profile lifted by recent arrival of TAPANAPPA and Peppertree.

Wynns Coon, SA r w ★★★★ (SHIRAZ) 55' 63 86' 90' 91' 94' 96' 98 99' 02 04' 05' 06' 09' (CAB SAUV) 57' 60' 82' 85' 86' 90' 91' 94' 96' 98' 00 02 04' 05' 06' 07' 08' 09' TWE-owned COONAWARRA classic. RIES, CHARD, Shiraz and *Cab Sauv* are all v.gd, esp Black Label Cab Sauv and *John Riddoch Cab Sauv*. Recent single-v'yd releases add lustre.

Looking for more information on grapes? Try the "Grapes" section on pp.16–26.

Yabby Lake Mor Pen, Vic r w ★★★ Joint venture between movie magnate Robert Kirby, Larry McKenna and Tod Dexter. Quality on sharp rise since winemaker Tom Carson arrived. Single-site PINOT N and SHIRAZ excellent.

Yalumba Barossa V, SA, SA r w sp ★★★ 163 years young, family-owned. Showing considerable verve. *Full spectrum of high-quality wines*, from budget to elite single-v'yd. In outstanding form. Entry-level Y Series excellent value.

Yarra Valley Vic Historic area nr Melbourne. Growing emphasis on v. successful PINOT N, CHARD, SHIRAZ, sparkling.

Yarra Yarra Yarra V, Vic r w ★★★ Increased to 7ha, giving greater access to fine SEM/SAUV BL and CAB SAUV, each in classic Bordeaux style.

Yarra Yering Yarra V, Vic r w ★★★★ (Dry Reds) 80' 81' 82' 83 84 85' 90' 91' 93' 94 97' 99' 00' 01' 02' 04' 05' 06' 08' 09' Best-known Lilydale boutique winery. Esp racy, powerful PINOT N; deep, herby CAB SAUV (Dry Red No 1); SHIRAZ (Dry Red No 2). Luscious, daring flavours in red and white. Much-admired founder/owner Bailey Carrodus died in 2008. Acquired in 2009 by KAESLER.

Yellow Tail NSW See CASELLA.

Yeringberg Yarra V, Vic r w ★★★ (MARSANNE) 91' 92 94' 95 97 98 00 02' 04 05 06' 09' (CAB SAUV) 77' 80 81' 84' 88' 90 97' 98 00 04 05' 06' 08' Dreamlike historic estate still in the hands of founding family. Makes small quantities of v.-high-quality Marsanne, ROUSSANNE, CHARD, CAB SAUV, PINOT N.

Yering Station/Yarrabank Yarra V, Vic r w sp ★★★ On site of Victoria's first v'yd; replanted after 80-yr gap. Yering Station table wines (Res CHARD, PINOT N, SHIRAZ and VIOGNIER); Yarrabank (esp fine sparkling wines in joint venture with Champagne Devaux).

Zema Estate Coon, SA r ★ One of the last bastions of hand-pruning in COONAWARRA. Powerful, straightforward reds. Serviceable of late.

New Zealand

Abbreviations used in the text:

Auck	Auckland
B of P	Bay of Plenty
Cant	Canterbury
C Ot	Central Otago
Gis	Gisborne
Hawk	Hawke's Bay
Hend	Henderson
Marl	Marlborough
Mart	Martinborough
Nel	Nelson
Waih	Waiheke Island
Waip	Waipara
Wair	Wairarapa

New Zealand presents a more complex picture than its image as a purveyor of herbaceous Sauvignon Blanc might suggest. And it needs to: Sauvignon is NZ's flagship wine, but can be somewhat predictable, and the best producers are looking for ways of appealing to consumers who want something more interesting. A touch of barrel fermentation – say, five to ten per cent – is one way; limiting your crops so your wine can start to reflect its terroir is another. Pinot Noir is the next winner, with Central Otago and Martinborough making juicy wines of real presence. Syrah is the coming thing, superb in Hawke's Bay; and now Grüner Veltliner is stirring up interest. 2011 even brought the first Albariño. But overproduction is a problem. The 2011 harvest was even bigger than the previous record, set in 2008 and equalled in 2009. Prices are coming down. The truth is that the world doesn't need any more wine, especially Sauvignon.

Recent vintages

2011 Biggest-ever harvest. Summer combined extreme heat in many regions with serious floods. Regions in the middle of the country – including Marlborough – fared best; elsewhere, a stiff test of grape-growing and winemaking skills.

2010 Aromatic, strongly flavoured Marlborough Sauv Bl with firm acid spine. Hawke's Bay had outstanding Chard.

2009 Aromatic, intense and zingy Marlborough Sauv Bl and concentrated, ripe Hawke's Bay reds. Central Otago frosty and cool, with variable Pinot N.

Akarua C Ot r (p) (w) ★★ Respected producer at Bannockburn. Powerful, rich Res PINOT N, impressive mid-tier Pinot N; v.gd, drink-young style Rua. Fresh, racy CHARD, intense RIES and scented, full-bodied PINOT GR.

Allan Scott Marl r w sp ★★ Medium-sized family producer. Gd slightly sweet RIES; elegant, skilfully oaked CHARD; tropical-fruit-flavoured SAUV BL; sturdy, spicy PINOT N. Recent focus on single-v'yd, organic and sparkling wines.

Alpha Domus Hawk r w ★★ V.gd CHARD, VIOGNIER. Concentrated, Bordeaux-style reds, esp savoury MERLOT-based The Navigator, and notably dark, rich CAB SAUV-based The Aviator. Top wines labelled AD (superb Noble Selection from SEM). Everyday range, The Pilot.

Amisfield C Ot r p w ★★ Impressive, fleshy, smooth PINOT GR; tense, minerally RIES (dr sw); lively, ripe SAUV BL; classy Pinot Rosé and floral, complex PINOT N (Rocky Knoll is Rolls-Royce model). Lake Hayes is lower-tier label.

Ara Marl r w ★★ Huge v'yd in Waihopai Valley for SAUV BL and PINOT N. Dry, minerally wines, full of interest. Top-tier: Select Blocks; mid-tier: Single Estate. 3rd-tier Pathway wines gd value. New winemaker in 2011, Jeff Clarke (ex-Montana).

Astrolabe Marl r w ★★ Label part-owned by winemaker Simon Waghorn. Best-known for rich, harmonious Voyage SAUV BL. Also gd PINOT GR, RIES, CHARD, PINOT N. Second label: Durvillea.

Looking for more information on grapes? Try the "Grapes" section on pp.16–26.

Ata Rangi Mart r (p) (w) ★★★ Small, highly respected. *Outstanding Pinot N* (05 06' 07 08 09') is one of NZ's greatest, cellaring well for a decade. V.gd young-vine Crimson PINOT N. Rich, concentrated Craighall CHARD and Lismore PINOT GR.

Auckland Largest city (northern, warm) in NZ with 2% of v'yd area. Nearby wine districts are Henderson, Huapai, Kumeu (long established) and newer (since 1980s) Matakana, Clevedon, Waiheke Island. Often classy Bordeaux-style reds, bold, ripe SYRAH and gd, underrated CHARD.

Auntsfield Marl r w ★★ Excellent wines from site of the region's first v'yd, planted in 1873, uprooted in 1931 and replanted 1999. Strong, tropical-fruit-flavoured SAUV BL (partly barrel-fermented); fleshy, peachy, rich CHARD; sturdy, dense PINOT N (Heritage is esp lush, powerful).

Awatere Valley Marl Key subregion, with few wineries but huge v'yd area (more than Hawke's Bay). Slightly cooler and drier than the larger WAIRAU VALLEY, with racy, herbaceous, minerally SAUV BL and scented, often slightly leafy PINOT N.

Babich Hend r w ★★·★★★ Sizeable family firm (1916). HAWKE'S BAY, MARLBOROUGH v'yds. Refined, age-worthy, single-v'yd Irongate CHARD (07', 08,10) and Irongate CAB/MERLOT/CAB FR (09', 07' 05'). Ripe, dry Marlborough SAUV BL is big seller. Mid-tier Winemaker's Res. Flagship: The Patriarch (bold red blend).

Bald Hills C Ot r (p) (w) ★★ Bannockburn v'yd with crisp, dry PINOT GR; floral, full-bodied, slightly sweet RIES and generous, savoury, complex PINOT N. Delicious, drink-young Pinot N, 3 Acres.

Bell Hill Cant r w ★★★ Tiny, elevated v'yd on limestone, owned by Marcel GIESEN and Sherwyn Veldhuizen. Strikingly rich, finely textured CHARD and gorgeously scented, powerful, velvety PINOT N. Second label: Old Weka Pass.

Bilancia Hawk r (w) ★★ Small producer of classy SYRAH (incl brilliant, powerful, nutty, spicy La Collina 09' 07) and PINOT GR (Res is richer, sweeter.) La Collina White is VIOGNIER/GEWURZ (powerful apricot, spice flavours).

Blackenbrook Nel (r) w ★★ Small winery with excellent aromatic whites, esp highly perfumed, rich GEWURZ, PINOT GR. Punchy SAUV BL; fleshy, supple Res PINOT N; v. promising MONTEPULCIANO. Second label: St Jacques.

Borthwick Wair r w ★★ Lively, tropical-fruit SAUV BL; rich, dryish RIES; peachy, toasty CHARD; fleshy, dry PINOT GR; deep-coloured, perfumed, muscular PINOT N.

Brancott Estate Marl r w ★·★★★ Brand formerly used by PERNOD RICARD NZ only in the USA, as a substitute for Montana, but since 2010 has replaced the Montana brand worldwide. Top wines: Letter Series (eg. "B" Brancott SAUV BL). Biggest-selling: crisp, grassy MARLBOROUGH Sauv Bl (one million cases per year); floral, smooth, easy-drinking South Island PINOT N.

Brightwater Nel (r) w ★★ Impressive whites, esp crisp, flavour-packed SAUV BL; fresh, pure, medium-dry RIES; lively, citrussy, gently oaked CHARD and rich, gently sweet PINOT GR. Top wines labelled Lord Rutherford.

Brookfields Hawk r w ★★ Excellent "gold label" CAB SAUV/MERLOT; gd CHARD, PINOT GR, GEWURZ and SYRAH (esp powerful, spicy Hillside Syrah). Sturdy, satisfying, mid-priced Burnfoot Merlot and Ohiti Cab Sauv.

Cable Bay Waih r p w ★★ Mid-sized producer with v. refined Waiheke CHARD; sturdy, complex VIOGNIER and outstanding, bold yet stylish SYRAH. Subtle, fine-textured Marlborough SAUV BL. Second label: Selection (formerly Culley).

Canterbury NZ's fourth-largest wine region; almost all top v'yds are in warm, sheltered Waipara district. SAUV BL is most heavily planted, but greatest success with RIES and PINOT N. Emerging strengths in GEWURZ and PINOT GR.

Carrick C Ot r w ★★ Bannockburn winery with crisp, flavourful whites (PINOT GR, SAUV BL, CHARD), excellent RIES (dr sw s/sw) and densely packed PINOT N, built to last. Drink-young style Unravelled Pinot N is also sturdy and rich.

Central Otago (r) 09 10 (w) 09 10 Cool, relatively low rainfall, mountainous region (now NZ's fifth-largest) in southern South Island. Centre is Queenstown. Scented, crisp RIES and PINOT GR; PINOT N notably perfumed and silky, with plenty of drink-young charm. Promising Champagne-style sparkling.

Chard Farm C Ot r w ★★ Rich, citrussy, medium RIES, fleshy, oily PINOT GR and typically perfumed, midweight, supple PINOT N (River Run: floral, charming; Matá-Au more complex). Also light, smooth Rabbit Ranch Pinot N.

Church Road Hawk r w ★★→★★★ PERNOD RICARD NZ winery with deep Hawke's Bay roots. Rich, refined CHARD; ripe, oak-aged SAUV BL; elegant, Bordeaux-like MERLOT/CAB SAUV (v.gd value). Top-flight Res wines; prestige claret-style red TOM (02' 07'). Mid-priced Cuve range is superb quality and value.

Churton Marl r w ★★★ Subtle, complex, finely textured SAUV BL; sturdy, creamy VIOGNIER and fragrant, spicy, harmonious PINOT N (esp The Abyss – oldest vines, greater depth).

Clearview Hawk r p w ★★→★★★ Impressive oak-fermented Res SAUV BL; hedonistic, lush, super-charged Res CHARD; dark, rich Res CAB FR, Enigma (MERLOT-based), Old Olive Block (CAB SAUV blend). Second-tier: Beachhead, Cape Kidnappers.

Clifford Bay Marl r w ★★→★★★ Attractive, affordable whites – SAUV BL is best, with fresh, racy gooseberry and lime; floral, smooth PINOT N. Linked to VAVASOUR.

Clos Henri Marl r w ★★→★★★ Established by Henri Bourgeois of Sancerre. Delicious, weighty, rounded SAUV BL (grown in stony soils and partly barrel-fermented), one of NZ's finest; vibrant, supple PINOT N (clay soils). Second label (based on soil type): Bel Echo. Third label (based on young vines): Petit Clos.

Clos Marguerite Marl r w ★★ Single-v'yd AWATERE VALLEY wines. Unusually sweet-fruited, minerally, long SAUV BL is the star; also mid-weight, savoury PINOT N.

Cloudy Bay Marl r w ★★★ Large-volume SAUV BL (weighty, dry, finely textured; since 2010, some barrel-ageing) – NZ's most famous wine. CHARD (robust, complex, crisp) and PINOT N (floral, supple) all classy. Pelorus vintage sparkling (toasty, rich, elegant), Chard-pred NV. Rarer GEWURZ, Late Harvest RIES, barrel-aged, medium-dry Ries and Te Koko (oak-aged Sauv Bl) now best. Owned by LVMH.

Constellation New Zealand Auck r w ★→★★ NZ's second-largest wine company, previously the Nobilo Wine Group, now owned by US-based Constellation Brands. Nobilo MARLBOROUGH SAUV BL (fresh, ripe, tropical) is now the biggest-selling Sauv Bl in the USA. Superior varietals labelled Nobilo Icon (weighty and ripely herbaceous Sauv Bl esp impressive); v.gd Drylands Sauv Bl. *See* KIM CRAWFORD, MONKEY BAY, SELAKS.

Cooper's Creek Auck r w ★★ Extensive range of gd-value wines from four regions. Excellent Swamp Res CHARD; v.gd SAUV BL, RIES; MERLOT; top-value VIOGNIER. SV (Select V'yd) range is mid-tier. NZ's first ARNEIS (2006), first GRÜNER VELTLINER (2008), first ALBARIÑO (2011).

Corbans Auck r w ★→★★★ Former PERNOD RICARD NZ brand, sold in 2010 to brewer Lion (owner of WITHER HILLS) and its joint venture partner Indevin. Best: Cottage Block, Private Bin. Quality from basic to outstanding. Quiet lately.

Craggy *Range* Hawk r w ★★→★★★ Mid-sized winery with v'yds in HAWKE'S BAY and MARTINBOROUGH. V. stylish CHARD, PINOT N; excellent mid-range MERLOT and SYRAH from GIMBLETT GRAVELS; strikingly dense, ripe Sophia (Merlot), The Quarry (CAB SAUV) and Le Sol (SYRAH 09' 08 07'). Most recent reds are more supple, refined. Cheaper regional blends labelled Wild Rock.

Darling, The Marl ★★ Winemaker Chris Darling and viticulturist Bart Arnst (ex-SERESIN) produce organic SAUV BL (rich, ripe, partly barrel-fermented) and v.gd PINOT GR, GEWURZ, PINOT N.

Delegat's Auck r w ★★ V. large company (two million cases per year), still controlled by brother-and-sister team, Jim and Rose Delegat. V'yds and other big wineries in HAWKE'S BAY and MARLBOROUGH. Res CHARD and CAB SAUV/MERLOT offer v.gd quality and value. Hugely successful OYSTER BAY brand.

Delta Marl r w ★★ Owned by consultant-winemaker Matt Thomson, UK importer David Gleave and others. Vibrant, tropical-fruit-flavoured, single-v'yd SAUV BL and floral, silky PINOT N. Top label: Hatter's Hill (richer, more new oak).

Destiny Bay Waih r ★★★ Expatriate Americans make Bordeaux-style reds: lush, brambly, silky. Flagship is substantial, deep, savoury Magna Praemia (mostly CAB SAUV). Mid-tier: Mystae. Destinae has drink-young appeal. All classy, high-priced.

Deutz Auck sp ★★★ Champagne house gives its name to fine sparkling from MARLBOROUGH by PERNOD RICARD NZ. NV is lively, yeasty and intense (min 2 yrs on lees). Vintage Blanc de Blancs is finely focused, citrussy, piercing (NZ's most awarded bubbly). Rosé is crisp, yeasty and strawberryish. Prestige is CHARD-pred, v. classy (07).

Distant Land Auck r w ★→★★ Newish brand from old family winery. Best are crisp, strong MARLBOROUGH SAUV BL; well-spiced GEWURZ and scented, rich, nectarine- and pear-flavoured Marlborough PINOT GR.

Dog Point Marl r w ★★ Grower Ivan Sutherland and winemaker James Healy (both ex-CLOUDY BAY) make unusually complex, oak-aged SAUV BL (Section 94), CHARD (subtle, layered) and PINOT N (one of region's best.) Also limey, smooth, unoaked Sauv Bl.

Dry River Mart r w ★★★ Small winery, now American-owned. Elegant, long-lived CHARD, RIES and PINOT GR (NZ's first outstanding Pinot Gr), GEWURZ; gorgeous late-harvest whites; floral, v. sweet-fruited and slowly evolving PINOT N (03' 05 06' 07 08 09).

Elephant Hill Hawk r (p) w ★★ German-owned coastal v'yd and winery at Te Awanga. Sophisticated wines: v. pure VIOGNIER; rich and vibrant CHARD; highly scented, delicate PINOT GR and floral, supple SYRAH.

Escarpment Mart r w ★★ Sturdy, Alsace-like PINOT GR; fleshy, soft CHARD; complex, concentrated PINOT N from Larry McKenna, ex-MARTINBOROUGH V'YD. Top label: Kupe. Single-v'yd, old-vine reds launched from 2006. Martinborough Pinot N is district label. The Edge Pinot Noir: drink young.

Esk Valley Hawk r p w ★★→★★★ Owned by VILLA MARIA. Some of NZ's most voluptuous MERLOT-based reds (esp Winemakers Res 09' 07' 06'); excellent Merlot/MALBEC Rosé; v. satisfying CHARD, CHENIN BL and MARLBOROUGH SAUV BL. Flagship red: The Terraces (super-charged, single-v'yd blend, Malbec/Merlot/CAB FR 09' 06' 04' 02').

Fairhall Downs Marl r w ★★ Single-v'yd wines from elevated site. Weighty, dry PINOT GR; peachy, nutty, full-flavoured CHARD; rich, sweet-fruited SAUV BL (Hugo is complex, oak-aged style); perfumed, smooth PINOT N. Second label: Torea.

Felton Road C Ot r w ★★★ Star winery in warm Bannockburn. Bold, supple, graceful PINOT N Block 3 and 5 (06' 07 08' 09 10'); light, intense RIES (dr s/sw) outstanding; excellent CHARD (esp Block 2) and regular Pinot N. Superb *Cornish Point Pinot N* from nearby v'yd.

Forrest Marl r p w ★★ Mid-size winery with v. wide range. Gd SAUV BL and RIES; gorgeous botrytized Ries; flavour-crammed Hawke's Bay Newton/Forrest Cornerstone (Bordeaux red blend). Distinguished flagship range, John Forrest Collection. Popular low-alcohol Ries The Doctors.

Foxes Island Marl r w ★★ Smallish producer. rich, smooth CHARD, finely textured SAUV BL, scented, rich RIES and elegant, supple PINOT N. Gd, large-volume Sauv Bl and Pinot N under Fox Junior brand.

Framingham Marl r p w ★★ Owned by Sogrape (*see* Portugal). Fine, aromatic whites: intense, zesty RIES (esp rich Classic) from 30-yr-old vines. Lush, slightly sweet PINOT GR, GEWURZ. Subtle, dry SAUV BL. Scented, silky PINOT N. F-Series (rare, "innovative" wines, incl several outstanding sweet Ries).

Fromm Marl r w ★★★ Initially powerful, tannic, now more charming reds. Sturdy, long-lived PINOT N, esp Fromm V'yd (firmly structured, 09' 05') and Clayvin V'yd (rich, elegant, 08 07'). Also stylish, citrussy, minerally Clayvin CHARD. Earlier-drinking La Strada range also v.gd.

Sir George Fistonich, owner of Villa Maria, is NZ's only wine knight.

Gibbston Valley C Ot r p w ★★ Pioneer winery with popular restaurant. Strength is PINOT N – esp rich, complex CENTRAL OTAGO blend and robust, exuberantly fruity Res (09'). Superb single-v'yd reds (School House, China Terrace). Racy whites, esp zingy, medium-dry RIES and scented, full-bodied PINOT GR.

Giesen Cant r w ★→★★ Large family winery. Most is fresh, tangy MARLBOROUGH SAUV BL. Also weighty The Brothers Sauv Bl and barrel-fermented The August Sauv Bl. Fast-improving PINOT N (esp The Brothers).

Gimblett Gravels Hawk Defined area (800ha+ planted), with v. free-draining soils noted for rich Bordeaux-style reds (mostly MERLOT-pred) and fragrant, vibrant SYRAH. Best of both are world-class. Also powerful, age-worthy CHARD, VIOGNIER.

Gisborne Gis (r) 09' 10' (w) 10' NZ's third-largest region, although not expanding. Abundant sunshine and rain, with fertile soils. Key strength is CHARD (deliciously fragrant and soft in youth, but the best mature well). Excellent GEWURZ, VIOGNIER; MERLOT, PINOT GR more variable.

Gladstone Wair r w ★★ Tropical SAUV BL; weighty, partly oak-aged PINOT GR; gd dry RIES; classy VIOGNIER; v. graceful PINOT N under top label, Gladstone; 12,000 Miles is lower-priced brand.

Grasshopper Rock C Ot r ★★ Estate-grown at Alexandra. One of the subregion's finest reds: strong cherry and herb flavours, nutty oak and savoury complexity.

Greenhough Nel r w ★★→★★★ One of region's top producers, with immaculate RIES, SAUV BL, CHARD, PINOT N. Top label: Hope V'yd (complex Chard; powerful, old-vine PINOT BL; mushroomy Pinot N).

Greystone Waip r w ★★ Emerging star with v. classy, aromatic whites (RIES, GEWURZ, PINOT GR – all rich, finely textured); fast-improving CHARD and SAUV BL; promising PINOT N.

Greywacke Marl r w ★★ Label of Kevin Judd, ex-CLOUDY BAY. Named after a soil type. Tight, elegant SAUV BL; weighty, complex CHARD; fleshy PINOT GR; gently sweet RIES and silky PINOT N.

Grove Mill Marl r w ★★ Attractive whites, incl v.gd, punchy SAUV BL and slightly sweet

PINOT GR, RIES. Reds less exciting. Gd-value lower-tier Sanctuary brand. Reported a loss of over $NZ3 million in 2011.

Hans Herzog Marl r w ★★★ Power-packed, classy and long-lived MERLOT/CAB SAUV (the region's greatest); MONTEPULCIANO; PINOT N; sturdy, dry VIOGNIER and PINOT GR; fleshy, oak-aged SAUV BL. Dense, dark ZWEIGELT. Sold under Hans brand in Europe and the USA.

Hawke's Bay (r) 07' 08 09' 10' (w) 10' NZ's 2nd-largest region. Long history of winemaking in sunny, warm climate; shingly and heavier soils. Full and rich MERLOT and CAB SAUV-based reds in gd vintages; SYRAH a fast-rising star; powerful CHARD; ripe, rounded SAUV BL (suits oak); NZ's best VIOGNIER. Central Hawke's Bay (elevated, cooler) suits PINOT N.

Highfield Marl r w sp ★★ Light, intense RIES, citrussy, mealy CHARD; immaculate SAUV BL and generous, savoury PINOT N. Elstree sparkling variable lately; can be Champagne-like. Second label: Paua.

Hunter's Marl r p w sp ★★→★★★ Pioneering (since 1982) medium-sized winery, with classic SAUV BL. Fine, gently-oaked CHARD. Excellent sparkling (MiruMiru), RIES, GEWURZ; elegant PINOT N. Whites esp gd value.

Invivo Auck r w ★★ Energetic young company with nettley, minerally MARLBOROUGH SAUV BL; fruit-packed CENTRAL OTAGO PINOT N. Second label: Brams Run.

Isabel Estate Marl r w ★→★★ Family estate with formerly outstanding PINOT N, SAUV BL and CHARD. Lately less exciting. Crisp, dryish PINOT GR; strong, dry RIES.

Jackson Estate Marl r w ★★ Rich, ripe Stich SAUV BL is consistently outstanding; attractive, gently oaked CHARD and classy, sweet-fruited PINOT N (esp top-tier, deep Gum Emperor Pinot N).

Johanneshof Marl (r) w sp ★★ Small winery with perfumed, gently sweet GEWURZ (one of NZ's finest); v.gd RIES and PINOT GR. Excellent botrytis Ries and late-harvest Gewurz.

Jules Taylor Marl r p w ★★ Growing volume of creamy PINOT GR, concentrated SAUV BL and floral PINOT N.

Julicher Mart r w ★★ Small producer with gd whites (CHARD, PINOT GR, RIES and SAUV BL); distinguished, savoury PINOT N (99 Rows is 2nd tier Pinot N and v.gd value).

Kim Crawford Hawk ★★ Part of US-based CONSTELLATION empire. Easy-drinking wines, incl fresh, plummy MERLOT; lightly oaked PINOT N; scented Marlborough SAUV BL (large volume, but high quality.) Top range SP (Small Parcel).

Kumeu River Auck (r) w ★★→★★★ Rich, refined Kumeu Estate CHARD (10') single-v'yd *Mate's V'yd Chard* (08 10) even more opulent. Both among NZ's greatest. Weighty, floral PINOT GR and sturdy PINOT N. Satisfying lower-tier Chard – Kumeu River Village.

Lake Chalice Marl (r) w ★★ Medium-sized producer with vibrant, creamy CHARD and

---

Hot off the presses

Think NZ wine – think punchy, zesty SAUV BL or more recently, enticingly floral and supple PINOT N. Of the hundreds of brand-new labels released in the past year, most were based on Sauv Bl, PINOT GR, Pinot N or SYRAH. However, there is rising interest in other grape varieties: ARNEIS, GRÜNER VELTLINER, VERDELHO, Sauvignon Gris, TEMPRANILLO, DOLCETTO and MONTEPULCIANO. The hot new wine style is sparkling Sauv Bl. Mount Riley in 2000 was the country's first winery to put bubbles in Sauv Bl, but until recently attracted few imitators. Suddenly, sparkling Sauvs are everywhere. A convenient way to shift surplus stocks of Sauv Bl, the wines are typically fresh and simple, with tropical-fruit flavours, crisp and lively.

incisive, slightly sweet RIES; gd SAUV BL (esp intense, zingy The Raptor). Platinum premium label. Second label: The Nest.

Lawson's Dry Hills Marl (r) (p) w ★★→★★★ Weighty wines with intense flavours. Complex, lightly oaked SAUV BL and exotic, sturdy GEWURZ. Dry, toasty, bottle-aged RIES. Top-end range: The Pioneer.

Over 90 per cent of NZ wines are now sealed with screwcaps.

Lindauer Auck ★★ A huge sparkling brand, esp bottle-fermented, low-priced Lindauer Brut, sold in 2010 by PERNOD RICARD NZ to Lion. Latest releases still gd.

Lowburn Ferry C Ot r ★★ PINOT N specialist. Flagship is The Ferryman (elegant, feminine). Also Home Block (fleshy, silky); Skeleton Creek (not estate-grown, but concentrated and complex).

Mahi Marl r w ★★ Stylish and complex wines from Brian Bicknell, ex-SERESIN winemaker. Finely textured SAUV BL (partly oak-aged), CHARD and PINOT N.

Man O' War Auck r w ★★ Largest v'yd on Waiheke Island. Dense, Bordeaux-style reds (esp Ironclad) and powerful, spicy, firm Dreadnought SYRAH.

Margrain Mart r w sp ★★ Small winery with tightly structured, age-worthy CHARD, RIES, PINOT GR, GEWURZ and PINOT N. Classy sparkling La Michelle (biscuity, v. dry). River's Edge is early-drinking.

Marisco Marl r w ★★ Latest venture of Brent Marris, ex-WITHER HILLS. Medium-sized, Waihopai Valley producer with two brands: The Ned and (latterly) The Kings Series. Well-regarded SAUV BL, CHARD, PINOT GR and PINOT N.

Marlborough (r) 10' 09' (w) 11 NZ's largest region by far (60% of all plantings) at the top of South Island. Warm, sunny days and cold nights give aromatic, crisp whites. Intense SAUV BL, from sharp, green capsicum to ripe tropical fruit. Fresh, limey RIES (recent wave of low-alcohol wines); some of NZ's best PINOT GR and GEWURZ; CHARD is leaner, crisper than HAWKE'S BAY. High-quality sparkling and botrytized Ries. PINOT N underrated – top examples (from clay hillsides) among NZ's finest.

Martinborough (r) 08' 09 10 (w) 09 10' Small, high-quality area in south WAIRARAPA (foot of North Island). Warm summers, dry autumns, gravelly soils. Success with several white grapes (incl MARLBOROUGH-like SAUV BL) but acclaimed since mid-late 1980s for sturdy, rich, long-lived PINOT N.

Martinborough Vineyard Mart r (p) (w) ★★★ Distinguished small winery; famous PINOT N (07' 10'), cherryish, spicy. Rich, biscuity CHARD; intense RIES; rich, medium-dry PINOT GR. Also single-v'yd Burnt Spur and drink-young Te Tera ranges (top-value Pinot N).

Matahiwi Wair r w ★→★★ One of region's larger wineries. Top-range Holly incl rich CHARD; nutty, barrel-fermented SAUV BL; generous, savoury PINOT N. Second label: Mt Hector.

Matua Valley Auck r w ★→★★ Producer of NZ's first SAUV BL in 1974. Once prestigious, family-run producer, now owned by Treasury Wine Estates, with v'yds in four regions. GISBORNE (esp Judd CHARD), HAWKE'S BAY and MARLBOROUGH wines; most pleasant, easy-drinking. Shingle Peak Sauv Bl top value. New range of high-priced, single-v'yd wines, incl bold Matheson MERLOT, MALBEC.

Mills Reef B of P r w ★★→★★★ Impressive wines from HAWKE'S BAY grapes, incl finely crafted CHARD. Top Elspeth range incl powerful Bordeaux-style reds and SYRAH (now more refined, supple). Res range reds also concentrated, fine-value.

Millton Gis r p w ★★★ Region's top winery; wines certified organic. Hill-grown single-v'yd Clos de Ste Anne range (CHARD, CHENIN BL, VIOGNIER, SYRAH, PINOT N) is concentrated, characterful. Rich, long-lived **Chenin Bl** is NZ's finest (honeyed in wetter vintages; tight, pure in drier yrs). Riverpoint V'yd Viognier classy and gd value.

Misha's C Ot r w ★★ Large v'yd at Bendigo. Consistently classy GEWURZ, PINOT GR, RIES (medium Limelight and medium-dry Lyric); vibrant, tangy SAUV BL; savoury, complex PINOT N.

Mission Hawk r p w ★★ NZ's oldest wine producer, vines first planted in 1851, first sales in the 1890s – still run by Catholic Society of Mary. Solid, increasingly gd varietals: creamy-smooth CHARD and fruit-driven SYRAH are top-value. Res range incl: gd Bordeaux-style reds, Syrah, oak-aged SAUV BL and CHARD. Top label: Jewelstone (v. classy Chard and CAB/MERLOT 09').

Mondillo C Ot r w ★★ Rising star at Bendigo with scented, citrussy, slightly sweet RIES and enticingly floral, weighty, tasty PINOT N.

Monkey Bay r w ★ CONSTELLATION NZ brand, modestly priced and popular in the USA. Easy-drinking, dryish CHARD; crisp, gently sweet SAUV BL; light PINOT GR and fresh, fruity MERLOT.

Montana Auck ★→★★★ The former key brand of PERNOD RICARD NZ, replaced internationally in 2010 by BRANCOTT ESTATE.

Morton Estate B of P ★→★★ r w sp Mid-size producer with v'yds in HAWKE'S BAY and MARLBOROUGH. Refined Black Label CHARD. White Label Chard and Premium Brut gd and top value; ditto VIOGNIER and PINOT GR. Reds less exciting.

Mount Riley Marl r w ★★ Medium-sized family producer. Punchy, gd-value SAUV BL; finely textured PINOT GR; easy-drinking PINOT N. Top range is Seventeen Valley (elegant, complex CHARD and oak-aged Sauv Bl).

Mt Difficulty C Ot r p w ★★ Quality producer in relatively warm Bannockburn. Refined, intense PINOT N – Roaring Meg for early consumption; Single-v'yd Pipeclay Terrace dense, lasting. Classy whites (RIES, PINOT GR) and satisfying rosé.

Muddy Water Waip r p w ★★→★★★ Small, high-quality producer with intense RIES (among NZ's best), minerally CHARD and savoury, notably complex PINOT N (esp Slowhand, based on oldest, low-yielding vines). Sold in 2011 to GREYSTONE.

Looking for more information on grapes? Try the "Grapes" section on pp.16–26.

Mud House Cant r w ★★ Large WAIPARA-based winery. Brands incl: Mud House (top range, Swan), Hay Maker (lower tier), Waipara Hills. Punchy, herbaceous Marlborough SAUV BL is classy and top-value; intense, racy Waipara RIES.

Nautilus Marl r w ★★ Medium-sized, v. reliable range of distributors Négociants (NZ), owned by S Smith & Sons (see Yalumba, Australia). Top wines incl: stylish SAUV BL (released with bottle-age), savoury PINOT N, Alsace-style PINOT GR; and fragrant, classy sparkler. Mid-tier: Opawa. Lower tier: Twin Islands.

Nelson (r) 09 10 (w) 10' Smallish region west of MARLBOROUGH; climate wetter but equally sunny. Clay soils of Upper Moutere hills and silty Waimea plains. Strengths in aromatic whites, esp RIES, SAUV BL, PINOT GR, GEWURZ; plus gd (sometimes outstanding) CHARD and PINOT N.

Neudorf Nel r p w ★★★ A top small winery. Powerful, mineral Moutere CHARD (09 10') one of NZ's greatest; superb, savoury Moutere PINOT N (esp Home V'yd 09 10). SAUV BL, PINOT GR and RIES also top-flight.

Ngatarawa Hawk r w ★★→★★★ A mid-sized producer. Top Alwyn range, incl powerful CHARD; dark, generous MERLOT/CAB and honey-sweet Noble Harvest RIES. Mid-range Glazebrook also excellent. Stables range is gd value.

No. 1 Family Estate Marl sp ★★ Family-owned firm of Daniel Le Brun, ex-Champagne but MARLBOROUGH-based since 1980. Specialist in sparkling wine, esp refined, tight-knit, NV Blanc de Blancs, Cuvée No 1. Cuvée No 8: lemony, toasty apéritif.

Nobilo Marl See CONSTELLATION NZ.

Obsidian Waih r w ★ V. stylish Bordeaux blend (The Obsidian), VIOGNIER, CHARD, SYRAH and TEMPRANILLO under top brand Obsidian. Gd-value Waiheke reds (incl MERLOT, Syrah, MONTEPULCIANO) under second-tier Weeping Sands label.

Oyster Bay Marl r w ★★ From DELEGAT'S, this is a marketing triumph, with sales exceeding 1.5 million cases (incl the no. 1 white-wine spot in Australia). Vibrant fruit-driven wines from SAUV BL, CHARD, PINOT N, MERLOT.

Palliser Mart r w ★★ →★★★ One of the district's largest and best. Superb, tropical-fruit SAUV BL, excellent CHARD, RIES, PINOT GR, bubbly, PINOT N. Top wines: Palliser Estate. Lower tier: Pencarrow (great-value, rising share of output).

Pask, C J Hawk r w ★★ Mid-size winery, extensive v'yds in GIMBLETT GRAVELS. SYRAH, CAB SAUV and MERLOT-based reds under middle-tier Gimblett Road label offer great value; CHARD and VIOGNIER, too. Top Declaration range less convincing. Roy's Hill: everyday drinking.

Pasquale r w ★★ Expat Italian Antonio Pasquale makes v.gd aromatic whites (RIES, GEWURZ and Alma Mater: PINOT GR/Gewurz/Ries) and floral, fresh PINOT N from Waitaki Valley (North Otago) and Hakataramea Valley (South Canterbury).

Passage Rock Waih r w ★★ Powerful, opulent SYRAH, esp Res (Waiheke's most awarded wine 10' 08). Gd Bordeaux-style reds, whites solid (esp VIOGNIER).

Pegasus Bay Waip r w ★★★ Pioneer family firm with distinguished range: taut, cool-climate CHARD; complex, oaked SAUV BL/SEM; rich, zingy, medium RIES and lemon-scented Bel Canto Ries Dry; lush, silky PINOT N (esp old-vine Prima Donna). Second label: Main Divide (gd value).

Peregrine C Ot r w ★★ Crisp, concentrated whites (esp RIES with various degrees of sweetness), and rich, silky PINOT N. Saddleback Pinot N esp gd value.

Pernod Ricard NZ Auck r p w ★→★★★ NZ wine giant, formerly MONTANA. Sold CORBANS and LINDAUER brands in 2010 and dropped Montana brand in favour of BRANCOTT ESTATE. Wineries in AUCKLAND, HAWKE'S BAY and MARLBOROUGH. Extensive co-owned v'yds for MARLBOROUGH whites, incl top-value Brancott Estate SAUV BL. Strength in sparkling, esp DEUTZ Marlborough Cuvée. Elegant CHURCH ROAD reds and quality CHARD. Other key brands incl: STONELEIGH (tropical fruit-flavoured Sauv Bl) and Triplebank (vibrant, racy AWATERE VALLEY wines). Camshorn is gd Waipara RIES and PINOT N.

Pisa Range C Ot r (w) ★★ Former diplomat Warwick Hawker and wife Jenny run small v'yd with powerful, arrestingly rich Black Poplar PINOT N and crisp, dry PINOT GR.

Puriri Hills Auck r p ★★ Silky, seductive MERLOT-based reds from Clevedon. Res esp rich and plump, with more new oak. Classy, blend "Pope" incl one-third CARMENÈRE.

Pyramid Valley Cant r w ★★ Tiny v'yd at Waikari. Estate-grown, floral, middleweight PINOT N (Angel Flower and Earth Smoke). Classy Growers Collection wines from other regions.

Quartz Reef C Ot r w ★★ Small, quality producer with crisp, citrussy PINOT GR; deep, spicy PINOT N (Bendigo Estate V'yd esp concentrated); *Champagne-like sparkler* (vintage esp gd).

Rippon Vineyard C Ot r w ★★ Stunning v'yd on shores of Lake Wanaka. Scented, "feminine" Mature Vine PINOT N. Jeunesse Pinot N from younger vines; powerful, complex Tinker's Field Pinot N (from oldest vines). Slowly evolving whites, esp outstanding, steely, minerally RIES.

Rockburn C Ot r p w ★★ Crisp, racy CHARD, PINOT GR, GEWURZ, RIES, SAUV BL. Fragrant, rich PINOT N is best and an emerging star – Twelve Barrels Pinot N shows compelling density.

Sacred Hill Hawk r w ★★ →★★★ Mid-size producer, partly Chinese-owned. Distinguished Riflemans CHARD (powerful but refined). Dark, long-lived Brokenstone MERLOT, Helmsman CAB/Merlot and Deer Stalkers SYRAH from GIMBLETT GRAVELS. Punchy MARLBOROUGH SAUV BL. Halo: middle-tier. Other brands: Gunn Estate, Wild South (gd-value Marlborough range).

Saint Clair Marl r p w ★★ →★★★ Largest family-owned producer in the region with extensive v'yds. Acclaimed SAUV BL – esp impressive, great-value regional blend and intense Wairau Res. Easy-drinking RIES, CHARD, MERLOT and PINOT N. Rich Res Chard, Merlot, Pinot N. Bewildering array of classy, second-tier Pioneer Block wines (incl 9 Sauv Bls). Vicar's Choice is lower tier.

Seifried Estate Nel r w ★★ The region's largest winery. Aromatic, medium-dry RIES and GEWURZ; now also gd value, often excellent SAUV BL and CHARD. Best: Winemakers Collection (also sold under Aotea brand). Old Coach Road is third tier. Plain reds.

Selaks Marl r w ★→★★ Old producer of Croatian origin, now a brand of CONSTELLATION NZ. Moderately priced MARLBOROUGH whites called Premium Selection. Top: Founders Res. Mid-tier, Winemaker's Favourite excellent quality/value, esp rich, creamy HAWKE'S BAY CHARD and pungent, nettley SAUV BL.

Seresin Marl r w ★★→★★★ Medium-sized winery, established by film producer Michael Seresin. Stylish and concentrated SAUV BL (certified organic), CHARD, PINOTS N and GR, RIES. Second tier: Momo (gd-quality/value). Overall, complex and finely textured wines.

Sileni Hawk r p w ★★ Medium-sized producer, with classy CHARD, MERLOT and MARLBOROUGH SAUV BL. Top wines: rare EV (Exceptional Vintage), then a range with individual names (incl lush Chard, The Lodge), then Cellar Selection (easy-drinking Merlot). Rich, smooth Marlborough Sauv Bl (esp The Straits).

Spy Valley Marl r p w ★★→★★★ High-achieving company with extensive v'yds. Richly flavoured aromatic whites (RIES, GEWURZ, PINOT GR) and v.gd SAUV BL, CHARD, MERLOT/MALBEC and PINOT N; all priced right. Superb top selection: Envoy (incl rich, subtle Chard and Mosel-like Ries). Second label: Satellite.

Staete Landt Marl r w ★★ Dutch immigrants producing refined CHARD, SAUV BL and PINOT GR; graceful PINOT N. Promising VIOGNIER, SYRAH. Second label: Map Maker.

Lamb from the Central Otago hills is some of the best you'll ever taste.

Stonecroft Hawk r w ★★ Small winery. NZ's first serious SYRAH (since 1989), more Rhône than Oz. Reputation for outstanding CHARD, rich Old-Vine GEWURZ. New ownership since 2010.

Stoneleigh Marl r p w ★★ Owned by PERNOD RICARD NZ. Gd, large-volume MARLBOROUGH whites (incl: punchy, tropical SAUV BL; generous PINOT GR; refined RIES and creamy-smooth CHARD); fast-improving, savoury PINOT N. New mid-tier range: Latitude. Top wines: Rapaura Series.

Stonyridge Waih r w ★★★ Boutique winery. Famous for exceptional, CAB SAUV-based red, Larose (04' 05' 06 07 08' 09, 10'), one of NZ's greatest. Airfield is little brother of Larose. Also powerful, dense Rhône-style Pilgrim and super-charged Luna Negra MALBEC. Second label: Fallen Angel.

Te Awa Hawk r w ★★ US-owned estate v'yd, with reputation for Bordeaux-like MERLOT-based reds. Recent premium Kidnapper Cliffs range: classy CHARD; concentrated, silky Ariki (mostly Merlot); bold, peppery PINOTAGE; elegant SYRAH. Now linked to DRY RIVER.

Te Kairanga Mart r w ★→★★ One of district's largest wineries; chequered history of early quality issues and lately financial problems. Purchased in 2011 by American Bill Foley (*see* box, opposite), who is keen to elevate quality. Moderately complex Estate PINOT N has been gd value; Estate RIES is strong and tangy.

Te Mata Hawk r w ★★★→★★★★ Prestigious winery (first vintage 1895). Coleraine (MERLOT/CAB SAUV/CAB F blend) (98' 00 02 04 05' 06' 07' 08 09') is NZ's closest parallel to great Bordeaux; *Awatea Cab/Merlot* also classy and more forward. Bullnose SYRAH among NZ's finest. Rich, elegant Elston CHARD. Woodthorpe V'yd range for early drinking (v.gd and great-value Chard, SAUV BL, GAMAY Noir – NZ's only – Merlot/Cab, Syrah/VIOGNIER).

NEW ZEALAND

Terra Sancta C Ot r (w) ★★ Originally Olssens. Bannockburn's first v'yd, founded 1991, recently sold and renamed. Consistently attractive PINOT N. Smooth, rich Jackson Barry is mid-tier; top wine is bold Slapjack Creek Res Pinot N.

TerraVin Marl r w ★★ Weighty, dry, tropical SAUV BL (single v'yd, more oak), but real focus is rich, complex PINOT N, esp Hillside Res (now multi-site) and Eaton Family V'yd. Among region's best reds.

Foley's empire

What do VAVASOUR, Goldwater, Dashwood, Redwood Pass and CLIFFORD BAY in MARLBOROUGH have in common with MARTINBOROUGH's Te Kairanga, luxury Wharekauhau Lodge and wine distributor, EuroVintage? All are parts of the fast-expanding wine-based empire of entrepreneurial billionaire Bill Foley, who built his fortune in title insurance and also owns ten wineries in California and Washington State. Foley, whose goal is to "bring financial discipline to the wine industry", made his first move in NZ in 2009. His involvement (focus on SAUV BL, PINOT N) is expected to boost the profile of NZ in the USA.

Te Whau Waih ★★→★★★ Tiny, acclaimed v'yd and restaurant. Ripe, complex CHARD and savoury, mostly CAB SAUV blend, The Point (05' 08') *Now also Northern Rhône-like Syrah.*

Tiki Marl w ★★ McKean family owns extensive v'yds in MARLBOROUGH and Waipara. Winemaker is Evan Ward (ex-MORTON). Punchy, expressive, easy-drinking SAUV BL. Second label: Maui.

Tohu r w ★★ Maori-owned venture with extensive v'yds. Racy, gd-value SAUV BL (Mugwi is oak-aged); strong, medium-dry RIES; citrussy, creamy, unoaked CHARD and moderately complex PINOT N – all from MARLBOROUGH. Scented and weighty NELSON PINOT GR.

Trinity Hill Hawk r p w ★★→★★★ Innovative winery with concentrated reds (Bordeaux-style The Gimblett is rich, refined, v.gd value) and stylish "black label" CHARD. Exceptional Homage SYRAH is muscular and dense. Impressive, plummy TEMPRANILLO. Scented, soft PINOT GR and VIOGNIER among NZ's best. HAWKE'S BAY SAUV BL: fresh, frisky, gd value.

Tupari Marl w ★★ Single-v'yd AWATERE VALLEY wines made by Glenn Thomas (ex-VAVASOUR). Authoritative SAUV BL (drive, delicacy, depth); classy dry RIES; scented, vibrant PINOT GR.

Two Paddocks C Ot r ★★ Actor Sam Neill makes several PINOT N, incl First Paddock (more herbal, from cool Gibbston), Last Chance (riper, from warmer Alexandra).

Two Rivers Marl ★★ Convergence SAUV BL – classy, deep wine from Wairau and AWATERE VALLEYS. V.gd CHARD, PINOT GR, RIES, PINOT N (floral, supple).

Unison Hawk r (w) ★★ Dark, spicy blends of MERLOT, CAB SAUV, SYRAH. Selection label is oak-aged the longest (07'). Also fragrant, fleshy Syrah and "serious" dry rosé. New owners since 2008.

Vavasour Marl r w ★★ Based in AWATERE VALLEY. Immaculate, intense CHARD and pure, nettley SAUV BL; v. promising PINOTS N and GR. Vavasour Awatere Valley is top label; Dashwood is regional blend (aromatic, vibrant Sauv Bl is top value). Linked to Goldwater and TE KAIRANGA.

Vidal Hawk r w ★★→★★★ Part of VILLA MARIA. Distinguished Legacy Series (previously Res) CHARD (fragrant, tight and long) and MERLOT/CAB SAUV (intense and complex). Middle-tier: Res Series. Lower-tier: White Series Merlot/Cab Sauv is outstanding value. Impressive SYRAH (esp Legacy.) Excellent MARLBOROUGH SAUV BL, RIES and PINOT N. Also strength in VIOGNIER: East Coast is top-value.

Villa Maria Auck r p w ★★→★★★ NZ's largest family-owned wine company, VIDAL and ESK VALLEY. Exceptional track record in competitions. Top ranges: Res (express regional character) and Single V'yd (reflect individual sites); Cellar Selection: mid-tier (less oak) is often v.gd; third-tier Private Bin wines can be excellent and gd value (esp SAUV BL, but also GEWURZ, PINOT GR, VIOGNIER, PINOT N). Thornbury brand: rich, soft MERLOT and v. perfumed, supple Pinot N.

Vinoptima Gis w ★★→★★★ Small GEWURZ specialist, owned by Nick Nobilo (ex-NOBILO Wines). Top vintages (06') are pricey but full of power and personality. Also gorgeous Noble Late-Harvest.

Voss Mart r w ★★ Small, respected producer of PINOT N (perfumed, weighty); RIES (dryish, citrus) and Res CHARD (lush, complex).

Waimea Nel r p w ★★ One of region's best white producers. Punchy SAUV BL; rich, rounded PINOT GR; vibrant VIOGNIER; v.gd RIES (Classic is honeyed, medium style). Reds solid but less exciting. Top range: Bolitho SV. Spinyback range: DYA.

Waipara Hills Cant r w ★★ A key brand of MUD HOUSE. Ripe, tropical MARLBOROUGH SAUV BL (compared to more herbaceous Mud House Sauv Bl); top-flight Waipara RIES and PINOT GR. Equinox and Southern Cross Selection are top ranges. Next tier: Soul of the South.

Waipara Springs Cant r w ★★ Small producer of strong, racy RIES (dry and medium), gd SAUV BL, GEWURZ and CHARD. Impressive top range: Premo, incl fragrant, concentrated PINOT N from district's oldest Pinot N vines.

Wairarapa NZ's fifth-largest wine region. *See* MARTINBOROUGH. Also incl Gladstone subregion in the north (slightly higher, cooler, wetter). Driest, coolest region in North Island; strength in whites and PINOT N (full-bodied, spicy).

Wairau River Marl r p w ★★ Racy SAUV BL; full-bodied, rounded PINOT GR; mouthfilling GEWURZ; promising VIOGNIER; gently sweet Summer RIES, finely crafted PINOT N. Res is top label.

Wairau Valley Marl MARLBOROUGH's largest and oldest subregion (v'yds since 1873), still with most of the region's wineries. Three important side valleys to the south: Brancott, Omaka and Waihopai. SAUV BL grown on the stony, silty plains, PINOT N on the clay-based, north-facing slopes to the south.

Waitaki Valley Ot Emerging district in North Otago. Limestone soils; cool, frost-prone climate. V. promising PINOT N, PINOT GR and RIES.

Whitehaven Marl r w ★★ Medium-sized producer. Pure, harmonious SAUV BL is top-value. Rich, soft GEWURZ; citrussy, slightly buttery CHARD and full-of-charm PINOT N. Gallo (*see* California) is part-owner. Top range: Greg (named after co-founder Greg White).

Wither Hills Marl r w ★★→★★★ Large producer, owned since 2002 by Lion. V. popular gooseberry/lime SAUV BL. Generous CHARD and smooth PINOT N. Latest vintages less oaky. Intense single-v'yd Rarangi Sauv Bl (racy, long); scented, poised PINOT GR. Other brands: Shepherds Ridge, Two Tracks.

Wooing Tree C Ot r p w ★★ Single-v'yd producer at Cromwell. Pale strawberry- and spice-flavoured rosé. Bold PINOT N (Beetle Juice Pinot N less new oak). Sandstorm Res, low-yielding vines, oak-aged longer.

Yealands Marl r p w ★★ Privately owned v'yd, one of NZ's biggest, in AWATERE VALLEY. Top wines labelled Estate: SAUV BL, vibrant, herbaceous, pure; RIES, tight, citrussy; PINOT N, floral, supple. Second-tier: Peter Yealands. Full Circle in plastic bottles.

South Africa

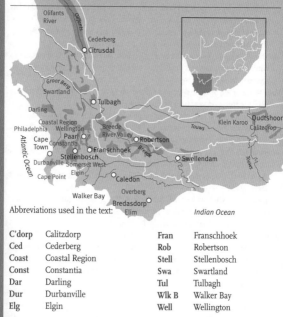

Abbreviations used in the text:

C'dorp	Calitzdorp	Fran	Franschhoek
Ced	Cederberg	Rob	Robertson
Coast	Coastal Region	Stell	Stellenbosch
Const	Constantia	Swa	Swartland
Dar	Darling	Tul	Tulbagh
Dur	Durbanville	Wlk B	Walker Bay
Elg	Elgin	Well	Wellington

The talk around South African wines is of terroir, and matching the vine variety to the place. There is no more basic measure. How long will this take? And how will they know when they've got there? The second question is easier to answer: in Bordeaux, they're still doing it – after several hundred years. In Burgundy there are only two varieties, essentially, but they're still changing their minds about individual plots. It's an open-ended game, in which an infinity of precision is possible.

In SA, we're seeing more and more wines with a real sense of place. Even so, some say it's too early to talk of terroir, and a study of Pinotage in specific terroirs had to be abandoned because so many producers didn't bother to take part. Chenin Blanc, the bedrock vine of the Cape, can reveal its terroir with razor-sharp focus, but few in SA reflect more than good intentions. If you want some real local character, however – of *fynbos*, of rock, of salt sea air – then try SA Syrah.

The potential is certainly there. In Swartland, possibly the most fashionable area of SA currently, the soil is fantastically varied. There's decomposed granite, slate, chalk, clay with iron, and alluvial soils, all in the same region. Winemakers are starting to match Syrah, Grenache and Mourvèdre to the decomposed granite, starting to talk of Graves and Pessac-Léognan in relation to the alluvial soils. All this will take time, and everybody will change their minds several times over during the journey. But they're on their way.

Recent vintages

2011 Another challenging and variable season. As with 2010, producer track record more than vintage generalizations should guide buying and cellaring decisions.

2010 A mixed bag, later-ripening varieties (reds and whites) generally performing best.

2009 South Africa's 350th harvest and one of its best. Stellar whites, most reds.

2008 Challenging but cool; ripe yet elegant wines – lower-than-usual alcohol.

2007 Sturdy whites for keeping; soft, easy reds for earlier drinking.

2006 Trouble-free season, average yields; sound wines – more modest alcohol.

Note: Most dry whites are best drunk within two to three years.

Anthonij Rupert Wines W Cape r w ★→★★★ Evolving wine portfolio named after brand-owner Johann Rupert's late brother. Flagship Anthonij Rupert range with emphatic reds; old-vines bottlings under Cape of Good Hope label; Italianate Terra del Capo trio; early-drinking Protea label.

Anwilka Stell r ★★→★★★ Local partner Lowell Jooste (KLEIN CONSTANTIA) with Bordeaux's Bruno Prats and Hubert de Boüard. Flagship is SHIRAZ/CAB SAUV blend Anwilka (05 06 07 08 09'); second wine is Ugaba.

Ashbourne See HAMILTON RUSSELL.

Ataraxia Wines W Cape r w ★★★ Kevin Grant and partners' young v'yds in Hemel-en-Aarde Ridge WARD; acclaimed CHARD, SAUV BL and Serenity red. Given Grant's record at HAMILTON RUSSELL, much is expected from forthcoming PINOT N.

Avondale Bio-LOGIC & Organic Wines Paarl r (p) w (sp) ★★→★★★ Family-owned eco-pioneer's restructured range incl Bordeaux- and Rhône-style reds, scented Rosé, VIOGNIER blend and wooded CHENIN BL.

Axe Hill C'dorp r br sw ★★→★★★ Noted Port-style exponent (Cape Vintage, mainly TOURIGA NACIONAL 01 02' 03' 04 05' 06 07 08 09) now also offers unfortified SHIRAZ and Port-grape blend, Machado.

Badenhorst Family Wines Coast r (p) w ★★→★★★ SWARTLAND-based cousins Hein and Adi Badenhorst (latter ex-RUSTENBERG) vinify mainly Mediterranean grapes under serious but light-hearted and -textured A A Badenhorst and Secateurs labels.

Bamboes Bay Tiny (5ha) maritime WARD in OLIFANTS RIVER REGION. Fryer's Cove first and still only winery, with racy SAUV BL and promising PINOT N.

Beaumont Wines Wlk B r (p) w (br sw) ★→★★★ Rustic family estate at Bot River, home to expressive CHENIN BL, PINOTAGE, varietal and blended MOURVÈDRE, and Bordeaux-blend red Ariane.

Bellingham W Cape r (p) w ★→★★★ Enduring DGB brand with limited-release Bernard Series and larger-volume, easy-drinking Legends, Fusion, Blends and Insignia ranges.

Beyerskloof Stell r (p) (w) (br) (sp) ★→★★★ SA's top PINOTAGE producer. Nine versions on offer, incl superlative Diesel (06 07' 08' 09) and various CAPE BLENDS. Also classically styled Bordeaux-style red, Field Blend (00 01 02 03' 04 05 07).

Biodynamic Anthroposophic mode of wine-growing practised by small, expanding group, incl: Andreas, AVONDALE, Botanica, EDGEBASTON, FABLE, Farm 1120, Heron Ridge, Oldenburg, Porseleinberg, REYNEKE, WATERKLOOF. See also ORGANIC.

Black Economic Empowerment (BEE) Initiative aimed at increasing wine industry ownership and participation by previously disadvantaged groups. Since the late 1990s, with pioneers New Beginnings and Fairvalley, black-owned or part-black-owned cellars have increased steadily, incl majors like BOSCHENDAL, CONSTANTIA UITSIG and KWV. Other quality labels incl: Epicurean, Howard Booysen, Land of Hope (THE WINERY OF GOOD HOPE), SOLMS-DELTA, Thandi, Thokozani, Tukulu (DISTELL), Vins d'Orrance.

Boekenhoutskloof Winery W Cape r (w) (sw) ★★→★★★★ Consistently excellent producer specializing in unfiltered, native-yeast ferments. Spicy SYRAH (01' 02' 03 04' 05 06' 07 08 09'); intense, minerally CAB SAUV (01' 02' 03 04' 05 06' 07' 08' 09'). Also fine SÉM, Mediterranean-style red The Chocolate Block, and gd-value labels Porcupine Ridge and Wolftrap.

Bon Courage Estate Rob r (p) w (br) sw sp ★★→★★★ Extensive family-grown range led by Inkará reds, stylish MCC, and outstanding RIES and MUSCAT desserts.

Boplaas Family Vineyards W Cape r w br (sp) ★→★★★ Best-known for Port styles, esp Vintage Res (99' 01 03 04' 05' 06' 07' 08 09') and Cape Tawny. Expanded Cool Bay (unfortified) range from ocean-facing v'yds.

Boschendal Wines W Cape r (p) w sp ★★→★★★ Famous old estate showing new elan under DGB ownership. Calling cards: SHIRAZ, SAUV BL, Bordeaux/SHIRAZ Grand Res and MCC.

Bot River *See* WALKER BAY.

Bouchard Finlayson W Cape r w ★★→★★★★ V. fine PINOT N grower. Galpin Peak (01 02' 03 04 05 07 08 09 10), barrel selection Tête de Cuvée (99 01' 03' 05' 07 09 10) and Unfiltered Limited Edition (07). Impressive CHARD, SAUV BL and exotic red blend Hannibal.

Breedekloof Large (12,500ha) inland district in Breede River Valley REGION producing mainly bulk wine. Notable exceptions: Avondrood, Bergsig, Deetlefs, Mtn Oaks, Du Preez, Merwida and Opstal; Du Toitskloof Winery welded to gd-value award podiums.

Buitenverwachting Coast r (p) w (sw) (sp) ★★→★★★ Classy family v'yds, cellar and restaurant; standout SAUV BL, CAB FR, restrained Bordeaux blend Christine (00 01' 02 03 04 06 07 08), aromatic MUSCAT dessert "1769".

Calitzdorp DISTRICT in KLEIN KAROO REGION, climatically similar to the Douro and known for Port styles. Best: AXE HILL, BOPLAAS, DE KRANS, Peter Bayly, Quinta do Sul.

Cape Agulhas *See* ELIM.

Cape Blend Usually a red blend with proportion of PINOTAGE. Top examples incl: BEYERSKLOOF, GRAHAM BECK, GRANGEHURST, KAAPZICHT, MEINERT, Post House, SIMONSIG, SPIER, WARWICK, Windmeul.

Cape Chamonix Wine Farm Fran r w (sp) ★★→★★★ Recent vintages confirm excellence of these winemaker-run mtn v'yds. Individual and v.gd PINOT N, PINOTAGE, CHARD, SAUV BL, Chard MCC and Bordeaux-blend red Troika.

Cape Point Tiny (32ha) maritime DISTRICT on southern tip of Cape Peninsula. Mainly white grapes. Sole winery CAPE POINT V'YDS consistent star performer despite viticultural challenges.

Sutherland-Karoo is SA's coolest wine area: average annual temperature is 11°C.

Cape Point Vineyards W Cape (r) w ★→★★★★ One of SA's most exciting producers. Complex SAUV BL/SÉM blend Isliedh, racy CHARD and thrilling SAUV BL; gd-value Splattered Toad label helps save endangered amphibians.

Cape South Coast New appellation in WINE OF ORIGIN system, combining standalone DISTRICTS CAPE AGULHAS, Overberg, Plettenberg Bay and WALKER BAY, plus Swellendam (previously part of Breede River Valley) into ocean-influenced, cool-climate "umbrella" REGION.

Cape Winemakers Guild (CWG) Independent, invitation-only association of 43 top growers. Stages benchmarking annual auction of limited premium bottlings and, via a trust, provides development aid to wineland schoolchildren, education bursaries and mentorship for just-graduated winemakers.

Cederberg WARD in remote Cederberg Mts. Just 70ha, now mainly white varieties, among highest in SA. Relative newcomer Driehoek and established star CEDERBERG PRIVATE CELLAR are sole producers.

Cederberg Private Cellar r w (p) (sp) ★★→★★★ Combines high-altitude minerality with intense flavour in SHIRAZ, CAB SAUV, SAUV BL, SÉM, CHENIN BL, rare Bukettraube.

Central Orange River Formerly "Lower Orange". Standalone inland "super WARD" (12,000ha) straddling Gariep (Orange) River: hot, dry, dependent on irrigation; mainly white wines, fortified. Major producer is Orange River Wine Cellars.

Coastal Large (31,000ha) REGION, incl sea-influenced DISTRICTS of CAPE POINT, DARLING, Tygerberg, ST'BOSCH, SWARTLAND, inland FRANSCHHOEK VALLEY, PAARL and TULBAGH.

Colmant Cap Classique & Champagne sp ★★★ Exciting new Franschhoek *méthode traditionnelle* sparkling specialist. Currently a trio of MCC: Res, Rosé (PINOT N/CHARD) and Chard; all Brut, NV and excellent.

Company of Wine People, The W Cape r (p) w (sw) (sp) ★→★★★ 3.8-million-cases-a-yr operation nr STELLENBOSCH with 60+ labels in 13 ranges. Best is Kumkani; also well-priced easy-drinkers in Arniston Bay, Versus and Welmoed lines.

Constantia Cool, scenic WARD in Constantiaberg foothills and SA's original fine-wine-growing area, revitalized in recent yrs by GROOT and KLEIN CONSTANTIA, BUITENVERWACHTING, Constantia Glen, CONSTANTIA UITSIG, Eagles' Nest, STEENBERG. New kids Beau Constantia and Constantia Mist worth watching.

Constantia Uitsig Const (r) w (br) (sp) ★★★ Premium v'yds and tourist destination, partly black-owned. Mainly white wines and MCC, all excellent, carefully crafted.

Creation Wines Wlk B r w ★★→★★★ Elegant modernity in family-owned/-vinified range, showcasing Bordeaux, Rhône and Burgundy varieties and blends. Varied, social-media-enabled cellar-door offering worth the detour.

Dalla Cia Wine & Spirit Company Stell r w ★★→★★★ Family patriarch Giorgio Dalla Cia vinifies a CAB SAUV, Bordeaux blend Giorgio, CHARD, SAUV BL and new PINOT N, and advises select clients like ambitious STELLENBOSCH start-up 4G Wines.

Danie de Wet *See* DE WETSHOF.

The cellar door revolution

Forget the traditional SA cellar door, with its tasting samples and cash till; now it's all about giving a "visitor experience". You're nobody if you don't have at least one of the following: hotel, guest lodge, wellness spa, fine-dining restaurant, art exhibition, jewellery salon, sculpted garden, bird hide, cricket oval, boule court, motor museum, play area for children, or shops selling anything from essential oils to eco-friendly linen. And you must have events and activities to suit every taste: trips in a Jaguar, music concerts, farmers' markets, guided slackpacking trails, tutored horse-riding tours, harvest festivals, wine pairings (chocolate, toffee, nougat, even biltong) and, just possibly, al fresco bathing in PINOTAGE.

Darling DISTRICT (2,800ha) around eponymous west coast town. Best v'yds in hilly Groenekloof WARD. Cloof, Darling Cellars, Groote Post, Ormonde and recent entrant Lanner Hill (formerly Tullie Family) bottle under own labels; most other fruit channelled into other brands.

De Grendel Wines W Cape r (p) w (sp) ★→★★★ Hillside property overlooking Table Bay, owned by Sir David Graaff. Crisp, layered PINOT N, Koetshuis SAUV BL and new VIOGNIER are stand-outs.

De Krans C'dorp r (p) w br (sw) ★→★★★ Family v'yds noted for rich, impressive Port styles (esp Vintage Res 01 02 03' 04' 05' 06' 07 08' 09'), fortified MUSCATS, and varietal bottlings of rarer grapes eg. TEMPRANILLO, TOURIGA NACIONAL.

De Toren Private Cellar Stell r ★★★ Consistently flavourful Bordeaux blend Fusion V (02 03' 04 05' 06' 07 08 09') and earlier-maturing MERLOT-based blend "Z".

De Trafford Wines Stell r (p) (w) (sw) ★★★★ Consistent boutique grower with international reputation for bold but elegant wines. Brilliant Bordeaux/SHIRAZ blend Elevation 393 (01 03' 04 05 06 07 08 09), CAB SAUV (01 03' 04 05 06 07 08 09) and SHIRAZ. Sijnn brand from new Malgas WARD showcases promising young maritime v'yds.

De Wetshof Estate Rob (r) (p) w (br) (sw) ★→★★★ Famed CHARD pioneer and exponent; seven versions, oaked and unwooded, under De Wetshof and Danie de Wet branding. Headed by powerful new DeW The Site.

Delaire Graff Estate W Cape r (p) w (br) (sw) ★★→★★★ International jeweller Laurence Graff's eyrie v'yds, winery and opulent tourist destination. Evolving line-up incl exceptional CAB SAUV Res.

Delheim Stell r (p) w (sw) (s/sw) ★★→★★★ An eco-minded family winery nr STELLENBOSCH. Acclaimed Vera Cruz SHIRAZ; age-worthy CAB SAUV Grand Res (00 01 03 04' 05 06 07' 08).

DGB W Cape Well-established WELLINGTON-based producer/wholesaler, with brands like BELLINGHAM/Bernard Series, BOSCHENDAL, Brampton and Douglas Green.

Diemersdal Estate W Cape r (p) w ★→★★★ Family firm with dynamic younger generation specializing in red blends, CHARD and SAUV BL. Exciting newer internet-inspired brand Sauvignon.com.

Diemersfontein Wines Well r w ★★→★★★ Family wine estate and guest lodge, noted for full-throttle styling esp PINOTAGE, CHENIN BL, VIOGNIER. BEE brand Thokozani.

Distell W Cape SA's biggest drinks company, headquartered in STELLENBOSCH. Owns many brands, spanning quality scales. Also interests in various top Stellenbosch wineries, incl STELLENZICHT, and in west coast BEE venture Tukulu.

District *See* GEOGRAPHICAL UNIT.

Durbanville Cool, hilly WARD (1,500ha) nr Cape Town, known for pungent SAUV BL and MERLOT. Corporate co-owned DURBANVILLE HILLS and many family farms. Also thriving *garagiste* community, incl Kronendal and Hermit on the Hill.

Durbanville Hills Dur r (p) w ★→★★★ Maritime-cooled v'yds co-owned by DISTELL and local growers. Best are single-v'yd and Rhinofields Res ranges.

Edgebaston Coast r w ★★→★★★ Finlayson family (GLEN CARLOU fame). V.gd "GS" CAB SAUV (05 '06 07 08), SHIRAZ, CHARD; classy early-ready Berry Box and Pepper Pot reds, and new Honey Pot white.

Elgin Cool-climate Overberg WARD, fast-developing upland; increasingly recognized for SAUV BL, CHARD, PINOT N, MERLOT and Bordeaux blends. Mainly family-owned boutique cellars, incl Almenkerk, Catherine Marshall, Elgin Vintners, Highlands Road, Iona, Oak Valley, PAUL CLUVER, SHANNON and the ebullient newcomer Spioenkop.

Elim Sea-breezy WARD (146ha) in southernmost DISTRICT, CAPE AGULHAS. Svelte SAUV BL, white blends and SHIRAZ from The Berrio, Black Oystercatcher, Land's End/ Hidden Valley, Strandveld and Zoetendal.

Ernie Els Wines Stell r ★★→★★★★ SA's star golfer's wine venture, led by big ticket Bordeaux red Ernie Els Signature (01 02' 03 04' 05 06 07' 08). Els' famously effortless swing gives name to Big Easy Red and new White. V.gd Guardian Peak range.

Estate Wine Official term for wines grown, made and bottled on "units registered for the production of estate wine". Not a quality designation.

Fable Wines r w ★★★ BIODYNAMIC grower and sibling of MULDERBOSCH, recently acquired by California's Terroir Capital and renamed from TULBAGH MTN V'YDS. Exceptional debut SHIRAZ (varietal and blend); textured white blend Jackal Bird.

Fairtrade The international Fairtrade network's sustainable development and empowerment objectives are embraced by a growing list of producers, incl big players such as African Terroir, THE COMPANY OF WINE PEOPLE, DISTELL, Origin,

Simonsvlei, SPIER, uniWines and Van Loveren; BEE wineries; and family-owned cellars such as The Berrio, Bosman Family/Appollis, Lorraine and StellenRust.

Fairview W Cape r (p) w (s/sw) (sw) ★→★★★★ Acquisition of a neighbour's brands has swelled dynamic and innovative owner Charles Back's smorgasbord of sensibly priced blended, varietal, single-v'yd and terroir-specific bottlings. They now incl: Fairview, Spice Route, *Goats do Roam*, La Capra, Seidelberg and De Leuwen Jagt. Also, via shareholding, Six Hats (FAIRTRADE) and Juno.

FirstCape Vineyards W Cape r (p) w (sp) DYA Biggest-selling SA wine brand in the UK. Joint venture of five local co-ops and UK's Brand Phoenix, with entry-level wines in seven ranges. Recent Discovery line-up incl non-SA wines.

Flagstone Winery W Cape r w (br) ★★→★★★ Medalled winery at Somerset West, owned by Australia's CHAMP Private Equity. Idiosyncratically named labels (eg. Writer's Block PINOTAGE, The Last Word Port) in top-end Flagstone and Knockon Wood, and early-ready Stumble V'yds ranges.

Fleur du Cap W Cape r w (sw) ★★→★★★ DISTELL premium label; incl v.gd Unfiltered Collection and racy botrytis Noble Late Harvest in Bergkelder Selection.

Franschhoek Valley French Huguenot-founded DISTRICT in COASTAL REGION. 1,400ha, mainly CAB SAUV, SAUV BL, SHIRAZ. Many wineries (and restaurants), incl ANTHONIJ RUPERT, Allée Bleue, BOEKENHOUTSKLOOF, BOSCHENDAL, COLMANT, CAPE CHAMONIX, Glenwood, Grande Provence, LA MOTTE, Lynx, Môreson, SOLMS-DELTA, Topiary.

Looking for more information on grapes? Try the "Grapes" section on pp.16–26.

Geographical Unit (GU) Largest of the four main WINE OF ORIGIN demarcations. Currently five GUs: Eastern, Northern and Western Cape, KwaZulu-Natal and recent Limpopo. The other WINE OF ORIGEN demarcations (in descending size): REGION, DISTRICT and WARD.

Glen Carlou Coast r w (sw) ★★→★★★ First-rate Donald Hess-owned winery, v'yds, fine-art gallery and restaurant nr PAARL. Spicy Syrah (02 03 04' 05 06 07); fine Bordeaux red Grand Classique (00 01 02 03 04 05 06' 07 08).

Glenelly Cellars W Cape r w ★★→★★★ Former Château Pichon-Lalande (Bordeaux) owner May-Eliane de Lencquesaing's v'yds, state-of-the-art cellar at STELLENBOSCH. Impressive flagships Lady May (Bordeaux red) and Grand Vin duo (Bordeaux/ SHIRAZ and new CHARD); ready-on-release Glass Collection.

Graham Beck Wines W Cape r (p) w sp (br) (sw) ★★→★★★ Front-ranker with 30+ labels, incl classy bubbles, varietal and blended reds/whites, topped by superb Cuvée Clive MCC, Ad Honorem CAB SAUV/SHIRAZ and new Chalkboard range.

Grangehurst Winery Stell r (p) ★★→★★★ Small, top red and, latterly, rosé specialist. V.gd CAPE BLEND Nikela (98 99 00 01 02 03 05), PINOTAGE (97 98 99 01 02 03').

Groot Constantia Estate Const r (p) w (br) (sw) (sp) ★★→★★★ Wines befitting a tourism hotspot in the Cape's original fine-wine-growing area. PINOTAGE, CHARD, Res SÉM/SAUV blend. Grand Constance revives CONSTANTIA tradition of world-class MUSCAT desserts.

Guardian Peak See ERNIE ELS.

Hamilton Russell Vineyards (HRV) Wlk B r w ★★★→★★★★ Burgundian-style specialist at Hermanus. Fine PINOT N (01' 03' 04 05 06 07 08 09 10); classy CHARD. Super SAUV BL, PINOTAGE, white blend Southern Right, Ashbourne labels.

Hartenberg Estate Stell r w ★★→★★★★ Consistent top performer. Trio of outstanding SHIRAZ: always serious Shiraz (01 02 03 04' 05 06 07 08), flagship single-site The Stork (03 04' 05' 06 07 08) and Gravel Hill; also fine MERLOT, CHARD, RIES.

Haskell Vineyards Stell r ★★★ American-owned v'yds and cellar receiving rave notices for pair of SYRAHS (Pillars and Aeon), red blends and new CHARD. Ever-improving sibling brand Dombeya.

Hemel-en-Aarde Trio of cool-climate WARDS in WALKER BAY DISTRICT (Hemel-en-Aarde

Valley, Upper Hemel-en-Aarde, Hemel-en-Aarde Ridge), producing outstanding PINOT N, CHARD, SAUV BL. ATARAXIA, BOUCHARD FINLAYSON, CREATION, HAMILTON RUSSELL and NEWTON JOHNSON are top names.

Hermanuspietersfontein Wingerde r (p) w ★★→★★★ Leading SAUV BL and Bordeaux red-blend specialist; creatively markets physical and historical connections with seaside resort Hermanus.

J C le Roux, The House of W Cape sp ★★ SA's largest sparkling-wine house, DISTELL owned. Best are PINOT N, Scintilla (CHARD/Pinot N) and new Brut NV, all MCC.

Jean Daneel Wines W Cape r w (br) (sp) ★★→★★★ Family winery at Napier; outstanding Signature Series, esp *Chenin Bl*, CAB SAUV/MERLOT/SHIRAZ; rare MCC sparkling from CHENIN BL.

Jordan Wine Estate Stell r (p) w ★★→★★★ Consistency, quality and value, from entry-level Bradgate and Chameleon lines to immaculate CWG Auction bottlings. Flagship Nine Yards CHARD; Bordeaux blend Cobblers Hill (00 01 03 04' 05' 06 07 08); CAB SAUV; MERLOT; SAUV BL (oaked and unwooded); RIES botrytis dessert.

J P Bredell Wines Stell (r) br ★★★ Best-known for Port styles, esp plush Bredell's Cape Vintage Res (97' 98' 00 01' 03' 07') and Late Bottled Vintage.

Kaapzicht Wine Estate Stell r (p) w (br) (sw) ★→★★★ Family winery; internationally acclaimed top range Steytler: Vision CAPE BLEND (01' 02' 03' 04 05' 06 07), PINOTAGE and Bordeaux red blend Pentagon.

Kanonkop Estate Stell r (p) ★★→★★★★ Grand local status past three decades, mainly with PINOTAGE (01 02 03' 04 05 06 07 08 09'), Bordeaux blend Paul Sauer (01 02 03 04' 05 06' 07 08), CAB SAUV. Second tier is Kadette (red, Pinotage Dry Rosé).

Ken Forrester Wines W Cape r (p) w sw ★★→★★★ Vintner/restaurateur Ken Forrester and grower Martin MEINERT collaboration. Three benchmark CHENIN BL: racy, dry Res; opulent, off-dry The FMC; sumptuous botrytis "T". Devilishly drinkable budget range, Petit.

Klein Constantia Estate Coast r (p) w sw (sp) ★★→★★★ Meticulously restored property, now US/UK-owned. Luscious (non-botrytis) Vin de Constance (00' 01 02' 04 05 06' 07) convincingly re-creates legendary 18th-century Constantia MUSCAT dessert. Also elegant Marlbrook blends, age-worthy RIES, classy SAUV BL and earlier-ready KC range.

Klein Karoo Semi-arid REGION (2,700ha) known for fortified, esp Port-style in CALITZDORP DISTRICT. Higher-lying Tradouw, Tradouw Highlands, Outeniqua and Upper Langkloof WARDS show promise with PINOT N, SHIRAZ and SAUV BL.

Kleine Zalze Wines W Cape r (p) w ★★→★★★ STELLENBOSCH-based star with brilliant CAB SAUV, SHIRAZ, CHENIN BL and SAUV BL in Family Res and V'yd Selection ranges; tasty and affordable Cellar Selection and Zalze line-ups.

Krone, The House of W Cape sp ★★★ Elegant Brut MCC, incl Borealis, Rosé and NV prestige cuvée Nicolas Charles Krone, from PINOT N/CHARD, made at TWEE JONGE GEZELLEN Estate in TULBAGH.

Kumala W Cape r (p) w DYA Hugely successful export label and sibling brand to premium FLAGSTONE and entry-level Fish Hoek, all owned via Accolade Wines SA by Sydney-based CHAMP Private Equity. Immediately drinkable wines showing improving form.

KwaZulu-Natal Province and demarcated GEOGRAPHICAL UNIT on country's east coast; summer rain; subtropical or tropical climate in coastal areas; cooler, hilly central Midlands plateau home to nascent fine-wine industry led by Abingdon Estate.

KWV W Cape r (p) w (br) (s/sw) (sw) (sp) ★→★★★ Formerly the national wine co-op and controlling body, today a partly black-owned listed group based in PAARL. 90+ reds, whites, sparkling, Port styles and fortified desserts in 15 ranges. Best are Cathedral Cellar; Laborie; and KWV Mentors, Heritage and Res. Café Culture "coffee" PINOTAGE and new BerRaz sweet SHIRAZ target pop palate.

Lamberts Bay West coast WARD (22ha) close by Atlantic. Trenchant SAUV BL, promising SHIRAZ; Sir Lambert, local joint venture with DIEMERSDAL, a cracker.

Lammershoek Winery Swa r (p) w (sw) ★★→★★★ Traditionally vinified, deep-flavoured Rhône-style blends and CHENIN BL that epitomize SWARTLAND warmth and concentration. New younger-vines LAM quartet overdelivers.

La Motte W Cape r w (sp) ★★→★★★ Increasingly ORGANIC venture by the Rupert family, based at FRANSCHHOEK. Fine, distinctive SHIRAZ/VIOGNIER, SAUV BL and Shiraz/GRENACHE in flagship Pierneef Collection; improving MCC.

Lanzerac Stell r (p) w ★★★ Venerable property (incl luxury hotel) long associated with PINOTAGE (1st vintage 1959) and dry Rosé. Sister farm to LOURENSFORD.

L'Avenir Vineyards W Cape r (p) w (sp) ★→★★★ AdVini-owned v'yds and tourist hotspot nr STELLENBOSCH, vinifying SA stalwarts PINOTAGE and CHENIN BL with Gallic panache, esp in flagship Icon range.

Le Riche Wines Stell r (w) ★★★ Fine CAB SAUV-based boutique wines, hand-crafted by respected Etienne le Riche and family. Also v.gd CHARD.

SA's oldest vine, a Crouchen Blanc in central Cape Town, is over 240 years old.

Lourensford Wine Estate W Cape r (p) w (sw) (sp) ★★→★★★ Sibling to LANZERAC, rejuvenated and refocused on SHIRAZ, CAB SAUV, CHARD, SAUV BL and VIOGNIER. Best in Lourensford and "1700" ranges. River Garden is entry-level label.

Meerlust Estate Stell r w ★★★★ Prestigious v'yds and cellar, probably SA's best-known quality red label. Hallmark elegance and restraint in flagship Rubicon (99 00 01' 03' 04 05 06 07'), one of Cape's first Bordeaux blends; also excellent MERLOT, CAB SAUV, CHARD and PINOT N.

Meinert Wines Coast r (p w) ★★→★★★ Producer/consultant Martin Meinert noted for two fine blends, Devon Crest (Bordeaux) and Synchronicity (Bordeaux/PINOTAGE). New White MERLOT one of only two in SA.

Méthode Cap Classique (MCC) EU-friendly name for bottle-fermented sparkling, one of SA's major success stories. 140 labels with annual sales of 2.3 million bottles. Ambeloui, BON COURAGE, BOSCHENDAL, Cabrière, COLMANT, CONSTANTIA UITSIG, newcomer Francois la Garde, *Graham Beck*, J C LE ROUX, KRONE, Silverthorn, SIMONSIG, *Steenberg*, *Tanzanite*, Topiary, VILLIERA, Weltevrede.

Morgenhof Wine Estate Stell r (p) w (br) (sw) (s/sw) ★→★★★ 1692 property revitalized by Anne Cointreau (of Cognac/liqueur family). Bordeaux red blend The Morgenhof Estate and CHENIN BL. Gd everyday Fantail range.

Morgenster Estate Stell r (p) ★★→★★★ Prime Italian-owned wine and olive farm, advised by Bordelais Pierre Lurton (Cheval Blanc). Classic Bordeaux red blend Morgenster (00 01 03 04 05' 06' 08 09); second label Lourens River Valley. SANGIOVESE and NEBBIOLO blends in Italian Collection; new Bordeaux white blend.

Mulderbosch Vineyards W Cape r (p) w (sw) ★★→★★★ STELLENBOSCH winery owned by California investment group Terroir Capital. Individualistic SAUV BL, just-dry and botrytis; wood-fermented CHARD; high-priced CHENIN BL Small Change.

Mullineux Family Wines Swa r w sw ★★★ Rising-star husband-and-wife team Chris and Andrea Mullineux, specializing in smart, generous, carefully made SYRAH, Rhône-style blends (r w) and CHENIN BL.

Mvemve Raats Stell r ★★★ Mzokhona Mvemve, SA's 1st university-qualified black winemaker, and Bruwer RAATS vinify acclaimed Bordeaux red De Compostella.

Nederburg Wines W Cape r (p) w sw s/sw sp ★→★★★★ Among SA's biggest (1.4 million cases) and best-known brands, DISTELL-owned. Exceptional Ingenuity Red (05 06 07' 08) and White; excellent Manor House label; reliable Winemaster's Reserves, incl enduring Edelrood and Baronne reds. Also low-price quaffers, still and sparkling. Small, sometimes stellar Private Bins for annual Nederburg Auction, incl CHENIN BL botrytis *Edelkeur* (02 03' 04' 05 06 07' 08 09' 10').

Neil Ellis Wines Coast r w ★★★→★★★★ Veteran winemaker Neil Ellis sources cooler-climate parcels for site expression. Top V'yd Selection CAB SAUV (99 00' 01 03 04' 05 06 07), SYRAH, SAUV BL, PINOTAGE and sensational old-vine GRENACHE Noir from Piekenierskloof WARD.

Newton Johnson Vineyards r (p) w ★★→★★★ Cellar and restaurant in scenic Upper HEMEL-EN-AARDE. Outstanding PINOT N, *Chard*, SAUV BL and Rhône reds, from own and partner v'yds. Widely sourced entry-level brand Felicité.

Olifants River West coast REGION. Warm valley floors, conducive to ORGANIC cultivation; cooler, fine-wine-favouring sites in mtn WARD Piekenierskloof; BAMBOES BAY, Koekenaap nr the Atlantic.

Organic Quality variable, but producers with track records incl AVONDALE, Bon Cap, FABLE, Groot Parys, Laibach, Mtn Oaks, REYNEKE, Stellar, Tukulu, Upland and Waverley. Lazanou one to watch. *See also* BIODYNAMIC.

Outeniqua *See* KLEIN KAROO.

Paarl Town and demarcated wine district 50km+ northeast of Cape Town. 14,000ha. Diverse styles, approaches; best results with Mediterranean varieties (r w), CAB SAUV, PINOTAGE. For a fresh take, try: Anura, Arra, Ayama, Boer & Brit, Joostenberg, La Ferme Derik, Le Joubert, Mellasat, Mont Destin, Mooi Bly, Noble Hill, Perdeberg, Ridgeback, Rhebokskloof, Scali, Vondeling, Windmeul.

Paul Cluver Estate Wines Elg r w (s/sw) sw ★★★→★★★★ Appellation's leading winery, Cluver family-owned; convincing PINOT N, elegant CHARD, always *gorgeous Gewurz*, RIES (botrytis 03' 04 05' 06' 07 08' 09 10), and two crisp s/sw versions.

Quoin Rock Winery W Cape r w (sp) (sw) ★★★ Classically styled SYRAH, MERLOT, white flagship Oculus, SAUV BL The Nicobar and new SHIRAZ blend The Centaur.

Raats Family Wines Coast r w ★★→★★★ CAB FR and two pure-fruited CHENIN BL, oaked and unwooded, vinified by STELLENBOSCH-based Bruwer Raats, also a partner in boutique-scale MVEMVE RAATS.

Region *See* GEOGRAPHICAL UNIT.

Reyneke Wines Coast r w ★★★ Organic and biodynamic producer recently showing much-improved form, esp with Res Red (mainly SHIRAZ) and White (SAUV BL).

Rijk's Coast r w ★★→★★★ TULBAGH pioneer vinifying/marketing both as "Estate" and "Private Cellar". New lightly wooded Touch of Oak trio part of refocus on SHIRAZ, PINOTAGE, CHENIN BL.

Robertson District Low-rainfall inland valley; 13,500ha; lime soils; conducive climate for ORGANIC production. Historically gd CHARD, dessert styles (notably MUSCAT); more recently SAUV BL, SHIRAZ, CAB SAUV; many family boutiques (incl tyros Esona, Le Roux & Fourie); major cellars: BON COURAGE, DE WETSHOF, GRAHAM BECK, Rietvallei, ROBERTSON WINERY, Rooiberg, SPRINGFIELD, Weltevrede, Zandvliet.

Robertson Winery Rob r (p) w (br) sw s/sw ★→★★ Consistency and gd value from co-op-scale winery. Best is No 1 Constitution Rd SHIRAZ; also v.gd V'yd Selection.

Rudera Wines Elg, Stell, Wlk B r w (sw) ★★→★★★ Hailed for consistently excellent CHENIN BL (dry/semi-dry and botrytis), CAB SAUV, SYRAH. Second label: Halala/Lula.

Rupert & Rothschild Vignerons W Cape r w ★★★ Top v'yds and cellar nr PAARL owned by the Rupert family and Baron Benjamin de Rothschild. Impressive Bordeaux blend Baron Edmond (98 00 01 03' 04 05 07 08); CHARD Baroness Nadine is a deep-flavoured classic.

Rustenberg Wines W Cape r w (sw) ★★→★★★★ Prestigious family winery nr STELLENBOSCH. Flagship is CAB SAUV Peter Barlow (99' 01' 03 04 05 06 07 08). Outstanding Bordeaux red blend John X Merriman; savoury SYRAH; single-v'yd Five Soldiers CHARD; rare ROUSSANNE (varietal and blend).

Rust en Vrede Estate Stell r w ★★★ Powerful, showy offering features pricey single-v'yd SYRAH and limited-release SHIRAZ/CAB SAUV blend "1694 Classification".

Sadie Family Wines Swa r w ★★★★ Organically grown, traditionally made Columella

(SHIRAZ/MOURVÈDRE) (01 02' 03 04 05' 06 07' 08 09') a Cape benchmark; complex, intriguing multi-variety white Palladius; newer Ouwingerdreeks, site-specific wines from venerable vines. Star winemaker Eben Sadie also grows the rated Sequillo Red and White with Cape Wine Master Cornel Spies.

Saronsberg Cellar Coast r (p) w (sw) (sp) ★→★★★ Art-adorned TULBAGH showplace with awarded Bordeaux reds, Rhône (r w) varieties and blends, and new CHARD MCC in eponymous and Provenance ranges.

Saxenburg Stell r (p) w (sw) (sp) ★★→★★★ Swiss-owned v'yds, winery and restaurant. Roundly oaked reds, SAUV BL and CHARD in high-end Private Collection; premium-priced flagship SHIRAZ Select (00 01 02 03' 05' 06' 07').

Secateurs *See* BADENHORST FAMILY.

Sequillo *See* SADIE FAMILY.

Shannon Vineyards Elg r w (sw) ★★★ Exemplary MERLOT, PINOT N, SAUV BL and rare botrytis Pinot N, grown in ELGIN by brothers James and Stuart Downes, and vinified at NEWTON JOHNSON.

Simonsig Wine Estate W Cape r w (sw) (s/sw) sp ★→★★★ Consistency and value among hallmarks of Malan family winery nr STELLENBOSCH. Extensive but serious top-end, incl Merindol SYRAH (01 02' 03 04 05 06 07 08), Red Hill PINOTAGE (01 02 03' 04 05 06 07' 08 09). First (42 yrs ago) with an MCC, Kaapse Vonkel.

Solms-Delta W Cape r (p) w (br) (sp) ★★→★★★ Historic Franschhoek estate, partly staff-owned; delightfully different wines: Amarone-style SHIRAZ Africana, sophisticated dry rosé Lekkerwijn, musky white blend Koloni, *pétillant* Cape Jazz SHIRAZ.

Southern Right *See* HAMILTON RUSSELL.

Spice Route Winery Dar, Swa r w ★★→★★★ Charles Back (FAIRVIEW)-owned pioneer of Swartland DISTRICT; Rhône-style reds, esp spicy Chakalaka blend; also perfumed VIOGNIER. Non-Rhône offerings incl v.gd CHENIN BL and PINOTAGE.

Spier W Cape r (p) w (sp) ★→★★★ Serious, multi-awarded player (one million+ cases per year) headquartered nr STELLENBOSCH. Flagship is brooding CAPE BLEND Frans K Smit (04 05' 06' 07); Spier and Savanha brands, each with tiers of quality, show meticulous wine-growing.

Springfield Estate Rob r w ★★→★★★ Cult winemaker Abrie Bruwer. Traditionally vinified pairs of CAB SAUV (Méthode Ancienne and Whole Berry), CHARD (Méthode Ancienne and Wild Yeast) and SAUV BL (Special Cuvée and Life from Stone), all oozing class, personality.

Steenberg Vineyards W Cape r w (sp) ★→★★★★ Top winery, v'yds and chic cellar door, known for arresting SAUV BL, Sauv Bl/SÉM blends and, increasingly, *MCC*. Fine reds incl rare varietal NEBBIOLO.

Stellenbosch University town and demarcated wine DISTRICT (14,100ha). Heart of wine industry – Napa of SA. Many top estates, esp for reds, tucked into mtn valleys and foothills; extensive wine tasting, accommodation, fine-dining options.

Stellenzicht Vineyards Stell r w ★→★★★ DISTELL co-owned winery and v'yds scaling Helderberg Mtn; excellent SYRAH, SÉM Res, PINOTAGE; quirky new No Added Sulphites (r w). Standalone value brand Hill & Dale.

Swartland Increasingly acclaimed warm-climate DISTRICT in COASTAL REGION; 11,400ha of mainly shy-bearing, unirrigated bush vines producing concentrated, hearty but fresh wines. BADENHORST/Secateurs, LAMMERSHOEK, MULLINEUX, SADIE FAMILY/Sequillo, SPICE ROUTE, newcomer Porseleinberg; gd-value Riebeek Cellars and Swartland Winery.

Thelema Mountain Vineyards W Cape r w (s/sw) ★★→★★★★ Pioneer of SA's modern wine revival, still top of game with *Cab Sauv* (00' 03 04 05 06 07 08), The Mint CAB SAUV (05 06' 07 08 09) *et al*. Sutherland range from ELGIN v'yds charts fresh course (eg. PINOT N, ROUSSANNE/VIOGNIER).

Tokara W Cape r (p) w (sw) ★★→★★★★ Wine, food and art showcase overlooking

STELLENBOSCH. V'yds in ELGIN, WALKER BAY. Gorgeous Director's Res blends; pure, elegant CHARD, SAUV BL. Winemaker Miles Mossop's proprietary label also excellent.

Tulbagh Inland DISTRICT historically associated with white wine and bubbly, now also with beefy reds, some sweeter styles and ORGANIC. 1,300ha. KRONE, RIJK'S, SARONSBERG, FABLE WINES, Waverley Organic.

Tulbagh Mountain Vineyards See FABLE WINES.

Twee Jonge Gezellen See KRONE.

Vergelegen Wines W Cape r w ★★→★★★★ Historic mansion; immaculate v'yds and wines, serially awarded cellar door at Somerset West; owned by Anglo American plc. Flagships are powerful single-v'yd CAB SAUV "V" (01' 03 04 05 06 07), lower-keyed but still sumptuous Bordeaux "Red", and mineral *Sauv Bl/Sém "White"*.

Vilafonté Paarl r ★★★ California's acclaimed Zelma Long (ex-Simi winemaker) and Phil Freese (ex-Mondavi viticulturalist) partnering WARWICK's Mike Ratcliffe. Two superb Bordeaux blends: firmly structured Series C, fleshier Series M.

Villiera Wines W Cape r w sp (br) (sw) ★★→★★★ Grier family v'yds and winery with excellent quality/value range. Cream of the crop: Bordeaux red Monro; Bush Vine SAUV BL; Traditional CHENIN BL; five MCC bubblies (incl no-sulphur-added Brut Natural). Boutique-scale Domaine Grier nr Perpignan.

Walker Bay Small (900ha), fast-developing and highly reputed DISTRICT, with sub-appellations HEMEL-EN-AARDE, Bot River and Sunday's Glen. PINOT N, SHIRAZ, CHARD and SAUV BL are standouts. Top producers incl: ATARAXIA, BEAUMONT, BOUCHARD FINLAYSON, CREATION, HAMILTON RUSSELL, HERMANUSPIETERSFONTEIN, NEWTON JOHNSON, Luddite, Raka, Springfontein, Sumaridge.

Ward The smallest of the WINE OF ORIGIN demarcations. See GEOGRAPHICAL UNITS.

Warwick Estate W Cape r w ★★★ Tourist-cordial Ratcliffe family farm on STELLENBOSCH outskirts. V. fine red blends Trilogy (aka Estate Res), First Lady, Three Cape Ladies; savoury SYRAH; opulent CHARD.

Waterford Estate W Cape r (p) w (sw) ★★→★★★ Classy family winery nr STELLENBOSCH; award-winning cellar door. Savoury SHIRAZ (01 02' 03 04 05 06 07 08), mineral CAB SAUV (01 02 03' 04 05 06 07 08), pricey Cab Sauv-based flagship The Jem. New Library Collection is highly potable record of experimentation with blends.

Waterkloof Stell r (p) w ★→★★★ British wine importer Paul Boutinot's v'yds, winery and cantilevered cellar door nr Somerset West. BIODYNAMIC viticulture and natural/traditional vinification. Flagships are Waterkloof and Circumstance ranges; also characterful, gd-value False Bay and Peacock Ridge lines.

Wellington Historic, warm-climate WARD (4,300ha), abutting PAARL. Traditionally source of grapes for some famous (and not-so-storied) names, but in-house vinification is increasing along with local and overseas recognition. Andreas, Bosman Family, DIEMERSFONTEIN, Doolhof, Dunstone, Lazanou Organic, Linton Park, Mischa, Mont du Toit, Nabygelegen, Napier and Schalk Burger.

Wine of Origin (WO) SA's "AC" but without French crop yield, etc. restrictions. Certifies vintage, variety, area of origin. New opt-in "sustainability" certification guarantees eco-sensitive production from grape to glass. See GEOGRAPHICAL UNIT.

Winery of Good Hope, The W Cape r w (sw) ★★→★★★ Polished STELLENBOSCH producer as eclectic as its Australian-French-SA ownership. Creative, compatible blend of styles, influences, varieties and terroirs (eg. Bordeaux, Burgundy, Rhône, Loire, Stellenbosch, SWARTLAND, sometimes in the same bottle!) in eponymous, Radford Dale, Vinum, Black Rock and Land of Hope line-ups.

Zorgvliet Wines r (p) w (sp) ★→★★★ STELLENBOSCH-based vinous arm of luxury lifestyle group Zorgvliet Portfolio. Extensive Zorgvliet and Silver Myn ranges incl rare Bordeaux/TANNAT blend Richelle.

Worcester DISTRICT with mostly co-ops producing bulk wine; exceptions are Conradie Family, Eagle's Cliff and Alvi's Drift.

Sparkling wines:

Champagne and other bubbles

Why make wine sparkling? To begin with, it happened willy-nilly. In cool northerly climates, if you pick grapes late the fermentation might not be completely finished before winter sets in. A gentle effervescence remains in the wine. The bubbles feel lively on the tongue; the wine seems more aromatic, since the bubbles do an effective job of whooshing aromas towards your nose. And alcohol: people are instantly more talkative, more celebratory. Even Dom Pérignon, whose initial aim had been to turn the wines of chilly Champagne, with their natural tendency to sparkle, into still wines as sober and respectable as those of Burgundy, had to admit that fizz was fun.

The international aristocracy agreed, and sparkling wine quickly became fashionable. Usually it was called Champagne, and some of it was. But the wine region of Champagne had yet to be legally defined, and "Champagne" was as likely to come from Saumur or even the Crimea as Reims or Épernay.

It was also more likely to be drunk with food than purely for celebrations. In the 19th century, the great age of Champagne, when the number of houses multiplied and most of today's great brands established their reputations, Champagne was vintage. It was a bigger, weightier wine than now, and it was routinely drunk with dinner. Non-vintage Champagne didn't appear until the 1920s, with Bollinger and Ayala politely disputing who was first.

Now almost every wine region in the world makes sparkling wine, and a massive 1.6 billion bottles are consumed each year, of which 360 million are Champagne. That leaves a lot of sparkling wine that is not Champagne. We can't look at all the alternatives to Champagne in this supplement, so we're going to focus on the best. And who knows? There may even be a few surprises.

The resurgence of rosé has
reached the world of sparkling wine.

The geography of fizz
A cool-climate phenomenon

You can make sparkling wine anywhere in the world, in any climate. All you need is some rather expensive kit: Champagne and other traditional method sparkling wines, for all that the Champenois like to stress the antiquity of their cellars, is a thoroughly modern, industrial technique, mostly carried out on an industrial scale.

The best sparkling wines, however, come from cool climates, and all over the world, makers of sparkling wines seek out the chilliest planting spots for fizz. Or at least, for fizz made in the image of Champagne, even if not precisely its likeness. The rich, ripe sparkling Shiraz of Australia is the exception – and perhaps as far stylistically from Champagne as it is possible to get.

The reason is that the best base wine for good fizz is lean, mean and barely ripe. That's not how the Champenois put it, naturally, and it's perfectly true that the best vintages in Champagne are the warmer, riper ones. But you need acidity in sparkling wine: lots of it. The young still wines of Champagne are a gift to dentists, and even in the warmest, ripest years you would seldom want to drink them as they are. The ideal base wine is ten to 10.5 degrees potential alcohol; compare that to most still table wines, which are 13.5 to 14 degrees or more these days. That's an enormous difference in ripeness.

Champagne gains the rest of its alcohol from the second fermentation, but even then it's still quite lean. Age rounds it out, both the slow oxidation of bottle-age and the altogether different effects of ageing on the lees between the second